FINANCIAL R
UNDER THE
PROCEDURE RULES

Mr Justice Moor

Mr Justice Moor

FINANCIAL REMEDIES UNDER THE FAMILY PROCEDURE RULES

Commentary, Rules and Practice Directions for
FAMILY PROCEEDINGS
SENIOR COURTS OF ENGLAND AND WALES
COUNTY COURTS, ENGLAND AND WALES
MAGISTRATES' COURTS, ENGLAND AND WALES

CLASS
LEGAL

Class Legal
Owl House, Carr Farm, Cadney, BRIGG,
Lincolnshire, DN20 9HP, UK
Tel: 01652 652222 Fax: 01652 651050
DX 24360 Brigg
Email: Info@ClassLegal.com
Website: www.ClassLegal.com

Class Legal is an imprint of Class Publishing Ltd, a company registered in England No. 2993127. VAT No: GB 503 5208 87

Registered Office: 7 Melrose Terrace, London W6 7RL, UK

First published 2011

ISBN: 978-1-85959-341-7   e-book: 978-1-85959-342-4

A CIP Catalogue for this book is available from the British Library

Typeset by: Stephen Theaker

Printed and bound by: Good News Digital Books

Contents

Updates

Updates to the Commentary in this book are available using any of the methods listed below

1. Visit www.familyprocedure.com

The Commentary in this book will be updated on the accompanying website:

www.familyprocedure.com

Access to the site is included in the price for all purchasers of the book.

You will need to enter your unique personal access code as printed below when registering with the site

boo830013

NOTE: This code is for your use only, and may not be passed on or used by any other person. Registering on the site will deem you to have accepted the terms and conditions applying to use of your code. Any suspected abuse will result in access to the site being denied.

2. @eGlance

The Commentary and source texts in this book are adapted from the @eGlance software also available from Class Legal. The software is regularly updated and is self-contained, so that once installed on your PC you can be confident that you have the latest resources with you. This program includes not only amendments and additions to the Rules and PDs and the latest edition of the Commentary, but also an array of tools, calculators and report-printing features inspired by the industry bible, *At A Glance*.

If you bought this book from Class Legal you can upgrade your purchase to include a 12-month subscription to @eGlance for an additional £55 (normally £85) – saving £30 on the total price.

To order, call Class Legal on 01652 652 222 or order online at www.classlegal.com and enter the code you use to access the www.familyprocedure.com website when prompted.

3. Sign up for our free monthly email newsletter

News of latest changes to the Rules will be set out in our monthly email. The email also includes case law updates and other practice news.

You can sign up for the email on our website – www.classlegal.com – or by sending an email with the subject 'subscribe' to list@classlegal.com

Overview

Commentary:
OVERVIEW

The Family Procedure Rules 2010 (FPR) represent the greatest overhaul of practice and procedure in relation to family justice in two decades. The FPR is a new and comprehensive code intended to unify, rationalise, modernise and harmonise the previously diverse rules in operation in relation to different aspects of family law. It is important, however, to bear in mind that none of the underlying statutory material has been amended – so the substantive law remains the same.

The structure of the FPR will be familiar to all practitioners who have dealt with the CPR, comprising as it does individually numbered Parts by and large supplemented by correspondingly numbered and lettered Practice Directions: 'PD #A', 'PD #B' etc. whereby meat is hung on the generally desiccated bones of the primary rules. Unsurprisingly the FPR reflects not only the structure of the CPR but also, subject to necessary adaptations, the contents of that code.

The FPR replaces *all* previous rules, all but a few practice directions and precedent derived from the authorities – although many of the new rules replicate the old rules, and many of the new Practice Directions (PDs) are more or less modified versions of the old practice directions melded with appropriate modifications from the CPR. It is however anticipated that much of the earlier judicial thinking in relation to procedural best practice will have been swept away by the comprehensive nature of the new code. The main exception is that all existing Guidance (as opposed to Directions) issued by the President of the Family Division remains in place. Those PDs from the former era which survive (see the unnumbered PD devoted to them to be found at the very end of the work) are limited in number and in many cases appear archaic in form and content. (A notable exception to those criticisms is the well known and much loved '"Bundles" Direction' now relabelled PD 27A.)

The FPR are comprehensive in the sense that they are free-standing, although in relation to Costs (**Part 28**) and Enforcement (**Part 33**) CPR rule extracts (usually with adaptive amendment en route of the unhelpful 'for this read that' variety) are applied rather than being incorporated line by line into the corpus of the 2010 Rules. This is a missed opportunity: no doubt what seemed sound reasons for this referential (though not markedly reverential) approach succeeded in neutralising in this regard one of the objectives of the new assemblage which was to make all relevant rules accessible. That would seem to connote that they might be in the same place, rather than involving an obstacle course and a cumbrous filtration process to adapt them to their FPR habitat. Cost and volume cannot have been considerations: the Rules and the PDs relevant to financial remedies as reproduced in this volume weigh in at some 348 pages, there are approximately 100 further pages on topics not relevant to financial remedies, and the Rules alone in printed form cost £31.75.

The FPR will apply to all proceedings falling under the broad umbrella of family law (but with the exception of quasi-family civil proceedings which are heard in family courts, such as applications under the Trusts of Land and Appointment of Trustees Act 1996 (TOLATA) and, oddly, proceedings under the Inheritance (Provision for Family and Dependants) Act 1975 to which the CPR will continue to apply) at all judicial levels.

Perhaps the most urgently significant provisions for practitioners are those contained in **Part 36**, and in particular *PD 36A – Transitional Arrangements*. Unlike other recently introduced reforms there is no time to prepare for a soft landing. Essentially the FPR will apply to *all* proceedings, regardless of their date of commencement, with effect from the first time that a case is in court on or after 6 April 2011, although any directions made under the old procedures prior to such an attendance in court will continue to apply and should be complied with according to the old rules. While the court has a discretion to direct that the old rules should continue to apply to a case, or to an aspect of a case, the general principle and presumption is that the (new) FPR will henceforward apply.

So far as users of this publication are concerned the good news is that the essential practice in relation to what used to be called 'ancillary relief law', but which is henceforward to be known as 'financial remedies law' and which is contained in **Part 9** is *largely* unaltered. There will still be First Appointments, prior to which the parties will exchange their Form E (only minutely modified) and the other familiar documents: statements of issues, chronologies, proposed directions etc. Disclosure will continue to be by Answers to Questionnaire – although these will now have to be verified by a statement of truth, rendering anyone supplying knowingly false information liable to sanctions for contempt (see **Part 17**). A subsequent Questionnaire may be permitted by the court after the answers to the first have been received. There will usually be an FDR – though the emphasis of the mandatory requirement to list such a hearing has been slightly weakened, perhaps in deference to the anticipated increase in the number of cases in which ADR of one kind or another, which may include something akin to an FDR, will already have been tried and failed pursuant to the new **Part 3** under which the court will encourage, even to the point of compelling, an attempt at ADR.

Part 9 contains slightly different codes, under Chapter 4 (FPR rules 9.12 to 9.17) in respect of proceedings in the High Court and county court, and under Chapter 5 (FPR rules 9.18 to 9.23) in respect of proceedings in the magistrates' court, and different versions of the Forms are prescribed for magistrates' court proceedings.

The even better news for our readers is that the unifying nature of the FPR means that the familiar procedures from 'ancillary relief' are applied, with necessary but mostly minor amendments, to those other areas of practice such as applications for provision for the children of unmarried parents under section 15 of and Schedule 1 to the Children Act 1989, for provision following a foreign divorce under Part 3 of the Matrimonial and Family Proceedings Act 1984, or for provision during a separation – whether under sections 27, 35 or 10(2) of the Matrimonial Causes Act 1973: in each of which an essentially similar financial investigation and ultimate discretionary exercise is undertaken. Naturally the rules applicable as between married couples and those in same sex Civil Partnerships are completely harmonised.

PD 9A (which unlike most of the rest of the FPR does not, except where context requires, apply to proceedings in a magistrates' court), incorporates a pre-action protocol encouraging mediation and/or a collaborative law approach, discouraging pre-application disclosure, giving guidance on the tone, if not the content, of a 'first letter' and generally exhorting practitioners not to raise the temperature between the parties. It will be interesting to see whether failure to adhere to that guidance will have any more impact on the court's approach to proceedings than failure to follow the corresponding guidance under the old protocol.

PD 22A and **PD 27A** give detailed instructions for the preparation of bundles in respect of written evidence (including exhibits to Form E) and court bundles for trial respectively. The latter simply replicates the current (27 July 2006) '"Bundles" Direction' but it can be anticipated that the courts, or at least some of them, may be less tolerant of breaches than hitherto. **PD 27B** and **27C** deal with the attendance of the media at family proceedings in the High Court and county court, and in the magistrates' court respectively in accordance with the 'old' practice directions.

However the bad news, at least while practitioners adjust and adapt to the regime, is that much has changed. Overall, and in general, for the better – but it will still take some getting used to.

As part of the modernisation process the term 'financial remedy' will embrace all of the orders which might previously have been made in ancillary relief proceedings (including not only periodical payments, lump sums etc, but also avoidance of disposition orders, variation of trusts and so on), as well as the kinds of order which might be made on the applications referred to above.

Almost all applications must now be made in accordance with **Part 18** and in the Form(s) prescribed in **PD 5A**, and which in most cases must be served on the other party not less than **7 days** before any hearing, and in the case of an application for an interim financial remedy, not less than **14 days** before any hearing. Hearings without notice can only, as previously, be made in cases of real urgency or where it is necessary to make the application without notice so as not to defeat its purpose. The very few types of application not governed by **Part 18** must be issued in accordance with **Part 19**. Interim remedies, including freezing orders and search orders, are governed by **Part 20**, and are made in accordance with **Part 18**.

Although there has been an attempt, some would suggest misguidedly, to modernise some of the older language (e.g. the much publicised substitution of 'application for a matrimonial order' for 'divorce petition'), technical issues have resulted in the highly undesirable coexistence of the old and new terms under the FPR. While there might be something to be said for dispensing with 'decree nisi' and 'decree absolute' (a) the MCA 1973 continues to provide for the dissolution of a marriage by a 'decree', and (b) surely 'conditional decree' and 'final decree', or even 'conditional divorce' and 'final divorce', would be more user-friendly terms than 'conditional order' and 'final order' which could easily be misunderstood as referring to some other kind of order within the proceedings. Some language changes are welcome, and already in common use: 'permission' replaces 'leave' and 'affidavits' have, at least in most situations, given way to 'statements of truth' (themselves dealt with under **Part 17** and in particular **PD 17A** – the most significant element of which is that almost all documents, which contain any assertions of fact, must be verified by a statement of truth. Such verification may be signed by the party, the person making the statement or assertion, or, except in relation to a witness statement, by the party's lawyer. Note that the lawyer is signing on behalf of the client and verifying the client's, and not their own, assertion of the truthfulness of the document. The exceptions are a petition/application for a matrimonial order and an answer thereto (which do not require any such verification) and a Form E (which must still be sworn).

Rules on service (**Part 6**) are significantly modernised save in relation to petitions/applications for a matrimonial order, so as to permit service by fax (in any case where a fax number appears on solicitors' notepaper), by email (where there is an email address on notepaper unless specifically accompanied by a disclaimer against service by that means), by DX and by other means. The prohibition on Sunday service is abolished in respect of petitions/applications for a matrimonial order. Permission is no longer required for service of any documents out of the jurisdiction.

Enforcement receives something of a shake-up, including the very welcome simplification of the enforcement of undertakings as if they were orders, under **Part 33**. Perhaps the greatest innovation is the application for an order 'for such method of enforcement as the court may consider appropriate' under rule 33.3(2)(b) relieving would-be enforcers, at least in the first place, from the responsibility of committing themselves to what may prove to be an inappropriate recovery mechanism. **PD 33A** includes exact wording to be included on orders containing undertakings, different wording where the undertaking is to pay money, and a requirement that those giving undertakings sign a statement confirming both that they have given the undertaking(s) and that they understand that they risk imprisonment if found to have broken their promises to the court.

All appeals, except against an order involving loss of liberty, now require permission (**Part 30**) – including an appeal from District Judge to Judge, at all levels, and all appeals are by way of a review of the first instance decision rather than by way of a rehearing, save where in the interests of justice a rehearing is required. In short, appeals are harmonised with the procedure under CPR Part 52. An appeal is the only route by which an order – including a consent order – can be challenged, whether on grounds of misrepresentation, a *Barder* event or otherwise. The time for filing an appellant's notice is 21 days after the decision appealed against, although the court may direct a different period. Note that the parties cannot agree between themselves to extend time.

The Family Procedure Rules 2010

STATUTORY INSTRUMENTS
2010 No. 2955 (L.17)
FAMILY PROCEEDINGS
SENIOR COURTS OF ENGLAND AND WALES
COUNTY COURTS, ENGLAND AND WALES
MAGISTRATES' COURTS, ENGLAND AND WALES
Made – 13th December 2010
Laid before Parliament 17th December 2010
Coming into force – 6th April 2011

The Family Procedure Rule Committee makes the following rules in exercise of the powers conferred by sections 75 and 76 of the Courts Act 2003[1], section 18(1) of the Maintenance Orders (Reciprocal Enforcement) Act 1972[2], sections 12 and 48 of the Civil Jurisdiction and Judgments Act 1982[3], sections 10 and 24 of the Child Abduction and Custody Act 1985[4], section 97(1) of the Children Act 1989[5], section 54(1) of the Access to Justice Act 1999[6], sections 52(7), 102, 109(2) and 141(1) and (3) of the Adoption and Children Act 2002[7], after consulting in accordance with section 79 of the Courts Act 2003[8].

These rules may be cited as the Family Procedure Rules 2010 and shall come into force on 6th April 2011.

Part 1

Commentary on Part 1:
OVERRIDING OBJECTIVE

Part 1 is the counterpart of CPR Part 1. It concerns the now numinous 'overriding objective'. Of course reams have been written and manifold cases decided on the CPR overriding objective since its emergence into the brave new world of reformed civil justice on 26 April 1999. See, for example, Section 11 of Volume 2 of *Civil Procedure 2010* (Sweet & Maxwell). Interestingly, when Hong Kong SAR came to embrace these reforms on 2 April 2009 the 'overriding objective' became the 'underlying objectives' which is in a way a more accurate description of the effect of the Rules, for they cannot, of course, override the statutory powers and duties applicable to the cause in hand.

The CPR overriding objective has been present as a governing feature of ancillary relief procedure since 5 June 2000. Old rule 2.51D provided that:

2.51D The overriding objective

(1) The ancillary relief rules are a procedural code with the overriding objective of enabling the court to deal with cases justly.

(2) Dealing with a case justly includes, so far as is practicable—

    (a) ensuring that the parties are on an equal footing;

    (b) saving expense;

    (c) dealing with the case in ways which are proportionate—

        (i) to the amount of money involved;

        (ii) to the importance of the case;

        (iii) to the complexity of the issues; and

        (iv) to the financial position of each party;

    (d) ensuring that it is dealt with expeditiously and fairly; and

    (e) allotting to it an appropriate share of the court's resources, while taking into account the need to allot resources to other cases.

(3) The court must seek to give effect to the overriding objective when it—

    (a) exercises any power given to it by the ancillary relief rules; or

    (b) interprets any rule.

(4) The parties are required to help the court to further the overriding objective.

(5) The court must further the overriding objective by actively managing cases.

(6) Active case management includes—

    (a) encouraging the parties to co-operate with each other in the conduct of the proceedings;

    (b) encouraging the parties to settle their disputes through mediation, where appropriate;

    (c) identifying the issues at an early date;

    (d) regulating the extent of disclosure of documents and expert evidence so that they are proportionate to the issues in question;

    (e) helping the parties to settle the whole or part of the case;

    (f) fixing timetables or otherwise controlling the progress of the case;

    (g) making use of technology; and

    (h) giving directions to ensure that the trial of a case proceeds quickly and efficiently.

The concept of applying the overriding objective in financial applications is therefore well established.

The overriding objective of these FPR, framed in very similar language to their CPR counterpart, is of course intended to cover all family applications and not merely financial ones. Rule 1.1(1) states 'these rules are a new procedural code with the overriding objective of enabling the court to deal with cases justly, **having regard to any welfare issues involved**'. The highlighted phrase does not appear in CPR rule 1.1(1), and points up the differences in nature between civil and family proceedings.

It is interesting, but probably not very significant, to note what is now omitted from the old ancillary relief rule, and what is now included but which was previously absent.

Omitted is the requirement to deal with the case in ways which are proportionate to the amount of money involved and to the financial position of each party. These objectives appear in CPR rule 1.1(2)(c). While this omission is probably accounted for by the need to make the objective all-embracing and not money-specific, it is perhaps a pity that these obvious factors have fallen by the wayside. It is considered that the court should still have these considerations very much at the forefront of its mind when managing the case.

Included in the new overriding objective, but previously absent from old rule 2.51D, are the case-management tools of:

- identifying at an early stage who should be a party to the proceedings;
- deciding promptly the procedure to be followed in the case;
- deciding the order in which issues are to be resolved;
- considering whether the likely benefits of taking a particular step justify the cost of taking it;
- dealing with as many aspects of the case as it can on the same occasion; and
- dealing with the case without the parties needing to attend at court.

These are valuable additions to the old code and should be clearly borne in mind by the court (and indeed the parties and their lawyers) when the case is managed.

Although the CPR overriding objective was not directly applicable to family proceedings, save for proceedings under the Inheritance (Provision for Family and Dependants) Act 1975 and TOLATA, it was regularly applied in spirit if not to the letter. See, for example, *AA v NA and others* [2010] 2 FLR 1173 at [34] where it was said:

> While it is true that, strictly speaking, the [CPR] overriding objective does not apply to family proceedings, I am quite sure that their spirit, if not their letter, should be borne firmly in mind when deciding whether or not to order a rehearing.

The imperative of avoiding a multiplicity of proceedings is enshrined in section 49(2) of the Senior Courts Act 1981 (formerly the Supreme Court Act 1981 before its banal and ageist renaming, re-enacting section 43 of the Judicature Act 1925) which provides that:

> Every ... court shall ... so exercise its jurisdiction in every cause or matter before it as to secure that, as far as possible, all matters in dispute between the parties are completely and finally determined, and all multiplicity of legal proceedings with respect to any of those matters is avoided.

This is a key statutory rule, often overlooked in family proceedings. It is to be hoped that robust application of the overriding objective will ensure that it is applied rigorously.

PART 1: OVERRIDING OBJECTIVE

The overriding objective

1.1.—(1) These rules are a new procedural code with the overriding objective of enabling the court to deal with cases justly, having regard to any welfare issues involved.

(2) Dealing with a case justly includes, so far as is practicable—

(a) ensuring that it is dealt with expeditiously and fairly;
(b) dealing with the case in ways which are proportionate to the nature, importance and complexity of the issues;
(c) ensuring that the parties are on an equal footing;
(d) saving expense; and
(e) allotting to it an appropriate share of the court's resources, while taking into account the need to allot resources to other cases.

Application by the court of the overriding objective

1.2. The court must seek to give effect to the overriding objective when it—

(a) exercises any power given to it by these rules; or
(b) interprets any rule.

Duty of the parties

1.3. The parties are required to help the court to further the overriding objective.

Court's duty to manage cases

1.4.—(1) The court must further the overriding objective by actively managing cases.

(2) Active case management includes—

(a) encouraging the parties to co-operate with each other in the conduct of the proceedings;
(b) identifying at an early stage—
    (i) the issues; and
    (ii) who should be a party to the proceedings;
(c) deciding promptly—
    (i) which issues need full investigation and hearing and which do not; and
    (ii) the procedure to be followed in the case;
(d) deciding the order in which issues are to be resolved;
(e) encouraging the parties to use an alternative dispute resolution procedure if the court considers that appropriate and facilitating the use of such procedure;
(f) helping the parties to settle the whole or part of the case;
(g) fixing timetables or otherwise controlling the progress of the case;

(h) considering whether the likely benefits of taking a particular step justify the cost of taking it;

(i) dealing with as many aspects of the case as it can on the same occasion;

(j) dealing with the case without the parties needing to attend at court;

(k) making use of technology; and

(l) giving directions to ensure that the case proceeds quickly and efficiently.

Part 2

Commentary on Part 2:
APPLICATION AND INTERPRETATION OF THE RULES

Part 2 is the counterpart to CPR Part 2 and deals with the application and interpretation of the rules. Omitted from *@eGlance* are those rules which have no conceivable relevance to financial applications, namely rule 2.4 (Modification of rules in application to serial numbers etc), rule 2.6 (Powers of the single justice to perform functions under the 1989 Act, the 1996 Act, the 2002 Act and the Childcare Act 2006) and rule 2.7 (Single justice's power to refer to a magistrates' court).

The remainder of the rules are largely self-explanatory. Rule 2.2 introduces the glossary of terms found at the end of the FPR. Rule 2.3 supplies a lengthy list of interpretations.

A **financial remedy** is defined as:

(a) a financial order (as to which see *below*);
(b) an order under Schedule 1 to the Children Act 1989;
(c) an order under Part 3 of the Matrimonial and Family Proceedings Act 1984;
(d) an order under Schedule 7 to the Civil Partnership Act 2004;
(e) an order under section 27 of the Matrimonial Causes Act 1973;
(f) an order under Part 9 of Schedule 5 to the Civil Partnership Act 2004;
(g) an order under section 35 of the Matrimonial Causes Act 1973;
(h) an order under para 69 of Schedule 5 to the Civil Partnership Act 2004;
(i) an order under Part 1 of the Domestic Proceedings and Magistrates' Courts Act 1978;
(j) an order under Schedule 6 to the Civil Partnership Act 2004;
(k) an order under section 10(2) of the Matrimonial Causes Act 1973; or
(l) an order under section 48(2) of the Civil Partnership Act 2004

A **financial order** is defined as:

(a) an avoidance of disposition order;

(b) an order for maintenance pending suit;

(c) an order for maintenance pending the outcome of proceedings;

(d) an order for periodical payments or lump sum provision as mentioned in section 21(1) of the Matrimonial Causes Act 1973, except an order under section 27(6) of that Act;

(e) an order for periodical payments or lump sum provision as mentioned in paragraph 2(1) of Schedule 5 to the Civil Partnership Act 2004, made under Part 1 of Schedule 5 to that Act;

(f) a property adjustment order;

(g) a variation order;

(h) a pension sharing order; or

(i) a pension compensation sharing order.

A **matrimonial order** is defined as:

(a) a decree of divorce made under section 1 of the Matrimonial Causes Act 1973;

(b) a decree of nullity made on one of the grounds set out in sections 11 or 12 of the Matrimonial Causes Act 1973; or

(c) a decree of judicial separation made under section 17 of the Matrimonial Causes Act 1973.

Rule 2.5 specifies the general commonality of functions enjoyed by judges of all levels, but prescribes that only a full-time High Court Judge may try an application for a declaration of incompatibility under section 4 of the Human Rights Act 1998.

Rule 2.8 allows the court to deal with a case at any place that it considers appropriate. Examples have included hospitals, prisons and cafeteria (following the evacuation of the court building on account of fire or bomb threat). Rule 4.1(3)(e) permits the court 'to hold a hearing and receive evidence by telephone or by using any other method of direct oral communication'.

These rules also cover the out-of-hours judge hearing an application at his home or on the golf course (although such applications by telephone from unrepresented litigants are not countenanced: PD 20A, para 4.5(d)).

Procedures and directions in relation to telephone hearings are contained in PD 18A, para 8.

As to hearing evidence by video link 'or by other means', rule 22.3 is to the same effect as rule 4.1(3)(e). Extensive guidance for video-conferencing is curiously sited within *PD 22A – Written Evidence (Annex 3)*.

Rules 2.9 and 2.10 contain the familiar rules concerning the computation of time.

PART 2: APPLICATION AND INTERPRETATION
OF THE RULES

Application of these Rules

2.1.—(1) Unless the context otherwise requires, these rules apply to family proceedings in—

(a) the High Court;
(b) a county court; and
(c) a magistrates' court.

(2) Nothing in these rules is to be construed as—

(a) purporting to apply to proceedings in a magistrates' court which are not family proceedings within the meaning of section 65 of the Magistrates' Courts Act 1980[9] or
(b) conferring upon a magistrate a function which a magistrate is not permitted by statute to perform.

The glossary

2.2.—(1) The glossary at the end of these rules is a guide to the meaning of certain legal expressions used in the rules, but is not to be taken as giving those expressions any meaning in the rules which they do not have in the law generally.

(2) Subject to paragraph (3), words in these rules which are included in the glossary are followed by "GL".

(3) The word "service", which appears frequently in the rules, is included in the glossary but is not followed by "GL".

Interpretation

2.3.—(1) In these rules—

"the 1973 Act" means the Matrimonial Causes Act 1973[10];

"the 1978 Act" means the Domestic Proceedings and Magistrates' Courts Act 1978[11];

"the 1980 Hague Convention" means the Convention on the Civil Aspects of International Child Abduction which was signed at The Hague on 25 October 1980;

"the 1984 Act" means the Matrimonial and Family Proceedings Act 1984[12];

"the 1986 Act" means the Family Law Act 1986[13];

"the 1989 Act" means the Children Act 1989;

"the 1990 Act" means the Human Fertilisation and Embryology Act 1990[14];

"the 1991 Act" means the Child Support Act 1991[15];

"the 1996 Act" means the Family Law Act 1996[16];

"the 1996 Hague Convention" means the Convention on Jurisdiction, Applicable Law, Recognition, Enforcement and Co-Operation in Respect of Parental Responsibility and Measures for the Protection of Children;

"the 2002 Act" means the Adoption and Children Act 2002;

"the 2004 Act" means the Civil Partnership Act 2004;

"the 2005 Act" means the Mental Capacity Act 2005[17];

"the 2008 Act" means the Human Fertilisation and Embryology Act 2008[18];

"adoption proceedings" means proceedings for an adoption order under the 2002 Act;

"Allocation Order" means any order made by the Lord Chancellor under Part 1 of Schedule 11 to the 1989 Act;

"alternative dispute resolution" means methods of resolving a dispute, including mediation, other than through the normal court process;

"application form" means a document in which the applicant states his intention to seek a court order other than in accordance with the Part 18 procedure;

"application notice" means a document in which the applicant states his intention to seek a court order in accordance with the Part 18 procedure;

"Assembly" means the National Assembly for Wales;

"bank holiday" means a bank holiday under the Banking and Financial Dealings Act 1971[19]—

(a) for the purpose of service of a document within the United Kingdom, in the part of the United Kingdom where service is to take place; and
(b) for all other purposes, in England and Wales.

"business day" means any day other than—

(a) a Saturday, Sunday, Christmas Day or Good Friday; or
(b) a bank holiday;

"care order" has the meaning assigned to it by section 31(11) of the 1989 Act;

"CCR" means the County Court Rules 1981, as they appear in Schedule 2 to the CPR;

"child" means a person under the age of 18 years who is the subject of the proceedings; except that—

(a) in adoption proceedings, it also includes a person who has attained the age of 18 years before the proceedings are concluded; and
(b) in proceedings brought under the Council Regulation, the 1980 Hague Convention or the European Convention, it means a person under the age of 16 years who is the subject of the proceedings;

"child of the family" has the meaning given to it by section 105(1) of the 1989 Act;

"children and family reporter" means an officer of the Service or a Welsh family proceedings officer who has been asked to prepare a welfare report under section 7(1)(a) of the 1989[20] Act or section 102(3)(b) of the 2002 Act;

"children's guardian" means—

(a) in relation to a child who is the subject of and a party to specified proceedings or proceedings to which Part 14 applies, the person appointed in accordance with rule 15.3(1); and

(b) in any other case, the person appointed in accordance with rule 15.4;

"civil partnership order" means one of the orders mentioned in section 37 of the 2004 Act;

"civil partnership proceedings" means proceedings for a civil partnership order;

"civil partnership proceedings county court" means a county court so designated by the Lord Chancellor under section 36A of the 1984 Act[21];

"civil restraint order" means an order restraining a party—

(a) from making any further applications in current proceedings (a limited civil restraint order);

(b) from making certain applications in specified courts (an extended civil restraint order); or

(c) from making any application in specified courts (a general civil restraint order);

"Commission" means the Child Maintenance and Enforcement Commission;

"consent order" means an order in the terms applied for to which the respondent agrees;

"contact order" has the meaning assigned to it by section 8(1) of the 1989 Act;

"the Council Regulation" means Council Regulation (EC) No 2201/2003 of 27 November 2003 on jurisdiction and the recognition and enforcement of judgments in matrimonial matters and in matters of parental responsibility;

"court" means, subject to any rule or other enactment which provides otherwise, the High Court, a county court or a magistrates' court;

(rule 2.5 relates to the power to perform functions of the court.)

"court of trial" means—

(a) in proceedings under the 1973 Act, a divorce county court designated by the Lord Chancellor as a court of trial pursuant to section 33(1) of the 1984 Act[22]; or

(b) in proceedings under the 2004 Act, a civil partnership proceedings county court designated by the Lord Chancellor as a court of trial pursuant to section 36A(1)(b) of the 1984 Act; and in proceedings under the 1973 Act pending in a divorce county court or proceedings under the 2004 Act pending in a civil partnership proceedings county court, the principal registry is treated as a court of trial having its place of sitting at the Royal Courts of Justice;

"court officer" means—

(a) in the High Court or in a county court, a member of court staff; and
(b) in a magistrates' court, the designated officer;

("designated officer" is defined in section 37(1) of the Courts Act 2003.)
"CPR" means the Civil Procedure Rules 1998;
"deputy" has the meaning given in section 16(2)(b) of the 2005 Act;
"designated county court" means a court designated as—

(a) a divorce county court;
(b) a civil partnership proceedings county court; or
(c) both a divorce county court and a civil partnership proceedings county court;

"detailed assessment proceedings" means the procedure by which the amount of costs is decided in accordance with Part 47 of the CPR;
"directions appointment" means a hearing for directions;
"district judge"—

(a) in relation to proceedings in the High Court, includes a district judge of the principal registry and in relation to proceedings in a county court, includes a district judge of the principal registry when the principal registry is treated as if it were a county court;
(b) in relation to proceedings in a district registry or a county court, means the district judge or one of the district judges of that registry or county court, as the case may be;

"district registry" means—

(a) in proceedings under the 1973 Act, any district registry having a divorce county court within its district;
(b) in proceedings under the 2004 Act, any district registry having a civil partnership proceedings county court within its district; and
(c) in any other case, any district registry having a designated county court within its district;

"divorce county court" means a county court so designated by the Lord Chancellor pursuant to section 33(1) of the 1984 Act, including the principal registry when it is treated as a divorce county court;
"the European Convention" means the European Convention on Recognition and Enforcement of Decisions concerning Custody of Children and on the Restoration of Custody of Children which was signed in Luxembourg on 20 May 1980;

"filing", in relation to a document, means delivering it, by post or otherwise, to the court office;

"financial order" means—

(a) an avoidance of disposition order;
(b) an order for maintenance pending suit;
(c) an order for maintenance pending outcome of proceedings;
(d) an order for periodical payments or lump sum provision as mentioned in section 21(1) of the 1973 Act [23], except an order under section 27(6) of that Act[24];
(e) an order for periodical payments or lump sum provision as mentioned in paragraph 2(1) of Schedule 5 to the 2004 Act, made under Part 1 of Schedule 5 to that Act;
(f) a property adjustment order;
(g) a variation order;
(h) a pension sharing order; or
(i) a pension compensation sharing order;

("variation order", "pension compensation sharing order" and "pension sharing order" are defined in rule 9.3.)

"financial remedy" means—

(a) a financial order;
(b) an order under Schedule 1 to the 1989 Act;
(c) an order under Part 3 of the 1984 Act;
(d) an order under Schedule 7 to the 2004 Act;
(e) an order under section 27 of the 1973 Act;
(f) an order under Part 9 of Schedule 5 to the 2004 Act;
(g) an order under section 35 of the 1973 Act[25];
(h) an order under paragraph 69 of Schedule 5 to the 2004 Act;
(i) an order under Part 1 of the 1978 Act;
(j) an order under Schedule 6 to the 2004 Act;
(k) an order under section 10(2) of the 1973 Act[26]; or
(l) an order under section 48(2) of the 2004 Act;

"hearing" includes a directions appointment;

"hearsay" means a statement made, otherwise than by a person while giving oral evidence in proceedings, which is tendered as evidence of the matters stated, and references to hearsay include hearsay of whatever degree;

"inherent jurisdiction" means the High Court's power to make any order or determine any issue in respect of a child, including in wardship proceedings, where it would be just and equitable to do so unless restricted by legislation or case law;

(Practice Direction 12D (Inherent Jurisdiction (including Wardship Proceedings)) provides examples of inherent jurisdiction proceedings.)

"judge", in the High Court or a county court, means, unless the context requires otherwise, a judge, district judge or a person authorised to act as such;

"jurisdiction" means, unless the context requires otherwise, England and Wales and any part of the territorial waters of the United Kingdom adjoining England and Wales;

"justices' clerk" has the meaning assigned to it by section 27(1) of the Courts Act 2003[27];

"legal representative" means a—

(a) barrister;
(b) solicitor;
(c) solicitor's employee;
(d) manager of a body recognised under section 9 of the Administration of Justice Act 1985[28]; or
(e) person who, for the purposes of the Legal Services Act 2007[29], is an authorised person in relation to an activity which constitutes the conduct of litigation (within the meaning of the Act),

who has been instructed to act for a party in relation to proceedings;

"litigation friend" has the meaning given—

(a) in relation to a protected party, by Part 15; and
(b) in relation to a child, by Part 16;

"matrimonial cause" means proceedings for a matrimonial order;

"matrimonial order" means—

(a) a decree of divorce made under section 1 of the 1973 Act[30];
(b) a decree of nullity made on one of the grounds set out in sections 11 or 12 of the 1973 Act[31];
(c) a decree of judicial separation made under section 17 of the 1973 Act[32];

"note" includes a record made by mechanical means;

"officer of the Service" has the meaning given by section 11(3) of the Criminal Justice and Court Services Act 2000;

"order" includes directions of the court;

"order for maintenance pending outcome of proceedings" means an order under paragraph 38 of Schedule 5 to the 2004 Act;

"order for maintenance pending suit" means an order under section 22 of the 1973 Act[33];

"parental order proceedings" has the meaning assigned to it by rule 13.1;

"parental responsibility" has the meaning assigned to it by section 3 of the 1989 Act;

"placement proceedings" means proceedings for the making, varying or revoking of a placement order under the 2002 Act;

"principal registry" means the principal registry of the Family Division of the High Court;

"proceedings" means, unless the context requires otherwise, family proceedings as defined in section 75(3) of the Courts Act 2003;

"professional acting in furtherance of the protection of children" includes—

(a) an officer of a local authority exercising child protection functions;
(b) a police officer who is—
    (i) exercising powers under section 46 of the Act of 1989; or
    (ii) serving in a child protection unit or a paedophile unit of a police force;
(c) any professional person attending a child protection conference or review in relation to a child who is the subject of the proceedings to which the information regarding the proceedings held in private relates; or
(d) an officer of the National Society for the Prevention of Cruelty to Children;

"professional legal adviser" means a—

(a) barrister;
(b) solicitor;
(c) solicitor's employee;
(d) manager of a body recognised under section 9 of the Administration of Justice Act 1985; or
(e) person who, for the purposes of the Legal Services Act 2007, is an authorised person in relation to an activity which constitutes the conduct of litigation (within the meaning of that Act),

who is providing advice to a party but is not instructed to represent that party in the proceedings;

"property adjustment order" means—

(a) in proceedings under the 1973 Act, any of the orders mentioned in section 21(2) of that Act;
(b) in proceedings under the 1984 Act, an order under section 17(1)(a)(ii) of that Act;
(c) in proceedings under Schedule 5 to the 2004 Act, any of the orders mentioned in paragraph 7(1); or
(d) in proceedings under Schedule 7 to the 2004 Act, an order for property adjustment under paragraph 9(2) or (3);

"protected party" means a party, or an intended party, who lacks capacity (within the meaning of the 2005 Act) to conduct proceedings;

"reporting officer" means an officer of the Service or a Welsh family proceedings officer appointed to witness the documents which signify a parent's or guardian's consent to the placing of the child for adoption or to the making of an adoption order or a section 84 order;

"risk assessment" has the meaning assigned to it by section 16A(3) of the 1989 Act;

"Royal Courts of Justice", in relation to matrimonial proceedings pending in a divorce county court or civil partnership proceedings pending in a civil partnership proceedings county court, means such place as may be specified in directions given by the Lord Chancellor pursuant to section 42(2)(a)[34] of the 1984 Act;

"RSC" means the Rules of the Supreme Court 1965 as they appear in Schedule 1 to the CPR;

"section 8 order" has the meaning assigned to it by section 8(2) of the 1989 Act;

"section 84 order" means an order made by the High Court under section 84 of the 2002 Act giving parental responsibility prior to adoption abroad;

"section 89 order" means an order made by the High Court under section 89 of the 2002 Act—

(a) annulling a Convention adoption or Convention adoption order;
(b) providing for an overseas adoption or determination under section 91 of the 2002 Act to cease to be valid; or
(c) deciding the extent, if any, to which a determination under section 91 of the 2002 Act has been affected by a subsequent determination under that section;

"Service" has the meaning given by section 11 of the Criminal Justice and Court Services Act 2000;

"the Service Regulation" means Regulation (EC) No. 1393/2007 of the European Parliament and of the Council of 13 November 2007 on the service in the Member States of judicial and extrajudicial documents in civil or commercial matters (service of documents), and repealing Council Regulation (EC) No. 1348/2000, as amended from time to time and as applied by the Agreement made on 19 October 2005 between the European Community and the Kingdom of Denmark on the service of judicial and extrajudicial documents in civil and commercial matters;

"specified proceedings" has the meaning assigned to it by section 41(6) of the 1989 Act and rule (4);

"welfare officer" means a person who has been asked to prepare a report under section 7(1)(b) of the 1989 Act[35];

"Welsh family proceedings officer" has the meaning given by section 35(4) of the Children Act 2004.

(2) In these rules a reference to—

(a) an application for a matrimonial order or a civil partnership order is to be read as a reference to a petition for—

(i) a matrimonial order;
(ii) a decree of presumption of death and dissolution of marriage made under section 19 of the 1973 Act[36]; or
(iii) a civil partnership order,
and includes a petition by a respondent asking for such an order;

(b) "financial order" in matrimonial proceedings is to be read as a reference to "ancillary relief";

(c) "matrimonial proceedings" is to be read as a reference to a matrimonial cause or proceedings for an application for a decree of presumption of death and dissolution of marriage made under section 19 of the 1973 Act.

(3) Where these rules apply the CPR, they apply the CPR as amended from time to time.

Modification of rules in application to serial numbers etc.

* * * * *

Power to perform functions conferred on the court by these rules and practice directions

2.5.—(1) Where these rules or a practice direction provide for the court to perform any function then, except where any rule or practice direction, any other enactment or any directions made by the President of the Family Division under section 9 of the Courts and Legal Services Act 1990[37], provides otherwise, that function may be performed—

(a) in relation to proceedings in the High Court or in a district registry, by any judge or district judge of that Court including a district judge of the principal registry;

(b) in relation to proceedings in a county court, by any judge or district judge including a district judge of the principal registry when the principal registry is treated as if it were a county court; and

(c) in relation to proceedings in a magistrates' court—
   (i) by any family proceedings court constituted in accordance with sections 66 and 67 of the Magistrates' Courts Act 1980[38]; or
   (ii) by a single justice of the peace who is a member of the family panel in accordance with Practice Direction 2A.

(The Justices' Clerks Rules 2005 make provision for a justices' clerk or assistant clerk to carry out certain functions of a single justice of the peace.)

(2) A deputy High Court judge and a district judge, including a district judge of the principal registry, may not try a claim for a declaration of incompatibility in accordance with section 4 of the Human Rights Act 1998[39].

* * * * *

Court's discretion as to where it deals with cases

2.8. The court may deal with a case at any place that it considers appropriate.

Computation of time

2.9.—(1) This rule shows how to calculate any period of time for doing any act which is specified—

(a) by these rules;

(b) by a practice direction; or

(c) by a direction or order of the court.

(2) A period of time expressed as a number of days must be computed as clear days.

(3) In this rule "clear days" means that in computing the numbers of days—

(a) the day on which the period begins; and

(b) if the end of the period is defined by reference to an event, the day on which that event occurs,

are not included.

(4) Where the specified period is 7 days or less and includes a day which is not a business day, that day does not count.

(5) When the period specified—

(a) by these rules or a practice direction; or

(b) by any direction or order of the court,

for doing any act at the court office ends on a day on which the office is closed, that act will be in time if done on the next day on which the court office is open.

Dates for compliance to be calendar dates and to include time of day

2.10—(1) Where the court makes an order or gives a direction which imposes a time limit for doing any act, the last date for compliance must, wherever practicable—

(a) be expressed as a calendar date; and

(b) include the time of day by which the act must be done.

(2) Where the date by which an act must be done is inserted in any document, the date must, wherever practicable, be expressed as a calendar date.

(3) Where "month" occurs in any order, direction or other document, it means a calendar month.

Part 3

Commentary on Part 3:
ALTERNATIVE DISPUTE RESOLUTION: THE COURT'S POWERS

Part 3, which contains the court's powers to encourage the parties to espouse alternative dispute resolution (ADR) and to facilitate its use, has no direct counterpart in the CPR. It is complementary to the overriding objective which rule 1.4(1) and (2) provides that the court must further 'by actively managing cases', to include 'encouraging the parties to use an alternative dispute resolution procedure if the court considers that appropriate and facilitating the use of such procedure'. This, of course, directly corresponds to CPR rule 1.4(2)(e).

There was considerable debate as to whether the CPR contained a specific power to oblige litigants to use ADR against their will, a debate that was finally resolved by the judgments of the Court of Appeal in *Halsey v Milton Keynes General NHS Trust* [2004] 1 WLR 3002, which decided that there was no such power. However, pursuant to the relevant CPR Practice Direction a form of order, known as an 'Ungley Order', is commonly made as part of routine case management. It (a) requires the parties to consider whether the case is capable of resolution by ADR, (b) and that any party who considers that ADR is unsuitable must justify his stance in a witness statement filed 'without prejudice save as to costs', and (c) specifies that the court will consider that statement after reaching its decision when considering whether to making an adverse costs order should it conclude that the case was in fact suitable for ADR. It is reasonable to suppose that that practice may be adopted and such orders made in family proceedings under Part 3 and the associated *Practice Direction 3A – Pre-application protocol for mediation information and assessment* (below).

Rule 3.2 specifically requires the court at every stage of the proceedings to consider whether ADR is appropriate.

Rule 3.3(1) allows the court to adjourn proceedings not only for such resolution to take place but also to enable the parties to obtain information and advice about it. The court can take such steps on its own initiative.

In *Al-Khatib v Masry* [2005] 1 FLR 381 Thorpe LJ stated, when approving a mediated compromise of an appeal, that that there is no case, however conflicted, which is not potentially open to successful mediation, even if mediation has not been attempted or has failed during the trial process.

Thorpe LJ went on to emphasise how vital it is for there to be judicial supervision of the process of mediation. Thus rule 3.3(3) specifically requires the court to be kept informed of the progress of the ADR process.

In *S v P (Settlement By Collaborative Law Process)* [2008] 2 FLR 2040 Coleridge J, with the agreement of the President, devised a short-cut procedure for the making of a consent order following an agreement reached under the collaborative law process. The application for approval of such a draft consent order may be dealt with in the 'urgent without notice' High Court applications list. A full day's notice must be given to the clerk of the High Court judge in front of whom it is proposed to list the case: such notice may be given by telephone. The clerk of the rules should be informed that this is taking place. Use of the shortcut process is always subject to the consent of the urgent application judge. However, provided every aspect of the documentation is agreed, the hearing is not expected to last more than 10 minutes, and the documentation has been lodged with the judge the night before the hearing, this process has been approved by the President for use by those who achieve collaborative law agreements, in order to provide as much encouragement as possible to people to resolve their difficulties in this civilised and sensible way.

There is no suggestion that this procedure will be affected by the new Rules regime.

It remains to be seen whether a similar streamlined procedure may be developed for cross-border mediated settlements so as to comply with the requirements of Part 35 *below*.

The associated *Practice Direction 3A – Pre-application protocol for mediation information and assessment* goes considerably further than the terms of Part 3 and could be viewed as seeking to coerce the use of ADR. It reflects the belief of the present government that mediation should be a mandatory step in most family cases before proceedings are initiated. It states that all potential applicants for a court order in relevant family proceedings will be expected, before making their application, to have followed the steps set out in the Protocol which is contained in the PD. Relevant family proceedings are defined for the purposes of this PD to include almost all applications for a financial remedy (the exceptions being applications for enforcement or avoidance of disposition), and almost all private law children applications.

The Protocol requires a potential applicant, except in certain specified circumstances, to consider with a mediator whether the dispute may be capable of being resolved. The specified circumstances include cases where the mediator is satisfied that mediation is not suitable because another party to the dispute is unwilling to attend a Mediation Information and Assessment Meeting and to consider mediation; if the mediator determines that the case is not suitable for a Mediation Information and Assessment Meeting; where a party has made an allegation of domestic violence against another party and this has resulted in a police investigation or the issuing of civil proceedings for the protection of any party within the last 12 months; where a party is bankrupt; where the whereabouts of the other party are unknown to the applicant; where the prospective application is for an order in relevant family proceedings which are already in existence and are continuing; and where the prospective application is urgent, meaning there is a risk to the life, liberty or physical safety of the applicant or his or her family or his or her home, or where any delay caused by attending a Mediation Information and Assessment Meeting would cause a risk of significant harm to a child, a significant risk of a miscarriage of justice, unreasonable hardship to the applicant or irretrievable problems in dealing with the dispute (such as an irretrievable loss of significant evidence); and where the applicant (or the applicant's solicitor) contacts three mediators within 15 miles of the applicant's home and none is able to conduct a Mediation Information and Assessment Meeting within 15 working days of the date of contact.

Under the Protocol the court will expect all applicants to have complied with its terms before commencing proceedings and will expect any respondent to have attended a Mediation Information and Assessment Meeting, if invited to do so. If court proceedings are taken, the court will wish to know at the first hearing whether mediation has been considered by the parties. In considering the conduct of any relevant family proceedings, the court will take into account any failure to comply with the Protocol and may refer the parties to a meeting with a mediator before the proceedings continue further.

There is implicit in this language the threat that non-compliance with the Protocol may result in adverse costs orders.

It should be noted that the PRFD runs its own mediation scheme whereby arrangements have been established with effect from 1st November 2010 for mediators to be present at court to enable parties to obtain mediation services. The telephone number on which mediators can be contacted is 020 7947 7033. The mediators will normally be based in Room 6.22 on the 6th floor of First Avenue House.

Reference should also be made to Part 35: Mediation Directive and to its Practice Direction 35A which apply to those mediated 'cross-border disputes' which are subject to the EU Mediation Directive (Directive 2008/52/EC of the European Parliament and of the Council of 21 May 2008 on certain aspects of mediation in civil and commercial matters).

Cross-border disputes are defined by article 2 of the Directive.

PART 3: ALTERNATIVE DISPUTE RESOLUTION: THE COURT'S POWERS

Scope of this Part

3.1.—(1) This Part contains the court's powers to encourage the parties to use alternative dispute resolution and to facilitate its use.

(2) The powers in this Part are subject to any powers given to the court by any other rule or practice direction or by any other enactment or any powers it may otherwise have.

Court's duty to consider alternative dispute resolution

3.2. The court must consider, at every stage in proceedings, whether alternative dispute resolution is appropriate.

When the court will adjourn proceedings or a hearing in proceedings

3.3.—(1) If the court considers that alternative dispute resolution is appropriate, the court may direct that the proceedings, or a hearing in the proceedings, be adjourned for such specified period as it considers appropriate—

(a) to enable the parties to obtain information and advice about alternative dispute resolution; and

(b) where the parties agree, to enable alternative dispute resolution to take place.

(2) The court may give directions under this rule on an application or of its own initiative.

(3) Where the court directs an adjournment under this rule, it will give directions about the timing and method by which the parties must tell the court if any of the issues in the proceedings have been resolved.

(4) If the parties do not tell the court if any of the issues have been resolved as directed under paragraph (3), the court will give such directions as to the management of the case as it considers appropriate.

(5) The court or court officer will—

(a) record the making of an order under this rule; and

(b) arrange for a copy of the order to be served as soon as practicable on the parties.

(6) Where the court proposes to exercise its powers of its own initiative, the procedure set out in rule 4.3(2) to (6) applies.

(By rule 4.1(7), any direction given under this rule may be varied or revoked.)

PRACTICE DIRECTION 3A – PRE-APPLICATION PROTOCOL FOR MEDIATION INFORMATION AND ASSESSMENT

This Practice Direction supplements FPR Part 3

[**Editors' note:** Form FM1 (which in family proceedings relevant to this PD and Pre-action Protocol must be completed and signed by the applicant or the applicant's solicitor) is not reproduced in **@eGlance**, but may be obtained from magistrates' courts, county courts or the High Court or online.]

1. Introduction

1.1 This Practice Direction applies where a person is considering applying for an order in family proceedings of a type specified in Annex B (referred to in this Direction as "relevant family proceedings").

1.2 Terms used in this Practice Direction and the accompanying Pre-action Protocol have the same meaning as in the FPR.

1.3 This Practice Direction is supplemented by the following Annexes:

(i) Annex A: The Pre-application Protocol ("the Protocol"), which sets out steps which the court will normally expect an applicant to follow before an application is made to the court in relevant family proceedings;

(ii) Annex B: Proceedings which are "relevant family proceedings" for the purposes of this Practice Direction; and

(iii) Annex C: Circumstances in which attendance at a Mediation Information and Assessment Meeting is not expected.

2. Aims

2.1 The purpose of this Practice Direction and the accompanying Protocol is to:

(a) supplement the court's powers in Part 3 of the FPR to encourage and facilitate the use of alternative dispute resolution;

(b) set out good practice to be followed by any person who is considering making an application to court for an order in relevant family proceedings; and

(c) ensure, as far as possible, that all parties have considered mediation as an alternative means of resolving their disputes.

3. Rationale

3.1 There is a general acknowledgement that an adversarial court process is not always best-suited to the resolution of family disputes, particularly private law disputes between parents relating to children, with such disputes often best resolved through discussion and agreement, where that can be managed safely and appropriately.

3.2 Litigants who seek public funding for certain types of family proceedings are (subject to some exceptions) already required to attend a meeting with a mediator as a pre-condition of receiving public funding.

3.3 There is growing recognition of the benefits of early information and advice about mediation and of the need for those wishing to make an application to court, whether publicly-funded or otherwise, to consider alternative means of resolving their disputes, as appropriate.

3.4 In private law proceedings relating to children, the court is actively involved in helping parties to explore ways of resolving their dispute. The Private Law Programme, set out in Practice Direction 12B, provides for a first hearing dispute resolution appointment ('FHDRA'), at which the judge, legal advisor or magistrates, accompanied by an officer from Cafcass (the Children and Family Court Advisory and Support Service), will discuss with parties both the nature of their dispute and whether it could be resolved by mediation or other alternative means and can give the parties information about services which may be available to assist them. The court should also have information obtained through safeguarding checks carried out by Cafcass, to ensure that any agreement between the parties, or any dispute resolution process selected, is in the interests of the child and safe for all concerned.

3.5 Against that background, it is likely to save court time and expense if the parties take steps to resolve their dispute without pursuing court proceedings. Parties will therefore be expected to explore the scope for resolving their dispute through mediation before embarking on the court process.

4. The Pre-application Protocol

4.1 To encourage this approach, all potential applicants for a court order in relevant family proceedings will be expected, before making their application, to have followed the steps set out in the Protocol. This requires a potential applicant, except in certain specified circumstances, to consider with a mediator whether the dispute may be capable of being resolved through mediation. The court will expect all applicants to have complied with the Protocol before commencing proceedings and (except where any of the circumstances in Annex C applies) will expect any respondent to have attended a Mediation Information and Assessment Meeting, if invited to do so. If court proceedings are taken, the court will wish to know at the first hearing whether mediation has been considered by the parties. In considering the conduct of any relevant family proceedings, the court will take into account any failure to comply with the Protocol and may refer the parties to a meeting with a mediator before the proceedings continue further.

4.2 Nothing in the Protocol is to be read as affecting the operation of the Private Law Programme, set out in Practice Direction 12B, or the role of the court at the first hearing in any relevant family proceedings.

Annex A: The Pre-application Protocol

1. This Protocol applies where a person ("the applicant") is considering making an application to the court for an order in relevant family proceedings.

2. Before an applicant makes an application to the court for an order in relevant family proceedings, the applicant (or the applicant's solicitor) should contact a family mediator to arrange for the applicant to attend an information meeting about family mediation and other forms of alternative dispute resolution (referred to in this Protocol as "a Mediation Information and Assessment Meeting").

3. An applicant is not expected to attend a Mediation Information and Assessment Meeting where any of the circumstances set out in Annex C applies.

4. Information on how to find a family mediator may be obtained from local family courts, from the Community Legal Advice Helpline – CLA Direct (0845 345 4345) or at www.direct.gov.uk.

5. The applicant (or the applicant's solicitor) should provide the mediator with contact details for the other party or parties to the dispute ("the respondent(s)"), so that the mediator can contact the respondent(s) to discuss that party's willingness and availability to attend a Mediation Information and Assessment Meeting.

6. The applicant should then attend a Mediation Information and Assessment Meeting arranged by the mediator. If the parties are willing to attend together, the meeting may be conducted jointly, but where necessary separate meetings may be held. If the applicant and respondent(s) do not attend a joint meeting, the mediator will invite the respondent(s) to a separate meeting unless any of the circumstances set out in Annex C applies.

7. A mediator who arranges a Mediation Information and Assessment Meeting with one or more parties to a dispute should consider with the party or parties concerned whether public funding may be available to meet the cost of the meeting and any subsequent mediation. Where none of the parties is eligible for, or wishes to seek, public funding, any charge made by the mediator for the Mediation Information and Assessment Meeting will be the responsibility of the party or parties attending, in accordance with any agreement made with the mediator.

8. If the applicant then makes an application to the court in respect of the dispute, the applicant should at the same time file a completed Family Mediation Information and Assessment Form (Form FM1) confirming attendance at a Mediation Information and Assessment Meeting or giving the reasons for not attending.

9. The Form FM1, must be completed and signed by the mediator, and counter-signed by the applicant or the applicant's solicitor, where either

(a) the applicant has attended a Mediation Information and Assessment Meeting; or

(b) the applicant has not attended a Mediation Information and Assessment Meeting and

    (i) the mediator is satisfied that mediation is not suitable because another party to the dispute is unwilling to attend a Mediation Information and Assessment Meeting and consider mediation;

    (ii) the mediator determines that the case is not suitable for a Mediation Information and Assessment Meeting; or

    (iii) a mediator has made a determination within the previous four months that the case is not suitable for a Mediation Information and Assessment Meeting or for mediation.

10. In all other circumstances, the Form FM1 must be completed and signed by the applicant or the applicant's solicitor.

11. The form may be obtained from magistrates' courts, county courts or the High Court or from www.direct.gov.uk.

Annex B: Proceedings which are "relevant family proceedings" for the purposes of this Practice Direction

1. Private law proceedings relating to children, except:

– proceedings for an enforcement order, a financial compensation order or an order under paragraph 9 or Part 2 of Schedule A1 to the Children Act 1989;

– any other proceedings for enforcement of an order made in private law proceedings; or

– where emergency proceedings have been brought in respect of the same child(ren) and have not been determined.

("Private law proceedings" and "emergency proceedings" are defined in Rule 12.2)

2. Proceedings for a financial remedy, except:

– Proceedings for an avoidance of disposition order or an order preventing a disposition;

– Proceedings for enforcement of any order made in financial remedy proceedings.

("Financial remedy" is defined in Rule 2.3(1) and "avoidance of disposition order" and "order preventing a disposition" are defined in Rule 9.3(1))

Annex C: A person considering making an application to the court in relevant family proceedings is not expected to attend a Mediation Information and Assessment Meeting before doing so if any of the following circumstances applies:

1. The mediator is satisfied that mediation is not suitable because another party to the dispute is unwilling to attend a Mediation Information and Assessment Meeting and consider mediation.

2. The mediator determines that the case is not suitable for a Mediation Information and Assessment Meeting.

3. A mediator has made a determination within the previous four months that the case is not suitable for a Mediation Information and Assessment Meeting or for mediation.

4. *Domestic abuse*

Any party has, to the applicant's knowledge, made an allegation of domestic Violence against another party and this has resulted in a police investigation or the issuing of civil proceedings for the protection of any party within the last 12 months.

5. *Bankruptcy*

The dispute concerns financial issues and the applicant or another party is bankrupt.

6. The parties are in agreement and there is no dispute to mediate.

7. The whereabouts of the other party are unknown to the applicant.

8. The prospective application is for an order in relevant family proceedings which are already in existence and are continuing.

9. The prospective application is to be made without notice to the other party.

10. Urgency

The prospective application is urgent, meaning:

(a) there is a risk to the life, liberty or physical safety of the applicant or his or her family or his or her home; or

(b) any delay caused by attending a Mediation Information and Assessment Meeting would cause a risk of significant harm to a child, a significant risk of a miscarriage of justice, unreasonable hardship to the applicant or irretrievable problems in dealing with the dispute (such as an irretrievable loss of significant evidence).

11. There is current social services involvement as a result of child protection concerns in respect of any child who would be the subject of the prospective application.

12. A child would be a party to the prospective application by virtue of Rule 12.3(1).

13. The applicant (or the applicant's solicitor) contacts three mediators within 15 miles of the applicant's home and none is able to conduct a Mediation Information and Assessment Meeting within 15 working days of the date of contact.

* * * * *

Part 4

Commentary on Part 4:
GENERAL CASE MANAGEMENT POWERS

Part 4 seeks to set out and specify the court's General Case Management Powers as compendiously as possible. Such a compendium is an innovation although the obligation to case-manage ancillary relief cases was, of course, explicitly mandated under the overriding objective applicable to such cases under the old FPR 1991 rule 2.51D(5) and (6). Moreover, under the former rule 2.61D(1) what was required was that *'the first appointment must be conducted with the objective of defining the issues and saving costs'*. (This is replicated in rule 9.15(1).) So the concept of detailed, specific, active case-management is nothing new.

Part 4 is the direct counterpart to CPR Part 3. There has been a deal of jurisprudence on the interpretation of the identical language used in CPR Part 3. Unsurprisingly, the dominant theme has been that in deciding whether, and if so how, to exercise any particular power the court must take into account the overriding objective to deal with cases justly: see, for example, *Sayers v Clarke Walker* [2002] 1 WLR 3095, CA.

General powers of management
Rule 4.1 should be regarded as a particularisation of the duty in rule 1.4(1) to further the overriding objective by actively managing cases. The specification of that duty in rule 1.4(2)(a) to (l) should be regarded as amplified and mechanized by Part 4, rather than being in any way in conflict with it because of the use of different language.

The list of powers set forth in rule 4.1(3) again contains almost nothing new, but their assembly in one place and the forcefulness of the language used will no doubt act as a spur to judges to achieve the greatest degree of efficiency possible. An interesting specific power is (e) *'to hold a hearing and receive evidence by telephone or by using any other method of direct oral communication'*. This would seem to suggest that hearings by Skype are acceptable, but probably not by Twitter. Note should be made of (o) which allows the court to *'take any other step or make any other order for*

the purpose of managing the case and furthering the overriding objective'.
Thus is the fertile imagination of the judge in question engaged.

Joinder

Perhaps curiously, the power to order joinder of a party is not listed in rule
4.1(3), although the question of who should be a party is explicitly specified
as an aspect of active case management in rule 1.4(2)(b)(ii). In the cases of
Gourisaria v Gourisaria [2010] EWCA Civ 1019 and *Goldstone v
Goldstone* [2011] EWCA Civ 39 the Court of Appeal has given
comprehensive guidance on the principles and procedure to be applied on
an application to join a third party to a financial order application. In the
latter case Hughes LJ considered the impact of these (then forthcoming)
FPR 2010 and stated at [71]:

> It should be recorded that with effect from 6 April 2011 the rules position will
> change with the introduction of the new Family Procedure Rules 2010 in place
> of the existing Family Proceedings Rules 1991. The 2010 rules remove the
> default application to family proceedings of the RSC. They are plainly
> modelled generally on the CPR, and include a re-statement (in slightly
> different terms) of the overriding objective, but the CPR continue not to apply
> directly to family proceedings. After 6 April 2011, the provisions of RSC O
> 11 and O 15 r 6 will therefore not be applicable to a case such as the present,
> and nor will CPR 19.2 or 6.36 and its associated Practice Direction. It appears
> that the new 2010 Rules contemplate that the joinder of parties be
> accomplished according to the broad discretionary case management powers
> contained in the overriding objective, viz: 1.4(2)(b)(ii) which makes clear that
> that objective includes the duty to decide an early stage who should be a party
> to the proceedings; see also 4.1(3)(o) and Part 18. Since the 2010 rules say
> nothing about the principles on which joinder of third parties (onshore or
> offshore) should be exercised, it may be that courts will have recourse by
> analogy to the principles contained in CPR 19.2 and 6.36 with its Practice
> Direction 6B. The final resolution of that issue must however await a decision
> on the point.

Altering time limits

By rule 4.1(3)(a) the court is empowered to extend or shorten time limits.
In *Roberts v Momentum Services Ltd* [2003] 1 WLR 1577 the Court of
Appeal considered the corresponding CPR rule 3.1(2)(a) and held that it
would rarely be appropriate to dismiss an application for an extension of
time on the ground that the claim is weak unless the court is able to
conclude that an application to strike out (under CPR rule 3.4, reflected in
FPR rule 4.4) or for summary judgment (under CPR Part 24) would
succeed.

The Court of Appeal has held in *Keen Philips (A Firm) v Field* [2007] 1
WLR 686 that the general powers to extend time periods are not cut down
by CPR rule 3.8 (FPR rule 4.5) which stipulates that sanctions are to have

effect unless the defaulting party obtains relief under CPR rule 3.9 (FPR rule 4.6: see **Sanctions and relief therefrom** *below*).

Consolidation

The Court is given power under FPR rule 4.1(3)(h) to consolidate claims. The effect of such an order is to combine two or more claims so that they will proceed thereafter as one claim. In financial order proceedings it is not uncommon for there to be parallel third party claims, for example by a company against a party – see for example *Ben Hashem v Ali Shayif and Radfan Ltd* [2009] 2 FLR 896.

We suggest that the Court should be wary of consolidating such claims; rather, the better direction should be for the claims to be heard together by the same judge sequentially as part of one overall hearing. The reason is that otherwise a direction or step specific to one claim becomes common to the other, for which it may be inappropriate.

Conditions

Rule 4.1(4) states that where the court makes an order it may make it subject to conditions (including a condition that a sum of money be paid into court), and may specify the consequence of failure to comply with the order or a condition. An interesting example of a condition being imposed under CPR rule 3.1(3) other than for a payment into court is *Price v Price* [2003] 3 All ER 311 where a dilatory personal injury claimant who had failed to supply particulars of claim for 15 months was granted an extension of time subject to the condition that he would only be allowed to rely in support of his claim for compensation on the medical evidence available as at the date of issue of his claim form.

Court acting on its own initiative

Rule 4.3 allows the court to exercise its powers of its own initiative (except where an enactment provides otherwise), and without a hearing. This power was always present, even if tacit and seldom used. Its express inclusion, with safeguards permitting such orders to be challenged, may prove to be significant. Perhaps more orders will be made proactively from the judge's desktop in pursuit of a fairer allocation of the court's resources.

Power to strike out a statement of case

Rule 4.4 contains the court's powers to strike out a statement of case. By rule 4.1(1) a statement of case is the whole, or part of, an application form or an answer. By rule 2.3 'application form' means 'a document in which the applicant states his intention to seek a court order other than in accordance with the Part 18 procedure', and by rule 7.12(8) an answer is the familiar (and still traditionally named) defence to an 'application for a matrimonial order' (previously known as a 'petition') for divorce, judicial separation or nullity.

Part 18 is the prescribed procedure (a) where the application is made in the course of existing proceedings; or (b) to start proceedings except where some other Part of the FPR prescribes the procedure to start proceedings; or (c) in connection with proceedings which have been concluded. For such applications the procedure stipulated by PD 18A is essentially summary (and may involve no hearing at all). See Commentary on Part 18 *below*. Therefore for such applications a strike-out procedure is unnecessary.

The strike-out procedure is reserved in effect for originating applications, whether for divorce, financial remedy applications (including what were previously known as applications for ancillary relief but which are now known as financial order applications), or private law children applications (public law applications and adoption and placement applications are excluded), and for appeals.

A strike-out procedure is relatively unfamiliar territory in ancillary relief, although not unknown (see, for example *P v P (Consent Order: Appeal Out of Time)* [2002] 1 FLR 743). The power remained to strike out a pleading (RSC Order 18, rule 19) and to strike out all or part of an affidavit on the ground that it was scandalous irrelevant or otherwise oppressive (RSC Order 41, rule 4). Under the former the power was restricted to situations where the pleading disclosed no reasonable cause of action or defence; or was scandalous, frivolous or vexatious; or may prejudice embarrass or delay the fair trial of the action; or was otherwise an abuse of the process of the court. It has been long established that only in 'plain and obvious cases' should recourse be had to this summary power (see *Hubbock v Wilkinson* [1899] 1 QB 86 per Lindley MR).

The new procedure is framed more widely (particularly in the accompanying explanatory PD 4A) and is given central prominence. It must be anticipated that its use will become frequent, if not commonplace, particularly having regard to the volume of uninformed and spurious applications made by litigants in person (in particular), a phenomenon that can only increase having regard to the Government's legal aid reform proposals.

The basic rule is not dissimilar to the old RSC Order 18, rule 19. Rule 4.4(1) provides that the Court may order a strike-out on the ground that that the statement of case (a) discloses no reasonable grounds for bringing or defending the application; or (b) that the statement of case is an abuse of the court's process or is otherwise likely to obstruct the just disposal of the proceedings; or (c) that there has been a failure to comply with a rule, practice direction or court order; or (d) in relation to applications for matrimonial and civil partnership orders and answers to such applications, that the parties to the proceedings consent. Section 2 of PD 4A gives interesting examples of each category. As to the first (statement of case discloses no reasonable cause of action) it cites situations where the case sets out no facts indicating what the application is about; or which is incoherent and makes no sense; or which fails to disclose any legally recognisable application against the respondent. An answer may fall within this category where it consists of a bare denial or otherwise sets out no coherent statement of facts. An application may fall within the second category (abuse of process) where it cannot be justified, for example because it is frivolous, scurrilous or obviously ill-founded. These examples are widely framed indeed.

It should be noted that under paras 3.1 to 3.5 and 4.1 to 4.5 of the PD a court officer can take a suspect application or answer which a party seeks to issue straight to a judge for immediate disposal with or without a hearing. Perhaps this will lead to a reduction in the volume of unmeritorious and/or nonsensical applications with which courts are increasingly plagued.

The authorities on the corresponding CPR rule 3.4 echo the words of the Master of the Rolls in 1899. As Clarke LJ put it in *Asiansky Television Ltd v Bayer Rosin* [2001] EWCA Civ 1792:

> it is necessary to concentrate on the intrinsic justice of a particular case ... It is important that the judge exercising his discretion should consider alternative possibilities short of striking out.

There have been authorities, both domestic and from Strasbourg, considering whether a strike out breaches the right of access to a court under ECHR Article 6(1). From the highwater mark of *Osman v UK* [2000] 29 EHRR 245, [1999] 1 FLR 193, where such breach was found, the position now appears to be that a court should not be discouraged by fear of breach of the Convention from summarily dismissing cases which have no real prospect of success.

Debarring orders

There have been civil cases where a party's litigation conduct has been so abysmal that he has been held to forfeit his right to a trial: see *Arrow Nominees Inc v Blackledge* [2000] 2 BCLC 167, CA where documents were forged in the disclosure process and perjured evidence given. It is hard (although not impossible), given the inquisitorial duty imposed on a court trying a financial order application, to see an equivalent approach being applied under the FPR. Such a step would be exceedingly rare, and probably confined to those situations where the *Hadkinson v Hadkinson* [1952] P 285 debarring principle is applied in respect of a contemnor. Even in gross cases the Court is much more likely to impose terms on participation rather than to debar the litigant: see, for example, *Mubarak v Mubarik (No 4)* [2004] 2 FLR 932 and *Mubarak v Mubarik (No 5) (Contempt in Failure to Pay Lump Sum: Standard of Proof)* [2007] 1 FLR 722.

A recent decision summarising the *Hadkinson* jurisprudence is *C v C (Appeal: Hadkinson Order)* [2010] EWHC 1656 (Fam), [2011] 1 FLR 434, where Eleanor King J stated:

When considering the *Hadkinson* criteria, I bear in mind the draconian nature of the *Hadkinson* order, that the power must be exercised judicially, sparingly and proportionately.

In that case the husband, who was in defiant contempt, had strict conditions imposed on his appeal (£1m was to be placed into a joint solicitors' account). A debarring order was not made (nor even sought).

A debarring order must be regarded as the ultimate nuclear option, and in the inquisitorial field of family law the words of Laddie J in *Re Swaptronics Ltd* [1998] All ER (D) 407, ChD at [20] are surely particularly apt:

> I can see no need for an additional power to prohibit a party who is obdurately in contempt, *by reason of his contempt,* from enforcing his civil rights or from defending himself against civil claims made against him. A person guilty of the most disgraceful and persistent crimes is not prevented by reason of those activities from enforcing or defending civil litigation. That is so even if he is continuing to threaten to commit a criminal act. If a persistent and serious criminal is allowed to litigate, why should a person in contempt of court be prevented from doing so? I can not see why it is necessary to treat him as a pariah because he has offended a court. It is all too easy for a court to be impressed by its own status. Sir Robert Megarry's *Miscellany-at-Law* records that in 1631 a litigant who threw a brickbat at a judge, but missed, had his right hand chopped off and nailed to the gibbet on which he was thereafter hanged in the presence of the court. I am not sure what would have happened to him had his aim been better. In any event, we have come a long way since then. The courts need powers of punishment with which to enforce their orders. The ones they have at present are adequate. They do not need a power which deprives a litigant of his right to litigate. Indeed it seems to me that were the courts to refuse to allow those in contempt access to the courts simply on the grounds that they are in contempt, they could well be acting in breach of the provisions of Article 6.1 of the European Convention on Human Rights which entitles everyone to the determination of his civil rights by means of a fair and public hearing before an independent and impartial tribunal. The 'everyone' in that Article is not subject to an exception in respect of people who are guilty of serious offences or contempt of court.

Other abusive applications

A plain instance where the power will be exercised is where the application in question is an attempt to re-litigate issues that have already been decided by a court of competent jurisdiction. The ancient rule in *Henderson v Henderson* (1843) 3 Hare 100, applies equally to domestic proceedings: see *Ganesmoorthy v Ganesmoorthy* [2003] 3 FCR 167.

There are many civil authorities on abusive applications justifying strike out which are of doubtful applicability to a court inquiring into the appropriate financial provision between spouses.

Sanctions and relief therefrom

Rules 4.5 and 4.6 are an innovation and are the direct counterpart of CPR rules 3.8 and 3.9. In a way they are statements of the obvious. A sanction imposed by a rule, practice direction or order is valid but a party in default may apply for relief. In deciding whether to grant relief the court must take into account the self-evident matters listed in rule 4.6(1). A number of cases under CPR rule 3.9 have emphasised that when considering an application for relief the court must systematically go through the list in that rule, but the list is not exhaustive: all the circumstances must be considered.

A swathe of the civil cases are concerned with the grant of relief from sanctions for failing to comply with an 'unless' order. It must be doubted whether in the inquisitorial field of financial applications an order should be made which debars a party from further participation: see the *Mubarak* decisions cited *above*, where conditions were imposed. Were equivalent orders to be made today the contemnor would be obliged to seek relief under rule 4.6 were he to seek to escape the effect of those conditions.

A refusal to grant relief from a debarring sanction will not contravene ECHR article 6(1) provided that it is proportionate and for a legitimate purpose: see *Momson v Azeez* [2009] EWCA Civ 202.

Rectification of errors of procedure

Until now family proceedings have not had the benefit of an equivalent to CPR rule 3.10. Under the old RSC there was, of course, the slip rule in Order 20, rule 11 permitting correction of clerical errors or slips in orders or judgments, as well as the very rarely used Order 20, rule 8 which permitted the court of its own motion to direct any document in the proceedings to be amended. The slip rule lives on in FPR rule 29.6.

Proceedings under the Inheritance (Provision for Family and Dependants) Act 1975 are subject to the CPR, and an example of the invocation of CPR rule 3.10 is *Hannigan v Hannigan* [2000] 2 FCR 650 where a widow had issued her claim on an obsolete form under the CCR rather than using the CPR Part 8 procedure. The claim was struck out but the Court of Appeal restored the claim, applying rule 3.10. Brooke LJ held that in deciding whether to exercise the discretion to rectify regard should be had to the matters set out in CPR rule 3.9 (mirrored in FPR rule 4.6).

Civil Restraint Orders (CRO)

FPR rule 4.8 and Practice Direction 4B specify the power of the court to make a CRO, and the procedure for and consequences of making such an order. It is a direct counterpart of CPR rule 3.11 and its associated PD which since 1 October 2004 have placed on a statutory footing the inherent jurisdiction of the court to prevent abuse of its process by vexatious litigants by making a *Grepe v Loam* (1887) 37 Ch D 168 order.

While such orders are unfamiliar territory in the world of application for financial orders, they are well known in children's cases. Section 91(14) of the Children Act 1989 provides the power to make an order preventing further applications in respect of a child without the leave of the court. In *Re P (Section 91(14) Guidelines) (Residence and Religious Heritage)* [1999] 2 FLR 573 Butler-Sloss LJ gave guidelines which sought to strike the delicate balance between the welfare of the child and the right of access of a litigant to the court. PD 4B emphasises that the powers of the court to make civil restraint orders are separate from and do not replace the powers given to the court by section 91(14).

PD 4A follows its CPR counterpart and specifies that the court may make a limited, extended or general CRO. Only a High Court Judge may make an extended or general CRO.

A limited order may be sought where a party has made two or more applications which are totally without merit. Where the court makes a limited CRO order, the party against whom the order is made will be restrained from making any further applications in the proceedings in which the order is made without first obtaining the permission of a judge identified in the order.

An extended order may be sought where a party has persistently made applications which are totally without merit. When the court makes an extended civil restraint order, the party against whom the order is made is restrained from making applications in any court concerning any matter involving or relating to or touching upon or leading to the proceedings in which the order is made without first obtaining the permission of a judge identified in the order.

A general order (which is the ultimate nuclear option) may be sought where the party against whom the order is made persists in making applications which are totally without merit, in circumstances where an extended civil restraint order would not be sufficient or appropriate. Where the court makes a general civil restraint order, the party against whom the order is made is restrained from making any application in any court without first obtaining the permission of a judge identified in the order.

In each instance there are rights to apply, with permission, to vary, discharge or appeal the order. The procedure for obtaining such an order is fully prescribed in the PD and should be carefully noted.

It remains to be seen how extensively use will be made of these powers.

PART 4: GENERAL CASE MANAGEMENT POWERS

The court's general powers of management

4.1.—(1) In this Part, "statement of case" means the whole or part of, an application form or answer.

(2) The list of powers in this rule is in addition to any powers given to

the court by any other rule or practice direction or by any other enactment or any powers it may otherwise have.

(3) Except where these rules provide otherwise, the court may—

(a) extend or shorten the time for compliance with any rule, practice direction or court order (even if an application for extension is made after the time for compliance has expired);

(b) make such order for disclosure and inspection, including specific disclosure of documents, as it thinks fit;

(c) adjourn or bring forward a hearing;

(d) require a party or a party's legal representative to attend the court;

(e) hold a hearing and receive evidence by telephone or by using any other method of direct oral communication;

(f) direct that part of any proceedings be dealt with as separate proceedings;

(g) stay the whole or part of any proceedings or judgment either generally or until a specified date or event;

(h) consolidate proceedings;

(i) hear two or more applications on the same occasion;

(j) direct a separate hearing of any issue;

(k) decide the order in which issues are to be heard;

(l) exclude an issue from consideration;

(m) dismiss or give a decision on an application after a decision on a preliminary issue;

(n) direct any party to file and serve an estimate of costs; and

(o) take any other step or make any other order for the purpose of managing the case and furthering the overriding objective.

(Rule 21.1 explains what is meant by disclosure and inspection.)

(4) When the court makes an order, it may—

(a) make it subject to conditions, including a condition to pay a sum of money into court; and

(b) specify the consequence of failure to comply with the order or a condition.

(5) Where the court gives directions it will take into account whether or not a party has complied with any relevant pre-action protocol.

(6) A power of the court under these rules to make an order includes a power to vary or revoke the order.

(7) Any provision in these rules—

(a) requiring or permitting directions to be given by the court is to be taken as including provision for such directions to be varied or revoked; and

(b) requiring or permitting a date to be set is to be taken as including provision for that date to be changed or cancelled.

(8) The court may not extend the period within which a section 89 order must be made.

Court officer's power to refer to the court

4.2. Where a step is to be taken by a court officer—

    (a) the court officer may consult the court before taking that step;

    (b) the step may be taken by the court instead of the court officer.

Court's power to make order of its own initiative

4.3.—(1) Except where an enactment provides otherwise, the court may exercise its powers on an application or of its own initiative.

(Part 18 sets out the procedure for making an application.)

(2) Where the court proposes to make an order of its own initiative—

    (a) it may give any person likely to be affected by the order an opportunity to make representations; and

    (b) where it does so it must specify the time by and the manner in which the representations must be made.

(3) Where the court proposes—

    (a) to make an order of its own initiative; and

    (b) to hold a hearing to decide whether to make the order,

it must give each party likely to be affected by the order at least 5 days' notice of the hearing.

(4) The court may make an order of its own initiative without hearing the parties or giving them an opportunity to make representations.

(5) Where the court has made an order under paragraph (4)—

    (a) a party affected by the order may apply to have it set aside, varied or stayed; and

    (b) the order must contain a statement of the right to make such an application.

(6) An application under paragraph (5)(a) must be made—

    (a) within such period as may be specified by the court; or

    (b) if the court does not specify a period, within 7 days beginning with the date on which the order was served on the party making the application.

(7) If the High Court or a county court of its own initiative strikes out a statement of case or dismisses an application (including an application for permission to appeal) and it considers that the application is totally without merit—

    (a) the court's order must record that fact; and

(b) the court must at the same time consider whether it is appropriate to make a civil restraint order.

Power to strike out a statement of case

4.4.—(1) Except in proceedings to which Parts 12 to 14 apply, the court may strike out a statement of case if it appears to the court—

(a) that the statement of case discloses no reasonable grounds for bringing or defending the application;

(b) that the statement of case is an abuse of the court's process or is otherwise likely to obstruct the just disposal of the proceedings;

(c) that there has been a failure to comply with a rule, practice direction or court order; or

(d) in relation to applications for matrimonial and civil partnership orders and answers to such applications, that the parties to the proceedings consent.

(2) When the court strikes out a statement of case it may make any consequential order it considers appropriate.

(3) Where—

(a) the court has struck out an applicant's statement of case;

(b) the applicant has been ordered to pay costs to the respondent; and

(c) before paying those costs, the applicant starts another application against the same respondent, arising out of facts which are the same or substantially the same as those relating to the application in which the statement of case was struck out,

the court may, on the application of the respondent, stay that other application until the costs of the first application have been paid.

(4) Paragraph (1) does not limit any other power of the court to strike out a statement of case.

(5) If the High Court or a county court strikes out an applicant's statement of case and it considers that the application is totally without merit—

(a) the court's order must record that fact; and

(b) the court must at the same time consider whether it is appropriate to make a civil restraint order.

Practice Direction 4A supplements FPR Part 4, rule 4.4 (Power to strike out a statement of case)

Sanctions have effect unless defaulting party obtains relief

4.5.—(1) Where a party has failed to comply with a rule, practice direction or court order, any sanction for failure to comply imposed by the rule, practice direction or court order has effect unless the party in default applies for and obtains relief from the sanction.

(Rule 4.6 sets out the circumstances which the court may consider on an application to grant relief from a sanction.)

(2) Where the sanction is the payment of costs, the party in default may only obtain relief by appealing against the order for costs.

(3) Where a rule, practice direction or court order—

(a) requires a party to do something within a specified time; and
(b) specifies the consequence of failure to comply,

the time for doing the act in question may not be extended by agreement between the parties.

Relief from sanctions

4.6.—(1) On an application for relief from any sanction imposed for a failure to comply with any rule, practice direction or court order the court will consider all the circumstances including—

(a) the interests of the administration of justice;
(b) whether the application for relief has been made promptly;
(c) whether the failure to comply was intentional;
(d) whether there is a good explanation for the failure;
(e) the extent to which the party in default has complied with other rules, practice directions, court orders and any relevant pre-action protocol;
(f) whether the failure to comply was caused by the party or the party's legal representative;
(g) whether the hearing date or the likely hearing date can still be met if relief is granted;
(h) the effect which the failure to comply had on each party; and
(i) the effect which the granting of relief would have on each party or a child whose interest the court considers relevant.

(2) An application for relief must be supported by evidence.

General power of the court to rectify matters where there has been an error of procedure

4.7. Where there has been an error of procedure such as a failure to comply with a rule or practice direction—

(a) the error does not invalidate any step taken in the proceedings unless the court so orders; and
(b) the court may make an order to remedy the error.

Power of the court to make civil restraint orders

4.8. Practice Direction 4B sets out—

(a) the circumstances in which the High Court or a county court has the power to make a civil restraint order against a party to proceedings;

(b) the procedure where a party applies for a civil restraint order against another party; and

(c) the consequences of the court making a civil restraint order.

PRACTICE DIRECTION 4A – STRIKING OUT A STATEMENT OF CASE

This Practice Direction supplements FPR Part 4, rule 4.4
(Power to strike out a statement of case)

Introduction

1.1 Rule 4.4 enables the court to strike out the whole or part of a statement of case which discloses no reasonable grounds for bringing or defending the application (rule 4.4(1)(a)), or which is an abuse of the process of the court or otherwise likely to obstruct the just disposal of the proceedings (rule 4.4(1)(b)). These powers may be exercised on an application by a party or on the court's own initiative.

1.2 This practice direction sets out the procedure a party should follow to make an application for an order under rule 4.4.

Examples of cases within the rule

2.1 The following are examples of cases where the court may conclude that an application falls within rule 4.4(1)(a)—

(a) those which set out no facts indicating what the application is about;

(b) those which are incoherent and make no sense;

(c) those which contain a coherent set of facts but those facts, even if true, do not disclose any legally recognisable application against the respondent.

2.2 An application may fall within rule 4.4(1)(b) where it cannot be justified, for example because it is frivolous, scurrilous or obviously ill-founded.

2.3 An answer may fall within rule 4.4(1)(a) where it consists of a bare denial or otherwise sets out no coherent statement of facts.

2.4 A party may believe that it can be shown without the need for a hearing that an opponent's case has no real prospect of success on the facts, or that the case is bound to succeed or fail, as the case may be, because of a point of law (including the construction of a document). In such a case the party concerned may make an application under rule 4.4.

2.5 The examples set out above are intended only as illustrations.

2.6 Where a rule, practice direction or order states 'shall be struck out or dismissed' or 'will be struck out or dismissed' this means that the order striking out or dismissing the proceedings will itself bring the proceedings to an end and that no further order of the court is required.

Applications which appear to fall within rule 4.4(1)(a) or (b)

3.1 A court officer who is asked to issue an application form but believes the application may fall within rule 4.4(1)(a) or (b) should issue the application form, but may then consult the court (under rule 4.2) before returning the form to the applicant or taking any other step to serve the respondent. The court may of its own initiative make an immediate order designed to ensure that the application is disposed of or (as the case may be) proceeds in a way that accords with the rules.

3.2 The court may allow the applicant a hearing before deciding whether to make such an order.

3.3 Orders the court may make include—

(a) an order that the application be stayed until further order;
(b) an order that the application form be retained by the court and not served until the stay is lifted;
(c) an order that no application by the applicant to lift the stay be heard unless the applicant files such further documents (for example a witness statement or an amended application form) as may be specified in the order.

3.4 Where the court makes any such order or, subsequently, an order lifting the stay, it may give directions about the service on the respondent of the order and any other documents on the court file.

3.5 The fact that the court allows an application referred to it by a court officer to proceed does not prejudice the right of any party to apply for any order against the applicant.

Answers which appear to fall within rule 4.4(1)(a) or (b)

4.1 A court officer may similarly consult the court about any document filed which purports to be an answer and which the officer believes may fall within rule 4.4 (1)(a) or (b).

4.2 If the court decides that the document falls within rule 4.4(1)(a) or (b) it may on its own initiative make an order striking it out. Where the court does so it may extend the time for the respondent to file a proper answer.

4.3 The court may allow the respondent a hearing before deciding whether to make such an order.

4.4 Alternatively the court may make an order requiring the respondent within a stated time to clarify the answer or to give additional information about it. The order may provide that the answer will be struck out if the respondent does not comply.

4.5 The fact that the court does not strike out an answer on its own initiative does not prejudice the right of the applicant to apply for any order against the respondent.

General provisions

5.1 The court may exercise its powers under rule 4.4(1)(a) or (b) on application by a party to the proceedings or on its own initiative at any time.

5.2 Where the court at a hearing strikes out all or part of a party's statement of case it may enter such judgment for the other party as that party appears entitled to.

Applications for orders under rule 4.4(1)

6.1 Attention is drawn to Part 18 (Procedure for Other Applications in Proceedings) and to the practice direction that supplements it. The practice direction requires all applications to be made as soon as possible.

6.2 While many applications under rule 4.4(1) can be made without evidence in support, the applicant should consider whether facts need to be proved and, if so, whether evidence in support should be filed and served.

* * * * *

PRACTICE DIRECTION 4B – CIVIL RESTRAINT ORDERS

This Practice Direction supplements FPR rule 4.8

Introduction

1.1 This practice direction applies where the court is considering whether to make—

(a) a limited civil restraint order;
(b) an extended civil restraint order; or
(c) a general civil restraint order,

against a party who has made applications which are totally without merit.

Rules 4.3(7), 4.4(5) and 18.13 provide that where a statement of case or application is struck out or dismissed and is totally without merit, the court order must specify that fact and the court must consider whether to make a civil restraint order. Rule 30.11(5) makes similar provision where the appeal court refuses an application for permission to appeal, strikes out an appellant's notice or dismisses an appeal.

The powers of the court to make civil restraint orders are separate from and do not replace the powers given to the court by section 91(14) of the Children Act 1989.

Limited civil restraint orders

2.1 A limited civil restraint order may be made by a judge of the High Court or a county court where a party has made 2 or more applications which are totally without merit.

2.2 Where the court makes a limited civil restraint order, the party against whom the order is made—

(a) will be restrained from making any further applications in the proceedings in which the order is made without first obtaining the permission of a judge identified in the order;

(b) may apply for amendment or discharge of the order, but only with the permission of a judge identified in the order; and

(c) may apply for permission to appeal the order and if permission is granted, may appeal the order.

2.3 Where a party who is subject to a limited civil restraint order—

(a) makes a further application in the proceedings in which the order is made without first obtaining the permission of a judge identified in the order, such application will automatically be dismissed—
    (i) without the judge having to make any further order; and
    (ii) without the need for the other party to respond to it; and

(b) repeatedly makes applications for permission pursuant to that order which are totally without merit, the court may direct that if the party makes any further application for permission which is totally without merit, the decision to dismiss the application will be final and there will be no right of appeal, unless the judge who refused permission grants permission to appeal.

2.4 A party who is subject to a limited civil restraint order may not make an application for permission under paragraphs 2.2(a) or (b) without first serving notice of the application on the other party in accordance with paragraph 2.5.

2.5 A notice under paragraph 2.4 must—

(a) set out the nature and grounds of the application; and

(b) provide the other party with at least 7 days within which to respond.

2.6 An application for permission under paragraphs 2.2(a) or (b)—

(a) must be made in writing;

(b) must include the other party's written response, if any, to the notice served under paragraph 2.4; and

(c) will be determined without a hearing.

2.7 An order under paragraph 2.3(b) may only be made by a High Court judge but not a district judge.

2.8 Where a party makes an application for permission under paragraphs

2.2(a) or (b) and permission is refused, any application for permission to appeal—

(a) must be made in writing; and
(b) will be determined without a hearing.

2.9 A limited civil restraint order—

(a) is limited to the particular proceedings in which it is made;
(b) will remain in effect for the duration of the proceedings in which it is made, unless the court orders otherwise; and
(c) must identify the judge or judges to whom an application for permission under paragraphs 2.2(a), 2.2(b) or 2.8 should be made.

Extended civil restraint orders
3.1 An extended civil restraint order may be made by a judge of the High Court but not a district judge where a party has persistently made applications which are totally without merit.

3.2 Unless the court orders otherwise, where the court makes an extended civil restraint order, the party against whom the order is made—

(a) will be restrained from making applications in any court concerning any matter involving or relating to or touching upon or leading to the proceedings in which the order is made without first obtaining the permission of a judge identified in the order;
(b) may apply for amendment or discharge of the order, but only with the permission of a judge identified in the order; and
(c) may apply for permission to appeal the order and if permission is granted, may appeal the order.

3.3 Where a party who is subject to an extended civil restraint order—

(a) makes an application in a court identified in the order concerning any matter involving or relating to or touching upon or leading to the proceedings in which the order is made without first obtaining the permission of a judge identified in the order, the application will automatically be struck out or dismissed—
  (i) without the judge having to make any further order; and
  (ii) without the need for the other party to respond to it; and
(b) repeatedly makes applications for permission pursuant to that order which are totally without merit, the court may direct that if the party makes any further application for permission which is totally without merit, the decision to dismiss the application will be final and there will be no right of appeal, unless the judge who refused permission grants permission to appeal.

3.4 A party who is subject to an extended civil restraint order may not make an application for permission under paragraphs 3.2(a) or (b) without first serving notice of the application on the other party in accordance with paragraph 3.5.

3.5 A notice under paragraph 3.4 must—

(a) set out the nature and grounds of the application; and
(b) provide the other party with at least 7 days within which to respond.

3.6 An application for permission under paragraphs 3.2(a) or (b)—

(a) must be made in writing;
(b) must include the other party's written response, if any, to the notice served under paragraph 3.4; and
(c) will be determined without a hearing.

3.7 An order under paragraph 3.3(b) may only be made by a High Court judge but not a district judge.

3.8 Where a party makes an application for permission under paragraphs 3.2(a) or (b) and permission is refused, any application for permission to appeal—

(a) must be made in writing; and
(b) will be determined without a hearing.

3.9 An extended civil restraint order—

(a) will be made for a specified period not exceeding 2 years;
(b) must identify the courts in which the party against whom the order is made is restrained from making applications; and
(c) must identify the judge or judges to whom an application for permission under paragraphs 3.2(a), 3.2(b) or 3.8 should be made.

3.10 The court may extend the duration of an extended civil restraint order, if it considers it appropriate to do so, but the duration of the order must not be extended for a period greater than 2 years on any given occasion.

General civil restraint orders

4.1 A general civil restraint order may be made by a judge of the High Court but not a district judge where, the party against whom the order is made persists in making applications which are totally without merit, in circumstances where an extended civil restraint order would not be sufficient or appropriate.

4.2 Unless the court otherwise orders, where the court makes a general civil restraint order, the party against whom the order is made—

(a) will be restrained from making any application in any court without first obtaining the permission of a judge identified in the order;
(b) may apply for amendment or discharge of the order, but only with the permission of a judge identified in the order; and

(c) may apply for permission to appeal the order and if permission is granted, may appeal the order.

4.3 Where a party who is subject to a general civil restraint order—

(a) makes an application in any court without first obtaining the permission of a judge identified in the order, the application will automatically be struck out or dismissed—

    (i) without the judge having to make any further order; and

    (ii) without the need for the other party to respond to it; and

(b) repeatedly makes applications for permission pursuant to that order which are totally without merit, the court may direct that if the party makes any further application for permission which is totally without merit, the decision to dismiss that application will be final and there will be no right of appeal, unless the judge who refused permission grants permission to appeal.

4.4 A party who is subject to a general civil restraint order may not make an application for permission under paragraphs 4.2(a) or (b) without first serving notice of the application on the other party in accordance with paragraph 4.5.

4.5 A notice under paragraph 4.4 must—

(a) set out the nature and grounds of the application; and

(b) provide the other party with at least 7 days within which to respond.

4.6 An application for permission under paragraphs 4.2(a) or (b)—

(a) must be made in writing;

(b) must include the other party's written response, if any, to the notice served under paragraph 4.4; and

(c) will be determined without a hearing.

4.7 An order under paragraph 4.3(b) may only be made by a High Court judge but not a district judge.

4.8 Where a party makes an application for permission under paragraphs 4.2(a) or (b) and permission is refused, any application for permission to appeal—

(a) must be made in writing; and

(b) will be determined without a hearing.

4.9 A general civil restraint order—

(a) will be made for a specified period not exceeding 2 years;

(b) must identify the courts in which the party against whom the order is made is restrained from making applications; and

(c) must identify the judge or judges to whom an application for permission under paragraphs 4.2(a), 4.2(b) or 4.8 should be made.

4.10 The court may extend the duration of a general civil restraint order, if it considers it appropriate to do so, but the duration of the order must not be extended for a period greater than 2 years on any given occasion.

General

5.1 The other party or parties to the proceedings may apply for any civil restraint order.

5.2 An application under paragraph 5.1 must be made using the procedure in Part 18 unless the court otherwise directs and the application must specify which type of civil restraint order is sought.

* * * * *

Part 5

Commentary on Part 5:
FORMS AND START OF PROCEEDINGS

Part 5 (Forms and Start of Proceedings) is the counterpart to CPR Part 4 (Forms) and Part 7 (How to Start Proceedings – the Claim Form). It is significantly less extensive than its CPR counterparts.

Rule 5.1 simply requires that for the purposes of financial applications the Forms referred to in a Practice Direction must be used in the cases to which they apply. Interestingly rule 5.1(2) allows a Form to be varied by the court or a party if the variation *is required by the circumstances of a particular case*, and rule 5.1(4) states that where the rules require a Form to be sent by the court or by a party for another party to use it must be sent without any variation *except such as is required by the circumstances of the particular case*. Although some degree of circumstantial flexibility is commendable, it no doubt would not extend so far as to permit a party to omit those parts of Form E which he or she might unilaterally decide were irrelevant to his or her case, or which he or she would prefer not to answer.

The Practice Direction

PD 5A lists the Forms to be used in family proceedings. Again, alteration to the Forms is allowed in that they may be modified *as the circumstances require*, provided that all essential information, especially information or guidance which the Form gives to the recipient, is included; or they may be expanded to include additional pages where that may be necessary, provided that any additional pages are also verified by a statement of truth.

The FPR 2010 Forms are not reproduced within *@eGlance*, but may be conveniently accessed, completed online and/or downloaded.

The Form E family

We are happy to announce additions to the Form E family: two offspring, more modestly proportioned but of course just as perfectly-Formed as their sire, each take the centre of their own defined stage.

Form E1 has been devised, and by virtue of PD 5A must be used, for all applications for a *financial remedy* other than an application for a *financial order* (i.e. other than old style ancillary relief: see the rule 2.3 definitions conveniently side by side at the Commentary on Part 2 *above*) and **other than** an application for an order under Part 3 of the Matrimonial and Family Proceedings Act 1984 (financial relief after foreign decree/dissolution etc.).

The archetypal Form E, well-known and loved and of itself the progenitor of some case-law (*GW v RW (Financial Provision: Departure from Equality)* [2003] 2 FLR 108; *W v W (Financial Provision: Form E)* [2004] 1 FLR 494) has been updated to incorporate references to the Pension Protection Fund and PPF compensation but otherwise survives the generational change to the new FPR unscathed, save in one curious detail (see *below*). Form E is henceforth to be used on applications for financial statements for a financial order or for financial relief after an overseas divorce/dissolution etc.) in the county or High Court.

Form E2 has been devised and is to be used on applications for a financial remedy in the magistrates' court.

Forms E1 and E2 will join the cast of the hardy and perennially popular favourite **Quantum and Quantum Pro**, the Form E and Ancillary Relief package.

Apart from some cosmetic changes to the front page Form E is unchanged. It had been mooted during the drafting and consultation process that Form E would no longer be sworn, but rather verified by a simple declaration of truth. Against that eventuality the old minatory statement printed on the front of the Form, warning of the possibility of criminal proceedings for perjury, needed to be changed, and the new Form E now states that:

> If you are found to have been deliberately untruthful, criminal proceedings may be brought against you for fraud under the Fraud Act 2006.

However, it was ultimately decided to maintain the requirement that the Form E should be sworn.

In *R v K* [2009] EWCA Crim 1640, [2010] 1 FLR 807 the Court of Appeal held that no privilege against incrimination was available when completing a Form E, but that no material thereby compulsorily disclosed could be used in a criminal prosecution, in that case for tax offences.

Other provisions

Para 2.1 of the PD deals with the Forms to be used for committal proceedings. Where the existing proceedings are matrimonial or civil partnership proceedings, or financial remedy proceedings, an application for committal must be commenced by filing a Form D11 under Part 18 in those proceedings.

Rule 5.3 states that proceedings are started when a court officer issues an application at the request of the applicant on the date entered in the application form by the court officer.

Transitional provisions

Part 36 sets out the transitional provisions which take effect from 6 April 2011.

The following paragraphs from the accompanying PD 36A relate to proceedings where originating process has been filed under 'the previous rules' (as set out in para 1.2):

Where the previous rules will normally apply

General principle

3.1 Where an initiating step has been taken in a case before 6th April 2011, in particular a step using forms or other documentation required by the previous rules, the case will proceed in the first instance under the previous rules. Where a party must take a step in response to something done by another party in accordance with the previous rules, that step must also be in accordance with those rules.

... but when proceedings come before a court (whether at a hearing or on paper) for the first time on or after 6th April 2011 then, as described in para 4.4 of PD 36A, the court may direct how the FPR are to apply to the proceedings and may disapply certain provisions of the FPR. The court may also give case management directions. The general presumption will be that the FPR will apply to the proceedings from then on unless the court directs or that PD provides otherwise.

Responding to old process

3.2 A party who is served with an old type of originating process (for example, an originating summons) on or after 6th April 2011 must respond in accordance with the previous rules and the instructions on any forms received.

Filing and service of pleadings where old process served

3.3 Where a case has been begun by an old type of originating process (whether served before or after 6th April 2011), filing and service of pleadings will continue according to the previous rules.

... and the following provisions set out (in relation to Forms) the general principles which will be required post-implementation of FPR 2010:

Where the FPR will normally apply

General principle

4.1 Where a new step is to be taken in any existing proceedings on or after 6th April 2011, it is to be taken under the FPR.

Part 1 (Overriding objective) to apply

4.2 ...

Issuing of application forms after the FPR come into force

4.3 (1) The general rule is that—

(a) only application forms under the FPR will be issued by the court on or after 6th April 2011; and

(b) if a request to issue an old type of form or originating process (summons, etc.) is received at the court on or after 6th April 2011, it will be returned unissued.

(2) By way of exception to the general rule, the court may in cases of urgency direct that the form or process is to be issued as if the request to issue it had been a request to issue an application form under the FPR and, if it does so, the court may make such supplementary directions as it considers appropriate.

It remains (as at the time of preparation of this Commentary) to be seen how generally available the new Forms will be at courts and to the professions and the public generally on and indeed before (for Forms are not always completed in a day) implementation date; and (perhaps concomitantly) what degree of urgency will be required before the court applies the moderating provisions of para 4.3(2).

PART 5: FORMS AND START OF PROCEEDINGS

Forms

5.1.—(1) Subject to rule 14.10(2) and (3), the forms referred to in a practice direction, shall be used in the cases to which they apply.

(2) A form may be varied by the court or a party if the variation is required by the circumstances of a particular case.

(3) A form must not be varied so as to leave out any information or guidance which the form gives to the recipient.

(4) Where these rules require a form to be sent by the court or by a party for another party to use, it must be sent without any variation except such as is required by the circumstances of the particular case.

Documents to be attached to a form

5.2. Subject to any rule or practice direction, unless the court directs otherwise, a form must have attached to it any documents which, in the form, are—

(a) stated to be required; or
(b) referred to.

Proceedings are started by issue of application form

5.3.—(1) Proceedings are started when a court officer issues an application at the request of the applicant.

(2) An application is issued on the date entered in the application form by the court officer.

(Rule 29.7 requires an application form to be authenticated with the stamp of the court when it is issued)

PRACTICE DIRECTION 5A – FORMS

This Practice Direction supplements FPR Part 5, rule 5.1 (Forms)

Scope and interpretation

1.1 This Practice Direction lists the forms to be used in family proceedings on or after 6th April 2011. Table 1 lists the forms against the part of the FPR to which they are relevant, and Table 2 lists the forms individually with their description.

1.2 The forms may be—

(a) modified as the circumstances require, provided that all essential information, especially information or guidance which the form gives to the recipient, is included;

(b) expanded to include additional pages where that may be necessary, provided that any additional pages are also verified by a statement of truth.

1.3 Any reference in family proceedings forms to a Part, rule or Practice Direction is to be read as a reference to the equivalent Part, rule or Practice Direction in the FPR and any reference to a Practice Direction in any CPR form used in family proceedings is to be read as a reference to the equivalent Practice Direction in the FPR.

Forms for committal applications

2.1 Rule 33.1(2) applies Part 50 of, and Schedules 1 and 2 to the CPR, in so far as they are relevant and with necessary modification (including the modification referred to in rule 33.7), to an application made in the High Court and a county court to enforce an order made in family proceedings. The CPR Practice Direction "RSC52 and CCR 29-Committal Applications" therefore applies with necessary modifications to the enforcement of such an order. The form to be used for a committal application is set out in that Practice Direction. Accordingly, where a committal application is made in existing proceedings, it must be commenced by filing an application notice under Part 18 in those proceedings (a form C2 where there are existing proceedings under the Children Act 1989, a form D11 where the existing proceedings are matrimonial or civil partnership proceedings, financial remedy proceedings and proceedings under Part 8 or otherwise a form FP2).Otherwise a committal application must be commenced by the issue of a Part 19 application notice (a form FP1).

Other Forms

3.1 Other forms may be authorised by practice directions.

Table 1: Index to forms

FPR Part	Forms
Part 3 Alternative Dispute Resolution (Family Mediation)	FM1
Part 6 Service	C9, D5, D89, FL415, FP6
Part 7 Matrimonial and Civil Partnership Proceedings	[non-financial]
Part 8 Miscellaneous Applications	D50, D50A, D50B, D50C, D50D, D50E, D50F, D50G, D50H, D50J, D50K
Part 8 Chapter 5 Applications for declarations	[non-financial]
Part 9 Applications for a Financial Remedy	Form A, Form A1, Form A2, Form B, Form E, Form E Notes, Form E1, Form E2, Form F, Form I, Form P, Form P1, Form P2, Form PPF, Form PPF1, Form PPF2
Part 10 Applications under Part 4 of the Family Law Act 1996	[non-financial]
Part 11 Applications under Part 4A of the Family Law Act 1996	[non-financial]
Part 12 Applications in respect of children	[non-financial]
Part 13 Applications under section 54 of Human Fertilisation and Embryology Act 2008	[non-financial]
Part 14 Adoption	[non-financial]
Part 15 Representation of Protected Parties	FP9
Part 16 Representation of children	FP9
Part 18 Applications in proceedings	C2, D11, FP2
Part 19 Alternative Procedure for applications	FP1, FP1A, FP1B, FP3, FP5
Part 22 Evidence	N285
Part 24 Witnesses	FP25
Part 26 Notification of change of solicitor	FP8
Part 28 Costs	D252, D254, D258,

	D258A, D258B, D258C, D259, Form H, Form H1, N260
Part 30 Appeals	N161, N161A, N161B, N162, N162A, N162, N164
Part 31 Registration of Orders under the Council Regulation, The Civil Partnership (Jurisdiction and Recognition of Judgements) Regulations 2005 and under the Hague Convention 1996	[non-financial]
Part 32 Registration and Enforcement of Orders	D151
Part 33 Enforcement	D62, N56, N323, N336, N337, N349, N379, N380
Part 34 Reciprocal Enforcement of Maintenance Orders	REMO 1, REMO 2

Table 2: List of Forms

[Editors' note: excluding those of no relevance in financial cases.]

Number	*Name*
D50	Notice of application on ground of failure to provide maintenance or for alteration of maintenance agreement during parties' lifetime
D50A	Notice of proceedings and acknowledgement of service – maintenance/property proceedings
D50B	Application under Section 17 of the Married Women's Property Act 1882/Section 67 of the Civil Partnership Act 2004/Application to transfer a tenancy under the Family Law Act 1996 Part IV
D50C	Application on ground of failure to provide maintenance
D50D	Application for alteration of maintenance agreement after the death of one of the parties
D50E	Application for permission to apply for financial relief after overseas divorce/dissolution etc under section 13 of the Matrimonial and Family Proceedings Act 1984 / paragraph 4 of Schedule 7 to the Civil Partnership Act 2004
D50F	Application for financial relief after overseas divorce etc under section 12 of the Matrimonial and Family Proceedings Act 1984/paragraph 4 to Schedule 7 to the Civil Partnership Act 2004
D50G	Application to prevent transactions intended to defeat prospective applications for financial relief

D50H	Application for alteration of maintenance agreement during parties lifetime
D50J	Application for an order preventing avoidance under section 32L of the Child Support Act 1991
D50K	Notice of Application for Enforcement by such method of enforcement as the court may consider appropriate
D62	Request for issue of Judgment Summons
D81	Statement of inform'n for a Consent Order in rel'n to a financial remedy
D89	Request for personal service by a court bailiff
D151	Application for registration of maintenance order in a magistrates' court
D180	Concerning judgements in matrimonial matters
D252	Notice of commencement of assessment of bill of costs.
D254	Request for a default costs certificate
D258	Request for a detailed assessment of hearing
D258A	Request for detailed assessment (legal aid only)
D258B	Request for detailed assessment (Costs payable out of a fund other than the Community Legal Service Fund)
D258C	Request for detailed assessment hearing pursuant to an order under Part III of the Solicitors Act 1974
D259	Notice of appeal against a detailed assessment (divorce)
FM1	Family Mediation Information and Assessment Form FM1
Form A	Notice of [intention to proceed with] an application for a financial order (**NOTE: This form should be used whether the applicant is proceeding with an application in the petition or making a free standing application**)
Form A1	Notice of [intention to proceed with] an application for a financial remedy (other than a financial order) in the county or high court
Form A2	Notice of [intention to proceed with] an application for a financial remedy in the magistrates court
Form B	Notice of an application to consider the financial position of the Respondent after the divorce/dissolution
Form E	Financial Statement for a financial order or for financial relief after an over seas divorce or dissolution etc
Form E Notes	Form E (Financial Statement for a financial order or for financial relief after an overseas divorce or dissolution etc) Notes for guidance
Form E1	Financial Statement for a financial remedy (other than a financial order or financial relief after an overseas divorce/dissolution etc) in the county or high court

Form E2	Financial Statement for a financial remedy in the magistrates court
Form F	Notice of allegation in proceedings for financial remedy
Form H	Estimate of costs (financial remedy)
Form H1	Statement of Costs (financial remedy)
Form I	Notice of request for periodical payments order at the same rate as order for interim maintenance pending outcome of proceeding
Form P	Pension inquiry form
Form P1	Pension sharing annex
Form P2	Pension attachment annex
Form PPF	Pension Protection Fund Inquiry Form
Form PPF 1	Pension Protection Fund sharing annex
Form PPF 2	Pension Protection Fund attachment annex
FP1	Application under Part 19 of the Family Procedure Rules 2010
FP1A	Application under Part 19 of the Family Procedure Rules 2010 Notes for applicant on completing the application (Form FP1)
FP1B	Application under Part 19 of the Family Procedure Rules 2010 Notes for respondent
FP2	Application notice Part 18 of the Family Procedure Rules 2010
FP3	Application for injunction (General form)
FP5	Acknowledgment of service Application under Part 19 of the Family Procedure Rules 2010
FP6	Certificate of service
FP8	Notice of change of solicitor
FP9	Certificate of suitability of litigation friend
FP25	Witness Summons
N56	Form for replying to an attachment of earnings application (statement of means)
N161	Appellant's Notice
N161A	Guidance Notes on Completing the Appellant's Notice
N161B	Important Notes for Respondents
N162	Respondent's Notice
N162A	Guidance Notes for Completing the Respondent's Notice
N163	Skeleton Argument
N164	Appellant's Notice
N260	Statement of costs (summary assessment)
N285	General Affidavit

N323	Request for Warrant of Execution
N336	Request and result of search in the attachment of earnings index
N337	Request for attachment of earnings order
N349	Application for a third party debt order
N379	Application for a charging order on land or property
N380	Application for charging order on securities
REMO 1	Notice of Registration

* * * * *

Part 6

Commentary on Part 6:
SERVICE

Under the old regime the rules about service were scattered throughout FPR 1991 and were neither uniform nor integrated. They are combined within and replaced by a single code which is directly modelled on CPR Part 6. *@eGlance* reproduces only those rules potentially relevant to applications for a financial remedy and thus omits Chapter 2 which deals with service of what used to be called petitions for divorce etc. (now called 'applications for a matrimonial order or civil partnership order').

Service in the United Kingdom

Chapter 3 of Part 6 deals with service in the United Kingdom of documents other than an application for a matrimonial order or civil partnership order. It is the direct counterpart of CPR Part 6 Chapter II. Practice Direction 6A supplements, amplifies and explains Chapter 3.

The rules and the accompanying PD 6A are largely self-explanatory, although the following points should be noted.

Chapter 3 applies to service in the United Kingdom, which means England and Wales, Scotland and Northern Island. It does not extend to the Isle of Man, the Channel Islands, or British Dependant Territories.

Rule 6.23(d) permits service by 'fax or other means of electronic communication in accordance with Practice Direction 6A'. Lest it be thought that this allows applications to be routinely served via Twitter, Facebook or SMS, reference should be made to PD 6A para 4.2 which provides that 'the party who is to be served [or his solicitor] must previously have indicated in writing to the party serving:

(i) that the party to be served [or his solicitor] is willing to accept service by fax or other electronic means; and

(ii) the fax number, e-mail address or other electronic identification to which it must be sent'.

Willingness to accept service electronically can be taken as read where a fax number or an e-mail address is set out on the writing paper of the solicitor acting for the party to be served but in the case of an e-mail address the writing paper must state that the e-mail address may be used for service.

Similarly willingness to accept service electronically is treated as given where a fax number, e-mail address or electronic identification is set out on a statement of case or an answer to a claim filed with the court. What 'electronic identification' signifies is not explained, but it is unlikely to be intended to refer to a Twitter or Facebook identity or page.

As is well known electronic documents (particularly those in scanned .pdf format) may be of vast size running to tens of megabytes. Thus PD 6A para 4.3 provides that where a party intends to serve a document by electronic means (other than by fax) that party must first ask the party who is to be served whether there are any limitations to the recipient's agreement to accept service by such means (for example, the format in which documents are to be sent and the maximum size of attachments that may be received).

It is very important that willingness to accept service is clearly established. Failure to do so will render electronic service invalid, and the court will not make an order under rule 6.36 dispensing with service in such circumstances: see *Kuenyehia v International Hospitals Group* [2006] EWCA Civ 21.

In relation to deemed willingness to accept service electronically a clear distinction must be drawn between a party and his solicitor. If a party acts in person willingness cannot be inferred from the appearance of his fax number on his stationery: *Molins plc v GD SpA* [2000] 1 WLR 1741, CA, nor (by parity of reasoning one presumes) from the appearance there of an email address or website.

By rule 6.34 if a document is served electronically by fax or email or 'other electronic transmission' (whatever that may be) completed or sent by 4.30 p.m. on a given business day it is deemed served that day; but if later than 4.30 p.m. it is deemed served on the following business day.

Rule 6.36 provides for the court to dispense with service of any document. Its counterpart is CPR rule 6.28. There is a deal of jurisprudence on the topic largely concerned with whether this rule can be used to circumvent statutory time limits for the commencement of claims. The answer is almost invariably 'no'. This is of potential relevance in only very few family cases, as such time limits do not generally apply – one example is section 4 of the Inheritance (Provision for Family and Dependants) Act 1975 which imposes a time limit for the commencement of proceedings of 6 months from the date when representation with respect to the deceased's estate is first taken out.

Service on protected parties

In a number of places there is reference to service on a protected party, to be read with Part 15 which concerns representation of protected parties. A protected party is defined in rule 2.3 as a party, or an intended party, who lacks capacity (within the meaning of the Mental Capacity Act 2005) to conduct proceedings. By section 2(1) of the Mental Capacity Act 2005 a person lacks capacity in relation to a matter if at the material time he is unable to make a decision for himself in relation to the matter because of an impairment of, or a disturbance in the functioning of, the mind or brain. Section 3 of the 2005 Act amplifies the meaning of 'inability to make decisions'.

Disclosure of addresses by government departments

The *Practice Direction (Disclosure of Addresses by Government Departments)* dated 20 July 1995, amending the Practice Direction of 13th February 1989, remains in force and is now numbered PD 6C.

Service out of the jurisdiction

Chapter 4 of Part 6 deals with service out of the jurisdiction. It is the direct counterpart of CPR Part 6, Chapter 3. Practice Direction 6B supplements, amplifies and explains Chapter 4.

The rules and the PD are largely self-explanatory, although the following points should be noted.

The rules permit service out of the jurisdiction in a variety of ways depending on the country or territory where service is to be effected. Permission from the court is not required for service out of the jurisdiction of any document required by FPR 2010 to be served: rule 6.41.

EU member states

For such countries, including in this instance Denmark (by separate agreement), service must be effected by the means prescribed in the EU Service Regulation. Here, the prescribed standard request form (to be found in English and the other EU languages in the Annex at the end of the Regulation) must be used and documents forwarded to the Senior Master of the QB Division for onward transmission.

Non-EU Hague Convention Countries

For those countries, other than EU member states, which are parties to the Hague Convention of 15 November 1965 on the Service Abroad of Judicial and Extrajudicial Documents in Civil or Commercial Matters service may be effected through the authority designated under the Hague Convention in respect of that country; or, if the law of that country permits (i) through the judicial authorities of that country; or (ii) through a British Consular authority in that country (rule 6.45(1)). The countries are Albania, Argentina, Australia, Belarus, Bosnia and Herzegovina, Canada, People's Republic of China, Croatia, Egypt, Iceland, India, Israel, Japan, South Korea, Mexico, Monaco, Norway, Russia, Serbia, Sri Lanka, Switzerland, FYR Macedonia, Turkey, Ukraine, United States of America and Venezuela.

Countries which are not party to the Hague Convention (but not those non-Hague countries referred to in the next paragraph)

Here, by rules 6.45(2) and 6.43(3)(b) service is to be effected if the law of that country so permits through the government of that country (where that government is willing to serve documents); or through a British Consular authority there; or by any method permitted by the law of that country.

Non-Hague Commonwealth States, the Isle of Man, the Channel Islands and British Dependent Territories

Here, by rule 6.45(3) service must be effected by any method permitted by rule 6.43(3) unless PD 6B provides otherwise. PD 6B para 4.1 draws attention to the requirement of certain Non-Hague Commonwealth States to serve instead in accordance with rule 6.45(1)(b)(i) through the country's judicial authorities. A list is available from the Foreign Process Section (Room E02) at the Royal Courts of Justice.

The Practice Direction 6B sets out in a Table the number of days allowed for acknowledging service to an application form or notice for every country and territory in the world. The shortest period is 21 days, for Scotland and Northern Ireland, all EU and some other European and Eurasian states.

The longest, no fewer than 41 days, is reserved uniquely for the Cocos (Keeling) Islands, a territory of Australia located in the Indian Ocean southwest of Christmas Island and approximately midway between Australia and Sri Lanka. According to Wikipedia the territory consists of two atolls and 27 coral islands, of which two, West Island and Home Island, are inhabited by a population totalling approximately 600. Queen Victoria granted the islands in perpetuity to the Clunies-Ross family in 1886. On 23 November 1955, the islands were transferred to Australian control under the Cocos (Keeling) Islands Act 1955 (an Australian Act) pursuant to the Cocos Islands Act 1955 (a UK Act). In the 1970s, the Australian government's dissatisfaction with the Clunies-Ross feudal style of rule of the island increased. In 1978, Australia forced the family to sell the islands for the sum of A$6.25m, using the threat of compulsory acquisition. By agreement, the family retained ownership of Oceania House, their home on the island. However, in 1983 the Australian government reneged on this agreement, and told John Clunies-Ross that he should leave the Cocos. The following year the High Court of Australia ruled that the expropriation of Oceania House was unlawful, but the Australian government ordered that no government business was to be granted to his shipping company, an action that contributed to his bankruptcy.

PART 6: SERVICE

CHAPTER 1: SCOPE OF THIS PART AND INTERPRETATION

Part 6 rules about service apply generally

6.1. This Part applies to the service of documents, except where—

(a) another Part, any other enactment or a practice direction makes a different provision; or
(b) the court directs otherwise.

Interpretation

6.2. In this Part "solicitor" includes any person who, for the purposes of the Legal Services Act 2007, is an authorised person in relation to an activity which constitutes the conduct of litigation (within the meaning of that Act).

CHAPTER 2: SERVICE OF THE APPLICATION FOR A MATRIMONIAL ORDER OR CIVIL PARTNERSHIP ORDER IN THE JURISDICTION

* * * * *

CHAPTER 3: SERVICE OF DOCUMENTS OTHER THAN AN APPLICATION FOR A MATRIMONIAL ORDER OR CIVIL PARTNERSHIP ORDER IN THE UNITED KINGDOM

Method of service

6.23. A document may be served by any of the following methods—

(a) personal service, in accordance with rule 6.25;
(b) first class post, document exchange or other service which provides for delivery on the next business day, in accordance with Practice Direction 6A;
(c) leaving it at a place specified in rule 6.26; or
(d) fax or other means of electronic communication in accordance with Practice Direction 6A.

(Rule 6.35 provides for the court to permit service by an alternative method or at an alternative place.)

Who is to serve

6.24.—(1) A party to proceedings will serve a document which that party has prepared, or which the court has prepared or issued on behalf of that party, except where—

(a) a rule or practice direction provides that the court will serve the document; or

(b) the court directs otherwise.

(2) Where a court officer is to serve a document, it is for the court to decide which method of service is to be used.

(3) Where the court officer is to serve a document prepared by a party, that party must provide a copy for the court and for each party to be served.

Personal service

6.25.—(1) Where required by another Part, any other enactment, a practice direction or a court order, a document must be served personally.

(2) In other cases, a document may be served personally except where the party to be served has given an address for service under rule 6.26(2)(a).

(3) A document is served personally on an individual by leaving it with that individual.

Address for service

6.26.—(1) A party to proceedings must give an address at which that party may be served with documents relating to those proceedings.

(2) Subject to paragraph (4), a party's address for service must be—

(a) the business address either within the United Kingdom or any other EEA state of a solicitor acting for the party to be served; or

(b) where there is no solicitor acting for the party to be served, an address within the United Kingdom at which the party resides or carries on business.

("EEA state" is defined in Schedule 1 to the Interpretation Act 1978)

(3) Where there is no solicitor acting for the party to be served and the party does not have an address within the United Kingdom at which that party resides or carries on business, the party must, subject to paragraph (4), give an address for service within the United Kingdom.

(4) A party who—

(a) has been served with an application for a matrimonial or civil partnership order outside the United Kingdom; and

(b) apart from acknowledging service of the application, does not take part in the proceedings, need not give an address for service within the United Kingdom.

(5) Any document to be served in proceedings must be sent, or transmitted to, or left at, the party's address for service unless it is to be served personally or the court orders otherwise.

(6) Where, in accordance with Practice Direction 6A, a party indicates or is deemed to have indicated that they will accept service by fax, the fax number given by that party must be at the address for service.

(7) Where a party indicates in accordance with Practice Direction 6A, that they will accept service by electronic means other than fax, the e-mail address or electronic identification given by that party will be deemed to be at the address for service.

(8) This rule does not apply where an order made by the court under rule 6.35 (service by an alternative method or at an alternative place) specifies where a document may be served.

Change of address for service

6.27. Where the address for service of a party changes, that party must give notice in writing of the change, as soon as it has taken place, to the court and every other party.

Service of an application form commencing proceedings on children and protected parties

6.28.—(1) This rule applies to the service of an application form commencing proceedings other than an application for a matrimonial or civil partnership order.

(2) An application form commencing proceedings which would otherwise be served on a child or protected party must be served—

(a) where the respondent is a child, in accordance with rule 6.14(1); and
(b) where the respondent is a protected party, in accordance with rule 6.14(2).

Service of other documents on or by children and protected parties where a litigation friend has been or will be appointed

6.29.—(1) This rule applies to—

(a) a protected party; or
(b) a child to whom the provisions of rule 16.5 and Chapter 5 of Part 16 apply (litigation friends).

(2) An application for an order appointing a litigation friend where a protected party or child has no litigation friend must be served in accordance with rule 15.8 or rule 16.13 as the case may be.

(3) Any other document which would otherwise be served on or by a child or protected party must be served on or by the litigation friend conducting the proceedings on behalf of the child or protected party.

Service on or by children where a children's guardian has been or will be appointed under rule 16.4

6.30.—(1) This rule applies to a child to whom the provisions of rule 16.4 and Chapter 7 apply.

(2) An application for an order appointing a children's guardian where a child has no children's guardian must be served in accordance with rule 16.26.

(3) Any other document which would otherwise be served on or by a child must be served on or by the children's guardian conducting the proceedings on behalf of the child.

Service on or by children where a children's guardian has been appointed under rule 16.3

6.31.—(1) This rule applies where a children's guardian has been appointed for a child in accordance with rule 16.3.

(2) Any document which would otherwise be served on the child must be served on—

    (a) the solicitor appointed by the court in accordance with section 41(3) of the 1989 Act; and

    (b) the children's guardian.

(3) Any document which would otherwise be served by the child must be served by—

    (a) the solicitor appointed by the court in accordance with section 41(3) of the 1989 Act or by the children's guardian; or

    (b) if no solicitor has been appointed as mentioned in paragraph (a), the children's guardian.

Supplementary provisions relating to service on children and protected parties

6.32.—(1) The court may direct that a document be served on a protected party or child or on some person other than a person upon whom it would be served under rules 6.28 to 6.31 above.

(2) The court may direct that, although a document has been sent or given to someone other than a person upon whom it should be served under rules 6.28 to 6.31 above, the document is to be treated as if it had been properly served.

(3) This rule and rules 6.28 to 6.31 do not apply where the court has made an order under rule 15.6 allowing a child to conduct proceedings without a children's guardian or litigation friend.

Supplementary provision relating to service on children

6.33.—(1) This rule applies to proceedings to which Part 12 applies.

(2) Where a rule requires—

(a) a document to be served on a party;

(b) a party to be notified of any matter; or

(c) a party to be supplied with a copy of a document,

in addition to the persons to be served in accordance with rules 6.28 to 6.32, the persons or bodies mentioned in paragraph (3) must be served, notified or supplied with a copy of a document, as applicable, unless the court directs otherwise.

(3) The persons or bodies referred to in paragraph (2) are—

(a) such of the following who are appointed in the proceedings—
　(i)　the children's guardian (if the children's guardian is not otherwise to be served);
　(ii)　the welfare officer;
　(iii) the children and family reporter;
　(iv) the officer of the Service, Welsh family proceedings officer or local authority officer acting under a duty referred to in rule 16.38; and

(b) a local authority preparing a report under section 14A(8) or (9) of the 1989 Act.

Deemed service

6.34. A document, other than an application for a matrimonial or civil partnership order, served in accordance with these rules or a practice direction is deemed to be served on the day shown in the following table—

Method of service	Deemed day of service
First class post (or other service which provides for delivery on the next business day)	The second day after it was posted, left with, delivered to or collected by the relevant service provider, provided that day is a business day; or, if not, the next business day after that day.
Document exchange	The second day after it was left with, delivered to or collected by the relevant service provider, provided that day is a business day; or, if not, the next business day after that day.
Delivering the document to or leaving it at a permitted address.	If it is delivered to or left at the permitted address on a business day before 4.30p.m., on that day; or in any other case, on the next business day after that day.
Fax.	If the transmission of the fax is completed on a business day before 4.30p.m., on that day; or, in any other case, the next business day after the day on which it was transmitted.
Other electronic method.	If the e-mail or other electronic transmission is sent on a business day before 4.30p.m., on that

	day; or in any other case, on the next business day after the day on which it was sent.
Personal service	If the document is served personally before 4.30p.m. on a business day, on that day; or, in any other case, on the next business day after that day.

(Practice Direction 6A contains examples of how the date of deemed service is calculated.)

Service by an alternative method or at an alternative place

6.35. Rule 6.19 applies to any document in proceedings as it applies to an application for a matrimonial or civil partnership order and reference to the respondent in that rule is modified accordingly.

Power to dispense with service

6.36. The court may dispense with the service of any document which is to be served in proceedings.

Certificate of service

6.37.—(1) Where a rule, practice direction or court order requires a certificate of service, the certificate must state the details set out in the following table—

Method of service	*Details to be certified*
Personal service.	Date and time of personal service and method of identifying the person served.
First class post, document exchange or other service which provides for delivery on the next business day.	Date of posting, leaving with, delivering to or collection by the relevant service provider.
Delivery of document to or leaving it at a permitted place.	Date and time when the document was delivered to or left at the permitted place.
Fax.	Date and time of completion of transmission.
Other electronic method	Date and time of sending the email or other electronic transmission.
Alternative method or place permitted by court	As required by the court.

(2) An applicant who is required to file a certificate of service of an application form must do so at or before the earlier of—

(a) the first directions appointment in; or

(b) the hearing of,

the proceedings unless a rule or practice direction provides otherwise.

(Rule 17.2 requires a certificate of service to contain a statement of truth.)

Notification of outcome of service by the court
6.38. Where—

- (a) a document to be served by a court officer is served by post or other service which provides for delivery on the next working day; and
- (b) the document is returned to the court,

the court officer will send notification to the party who requested service that the document has been returned.

Notification of non-service by bailiff
6.39. Where—

- (a) the bailiff is to serve a document; and
- (b) the bailiff is unable to serve it,

the court officer must send notification to the party who requested service.

Practice Direction 6A supplements FPR Part 6, Chapters 2 and 3 (Service within the jurisdiction)

CHAPTER 4: SERVICE OUT OF THE JURISDICTION

Scope and interpretation
6.40.—(1) This Chapter contains rules about—

- (a) service of application forms and other documents out of the jurisdiction; and
- (b) the procedure for service.

("Jurisdiction" is defined in rule 2.3.)

(2) In this Chapter—

"application form" includes an application notice;

"Commonwealth State" means a State listed in Schedule 3 to the British Nationality Act 1981;[(40)]and

"the Hague Convention" means the Convention on the service abroad of judicial and extra-judicial documents in civil or commercial matters signed at the Hague on November 15, 1965.

Permission to serve not required
6.41. Any document to be served for the purposes of these rules may be served out of the jurisdiction without the permission of the court.

Period for acknowledging service or responding to application where application is served out of the jurisdiction

6.42.— This rule applies where, under these rules, a party is required to file—

(a) an acknowledgment of service; or
(b) an answer to an application,

and sets out the time period for doing so where the application is served out of the jurisdiction.

(2) Where the applicant serves an application on a respondent in—

(a) Scotland or Northern Ireland; or
(b) a Member State or Hague Convention country within Europe,

the period for filing an acknowledgment of service or an answer to an application is 21 days after service of the application.

(3) Where the applicant serves an application on a respondent in a Hague Convention country outside Europe, the period for filing an acknowledgment of service or an answer to an application is 31 days after service of the application.

(4) Where the applicant serves an application on a respondent in a country not referred to in paragraphs (2) and (3), the period for filing an acknowledgment of service or an answer to an application is set out in Practice Direction 6B.

Method of service – general provisions

6.43.—(1) This rule contains general provisions about the method of service of an application for a matrimonial or civil partnership order, or other document, on a party out of the jurisdiction.

Where service is to be effected on a party in Scotland or Northern Ireland

(2) Where a party serves an application form or other document on a party in Scotland or Northern Ireland, it must be served by a method permitted by Chapter 2 (and references to "jurisdiction" in that Chapter are modified accordingly) or Chapter 3 of this Part and rule 6.26(5) applies.

Where service is to be effected on a respondent out of the United Kingdom

(3) Where the applicant wishes to serve an application form, or other document, on a respondent out of the United Kingdom, it may be served by any method—

(a) provided for by—
    (i) rule 6.44 (service in accordance with the Service Regulation);
    (ii) rule 6.45 (service through foreign governments, judicial authorities and British Consular authorities); or

(b) permitted by the law of the country in which it is to be served.

(4) Nothing in paragraph (3) or in any court order authorises or requires any person to do anything which is contrary to the law of the country where the application form, or other document, is to be served.

(Practice Direction 6A contains relevant provisions supplementing rule 6.43(2) in relation to the method of service on a party in Scotland or Northern Ireland.)

Service in accordance with the Service Regulation

6.44.—(1) This rule applies where the applicant wishes to serve the application form, or other document, in accordance with the Service Regulation.

(2) The applicant must file—

(a) the application form or other document;
(b) any translation; and
(c) any other documents required by the Service Regulation.

(3) When the applicant files the documents referred to in paragraph (2), the court officer will—

(a) seal, or otherwise authenticate with the stamp of the court, the copy of the application form; and
(b) forward the documents to the Senior Master of the Queen's Bench Division.

(The Service Regulation is annexed to Practice Direction 6B.)

(Article 20(1) of the Service Regulation provides that the Regulation prevails over other provisions contained in any other agreement or arrangement concluded by Member States.)

Service through foreign governments, judicial authorities and British Consular authorities

6.45.—(1) Where the applicant wishes to serve an application form, or other document, on a respondent in any country which is a party to the Hague Convention, it may be served—

(a) through the authority designated under the Hague Convention in respect of that country; or
(b) if the law of that country permits—
    (i) through the judicial authorities of that country; or
    (ii) through a British Consular authority in that country.

(2) Where the applicant wishes to serve an application form, or other document, on a respondent in any country which is not a party to the Hague Convention, it may be served, if the law of that country so permits—

(a) through the government of that country, where that government is willing to serve it; or

(b) through a British Consular authority in that country.

(3) Where the applicant wishes to serve an application form, or other document, in—

(a) any Commonwealth State which is not a party to the Hague Convention;

(b) the Isle of Man or the Channel Islands; or

(c) any British Overseas Territory,

the methods of service permitted by paragraphs (1)(b) and (2) are not available and the applicant or the applicant's agent must effect service on a respondent in accordance with rule 6.43 unless Practice Direction 6B provides otherwise.

(4) This rule does not apply where service is to be effected in accordance with the Service Regulation.

(A list of British overseas territories is reproduced in Practice Direction 6B.)

Procedure where service is to be through foreign governments, judicial authorities and British Consular authorities

6.46.—(1) This rule applies where the applicant wishes to serve an application form, or other document, under rule 6.45(1) or (2).

(2) Where this rule applies, the applicant must file—

(a) a request for service of the application form, or other document, by specifying one or more of the methods in rule 6.45(1) or (2);

(b) a copy of the application form or other document;

(c) any other documents or copies of documents required by Practice Direction 6B; and

(d) any translation required under rule 6.47.

(3) When the applicant files the documents specified in paragraph (2), the court officer will—

(a) seal, or otherwise authenticate with the stamp of the court, the copy of the application form or other document; and

(b) forward the documents to the Senior Master of the Queen's Bench Division.

(4) The Senior Master will send documents forwarded under this rule—

(a) where the application form, or other document, is being served through the authority designated under the Hague Convention, to that authority; or

(b) in any other case, to the Foreign and Commonwealth Office with a request that it arranges for the application form or other document to be served.

(5) An official certificate which—

(a) states that the method requested under paragraph (2)(a) has been performed and the date of such performance;

(b) states, where more than one method is requested under paragraph (2)(a), which method was used; and

(c) is made by—

    (i) a British Consular authority in the country where the method requested under paragraph (2)(a) was performed;

    (ii) the government or judicial authorities in that country; or

    (iii) the authority designated in respect of that country under the Hague Convention,

is evidence of the facts stated in the certificate.

(6) A document purporting to be an official certificate under paragraph (5) is to be treated as such a certificate, unless it is proved not to be.

Translation of application form or other document

6.47.—(1) Except where paragraphs (4) and (5) apply, every copy of the application form, or other document, filed under rule 6.45 (service through foreign governments, judicial authorities and British Consular authorities) must be accompanied by a translation of the application form or other document.

(2) The translation must be—

(a) in the official language of the country in which it is to be served; or

(b) if there is more than one official language of that country, in any official language which is appropriate to the place in the country where the application form or other document is to be served.

(3) Every translation filed under this rule must be accompanied by a statement by the person making it that it is a correct translation, and the statement must include that person's name, address and qualifications for making the translation.

(4) The applicant is not required to file a translation of the application form, or other document, filed under rule 6.45 where it is to be served in a country of which English is an official language.

(5) The applicant is not required to file a translation of the application form or other document filed under rule 6.45 where—

(a) the person on whom the document is to be served is able to read and understand English; and

(b) service of the document is to be effected directly on that person.

(This rule does not apply to service in accordance with the Service

Regulation which contains its own provisions about the translation of documents.)

Undertaking to be responsible for expenses of the Foreign and Commonwealth Office

6.48 Every request for service filed under rule 6.46 (procedure where service is to be through foreign governments, judicial authorities etc.) must contain an undertaking by the person making the request—

(a) to be responsible for all expenses incurred by the Foreign and Commonwealth Office or foreign judicial authority; and

(b) to pay those expenses to the Foreign and Commonwealth Office or foreign judicial authority on being informed of the amount.

Practice Direction 6B supplements FPR Part 6, Chapter 4 (Service out of the jurisdiction)

PRACTICE DIRECTION 6A – SERVICE WITHIN THE JURISDICTION

This Practice Direction Supplements FPR Part 6, Chapters 2 (applications for a matrimonial order or civil partnership order) and Chapter 3 (service of other documents)

Contents of this Practice Direction

* * * * *

General Provisions

Scope of this Practice Direction

1.1 This Practice Direction supplements the following provisions of Part 6—

(a) Chapter 2 (service of the application for a matrimonial order or civil partnership order in the jurisdiction);

(b) Chapter 3 (service of documents other than an application for a matrimonial order or civil partnership order in the United Kingdom); and

(c) rule 6.43(2) in relation to the method of service on a party in Scotland or Northern Ireland.

(Practice Direction B supplementing Part 6 contains provisions relevant to service on a party in Scotland or Northern Ireland, including provisions about the period for responding to an application notice.)

When service may be by document exchange

2.1 Subject to the provisions of rule 6.4 (which provides when an application for a matrimonial or civil partnership order may be served by document exchange) service by document exchange (DX) may take place only where—

(a) the address at which the party is to be served includes a numbered box at a DX; or

(b) the writing paper of the party who is to be served or of the solicitor acting for that party sets out a DX box number; and

(c) the party or the solicitor acting for that party has not indicated in writing that they are unwilling to accept service by DX.

How service is effected by post, an alternative service provider or DX

3.1 Service by post, DX or other service which provides for delivery on the next business day is effected by—

(a) placing the document in a post box;

(b) leaving the document with or delivering the document to the relevant service provider; or

(c) having the document collected by the relevant service provider.

Service by fax or other electronic means

4.1 This paragraph applies to the service of a document other than an application for a matrimonial or civil partnership order and documents in adoption proceedings and parental order proceedings.

4.2 Subject to the provisions of rule 6.26(6) and (7), where a document is to be served by fax or other electronic means—

    (a) the party who is to be served or the solicitor acting for that party must previously have indicated in writing to the party serving—

        (i) that the party to be served or the solicitor is willing to accept service by fax or other electronic means; and

        (ii) the fax number, e-mail address or other electronic identification to which it must be sent; and

    (b) the following are to be taken as sufficient written indications for the purposes of paragraph 4.2(a)—

        (i) a fax number set out on the writing paper of the solicitor acting for the party to be served;

        (ii) an e-mail address set out on the writing paper of the solicitor acting for the party to be served but only where it is stated that the e-mail address may be used for service; or

        (iii) a fax number, e-mail address or electronic identification set out on a statement of case or an answer to a claim filed with the court.

4.3 Where a party intends to serve a document by electronic means (other than by fax) that party must first ask the party who is to be served whether there are any limitations to the recipient's agreement to accept service by such means (for example, the format in which documents are to be sent and the maximum size of attachments that may be received).

4.4 Where a document is served by electronic means, the party serving the document need not in addition send or deliver a hard copy.

Service on members of the Regular Forces and United States Air Force

5.1 The provisions that apply to service on members of the regular forces (within the meaning of the Armed Forces Act 2006) and members of the United States Air Force are annexed to this practice direction.

Application for an order for service by an alternative method or at an alternative place

6.1 An application in the High Court or a county court for an order under rule 6.19 may be made without notice.

6.2 Where an application for an order under rule 6.19 is made before the document is served, the application must be supported by evidence stating—

    (a) the reason why an order is sought;

    (b) what alternative method or place is proposed; and

    (c) why the applicant believes that the document is likely to reach the person to be served by the method or at the place proposed.

6.3 Where the application for an order is made after the applicant has taken steps to bring the document to the attention of the person to be served by an alternative method or at an alternative place, the application must be supported by evidence stating—

(a) the reason why the order is sought;

(b) what alternative method or alternative place was used;

(c) when the alternative method or place was used; and

(d) why the applicant believes that the document is likely to have reached the person to be served by the alternative method or at the alternative place.

6.4 Examples—

(a) an application to serve by posting or delivering to an address of a person who knows the other party must be supported by evidence that if posted or delivered to that address, the document is likely to be brought to the attention of the other party;

(b) an application to serve by sending a SMS text message or leaving a voicemail message at a particular telephone number saying where the document is must be accompanied by evidence that the person serving the document has taken, or will take, appropriate steps to ensure that the party being served is using that telephone number and is likely to receive the message.

Applications for an order to dispense with service

7.1 An application in the High Court or a county court for an order under rule 6.36 (power to dispense with service) may be made without notice.

Deemed service of a document other than an application for a matrimonial or civil partnership order

8.1 Rule 6.34 contains provisions about deemed service of a document other than an application for a matrimonial or civil partnership order. Examples of how deemed service is calculated are set out below.

Example 1

8.2 Where the document is posted (by first class post) on a Monday (a business day), the day of deemed service is the following Wednesday (a business day).

Example 2

8.3 Where the document is left in a numbered box at the DX on a Friday (a business day), the day of deemed service is the following Monday (a business day).

Example 3

8.4 Where the document is sent by fax on a Saturday and the transmission of that fax is completed by 4.30 p.m. on that day, the day of deemed service is the following Monday (a business day).

Example 4

8.5 Where the document is served personally before 1.30 p.m on a Sunday, the day of deemed service is the next day (Monday, a business day).

Example 5
8.6 Where the document is delivered to a permitted address after 4.30 p.m. on the Thursday (a business day) before Good Friday, the day of deemed service is the following Tuesday (a business day) as the Monday is a bank holiday.

Example 6
8.7 Where the document is posted (by first class post) on a bank holiday Monday, the day of deemed service is the following Wednesday (a business day).

Service of application on children and protected parties
9.1 Rule 16.14(1) and (2) are applied to service of an application form (other than an application for a matrimonial or civil partnership order) commencing proceedings on children and protected parties by rule 6.28. Rule 6.14(7) makes provision as to how an application form must be served where the respondent is a child or protected party. A document served in accordance with rule 6.14(7) must be endorsed with the following notice which is set out in Form D5—

Important Notice

The contents or purport of this document are to be communicated to the Respondent

[or as the case may be], [full name of Respondent]

if s/he is over 16 [add if the person to be served lacks capacity within the meaning of the Mental Capacity Act 2005 to conduct the proceedings] unless you are satisfied [after consultation with the responsible medical officer within the meaning of the Mental Health Act 1983 or, if s/he is not liable to be detained or subject to guardianship under that Act, his/her medical attendant]* that communication will be detrimental to his/her mental condition].

Provisions relating to applications for matrimonial and civil partnership orders

* * * * *

Annex

Service on Members of the Regular Forces
1. The following information is for litigants and legal representatives who wish to serve legal documents in civil proceedings in the courts of England and Wales on parties to the proceedings who are (or who, at the material time, were) members of the regular forces (as defined in the Armed Forces Act 2006).

2. The proceedings may take place in the county court or the High Court, and the documents to be served may be claim forms, interim application notices and pre-action application notices. Proceedings for divorce or maintenance and proceedings in the Family Courts generally are subject to special rules as to service which are explained in a practice direction issued by the Senior District Judge of the Principal Registry on 26 June 1979.

(Now see *Practice Direction 1 Maintenance Orders: Service Personnel: 2 Disclosure of Addresses* (1995) 2 FLR 813.)

3. In this Annex, the person wishing to effect service is referred to as the 'claimant' and the member of the regular forces to be served is referred to as 'the member'; the expression 'overseas' means outside the United Kingdom.

Enquiries as to address

4. As a first step, the claimant's legal representative will need to find out where the member is serving, if this is not already known. For this purpose the claimant's legal representative should write to the appropriate officer of the Ministry of Defence as specified in paragraph 10 below.

5. The letter of enquiry should in every case show that the writer is a legal representative and that the enquiry is made solely with a view to the service of legal documents in civil proceedings.

6. In all cases the letter must give the full name, service number, rank or rate, and Ship, Arm or Trade, Regiment or Corps and Unit or as much of this information as is available. Failure to quote the service number and the rank or rate may result either in failure to identify the member or in considerable delay.

7. The letter must contain an undertaking by the legal representative that, if the address is given, it will be used solely for the purpose of issuing and serving documents in the proceedings and that so far as is possible the legal representative will disclose the address only to the court and not to the claimant or to any other person or body. A legal representative in the service of a public authority or private company must undertake that the address will be used solely for the purpose of issuing and serving documents in the proceedings and that the address will not be disclosed so far as is possible to any other part of the legal representative's employing organisation or to any other person but only to the court. Normally on receipt of the required information and undertaking the appropriate office will give the service address.

8. If the legal representative does not give the undertaking, the only information that will be given is whether the member is at that time serving in England or Wales, Scotland, Northern Ireland or overseas.

9. It should be noted that a member's address which ends with a British Forces Post Office address and reference (BFPO) will nearly always indicate that the member is serving overseas.

10. The letter of enquiry should be addressed as follows—

(a) Royal Navy and Royal Marine Officers, Ratings and Other Ranks
Director Naval Personnel
Fleet Headquarters
MP 3.1
Leach Building
Whale Island
Portsmouth
Hampshire
PO2 8BY

(b) Army Officers and other Ranks—
Army Personnel Centre
Disclosures 1
MP 520
Kentigern House
65 Brown Street
Glasgow
G2 8EX

(c) Royal Air Force Officers and Other Ranks—
Manning 22E
RAF Disclosures
Room 221B
Trenchard Hall
RAF Cranwell
Sleaford
Lincolnshire
NG34 8HB

Assistance in serving documents on members
11. Once the claimant's legal representative has ascertained the member's address, the legal representative may use that address as the address for service by post, in cases where this method of service is allowed by the Civil Procedure Rules. There are, however, some situations in which service of the proceedings, whether in the High Court or in the county court, must be effected personally; in these cases an appointment will have to be sought, through the Commanding Officer of the Unit, Establishment or Ship concerned, for the purpose of effecting service. The procedure for obtaining an appointment is described below, and it applies whether personal service is to be effected by the claimant's legal representative or the legal representative's agent or by a court bailiff, or, in the case of proceedings served overseas (with the leave of the court) through the British Consul or the foreign judicial authority.

12. The procedure for obtaining an appointment to effect personal service is by application to the Commanding Officer of the Unit, Establishment or Ship in which the member is serving. The Commanding

Officer may grant permission for the document server to enter the Unit, Establishment or Ship but if this is not appropriate the Commanding Officer may offer arrangements for the member to attend at a place in the vicinity of the Unit, Establishment or Ship in order that the member may be served. If suitable arrangements cannot be made the legal representative will have evidence that personal service is impracticable, which may be useful in an application for service by an alternative method or at an alternative place.

General

13. Subject to the procedure outlined in paragraphs 11 and 12, there are no special arrangements to assist in the service of legal documents when a member is outside the United Kingdom. The appropriate office will, however, give an approximate date when the member is likely to return to the United Kingdom.

14. It sometimes happens that a member has left the regular forces by the time an enquiry as to address is made. If the claimant's legal representative confirms that the proceedings result from an occurrence when the member was in the regular forces and the legal representative gives the undertaking referred to in paragraph 7, the last known private address after discharge will normally be provided. In no other case, however, will the Ministry of Defence disclose the private address of a member of the regular forces.

Service on Members of United States Air Force

15. In addition to the information contained in the memorandum of 26 July 1979, and after some doubts having been expressed as to the correct procedure to be followed by persons having civil claims against members of the United States Air Force in England and Wales, the Lord Chancellor's Office (as it was then) issued the following notes for guidance with the approval of the appropriate United States authorities.

16. Instructions have been issued by the United States authorities to the commanding officers of all their units in England and Wales that every facility is to be given for the service of documents in civil proceedings on members of the United States Air Force. The proper course to be followed by a creditor or other person having a claim against a member of the United States Air Force is for that person to communicate with the commanding officer or, where the unit concerned has a legal officer, with the legal officer of the defendant's unit requesting the provision of facilities for the service of documents on the defendant. It is not possible for the United States authorities to act as arbitrators when a civil claim is made against a member of their forces. It is, therefore, essential that the claim should either be admitted by the defendant or judgment should be obtained on it, whether in the High Court or a county court. If a claim has been admitted or judgment has been obtained and the claimant has failed to obtain satisfaction within a reasonable period, the claimant's proper course is then

to write to: Office of the Staff Judge Advocate, Headquarters, Third Air Force, R.A.F. Mildenhall, Suffolk, enclosing a copy of the defendant's written admission of the claim or, as the case may be, a copy of the judgment. Steps will then be taken by the Staff Judge Advocate to ensure that the matter is brought to the defendant's attention with a view to prompt satisfaction of the claim.

* * * * *

PRACTICE DIRECTION 6B – SERVICE OUT OF THE JURISDICTION

This Practice Direction Supplements FPR Part 6, Chapter 4

Contents of this Practice Direction

Scope of this Practice Direction

1.1 This Practice Direction supplements Chapter 4 (service out of the jurisdiction) of Part 6.

(Practice Direction 6A contains relevant provisions supplementing rule 6.43(2) in relation to the method of service on a party in Scotland or Northern Ireland.)

Service in other Member States of the European Union

2.1 Where service is to be effected in another Member of State of the European Union, the Service Regulation applies.

2.2 The Service Regulation is Regulation (EC) No. 1393/2007 of the European Parliament and of the Council of 13 November 2007 on the service in the Member States of judicial and extrajudicial documents in civil or commercial matters (service of documents), and repealing Council Regulation (EC) no. 1348/2000, as amended from time to time and as applied by the Agreement made on 19 October 2005 between the European

Community and the Kingdom of Denmark on the service of judicial and extrajudicial documents in civil and commercial matters.

2.3 The Service Regulation is annexed to this Practice Direction. (Article 20(1) of the Service Regulation provides that the Regulation prevails over other provisions contained in bilateral or multilateral agreements or arrangements concluded by the Member of States and in particular Article IV of the protocol to the Brussels Convention of 1968 and the Hague Convention of 15 November 1965)

Documents to be filed under rule 6.46(2)

3.1 A duplicate of—

(a) the application form or other document to be served under rule 6.45(1) or (2);
(b) any documents accompanying the application or other document referred to in paragraph (a); and
(c) any translation required by rule 6.47;

must be provided for each party to be served out of the jurisdiction, together with forms for responding to the application.

3.2 Some countries require legalisation of the document to be served and some require a formal letter of request which must be signed by the Senior Master. Any queries on this should be addressed to the Foreign Process Section (Room E02) at the Royal Courts of Justice.

Service in a Commonwealth State or British Overseas Territory

4.1 The judicial authorities of certain Commonwealth States which are not a party to the Hague Convention require service to be in accordance with rule 6.45(1)(b)(i) and not 6.45(3). A list of such countries can be obtained from the Foreign Process Section (Room E02) at the Royal Courts of Justice.

4.2 The list of British overseas territories is contained in Schedule 6 to the British Nationality Act 1981. For ease of reference these are—

(a) Anguilla;
(b) Bermuda;
(c) British Antarctic Territory;
(d) British Indian Ocean Territory;
(e) Cayman Islands;
(f) Falkland Islands;
(g) Gibraltar;
(h) Montserrat;
(i) Pitcairn, Henderson, Ducie and Oeno Islands;
(j) St. Helena, Ascension and Tristan da Cunha;
(k) South Georgia and the South Sandwich Islands;
(l) Sovereign Base Areas of Akrotiri and Dhekelia;

(m) Turks and Caicos Islands;
(n) Virgin Islands.

Period for responding to an application form
5.1 Where rule 6.42 applies, the period within which the respondent must file an acknowledgment of service or an answer to the application is the number of days listed in the Table after service of the application.

5.2 Where an application is served out of the jurisdiction any statement as to the period for responding to the claim contained in any of the forms required by the Family Procedure Rules to accompany the application must specify the period prescribed under rule 6.42.

Service of application notices and orders
6.1 The provisions of Chapter 4 of Part 6 (special provisions about service out of the jurisdiction) also apply to service out of the jurisdiction of an application notice or order.

6.2 Where an application notice is to be served out of the jurisdiction in accordance with Chapter 4 of Part 6 the court must have regard to the country in which the application notice is to be served in setting the date for the hearing of the application and giving any direction about service of the respondent's evidence.

Period for responding to an application notice
7.1 Where an application notice or order is served out of the jurisdiction, the period for responding is 7 days less than the number of days listed in the Table.

Further information
8.1 Further information concerning service out of the jurisdiction can be obtained from the Foreign Process Section, Room E02, Royal Courts of Justice, Strand, London WC2A 2LL (telephone 020 7947 6691).

TABLE

Place or country	Number of days
Afghanistan	23
Albania	25
Algeria	22
Andorra	21
Angola	22
Anguilla	31
Antigua and Barbuda	23
Antilles (Netherlands)	31
Argentina	22
Armenia	21
Ascension Island	31
Australia	25
Austria	21
Azerbaijan	22
Azores	23
Bahamas	22
Bahrain	22
Balearic Islands	21
Bangladesh	23
Barbados	23
Belarus	21

Belgium	21	Costa Rica	23
Belize	23	Croatia	21
Benin	25	Cuba	24
Bermuda	31	Cyprus	31
Bhutan	28	Czech Republic	21
Bolivia	23	Denmark	21
Bosnia and Herzegovina	21	Djibouti	22
Botswana	23	Dominica	23
Brazil	22	Dominican Republic	23
British Virgin Islands	31	East Timor	25
Brunei	25	Ecuador	22
Bulgaria	23	Egypt	22
Burkina Faso	23	El Salvador	25
Burma	23	Equatorial Guinea	23
Burundi	22	Eritrea	22
Cambodia	28	Estonia	21
Cameroon	22	Ethiopia	22
Canada	22	Falkland Islands and	31
Canary Islands	22	Dependencies	
Cape Verde	25	Faroe Islands	31
Caroline Islands	31	Fiji	23
Cayman Islands	31	Finland	24
Central African Republic	25	France	21
Chad	25	French Guyana	31
Chile	22	French Polynesia	31
China	24	French West Indies	31
China (Hong Kong)	31	Gabon	25
China (Macau)	31	Gambia	22
China (Taiwan)	23	Georgia	21
China (Tibet)	34	Germany	21
Christmas Island	27	Ghana	22
Cocos (Keeling) Islands	41	Gibraltar	31
Colombia	22	Greece	21
Comoros	23	Greenland	31
Congo (formerly	25	Grenada	24
Congo Brazzaville		Guatemala	24
or French Congo)		Guernsey	21
Congo (Democratic	25	Guinea	22
Republic)		Guinea-Bissau	22
Corsica	21	Guyana	22

Haiti	23	Malaysia	24
Holland (Netherlands)	21	Maldives	26
Honduras	24	Mali	25
Hungary	22	Malta	21
Iceland	22	Mariana Islands	26
India	23	Marshall Islands	32
Indonesia	22	Mauritania	23
Iran	22	Mauritius	22
Iraq	22	Mexico	23
Ireland (Republic of)	21	Micronesia	23
Ireland (Northern)	21	Moldova	21
Isle of Man	21	Monaco	21
Israel	22	Mongolia	24
Italy	21	Montenegro	21
Ivory Coast	22	Montserrat	31
Jamaica	22	Morocco	22
Japan	23	Mozambique	23
Jersey	21	Namibia	23
Jordan	23	Nauru	36
Kazakhstan	21	Nepal	23
Kenya	22	Netherlands	21
Kiribati	23	Nevis	24
Korea (North)	28	New Caledonia	31
Korea (South)	24	New Zealand	26
Kosovo	21	New Zealand Island Territories	50
Kuwait	22	Nicaragua	24
Kyrgyzstan	21	Niger (Republic of)	25
Laos	30	Nigeria	22
Latvia	21	Norfolk Island	31
Lebanon	22	Norway	21
Lesotho	23	Oman (Sultanate of)	22
Liberia	22	Pakistan	23
Libya	21	Palau	23
Liechtenstein	21	Panama	26
Lithuania	21	Papua New Guinea	26
Luxembourg	21	Paraguay	22
Macedonia	21	Peru	22
Madagascar	23	Philippines	23
Madeira	31		
Malawi	23		

Pitcairn, Henderson, Ducie and Oeno Islands	31	South Shetlands	21
Poland	21	Spain	21
Portugal	21	Spanish Territories of North Africa	31
Portuguese Timor	31	Sri Lanka	23
Puerto Rico	23	Sudan	22
Qatar	23	Surinam	22
Reunion	31	Swaziland	22
Romania	22	Sweden	21
Russia	21	Switzerland	21
Rwanda	23	Syria	23
Sabah	23	Tajikistan	21
St. Helena	31	Tanzania	22
St. Kitts and Nevis	24	Thailand	23
St. Lucia	24	Togo	22
St. Pierre and Miquelon	31	Tonga	30
St. Vincent and the Grenadines	24	Trinidad and Tobago	23
		Tristan Da Cunha	31
Samoa (U.S.A. Territory) (See also Western Samoa)	30	Tunisia	22
		Turkey	21
San Marino	21	Turkmenistan	21
Sao Tome and Principe	25	Turks & Caicos Islands	31
Sarawak	28	Tuvalu	23
Saudi Arabia	24	Uganda	22
Scotland	21	Ukraine	21
Senegal	22	United Arab Emirates	22
Serbia	21	United States of America	22
Seychelles	22	Uruguay	22
Sierra Leone	22	Uzbekistan	21
Singapore	22	Vanuatu	29
Slovakia	21	Vatican City State	21
Slovenia	21	Venezuela	22
Society Islands (French Polynesia)	31	Vietnam	28
		Virgin Islands – U.S.A	24
Solomon Islands	29	Wake Island	25
Somalia	22	Western Samoa	34
South Africa	22	Yemen (Republic of)	30
South Georgia (Falkland Island Dependencies)	31	Zaire	25
		Zambia	23
South Orkneys	21	Zimbabwe	22

Annex – Service Regulation (Rule 6.44)

http://www.justice.gov.uk/civil/procrules_fin/contents/form_section_
images/practice_directions/pd6b_pdf_eps/pd6b_ecreg2007.pdf

* * * * *

PRACTICE DIRECTION 6C – DISCLOSURE OF ADDRESSES BY GOVERNMENT DEPARTMENTS

[**Editors' note:** for all obsolete references to 'registrar' read 'district judge'.]

13 February 1989 [as amended by Practice Direction 20 July 1995]

The arrangements set out in the Registrar's Direction, *Disclosure of Addresses by Government Departments* of 26 April 1988 ([1988] 2 FLR 183; [1988] Fam. Law 360; [1988] 2 All ER 573; [1988] 1 WLR 638), whereby the court may request the disclosure of addresses by government departments have been further extended.

These arrangements will now cover—

(a) tracing the address of a person in proceedings against whom another person is seeking to obtain or enforce an order for financial provision either for himself or herself or for the children of the former marriage; and,

(b) tracing the whereabouts of a child, or the person with whom the child is said to be, in proceedings under the Child Abduction and Custody Act 1985 or in which a custody order, as defined in Part I of the Family Law Act 1986, is being sought or enforced.

Requests for such information will be made officially by the registrar. The request, in addition to giving the information mentioned below, should certify—

(1) *In financial provision applications* either (a) that a financial provision order is in existence, but cannot be enforced because the person against whom the order has been made cannot be traced; or (b) that the applicant has filed or issued a notice, petition or originating summons containing an application for financial provision which cannot be served because the respondent cannot be traced.

A 'financial provision order' means any order made under ss. 23, 24, 24A and 27 of the Matrimonial Causes Act 1973 or the variations of any order made under s. 31 of the 1973 Act, and any periodical payments or lump sum order made under s. 6 of the Family Law Reform Act 1969, the Guardianship of Minors Act 1971, s. 34 of the Children Act 1975 and any order registered in the High Court under the Maintenance Orders (Facilities for Enforcement) Act 1920, the Maintenance Orders Act 1950 and the Maintenance Orders Act 1958, and any order made under s. 17 of the Matrimonial and Family Proceedings Act 1984.

(2) *In wardship proceedings* that the child is the subject of wardship proceedings and cannot be traced, and is believed to be with the person whose address is sought.

(3) *In custody proceedings* that the child is the subject of custody proceedings and cannot be traced, and is believed to be with the person whose address is sought.

The following notes set out the information required by those departments which are likely to be of the greatest assistance to an applicant.

Department of Social Security
1. The department most likely to be able to assist is the Department of Social Security, whose records are the most comprehensive and complete. The possibility of identifying one person amongst so many will depend on the particulars given. An address will not be supplied by the department unless it is satisfied from the particulars given that the record of the person has been reliably identified.

The applicant or his solicitor should therefore be asked to supply as much as possible of the following information about the person sought —

  (i)   National Insurance number;
  (ii) surname;
  (iii) forenames in full;
  (iv) date of birth (or, if not known, approximate age);
  (v) last known address, with date when living there;
  (vi) any other known address(es) with dates;
  (vii) if the person sought is a war pensioner, his war pension and service particulars (if known);

and in applications for financial provision—

(viii) the exact date of the marriage and the wife's forenames.

Enquiries should be sent by the registrar to:
Department of Social Security
N1CB
Special Section A
Newcastle upon Tyne
NE98 1YU

The department will be prepared to search if given full particulars of the person's name and date of birth, but the chances of accurate identification are increased by the provision of more identifying information. Second requests for records to be searched, provided that a reasonable interval has elapsed, will be met by the Department of Social Security.

Supplementary Benefit/Income Support

Where, in the case of applications for financial provision, the wife is or has been in receipt of supplementary benefit income support, it would be advisable in the first instance to make enquiries of the manager of the local Social Security office for the area in which she resides in order to avoid possible duplication of enquiries.

Office of Population Censuses and Surveys National Health Service Central Register

[**Editors' note:** now the Office for National Statistics.]

2. The Office of Population Censuses and Surveys administers the National Health Service Central Register for the Department of Health. The records held in the Central Register include individuals' names, with dates of birth and National Health Service number, against a record of the Family Practitioner Committee area where the patient is currently registered with a National Health Service doctor. The Central Register does not hold individual patients' addresses, but can advise courts of the last Family Practitioner Committee area registration. Courts can then apply for information about addresses to the appropriate Family Practitioner Committee for independent action.

When application is made for the disclosure of Family Practitioner Committee area registrations from these records the applicant or his solicitor should supply as much as possible of the following information about the person sought—

(i) National Health Service number;
(ii) surname;
(iii) forenames in full;
(iv) date of birth (or, if not known, approximate age);
(v) last known address;
(vi) mother's maiden name.

Enquiries should be sent by the registrar to:

Office of Population Censuses and Surveys
National Health Service Central Register
Smedley Hydro
Trafalgar Road
Southport
Merseyside
PR 8 2HH

Passport Office

3. If all reasonable enquiries, including the aforesaid methods, have failed to reveal an address, or if there are strong grounds for believing that the person sought may have made a recent application for a passport, enquiries may be made to the Passport Office. The applicant or his solicitor should

provide as much of the following information about the person as possible—

(i)   surname;
(ii)   forenames in full;
(iii)   date of birth (or, if not known, approximate age);
(iv)   place of birth
(v)   occupation;
(vi)   whether known to have travelled abroad, and, if so, the destination and dates;
(vii)   last known address, with date living there;
(viii) any other known address(es), with dates.

The applicant or his solicitor must also undertake in writing that information given in response to the enquiry will be used solely for the purpose for which it was requested, i.e. to assist in tracing the husband in connection with the making or enforcement of a financial provision order or in tracing a child in connection with custody or wardship proceedings, as the case may be.

Enquiries should be sent to:

The Chief Passport Officer
Passport Department
Home Office
Clive House
Petty France
London
SW1H 9HD

Ministry of Defence

4. In cases where the person sought is known to be serving or to have recently served in any branch of H.M. Forces, the solicitor representing the applicant may obtain the address for service of financial provision or custody and wardship proceedings direct from the appropriate service department.

In the case of army servicemen, the solicitor can obtain a list of regiments and of the various manning and record offices from the Officer in Charge, Central Manning Support Office, Higher Barracks, Exeter, EC4 4ND.

The solicitor's request should be accompanied by a written undertaking that the address will be used for the purpose of service of process in those proceedings and that so far as is possible the solicitor will disclose the address only to the court and not to the applicant or any other person, except in the normal course of the proceedings.

Alternatively, if the solicitor wishes to serve process on the person's commanding officer under the provisions contained in s. 101 of the Naval Act 1957, s. 153 of the Army Act 1955 and s. 153 of the Air Force Act 1955 (all of which as amended by s. 62 of the Armed Forces Act 1971) he may obtain that officer's address in the same way.

Where the applicant is acting in person the appropriate service department is prepared to disclose the address of the person sought, or that of his commanding officer, to a registrar on receipt of an assurance that the applicant has given an undertaking that the information will be used solely for the purpose of serving process in the proceedings.

In all cases, the request should include details of the person's full name, service number, rank or rating, and his ship, arm or trade, corps regiment or unit or as much of this information as is available. The request should also include details of his date of birth, or, if not known, his age, his date of entry into the service and, if no longer serving, the date of discharge, and any other information, such as his last known address. Failure to quote the service number and the rank or rating may result in failure to identify the serviceman or at least in considerable delay.

Enquiries should be addressed as follows—

(a)

Officers of Royal Navy and Women's Royal Naval Service	The Naval Secretary, Room 161, Victory Building, HM Naval Base, Hants, PO1 3LS
Ratings in the Royal Navy, WRNS Ratings, QUARNNS Ratings	Captain, Naval Drafting, Centurion Building, Grange Road, Gosport, Hants, PO13 9XA
RN Medical and Dental Officers	The Medical Director, General (Naval), Room 114, Victory Building, HM Naval Base, Portsmouth, Hants, PO1 3LS
Officers of Queen Alexandra's Royal Naval Nursing Service	The Matron-in-Chief, QARNNS, Room 129, Victory Building, HM Naval Base, Portsmouth, Hants, PO1 3LS
Naval Chaplains	Director General, Naval Chaplaincy Service, Room 201, Victory Building, HM Naval Base, Portsmouth, Hants, PO1 3LS

(b)

Royal Marine Officers	The Naval Secretary, Room 161, Victory Building, HM Naval Base, Portsmouth, Hants, PO1 3LS

Royal Marine Ranks

HQRM, (DRORM), West
Battery, Whale Island,
Portsmouth, Hants, PO2 8DX

(c)

Army Officers (including WRAC
and QARANC)

Army Officer, Documentation
Office, Index Department, Room
F7, Government Buildings,
Stanmore, Middlesex

Other Ranks, Army

The Manning and Record Office
which is appropriate to the
Regiment or Corps.

(d)

Royal Air Force Officers and
other Ranks, Women's Royal
Air Force Officers and Other
Ranks (including PMRAFNS)

Ministry of Defence, RAF
Personnel, Management 2b1 (a),
(RAF), Building 248, RAF
Innsworth, Gloucester, GL3 1EZ

General Notes

Records held by other departments are less likely to be of use, either because of their limited scope or because individual records cannot readily be identified. If, however, the circumstances suggest that the address may be known to another department, application may be made to it by the registrar, all relevant particulars available being given.

When the department is able to supply the address of the person sought to the registrar, it will be passed on by him to the applicant's solicitor (or, in proper cases, direct to the applicant if acting in person) on an understanding to use it only for the purpose of the proceedings.

Nothing in this practice direction affects the service in matrimonial causes of petitions which do not contain any application for financial provision, etc. The existing arrangements whereby the Department of Social Security will at the request of the solicitor forward a letter by ordinary post to a party's last known address remain in force in such cases.

* * * * *

Part 7

Commentary on Part 7, rules 7.27 and 7.29:
PROCEDURE FOR APPLICATIONS IN MATRIMONIAL AND CIVIL PARTNERSHIP PROCEEDINGS

Part 7 is entitled 'procedure for applications in matrimonial and civil partnership proceedings' and is principally concerned with the procedure for divorce, nullity and judicial separation applications (and their civil partnership equivalents). Therefore only two of the Part 7 rules are reproduced here as relevant to the law, practice or procedure applicable to financial remedy applications.

It may be remarked (very much in passing) however that, notwithstanding a determined effort to eradicate all traditional language, historical vestiges linger on with references to decree nisi and absolute and even, in rule 7.26, to the procedure for medical examination in nullity cases alleging incapacity or wilful refusal to consummate, no doubt to establish whether that 19th century musical hall stalwart *Vera Copula* is still in the house.

Two rules have tangential relevance to financial remedy applications. Rule 7.27(1) addresses the situation if the court (when certifying and giving directions in an undefended suit under what used to be called the special procedure, or when otherwise giving case management directions in a defended suit) becomes aware that there are overseas proceedings continuing which may affect the validity or subsistence of the marriage or civil partnership in question. In that event, where the court considers that there is a question whether the suit should be stayed under para 9 of Schedule 1 to the Domicile and Matrimonial Proceedings Act 1973 then, not very surprisingly, it must give directions for the hearing of the question whether the proceedings should indeed be stayed. This may have the effect of pausing pending financial remedy proceedings or bringing them to an abrupt and inconclusive halt.

Similarly, by rule 7.27(2) if at any time it appears to the court that it does not have jurisdiction to hear the main suit by virtue of Arts 16 to 19 of the Council Regulation (Brussels II revised: *seisin*, enquiries as to jurisdiction or admissibility, *lis pendens* and dependent actions), or that it is or may be required to stay the proceedings under those provisions, then the court must stay the proceedings and fix a date for determination of the question of jurisdiction. This may have a similar effect on any pending financial remedy proceedings.

Rule 7.29 addresses the financial remedy that is the now almost totally obsolete application under section 10(2) and (3) of the Matrimonial Causes Act 1973 and its almost certainly never yet encountered equivalent under section 48(2) of the Civil Partnership Act 2004 for consideration of the financial position of the respondent in a 2- or 5-year separation divorce case (or its civil partnership equivalent). Where the court makes absolute a decree nisi (or makes a final order under the 2004 Act) following such a consideration then it must make a written record of its reasons.

PART 7: PROCEDURE FOR APPLICATIONS IN MATRIMONIAL AND CIVIL PARTNERSHIP PROCEEDINGS

* * * * *

CHAPTER 3: HOW THE COURT DETERMINES MATRIMONIAL AND CIVIL PARTNERSHIP PROCEEDINGS

* * * * *

Stay of proceedings
7.27.—(1) Where—

(a) the court is considering an application in accordance with rule 7.20 or gives directions under rule 7.22;

[Comment: 7.20 (What the court will do on an application for a decree nisi, a conditional order, a decree of judicial separation or a separation order) and 7.22 (What the court must do for the case management hearing) relate to matrimonial and civil partnership proceedings and are not here reproduced.]

(b) it appears to the court that there are proceedings continuing in any country outside England and Wales which are in respect of the marriage or civil partnership in question or which are capable of affecting its validity or subsistence; and

(c) the court considers that the question whether the proceedings should be stayed under paragraph 9 of Schedule 1 to the Domicile and Matrimonial Proceedings Act 1973[41] or, for civil partnership proceedings, under rules made under sections 75 and 76 of the Courts Act 2003,

the court must give directions for the hearing of that question.

(2) Where at any time after the making of an application under this Part it appears to the court in matrimonial proceedings that, under Articles 16 to 19 of the Council Regulation, the court does not have jurisdiction to hear the application and is or may be required to stay the proceedings, the court will—

(a) stay the proceedings; and
(b) fix a date for a hearing to determine the questions of jurisdiction and whether there should be a further stay or other order.

(3) The court must give reasons for its decision under Articles 16 to 19 of the Council Regulation and, where it makes a finding of fact, state such finding of fact.

(4) An order under Article 17 of the Council Regulation that the court has no jurisdiction over the proceedings will be recorded by the court or the court officer in writing.

(5) The court may, if all parties agree, deal with any question about the jurisdiction of the court without a hearing.

CHAPTER 4: COURT ORDERS

* * * * *

Applications under section 10(2) of 1973 Act or section 48(2) of 2004 Act
7.29. Where the court makes—

(a) in the case of divorce, a decree absolute following an application under section 10(2) of the 1973 Act; or
(b) in the case of dissolution, a final order following an application under section 48(2) of the 2004 Act,

it must make a written record of the reasons for deciding to make that decree absolute or final order.

* * * * *

Part 8

Commentary on Part 8:
PROCEDURE FOR MISCELLANEOUS APPLICATIONS

Part 8 deals with the procedure to be applied for certain specific applications. Omitted from *@eGlance* and from consideration in this Commentary are those Chapters in Part 8 which have no relevance to financial remedy applications. These are Chapter 2 (Application for corrected gender recognition certificate); Chapter 5 (Declarations as to marital status, as to civil partnership status, of parentage, of legitimacy or legitimation, and as to adoptions effected overseas); and Chapter 9 (Application for consent to marriage of a child or to registration of civil partnership of a child).

Those chapters with a financial dimension are:

- Chapter 3: Application under Matrimonial Causes Act 1973, section 36 or para 73 of Schedule 5 to the Civil Partnership Act 2004 for alteration of maintenance agreement after death of one party.
- Chapter 4: Application under Married Women's Property Act 1882, section 17 or section 66 of the Civil Partnership Act 2004 for a question as to property to be decided in summary way.
- Chapter 6: Application under section 13 of the Matrimonial and Family Proceedings Act 1984 or para 4 of Schedule 7 to the Civil Partnership Act 2004 for permission to apply for a financial remedy after overseas proceedings.
- Chapter 7: Application for the transfer of a tenancy under section 53 of, and Schedule 7 to the Family Law Act 1996.
- Chapter 8: Applications for orders preventing avoidance under section 32L of the Child Support Act 1991.

An application under Part 3 of the Matrimonial and Family Proceedings Act 1984 (or its civil partnership equivalent) must be made in accordance with the Part 18 procedure. Otherwise these applications must be made in accordance with the more summary Part 19 procedure applicable where a substantial dispute of fact is unlikely to be involved. A further exception from the Part 18 procedure is that an application under section 17 of the Married Women's Property Act 1882 (or its civil partnership equivalent) which is made *within* an application for a financial order must be made in accordance with the Part 18 procedure; whereas a free-standing application must be made under the Part 19 procedure. Other exceptions from the requirement to commence under the Part 18 procedure are noted *below*.

Chapter 3: Application under Matrimonial Causes Act 1973, section 36 or para 73 of Schedule 5 to the Civil Partnership Act 2004 for alteration of a maintenance agreement after death of one party

FPR 2010 rules 8.1 to 8.11 gather into one place rules that were previously scattered throughout the old FPR and indeed the RSC and CCR (see FPR 1991 rules 3.3, 3.5, 10.10, Appendix 4 (paras 4, 7, 8 and 9(4) to (7)); RSC Order 15 generally and Order 15 rule 13; and CCR Order 5 generally and Order 5 rule 6, and Order 48 rules 3(1), (7) and (9)).

The 2010 rules do not materially alter the old prescription. The application must if issued in a county court be in the divorce county court where the deceased resided at the date of death (with default positions if he resided overseas at the date of death).

The FPR 1991 Appendix 4, para 9(7) (applied by *ibid.* rule 3.5(1)(c)) stated that 'the hearing ... must, unless the court otherwise directs, take place in chambers'. The new FPR rule 8.11 is headed 'hearings may be in private' and states 'the Court may decide to hear any application to which this Chapter applies in private'. This subtle change of language appears to signify that the default position now is a hearing in open court, rather than in private.

By FPR Part 5 and PD 5A, Form D50D must be used for making the application.

Chapter 4: Application under 17 of the Married Women's Property Act 1882 or section 66 of the Civil Partnership Act 2004 for a question as to property to be decided in summary way

FPR 2010 rules 8.12 to 8.17 gather into one place and restate without material alteration the former rules 3.6, 3.7, and Appendix 4, para 9(7) and (9).

As stated *above*, the Part 18 procedure must be used if the application is made within any proceedings for a financial order; whereas a free-standing application must be made under the Part 19 procedure.

Rule 8.16 permits the grant of an injunction if, and only if, it is incidental or ancillary to the 'assistance' (formerly 'relief') sought by the applicant. Such an application must be made in accordance with the procedure in rule 19.4

By FPR 2010 Part 5 and PD 5A, Form D50B must be used for making the application.

Chapter 6: Application under section 13 of the Matrimonial and Family Proceedings Act 1984 or para 4 of Schedule 7 to the Civil Partnership Act 2004 for permission to apply for a financial remedy after overseas proceedings

FPR 2010 rules 8.23 to 8.28 restate former FPR rule 3.17, with some alterations, at least one of which may have been unintentional.

These rules deal only with the application for *permission*. If permission is granted then the substantive application is for a financial remedy (rule 2.3) and must be dealt with in accordance with the procedure specified in Part 9.

Rule 8.24(1) continues to require the application to be issued in the PRFD: save that by rule 8.24(2) if there is consent to the order and there are parallel proceedings for a financial remedy (other than a financial order) then the (consensual) permission application may be made in the court hearing the financial remedy application.

Rule 8.28 incorporates a significant innovation as to the level of judge who may hear the substantive application if permission is granted. Under the former FPR rule 3.18(8) the substantive application had to be determined by a High Court Judge. Now, the judge granting permission may direct that the substantive application be heard by a district judge of the PRFD.

The former FPR rule 3.17(1) explicitly required the application for permission (formerly 'leave') to be made ex parte (sic). The new rule 8.25 is ambiguously phrased. While it is headed 'Application to be made without notice' the text of the rule states that 'the court may grant an application made without notice if it appears to the court that there are good reasons for not giving notice'. This would suggest that the court had power to hear the application inter partes (to use traditional language). This seeming conflict was commented upon by Munby LJ in *Traversa v Freddi* [2011] EWCA Civ 81 at [57]:

> The wording of FPR 8.25 is slightly odd, for the requirement that the application for leave is to be made without notice appears only in the heading and not, at least explicitly, in the rule itself; and the wording of FPR 8.25(2) – '*if* the applicant makes an application without giving notice' (emphasis added) – might suggest that the applicant has a choice. But reading the rule in the context of both present practice and, more particularly, what Lord Collins said in *Agbaje*, it seems that what the new rules contemplate is an application which is to be made without notice but where the court has power to decline to make the order except at an inter partes hearing. This is borne out by FPR 8.26(b) which requires the court to 'give notice of the date of the hearing to the applicant' but not, it may be noted, to the respondent.

In that case the view of Mostyn J in *CG v IF* [2010] EWHC 1062 (Fam), [2010] 2 FLR 1790 that the court could adjourn a borderline case to be heard inter partes was trenchantly overruled. No reliance should now be placed on that decision: he was 'doubly wrong' in the opinions expressed at first instance. See also *Schofield v Schofield* [2011] EWCA Civ 174 at [13].

There is however a potential problem with that dictum of Munby LJ in *Traversa v Freddi* that the new rules when read 'in the context of both present practice and, more particularly, what Lord Collins said in *Agbaje*' contemplate 'an application which is to be made without notice but where the court has power to decline to make the order except at an inter partes hearing'. Rule 8.24(3) requires the application to be made in accordance with the Part 18 procedure. While rule 18.5(2) permits an application to be made without service of an application notice if permitted by a rule, practice direction, or the court, PD 18A para 5.1 stipulates that an application may be made without service of an application notice only *(a) where there is exceptional urgency; or (b) where the overriding objective is best furthered by doing so; or (c) by consent of all parties; or (d) with the permission of the court; or (e) where paragraph 4.9 applies; or (f) where a court order, rule or practice direction permits.* There is nothing in this list to suggest that an application for permission under section 13 should invariably be made ex parte.

In the decision of the Supreme Court of *Agbaje v Agbaje* [2010] UKSC 13, [2010] 1 FLR 1813, [2010] WLR 709 (SC) Lord Collins gave definitive guidance not only as to the test to be applied on considering an application for permission but also as to the propriety of the emerging practice of a party against whom permission had been granted ex parte applying on notice to set aside the grant of such permission. At [33] he stated:

> In the present context the principal object of the filter mechanism is to prevent wholly unmeritorious claims being pursued to oppress or blackmail a former spouse. The threshold is not high, but is higher than 'serious issue to be tried' or 'good arguable case' found in other contexts. It is perhaps best expressed by saying that in this context 'substantial' means 'solid.' Once a judge has given reasons for deciding at the *ex parte* stage that the threshold has been crossed, the approach to setting aside leave should be the same as the approach to setting aside permission to appeal in the Civil Procedure Rules, where (by contrast with the Family Proceedings Rules) there is an express power to set aside, but which may only be exercised where there is a compelling reason to do so: CPR rule 52.9(2). In practice in the Court of Appeal the power is only exercised where some decisive authority has been overlooked so that the appeal is bound to fail, or where the court has been misled: *Barings Bank plc v Coopers & Lybrand* [2002] EWCA Civ 1155; *Nathan v Smilovitch* [2007] EWCA Civ 759. In an application under section 13, unless it is clear that the respondent can deliver a knock-out blow, the court should use its case management powers to adjourn an application to set aside to be heard with the substantive application.

FPR 2010, rule 18.11 provides that a person who was not served with a copy of the application notice before an order was made may apply to have the order set aside or varied, and that such application must be made within 7 days beginning with the date on which the order was served on the person making the application. This will not enable a party against whom permission has been granted freely to revert to the practice of seeking a set-aside on an inter-partes hearing. In *Traversa v Freddi* Munby LJ stated at [58]:

> There are, however, two points which I wish to emphasise. The first is that if the court grants leave at a without notice hearing, any application to set aside in accordance with FPR rule 18.11 is to be dealt with as at present and in accordance with what Lord Collins said in *Agbaje*. Under the new rules, as under the old, unless the respondent can demonstrate that he has some 'knock-out' blow, his application to set aside the grant of permission, if not dismissed then and there, should be adjourned to be heard with the substantive application. The other is this. Whether the application for leave is dealt with at a without notice hearing or inter partes, the hearing should be given an appropriately short listing. Applications for leave or permission in this court and in the Administrative Court, even if listed inter partes, are customarily listed for 30 or at most 60 minutes. There is no reason why applications for leave under the 1984 Act cannot be dealt with justly and fairly – I quote the language of the new FPR 1.1 – within a similar timescale.

By rule 8.27 the permission application must be heard in private unless the court directs otherwise.

By Part 5 and PD 5A, Form D50E must be used for making the application. If permission is granted then by PD 5A the full Form E must be used in order to declare means: this is an innovation although in practice Form E was routinely ordered under the old regime. The substantive application must be made in Form D50F.

Chapter 7: Application for the transfer of a tenancy under section 53 of, and Schedule 7 to, the Family Law Act 1996

Rules 8.29 to 8.34 gather together the former FPR rule 3.6(7) to (9), 3.8(12) to (15) and Appendix 4 para 7 as they applied to an application for a transfer of a tenancy. Under the old regime the application had to be served on the landlord, and he (the landlord) was entitled to be heard. Now, the landlord will be made a party if he requests to become one (rule 8.32).

Rule 8.34 permits the grant of an injunction if, and only if, it is incidental or ancillary to the 'assistance' (formerly 'relief') sought by the applicant. Such an application must be made in accordance with the procedure in rule 19.4.

By FPR Part 5 and PD 5A, Form D50B must be used to make the application.

Chapter 8: Applications for orders preventing avoidance under section 32L of the Child Support Act 1991

Section 32L of the Child Support Act 1991 was inserted by section 24 of the Child Maintenance and Other Payments Act 2008 and was brought into force on 6 April 2010 by the Child Maintenance and Other Payments Act 2008 (Commencement No. 7) Order 2010. Section 32L provides an anti-avoidance measure very similar to that obtaining under section 37 of the Matrimonial Causes Act 1973.

Rules 8.36 to 8.40 provide the relevant procedural framework. By rule 8.37 the application must be made in the High Court. It may be heard by a district judge of the PRFD; a district judge of a district registry may only hear the application if a High Court Judge has so directed.

By section 32L(1) C-MEC may apply to the court (on the grounds that a person (a) has failed to pay an amount of child support maintenance, and (b) with the intention of avoiding payment of child support maintenance is about to make a disposition or to transfer out of the jurisdiction or otherwise deal with any property) for an order restraining the person from doing so. By rule 8.40(2) the court may make such an order without notice if it appears to the court that there are good reasons for not giving notice; but by rule 8.40(3) on such a without notice application the evidence in support of the application must state the reasons why notice has not been given. By rule 8.40(4) if the court grants such a without notice application (a) the order must include a provision allowing any respondent to apply to the court for an order to be reconsidered as soon as just and convenient at a full hearing; and (b) the applicant must, as soon as reasonably practicable, serve upon each respondent a copy of the order and a copy of the written evidence in support of the application.

By FPR Part 5 and PD 5A, Form D50J must be used for making the application.

PART 8: PROCEDURE FOR MISCELLANEOUS APPLICATIONS

CHAPTER 1: PROCEDURE

Procedure
8.1. Subject to rules 8.13 and 8.24, applications to which this Part applies must be made in accordance with the Part 19 procedure.

CHAPTER 2: APPLICATION FOR CORRECTED GENDER RECOGNITION CERTIFICATE

* * * * *

CHAPTER 3: APPLICATION FOR ALTERATION OF MAINTENANCE AGREEMENT AFTER DEATH OF ONE PARTY

Scope of this Chapter

8.6. The rules in this Chapter apply to an application under section 36 of the 1973 Act[42] or paragraph 73 of Schedule 5 to the 2004 Act to alter a maintenance agreement after the death of one of the parties.

Where to start proceedings

8.7.—(1) The application may be made in the High Court or a county court.

(2) Where the application is made in a county court it must be made in the divorce county court or civil partnership proceedings county court for the district in which—

(a) the deceased resided at the time of death; or
(b) if the deceased did not reside in England and Wales at the time of death—
    (i) the respondent or one of the respondents resides or carries on business; or
    (ii) where the respondent is the personal representative of the deceased, the deceased's estate is situated; or
(c) if neither nor applies—
    (i) the applicant resides or carries on business; or
    (ii) where the applicant is the personal representative of the deceased, the deceased's estate is situated.

Who the parties are

8.8.—(1) Where the applicant is—

(a) the surviving party to the agreement, the personal representative of the deceased must be a respondent;
(b) the personal representative of the deceased, the surviving party to the agreement must be a respondent.

(2) The court may at any time direct that—

(a) any person be made a party to proceedings; or

(b) a party be removed.

Representative parties

8.9.—(1) The court may, before or after the application has been filed at court, make an order appointing a person to represent any other person or persons in the application where the person or persons to be represented—

(a) are unborn;

(b) cannot be found;

(c) cannot easily be ascertained; or

(d) are a class of persons who have the same interest in an application and—

    (i) one or more members of that class are within sub-paragraphs (a), (b) or (c); or

    (ii) to appoint a representative would further the overriding objective.

(2) An application for an order under paragraph (1) may be made by—

(a) any person who seeks to be appointed under the order; or

(b) any party to the application.

(3) An application for an order under paragraph (1) must be served on—

(a) all parties to the application to alter the maintenance agreement, if that application has been filed at court;

(b) the person sought to be appointed, if that person is not the applicant or a party to the application; and

(c) any other person as directed by the court.

(4) The court's approval is required to settle proceedings in which a party is acting as a representative.

(5) The court may approve a settlement where it is satisfied that the settlement is for the benefit of all the represented persons.

(6) Unless the court directs otherwise, any order made on an application in which a party is acting as a representative—

(a) is binding on all persons represented in the proceedings; and

(b) may only be enforced by or against a person who is not a party with the permission of the court.

(7) An application may be brought by or against trustees, executors or administrators without adding as parties any persons who have a beneficial interest in the trust or estate and any order made on the application is binding on the beneficiaries unless the court orders otherwise.

Acknowledgment of service

8.10.—(1) A respondent who is a personal representative of the deceased must file with the acknowledgment of service a statement setting out—

(a) full particulars of the value of the deceased's estate for probate after providing for the discharge of the funeral, testamentary and administration expenses, debts and liabilities (including inheritance tax and interest); and

(b) the people (including names, addresses and details of any persons under disability) or classes of people beneficially interested in the estate and the value of their interests so far as ascertained.

(2) The respondent must file the acknowledgment of service and any statement required under this rule within 28 days beginning with the date on which the application is served.

Hearings may be in private

8.11. The court may decide to hear any application to which this Chapter applies in private.

CHAPTER 4: APPLICATION FOR QUESTION AS TO PROPERTY TO BE DECIDED IN SUMMARY WAY

Scope of this Chapter

8.12. The rules in this Chapter apply to an application under section 17 of the Married Women's Property Act 1882[43] or section 66 of the 2004 Act.

Procedure

8.13. Where an application for an order under section 17 of the Married Women's Property Act 1882[44] or section 66 of the 2004 Act is made in any proceedings for a financial order, the application must be made in accordance with the Part 18 procedure.

Where to start proceedings

8.14.—(1) The application may be made in the High Court or a county court.

(2) Where the application is made in a county court it must be made in the court—

(a) in which any matrimonial proceedings or civil partnership proceedings have been started or are intended to be started by the applicant or the respondent; or

(b) in the absence of any such proceedings, for the district in which the applicant or respondent resides.

(3) The application may be made to the principal registry as if it were a county court if—

(a) any matrimonial proceedings or civil partnership proceedings have been started there or are intended to be started there by the applicant or the respondent; and

(b) those proceedings are or will be treated as pending in a divorce county court or civil partnership proceedings county court.

Mortgagees as parties

8.15.—(1) Where particulars of a mortgage are provided with the application—

(a) the applicant must serve a copy of the application on the mortgagee; and

(b) the mortgagee may, within 14 days beginning with the date on which the application was received, file an acknowledgment of service and be heard on the application.

(2) The court must direct that a mortgagee be made a party to the proceedings where the mortgagee requests to be one.

Injunctions

8.16.—(1) The court may grant an injunction only if the injunction is ancillary or incidental to the assistance sought by the applicant.

(2) Applications for injunctive relief must be made in accordance with the procedure in rule 20.4 (how to apply for an interim remedy) and the provisions of rule 20.5 (interim injunction to cease if application is stayed) apply.

Application of other rules

8.17. Rule 9.24 applies where the court has made an order for sale under section 17 of the Married Women's Property Act 1882 or section 66 of the 2004 Act.

CHAPTER 5: DECLARATIONS

* * * * *

CHAPTER 6: APPLICATION FOR PERMISSION TO APPLY FOR A FINANCIAL REMEDY AFTER OVERSEAS PROCEEDINGS

Scope of this Chapter

8.23. Subject to rule 9.26(6), the rules in this Chapter apply to an application for permission to apply for a financial remedy under section 13 of the 1984 Act and paragraph 4 of Schedule 7 to the 2004 Act.

(Rule 9.26(6) enables the application for permission to apply for a financial remedy under section 13 of the 1984 Act or paragraph 4 of Schedule 7 to the 2004 Act to be heard at the same time as the application for a financial remedy under Part 3 of the 1984 Act or Schedule 7 to the 2004 Act where that application is an application for a consent order.)

Where and how to start proceedings

8.24.—(1) Subject to paragraph (2), the application must be made in the principal registry.

(2) Where rule 9.26(6) applies, the application must be made in the court hearing the application for a financial remedy.

(Rule 9.5(2) specifies the court where the application for the consent order should be filed.)

(3) The application must be made in accordance with the Part 18 procedure.

Application to be made without notice

8.25.—(1) The court may grant an application made without notice if it appears to the court that there are good reasons for not giving notice.

(2) If the applicant makes an application without giving notice, the applicant must state the reasons why notice has not been given.

Notification of hearing date

8.26. The court officer must—

(a) fix a date, time and place for the hearing of the application by a judge, but not a district judge; and
(b) give notice of the date of the hearing to the applicant.

Hearings to be in private unless the court directs otherwise

8.27. An application under this Chapter must be heard in private unless the court directs otherwise.

Direction that application be dealt with by a district judge of the principal registry

8.28. If the application is granted, the judge may direct that the application for a financial remedy under Part 3 of the 1984 Act or Schedule 7 to the 2004 Act may be heard by a district judge of the principal registry.

CHAPTER 7: APPLICATION FOR THE TRANSFER OF A TENANCY UNDER SECTION 53 OF, AND SCHEDULE 7 TO, THE 1996 ACT

Scope of this Chapter
8.29. This Chapter applies to an application for the transfer of a tenancy under section 53 of, and Schedule 7 to, the 1996 Act.

Where to start proceedings
8.30.—(1) Subject to paragraph (2), the application may be made in the High Court or a county court.

(2) The application must be made to the court in which any divorce, judicial separation, nullity or civil partnership proceedings are pending between the parties.

Service of the application
8.31.—(1) The court will serve a copy of the application on—

(a) the respondent; and
(b) the landlord (as defined by paragraph 1 of Schedule 7 to the 1996 Act[45]),

unless the court directs that the applicant must do so.

(2) Where service is effected by the applicant, the applicant must file a certificate of service.

Who the parties are
8.32. The court will direct that a landlord be made a party to the proceedings where the landlord requests to be one.

Orders for disclosure
8.33 Any party may apply to the court under rule 21.2 for an order that any person must attend an appointment before the court and produce any documents that are specified or described in the order.

Injunctions
8.34.—(1) The court may grant an injunction only if the injunction is ancillary or incidental to the assistance sought by the applicant.

(2) Applications for injunctive relief must be made in accordance with the procedure in rule 20.4 (how to apply for an interim remedy) and the provisions of rule 20.5 (interim injunction to cease if application is stayed) apply accordingly.

CHAPTER 8: APPLICATIONS FOR ORDERS PREVENTING AVOIDANCE UNDER SECTION 32L OF THE CHILD SUPPORT ACT 1991

Scope of this Chapter

8.35. Subject to rule 8.40, the rules in this Chapter apply to applications made under section 32L(1) and (2) of the 1991 Act[46].

Interpretation

8.36. In this Chapter—

"child support maintenance" has the meaning assigned to it in section 3(6) of the 1991 Act[47];

"reviewable disposition" has the meaning assigned to it in section 32L(5) of the 1991 Act.

Where to start proceedings

8.37.— The application must be made to the High Court and be filed in—

(a) the principal registry; or
(b) any district registry.

(2) The application may be heard by a judge but not a district judge except—

(a) a district judge of the principal registry of the Family Division; or
(b) a district judge in a district registry who is directed by a judge to hear the application.

(Section 32L(10)(a) of the 1991 Act defines "court" for the purposes of section 32L as being the High Court only.)

Who the parties are

8.38.—(1) The applicant to the proceedings is the Commission and the respondent is the person who has failed to pay child support maintenance.

(2) The court may at any time direct that—

(a) any person be made a party to proceedings; or
(b) a party be removed from the proceedings.

Service of the application

8.39.—(1) The applicant must serve the application and a copy of the applicant's written evidence on—

(a) any respondent;
(b) the person in whose favour the reviewable disposition is alleged to have been made; and
(c) such other persons as the court directs.

(2) Where an application includes an application relating to land, the applicant must serve a copy of the application on any—

(a) mortgagee;
(b) trustee of a trust of land or settlement; and
(c) other person who has an interest in the land,

of whom particulars are given in the application.

(3) Any person served under paragraph (2) may make a request to the court in writing, within 14 days beginning with the date of service of the application, for a copy of the applicant's written evidence.

(4) Any person who—

(a) is served with copies of the application and the applicant's written evidence under paragraph (1); or
(b) receives a copy of the applicant's written evidence following a request under paragraph (3),

may, within 14 days beginning with the date of service or receipt, file a statement in answer.

(5) A statement in answer filed under paragraph (4) must be verified by a statement of truth.

Applications without notice

8.40.—(1) This rule applies to an application under section 32L(1) of the 1991 Act.

(2) The court may grant an application made without notice if it appears to the court that there are good reasons for not giving notice.

(3) If the applicant makes an application without giving notice, the evidence in support of the application must state the reasons why notice has not been given.

(4) If the court grants an application under paragraph (2)—

(a) the order must include a provision allowing any respondent to apply to the court for an order to be reconsidered as soon as just and convenient at a full hearing; and
(b) the applicant must, as soon as reasonably practicable, serve upon each respondent a copy of the order and a copy of the written evidence in support of the application.

CHAPTER 9: APPLICATION FOR CONSENT TO MARRIAGE OF A CHILD OR TO REGISTRATION OF CIVIL PARTNERSHIP OF A CHILD

* * * * *

Part 9

Commentary on Part 9:
APPLICATIONS FOR A FINANCIAL REMEDY

Part 9 contains the key set of provisions for the procedure governing financial applications. It is not merely concerned with applications for a financial order (as applications for ancillary relief are now known) but provides rather for the full range of financial remedies available.

Definitions

Rule 2(3) defines a **financial remedy** as:

(a) a financial order;

(b) an order under Schedule 1 to the Children Act 1989;

(c) an order under Part 3 of the Matrimonial and Family Proceedings Act 1984 Act;

(d) an order under Schedule 7 to the Civil Partnership Act 2004;

(e) an order under section 27 of the Matrimonial Causes Act 1973;

(f) an order under Part 9 of Schedule 5 to the Civil Partnership Act 2004;

(g) an order under section 35 of the Matrimonial Causes Act 1973;

(h) an order under paragraph 69 of Schedule 5 to the Civil Partnership Act 2004;

(i) an order under Part 1 of the Domestic Proceedings and Magistrates' Courts Act 1978;

(j) an order under Schedule 6 to the Civil Partnership Act 2004;

(k) an order under section 10(2) of the Matrimonial Causes Act 1973; or

(l) an order under section 48(2) of the Civil Partnership Act 2004

A **financial order** is defined as:

(a) an avoidance of disposition order;

(b) an order for maintenance pending suit;

(c) an order for maintenance pending outcome of proceedings;

(d) an order for periodical payments or lump sum provision as mentioned in section 21(1) of the Matrimonial Causes Act 1973, except an order under section 27(6) of that Act;

(e) an order for periodical payments or lump sum provision as mentioned in paragraph 2(1) of Schedule 5 to the Civil Partnership Act 2004, made under Part 1 of Schedule 5 to that Act;

(f) a property adjustment order;

(g) a variation order;

(h) a pension sharing order; or

(i) a pension compensation sharing order.

Financial applications not covered by Part 9

It should be noted that a handful of applications with a financial dimension are not designated as a 'financial remedy'. These are:

(a) an application under section 36 of the Matrimonial Causes Act 1973 (or paragraph 73 of Schedule 5 to the Civil Partnership Act 2004) for alteration of a maintenance agreement after the death of one party;

(b) an application under section 17 of the Married Women's Property Act 1882 (or section 66 of the Civil Partnership Act 2004) for a question as to property to be decided in summary way;

(c) an application under section 13 of the Matrimonial and Family Proceedings Act 1984 (or paragraph 4 of Schedule 7 to the Civil Partnership Act 2004) for *permission* to apply for a financial remedy after overseas proceedings;

(d) an application for the transfer of a tenancy under section 53 of, and schedule 7 to, the Family Law Act 1996; and

(e) an application for an order preventing avoidance under section 32L of the Child Support Act 1991.

The procedure in relation to these applications is governed by Part 8, to which, and to the Commentary on which, reference should be made.

The ancillary relief rules resurrected

The essential scheme of Part 9, Chapter 4 (rules 9.12 to 9.17) is to take the familiar ancillary relief procedure found in FPR 1991, rules 2.51A to 2.71 (the former 'ancillary relief rules' as still available within *@eGlance* and as printed in editions of *At A Glance* until 2010–11), and to apply that procedure, with some minor modifications, to all applications for a financial remedy issued in the High Court or the county court.

The magistrates' court

Chapter 5 supplies the procedure for applications in the magistrates' court.

General

By rule 9.5 where an application for a matrimonial or civil partnership order (i.e. a divorce or its equivalent) has been made in a given court then an application for a financial remedy must be filed in that court.

As before, under rule 9.12 a first appointment (FA) will be fixed within 12 to 16 weeks after issue, and by rule 9.14 financial disclosure must be made 7 weeks before FA.

Form E has survived the generational change to the new FPR almost unscathed, and is henceforth to be used as the template for financial statements on applications for a *financial order* (i.e. old style ancillary relief: see the rule 2.3 definitions conveniently set out at the head of this Commentary), or for an order under Part 3 of the Matrimonial and Family Proceedings Act 1984 (for a financial order or for financial relief after an overseas divorce/dissolution etc.) in the county or High Court.

It should be noted that a truncated Form E, known as Form E1 (and perhaps to become known as Form E lite) has been devised, and must by virtue of PD 5A be used for all applications for a *financial remedy other than an application for a financial order,* and other than an application for an order under Part 3 of the Matrimonial and Family Proceedings Act 1984 (for a financial order or for financial relief after foreign decree/dissolution etc.).

The archetypal Form E, well-known and loved, is itself the progenitor of some case-law: *GW v RW (Financial Provision: Departure from Equality)* [2003] 2 FLR 108 and *W v W (Financial Provision: Form E)* [2004] 1 FLR 494. It is to be anticipated that no less a rigorous approach will be taken to the contents of the new Forms E1 and E2 (see **Magistrates' courts** *below*).

In *R v K* [2009] EWCA Crim 1640, [2010] 1 FLR 807 the Court of Appeal held that no privilege against incrimination was available when completing a Form E, but that no material thereby compulsorily disclosed could be used in a criminal prosecution, in that case for tax offences.

PD 22A applies to Forms E and E1. Note should be made of para 11.3 which requires that where an exhibit contains more than one document, a front page should be attached setting out a list of the documents contained in the exhibit. The list should contain the dates of the documents. Similarly para 13.1 stipulates that where an exhibit contains more than one document (a) the bundle should not be stapled but should be securely fastened in a way that does not hinder the reading of the documents; and (b) the pages should be numbered consecutively at bottom centre. Perhaps unsurprisingly para 13.2 requires that every page of an exhibit should be clearly legible; typed copies of illegible documents should be included, paginated with 'a' numbers.

Counsel of perfection (and perhaps more to the point solicitors of perfection and their assistants, paralegals, clerks, office juniors and secretaries) will welcome this guidance. It remains to be seen how many will honour it in the observance. An equally prescriptive set of requirements as to the presentation and preparation of witness statements is also to be found in PD 22A: see Commentary on Part 22 *below*.

As before, 14 days before the FA the parties must file and serve a concise statement of issues, a chronology, a questionnaire, and a notice specifying whether the FA can be used as a FDR.

An important innovation is to be found in para 4 of PD 9A which stipulates that the parties should, if possible, with a view to identifying and narrowing any issues between the parties, exchange and file with the court a summary of the case *agreed between the parties*; a schedule of assets *agreed between the parties*; and details of any directions that they seek, including, where appropriate, the name of any expert they wish to be appointed. Experience shows that negotiating agreement to such documents before the FA is extremely difficult and often impossible as they often involve many emotionally as well as practically important points of contention. It remains to be seen whether this exhortation will engender a cultural work practice change or (perhaps more to the point) a more conciliatory approach from clients.

A further change is the requirement in para 5.2 of PD 9A which requires a court-ordered reply to questionnaire to be verified by a statement of truth. As to the penalties for a false statement in a document verified by a statement of truth, see Commentary on Part 17 *below*.

Directions and Guidance

The Practice Direction of 27 July 2006 concerning Court Bundles and documents to be supplied therewith continues in force unaltered by virtue of the unnumbered *Practice Direction – Practice Directions relating to family proceedings in force before 6th April 2011 which support the Family Procedure Rules 2010*. The 2006 Direction now takes its place in the ranks of advancing Directions with the new style PD 27A: see PD 27A and Commentary on Part 27 *below*.

The President's Guidance of 1 December 2009 concerning the *Transfer of Financial Proceedings to a High Court Judge* remains in effect.

The Procedural Direction of 25 May 2000 [2000] 1 FLR 997 (hitherto reproduced in *At A Glance* and in previous editions of *@eGlance*) is now superseded, and no longer applies. Its substance is now covered within PD 9A and PD 25A.

The procedure of the court and its duties at the FA are unaltered and are found now in rule 9.15. Similarly, the procedure of the court and its duties at the FDR remain the same and are now set out in rule 9.17.

Modifications to FPR 1991 procedure

The inspection appointment procedure in 1991 rule 2.62(7) to (9) is not replicated in the 2010 Rules, but analogous relief is obtainable and the same objective served via rule 21.2 (orders for disclosure against a person not a party).

The former rule 2.53(2) (leave to apply for ancillary relief required where the petition or answer failed to include a prayer therefor) has been abrogated. Rule 9.4 now allows an application for a financial order to be made in an application for a matrimonial or civil partnership order or at any time thereafter.

The former rule 2.60 (requiring service of an allegation of adultery or improper association on a named person to be served on that third party) has also been abrogated, although, somewhat inconsistently, Form F, adapted for that purpose has survived: see **Forms**, *below*.

By PD 9A para 5.1 and 5.2 replies to questionnaire must now be endorsed with a statement of truth.

Under the old rule 2.61D(2)(c) the court 'must' refer a case to a FDR unless it decides that such a referral is not appropriate in the circumstances. In the new rule 9.15(4) this imperative is removed – the word 'must' has disappeared, and the steer to the court is expressed more neutrally. The rule now provides 'If the court decides that a referral to a FDR appointment is appropriate it must direct that the case be referred to a FDR appointment'. It is not thought that this nuanced change of emphasis will alter the practice of almost invariably ordering a FDR: it would be a highly exceptional case where the court dispenses with this 'key element in the procedure' (as it is described in PD 9A para 6.1). Examples would include those cases where the respondent is refusing to participate, or, arguably, egregious cases of alleged non-disclosure, but even such conflicted cases are capable of a mediated solution: see the commentary on Part 3.

Interim relief

Rule 9.7 requires an application for interim relief to be made in accordance with the Part 18 procedure, to which and to the Commentary upon which reference should be made. Part 18 is the standard procedure for making applications in the course of existing proceedings. It should be noted that by rule 18.9 the court may deal with an application without a hearing if it does not consider that a hearing would be appropriate.

While rule 9.7(1)(e) permits a party to apply for 'any other form of interim order', it should be noted that applications for injunctions and other forms of interim relief are specifically dealt with by Part 20, to which and to the Commentary to which reference should be made.

Costs in financial remedy proceedings

The former rule 2.71 (enshrining the general rule of no order as to costs in ancillary relief proceedings) is not repeated in Part 9: it is now to be found in rule 28.3: see that rule and Commentary on Part 28 *below*. Suffice to note here that the general 'no order' rule is extended to proceedings for a substantive order under Part 3 of the MFPA 1984 and to applications under section 10(2) of the MCA 1973 (and their CPA equivalents), but *no longer applies* to applications for an order for maintenance pending suit, an order for maintenance pending outcome of proceedings, an interim periodical payments order or any other form of interim order for the purposes of rule

9.7(1)(a), (b), (c) and (e). Oddly, the 'no order' rule continues to apply to interim variation orders.

This is a significant change designed to meet the complaint that the 'no order' rule effectively emasculated the economic value of many such orders. It is slightly surprising that the same distinction has not been carried through to variation orders, whether interim or final, where similar concerns have been raised, although PD 28A para 4.4 supplies a strong steer in favour of making orders for costs in such proceedings.

The no order rule *does not apply* to proceedings under Schedule 1 to the Children Act 1989; under section 27 of the Matrimonial Causes Act 1973 (failure to maintain); under section 35 of the Matrimonial Causes Act 1973 (alteration of maintenance agreement); or under the Domestic Proceedings and Magistrates Courts Act 1978 (or their CPA equivalents).

It should be noted that by rule 28.3(8) the prohibition on the use of *Calderbank* letters remains in place *only where the general rule remains in force*. It follows that *Calderbank* offers are admissible by virtue of rule 28.2 (which applies CPR rule 44.3(4)(c)) for those interim applications where the general rule has been disapplied, and for those other financial remedy proceedings referred to above where it does not apply.

Procedure in magistrates' courts
Chapter 5 contains the procedure governing applications made in the magistrates' court. A first hearing will be ordered. 14 days after issue of the application the parties must file and exchange an even more truncated version of Form E, Form E2. There is no FDR procedure.

Consequential powers and consent orders
Chapter 6 replicates the previous rules concerning the consequential powers of the court when making an order for sale of land.

Rule 9.26 restates the old familiar rules concerning consent orders. To these PD 9A paras 7.1 to 7.3 apply, to which reference should be made. The new Form to be completed for obtaining a consent order, Form D81, is somewhat expanded in comparison to its predecessor Form M1.

Estimates of costs and open proposals
Chapter 7 reproduces the familiar rules concerning estimates of costs and the obligation to make open proposals.

Pensions
Chapter 8 deals with pensions largely in the same terms as before, and Chapter 9 deals with (the very rare) pension protection fund compensation cases.

Pre-action protocol
PD 9A para 2.1 refers to the pre-action protocol contained in the Annex to that PD and states that the court expects the parties to comply with its

terms. Para 3.4 states that any breach of the pre-application protocol annexed to it will be taken into account by the court when deciding whether to depart from the general rule as to costs. The pre-action protocol largely replicates the old pre-action protocol although paras 3.8 to 3.14, which dealt with the instruction of experts, have been omitted, for reasons which are not clear.

Applications to set aside

An important change in procedure is the abolition of CCR Ord 37, rule 1, (which gave a judge power on application to order a rehearing where no error of the court at the hearing is alleged). Thus an appeal is now the only way to challenge (e.g. on *Barder* or non-disclosure grounds) an inter partes order which is otherwise valid: see Commentary on Part 30 *below*. This is consistent with the CPR approach. Cases suggesting that such applications could be heard at first instance, whether by issue of a writ (*Robinson v Robinson (Disclosure)* (1983) 4 FLR 102), or inter partes summons in the High Court (*Re C (Financial Provision: Leave to Appeal)* [1993] 2 FLR 799), or application under CCR Ord 37, rule 1 (*Benson v Benson (Deceased)* [1996] 1 FLR 692, *T v T (Consent Order: Procedure to Set Aside)* [1996] 2 FLR 640) are all now overreached.

Forms

By PD 5A the following Forms must be used in relation to applications and proceedings under Part 9:

Form A	Notice of [intention to proceed with] an application for a financial order
Form A1	Notice of [intention to proceed with] an application for a financial remedy (other than a financial order) in the county or high court
Form A2	Notice of [intention to proceed with] an application for a financial remedy in the magistrates court
Form B	Notice of an application to consider the financial position of the Respondent after the divorce/dissolution
Form E	Financial Statement for a financial order or for financial relief after an overseas divorce or dissolution etc
Form E1	Financial Statement for a financial remedy (other than a financial order or financial relief after an overseas divorce/dissolution etc) in the county or high court
Form E2	Financial Statement for a financial remedy in the magistrates court
Form F	Notice of allegation in proceedings for financial remedy
Form H	Estimate of costs (financial remedy)
Form H1	Statement of costs for final hearing (financial remedy)

Form I	Notice of request for periodical payments order at the same rate as order for interim maintenance pending outcome of proceeding
Form P	Pension inquiry form
Form P1	Pension sharing annex
Form P2	Pension attachment annex
Form PPF	Pension Protection Fund Inquiry Form
Form PPF 1	Pension Protection Fund sharing annex
Form PPF 2	Pension Protection Fund attachment annex

As before, Form A should be used whether the applicant is proceeding with an application in the petition or answer or is making a free-standing application.

As noted *above* the inclusion of Form F is possibly an oversight, since it relates to a non-existent rule now that the former rule 2.60 (which required notice of an allegation of adultery or other improper association against a named person to be given to that person) has not survived into Part 9 of FPR 2010.

Correspondances

The following Table sets out the correlation between FPR 1991 (as amended) and FPR 2010 (as promulgated).

FPR 1991	*Subject matter*	*FPR 2010*
2.51D	The overriding objective	Part 1
2.52	Right to be heard on ancillary questions	9.4
2.53	Application by petitioner or respondent for ancillary relief	9.4
2.54	Application by parent, guardian etc for ancillary relief in respect of children	9.10
2.57	Children to be separately represented on certain applications	9.11
2.59	Evidence on application for property adjustment or avoidance of disposition order	9.13
2.60	Service of statement in answer	abrogated
2.61	Information on application for consent order for financial relief	9.26
2.61A	Application for ancillary relief	9.12
2.61B	Procedure before the first appointment	9.14
2.61C	Expert evidence	Part 25
2.61D	The First Appointment	9.15, 9.16
2.61E	The FDR appointment	9.17
2.61F	Costs	9.27

PART 9: APPLICATIONS FOR A FINANCIAL REMEDY

CHAPTER 1: APPLICATION AND INTERPRETATION

Application
9.1. The rules in this Part apply to an application for a financial remedy.
("Financial remedy" and "financial order" are defined in rule 2.3)

Application of Magistrates' Courts Rules 1981
9.2 Unless the context otherwise requires, and subject to the rules in this Part, the following rules of the Magistrates' Courts Rules 1981[48] apply to proceedings in a magistrates' court which are family proceedings under section 65 of the Magistrates' Courts Act 1980—

(a) rule 39(6) (method of making periodical payments);
(b) rule 41 (revocation etc. of orders for periodical payments);
(c) rule 43 (service of copy of order);
(d) rule 44 (remission of sums due under order);
(e) rule 45 (duty of designated officer to notify subsequent marriage or

formation of civil partnership of person entitled to payments under a maintenance order);

(f) rule 48 (to whom payments are to be made);

(g) rule 49 (duty of designated officer to give receipt);

(h) rule 51 (application for further time);

(i) rule 62 (particulars relating to payment of lump sum under a magistrates' courts maintenance order etc. to be entered in register);

(j) rule 66 (register of convictions, etc.);

(k) rule 67 (proof of service, handwriting, etc.);

(l) rule 68 (proof of proceedings); and

(m) rule 69 (proof that magistrates' court maintenance orders, etc, have not been revoked, etc.).

Interpretation

9.3.—(1) In this Part—

"avoidance of disposition order" means—

(a) in proceedings under the 1973 Act, an order under section 37(2)(b) or (c) of that Act;

(b) in proceedings under the 1984 Act, an order under section 23(2)(b) or 23(3) of that Act[49];

(c) in proceedings under Schedule 5 to the 2004 Act, an order under paragraph 74(3) or (4); or

(d) in proceedings under Schedule 7 to the 2004 Act, an order under paragraph 15(3) or (4);

"the Board" means the Board of the Pension Protection Fund;

"FDR appointment" means a Financial Dispute Resolution appointment in accordance with rule 9.17;

"order preventing a disposition" means—

(a) in proceedings under the 1973 Act, an order under section 37(2)(a) of that Act;

(b) in proceedings under the 1984 Act, an order under section 23(2)(a) of that Act;

(c) in proceedings under Schedule 5 to the 2004 Act, an order under paragraph 74(2); or

(d) in proceedings under Schedule 7 to the 2004 Act, an order under paragraph 15(2);

"pension arrangement" means—

(a) an occupational pension scheme;

(b) a personal pension scheme;

(c) shareable state scheme rights;

(d) a retirement annuity contract;

(e) an annuity or insurance policy purchased, or transferred, for the purpose of giving effect to rights under an occupational pension scheme or a personal pension scheme; and

(f) an annuity purchased, or entered into, for the purpose of discharging liability in respect of a pension credit under section 29(1)(b) of the Welfare Reform and Pensions Act 1999 or under corresponding Northern Ireland legislation;

"pension attachment order" means—

(a) in proceedings under the 1973 Act, an order making provision under section 25B or 25C of that Act[50];

(b) in proceedings under the 1984 Act, an order under section 17(1)(a)(i) of that Act making provision equivalent to an order referred to in paragraph (a);

(c) in proceedings under Schedule 5 to the 2004 Act, an order making provision under paragraph 25 or paragraph 26; or

(d) in proceedings under Schedule 7 to the 2004 Act, an order under paragraph 9(2)[51] or (3) making provision equivalent to an order referred to in paragraph (c);

"pension compensation attachment order" means—

(a) in proceedings under the 1973 Act, an order making provision under section 25F of that Act;[52]

(b) in proceedings under the 1984 Act, an order under section 17(1)(a)(i) of that Act[53] making provision equivalent to an order referred in to paragraph (a);

(c) in proceedings under Schedule 5 to the 2004 Act, an order under paragraph 34A; and

(d) in proceedings under Schedule 7 to the 2004 Act, an order under paragraph 9(2) or (3) making provision equivalent to an order referred to in paragraph (c);

"pension compensation sharing order" means—

(a) in proceedings under the 1973 Act, an order under section 24E of that Act[54];

(b) in proceedings under the 1984 Act, an order under section 17(1)(c) of that Act;

(c) in proceedings under Schedule 5 to the 2004 Act, an order under paragraph 19A; and

(d) in proceedings under Schedule 7 to the 2004 Act, an order under paragraph 9(2) or (3)[55] making provision equivalent to an order referred to in paragraph (c);

"pension sharing order" means—

(a) in proceedings under the 1973 Act, an order making provision under section 24B of that Act[56];

(b) in proceedings under the 1984 Act, an order under section 17(1)(b) of that Act;

(c) in proceedings under Schedule 5 to the 2004 Act, an order under paragraph 15; or

(d) in proceedings under Schedule 7 to the 2004 Act, an order under paragraph 9(2) or (3) making provision equivalent to an order referred to in paragraph (c);

"pension scheme" means, unless the context otherwise requires, a scheme for which the Board has assumed responsibility in accordance with Chapter 3 of Part 2 of the Pensions Act 2004 (pension protection) or any provision in force in Northern Ireland corresponding to that Chapter;

"PPF compensation" has the meaning given to it—

(a) in proceedings under the 1973 Act, by section 21C of the 1973 Act[57];

(b) in proceedings under the 1984 Act, by section 18(7) of the 1984 Act; and

(c) in proceedings under the 2004 Act, by paragraph 19F of Schedule 5 to the 2004 Act;

"relevant valuation" means a valuation of pension rights or benefits as at a date not more than 12 months earlier than the date fixed for the first appointment which has been furnished or requested for the purposes of any of the following provisions—

(a) the Pensions on Divorce etc (Provision of Information) Regulations 2000[58];

(b) regulation 5 of and Schedule 2 to the Occupational Pension Schemes (Disclosure of Information) Regulations 1996[59] and regulation 11 of and Schedule 1 to the Occupational Pension Schemes (Transfer Value) Regulations 1996[60];

(c) section 93A or 94(1)(a) or (aa) of the Pension Schemes Act 1993[61];

(d) section 94(1)(b) of the Pension Schemes Act 1993 or paragraph 2(a) (or, where applicable, 2(b)) of Schedule 2 to the Personal Pension Schemes (Disclosure of Information) Regulations 1987[62];

(e) the Dissolution etc. (Pensions) Regulations 2005[63];

"variation order" means—

(a) in proceedings under the 1973 Act, an order under section 31 of that Act; or

(b) in proceedings under the 2004 Act, an order under Part 11 of Schedule 5 to that Act.

(2) References in this Part to a county court are to be construed, in

relation to proceedings for a financial order, as references to a divorce county court or a civil partnership proceedings county court, as the case may be.

CHAPTER 2: PROCEDURE FOR APPLICATIONS

When an Application for a financial order may be made
9.4. An application for a financial order may be made—

(a) in an application for a matrimonial or civil partnership order; or
(b) at any time after an application for a matrimonial or civil partnership order has been made.

Where to start proceedings
9.5.—(1) An application for a financial remedy must be filed—

(a) if there are proceedings for a matrimonial order or a civil partnership order which are proceeding in a designated county court, in that court; or
(b) if there are proceedings for a matrimonial order or a civil partnership order which are proceeding in the High Court, in the registry in which those proceedings are taking place.

(2) In any other case, in relation to the application set out in column 1 of the following table, column 2 sets out where the application must be filed.

Provision under which application is made	*Court where application must be filed*
Section 27 of the 1973 Act.[64]	Divorce county court.
Part 9 of Schedule 5 to the 2004 Act.	Civil partnership proceedings county court.
Part 3 of the 1984 Act.	Principal Registry or, in relation to an application for a consent order, a divorce county court.
Schedule 7 to the 2004 Act.	Principal Registry or, in relation to an application for a consent order, a civil partnership proceedings county court.
Section 35 of the 1973 Act.[65]	High Court, a divorce county court or a magistrates' court.

Paragraph 69 of Schedule 5 to the	High Court, a civil 2004 Act. partnership proceedings county court or a magistrates' court.
Schedule 1 to the 1989 Act.	High Court, designated county court or a magistrates' court.
Part 1 of the 1978 Act.	Magistrates' court.
Schedule 6 to the 2004 Act.	Magistrates' court.

(3) An application for a financial remedy under Part 3 of the 1984 Act, or Schedule 7 to the 2004 Act which is proceeding in the High Court must be heard by a judge, but not a district judge, of that court unless a direction has been made that the application may be heard by a district judge of the principal registry.

(Rule 8.28 enables a judge to direct that an application for a financial remedy under Part 3 of the 1984 Act or Schedule 7 to the 2004 Act may be heard by a district judge of the principal registry.)

Application for an order preventing a disposition

9.6.— The Part 18 procedure applies to an application for an order preventing a disposition.

(2) An application for an order preventing a disposition may be made without notice to the respondent.

("Order preventing a disposition" is defined in rule 9.3.)

Application for interim orders

9.7.—(1) A party may apply at any stage of the proceedings for—

  (a) an order for maintenance pending suit;
  (b) an order for maintenance pending outcome of proceedings;
  (c) an order for interim periodical payments;
  (d) an interim variation order; or
  (e) any other form of interim order.

(2) The Part 18 procedure applies to an application for an interim order.

(3) Where a party makes an application before filing a financial statement, the written evidence in support must—

  (a) explain why the order is necessary; and
  (b) give up to date information about that party's financial circumstances.

(4) Unless the respondent has filed a financial statement, the respondent must, at least 7 days before the court is to deal with the application, file a statement of his means and serve a copy on the applicant.

(5) An application for an order mentioned in paragraph (1) may be made without notice.

Application for periodical payments order at same rate as an order for maintenance pending suit

9.8.—(1) This rule applies where there are matrimonial proceedings and—

    (a) a decree nisi of divorce or nullity of marriage has been made;

    (b) at or after the date of the decree nisi an order for maintenance pending suit is in force; and

    (c) the spouse in whose favour the decree nisi was made has made an application for an order for periodical payments.

(2) The spouse in whose favour the decree nisi was made may apply, using the Part 18 procedure, for an order providing for payments at the same rate as those provided for by the order for maintenance pending suit.

Application for periodical payments order at same rate as an order for maintenance pending outcome of proceedings

9.9.—(1) This rule applies where there are civil partnership proceedings and—

    (a) a conditional order of dissolution or nullity of civil partnership has been made;

    (b) at or after the date of the conditional order an order for maintenance pending outcome of proceedings is in force;

    (c) the civil partner in whose favour the conditional order was made has made an application for an order for periodical payments.

(2) The civil partner in whose favour the conditional order was made may apply, using the Part 18 procedure, for an order providing for payments at the same rate as those provided for by, the order for maintenance pending the outcome of proceedings.

CHAPTER 3: APPLICATIONS FOR FINANCIAL REMEDIES FOR CHILDREN

Application by parent, guardian etc for financial remedy in respect of children

9.10.—(1) The following people may apply for a financial remedy in respect of a child—

    (a) a parent, guardian or special guardian of any child of the family;

    (b) any person in whose favour a residence order has been made with respect to a child of the family, and any applicant for such an order;

    (c) any other person who is entitled to apply for a residence order with respect to a child;

(d) a local authority, where an order has been made under section 31(1)(a) of the 1989 Act placing a child in its care;

(e) the Official Solicitor, if appointed the children's guardian of a child of the family under rule 16.24; and

(f) a child of the family who has been given permission to apply for a financial remedy.

(2) In this rule "residence order" has the meaning given to it by section 8(1) of the 1989 Act.

Children to be separately represented on certain applications

9.11.—(1) Where an application for a financial remedy includes an application for an order for a variation of settlement, the court must, unless it is satisfied that the proposed variation does not adversely affect the rights or interests of any child concerned, direct that the child be separately represented on the application.

(2) On any other application for a financial remedy the court may direct that the child be separately represented on the application.

(3) Where a direction is made under paragraph (1) or (2), the court may if the person to be appointed so consents, appoint—

(a) a person other than the Official Solicitor; or

(b) the Official Solicitor,

to be a children's guardian and rule 16.24(5) and (6) and rules 16.25 to 16.28 apply as appropriate to such an appointment.

CHAPTER 4: PROCEDURE IN THE HIGH COURT AND COUNTY COURT AFTER FILING AN APPLICATION

Duties of the court and the applicant upon issuing an application

9.12.—(1) When an application under this Part is issued in the High Court or in a county court—

(a) the court will fix a first appointment not less than 12 weeks and not more than 16 weeks after the date of the filing of the application; and

(b) subject to paragraph (2), within 4 days beginning with the date on which the application was filed, a court officer will—

(i) serve a copy of the application on the respondent; and

(ii) give notice of the date of the first appointment to the applicant and the respondent.

(2) Where the applicant wishes to serve a copy of the application on the respondent and on filing the application so notifies the court—

(a) paragraph (1)(b) does not apply;

(b) a court officer will return to the applicant the copy of the application and the notice of the date of the first appointment; and
(c) the applicant must,—
  (i) within 4 days beginning with the date on which the copy of the application is received from the court, serve the copy of the application and notice of the date of the first appointment on the respondent; and
  (ii) file a certificate of service at or before the first appointment.

(Rule 6.37 sets out what must be included in a certificate of service.)

(3) The date fixed under paragraph (1), or for any subsequent appointment, must not be cancelled except with the court's permission and, if cancelled, the court must immediately fix a new date.

Service of application on mortgagees, trustees etc

9.13.—(1) Where an application for a financial remedy includes an application for an order for a variation of settlement, the applicant must serve copies of the application on—

(a) the trustees of the settlement;
(b) the settlor if living; and
(c) such other persons as the court directs.

(2) In the case of an application for an avoidance of disposition order, the applicant must serve copies of the application on the person in whose favour the disposition is alleged to have been made.

(3) Where an application for a financial remedy includes an application relating to land, the applicant must serve a copy of the application on any mortgagee of whom particulars are given in the application.

(4) Any person served under paragraphs (1), (2) or (3) may make a request to the court in writing, within 14 days beginning with the date of service of the application, for a copy of the applicant's financial statement or any relevant part of that statement.

(5) Any person who—

(a) is served with copies of the application in accordance with paragraphs (1), (2) or (3); or
(b) receives a copy of a financial statement, or a relevant part of that statement, following an application made under paragraph (4),

may within 14 days beginning with the date of service or receipt file a statement in answer.

(6) Where a copy of an application is served under paragraphs (1), (2) or (3), the applicant must file a certificate of service at or before the first appointment.

(7) A statement in answer filed under paragraph (5) must be verified by a statement of truth.

Procedure before the first appointment

9.14.—(1) Not less than 35 days before the first appointment both parties must simultaneously exchange with each other and file with the court a financial statement in the form referred to in Practice Direction 5A.

(2) The financial statement must—

(a) be verified by an affidavit; and
(b) accompanied by the following documents only—
    (i) any documents required by the financial statement;
    (ii) any other documents necessary to explain or clarify any of the information contained in the financial statement; and
    (iii) any documents provided to the party producing the financial statement by a person responsible for a pension arrangement, either following a request under rule 9.30 or as part of a relevant valuation; and
    (iv) any notification or other document referred to in rule 9.37(2), (4) or (5) which has been received by the party producing the financial statement.

(3) Where a party was unavoidably prevented from sending any document required by the financial statement, that party must at the earliest opportunity—

(a) serve a copy of that document on the other party; and
(b) file a copy of that document with the court, together with a written explanation of the failure to send it with the financial statement.

(4) No disclosure or inspection of documents may be requested or given between the filing of the application for a financial remedy and the first appointment, except—

(a) copies sent with the financial statement, or in accordance with paragraph (3); or
(b) in accordance with paragraphs (5) and (6).

(Rule 21.1 explains what is meant by disclosure and inspection.)

(5) Not less than 14 days before the hearing of the first appointment, each party must file with the court and serve on the other party—

(a) a concise statement of the issues between the parties;
(b) a chronology;
(c) a questionnaire setting out by reference to the concise statement of issues any further information and documents requested from the other party or a statement that no information and documents are required; and
(d) a notice stating whether that party will be in a position at the first appointment to proceed on that occasion to a FDR appointment.

(6) Not less than 14 days before the hearing of the first appointment, the applicant must file with the court and serve on the respondent confirmation—

(a) of the names of all persons served in accordance with rule 9.13(1) to (3); and

(b) that there are no other persons who must be served in accordance with those paragraphs.

Duties of the court at the first appointment

9.15.—(1) The first appointment must be conducted with the objective of defining the issues and saving costs.

(2) At the first appointment the court must determine—

(a) the extent to which any questions seeking information under rule 9.14(5)(c) must be answered; and

(b) what documents requested under rule 9.14(5)(c) must be produced,

and give directions for the production of such further documents as may be necessary.

(3) The court must give directions where appropriate about—

(a) the valuation of assets (including the joint instruction of joint experts);

(b) obtaining and exchanging expert evidence, if required;

(c) the evidence to be adduced by each party; and

(d) further chronologies or schedules to be filed by each party.

(4) If the court decides that a referral to a FDR appointment is appropriate it must direct that the case be referred to a FDR appointment.

(5) If the court decides that a referral to a FDR appointment is not appropriate it must direct one or more of the following—

(a) that a further directions appointment be fixed;

(b) that an appointment be fixed for the making of an interim order;

(c) that the case be fixed for a final hearing and, where that direction is given, the court must determine the judicial level at which the case should be heard.

(By rule 3.3 the court may also direct that the case be adjourned if it considers that alternative dispute resolution is appropriate.)

(6) In considering whether to make a costs order under rule 28.3(5), the court must have particular regard to the extent to which each party has complied with the requirement to send documents with the financial statement and the explanation given for any failure to comply.

(7) The court may—

(a) where an application for an interim order has been listed for consideration at the first appointment, make an interim order;

(b) having regard to the contents of the notice filed by the parties under rule 9.14(5)(d), treat the appointment (or part of it) as a FDR appointment to which rule 9.17 applies;

(c) in a case where a pension sharing order or a pension attachment order is requested, direct any party with pension rights to file and serve a Pension Inquiry Form, completed in full or in part as the court may direct; and

(d) in a case where a pension compensation sharing order or a pension compensation attachment order is requested, direct any party with PPF compensation rights to file and serve a Pension Protection Fund Inquiry Form, completed in full or in part as the court may direct.

(8) Both parties must personally attend the first appointment unless the court directs otherwise.

After the first appointment

9.16.—(1) Between the first appointment and the FDR appointment, a party is not entitled to the production of any further documents except—

(a) in accordance with directions given under rule 9.15(2); or

(b) with the permission of the court.

(2) At any stage—

(a) a party may apply for further directions or a FDR appointment;

(b) the court may give further directions or direct that parties attend a FDR appointment.

The FDR appointment

9.17.—(1) The FDR appointment must be treated as a meeting held for the purposes of discussion and negotiation.

(2) The judge hearing the FDR appointment must have no further involvement with the application, other than to conduct any further FDR appointment or to make a consent order or a further directions order.

(3) Not less than 7 days before the FDR appointment, the applicant must file with the court details of all offers and proposals, and responses to them.

(4) Paragraph (3) includes any offers, proposals or responses made wholly or partly without prejudice, but paragraph (3) does not make any material admissible as evidence if, but for that paragraph, it would not be admissible.

(5) At the conclusion of the FDR appointment, any documents filed under paragraph (3), and any filed documents referring to them, must, at the request of the party who filed them, be returned to that party and not retained on the court file.

(6) Parties attending the FDR appointment must use their best endeavours to reach agreement on matters in issue between them.

(7) The FDR appointment may be adjourned from time to time.

(8) At the conclusion of the FDR appointment, the court may make an appropriate consent order.

(9) If the court does not make an appropriate consent order as mentioned in paragraph (8), the court must give directions for the future course of the proceedings including, where appropriate—

(a) the filing of evidence, including up to date information; and
(b) fixing a final hearing date.

(10) Both parties must personally attend the FDR appointment unless the court directs otherwise.

CHAPTER 5: PROCEDURE IN THE MAGISTRATES' COURT AFTER FILING AN APPLICATION

Duties of the court and the applicant upon filing an application

9.18.—(1) When an application for an order under this Part is issued in a magistrates' court—

(a) the court will fix a first hearing date not less than 4 weeks and not more than 8 weeks after the date of the filing of the application; and
(b) subject to paragraph (2), within 4 days beginning with the date on which the application was filed, a court officer will—
  (i) serve a copy of the application on the respondent;
  (ii) give notice of the date of the first hearing to the applicant and the respondent; and
  (iii) send a blank financial statement to both the applicant and the respondent.

(2) Where the applicant wishes to serve a copy of the application on the respondent and, on filing the application, so notifies the court—

(a) paragraph (1)(b) does not apply;
(b) a court officer will return to the applicant the copy of the application and the notice of the date of the first hearing; and
(c) the applicant must—
  (i) within 4 days beginning with the date on which the copy of the application is received from the court, serve the copy of the application and notice of the date of the first hearing on the respondent;
  (ii) send a blank financial statement to the respondent; and
  (iii) file a certificate of service at or before the first hearing.

(3) The date fixed under paragraph (1), or for any other subsequent hearing or appointment must not be cancelled except with the court's permission and, if cancelled, the court must immediately fix a new date.

Procedure before the first hearing

9.19.—(1) Not more than 14 days after the date of the issue of the application both parties must simultaneously exchange with each other and file with the court a financial statement referred to in Practice Direction 5A.

(2) The financial statement must—

(a) be verified by an affidavit; and
(b) contain the following documents only—
  (i) any documents required by the financial statement; and
  (ii) any other documents necessary to explain or clarify any of the information contained in the financial statement.

(3) Where a party was unavoidably prevented from sending any document required by the financial statement, that party must at the earliest opportunity—

(a) serve a copy of that document on the other party; and
(b) file a copy of that document with the court, together with a statement explaining the failure to send it with the financial statement.

(4) No disclosure or inspection of documents may be requested or given between the filing of the application for a financial remedy and the first hearing except copies sent with the financial statement or in accordance with paragraph (3).

(Rule 21.1 explains what is meant by disclosure and inspection.)

Power of the court to direct filing of evidence and set dates for further hearings

9.20. Unless the court is able to determine the application at the first hearing the court may direct that further evidence be filed and set a date for a directions hearing or appointment or final hearing.

Who the respondent is on an application under section 20 or section 20A of the 1978 Act([66]) or Part 6 of Schedule 6 to the 2004 Act

9.21. In relation to proceedings set out in column 1 of the following table, column 2 sets out who the respondents to those proceedings will be

Proceedings	*Respondent*
Application under section 20 of the 1978 Act, except an application for variation of an order.	The other party to the marriage; andwhere the order to which the application relates requires periodical payments to be made to,

Application under paragraphs 30 to 34 of Schedule 6 to the 2004 Act, except an application for variation of an order.	or in respect of, a child who is 16 years of age or over, that child. The other party to the civil partnership; and where the order to which the application relates requires periodical payments to be made to, or in respect of, a child who is 16 years of age or over, that child.
Application for the revival of an order under section 20A of the 1978 Act or paragraph 40 of Schedule 6 to the 2004 Act.	The parties to the proceedings leading to the order which it is sought to have revived.

Proceedings by or against a person outside England and Wales for orders under section 20 of the 1978 Act or paragraphs 30 to 34 of Schedule 6 to the 2004 Act other than proceedings for variation of orders

9.22.—(1) Subject to the provisions of this rule, the jurisdiction conferred on a court by virtue of section 20 of the 1978 Act or paragraphs 30 to 34 of Schedule 6 to the 2004 Act is exercisable when proceedings are brought by or against a person residing outside England and Wales.

(2) Subject to paragraph (3), where the court is satisfied that the respondent has been outside England and Wales for the whole of the period beginning one month before the making of the application and ending with the date of the hearing, it may proceed with the application provided that—

(a) the applicant provided the court with an address for service of the application and written notice of the hearing on the respondent; or

(b) the court is satisfied that the respondent has been made aware of the application and of the time and place appointed for the hearing otherwise than by service of the application upon the respondent by the court; and

(c) it is reasonable in all the circumstances to proceed in the absence of the respondent.

(3) The court must not make the order for which the application is made unless it is satisfied that—

(a) during the period of 6 months immediately preceding the making of the application the respondent was continuously outside England and Wales, or was not in England and Wales on more than 30 days; and

(b) having regard to any communication to the court in writing purporting to be from the respondent, it is reasonable in all the circumstances to do so.

(4) This rule does not apply in relation to proceedings to vary an order for periodical payments.

(Rules made under section 144 of the Magistrates' Courts Act 1980 make provision in respect of proceedings by or against a person outside England and Wales for variation of orders under section 20 of the 1978 Act or paragraphs 30 to 34 of Schedule 6 to the 2004 Act.)

Duty to make entries in the court's register

9.23.—(1) Where the designated officer for the court receives notice of any direction made in the High Court or a county court under section 28 of the 1978 Act[67] by virtue of which an order made by the court under that Act or the 2004 Act ceases to have effect, particulars of the direction must be entered in the court's register.

(2) Where—

(a) in proceedings under the 1978 Act, the hearing of an application under section 2 of that Act[68] is adjourned after the court has decided that it is satisfied of any ground mentioned in section 1[69]; or

(b) in proceedings under the 2004 Act, the hearing of an application under Part 1 of Schedule 6 to that Act is adjourned after the court has decided that it is satisfied of any ground mentioned in paragraph 1,

and the parties to the proceedings agree to the resumption of the hearing in accordance with section 31 of the 1978 Act by a court which includes justices who were not sitting when the hearing began, particulars of the agreement must be entered into the court's register.

CHAPTER 6: GENERAL PROCEDURE

Power to order delivery up of possession etc.

9.24.—(1) This rule applies where the court has made an order under—

(a) section 24A of the 1973 Act[70];
(b) section 17(2) of the 1984 Act;
(c) Part 3 of Schedule 5 to the 2004 Act; or
(d) paragraph 9(4) of Schedule 7 to the 2004 Act.

(2) When the court makes an order mentioned in paragraph (1), it may order any party to deliver up to the purchaser or any other person—

(a) possession of the land, including any interest in, or right over, land;
(b) receipt of rents or profits relating to it; or
(c) both.

Where proceedings may be heard

9.25.—(1) Paragraph (2) applies to an application—

(a) for a financial order;
(b) under Part 3 of the 1984 Act; or
(c) under Schedule 7 to the 2004 Act.

(2) An application mentioned in paragraph (1) must be heard—

(a) where the case is proceeding in the county court, at any court of trial; and
(b) where the case is proceeding in the High Court—
    (i) at the Royal Courts of Justice; or
    (ii) in matrimonial or civil partnership proceedings, any court at which sittings of the High Court are authorised.

(3) An application for an order under—

(a) section 27 of the 1973 Act[71]; or
(b) Part 9 of Schedule 5 to the 2004 Act,
must be heard in a court of trial or in the High Court.

(4) A court may transfer a case to another court exercising the same jurisdiction, either of its own initiative or on the application of one of the parties, if—

(a) the parties consent to the transfer;
(b) the court has held a hearing to determine whether a transfer should be ordered; or
(c) paragraph (5) applies.

(5) A court may transfer a case without a hearing if—

(a) the court has notified the parties in writing that it intends to order a transfer; and
(b) neither party has, within 14 days of the notification being sent, requested a hearing to determine whether a transfer should be ordered.

Applications for consent orders for financial remedy

9.26.—(1) Subject to paragraph (5) and to rule 35.2, in relation to an application for a consent order—

(a) the applicant must file two copies of a draft of the order in the terms sought, one of which must be endorsed with a statement signed by the respondent to the application signifying agreement; and
(b) each party must file with the court and serve on the other party, a statement of information in the form referred to in Practice Direction 5A.

(2) Where each party's statement of information is contained in one form, it must be signed by both the applicant and respondent to certify that they have read the contents of the other party's statement.

(3) Where each party's statement of information is in a separate form, the form of each party must be signed by the other party to certify that they have read the contents of the statement contained in that form.

(4) Unless the court directs otherwise, the applicant and the respondent need not attend the hearing of an application for a consent order.

(5) Where all or any of the parties attend the hearing of an application for a financial remedy the court may—

(a) dispense with the filing of a statement of information; and
(b) give directions for the information which would otherwise be required to be given in such a statement in such a manner as it thinks fit.

(6) In relation to an application for a consent order under Part 3 of the 1984 Act or Schedule 7 to the 2004 Act, the application for permission to make the application may be heard at the same time as the application for a financial remedy if evidence of the respondent's consent to the order is filed with the application.

(The following rules contain provision in relation to applications for consent orders – rule 9.32 (pension sharing order), rule 9.34 (pension attachment order), rule 9.41 (pension compensation sharing orders) and rule 9.43 (pension compensation attachment orders.)

CHAPTER 7: ESTIMATES OF COSTS

Estimates of Costs

9.27.—(1) Subject to paragraph (2), at every hearing or appointment each party must produce to the court an estimate of the costs incurred by that party up to the date of that hearing or appointment.

(2) Not less than 14 days before the date fixed for the final hearing of an application for a financial remedy, each party ("the filing party") must (unless the court directs otherwise) file with the court and serve on each other party a statement giving full particulars of all costs in respect of the proceedings which the filing party has incurred or expects to incur, to enable the court to take account of the parties' liabilities for costs when deciding what order (if any) to make for a financial remedy.

(3) This rule does not apply to magistrates' courts.

(Rule 28.3 makes provision for orders for costs in financial remedy proceedings.)

Duty to make open proposals

9.28.—(1) Not less than 14 days before the date fixed for the final hearing of an application for a financial remedy, the applicant must (unless the court directs otherwise) file with the court and serve on the respondent an open statement which sets out concise details, including the amounts involved, of the orders which the applicant proposes to ask the court to make.

(2) Not more than 7 days after service of a statement under paragraph (1), the respondent must file with the court and serve on the applicant an open statement which sets out concise details, including the amounts involved, of the orders which the respondent proposes to ask the court to make.

CHAPTER 8: PENSIONS

Application and interpretation of this Chapter

9.29.—(1) This Chapter applies

(a) where an application for a financial remedy has been made; and
(b) the applicant or respondent is the party with pension rights.

(2) In this Chapter—

(a) in proceedings under the 1973 Act and the 1984 Act, all words and phrases defined in sections 25D(3) and (4) of the 1973 Act[72] have the meaning assigned by those subsections;
(b) in proceedings under the 2004 Act—
  (i) all words and phrases defined in paragraphs 16(4) to (5) and 29 of Schedule 5 to that Act have the meanings assigned by those paragraphs; and
  (ii) "the party with pension rights" has the meaning given to "civil partner with pension rights" by paragraph 29 of Schedule 5 to the 2004 Act;
(c) all words and phrases defined in section 46 of the Welfare Reform and Pensions Act 1999[73] have the meanings assigned by that section.

What the party with pension rights must do when the court fixes a first appointment

9.30.—(1) Where the court fixes a first appointment as required by rule 9.12(1)(a) the party with pension rights must request the person responsible for each pension arrangement under which the party has or is likely to have benefits to provide the information referred to in regulation 2(2) of the Pensions on Divorce etc (Provision of Information) Regulations 2000.

(The information referred to in regulation 2 of the Pensions on Divorce etc (Provision of Information) Regulations 2000 relates to the valuation of pension rights or benefits.)

(2) The party with pension rights must comply with paragraph (1) within 7 days beginning with the date on which that party receives notification of the date of the first appointment.

(3) Within 7 days beginning with the date on which the party with pension rights receives the information under paragraph (1) that party must send a copy of it to the other party, together with the name and address of the person responsible for each pension arrangement.

(4) A request under paragraph (1) need not be made where the party with pension rights is in possession of, or has requested, a relevant valuation of the pension rights or benefits accrued under the pension arrangement in question.

Applications for pension sharing orders

9.31. Where an application for a financial remedy includes an application for a pension sharing order, or where a request for such an order is added to an existing application for a financial remedy, the applicant must serve a copy of the application on the person responsible for the pension arrangement concerned.

Applications for consent orders for pension sharing

9.32.—(1) This rule applies where—

(a) the parties have agreed on the terms of an order and the agreement includes a pension sharing order;
(b) service has not been effected under rule 9.31; and
(c) the information referred to in paragraph (2) has not otherwise been provided.

(2) The party with pension rights must—

(a) request the person responsible for the pension arrangement concerned to provide the information set out in Section C of the Pension Inquiry Form; and
(b) on receipt, send a copy of the information referred to in sub-paragraph (a) to the other party.

Applications for pension attachment orders

9.33.—(1) Where an application for a financial remedy includes an application for a pension attachment order, or where a request for such an order is added to an existing application for a financial remedy, the applicant must serve a copy of the application on the person responsible for the pension arrangement concerned and must at the same time send—

(a) an address to which any notice which the person responsible is required to serve on the applicant is to be sent;

(b) an address to which any payment which the person responsible is required to make to the applicant is to be sent; and

(c) where the address in sub-paragraph (b) is that of a bank, a building society or the Department of National Savings, sufficient details to enable the payment to be made into the account of the applicant.

(2) A person responsible for a pension arrangement who receives a copy of the application under paragraph (1) may, within 21 days beginning with the date of service of the application, request the party with the pension rights to provide that person with the information disclosed in the financial statement relating to the party's pension rights or benefits under that arrangement.

(3) If the person responsible for a pension arrangement makes a request under paragraph (2), the party with the pension rights must provide that person with a copy of the section of that party's financial statement that relates to that party's pension rights or benefits under that arrangement.

(4) The party with the pension rights must comply with paragraph (3)—

(a) within the time limited for filing the financial statement by rule 9.14(1); or

(b) within 21 days beginning with the date on which the person responsible for the pension arrangement makes the request,
whichever is the later.

(5) A person responsible for a pension arrangement who receives a copy of the section of a financial statement as required pursuant to paragraph (4) may, within 21 days beginning with the date on which that person receives it, send to the court, the applicant and the respondent a statement in answer.

(6) A person responsible for a pension arrangement who files a statement in answer pursuant to paragraph (5) will be entitled to be represented at the first appointment, or such other hearing as the court may direct, and the court must within 4 days, beginning with the date on which that person files the statement in answer, give the person notice of the date of the first appointment or other hearing as the case may be.

Applications for consent orders for pension attachment
9.34.—(1) This rule applies where service has not been effected under rule 9.33(1).

(2) Where the parties have agreed on the terms of an order and the agreement includes a pension attachment order, then they must serve on the person responsible for the pension arrangement concerned—

(a) a copy of the application for a consent order;

(b) a draft of the proposed order, complying with rule 9.35; and

(c) the particulars set out in rule 9.33(1).

(3) No consent order that includes a pension attachment order must be made unless either—

(a) the person responsible for the pension arrangement has not made any objection within 21 days beginning with the date on which the application for a consent order was served on that person; or

(b) the court has considered any such objection, and for the purpose of considering any objection the court may make such direction as it sees fit for the person responsible to attend before it or to furnish written details of the objection.

Pension sharing orders or pension attachment orders

9.35. An order for a financial remedy, whether by consent or not, which includes a pension sharing order or a pension attachment order, must—

(a) in the body of the order, state that there is to be provision by way of pension sharing or pension attachment in accordance with the annex or annexes to the order; and

(b) be accompanied by a pension sharing annex or a pension attachment annex as the case may require, and if provision is made in relation to more than one pension arrangement there must be one annex for each pension arrangement.

Duty of the court upon making a pension sharing order or a pension attachment order

9.36.—(1) A court which varies or discharges a pension sharing order or a pension attachment order, must send, or direct one of the parties to send—

(a) to the person responsible for the pension arrangement concerned; or

(b) where the Board has assumed responsibility for the pension scheme or part of it, the Board;

the documents referred to in paragraph (4).

(2) A court which makes a pension sharing order or pension attachment order, must send, or direct one of the parties to send to the person responsible for the pension arrangement concerned, the documents referred to in paragraph (4).

(3) Where the Board has assumed responsibility for the pension scheme or part of it after the making of a pension sharing order or attachment order but before the documents have been sent to the person responsible for the pension arrangement in accordance with paragraph (2), the court which makes the pension sharing order or the pension attachment order, must send, or direct one of the parties to send to the Board the documents referred to in paragraph (4).

(4) The documents to be sent in accordance with paragraph (1) to (3) are—

(a) in the case of—
   (i) proceedings under the 1973 Act, a copy of the decree of judicial separation;
   (ii) proceedings under Schedule 5 to the 2004 Act, a copy of the separation order;
   (iii) proceedings under Part 3 of the 1984 Act, a copy of the document of divorce, annulment or legal separation;
   (iv) proceedings under Schedule 7 to the 2004 Act, a copy of the document of dissolution, annulment or legal separation;
(b) in the case of divorce or nullity of marriage, a copy of the decree absolute under rule 7.31 or 7.32; or
(c) in the case of dissolution or nullity of civil partnership, a copy of the order making the conditional order final under rule 7.31 or 7.32; and
(d) a copy of the pension sharing order or the pension attachment order, or as the case may be of the order varying or discharging that order, including any annex to that order relating to that pension arrangement but no other annex to that order.

(5) The documents referred to in paragraph (1) must be sent—

(a) in proceedings under the 1973 Act and the 1984 Act, within 7 days beginning with the date on which—
   (i) the relevant pension sharing or pension attachment order is made; or
   (ii) the decree absolute of divorce or nullity or decree of judicial separation is made,
   whichever is the later; and
(b) in proceedings under the 2004 Act, within 7 days beginning with the date on which—
   (i) the relevant pension sharing or pension attachment order is made; or
   (ii) the final order of dissolution or nullity or separation order is made,
   whichever is the later.

Procedure where Pension Protection Fund becomes involved with the pension scheme

9.37.—(1) This rule applies where—

(a) rules 9.30 to 9.34 or 9.36 apply; and
(b) the party with the pension rights ("the member") receives or has received notification in compliance with the Pension Protection Fund (Provision of Information) Regulations 2005 ("the 2005 Regulations")[74]—
   (i) from the trustees or managers of a pension scheme, that there is an assessment period in relation to that scheme; or

(ii) from the Board that it has assumed responsibility for the pension scheme or part of it.

(2) If the trustees or managers of the pension scheme notify or have notified the member that there is an assessment period in relation to that scheme, the member must send to the other party, all the information which the Board is required from time to time to provide to the member under the 2005 Regulations including—

(a) a copy of the notification; and
(b) a copy of the valuation summary,
in accordance with paragraph (3).

(3) The member must send the information or any part of it referred to in paragraph (2)—

(a) if available, when the member sends the information received under rule 9.30(1); or
(b) otherwise, within 7 days of receipt.

(4) If the Board notifies the member that it has assumed responsibility for the pension scheme, or part of it, the member must—

(a) send a copy of the notification to the other party within 7 days of receipt; and
(b) comply with paragraph (5).

(5) Where paragraph (4) applies, the member must—

(a) within 7 days of receipt of the notification, request the Board in writing to provide a forecast of the member's compensation entitlement as described in the 2005 Regulations; and
(b) send a copy of the forecast of the member's compensation entitlement to the other party within 7 days of receipt.

(6) In this rule—

(a) "assessment period" means an assessment period within the meaning of Part 2 of the Pensions Act 2004; and
(b) "valuation summary" has the meaning assigned to it by the 2005 Regulations.

CHAPTER 9: PENSION PROTECTION FUND COMPENSATION

Application and interpretation of this Chapter
9.38.—(1) This Chapter applies—

(a) where an application for a financial remedy has been made; and

(b) the applicant or respondent is, the party with compensation rights.

(2) In this Chapter "party with compensation rights"—

(a) in proceedings under the 1973 Act and the 1984 Act, has the meaning given to it by section 25G(5) of the 1973 Act;
(b) in proceedings under the 2004 Act, has the meaning given to "civil partner with compensation rights" by paragraph 37(1) of Schedule 5 to the 2004 Act[75].

What the party with compensation rights must do when the court fixes a first appointment

9.39.—(1) Where the court fixes a first appointment as required by rule 9.12(1)(a) the party with compensation rights must request the Board to provide the information about the valuation of entitlement to PPF compensation referred to in regulations made by the Secretary of State under section 118 of the Pensions Act 2008.

(2) The party with compensation rights must comply with paragraph (1) within 7 days beginning with the date on which that party receives notification of the date of the first appointment.

(3) Within 7 days beginning with the date on which the party with compensation rights receives the information under paragraph (1) that party must send a copy of it to the other party, together with the name and address of the trustees or managers responsible for each pension scheme.

(4) Where the rights to PPF Compensation are derived from rights under more than one pension scheme, the party with compensation rights must comply with this rule in relation to each entitlement.

Applications for pension compensation sharing orders

9.40. Where an application for a financial remedy includes an application for a pension compensation sharing order or where a request for such an order is added to an existing application for a financial remedy, the applicant must serve a copy of the application on the Board.

Applications for consent orders for pension compensation sharing

9.41.—(1) This rule applies where—

(a) the parties have agreed on the terms of an order and the agreement includes a pension compensation sharing order;
(b) service has not been effected under rule 9.40; and
(c) the information referred to in paragraph (2) has not otherwise been provided.

(2) The party with compensation rights must—

(a) request the Board to provide the information set out in Section C of the Pension Protection Fund Inquiry Form; and

(b) on receipt, send a copy of the information referred to in sub-
paragraph (a) to the other party.

Applications for pension compensation attachment orders

9.42. Where an application for a financial remedy includes an application
for a pension compensation attachment order or where a request for such
an order is added to an existing application for a financial remedy, the
applicant must serve a copy of the application on the Board and must at the
same time send—

(a) an address to which any notice which the Board is required to serve
on the applicant is to be sent;

(b) an address to which any payment which the Board is required to
make to the applicant is to be sent; and

(c) where the address in sub-paragraph (b) is that of a bank, a building
society or the Department of National Savings, sufficient details to
enable the payment to be made into the account of the applicant.

Applications for consent orders for pension compensation attachment

9.43.—(1) This rule applies where service has not been effected under rule
9.42.

(2) Where the parties have agreed on the terms of an order and the
agreement includes a pension compensation attachment order, then they
must serve on the Board—

(a) a copy of the application for a consent order;

(b) a draft of the proposed order, complying with rule 9.44; and

(c) the particulars set out in rule 9.42.

Pension compensation sharing orders or pension compensation attachment orders

9.44. An order for a financial remedy, whether by consent or not, which
includes a pension compensation sharing order or a pension compensation
attachment order, must—

(a) in the body of the order, state that there is to be provision by way of
pension compensation sharing or pension compensation attachment
in accordance with the annex or annexes to the order; and

(b) be accompanied by a pension compensation sharing annex or a
pension compensation attachment annex as the case may require,
and if provision is made in relation to entitlement to PPF
compensation that derives from rights under more than one pension
scheme there must be one annex for each such entitlement.

Duty of the court upon making a pension compensation sharing order or a pension compensation attachment order

9.45.—(1) A court which makes, varies or discharges a pension compensation sharing order or a pension compensation attachment order, must send, or direct one of the parties to send, to the Board—

(a) in the case of—
   (i) proceedings under Part 3 of the 1984 Act, a copy of the document of divorce, annulment or legal separation;
   (ii) proceedings under Schedule 7 to the 2004 Act, a copy of the document of dissolution, annulment or legal separation;
(b) in the case of—
   (i) divorce or nullity of marriage, a copy of the decree absolute under rule 7.32 or 7.33;
   (ii) dissolution or nullity of civil partnership, a copy of the order making the conditional order final under rule 7.32 or 7.33;
(c) in the case of separation—
   (i) in the matrimonial proceedings, a copy of the decree of judicial separation;
   (ii) in civil partnership proceedings, a copy of the separation order; and
(d) a copy of the pension compensation sharing order or the pension compensation attachment order, or as the case may be of the order varying or discharging that order, including any annex to that order relating to that PPF compensation but no other annex to that order.

(2) The documents referred to in paragraph (1) must be sent—

(a) in proceedings under the 1973 Act and the 1984 Act, within 7 days beginning with the date on which—
   (i) the relevant pension compensation sharing or pension compensation attachment order is made; or
   (ii) the decree absolute of divorce or nullity or the decree of judicial separation is made,
   whichever is the later; and
(b) in proceedings under the 2004 Act, within 7 days beginning with the date on which—
   (i) the relevant pension compensation sharing or pension compensation attachment order is made; or
   (ii) the final order of dissolution or nullity or separation order is made,
   whichever is the later.

Practice Direction 9A supplements FPR Part 9 (Application for a financial remedy)

PRACTICE DIRECTION 9A – APPLICATION FOR A FINANCIAL REMEDY

This Practice Direction supplements FPR Part 9

Introduction

1.1 Part 9 of the Family Procedure Rules sets out the procedure applicable to the financial proceedings that are included in the definition of a "financial remedy".

1.2 The procedure is applicable to a limited extent to applications for financial remedies that are heard in magistrates' courts (namely, those under section 35 of the Matrimonial Causes Act 1973, paragraph 69 of Schedule 5 to the Civil Partnership Act 2004, Part I of the Domestic Proceedings and Magistrates' Courts Act 1978, Schedule 1 to the Children Act 1989 and Schedule 6 to the Civil Partnership Act 2004). However, unless the context otherwise requires, this Practice Direction does not apply to proceedings in a magistrates' court.

1.3 Where an application for a financial remedy includes an application relating to land, details of any mortgagee must be included in the application.

Pre-application protocol

2.1 The "pre-application protocol" annexed to this Direction outlines the steps parties should take to seek and provide information from and to each other prior to the commencement of any application for a financial remedy. The court will expect the parties to comply with the terms of the protocol.

Costs

3.1 Rule 9.27 applies in the High Court and county court. The rule requires each party to produce to the court, at every hearing or appointment, an estimate of the costs incurred by the party up to the date of that hearing or appointment.

3.2 The purpose of this rule is to enable the court to take account of the impact of each party's costs liability on their financial situations. Parties should ensure that the information contained in the estimate is as full and accurate as possible and that any sums already paid in respect of a party's financial remedy costs are clearly set out. Where relevant, any liability arising from the costs of other proceedings between the parties should continue to be referred to in the appropriate section of a party's financial statement; any such costs should not be included in the estimates under rule 9.27.

3.3 Rule 28.3 provides that the general rule in financial remedy proceedings is that the court will not make an order requiring one party to pay the costs of another party. However the court may make such an order at any stage of the proceedings where it considers it appropriate to do so because of the conduct of a party in relation to the proceedings.

3.4 Any breach of this practice direction or the pre-application protocol annexed to it will be taken into account by the court when deciding whether to depart from the general rule as to costs.

Procedure before the first appointment

4.1 In addition to the matters listed at rule 9.14(5), the parties should, if possible, with a view to identifying and narrowing any issues between the parties, exchange and file with the court—

(a) a summary of the case agreed between the parties;
(b) a schedule of assets agreed between the parties; and
(c) details of any directions that they seek, including, where appropriate, the name of any expert they wish to be appointed.

4.2 Where a party is prevented from sending the details referred to in (c) above, the party should make that information available at the first appointment.

Financial Statements and other documents

5.1 Practice Direction 22A (Written Evidence) applies to any financial statement filed in accordance with rules 9.14 or 9.19 and to any exhibits to a financial statement. In preparing a bundle of documents to be exhibited to or attached to a financial statement, regard must be had in particular to paragraphs 11.1 to 11.3 and 13.1 to 13.4 of that Direction. Where on account of their bulk, it is impracticable for the exhibits to a financial statement to be retained on the court file after the First Appointment, the court may give directions as to their custody pending further hearings.

5.2 Where the court directs a party to provide information or documents by way of reply to a questionnaire or request by another party, the reply must be verified by a statement of truth. Unless otherwise directed, a reply to a questionnaire or request for information and documents shall not be filed with the court.

(Part 17 and Practice Direction 17A make further provision about statements of truth)

Financial Dispute Resolution (FDR) Appointment

6.1 A key element in the procedure is the Financial Dispute Resolution (FDR) appointment. Rule 9.17 provides that the FDR appointment is to be treated as a meeting held for the purposes of discussion and negotiation. Such meetings have been developed as a means of reducing the tension which inevitably arises in family disputes and facilitating settlement of those disputes.

6.2 In order for the FDR to be effective, parties must approach the occasion openly and without reserve. Non-disclosure of the content of such meetings is vital and is an essential prerequisite for fruitful discussion directed to the settlement of the dispute between the parties. The FDR appointment is an important part of the settlement process. As a consequence of Re D (Minors) (Conciliation: Disclosure of Information) [1993] Fam 231, evidence of anything said or of any admission made in the course of an FDR appointment will not be admissible in evidence, except at the trial of a person for an offence committed at the appointment or in the very exceptional circumstances indicated in Re D.

6.3 Courts will therefore expect—

(a) parties to make offers and proposals;
(b) recipients of offers and proposals to give them proper consideration; and
(c) (subject to paragraph 6.4), that parties, whether separately or together, will not seek to exclude from consideration at the appointment any such offer or proposal.

6.4 Paragraph 6.3(c) does not apply to an offer or proposal made during alternative dispute resolution.

6.5 In order to make the most effective use of the first appointment and the FDR appointment, the legal representatives attending those appointments will be expected to have full knowledge of the case.

6.6 The rules do not provide for FDR appointments to take place during proceedings in magistrates' courts.

(Provision relating to experts in financial remedy proceedings is contained in the Practice Direction supplementing Part 25 of the FPR relating to Experts and Assessors in Family Proceedings)

Consent orders

7.1 Rule 9.26(1)(a) requires an application for a consent order to be accompanied by two copies of the draft order in the terms sought, one of which must be endorsed with a statement signed by the respondent to the application signifying the respondent's agreement. The rule is considered to have been properly complied with if the endorsed statement is signed by solicitors on record as acting for the respondent; but where the consent order applied for contains undertakings, it should be signed by the party giving the undertakings as well as by that party's solicitor.

(Provision relating to the enforcement of undertakings is contained in the Practice Direction 33A supplementing Part 33 of the FPR)

7.2 Rule 9.26(1)(b) requires each party to file with the court and serve on the other party a statement of information. Where this is contained in one form, both parties must sign the statement to certify that each has read the contents of the other's statement.

7.3 Rule 35.2 deals with applications for a consent order in respect of a financial remedy where the parties wish to have the content of a written mediation agreement to which the Mediation Directive applies made the subject of a consent order.

Section 10(2) of the Matrimonial Causes Act 1973 and section 48(2) of the Civil Partnership Act 2004

8.1 Where a respondent who has applied under section 10(2) of the Matrimonial Causes Act 1973, or section 48(2) of the Civil Partnership Act 2004, for the court to consider his or her financial position after a divorce or dissolution elects not to proceed with the application, a notice of withdrawal of the application signed by the respondent or by the respondent's solicitor may be filed without leave of the court. In this event a formal order dismissing or striking out the application is unnecessary. Notice of withdrawal should also be given to the applicant's solicitor.

8.2 An application under section 10(2) or section 48(2) which has been withdrawn is not a bar to making in matrimonial proceedings, the decree absolute and in civil partnership proceedings, the final order.

Maintenance Orders – registration in magistrates' courts

9.1 Where periodical payments are required to be made to a child under an order registered in a magistrates' court, section 62 of the Magistrates' Courts Act 1980 permits the payments to be made instead to the person with whom the child has his home. That person may proceed in his own name for variation, revival or revocation of the order and may enforce payment either in his own name or by requesting the designated officer of the court to do so.

9.2 The registration in a magistrates' court of an order made direct to a child entails a considerable amount of work. Accordingly, when the court is considering the form of an order where there are children, care should be taken not to make orders for payment direct where such orders would be of no benefit to the parties.

Pensions

10.1 The phrase "party with pension rights" is used in FPR Part 9, Chapter 8. For matrimonial proceedings, this phrase has the meaning given to it by section 25D(3) of the Matrimonial Causes Act 1973 and means "the party to the marriage who has or is likely to have benefits under a pension arrangement". There is a definition of "civil partner with pension rights" in paragraph 29 of Schedule 5 to the Civil Partnership Act 2004 which mirrors the definition of "party with pension rights" in section 25D(3) of the 1973 Act. The phrase "is likely to have benefits" in these definitions refers to accrued rights to pension benefits which are not yet in payment.

PPF Compensation

11.1 The phrase "party with compensation rights" is used in FPR Part 9, Chapter 9. For matrimonial proceedings, the phrase has the meaning given to it by section 25G(5) of the Matrimonial Causes Act 1973 and means the party to the marriage who is or is likely to be entitled to PPF compensation. There is a definition of "civil partner with compensation rights" in paragraph 37(1) of Schedule 5 to the Civil Partnership Act 2004 which mirrors the definition of "party with compensation rights" in section 25G(5). The phrase "is likely to be entitled to PPF Compensation" in those definitions refers to statutory entitlement to PPF Compensation which is not yet in payment.

Annex: pre-application protocol

Notes of guidance

Scope of the Protocol

1 This protocol is intended to apply to all applications for a financial remedy as defined by rule 2.3. It is designed to cover all classes of case, ranging from a simple application for periodical payments to an application for a substantial lump sum and property adjustment order. The protocol is designed to facilitate the operation of the procedure for financial remedy applications.

2 In considering the options of pre-application disclosure and negotiation, solicitors should bear in mind the advantage of having a court timetable and court managed process. There is sometimes an advantage in preparing disclosure before proceedings are commenced. However, solicitors should bear in mind the objective of controlling costs and in particular the costs of discovery and that the option of pre-application disclosure and negotiation has risks of excessive and uncontrolled expenditure and delay. This option should only be encouraged where both parties agree to follow this route and disclosure is not likely to be an issue or has been adequately dealt with in mediation or otherwise.

3 Solicitors should consider at an early stage and keep under review whether it would be appropriate to suggest mediation and/or collaborative law to the clients as an alternative to solicitor negotiation or court based litigation.

4 Making an application to the court should not be regarded as a hostile step or a last resort, rather as a way of starting the court timetable, controlling disclosure and endeavouring to avoid the costly final hearing and the preparation for it.

First letter

5 The circumstances of parties to an application for a financial remedy are so various that it would be difficult to prepare a specimen first letter. The request for information will be different in every case. However, the tone of the initial letter is important and the guidelines in paragraphs 14 and 15 should be followed. It should be approved in advance by the client. Solicitors writing to an unrepresented party should always recommend that he seeks independent legal advice and enclose a second copy of the letter to be passed to any solicitor instructed. A reasonable time limit for an answer may be 14 days.

Negotiation and Settlement

6 In the event of pre-application disclosure and negotiation, as envisaged in paragraph 12 an application should not be issued when a settlement is a reasonable prospect.

Disclosure

7 The protocol underlines the obligation of parties to make full and frank disclosure of all material facts, documents and other information relevant to the issues. Solicitors owe their clients a duty to tell them in clear terms of this duty and of the possible consequences of breach of the duty, which may include criminal sanctions under the Fraud Act 2006. This duty of disclosure is an ongoing obligation and includes the duty to disclose any material changes after initial disclosure has been given. Solicitors are referred to the Good Practice Guide for Disclosure produced by Resolution (obtainable from the Administrative Director, 366A Crofton Road, Orpington, Kent BR2 8NN) and can also contact the Law Society's Practice Advice Service on 0870 606 2522.

The Protocol

General principles

8 All parties must always bear in mind the overriding objective set out at rules 1.1 to 1.4 and try to ensure that applications should be resolved and a just outcome achieved as speedily as possible without costs being unreasonably incurred. The needs of any children should be addressed and safeguarded. The procedures which it is appropriate to follow should be conducted with minimum distress to the parties and in a manner designed to promote as good a continuing relationship between the parties and any children affected as is possible in the circumstances.

9 The principle of proportionality must be borne in mind at all times. It is unacceptable for the costs of any case to be disproportionate to the financial value of the subject matter of the dispute.

10 Parties should be informed that where a court is considering whether to make an order requiring one party to pay the costs of another party, it will take into account pre-application offers to settle and conduct of disclosure.

Identifying the issues

11 Parties must seek to clarify their claims and identify the issues between them as soon as possible. So that this can be achieved, they must provide full, frank and clear disclosure of facts, information and documents, which are material and sufficiently accurate to enable proper negotiations to take place to settle their differences. Openness in all dealings is essential.

Disclosure

12 If parties carry out voluntary disclosure before the issue of proceedings the parties should exchange schedules of assets, income, liabilities and other

material facts, using the financial statement as a guide to the format of the disclosure. Documents should only be disclosed to the extent that they are required by the financial statement. Excessive or disproportionate costs should not be incurred.

Correspondence

13 Any first letter and subsequent correspondence must focus on the clarification of claims and identification of issues and their resolution. Protracted and unnecessary correspondence and "trial by correspondence" must be avoided.

14 The impact of any correspondence upon the reader and in particular the parties must always be considered. Any correspondence which raises irrelevant issues or which might cause the other party to adopt an entrenched, polarised or hostile position is to be discouraged.

Summary

15 The aim of all pre-application proceedings steps must be to assist the parties to resolve their differences speedily and fairly or at least narrow the issues and, should that not be possible, to assist the court to do so.

* * * * *

PART 10: APPLICATIONS UNDER PART 4 OF THE FAMILY LAW ACT 1996

* * * * *

PART 11: APPLICATIONS UNDER PART 4A OF THE FAMILY LAW ACT 1996

* * * * *

PART 12: PROCEEDINGS RELATING TO CHILDREN EXCEPT PARENTAL ORDER PROCEEDINGS AND PROCEEDINGS FOR APPLICATIONS IN ADOPTION, PLACEMENT AND RELATED PROCEEDINGS

* * * * *

PART 13: PROCEEDINGS UNDER SECTION 54 OF THE HUMAN FERTILISATION AND EMBRYOLOGY ACT 2008

* * * * *

PART 14: PROCEDURE FOR APPLICATIONS IN ADOPTION, PLACEMENT AND RELATED PROCEEDINGS

* * * * *

Part 15

Commentary on Part 15:
REPRESENTATION OF PROTECTED PARTIES

Part 15 and PD 15A concern the representation of 'protected parties'.

Definition of protected party
A protected party is defined by rule 2.3 as a party, or an intended party, who lacks capacity (within the meaning of the Mental Capacity Act 2005) to conduct proceedings. By section 2(1) of the Mental Capacity Act 2005 a person lacks capacity in relation to a matter if at the material time he is unable to make a decision for himself in relation to the matter because of an impairment of, or a disturbance in the functioning of, the mind or brain. Section 3 of the 2005 Act amplifies the meaning of 'inability to make decisions'.

Requirement to have a litigation friend
By rule 15.2 a protected party must have a litigation friend to conduct proceedings on that party's behalf. Strasbourg jurisprudence has established that this requirement is unlikely to constitute an undue interference with the ECHR art 6(1) right of access to the court.

Children no longer dealt with in this Part
Part 9 of FPR 1991 dealt with the representation of children and protected together under the heading 'Disability'. Under CPR Part 21 children and protected parties are also dealt with together.

Under the new FPR 2010 the provisions concerning representation of children and protected parties are separated. The representation of children is now dealt with in Parts 16 and 14 (public law proceedings).

Counterpart to CPR Part 21
The language of rules 15.2 to 15.9 mirrors CPR rules 21.2 to 21.9, save that the references to children in the CPR are not carried forward into these Rules.

Continuance of old scheme, with modifications

The scheme of the former FPR 1991 Part 9 is continued, with some modifications. A protected party must sue or be sued by a litigation friend (as a 'next friend' and 'guardian ad litem' in old rule 9.2 are now conflated and renamed). If there is no person with authority as a deputy to defend the proceedings and there is no one else suitable and willing to act then the Official Solicitor will be, as before, the representative of final resort. Under PD 15A para 4.5 where it is sought to appoint the Official Solicitor provision must be made for payment of his charges. By rule 2.3(1) 'deputy' has the meaning given in section 16(2)(b) of the 2005 Act which provides that the court may appoint a person (a 'deputy') to make decisions on behalf of a person lacking capacity in relation to a matter or matters concerning the incapacitated person's personal welfare, or property and affairs.

Appointment of litigation friend without court order

Under the old regime a person other than a deputy or the Official Solicitor could only act as a guardian ad litem to *defend* proceedings (as opposed to a next friend who *initiated* proceedings) pursuant to an order of the court. This requirement no longer applies. Under rule 15.5 a person may without any court order become the litigation friend of a protected party whether as an initiator or a defender of family proceedings. If the litigation friend is a person with authority as a deputy to conduct the proceedings in the name of a protected party, or on that party's behalf, then he must file an official copy of the order, declaration or other document which confers that person's authority to act (rule 15.5(2)). Any other person, the Official Solicitor apart, must file a certificate of suitability which the proposed litigation friend has verified by a statement of truth (in Form FP9) stating that that person (a) can fairly and competently conduct proceedings on behalf of the protected party; (b) has no interest adverse to that of the protected party; and (c) undertakes to pay any costs which the protected party may be ordered to pay in relation to the proceedings, subject to any right that person may have to be repaid from the assets of the protected party (rules 15.5(4) and 15.4(3)).

It is desirable (and one would have thought obvious) that a person intending to act as a litigation friend of an intended protected party should so inform that party beforehand: *Masterman-Lister v Brutton & Co & Others* [2003] 1 WLR 1511.

Appointment of litigation friend by court order

The court may appoint a person (including the Official Solicitor) to be a litigation friend under rule 15.6. If the person proposed is not the Official Solicitor then the court must be satisfied that the conditions of suitability mentioned above are met (rule 15.6(6)). Under the CPR there are circumstances where this route must be followed; these do not apply under the FPR. A court-ordered appointment is therefore only likely to arise where no one volunteers to act as litigation friend under rule 15.5. In such circumstances the application must be made under Part 18 and must be supported by evidence (rule 15.6(4) and PD 15A para 4.1), although who should actually be filing the evidence in support where the court acts of its own initiative under rule 15.6(2) is obscure. The requirement of evidence in support does not mean that someone opposing the appointment is entitled as of right to file evidence disputing the proposed appointment: *Folks v Faizey* [2006] EWCA Civ 381.

Change of litigation friend

Unlike the position under the former FPR 1991 there is now explicit power to change a litigation friend under rule 15.7.

PART 15: REPRESENTATION OF PROTECTED PARTIES

Application of this Part

15.1. This Part contains special provisions which apply in proceedings involving protected parties.

Requirement for litigation friend in proceedings

15.2. A protected party must have a litigation friend to conduct proceedings on that party's behalf.

Stage of proceedings at which a litigation friend becomes necessary

15.3.—(1) A person may not without the permission of the court take any step in proceedings except—

(a) filing an application form; or
(b) applying for the appointment of a litigation friend under rule 15.6,

until the protected party has a litigation friend.

(2) If during proceedings a party lacks capacity (within the meaning of the 2005 Act) to continue to conduct proceedings, no party may take any step in proceedings without the permission of the court until the protected party has a litigation friend.

(3) Any step taken before a protected party has a litigation friend has no effect unless the court orders otherwise.

Who may be a litigation friend for a protected party without a court order

15.4.—(1) This rule does not apply if the court has appointed a person to be a litigation friend.

(2) A person with authority as a deputy to conduct the proceedings in the name of a protected party or on that party's behalf is entitled to be the

litigation friend of the protected party in any proceedings to which that person's authority extends.

(3) If there is no person with authority as a deputy to conduct the proceedings in the name of a protected party or on that party's behalf, a person may act as a litigation friend if that person—

(a) can fairly and competently conduct proceedings on behalf of the protected party;

(b) has no interest adverse to that of the protected party; and

(c) subject to paragraph (4), undertakes to pay any costs which the protected party may be ordered to pay in relation to the proceedings, subject to any right that person may have to be repaid from the assets of the protected party.

(4) Paragraph (3)(c) does not apply to the Official Solicitor.

("deputy" is defined in rule 2.3.)

How a person becomes a litigation friend without a court order

15.5.—(1) If the court has not appointed a litigation friend, a person who wishes to act as a litigation friend must follow the procedure set out in this rule.

(2) A person with authority as a deputy to conduct the proceedings in the name of a protected party or on that party's behalf must file an official copy of the order, declaration or other document which confers that person's authority to act.

(3) Any other person must file a certificate of suitability stating that that person satisfies the conditions specified in rule 15.4(3).

(4) A person who is to act as a litigation friend must file—

(a) the document conferring that person's authority to act; or

(b) the certificate of suitability,

at the time when that person first takes a step in the proceedings on behalf of the protected party.

(5) A court officer will send the certificate of suitability to every person on whom, in accordance with rule 6.28, the application form should be served.

(6) This rule does not apply to the Official Solicitor.

How a person becomes a litigation friend by court order

15.6.—(1) The court may, if the person to be appointed so consents, make an order appointing—

(a) a person other than the Official Solicitor; or

(b) the Official Solicitor,

as a litigation friend.

(2) An order appointing a litigation friend may be made by the court of its own initiative or on the application of—

(a) a person who wishes to be a litigation friend; or
(b) a party to the proceedings.

(3) The court may at any time direct that a party make an application for an order under paragraph (2).

(4) An application for an order appointing a litigation friend must be supported by evidence.

(5) Unless the court directs otherwise, a person appointed under this rule to be a litigation friend for a protected party will be treated as a party for the purpose of any provision in these rules requiring a document to be served on, or sent to, or notice to be given to, a party to the proceedings.

(6) Subject to rule 15.4(4), the court may not appoint a litigation friend under this rule unless it is satisfied that the person to be appointed complies with the conditions specified in rule 15.4(3).

Court's power to change litigation friend and to prevent person acting as litigation friend

15.7.—(1) The court may—

(a) direct that a person may not act as a litigation friend;
(b) terminate a litigation friend's appointment; or
(c) appoint a new litigation friend in substitution for an existing one.

(2) An application for an order or direction under paragraph (1) must be supported by evidence.

(3) Subject to rule 15.4(4), the court may not appoint a litigation friend under this rule unless it is satisfied that the person to be appointed complies with the conditions specified in rule 15.4(3).

Appointment of litigation friend by court order – supplementary

15.8.—(1) A copy of the application for an order under rule 15.6 or 15.7 must be sent by a court officer to—

(a) every person on whom, in accordance with rule 6.28, the application form should be served; and
(b) unless the court directs otherwise, the protected party.

(2) A copy of an application for an order under rule 15.7 must also be sent to—

(a) the person who is the litigation friend, or who is purporting to act as the litigation friend when the application is made; and
(b) the person, if not the applicant, who it is proposed should be the litigation friend.

Procedure where appointment of litigation friend comes to an end

15.9.—(1) When a party ceases to be a protected party, the litigation friend's appointment continues until it is brought to an end by a court order.

(2) An application for an order under paragraph (1) may be made by—

(a) the former protected party;
(b) the litigation friend; or
(c) a party.

(3) On the making of an order under paragraph (1), the court officer will send a notice to the other parties stating that the appointment of the protected party's litigation friend to act has ended.

Practice Direction 15A supplements FPR Part 15 (Protected parties)

* * * * *

PRACTICE DIRECTION 15A – PROTECTED PARTIES

This Practice Direction supplements FPR Part 15

General

1.1 A protected party must have a litigation friend to conduct proceedings on the protected party's behalf.

1.2 In the proceedings the protected party should be referred to in the title as "A.B. (by C.D. his/her litigation friend)".

Duties of the Litigation Friend

2.1 It is the duty of a litigation friend fairly and competently to conduct proceedings on behalf of a protected party. The litigation friend must have no interest in the proceedings adverse to that of the protected party and all steps and decisions the litigation friend takes in the proceedings must be taken for the benefit of the protected party.

Becoming a Litigation Friend without a court order

3.1 In order to become a litigation friend without a court order the person who wishes to act as litigation friend must—

(a) file an official copy of the order, declaration or other document which confers the litigation friend's authority as a deputy to conduct the proceedings in the name of a protected party or on his/her behalf; or
(b) file a certificate of suitability—
    (i) stating that the litigation friend consents to act;
    (ii) stating that the litigation friend knows or believes that the

[applicant][respondent] lacks capacity (within the meaning of the 2005 Act) to conduct proceedings;

(iii) stating the grounds of that belief and if the belief is based upon medical opinion attaching any relevant document to the certificate;

(iv) stating that the litigation friend can fairly and competently conduct proceedings on behalf of the protected party and has no interest adverse to that of the protected party;

(v) undertaking to pay any costs which the protected party may be ordered to pay in relation to the proceedings, subject to any right the litigation friend may have to be repaid from the assets of the protected party; and

(vi) which the litigation friend has verified by a statement of truth.

3.2 Paragraph 3.1 does not apply to the Official Solicitor.

3.3 The court officer will send the certificate of suitability to the person who is the attorney of a registered enduring power of attorney, donee of a lasting power of attorney or deputy or, if there is no such person, to the person with whom the protected party resides or in whose care the protected party is.

3.4 The court officer is not required to send the documents referred to in paragraph 3.1(b)(iii) when sending the certificate of suitability to the person to be served under paragraph 3.3.

3.5 The litigation friend must file either the certificate of suitability or the authority referred to in paragraph 3.1(a) at a time when the litigation friend first takes a step in the proceedings on behalf of the protected party.

Application for a court order appointing a litigation friend

4.1 An application for a court order appointing a litigation friend should be made in accordance with Part 18 and must be supported by evidence.

4.2 The court officer must serve the application notice—

(a) on the persons referred to in paragraph 3.3; and
(b) on the protected party unless the court directs otherwise.

4.3 The evidence in support must satisfy the court that the proposed litigation friend—

(a) consents to act;
(b) can fairly and competently conduct proceedings on behalf of the protected party;
(c) has no interest adverse to that of the protected party; and
(d) undertakes to pay any costs which the protected party may be ordered to pay in relation to the proceedings, subject to any right the litigation friend may have to be repaid from the assets of the protected party.

4.4 Paragraph 4.3(d) does not apply to the Official Solicitor.

4.5 The proposed litigation friend may be one of the persons referred to in paragraph 3.3 where appropriate, or otherwise may be the Official Solicitor. Where it is sought to appoint the Official Solicitor, provision must be made for payment of his charges.

Change of litigation friend and prevention of person acting as litigation friend

5.1 Where an application is made for an order under rule 15.7, the application must set out the reasons for seeking it and must be supported by evidence.

5.2 Subject to paragraph 4.4, if the order sought is substitution of a new litigation friend for an existing one, the evidence must satisfy the court of the matters set out in paragraph 4.3.

5.3 The court officer will serve the application notice on—

(a) the persons referred to in paragraph 3.3; and
(b) the litigation friend or person purporting to act as litigation friend.

Procedure where the need for a litigation friend has come to an end

6.1 Where a person who was a protected party regains or acquires capacity (within the meaning of the 2005 Act) to conduct the proceedings, an application under rule 15.9(2) must be made for an order under rule 15.9(1) that the litigation friend's appointment has ceased.

6.2 The application must be supported by the following evidence—

(a) a medical report or other suitably qualified expert's report indicating that the protected party has regained or acquired capacity (within the meaning of the 2005 Act) to conduct the proceedings; and
(b) a copy of any relevant order or declaration of the Court of Protection.

* * * * *

PART 16: REPRESENTATION OF CHILDREN AND REPORTS IN PROCEEDINGS INVOLVING CHILDREN

* * * * *

Part 17

Commentary on Part 17:
STATEMENTS OF TRUTH

Counterpart to CPR Part 22

Part 17 (which is supported by PD 17A) is the counterpart of CPR Part 22. The introduction of a requirement to verify certain documentary averments by a statement of truth was an innovation of the CPR. Previously the system permitted on the one hand unverified pleadings or, on the other, affidavit evidence. Affidavits of course required verification by a formal oath, breach of which carried the penalty of perjury. The old system naturally permitted considerable obfuscation and left open to the pleader the ability to advance flatly contradictory propositions which would have been impossible had the pleading required verification by affidavit. The CPR innovation fell short of this solution but devised the concept of verification by a statement of truth, penalty for breach of which may involve proceedings for contempt of court being taken (but not perjury). Whether that change has had the effect of eliminating the old vices must be highly doubtful.

The CPR scheme allows a statement of case to be amended under CPR Part 17. CPR rule 22.1(2) requires any such amendment to be verified by a statement of truth. Given that amendments can have the effect of putting a case in a totally different way it is difficult, at least in the civil sphere, to regard these statements of truth as being very much more than a fig leaf inadequately covering what are sometimes barefaced [sic] misrepresentations.

Definition of a statement of truth

Under rule 17.2(4) a statement of truth is, unsurprisingly, a statement by the party advancing the document or the person making the witness statement (as the case may be) that he believes the facts stated in the document are true. By virtue of PD 17A paras 2.1 and 2.2 that is precisely what the statement must say. In the case of any document other than a witness statement the statement of truth may be made not only by the party (or his litigation friend) but also by his legal representative (rule 17.2(6)(ii)).

PD 17A paras 3.5, 3.6 and 3.11 specify who may sign in relation to corporations and unincorporated bodies as follows:

- *Registered companies or corporations:* A director, the treasurer, secretary, chief executive, manager or other officer of the company or corporation. A 'manager' should have personal knowledge of the content of the document or to be responsible for those *who have that knowledge of the content.*
- *A corporation which is not a registered company:* In addition to those persons set out above, the major (sic, recto 'mayor'), chairman, president, chief executive of a local authority or town clerk or other similar officer of the corporation.
- *Partnerships:* Any of the partners, or a person having the management or control of the partnership business.
- *Trusts:* Where some or all of the trustees comprise a single party one, some or all of the trustees comprising the party. The legal representative of the trustees may also sign.

Documents which must be verified

Under rule 17.2(1) the following documents must be verified by a statement of truth:

- a statement of case, which by rule 4.1 means the whole or part of an application form, but by rule 17.1 does not include an application for a matrimonial order or a civil partnership order (formerly a 'petition') or an answer to such an application;
- a witness statement;
- an acknowledgement of service in a claim begun by the Part 19 procedure;
- a certificate of service;
- a statement of arrangements for children;
- a statement of information for a consent order filed under rule 9.26(1)(b); and
- any other document where a rule or practice direction requires it.

PD 17A para 1.4 expands this list to include:

- an application notice for—
  - a third party debt order (CPR Part 72 as modified by rule 33.24);
  - a hardship payment order (CPR Part 72 as modified by rule 33.24); or
  - a charging order (CPR Part 73 as modified by rule 33.25); and
- a notice of objections to an account being taken by the court, unless verified by an affidavit or witness statement.

Para 5.2 of PD 9A requires a court-ordered reply to questionnaire to be verified by a statement of truth.

It had been mooted during the drafting and consultation process that Form E would no longer be sworn, but rather verified by a declaration of truth. For that eventuality the old minatory statement printed on the front of the Form, warning of the possibility of criminal proceedings for perjury, needed to be changed, and the new Form E now states that:

> If you are found to have been deliberately untruthful, criminal proceedings may be brought against you for fraud under the Fraud Act 2006.

However, it was ultimately decided to maintain the requirement that the Form E should be sworn, thus preserving the sanction of proceedings for perjury (even though the warning no longer refers to this).

Penalties for false statements of truth

By Rule 17.6 proceedings for contempt of court may be brought against a person who makes, or causes to be made, a false statement in a document verified by a statement of truth without an honest belief in its truth. But such penalty proceedings may be brought only by the Attorney General or with the permission of the court, and the rule does not apply to breaches in a magistrates' court, where it would seem that false statements may be advanced with impunity (at least until sworn to in evidence by a witness).

Consequences of failure to verify

If a party fails to verify a statement of case then by rule 17.3(2) the court may strike it out. However by rule 17.3(1) the statement of case shall remain effective until and unless struck out but the party may not rely on the statement of case as evidence of any of the matters set out therein. Under PD 17A para 5.2 a party may apply to the court for an order that unless within such period as the court may specify the statement of case is verified by the service of a statement of truth, the statement of case be struck out. If such an order is made the usual order for costs will be that the costs be paid by the party who had failed to verify, 'in any event and immediately' (para 5.3: presumably intended to signify 'in the first instance').

By rule 17.4 if the maker of a witness statement fails to verify the witness statement by a statement of truth, the court may direct that it shall not be admissible as evidence.

PART 17: STATEMENTS OF TRUTH

Interpretation

17.1. In this Part "statement of case" has the meaning given to it in Part 4 except that a statement of case does not include an application for a matrimonial order or a civil partnership order or an answer to such an application.

(Rule 4.1 defines "statement of case" for the purposes of Part 4.)

Documents to be verified by a statement of truth

17.2.—(1) Subject to paragraph (9), the following documents must be verified by a statement of truth—

(a) a statement of case;

(b) a witness statement;

(c) an acknowledgement of service in a claim begun by the Part 19 procedure;

(d) a certificate of service;

(e) a statement of arrangements for children;

(f) a statement of information filed under rule 9.26(1)(b); and

(g) any other document where a rule or practice direction requires it.

(2) Where a statement of case is amended, the amendments must be verified by a statement of truth unless the court orders otherwise.

(3) If an applicant wishes to rely on matters set out in the application form or application notice as evidence, the application form or notice must be verified by a statement of truth.

(4) Subject to paragraph (5), a statement of truth is a statement that—

(a) the party putting forward the document;

(b) in the case of a witness statement, the maker of the witness statement; or

(c) in the case of a certificate of service, the person who signs the certificate,

believes the facts stated in the document are true.

(5) If a party is conducting proceedings with a litigation friend, the statement of truth in—

(a) a statement of case; or

(b) an application notice,

is a statement that the litigation friend believes the facts stated in the document being verified are true.

(6) The statement of truth must be signed by—

(a) in the case of a statement of case—
    (i) the party or litigation friend; or
    (ii) the legal representative on behalf of the party or litigation friend; and

(b) in the case of a witness statement or statement of arrangements for children, the maker of the statement.

(7) A statement of truth, which is not contained in the document which it verifies, must clearly identify that document.

(8) A statement of truth in a statement of case may be made by—

(a) a person who is not a party; or
(b) by two parties jointly,

where this is permitted by a practice direction.

(9) An application that does not contain a statement of facts need not be verified by a statement of truth.

(Practice Direction 17A sets out the form of statement of truth.)

Failure to verify a statement of case

17.3.—(1) If a party fails to verify that party's statement of case by a statement of truth—

(a) the statement of case shall remain effective unless struck out; but
(b) the party may not rely on the statement of case as evidence of any of the matters set out in it.

(2) The court may strike out a statement of case which is not verified by a statement of truth.

(3) Any party may apply for an order under paragraph (2).

Failure to verify a witness statement

17.4. If the maker of a witness statement fails to verify the witness statement by a statement of truth, the court may direct that it shall not be admissible as evidence.

Power of the court to require a document to be verified

17.5.—(1) The court may order a person who has failed to verify a document in accordance with rule 17.2 to verify the document.

(2) Any party may apply for an order under paragraph (1).

False statements

17.6.—(1) Proceedings for contempt of court may be brought against a person who makes, or causes to be made, a false statement in a document verified by a statement of truth without an honest belief in its truth.

(2) Proceedings under this rule may be brought only—

(a) by the Attorney General; or
(b) with the permission of the court.

(3) This rule does not apply to proceedings in a magistrates' court.

Practice Direction 17A supplements FPR Part 17 (Statements of truth).

PRACTICE DIRECTION 17A – STATEMENTS OF TRUTH

This Practice Direction supplements FPR Part 17

Documents to be verified by a statement of truth

1.1 Rule 17.2 sets out the documents which must be verified by a statement of truth.

1.2 If an applicant wishes to rely on matters set out in his application notice as evidence, the application notice must be verified by a statement of truth.

1.3 An expert's report should also be verified by a statement of truth. For the form of the statement of truth verifying an expert's report (which differs from that set out below), see the practice direction which supplements Part 25.

1.4 In addition, the following documents must be verified by a statement of truth—

(a) an application notice for—
  (i) a third party debt order (CPR Part 72 as modified by rule 33.24);
  (ii) a hardship payment order (CPR Part 72 as modified by rule 33.24); or
  (iii) a charging order (CPR Part 73 as modified by rule 33.25); and
(b) a notice of objections to an account being taken by the court, unless verified by an affidavit or witness statement.

1.5 The statement of truth may be contained in the document it verifies or it may be in a separate document served subsequently, in which case it must identify the document to which it relates.

1.6 Where the form to be used includes a jurat for the content to be verified by an affidavit, then a statement of truth is not required in addition.

1.7 In this Practice Direction, "statement of case" has the meaning given to it by rule 17.1.

Form of the statement of truth

2.1 The form of the statement of truth verifying a statement of case or an application notice should be as follows:

"[I believe] [the *(applicant or as may be)* believes] that the facts stated in this *[name document being verified]* are true."

2.2 The form of the statement of truth verifying a witness statement should be as follows:

"I believe that the facts stated in this witness statement are true."

2.3 Where the statement of truth is contained in a separate document, the document containing the statement of truth must be headed with the title of and court reference for the proceedings. The document being verified should be identified in the statement of truth as follows—

(a) application form: "the application form issued on [*date*]";
(b) statement of case: "the (application or answer as may be) served on [*name of party*] on [*date*]";
(c) application notice: "the application notice issued on [*date*] for [*set out the remedy sought*]";
(d) witness statement: "the witness statement filed on [*date*] or served on [*party*] on [*date*]".

Who may sign the statement of truth

3.1 In a statement of case or an application notice, the statement of truth must be signed by—

(a) the party or his litigation friend; or
(b) the legal representative of the party or litigation friend.

3.2 A statement of truth verifying a witness statement must be signed by the witness.

3.3 A statement of truth verifying a notice of objections to an account must be signed by the objecting party or his or her legal representative.

3.4 Where a document is to be verified on behalf of a company or corporation, subject to paragraph 3.7 below, the statement of truth must be signed by a person holding a senior position in the company or corporation. That person must state the office or position he or she holds.

3.5 Each of the following persons is a person holding a senior position:

(a) in respect of a registered company or corporation, a director, the treasurer, secretary, chief executive, manager or other officer of the company or corporation; and
(b) in respect of a corporation which is not a registered company, in addition to those persons set out in (a), the major, chairman, president, chief executive of a local authority or town clerk or other similar officer of the corporation.

3.6 Where the document is to be verified on behalf of a partnership, those who may sign the statement of truth are—

(a) any of the partners; or
(b) a person having the management or control of the partnership business.

3.7 Where a party is legally represented, the legal representative may sign the statement of truth on his or her behalf. The statement signed by the legal representative will refer to the client's belief, not his or her own. In signing he or she must state the capacity in which he or she signs and the name of his or her firm where appropriate.

3.8 Where a legal representative has signed a statement of truth, his or her signature will be taken by the court as his or her statement—

(a) that the client on whose behalf he or she has signed had authorised him or her to do so;
(b) that before signing he or she had explained to the client that in signing the statement of truth he or she would be confirming the client's belief that the facts stated in the document were true; and
(c) that before signing he or she had informed the client of the possible consequences to the client if it should subsequently appear that the client did not have an honest belief in the truth of those facts (see rule 17.6).

3.9 A legal representative who signs a statement of truth must print his or her full name clearly beneath his or her signature.

3.10 The individual who signs a statement of truth must sign in his or her own name and not that of his or her firm or employer.

3.11 The following are examples of the possible application of this practice direction describing who may sign a statement of truth verifying statements in documents other than a witness statement. These are only examples and not an indication of how a court might apply the practice direction to a specific situation.

Managing Agent

An agent who manages property or investments for the party cannot sign a statement of truth. It must be signed by the party or by the legal representative of the party.

Trusts

Where some or all of the trustees comprise a single party one, some or all of the trustees comprising the party may sign a statement of truth. The legal representative of the trustees may sign it.

Companies

Paragraphs 3.4 and 3.5 apply. The word "manager" will be construed in the context of the phrase "a person holding a senior position" which it is used to define. The court will consider the size of the company and the importance and nature of the proceedings. It would expect the manager signing the statement of truth to to have personal knowledge of the content of the document or to be responsible for those who have that knowledge of the content. A small company may not have a manager, apart from the directors, who holds a senior position. A large company will have many such managers. In a large company with specialist claims, insurance or legal departments the statement may be signed by the manager of such a department if he or she is responsible for handling the claim or managing the staff handling it.

Inability of persons to read or sign documents to be verified by a statement of truth

4.1 Where a document containing a statement of truth is to be signed by a person who is unable to read or sign the document, it must contain a certificate made by an authorised person.

4.2 An authorised person is a person able to administer oaths and take affidavits but need not be independent of the parties or their representatives.

4.3 The authorised person must certify—

(a) that the document has been read to the person signing it;
(b) that the person appeared to understand it and approved its content as accurate;
(c) that the declaration of truth has been read to that person;
(d) that that person appeared to understand the declaration and the consequences of making a false declaration; and
(e) that that person signed or made his mark in the presence of the authorised person.

4.4 The form of the certificate is set out at the Annex to this Practice Direction.

Consequences of failure to verify

5.1 If a statement of case is not verified by a statement of truth, the statement of case will remain effective unless it is struck out, but a party may not rely on the contents of a statement of case as evidence until it has been verified by a statement of truth.

5.2 Any party may apply to the court for an order that unless within such period as the court may specify the statement of case is verified by the service of a statement of truth, the statement of case will be struck out.

5.3 The usual order for the costs of an application referred to in paragraph 5.2 will be that the costs be paid by the party who had failed to verify, in any event and immediately.

Penalty

6.1 Rule 17.6 sets out the consequences of verifying a statement of case containing a false statement without an honest belief in its truth. Where a party alleges that a statement of truth is false, the party shall refer that allegation to the court dealing with the proceedings in which the statement of truth has been made.

6.2 On a reference under paragraph 6.1 the court may—

(a) exercise any of its powers under the FPR;
(b) initiate steps to consider if there is a contempt of court and, where there is, to punish it;

(Order 52 of the Rules of the Supreme Court and Order 29 of the County

Court Rules (Schedules 1 and 2 to the CPR) make provision where committal to prison is a possibility if contempt is proved.)

(c) direct the party making the allegation to refer the matter to the Attorney General with a request to him or her to consider whether he or she wishes to bring proceedings for contempt of court.

6.3 A request to the Attorney General must be made in writing and sent to the Attorney General's Office at 20 Victoria Street, London, SW1H 0NF. The request must be accompanied by a copy of the order directing that the matter be referred to the Attorney General and must—

(a) identify the statement said to be false; and
(b) explain—
    (i) why it is false; and
    (ii) why the maker knew it to be false at the time it was made; and
(c) explain why contempt proceedings would be appropriate in the light of the overriding objective in Part 1 of the FPR.

6.4 The practice of the Attorney General is to prefer an application that comes from the court, and so has received preliminary consideration by a judge or district judge, to one made direct to him or her by a party to the proceedings in which the alleged contempt occurred without prior consideration by the court. An application to the Attorney General is not a way of appealing against, or reviewing, the decision of the judge or district judge.

6.5 Where a party makes an application to the court for permission for that party to commence proceedings for contempt of court, it must be supported by written evidence containing the information specified in paragraph 6.3 and the result of the application to the Attorney General made by the applicant.

6.6 The FPR do not change the law of contempt or introduce new categories of contempt. A person applying to commence such proceedings should consider whether the incident complained of does amount to contempt of court and whether such proceedings would further the overriding objective in Part 1 of the FPR.

Annex

Certificate to be used where a person is unable to read or sign a document to be verified by a statement of truth

I certify that I [name and address of authorised person] have read the contents of this document and the declaration of truth to the person signing the document [if there are exhibits, add "and explained the nature and effect of the exhibits referred to in it"] who appeared to understand (a) the document and approved its content as accurate and (b) the declaration of truth and the consequences of making a false declaration, and made his or her mark in my presence.

* * * * *

Part 18

Commentary on Part 18:
PROCEDURE FOR OTHER APPLICATIONS IN PROCEEDINGS

The scope of Part 18

Part 18 (as supplemented by PD 18A) sets out the procedure to be followed when making an application within existing proceedings. It replaces the old summons (in the High Court) and notice of application (in the county court). It is also the prescribed procedure to start proceedings where no other Part of these rules prescribes the initiating procedure, or to make an application after proceedings have been concluded.

PD 18A makes clear that all applications for permission must be made under Part 18 except where specific provision is made in other Parts of the FPR for permission to be sought: see, for example, rule 30.3 which deals with permission to appeal. An example of a permission application that must be made under Part 18 is an application under para 11(3) of Schedule 1 to the Children Act 1989 for variation of a maintenance agreement following the death of one of the parties where more than 6 months has passed since the day on which representation in regard to the estate of the deceased was first taken out.

CPR counterpart

The CPR counterpart to Part 18 is Part 23.

Forms

By PD 5A the forms to be used are Forms C2, D11 and FP2. Form C2 is used for making an application in children proceedings; Form D11 is for applications in the main suit. Form FP2 appears to be designed for use in adoption proceedings. In the absence of any particularly apt Form the view is that parties should use Form D11 for making an application within financial remedy proceedings.

Content of application notice

In contrast to the former regime the application notice must include brief reasons or grounds why the applicant is seeking the order (rule 18.7(1)(b)).

Moreover, a draft of the order sought must be attached to the application notice (rule 18.7(2)). If the case is proceeding in the High Court and the draft order is unusually long or complex it should also be supplied in electronic form for use by the court office on such storage medium as shall be agreed with the judge or court staff (PD 18A para 14.1). The present almost invariable practice is for counsel to email the court associate or the judge's clerk with the agreed order after adjudication. The new regime now requires the requested order if long or complex to be emailed *before* the hearing.

If the applicant wishes to rely on the contents of the application notice as evidence in support of the application then the notice must be verified by a statement of truth (rule 17.2(3)). If the written evidence is separate from the application notice then, unsurprisingly, it must be filed with the notice (rule 18.8(2)).

Period of notice

The old rule that 2 clear days' notice must be given is swept away. By rule 18.8(b)(ii) 7 days' notice must be given. This only includes 'business days' as rule 2.9(4) provides 'where the specified period is 7 days or less and includes a day which is not a business day, that day does not count'. A business day is defined by rule 2.3(1) as any day other than a Saturday, Sunday, Christmas Day, Good Friday or a bank holiday. If the application is for an interim order in financial remedy proceedings (as defined by rule 9.7, but not including an application for an injunction, where rule 20 governs the position) then 14 days' notice must be given. Here, the period being longer than 7 days, non-business days are included.

Where insufficient notice has been given the court nonetheless has power to direct that sufficient notice has been given and to hear the application (rule 18.8(4)).

Reference to Judge

An application under Part 18 will be dealt with by a district judge but by PD 18A such application may be referred to a judge. If an applicant believes that the application should be heard by a judge then the notice should say so (PD 18A para 4.5)

Disposal without a hearing

The court is now given explicit power under rule 18.9 to dispose of an application without a hearing if it considers that a hearing would not be appropriate or where the parties have reached terms and have agreed that a hearing is unnecessary. In such an event the parties should so inform the court in writing and *each* should confirm that all evidence and other material on which he or she relies has been disclosed to the other parties to the application (PD 18A para 13.2).

The application notice must state whether or not a hearing is sought (PD para 3.2(e)).

Disposal with a hearing

If the court decides that a hearing is appropriate it may conduct it on the telephone (PD 18A para 18.1). If an applicant thinks such a hearing is appropriate he should say so in his application notice (para 8.2). Generally speaking such a request will not be granted unless all parties agree (para 8.3). Equally, the 'telephoning' party must agree to any other party being present in court (para 8.4). There are detailed rules as to the order in which people are to be connected to a conference call (para 8.5). If the parties wish the hearing to be by video then they must apply to the court for directions and PD 22A will apply (see Commentary on Part 22 *below*). It will be interesting to see whether disposals without a hearing, or telephone hearings, become more commonplace.

By rule 27.10 hearings under Part 18 will be in private.

Without notice hearings

If an order has been made 'without notice' (as an ex parte order must now be known) then by rules 18.10 and 18.11 the application notice and evidence in support must, unless the court otherwise directs, be served on all parties to the proceedings and must be endorsed with a statement of the right of any affected party to apply, within 7 days, to set the order aside. The right to apply to set aside exists (obviously) where the original order was made orally and without an application notice (*Tombstone Ltd v Raja* [2008] EWCA Civ 1444). Breach of the requirements of rule 18.10, whilst not to be condoned, will not invariably lead to the order being set aside. Proportionality must be observed: *Dadourian Group International Ltd v Simms* [2006] 1 WLR 2499.

By PD 18A para 5.1 an application may be made ex parte only where there is exceptional urgency; or where the overriding objective is best furthered by doing so; or by consent of all parties; or with the permission of the court; or where paragraph 4.9 applies; or where a court order, rule or practice direction permits. Para 4.9 provides that:

> Where a date for a hearing has been fixed, a party who wishes to make an application at that hearing but does not have sufficient time to file an application notice should as soon as possible inform the court (if possible in writing) and, if possible, the other parties of the nature of the application and the reason for it. That party should then make the application orally at the hearing.

As to the principles to be observed on making an application without notice see *Moat Housing Group-South Limited v Harris* [2006] QB 606, *FZ v SZ (ancillary relief; conduct; valuations)* [2010] EWHC 1630 (Fam), [2011] 1 FLR 64, *Arena Corporation v Schroeder* [2003] EWHC 1089 (Ch) and *ND v K P* [2011] EWHC 457 (Fam). Without notice relief should normally only be sought and granted 'where there is a well founded belief that the giving of notice would lead to irretrievable prejudice being caused to the applicant for relief'. An applicant for without notice relief is fixed with a high duty of candour, breach of which will, generally speaking, lead to the order being set aside and a refusal to exercise the discretion to re-grant.

Proceeding in a party's absence

Not very surprisingly by rule 18.12 the court may proceed where a party is absent.

Applications dismissed as being totally without merit

Rule 18.13 addresses the position where the court dismisses an application as being totally without merit. In this event the court must not only make a formal record of the finding in its order, but it must also consider exercising its powers under rule 4.8 and PD 4B to make a civil restraint order (see Commentary on Part 4 *above*).

Costs

PD 18A para 15.1 specifically reminds all concerned of the court's powers to assess costs summarily under CPR PD 44A.

PART 18: PROCEDURE FOR OTHER APPLICATIONS IN PROCEEDINGS

Types of application for which Part 18 procedure may be followed

18.1.—(1) The Part 18 procedure is the procedure set out in this Part.

(2) An applicant may use the Part 18 procedure if the application is made—

(a) in the course of existing proceedings;
(b) to start proceedings except where some other Part of these rules prescribes the procedure to start proceedings; or
(c) in connection with proceedings which have been concluded.

(3) Paragraph (2) does not apply—

(a) to applications where any other rule in any other Part of these rules sets out the procedure for that type of application;
(b) if a practice direction provides that the Part 18 procedure may not be used in relation to the type of application in question.

Applications for permission to start proceedings

18.2. An application for permission to start proceedings must be made to the court where the proceedings will be started if permission is granted.

Respondents to applications under this Part

18.3.—(1) The following persons are to be respondents to an application under this Part—

(a) where there are existing proceedings or the proceedings have been concluded—

(i) the parties to those proceedings; and

(ii) if the proceedings are proceedings under Part 11, the person who is the subject of those proceedings;

(b) where there are no existing proceedings—

(i) if notice has been given under section 44 of the 2002 Act (notice of intention to adopt or apply for an order under section 84 of that Act), the local authority to whom notice has been given; and

(ii) if an application is made for permission to apply for an order in proceedings, any person who will be a party to the proceedings brought if permission is granted; and

(c) any other person as the court may direct.

Application notice to be filed

18.4.—(1) Subject to paragraph (2), the applicant must file an application notice.

(2) An applicant may make an application without filing an application notice if—

(a) this is permitted by a rule or practice direction; or

(b) the court dispenses with the requirement for an application notice.

Notice of an application

18.5.—(1) Subject to paragraph (2), a copy of the application notice must be served on—

(a) each respondent;

(b) in relation to proceedings under Part 11, the person who is, or, in the case of an application to start proceedings, it is intended will be, the subject of the proceedings; and

(c) in relation to proceedings under Parts 12 and 14, the children's guardian (if any).

(2) An application may be made without serving a copy of the application notice if this is permitted by—

(a) a rule;

(b) a practice direction; or

(c) the court.

(Rule 18.8 deals with service of a copy of the application notice.)

Time when an application is made

18.6. When an application must be made within a specified time, it is so made if the court receives the application notice within that time.

What an application notice must include

18.7.—(1) An application notice must state—

(a) what order the applicant is seeking; and

(b) briefly, why the applicant is seeking the order.

(2) A draft of the order sought must be attached to the application notice.

(Part 17 requires an application notice to be verified by a statement of truth if the applicant wishes to rely on matters set out in his application as evidence.)

Practice Direction 18A, paragraph 3, sets out additional requirements in relation to application notices

Service of a copy of an application notice

18.8.—(1) Subject to rule 2.4, a copy of the application notice must be served in accordance with the provisions of Part 6—

(a) as soon as practicable after it is filed; and

(b) in any event—

    (i) where the application is for an interim order under rule 9.7 at least 14 days; and

    (ii) in any other case, at least 7 days;

    before the court is to deal with the application.

(2) The applicant must, when filing the application notice, file a copy of any written evidence in support.

(3) If a copy of an application notice is served by a court officer it must be accompanied by—

(a) a notice of the date and place where the application will be heard;

(b) a copy of any witness statement in support; and

(c) a copy of the draft order which the applicant has attached to the application.

(4) If—

(a) an application notice is served; but

(b) the period of notice is shorter than the period required by these rules or a practice direction,

the court may direct that, in the circumstances of the case, sufficient notice has been given and hear the application.

(5) This rule does not require written evidence—

(a) to be filed if it has already been filed; or

(b) to be served on a party on whom it has already been served.

Applications which may be dealt with without a hearing

18.9.—(1) The court may deal with an application without a hearing if—

(a) the court does not consider that a hearing would be appropriate; or

(b) the parties agree as to the terms of the order sought or the parties agree that the court should dispose of the application without a hearing and the court does not consider that a hearing would be appropriate.

(2) Where—

(a) an application is made for permission to make an application in proceedings under the 1989 Act; and

(b) the court refuses the application without a hearing in accordance with paragraph (1)(a),

the court must, at the request of the applicant, re-list the application and fix a date for a hearing.

(3) Paragraph (2) does not apply to magistrates' courts.

Service of application notice following court order where application made without notice

18.10.—(1) This rule applies where the court has disposed of an application which it permitted to be made without service of a copy of the application notice.

(2) Where the court makes an order, whether granting or dismissing the application, a copy of the application notice and any evidence in support must unless the court orders otherwise, be served with the order on—

(a) all the parties in proceedings; and

(b) in relation to proceedings under Part 11, the person who is, or, in the case of an application to start proceedings, it is intended will be, the subject of the proceedings.

(3) The order must contain a statement of the right to make an application to set aside or vary the order under rule 18.11.

Application to set aside or vary order made without notice

18.11.—(1) A person who was not served with a copy of the application notice before an order was made under rule 18.10 may apply to have the order set aside or varied.

(2) An application under this rule must be made within 7 days beginning with the date on which the order was served on the person making the application.

Power of the court to proceed in the absence of a party

18.12.—(1) Where the applicant or any respondent fails to attend the hearing of an application, the court may proceed in the absence of that person.

(2) Where—

(a) the applicant or any respondent fails to attend the hearing of an application; and

(b) the court makes an order at the hearing,

the court may, on application or of its own initiative, re-list the application.

(3) Paragraph (2) does not apply to magistrates' courts.

Dismissal of totally without merit applications

18.13. If the High Court or a county court dismisses an application (including an application for permission to appeal) and it considers that the application is totally without merit—

(a) the court's order must record that fact; and

(b) the court must at the same time consider whether it is appropriate to make a civil restraint order.

Practice Direction 18A supplements FPR Part 18 (Other applications in proceedings)

PRACTICE DIRECTION 18A – OTHER APPLICATIONS IN PROCEEDINGS

This Practice Direction supplements FPR Part 18

Application of Part 18

1.1 Part 18 makes general provision for a procedure for making applications. All applications for the court's permission should be made under this Part, with the exception of applications for permission for which specific provision is made in other Parts of the FPR, in which case the application should be made under the specific provision. Examples of where specific provision has been made in another Part of the FPR for applications for permission are rule 11.3 (Permission to apply for a forced marriage protection order) and rule 30.3 (Permission to appeal).

Reference to a judge

2.1 In the High Court or a county court a district judge may refer to a judge any matter which the district judge thinks should properly be decided by a judge, and the judge may either dispose of the matter or refer it back to the district judge.

Additional requirements in relation to application notices

3.1 In addition to the requirements set out in rule 18.7, the following requirements apply to the applications to which the respective paragraph refers.

3.2 An application notice must be signed and include—

(a) the title of the case (if available);
(b) the reference number of the case (if available);
(c) the full name of the applicant;
(d) where the applicant is not already a party, the applicant's address for service, including a postcode. Postcode information may be obtained from www.royalmail.com or the Royal Mail Address Management Guide; and
(e) either a request for a hearing or a request that the application be dealt with without a hearing.

3.3 An application notice relating to an application under section 42(6) of the Adoption and Children Act 2002 (permission to apply for an adoption order) ...

3.4 An application notice relating to an application in the High Court by a local authority for permission under section 100(3...

3.5 Where permission is required to take any step under the Children Act 1989 ...

3.6 In an application for permission to bring proceedings under Schedule 1 of the Children Act 1989, the draft application for the making of which permission is sought must be accompanied by a statement setting out the financial details which the person seeking permission believes to be relevant to the request and contain a declaration that it is true to the maker's best knowledge and belief, together with sufficient copies for one to be served on each respondent.

3.7 The provisions in Schedule 1 which require an application for permission to bring proceedings are—

(a) paragraph 7(2) – permission is required to make an application for variation of a secured periodical payments order after the death of the parent liable to make the payments if a period of 6 months has passed from the date on which representation in regard to that parent's estate is first taken out; and
(b) paragraph 11(3) – permission is required to make an application to alter a maintenance agreement following the death of one of the parties if a period of 6 months has passed beginning with the day on which representation in regard to the estate of the deceased is first taken out.

Other provisions in relation to application notices.
4.1 On receipt of an application notice containing a request for a hearing, unless the court considers that the application is suitable for consideration without a hearing, the court officer will, if serving a copy of the application

notice, notify the applicant of the time and date fixed for the hearing of the application.

4.2 On receipt of an application notice containing a request that the application be dealt with without a hearing, the court will decide whether the application is suitable for consideration without a hearing.

4.3 Where the court—

(a) considers that the application is suitable for consideration without a hearing; but
(b) is not satisfied that it has sufficient material to decide the application immediately,

it may give directions for the filing of evidence and will inform the applicant and the respondent(s) of its decision. (Rule 18.11 enables a party to apply for an order made without notice to be set aside or varied.)

4.4 Where the court does not consider that the application is suitable for consideration without a hearing—

(a) it may give directions as to the filing of evidence; and
(b) the court officer will notify the applicant and the respondent of the time, date and place for the hearing of the application and any directions given.

4.5 In the High Court or a county court if the application is intended to be made to a judge, the application notice should so state. In that case, paragraphs 4.2, 4.3 and 4.4 will apply as though references to the court were references to a judge.

4.6 Every application should be made as soon as it becomes apparent that it is necessary or desirable to make it.

4.7 Applications should, wherever possible, be made so that they are considered at any directions hearing or other hearing for which a date has been fixed or for which a date is about to be fixed.

4.8 The parties must anticipate that at any hearing (including any directions hearing) the court may wish to review the conduct of the case as a whole and give any necessary directions. They should be ready to assist the court in doing so and to answer questions the court may ask for this purpose.

4.9 Where a date for a hearing has been fixed, a party who wishes to make an application at that hearing but does not have sufficient time to file an application notice should as soon as possible inform the court (if possible in writing) and, if possible, the other parties of the nature of the application and the reason for it. That party should then make the application orally at the hearing.

Applications without service of application notice

5.1 An application may be made without service of an application notice only—

(a) where there is exceptional urgency;

(b) where the overriding objective is best furthered by doing so;

(c) by consent of all parties;

(d) with the permission of the court;

(e) where paragraph 4.9 applies; or

(f) where a court order, rule or practice direction permits.

Giving notice of an application

6.1 Unless the court otherwise directs or paragraph 5.1 of this practice direction applies, the application notice must be served as soon as practicable after it has been issued and, if there is to be a hearing, at least 7 days before the hearing date.

6.2 Where an application notice should be served but there is not sufficient time to do so, informal notification of the application should be given unless the circumstances of the application require no notice of the application to be given.

Pre-action applications

7.1 All applications made before proceedings are commenced should be made under this Part.

Telephone hearings

8.1 The court may direct that an application be dealt with by a telephone hearing.

8.2 The applicant should, if seeking a direction under paragraph 8.1, indicate this on the application notice. Where the applicant has not indicated such an intention but nevertheless wishes to seek a direction the request should be made as early as possible.

8.3 A direction under paragraph 8.1 will not normally be made unless every party entitled to be given notice of the application and to be heard at the hearing has consented to the direction.

8.4 No representative of a party to an application being heard by telephone may attend the court in person while the application is being heard unless the other party to the application has agreed that the representative may do so.

8.5 If an application is to be heard by telephone the following directions will apply, subject to any direction to the contrary—

(a) the applicant's legal representative is responsible for arranging the telephone conference for precisely the time fixed by the court. The telecommunications provider used must be one of the approved panel of service providers (see HMCS website at www.hmcourts-service.gov.uk);

(b) the applicant's legal representative must tell the operator the telephone numbers of all those participating in the conference call and the sequence in which they are to be called;

(c) it is the responsibility of the applicant's legal representative to ascertain from all the other parties whether they have instructed counsel and, if so the identity of counsel, and whether the legal representative and counsel will be on the same or different telephone numbers;

(d) the sequence in which those involved are to be called will be—
    (i) the applicant's legal representative and (if on a different number) his counsel;
    (ii) the legal representative (and counsel) for all other parties; and
    (iii) the judge or justices, as the case may be;

(e) each speaker is to remain on the line after being called by the operator setting up the conference call. The call may be 2 or 3 minutes before the time fixed for the application;

(f) when the judge has or justices have been connected the applicant's legal representative (or counsel) will introduce the parties in the usual way;

(g) if the use of a "speakerphone" by any party causes the court or any other party any difficulty in hearing what is said the judge or justices may require that party to use a hand held telephone;

(h) the telephone charges debited to the account of the party initiating the conference call will be treated as part of the costs of the application.

Video conferencing

9.1 Where the parties to a matter wish to use video conferencing facilities, and those facilities are available in the relevant court, the parties should apply to the court for directions. (Practice Direction 22A provides guidance on the use of video conferencing)

Note of proceedings

10.1 The court or court officer should keep, either by way of a note or a tape recording, brief details of all proceedings before the court, including the dates of the proceedings and a short statement of the decision taken at each hearing.

Evidence

11.1 The requirement for evidence in certain types of applications is set out in some of the rules in the FPR and practice directions. Where there is no specific requirement to provide evidence it should be borne in mind that, as a practical matter, the court will often need to be satisfied by evidence of the facts that are relied on in support of or for opposing the application.

11.2 The court may give directions for the filing of evidence in support of or opposing a particular application. The court may also give directions for the filing of evidence in relation to any hearing that it fixes on its own initiative. The directions may specify the form that evidence is to take and when it is to be served.

11.3. Where it is intended to rely on evidence which is not contained in the application itself, the evidence, if it has not already been served, should be served with the application.

11.4 Where a respondent to an application wishes to rely on evidence, that evidence must be filed in accordance with any directions the court may have given and a court officer will serve the evidence on the other parties, unless the court directs otherwise.

11.5 If it is necessary for the applicant to serve any evidence in reply the court officer will serve it on the other parties unless the court directs otherwise.

11.6 Evidence must be filed with the court as well as served on the parties.

11.7 The contents of an application notice may be used as evidence provided the contents have been verified by a statement of truth.

Consent orders

12.1 The parties to an application for a consent order must ensure that they provide the court with any material it needs to be satisfied that it is appropriate to make the order. Subject to any rule in the FPR or practice direction a letter will generally be acceptable for this purpose.

12.2 Where a judgment or order has been agreed in respect of an application where a hearing date has been fixed, the parties must inform the court immediately.

Other applications considered without a hearing

13.1 Where rule 18.9(1)(b) applies the court will treat the application as if it were proposing to make an order on its own initiative.

13.2 Where the parties agree that the court should dispose of the application without a hearing they should so inform the court in writing and each should confirm that all evidence and other material on which he or she relies has been disclosed to the other parties to the application.

Miscellaneous

14.1 If the case is proceeding in the High Court and the draft order is unusually long or complex it should also be supplied in electronic form on such storage medium as shall be agreed with the judge or court staff, for use by the court office.

14.2 Where rule 18.12 applies the power to re-list the application in rule 18.12(2) is in addition to any other powers of the court with regard to the order (for example to set aside, vary, discharge or suspend the order).

Costs

15.1 Attention is drawn to the CPR costs practice direction and, in particular, to the court's power to make a summary assessment of costs.

15.2 Attention is also drawn to rule 44.13(1) of the CPR which provides that if an order makes no mention of costs, none are payable in respect of the proceedings to which it relates.

* * * * *

Part 19

Commentary on Part 19:
ALTERNATIVE PROCEDURE FOR APPLICATIONS

Scope of Part 19

Part 19, supported by PD 19A, lays down the procedure to be used for cases where the Part 18 procedure does not apply and where:

(a) there is no form prescribed by a rule or referred to in Practice Direction 5A in which to make the application; or

(b) the applicant seeks the court's decision on a question which is unlikely to involve a substantial dispute of fact; or (c) a rule or practice direction requires or permits the use of the Part 19 procedure in relation to a specified type of proceedings.

By rule 19.2 there are three non-financial situations specifically prescribed for the use of the Part 19 procedure. These are applications under section 60(3) of the Adoption and Children Act 2002 (order to prevent disclosure of information to an adopted person); or under section 79(4) of the Adoption and Children Act 2002 (order for Registrar General to give any information referred to in section 79(3) of the 2002 Act); or under rule 14.21 (directions of High Court regarding fathers without parental responsibility).

There has been some debate as to whether there actually exist *any* applications with a financial context, other than those specifically prescribed within Part 8 (see Commentary on Part 8 *above*), which would or indeed could be made under Part 19. The only further type of application identified by PD 5A para 2.1 is a free-standing committal application i.e. one which is not made within existing proceedings. However, where contempt is committed otherwise than in the course of proceedings, the application is made to a QBD Divisional Court (CPR Sch 1, RSC Ord 52, rule 1), and is governed by the CPR. It would therefore not fall to be made under Part 19.

It is considered that an application for interim relief in aid of overseas substantive proceedings made pursuant to the Civil Jurisdiction and

Judgments Act 1982 (Interim Relief) Order 1997 (SI 1997 No. 302) would fall within Part 19. Research has not thus far identified any further financial application which does so.

PD 19A para 1.5 states that 'the types of application for which the Part 19 procedure may be used include an application for an order or direction which is unopposed by each respondent before the commencement of the proceedings and the sole purpose of the application is to obtain the approval of the court to the agreement'. It is impossible to conceive of a financial application being made in this way for this purpose. A consent order would always be made in the context of existing proceedings, even if the proceedings were initiated with the sole objective of obtaining such an order.

It is with these considerations in mind that these notes are sparse. If and when the detail of the Part 19 procedure needs to be addressed the rules and the PD are clear guides to what is required.

Forms
PD5A identifies the following forms for use under Part 19:

FP1	Application under Part 19 of the Family Procedure Rules 2010
FP1A	Application under Part 19 of the Family Procedure Rules 2010: Notes for applicant on completing the application (Form FP1)
FP1B	Application under Part 19 of the Family Procedure Rules 2010: Notes for respondent
FP3	Application for injunction (General form)
FP5	Acknowledgment of service of Application under Part 19 of the Family Procedure Rules 2010

Content of the application, and evidence
The rules contain provisions concerning the content of the Application, the filing and service of written evidence and as to evidence generally.

Dispute as to aptness of Part 19
By rule 19.9 a respondent who contends that the Part 19 procedure should not be used because (a) there is a substantial dispute of fact; *and* (b) the use of the Part 19 procedure is not required or permitted by a rule or practice direction, must state the reasons for that contention when filing the acknowledgment of service. In such a case when the court receives the acknowledgment of service and any written evidence, it will give directions as to the future management of the case. These may include using the court's powers (available to it 'at any stage') to direct that the application is to continue as if the applicant had not used the Part 19 procedure, and in such case to give any directions it considers appropriate: rule 19.1(3).

PART 19: ALTERNATIVE PROCEDURE FOR APPLICATIONS

Types of application for which Part 19 procedure may be followed

19.1.—(1) The Part 19 procedure is the procedure set out in this Part.

(2) An applicant may use the Part 19 procedure where the Part 18 procedure does not apply and—

    (a) there is no form prescribed by a rule or referred to in Practice Direction 5A in which to make the application;

    (b) the applicant seeks the court's decision on a question which is unlikely to involve a substantial dispute of fact; or

    (c) paragraph (5) applies.

(3) The court may at any stage direct that the application is to continue as if the applicant had not used the Part 19 procedure and, if it does so, the court may give any directions it considers appropriate.

(4) Paragraph (2) does not apply if a practice direction provides that the Part 19 procedure may not be used in relation to the type of application in question.

(5) A rule or practice direction may, in relation to a specified type of proceedings—

    (a) require or permit the use of the Part 19 procedure; and

    (b) disapply or modify any of the rules set out in this Part as they apply to those proceedings.

Applications for which the Part 19 procedure must be followed

19.2.—(1) The Part 19 procedure must be used in an application made in accordance with—

    (a) section 60(3) of the 2002 Act (order to prevent disclosure of information to an adopted person);

    (b) section 79(4) of the 2002 Act (order for Registrar General to give any information referred to in section 79(3) of the 2002 Act); and

    (c) rule 13.21 (directions of High Court regarding fathers without parental responsibility).

(2) The respondent to an application made in accordance with paragraph (1)(b) is the Registrar General.

Contents of the application

19.3. Where the applicant uses the Part 19 procedure, the application must state—

    (a) that this Part applies;

    (b) either—

        (i) the question which the applicant wants the court to decide; or

(ii) the order which the applicant is seeking and the legal basis of the application for that order;

(c) if the application is being made under an enactment, what that enactment is;

(d) if the applicant is applying in a representative capacity, what that capacity is; and

(e) if the respondent appears or is to appear in a representative capacity, what that capacity is.

(Part 17 requires a statement of case to be verified by a statement of truth.)

Issue of application without naming respondents

19.4.—(1) A practice direction may set out circumstances in which an application may be issued under this Part without naming a respondent.

(2) The practice direction may set out those cases in which an application for permission must be made by application notice before the application is issued.

(3) The application for permission—

(a) need not be served on any other person; and

(b) must be accompanied by a copy of the application which the applicant proposes to issue.

(4) Where the court gives permission, it will give directions about the future management of the application.

Acknowledgment of service

19.5.—(1) Subject to paragraph (2), each respondent must—

(a) file an acknowledgment of service within 14 days beginning with the date on which the application is served; and

(b) serve the acknowledgment of service on the applicant and any other party.

(2) If the application is to be served out of the jurisdiction, the respondent must file and serve an acknowledgment of service within the period set out in Practice Direction 6B.

(3) The acknowledgment of service must—

(a) state whether the respondent contests the application;

(b) state, if the respondent seeks a different order from that set out in the application, what that order is; and

(c) be signed by the respondent or the respondent's legal representative.

Consequence of not filing an acknowledgment of service

19.6.—(1) This rule applies where—

(a) the respondent has failed to file an acknowledgment of service; and

(b) the time period for doing so has expired.

(2) The respondent may attend the hearing of the application but may not take part in the hearing unless the court gives permission.

Filing and serving written evidence

19.7.—(1) The applicant must, when filing the application, file the written evidence on which the applicant intends to rely.

(2) The applicant's evidence must be served on the respondent with the application.

(3) A respondent who wishes to rely on written evidence must file it when filing the acknowledgment of service.

(4) A respondent who files written evidence must also, at the same time, serve a copy of that evidence on the other parties.

(5) Within 14 days beginning with the date on which a respondent's evidence was served on the applicant, the applicant may file further written evidence in reply.

(6) An applicant who files further written evidence must also, within the same time limit, serve a copy of that evidence on the other parties.

Evidence – general

19.8.—(1) No written evidence may be relied on at the hearing of the application unless—

(a) it has been served in accordance with rule 19.7; or
(b) the court gives permission.

(2) The court may require or permit a party to give oral evidence at the hearing.

(3) The court may give directions requiring the attendance for cross-examination of a witness who has given written evidence.

(Rule 22.1 contains a general power for the court to control evidence.)

Procedure where respondent objects to use of the Part 19 procedure

19.9.—(1) A respondent who contends that the Part 19 procedure should not be used because—

(a) there is a substantial dispute of fact; and
(b) the use of the Part 19 procedure is not required or permitted by a rule or practice direction,

must state the reasons for that contention when filing the acknowledgment of service.

(2) When the court receives the acknowledgment of service and any written evidence, it will give directions as to the future management of the case.

(Rule 19.7 requires a respondent who wishes to rely on written evidence to file it when filing the acknowledgment of service.)

(Rule 19.1(3) allows the court to make an order that the application continue as if the applicant had not used the Part 19 procedure.)

Practice Direction 19A supplements FPR Part 19 (Alternative procedure for applications)

PRACTICE DIRECTION 19A – ALTERNATIVE PROCEDURE FOR APPLICATIONS

This Practice Direction supplements FPR Part 19

Types of application in which Part 19 procedure must be used

1.1 An applicant must use the Part 19 procedure if the application is for an order under—

- (a) section 60(3) of the 2002 Act, to prevent disclosure of information to an adopted person;
- (b) section 79(4) of the 2002 Act, to require the Registrar General to provide information; or
- (c) rule 14.21 (Inherent jurisdiction and fathers without parental responsibility) in Part 14, to request directions of the High Court regarding fathers without parental responsibility.

Types of application in which Part 19 procedure may be used

1.2 An applicant may use the Part 19 procedure if Part 18 does not apply and if—

- (a) there is no prescribed form in which to make the application; or
- (b) the applicant seeks the court's decision on a question which is unlikely to involve a substantial dispute of fact.

1.3 An applicant may also use the Part 19 procedure if a practice direction permits or requires its use for the type of proceedings concerned.

1.4 The practice directions referred to in paragraph 1.3 may in some respects modify or disapply the Part 19 procedure and, where that is so, it is those practice directions, rather than this one, which must be complied with.

1.5 The types of application for which the Part 19 procedure may be used include an application for an order or direction which is unopposed by each respondent before the commencement of the proceedings and the sole purpose of the application is to obtain the approval of the court to the agreement.

1.6 Where it appears to a court officer that an applicant is using the Part 19 procedure inappropriately, the officer may refer the application to the court for consideration of the point.

1.7 The court may at any stage order the application to continue as if the applicant had not used the Part 19 procedure and, if it does so, the court will give such directions as it considers appropriate (see rule 19.1(3)).

The application

2.1 Where an applicant uses the Part 19 procedure, the application form referred to in Practice Direction 5A should be used and must state the matters set out in rule 19.3 and, if paragraphs 1.3 and 1.4 apply, must comply with the requirements of the practice direction in question. In particular, the application form must state that Part 19 applies. A Part 19 application form means an application form which so states.

2.2 An application—

(a) in accordance with rule 19.4, to ask the High Court for directions on the need to give a father without parental responsibility notice of the intention to place a child for adoption; or
(b) under section 60(3) of the 2002 Act for an order to prevent disclosure of information to an adopted person,

may be issued without naming a respondent.

Responding to the application

3.1 Where a respondent who wishes to respond to a Part 19 application is required to file an acknowledgement of service, that acknowledgement of service should be in form FP5 which is referred to in Practice Direction 5A but can, alternatively be given in an informal document such as a letter.

3.2 Rule 19.5 sets out provisions relating to an acknowledgement of service of a Part 19 application.

3.3 Rule 19.6 sets out the consequence of failing to file an acknowledgement of service.

3.4 A respondent who believes that the Part 19 procedure should not be used because there is a substantial dispute of fact or, as the case may be, because its use is not authorised by any rule in the FPR or any practice direction, must state the reasons for that belief in writing when filing the acknowledgement of service (see rule 19.9). If the statement of reasons includes matters of evidence, it should be verified by a statement of truth.

Managing the application

4.1 The court may give directions immediately a Part 19 application is issued either on the application of a party or of its own initiative. The directions may include fixing a hearing date where—

(a) there is no dispute; or
(b) where there may be a dispute, but a hearing date could conveniently be given.

4.2 Where the court does not fix a hearing date when the application is issued, it will give directions for the disposal of the application as soon as practicable after the respondent has acknowledged service of the application or, as the case may be, after the period for acknowledging service has expired.

4.3 Certain applications may not require a hearing.

4.4 The court may convene a directions hearing before giving directions.

Evidence

5.1 An applicant wishing to rely on written evidence should file it when the Part 19 application form is issued.

5.2 Evidence will normally be in the form of a witness statement or an affidavit but an applicant may rely on the matters set out in the application form provided it has been verified by a statement of truth.

(For information about statements of truth see Part 17 and Practice Direction 17A, and about written evidence see Part 22 and Practice Direction 22A.)

5.3 A respondent wishing to rely on written evidence should file it with the acknowledgement of service (see rule 19.7(3)).

5.4 Rule 19.7 sets out the times and provisions for filing and serving written evidence.

5.5 A party may apply to the court for an extension of time to serve and file evidence under rule 19.7 or for permission to serve and file additional evidence under rule 19.8(1).

(For information about applications see Part 18 and Practice Direction 18A.)

5.6 The parties may, subject to paragraphs 5.7 and 5.8, agree in writing on an extension of time for serving and filing evidence under rule 19.7(3) or rule 19.7(5).

5.7 An agreement extending time for a respondent to file evidence in reply under rule 19.7(3)—

(a) must be filed by the respondent at the same time as the acknowledgement of service; and

(b) must not extend time by more than 17 days after the respondent files the acknowledgement of service.

5.8 An agreement extending time for an applicant to file evidence in reply under rule 19.7(5) must not extend time to more than 28 days after service of the respondent's evidence on the applicant.

Hearing

6.1 The court may on the hearing date—

(a) proceed to hear the case and dispose of the application;

(b) give case management directions.

* * * * *

Part 20

Commentary on Part 20:
INTERIM REMEDIES AND SECURITY FOR COSTS

CPR counterparts

Part 20 is the counterpart to CPR Part 25. The following rules are near direct replications of their CPR counterparts:

	FPR	CPR
I. Interim Remedies		
Orders for interim remedies	20.2	25.1
Time when an order for an interim remedy may be made	20.3	25.2
How to apply for an interim remedy	20.4	25.3
Interim injunction to cease if application is stayed	20.5	25.10
II. Security For Costs		
Security for costs	20.6	25.12
Conditions to be satisfied	20.7	25.13
Security for costs of an appeal	20.8	25.15

The following CPR rules have not been replicated in the FPR:

	CPR
Application for an interim remedy where there is no related claim	25.4
Inspection of property before commencement or against a non-party	25.5
Interim payments – general procedure	25.6
Interim payments – conditions to be satisfied and matters to be taken into account	25.7
Powers of court where it has made an order for interim payment	25.8
Restriction on disclosure of an interim payment	25.9
Interim injunction to cease after 14 days if claim struck out	25.11
Security for costs other than from the claimant	25.14

Part 20 is supported by PD 20A, which in turn is modelled on CPR PD 25A.

The following paragraphs of PD 20A are near direct replications of their CPR PD 25A counterparts:

	FPR PD20A	*CPR PD25A*
	para	*para*
Scope and jurisdiction	1	1
Making an application	2	2
Evidence	3	3
Urgent applications and applications without notice	4	4
Orders for injunctions	5	5
Search Orders	6	7
Delivery up orders	7	8
Injunctions against third parties	8	9

The only paragraph in CPR PD 25A which is **not** replicated in FPR PD 20A is para 6, which provides:

CPR PD 25A

Freezing Injunctions

Orders to restrain disposal of assets worldwide and within England and Wales

6.1. An example of a Freezing Injunction is annexed to this practice direction

6.2. This example may be modified as appropriate in any particular case. In particular, the court may, if it considers it appropriate, require the applicant's solicitors, as well as the applicant, to give undertakings.

Scope

Rule 20.1 provides that this Part shall not apply in a magistrates' court.

Rule 20.2 sets out the list of interim remedies which may be ordered by the court. It is an exact replication of CPR rule 25.1 save that two sub-rules in the CPR list are **omitted** namely:

- an order under section 33 of the Senior Courts Act 1981 or section 52 of the County Courts Act 1984 (order for disclosure of documents or inspection of property before a claim has been made); and
- an order under Article 9 of Council Directive (EC) 2004/48 on the enforcement of intellectual property rights (order in intellectual property proceedings making the continuation of an alleged infringement subject to the lodging of guarantees).

The list in rule 20.2 is plainly an attempt to set out every conceivable form of interim remedy for which a party may wish to apply, although the draftsman of the original CPR scheme, replicated in the FPR, did not rule out the fertile imagination of an applicant to conjure up an application hitherto unimagined and possibly also unimaginable (although were the court to dream up a new form of relief it would implicitly assume that it had always existed but had lain fallow as part of the court's own inherent jurisdiction). Thus rule 20.2(3) (CPR rule 25.1(3)) provides that 'the fact that a particular kind of interim remedy is not listed in paragraph (1) does not affect any power that the court may have to grant that remedy'. The provision was apparently inserted in the CPR to make clear that the list was not intended to cut down the court's inherent jurisdiction, or to exclude powers granted by statute (for example to appoint a receiver under section 37 of the Senior Courts Act 1981). Plainly the list does not limit the power of the High Court in child-related proceedings to make location, passport or disclosure orders, but these powers are beyond the scope of this work.

The interim remedies most likely to be sought in financial remedy proceedings prior to judgment are those mentioned in rule 20.1(a), (b), (c), (f), (g), (h) and (j):

(a) an interim injunction;
(b) an interim declaration;
(c) an order—
    (i) for the detention, custody or preservation of relevant property...
(f) an order (referred to as a 'freezing injunction')—
    (i) restraining a party from removing from the jurisdiction assets located there; or
    (ii) restraining a party from dealing with any assets whether located within the jurisdiction or not;
(g) an order directing a party to provide information about the location of relevant property or assets or to provide information about relevant property or assets which are or may be the subject of an application for a freezing injunction;
(h) an order (referred to as a 'search order') under section 7 of the Civil Procedure Act 1997 (order requiring a party to admit another party to premises for the purpose of preserving evidence etc.);
(j) an order for a specified fund to be paid into court or otherwise secured, where there is a dispute over a party's right to the fund.

Interim injunctions

As this Commentary is primarily concerned with procedure, it is not intended as a comprehensive (or even limited) guide to the substantive law concerning injunctions generally, or the specific types of injunction mentioned in (c)(i) (orders for the detention, custody or preservation of relevant property); (f) and (g) (freezing injunctions – as *Mareva* orders must now be called – and orders for the consequential provision of information); (h) (search orders – as *Anton Piller* orders must now be called); and (j) (orders for disputed monies to be paid into court or otherwise secured).

The grant of an injunction is a discretionary remedy and the court must, of course, give effect to the overriding objective when exercising its discretionary powers (see Commentary on Part 1 *above* for the overriding objective). It is classic law that an injunction may only be granted in support of a legal or equitable right (*North London Railway Co v Great Northern Railway Co* (1883) 11 QBD 30, CA per Cotton LJ), but the definition of such a right has been vastly expanded since that decision and now extends to a right claimed in proceedings in a foreign court or arbitral body (see *Fourie v Le Roux and others* [2007] 1 WLR 320, HL per Lord Scott). By the Civil Jurisdiction and Judgments Act 1982 (Interim Relief) Order 1997 (SI 1997 No. 302) an application for interim relief in aid of overseas substantive proceedings may be made notwithstanding the absence of any cause of action in England and Wales, thus reversing the decision of the House of Lords in *The Siskina* [1977] 3 WLR 818.

The test to be applied in deciding whether to exercise the discretionary power to grant an injunction, whether generally or of a specific kind as mentioned in rule 20.1, is laid down in the famous and familiar case of *American Cyanamid v Ethicon* [1975] AC 396. Provided that a serious issue is identified to be tried the court must first ask whether monetary compensation would be an adequate remedy for a party affected by the grant of, or the failure to grant, an injunction. If the answer to that question is yes, then an injunction should be refused. In reaching the answer to that question the court plainly has to consider the availability of monetary compensation in a practical rather than a theoretical way: the court must consider whether the respondent is actually in a position to pay such compensation. If the answer to the question is no then the court must consider where the 'balance of convenience' lies. This balance has been described as posing the question 'which course carries the lower risk of injustice?'

Freezing injunctions and search orders

An application for a freezing injunction, and *a fortiori* a search order, is a serious matter with a potentially severe effect on the respondent. In *Fourie v Le Roux* (*above*) Lord Bingham of Cornhill stated:

> 2. *Mareva* (or freezing) injunctions were from the beginning, and continue to be, granted for an important but limited purpose: to prevent a defendant dissipating his assets with the intention or effect of frustrating enforcement of a prospective judgment. They are not a proprietary remedy. They are not granted to give a claimant advance security for his claim, although they may have that effect. They are not an end in themselves. They are a supplementary remedy, granted to protect the efficacy of court proceedings, domestic or foreign: see *Gee, Commercial Injunctions*, 5th ed (2004), pp 77–83.

> 3. In recognition of the severe effect which such an injunction may have on a defendant, the procedure for seeking and making *Mareva* injunctions has over the last three decades become closely regulated. I regard that regulation as beneficial and would not wish to weaken it in any way. The procedure

incorporates important safeguards for the defendant. One of those safeguards, by no means the least important, is that the claimant should identify the prospective judgment whose enforcement the defendant is not to be permitted, by dissipating his assets, to frustrate. The claimant cannot of course guarantee that he will recover judgment, nor what the terms of the judgment will be. But he must at least point to proceedings already brought, or proceedings about to be brought, so as to show where and on what basis he expects to recover judgment against the defendant.

A freezing injunction may be made under the High Court's inherent jurisdiction or under the statutory regime of section 37 of the MCA 1973 (and its equivalents under Part 3 of the MFPA 1984 and under the CPA 2004). There has been some debate whether there are differences to be discerned in the principles to be applied under the two regimes. In *ND v KP* [2011] EWHC 457 (Fam) Mostyn J attempted to resolve the debate. He held:

4. I want to begin this judgment, which is being given ex tempore and which I hope will be comparatively short, with some statements of principle. In ancillary relief proceedings there are two routes available to obtain a freezing order. An application can either be made under section 37 of the Matrimonial Causes Act 1973 or it can be made under the inherent jurisdiction. It was submitted by Mr Turner QC in a case called *Khreino v Khreino* [2000] FCR 80 CA that the effect of the decision of the House of Lords in *Richards v Richards* [1984] AC 174 was that the only permissible route was the statutory one, but that submission was rejected.

5. That said, it would be a strange state of affairs if either the procedure or the test applicable under the statutory mechanism differed materially from that which applies under the inherent jurisdiction. Under the statutory test the court can restrain the transaction if it is satisfied that the other party to the proceedings is, with the intention of defeating the claim for financial relief, about to make any disposition, or to transfer out of the jurisdiction, or otherwise deal with, any property. So under the statutory test there has to be identified by evidence an impending transaction, or at least the risk of an impending transaction taking place.

6. It is really not very different from the test that applies under the inherent jurisdiction. I quote from *Civil Procedure* otherwise known as the White Book at paragraph 25.1.25.5 which states, citing a decision of Sir Peter Pain of *O'Regan & Ors v Iambic Productions Ltd* (1989) 139 NLJ 1378, that the applicant should depose to objective facts from which it may be inferred that the respondent is likely to move assets or to dissipate them; unsupported statements or expressions of fear have little weight. The notes go on to say that great care should be taken in the presentation of evidence to the court so that the court can see not only whether the applicant has a good arguable case but also whether there is a real risk of dissipation of assets. A freezing order

should not be granted unless the applicant has established an appropriately strong case showing, amongst other things, that the respondent owns the assets concerned or has some interest in them. It is for the applicant to make out his case, and orders should not be granted simply because the respondent cannot show an immediate and obvious prejudice. That formulation is really not very different from the formulation in section 37 which I have recited above.

7. Indeed, it is mirrored by the comments in more vivid language of Thorpe LJ in the case of *Khreino* where he says this:

'Family Division judges day in day out exercise the inherent jurisdiction to grant injunctions to ensure that one spouse does not selfishly or irresponsibly salt away, squirrel away or spirit away family assets which may be in his name but which must be carefully preserved pending the ultimate judicial determination as to what proportion of that asset must be either transferred to or made available for the benefit of the applicant spouse.'

8. So whilst the words used are different the language all points in the same direction, namely that there must be a good case put before the court, supported by objective facts, that there is a likelihood of the movement, or the dissipation, or the spiriting away, or the salting away, or the squirreling away, or the making of a disposition, or the transfer, of assets, with the intention of defeating a claim. It all comes to the same thing.

9. What is to be emphasised is that in this country, unlike some other countries on the continent, we do not have a system of general *saisie conservatoire* whereby assets are automatically frozen pending the determination of a divorce claim. Indeed, one must remind oneself that the basic rule in this country is of separate property, and that is bolstered by Article 1 of Protocol 1 of the European Convention on Human Rights which says that every natural person is entitled to the peaceful enjoyment of his possessions. So, in order to obtain a freezing order there must be before the court a demonstration of objective facts that evidence the likelihood of the movement or dissipation of assets with the intention of defeating the applicant's claim. That is the first principle.

Interim declarations

In CPR rule 40.20 the court is given explicit power to make 'binding declarations whether or not any other remedy is claimed'. Thus the power to grant an interim declaration under CPR rule 25.1(b) is both necessary and obvious. There is no equivalent to CPR rule 40.20 in the FPR, but there are, of course, statutory powers to grant declarations as to marital status and the like (see Part 3 of the Family Law Act 1986). It is hard to envisage circumstances in financial remedy proceedings where an interim declaration would be apt; most circumstances can surely be covered by the grant of an interim injunction.

Procedure

An application for an interim remedy made within existing proceedings (as almost invariably will be the case) must be made in accordance with the Part 18 procedure (see Commentary on Part 18 *above*). Part 20, linked with Part 18, should be seen as a definitive code for the procedure governing the types of interim remedies mentioned in rule 20.1. It is not considered that rule 9.7(1)(e) (which allows a party to apply at any stage of financial remedy proceedings for 'any other form of interim order') is a reference to an interim remedy listed in rule 20.1 justifying any procedural treatment other than those prescribed in Parts 20 and 18. The only exception to the Part 18 procedure that is capable of being identified is a free-standing application for interim relief in aid of overseas substantive proceedings made pursuant to the Civil Jurisdiction and Judgments Act 1982 (Interim Relief) Order 1997 (SI 1997 No. 302). Such an application should be made under Part 19.

By rule 20.3 an order for an interim remedy may be made at any time, including before proceedings are started, and after judgment has been given (subject to any rule, practice direction or other enactment which provides otherwise). However, the court may grant an interim remedy before an application has been started *only* if the matter is urgent, or it is otherwise desirable to do so in the interests of justice. Where the court grants an interim remedy before an application has been started, it will normally give directions requiring an application to be started.

PD 20A para 2.2 requires that the application notice and evidence in support must be served as soon as practicable after issue and in any event *not less than 7 days before the court is due to hear the application* unless the court directs otherwise. Whenever possible a draft of the order sought should be filed with the application notice and an electronic version of the draft should also be available to the court in a format compatible with the word processing software used by the court and on such storage medium as shall be agreed by the court (para 2.4). This will enable the court officer to arrange for any amendments to be incorporated and for the order to be speedily prepared and sealed.

Form of order for an injunction

By PD 20A para 5.1(a) any order for an injunction, unless the court orders otherwise, *must* contain an undertaking by the applicant to the court to pay any damages which the respondent sustains which the court considers the applicant should pay. In contrast by para 5.2 the court is merely obliged to 'consider' whether to require an undertaking by the applicant to pay any damages sustained by a person other than the respondent, including another party to the proceedings or any other person who may suffer loss as a consequence of the order. Interestingly, this totally reverses the principles identified in *Re W (Family Division: without notice orders)* [2000] 2 FLR 927. In that case Munby J held that an undertaking in damages was not necessarily required as between spouses but would almost invariably be required as between an applicant spouse and a third party.

If the order is made without notice it must contain (i) an undertaking by the applicant to the court to serve on the respondent the application notice, evidence in support and any order made as soon as practicable and (ii) a return date for a further hearing at which the other party can be present.

PD 20A para 6 contains further provisions that must be included in a search order.

As stated above FPR PD 20A, unlike CPR PD 25A, does not furnish a model freezing injunction order or search order. Plainly, the CPR versions should continue to be used, with appropriate modifications.

Applications made without notice

As to the general rules about making applications without notice (as ex parte applications must now be called) see Part 18 and its Commentary *above.*

By PD 18A para 5.1 an application may be made without notice only where there is exceptional urgency; or where the overriding objective is best furthered by doing so; or by consent of all parties; or with the permission of the court; or where paragraph 4.9 applies; or where a court order, rule or practice direction permits.

Para 4.9 provides that 'where a date for a hearing has been fixed, a party who wishes to make an application at that hearing but does not have sufficient time to file an application notice should as soon as possible inform the court (if possible in writing) and, if possible, the other parties of the nature of the application and the reason for it. That party should then make the application orally at the hearing'.

By rule 20.4 the court may grant an interim remedy on an application made without notice if it appears to the court that there are good reasons for not giving notice. The evidence in support of the application must state the reasons why notice has not been given.

By PD 20A para 1.2 only High Court Judges and any other judge duly authorised may grant search orders and freezing injunctions. By contrast, a District Judge hearing an application under Part 18 for an order to the same effect as a freezing injunction under section 37 of the MCA 1973 may make an order under that umbrella and hanging on that hook. This strange paradox of mixed messages was present under the old regime, and continues.

By PD 20A para 4.2 urgent without notice applications are normally dealt with at a court hearing but cases of extreme urgency may be dealt with by telephone.

If the without notice application is made *after* the issue of an application notice then by PD 20A para 4.3 the application notice, evidence in support and a draft order, both hard copy and soft electronic version, should be filed with the court two hours before the hearing wherever possible. If the without notice application is made *before* the application notice has been issued, a draft order (both hard and soft) should be provided at the hearing, and the application notice and evidence in support must be filed with the court on the same or next working day or as ordered by the court.

By para 4.4 unless the court orders otherwise, either the applicant must undertake to the court to issue an application notice immediately or the court will give directions for the commencement of the application. In both instances, except in cases where it is essential that the respondent must not be aware of the application, the applicant should take steps to notify the respondent informally of the application.

Para 4.5 provides the procedure where an application is sought to be made outside normal working hours. The applicant should either telephone the Royal Courts of Justice on 020 7947 6000 to be put in contact with the clerk to the appropriate duty judge in the High Court (or the appropriate area Circuit Judge where known), or telephone the Urgent Court Business Officer of the appropriate Circuit who will contact the local duty judge. The application will be heard by telephone only where the applicant is acting by counsel or solicitors. Where the facility is available it is likely that the judge will require a draft order to be faxed or emailed to him. The application notice and evidence in support must be filed with the court on the same or next working day or as ordered, together with two copies of the order for sealing.

The President has given guidance on this subject (*President's Guidance in relation to out of hours hearings* [2011] 1 FLR 303) emphasising that such applications must be capable of being reduced to a faxed sheet of A4 (or its email equivalent) or a short telephone conversation. The *Guidance* also emphasises that in this context 'urgent' has a special meaning: 'it means cases in which an order of the court is required to regulate the position between the moment the order is made and the next available sitting of the court in conventional court hours – that is, usually, 10.30 on the following morning.'

By para 5.1(b) an order made without notice must contain an undertaking by the applicant to the court to serve on the respondent as soon as practicable the application notice, the evidence in support and any order made.

As to the principles to be observed on making an application without notice see *Moat Housing Group-South Limited v Harris* [2006] QB 606, *FZ v SZ (ancillary relief: conduct; valuations)* [2011] 1 FLR 64, *Arena Corporation v Schroeder* [2003] EWHC 1089 (Ch) and *ND v KP* [2011] EWHC 457 (Fam). Without notice relief should normally only be sought and granted 'where there is a well founded belief that the giving of notice would lead to irretrievable prejudice being caused to the applicant for relief': see *ND v KP* at [10] to [12]. An applicant for without notice relief is fixed with a high duty of candour, breach of which will, generally speaking, lead to the order being set aside and a refusal to exercise the discretion to re-grant: see *ND v KP* at [13] and [14].

Third parties affected by an order
If a third party did not attend the hearing at which the order was made and is subsequently served with the order, then by PD 20A para 8 if such a person requests a copy of any materials read by the court, including material prepared after the hearing at the direction of the court or in compliance with the order and/or a note of the hearing, then the applicant, or the applicant's legal representative, must comply promptly with the request unless the court directs otherwise.

Security for costs
Chapter 2 (rules 20.6 to 20.8) deals with security for costs. There is no associated PD, either in the FPR or the CPR.

By rule 20.6 a respondent to any application may apply under Chapter 2 of Part 20 for the applicant to give security for costs of the proceedings. The application must be supported by written evidence.

Unless an enactment permits the court to require security for costs, certain conditions must be satisfied, as specified in rule 20.7. Any of the following suffices:

- The applicant is resident out of the jurisdiction (but not resident in a Brussels Contracting State, a Lugano Contracting State or a Regulation State, as defined in section 1(3) of the Civil Jurisdiction and Judgments Act 1982 or a Member State bound by the Council Regulation);
- The applicant has changed address since the application was started with a view to evading the consequences of the litigation;
- The applicant failed to give an address in the application form, or gave an incorrect address in that form;
- The applicant has taken steps in relation to the applicant's assets that would make it difficult to enforce an order for costs against the applicant.

Content and form of order for security for costs
Where the court makes an order for security for costs it will determine the amount of security and direct the manner in which and the time within which the security must be given (rule 20.6(3)). The FPR does not furnish a model order, but recourse may be made to CPR Form PF44.

Security for costs of an appeal
By rule 20.8 the court may order security for costs of an appeal against an

appellant or a respondent who also appeals on the same grounds as it may order security for costs against an applicant as specified above. These rules apply equally to appeals from District Judge to Judge and to appeals from Judge to Court of Appeal, although in the latter instance the appeal court will be governed by CPR Part 25 rather than the FPR Part 20: see *Radmacher v Granatino* [2009] 1 FLR 1566, CA at [33] which case also offers an illustration of the practical exercise of the applicable principles. For the relevant considerations under the former FPR 1991 in connection with an appeal from District Judge to Judge see *C v C (Appeal, Hadkinson order)* [2011] 1 FLR 434.

PART 20: INTERIM REMEDIES AND SECURITY FOR COSTS

CHAPTER 1: INTERIM REMEDIES

Scope of this Part

20.1. The rules in this Part do not apply to proceedings in a magistrates' court.

Orders for interim remedies

20.2.—(1) The court may grant the following interim remedies—

(a) an interim injunction;

(b) an interim declaration;

(c) an order—

  (i) for the detention, custody or preservation of relevant property;

  (ii) for the inspection of relevant property;

  (iii) for the taking of a sample of relevant property;

  (iv) for the carrying out of an experiment on or with relevant property;

  (v) for the sale of relevant property which is of a perishable nature or which for any other good reason it is desirable to sell quickly; and

  (vi) for the payment of income from relevant property until an application is decided;

(d) an order authorising a person to enter any land or building in the possession of a party to the proceedings for the purposes of carrying out an order under sub-paragraph (c);

(e) an order under section 4 of the Torts (Interference with Goods) Act 1977[76] to deliver up goods;

(f) an order (referred to as a 'freezing injunction')—

    (i) restraining a party from removing from the jurisdiction assets located there; or

    (ii) restraining a party from dealing with any assets whether located within the jurisdiction or not;

(g) an order directing a party to provide information about the location of relevant property or assets or to provide information about relevant property or assets which are or may be the subject of an application for a freezing injunction;

(h) an order (referred to as a "search order") under section 7 of the Civil Procedure Act 1997[77] (order requiring a party to admit another party to premises for the purpose of preserving evidence etc.);

(i) an order under section 34 of the Senior Courts Act 1981[78] or section 53 of the County Courts Act 1984[79] (order in certain proceedings for disclosure of documents or inspection of property against a non-party);

(j) an order for a specified fund to be paid into court or otherwise secured, where there is a dispute over a party's right to the fund;

(k) an order permitting a party seeking to recover personal property to pay money into court pending the outcome of the proceedings and directing that, if money is paid into court, the property must be given up to that party;

(l) an order directing a party to prepare and file accounts relating to the dispute;

(m) an order directing any account to be taken or inquiry to be made by the court.

(2) In paragraph (1)(c) and (g), 'relevant property' means property (including land) which is the subject of an application or as to which any question may arise on an application.

(3) The fact that a particular kind of interim remedy is not listed in paragraph (1) does not affect any power that the court may have to grant that remedy.

Time when an order for an interim remedy may be made

20.3.—(1) An order for an interim remedy may be made at any time, including—

(a) before proceedings are started; and

(b) after judgment has been given.

(Rule 5.3 provides that proceedings are started when the court issues an application form.)

(2) However—

(a) paragraph (1) is subject to any rule, practice direction or other enactment which provides otherwise; and

   (b) the court may grant an interim remedy before an application has been started only if—
     (i) the matter is urgent; or
     (ii) it is otherwise desirable to do so in the interests of justice.

(3) Where the court grants an interim remedy before an application has been started, it will give directions requiring an application to be started.

(4) The court need not direct that an application be started where the application is made under section 33 of the Senior Courts Act 1981 or section 52 of the County Courts Act 1984[80] (order for disclosure, inspection etc. before starting an application).

How to apply for an interim remedy

20.4.—(1) The court may grant an interim remedy on an application made without notice if it appears to the court that there are good reasons for not giving notice.

(2) An application for an interim remedy must be supported by evidence, unless the court orders otherwise.

(3) If the applicant makes an application without giving notice, the evidence in support of the application must state the reasons why notice has not been given.

(Part 4 lists general case-management powers of the court.)

(Part 18 contains general rules about making an application.)

Interim injunction to cease if application is stayed
20.5. If—

   (a) the court has granted an interim injunction other than a freezing injunction; and
   (b) the application is stayed other than by agreement between the parties,

the interim injunction will be set aside unless the court orders that it should continue to have effect even though the application is stayed.

CHAPTER 2: SECURITY FOR COSTS

Security for costs
20.6.—(1) A respondent to any application may apply under this Chapter of this Part for security for costs of the proceedings.

(Part 4 provides for the court to order payment of sums into court in other circumstances.)

(2) An application for security for costs must be supported by written evidence.

(3) Where the court makes an order for security for costs, it will—

(a) determine the amount of security; and
(b) direct—
  (i) the manner in which; and
  (ii) the time within which,
  the security must be given.

Conditions to be satisfied

20.7.—(1) The court may make an order for security for costs under rule 20.6 if—

(a) it is satisfied, having regard to all the circumstances of the case, that it is just to make such an order; and
(b) either—
  (i) one or more of the conditions in paragraph (2) applies; or
  (ii) an enactment permits the court to require security for costs.
(2) The conditions are—

(a) the applicant is—
  (i) resident out of the jurisdiction; but
  (ii) not resident in a Brussels Contracting State, a Lugano Contracting State or a Regulation State, as defined in section 1(3) of the Civil Jurisdiction and Judgments Act 1982 or a Member State bound by the Council Regulation;
(b) the applicant has changed address since the application was started with a view to evading the consequences of the litigation;
(c) the applicant failed to give an address in the application form, or gave an incorrect address in that form;
(d) the applicant has taken steps in relation to the applicant's assets that would make it difficult to enforce an order for costs against the applicant.

(3) The court may not make an order for security for costs under rule 20.6 in relation to the costs of proceedings under the 1980 Hague Convention.

(Rule 4.4 allows the court to strike out a statement of case.)

Security for costs of an appeal

20.8. The court may order security for costs of an appeal against—

(a) an appellant;
(b) a respondent who also appeals,

on the same grounds as it may order security for costs against an applicant under this Part.

Practice Direction 20A supplements FPR Part 20 (Interim remedies)

PRACTICE DIRECTION 20A – INTERIM REMEDIES

This Practice Direction supplements FPR Part 20

Scope and jurisdiction

1.1 This Practice Direction does not apply to an order under section 48 (Powers to assist in discovery of children who may be in need of emergency protection), section 50 (Recovery of abducted children, etc.) of the Children Act 1989 or section 33(Power to order disclosure of child's whereabouts) or section 34 (Power to order recovery of child) of the Family Law Act 1986.

1.2 High Court Judges and any other judge duly authorised may grant 'search orders' and 'freezing injunctions' (see rules 20.2(1)(h) and 20.2(1)(f)).

1.3 In a case in the High Court, district judges have the power to grant injunctions—

(a) by consent;

(b) in connection with charging orders and appointments of receivers;

(c) in aid of execution of judgments.

1.4 In any other case any judge who has jurisdiction to conduct the hearing of the proceedings has the power to grant an injunction in those proceedings.

1.5. A district judge has the power to vary or discharge an injunction granted by any judge with the consent of all the parties.

Making an application

2.1 The application notice must state—

(a) the order sought; and

(b) the date, time and place of the hearing.

2.2 The application notice and evidence in support must be served as soon as practicable after issue and in any event not less than 7 days before the court is due to hear the application unless the court directs otherwise.

2.3 Where the court is to serve, sufficient copies of the application notice and evidence in support for the court and for each respondent should be filed for issue and service.

2.4 Whenever possible a draft of the order sought should be filed with the application notice and an electronic version of the draft should also be available to the court in a format compatible with the word processing software used by the court and on such storage medium as shall be agreed by the court. This will enable the court officer to arrange for any amendments to be incorporated and for the speedy preparation and sealing of the order.

Evidence

3.1 Applications for search orders and freezing injunctions must be supported by affidavit evidence.

3.2 Applications for other interim injunctions must be supported by evidence set out in either—

(a) a witness statement; or
(b) the application notice provided that it is verified by a statement of truth,

unless the court, an Act, a rule in the FPR or a practice direction requires evidence by affidavit.

3.3 The evidence must set out the facts on which the applicant relies for the application being made against the respondent, including all material facts of which the court should be made aware.

3.4 Where an application is made without notice to the respondent, the evidence must also set out why notice was not given.

(See Part 22 and the practice direction that supplements it for information about evidence.)

Urgent applications and applications without notice

4.1 These fall into two categories—

(a) applications where an application in proceedings has already been issued; and
(b) applications where an application in proceedings has not yet been issued,

and, in both cases, where notice of the application has not been given to the respondent.

4.2 These applications are normally dealt with at a court hearing but cases of extreme urgency may be dealt with by telephone.

4.3 In relation to applications dealt with at a court hearing after issue of an application form—

(a) the application notice, evidence in support and a draft order (as in paragraph 2.4) should be filed with the court two hours before the hearing wherever possible;
(b) if an application is made before the application notice has been issued, a draft order (as in paragraph 2.4) should be provided at the hearing, and the application notice and evidence in support must be filed with the court on the same or next working day or as ordered by the court; and
(c) except in cases where it is essential that the respondent must not be aware of the application, the applicant should take steps to notify the respondent informally of the application.

4.4 In relation to applications made before the issue of an application—

(a) in addition to the provisions set out at paragraph 4.3, unless the court orders otherwise, either the applicant must undertake to the court to issue an application notice immediately or the court will give directions for the commencement of the application (see rule 20.3(3));

(b) where possible the application should be served with the order for the injunction;

(c) an order made before the issue of an application should state in the title after the names of the applicant and respondent 'the Applicant and Respondent in Intended Proceedings'.

4.5 In relation to applications made outside normal working hours—

(a) the applicant should either—

   (i) telephone the Royal Courts of Justice on 020 7947 6000 to be put in contact with the clerk to the appropriate duty judge in the High Court (or the appropriate area Circuit Judge where known); or

   (ii) telephone the Urgent Court Business Officer of the appropriate Circuit who will contact the local duty judge;

(b) where the facility is available it is likely that the judge will require a draft order to be faxed to him;

(c) the application notice and evidence in support must be filed with the court on the same or next working day or as ordered, together with two copies of the order for sealing;

(d) injunctions will be heard by telephone only where the applicant is acting by counsel or solicitors.

Orders for injunctions

5.1 Any order for an injunction, unless the court orders otherwise, must contain—

(a) an undertaking by the applicant to the court to pay any damages which the respondent sustains which the court considers the applicant should pay;

(b) if the order is made without notice to any other party, an undertaking by the applicant to the court to serve on the respondent the application notice, evidence in support and any order made as soon as practicable;

(c) if the order is made without notice to any other party, a return date for a further hearing at which the other party can be present;

(d) if the order is made before filing the application notice, an undertaking to file and pay the appropriate fee on the same or next working day; and

(e) if the order is made before issue of an application in proceedings—

   (i) an undertaking to issue and pay the appropriate fee on the same or next working day; or

(ii) directions for the commencement of the application.

5.2 When the court makes an order for an injunction, it should consider whether to require an undertaking by the applicant to pay any damages sustained by a person other than the respondent, including another party to the proceedings or any other person who may suffer loss as a consequence of the order.

5.3 An order for an injunction made in the presence of all parties to be bound by it or made at a hearing of which they have had notice, may state that it is effective until final hearing or further order.

5.4 Any order for an injunction must set out clearly what the respondent must do or not do.

SEARCH ORDERS

Orders for the preservation of evidence and property
6.1 The following provisions apply to search orders in addition to those listed above.

The Supervising Solicitor
6.2 The Supervising Solicitor must be experienced in the operation of search orders. A Supervising Solicitor may be contacted either through the Law Society or, for the London area, through the London Solicitors Litigation Association.

Evidence
6.3 (1) The affidavit must state the name, firm and its address, and
   experience of the Supervising Solicitor, also the address of the premises and whether it is a private or business address.

(2) The affidavit must disclose very fully the reason the order is sought, including the probability that relevant material would disappear if the order were not made.

Service
6.4. (1) The order must be served personally by the Supervising Solicitor,
   unless the court directs otherwise, and must be accompanied by the evidence in support and any documents capable of being copied.

(2) Confidential exhibits need not be served but they must be made available for inspection by the respondent in the presence of the applicant's solicitors while the order is carried out and afterwards be retained by the respondent's solicitors on their undertaking not to permit the respondent—

(a) to see them or copies of them except in their presence; and
(b) to make or take away any note or record of them.

(3) The Supervising Solicitor may be accompanied only by the persons mentioned in the order.

(4) The Supervising Solicitor must explain the terms and effect of the order to the respondent in everyday language and advise the respondent—

(a) of the respondent's right to take legal advice, and to apply to vary or discharge the order; and
(b) that the respondent may be entitled to avail himself of—
    (i) legal professional privilege; and
    (ii) the privilege against self-incrimination.

(5) Where the Supervising Solicitor is a man and the respondent is likely to be an unaccompanied woman, at least one other person named in the order must be a woman and must accompany the Supervising Solicitor.

(6) The order may only be served between 9.30 a.m. and 5.30 p.m. Monday to Friday unless the court directs otherwise.

Search and custody of materials
6.5 (1) No material shall be removed unless clearly covered by the terms of the order.

(2) The premises must not be searched and no items shall be removed from them except in the presence of the respondent or a person who appears to be a responsible employee of the respondent.

(3) Where copies of documents are sought, the documents should be retained for no more than 2 days before return to the owner.

(4) Where material in dispute is removed pending hearing, the applicant's solicitors should place it in the custody of the respondent's solicitors on their undertaking to retain it in safekeeping and to produce it to the court when required.

(5) In appropriate cases the applicant should insure the material retained in the respondent's solicitors' custody.

(6) The Supervising Solicitor must make a list of all material removed from the premises and supply a copy of the list to the respondent.

(7) No material shall be removed from the premises until the respondent has had reasonable time to check the list.

(8) If any of the listed items exists only in computer readable form, the respondent must immediately give the applicant's solicitors effective access to the computers, with all necessary passwords, to enable them to be searched, and cause the listed items to be printed out.

(9) The applicant must take all reasonable steps to ensure that no damage is done to any computer or data.

(10) The applicant and his representatives may not themselves search the respondent's computers unless they have sufficient expertise to do so without damaging the respondent's system;

(11) the Supervising Solicitor shall provide a report on the carrying out of the order to the applicant's solicitors.

(12) As soon as the report is received the applicant's solicitors shall—

(a) serve a copy of it on the respondent; and

(b) file a copy of it with the court.

(13) Where the Supervising Solicitor is satisfied that full compliance with paragraph 6.5(7) and (8) above is impracticable, that Solicitor may permit the search to proceed and items to be removed without compliance with the impracticable requirements.

General

6.6 The Supervising Solicitor must not be an employee or member of the applicant's firm of solicitors.

6.7 If the court orders that the order need not be served by the Supervising Solicitor, the reason for so ordering must be set out in the order.

6.8 The search order must not be carried out at the same time as a police search warrant.

6.9 There is no privilege against self-incrimination in proceedings in which a court is hearing an application for an order under Part 4 or 5 of the Children Act 1989 (see section 98 of the Children Act 1989).

Delivery up orders

7.1 The following provision applies to orders, other than search orders, for delivery up or preservation of evidence or property where it is likely that such an order will be executed at the premises of the respondent or a third party.

7.2 In such cases the court will consider whether to include in the order for the benefit or protection of the parties similar provisions to those specified above in relation to injunctions and search orders.

Injunctions against third parties

8.1 The following provision applies to orders which will affect a person other than the applicant or respondent, who—

(a) did not attend the hearing at which the order was made; and
(b) is served with the order.

8.2 Where such a person served with the order requests—

(a) a copy of any materials read by the court, including material prepared after the hearing at the direction of the court or in compliance with the order; or
(b) a note of the hearing,

the applicant, or the applicant's legal representative, must comply promptly with the request, unless the court directs otherwise.

* * * * *

Part 21

Commentary on Part 21:
MISCELLANEOUS RULES ABOUT DISCLOSURE AND INSPECTION OF DOCUMENTS

A reading of Part 21 alone would suggest that it does no more than to extend the old FPR 1991 rule 2.62(7) to (9) inspection/production order procedure to all proceedings governed by FPR 2010. The augmenting PD 21A, however, takes the scope of the Part considerably further, and brings into play the concept of 'standard disclosure' so familiar to civil practitioners.

Definitions
For the purposes of Part 21 certain somewhat obvious definitions are supplied by rule 21.1. Thus a party 'discloses' a document by stating that the document exists or has existed. 'Inspection' of a document occurs when a party is permitted to inspect a document disclosed by another person. A 'document' means anything in which information of any description is recorded and 'copy' in relation to a document, means anything onto which information recorded in the document has been copied, by whatever means and whether directly or indirectly. It is to be supposed that indirect copying by unorthodox means might extend to dictating the contents of a document into a mobile telephone or tape recorder, but probably would not extend to memorising them.

Types of order for disclosure in family proceedings
Para 2 of PD 21A addresses the 'types of order for disclosure in family proceedings'. Para 2.1 defines 'standard disclosure' in proceedings other than those for a financial remedy. As noted in Commentary to Part 8 *above* there are a number of financial applications which are not proceedings for a 'financial remedy'. In these cases the normal order will be for 'standard disclosure' which requires each party to set out in a list all the documents material to the proceedings, of the existence of which that party is aware and which are or have been in that party's control.
Para 2.2 deals with disclosure in financial remedy proceedings, and

restates the well known principles and procedures set forth in Part 9 and PD 9A whereby the process of disclosure is staged so that, first, Form E is served together with the documents which are required to be attached to it. The second stage occurs by the parties requesting further disclosure of each other by a questionnaire served before the first appointment; which questionnaire can request both information and documents. With the court's permission, a further questionnaire can be served later in the proceedings.

Whether the procedure is for standard disclosure or the staged financial remedy disclosure the court may, by para 2.4, order 'specific disclosure', which is an order that a party must disclose documents or classes of documents specified in the order, or carry out a search to the extent stated in the order, or disclose any documents located as a result of that search.

Orders for disclosure against a person not a party

These powers are contained in rules 21.2 and 21.3. The CPR counterparts are rules 31.17 and 31.19.

Rule 21.2 is not intended to be an exhaustive statement of these powers, for by rule 21.2(7) the rule does not limit any other power which the court may have to order disclosure against a person who is not a party to proceedings

Rule 21.2 provides the essential procedure. It applies where an application is made to the court 'under any Act' for disclosure by a person who is not a party to the proceedings. By rule 21.2(3) the court will only make an order where disclosure is necessary in order to dispose fairly of the proceedings or to save costs. The principal statutory provisions under which such an order will be sought are section 34 of the Senior Courts Act 1981, section 53 of the County Courts Act 1984, the Bankers Books Evidence Act 1879 and the Evidence (Proceedings in Other Jurisdictions) Act 1975.

As under FPR 1991 r 2.62(8), an order must not compel a person to produce any document which that person could not be compelled to produce at the final hearing (rule 21.2(6)).

Procedure

As an application will be made within proceedings the procedure under Part 18 will apply (see Commentary on Part 18 *above*). However, the restrictions on without notice applications do not apply, as rule 21.2(2)(a) provides baldly that the application may be made without notice and must be supported by evidence.

Form and content of order

An order under this rule *must* specify the documents or the classes of documents which the respondent must disclose, and require the respondent, when making disclosure, to specify any of those documents (i) which are no longer in the respondent's control, or (ii) in respect of which the respondent claims a right or duty to withhold inspection (rule 21.2(4)). In addition the order *may* require the respondent to indicate what has happened to any documents which are no longer in the respondent's control, and may specify the time and place for disclosure and inspection (rule 21.2(5)).

Costs

Neither this rule nor Part 28 deals with the costs incurred by a non-party in meeting an application under this rule or in complying with an order. However CPR rule 48.1 deals with the costs incurred in connection with orders for disclosure against a person who is not a party. CPR rule 48.2 provides that the general rule is that the court will award the person against whom the order is sought his costs of the application, and of complying with any order made on the application. CPR rule 48.3 allows the court to displace the general rule and to make a different order where having regard to all the circumstances, including the extent to which it was reasonable for the person against whom the order was sought to oppose the application, and whether the parties to the application have complied with any relevant pre-action protocol. There is no reason to suppose that a different approach would be adopted in proceedings for a financial remedy. Indeed, under the current practice applicable to inspection appointments the normal rule is that the third party discloser has his costs paid on the indemnity basis, leaving open for later determination the liability as between the parties.

Claim to withhold inspection or disclosure of a document

Rule 21.3 incorporates CPR 31.19. It addresses alternative scenarios. The first is where a person seeks to withhold disclosure of a document on the ground that disclosure would damage the public interest. Such a person may apply, without notice, but with evidence, for an order permitting him to withhold (rule 21.3(1)). If the claim is upheld then, subject to contrary order, the order must not be served on any other person, and must not be open to inspection by any other person (rule 21.3(2)). Documents falling under this head are generally confidential state documents, and are very rarely going to be in play in financial remedy proceedings.

The second scenario is where person (A) wishes to claim a right or a duty to withhold inspection of a document, or part of a document. Under rule 21.3(3) and (4) he must state in writing to the person wishing to inspect the document (B) the right or duty claimed and the grounds on which that right or duty is claimed. Person B may apply to the court, with evidence, under rule 21.3(5) to decide whether such a claim made under paragraph should be upheld. An example of this scenario in operation is where there is a dispute as whether a document is or is not privileged: see for example, *C v C (Privilege)* [2008] 1 FLR 115

Where the court is deciding an application under the first or second scenarios it may require the person seeking to withhold disclosure or inspection of a document to produce that document to the court, and invite any person, whether or not a party, to make representations. In *C v C* at [67] it was said that 'the power the court undoubtedly has to examine the documents should be exercised very sparingly'.

This rule is not exhaustive and does not affect any rule of law which permits or requires a document to be withheld from disclosure or inspection on the ground that its disclosure or inspection would damage the public interest (rule 21.3(8)). In this connection in the context of cross-border mediations see Commentary on Part 35 *below*.

PART 21: MISCELLANEOUS RULES ABOUT DISCLOSURE AND INSPECTION OF DOCUMENTS

Interpretation

21.1.—(1) A party discloses a document by stating that the document exists or has existed.

(2) Inspection of a document occurs when a party is permitted to inspect a document disclosed by another person.

(3) For the purposes of disclosure and inspection—

(a) "document" means anything in which information of any description is recorded; and

(b) "copy" in relation to a document, means anything onto which information recorded in the document has been copied, by whatever means and whether directly or indirectly.

Orders for disclosure against a person not a party

21.2.—(1) This rule applies where an application is made to the court under any Act for disclosure by a person who is not a party to the proceedings.

(2) The application—

(a) may be made without notice; and

(b) must be supported by evidence.

(3) The court may make an order under this rule only where disclosure is necessary in order to dispose fairly of the proceedings or to save costs.

(4) An order under this rule must—

(a) specify the documents or the classes of documents which the respondent must disclose; and

(b) require the respondent, when making disclosure, to specify any of those documents—

(i) which are no longer in the respondent's control; or

(ii) in respect of which the respondent claims a right or duty to withhold inspection.

(5) Such an order may—

(a) require the respondent to indicate what has happened to any documents which are no longer in the respondent's control; and

(b) specify the time and place for disclosure and inspection.

(6) An order under this rule must not compel a person to produce any document which that person could not be compelled to produce at the final hearing.

(7) This rule does not limit any other power which the court may have to order disclosure against a person who is not a party to proceedings.

(Rule 35.3 contains provisions in relation to the disclosure and inspection of evidence arising out of mediation of cross-border disputes.)

Claim to withhold inspection or disclosure of a document

21.3.—(1) A person may apply, without notice, for an order permitting that person to withhold disclosure of a document on the ground that disclosure would damage the public interest.

(2) Unless the court otherwise orders, an order of the court under paragraph (1)—

(a) must not be served on any other person; and

(b) must not be open to inspection by any other person.

(3) A person who wishes to claim a right or a duty to withhold inspection of a document, or part of a document, must state in writing—

(a) the right or duty claimed; and

(b) the grounds on which that right or duty is claimed.

(4) The statement referred to in paragraph must be made to the person wishing to inspect the document.

(5) A party may apply to the court to decide whether a claim made under paragraph (3) should be upheld.

(6) Where the court is deciding an application under paragraph (1) or (5) it may—

(a) require the person seeking to withhold disclosure or inspection of a document to produce that document to the court; and

(b) invite any person, whether or not a party, to make representations.

(7) An application under paragraph (1) or (5) must be supported by evidence.

(8) This Part does not affect any rule of law which permits or requires a document to be withheld from disclosure or inspection on the ground that its disclosure or inspection would damage the public interest.

Practice Direction 21A supplements FPR Part 21 (Disclosure and inspection of documents)

PRACTICE DIRECTION 21A – DISCLOSURE AND INSPECTION

This Practice Direction supplements FPR Part 21

CHAPTER 1

ORDERS FOR DISCLOSURE AND INSPECTION OF DOCUMENTS

Interpretation

1.1 A party discloses a document by stating that the document exists or has existed. Inspection occurs when a party is permitted to inspect a document disclosed by another party.

1.2 For the purposes of disclosure and inspection in family proceedings—

"document" means anything in which information of any description is recorded and any copy of a document which contains a modification, obliteration or other marking or feature shall be treated as a separate document; and

"copy", in relation to a document, means anything on which information recorded in the document has been copied, by whatever means and whether directly or indirectly.

Types of order for disclosure in family proceedings

2.1 In family proceedings other than proceedings for a financial remedy, where the court orders disclosure, the normal order will be for disclosure by each party setting out, in a list or questionnaire, the documents material to the proceedings, of the existence of which that party is aware and which are or have been in that party's control. This process is known as "standard disclosure".

2.2 In proceedings for a financial remedy, the process of disclosure is staged. First, Form E (the financial statement referred to in rule 9.14(1)) is served together with the documents which are required to be attached to it. The second stage occurs by the parties requesting (further) disclosure of each other by a questionnaire served before the first appointment; the questionnaire can request both information and documents. With the court's permission, a further questionnaire can be served later in the proceedings.

2.3 In matrimonial and civil partnership proceedings, under rule 7.15, the court – either on its own initiative or on the application of the other party – may order a party to clarify any matter which is in dispute in the proceedings or give additional information in relation to any such matter, whether or not the matter is contained in or referred to in the application or in the answer.

2.4 In any family proceedings, the court may order "specific disclosure", which is an order that a party must—

(a) disclose documents or classes of documents specified in the order;
(b) carry out a search to the extent stated in the order; or
(c) disclose any documents located as a result of that search.

* * * * *

Part 22

Commentary on Part 22:
EVIDENCE

Part 22 deals with evidence generally, although hearsay evidence is dealt with in Part 23. PD 22A deals with written evidence, but also in its Annex 3 sets out extensive video conferencing guidance.

CPR counterparts
Part 22 is the counterpart to CPR Part 32 on which it is very closely modelled. The corresponding provisions are as follows:

	FPR	CPR
1. General Rules		
Power of court to control evidence	Rule 22.1	Rule 32.1
Evidence of witnesses – general rule	Rule 22.2	Rule 32.2
Evidence by video link or other means	Rule 22.3	Rule 32.3
Witness statements	Rule 22.4	Rules 32.4 and 32.8
Service of witness statements for use at the final hearing	Rule 22.5	Rule 32.4
Use at the final hearing of witness statements which have been served	Rule 22.6	Rule 32.5
Evidence at hearings other than the final hearing	Rule 22.7	Rule 32.6
Order for cross-examination	Rule 22.8	Rule 32.7
Witness summaries	Rule 22.9	Rule 32.9
Consequence of failure to serve witness statement	Rule 22.10	Rule 32.10
Cross-examination on a witness statement	Rule 22.11	Rule 32.11
Affidavit evidence	Rule 22.12	Rule 32.15
Form of affidavit	Rule 22.13	Rule 32.16
Affidavit made outside the jurisdiction	Rule 22.14	Rule 32.17
Notice to admit facts	Rule 22.15	Rule 32.18
Notice to admit or produce documents	Rule 22.16	Rule 32.19

Similarly, PD 22A is almost identical to CPR PD 32A.

The power to control evidence

Rule 22.1 supplies the governing far-reaching power of the court to control evidence. It may do so by giving directions as to the issues on which it requires evidence, the nature of the evidence which it requires to decide those issues, and the way in which the evidence is to be placed before the court. It may use its power to exclude evidence that would otherwise be admissible. It may permit a party to adduce evidence, or to seek to rely on a document, where he fails to comply with the rules in this Part. The court may limit cross-examination.

These powers should be seen as complementary to the general powers of case-management under Part 4 *above*. It is reasonable to anticipate that at a first appointment the court will not only give directions under Part 4 but will also make orders for the control of evidence, although orders under this Part will perhaps be more specifically and forcefully made at the pre-trial review or at the final hearing itself.

Non-contentious directions of this nature may be made in the open phase of the FDR; in the light of *Myerson v Myerson* [2009] 1 FLR 826 it would likely be inappropriate for the FDR judge to entertain opposed applications to exclude evidence or documents from the court process.

In cases proceeding under the CPR it is apparently not uncommon for applications to exclude inadmissible evidence (for example evidence that is said to be privileged) to be framed under the counterpart to rule 22.1 (CPR rule 32.1). This is slightly surprising, as the source of the court's power to exclude such evidence is plainly not to be found here. Rather, the focus of rule 22.1 is the exclusion of evidence that would otherwise be admissible in the interests of economy (both of time and costs). The exercise of this exclusionary power manifestly gives rise to the question of the engagement of Convention rights, although the margin of appreciation is plainly wide. It was said, admittedly a long time ago, that the court should be careful before refusing to look at a document which a party wishes it to read: see *De Haes v Belgium* (1998) 25 EHRR 1.

Examples where the court may apply the exclusionary rule with vigour might include attempts to introduce evidence as to credit, or hearsay evidence where no attempt has been made to comply with the rules in Part 23 (see Commentary on Part 23 below).

The power to limit cross-examination is a facet of the court's general power to timetable a case and derives from rule 4.1(3)(o) ('the court may take any other step or make any other order for the purpose of managing the case and furthering the overriding objective'). It is a commonplace, and good practice, at (or better before) the commencement of a trial for the parties to agree (or the court to impose) a trial timetable or template.

Written evidence

Before a hearing formal written evidence made by the parties or their witnesses will come into being. This may take several forms. In financial remedy proceedings the following forms of written evidence will be encountered:

- Form E (rule 9.14(1));
- Witness statements (rule 22.4);
- Witness summaries (rule 22.9);
- Affidavits (rules 22.12 and 22.13);
- Replies to questionnaire (rule 9.14(5)(c));
- Further chronologies or schedules (rule 9.15(3)(d));
- Answer to a Notice to Admit Facts (rule 22.15).

As already noted in Commentary on Part 9 *above*, **Form E** must be sworn. A **witness statement** is defined by rule 22.4 as 'a written statement signed by a person which contains the evidence which that person would be allowed to give orally'. It must be verified by a statement of truth (rule 17.2(1)(b) and PD 22A para 6.4). A witness statement must indicate (i) which of the statements in it are made from the maker's own knowledge and which are matters of information and belief, and (ii) the source for any matters of information and belief (para 4.3). For a lay witness it must begin by giving his or her full name and residential address (a professional witness may give the address at which he or she works). A party can escape revelation of his or her address by giving notice to the court under rule 29.1 (see Commentary on rule 29 *below*).

PD 22A sets out highly prescriptive rules regulating the form of a witness statement. These include the requirements that it must be produced on durable quality A4 paper with a 3.5 cm margin; be fully legible and normally typed on one side of the paper only; where possible, be bound securely in a manner which would not hamper filing; have the pages numbered consecutively as a separate document (or as one of several documents contained in a file); be divided into numbered paragraphs; have all numbers, including dates, expressed in figures; and give the reference to any document or documents mentioned either in the margin or in bold text in the body of the statement.

It can be safely assumed in light of the anticipated ingress of a throng of litigants in person in the wake of the Government's legal aid reforms that very few, if any, of these prescriptions will be complied with. Counsel of perfection (and perhaps more to the point solicitors of perfection and their assistants, paralegals, clerks, office juniors and secretaries) will welcome this guidance. It remains to be seen how many will honour it in the observance.

Also to be found in PD 22A is an equally prescriptive set of requirements as to the presentation and preparation of exhibits. Para 11.3 requires that where an exhibit contains more than one document, a front page should be attached setting out a list of the documents contained in the exhibit. The list should contain the dates of the documents. Similarly para 13.1 stipulates that where an exhibit contains more than one document (a) the bundle should not be stapled but should be securely fastened in a way that does not hinder the reading of the documents; and (b) the pages should be numbered consecutively at bottom centre. Perhaps unsurprisingly para 13.2 requires that every page of an exhibit should be clearly legible: typed copies of illegible documents should be included, paginated with 'a' numbers.

At a time when government is fleeing from the expense of what was once a Rolls Royce system of justice and of legal aid it is odd to find so much pandering for perfection even in the worthy cause of such scrupulous preparation of documentation for the convenience at trial of the hard-pressed judge. Even for high rollers who have re-cut their cloth, dispensed with their chauffeur and are now driven to be driven to court in a hansom the cost of this standard of excellence will come dear. For those who drive minis if at all the extra cost may push them over the curb. For their solicitors (especially in publicly funded cases, if they survive – the solicitors *and* the cases) no extra funding is likely to be available to pay for what in these circumstances might be thought extravagances.

Although not explicitly stated it is clear from the tenor of Part 22 that the principal method of giving evidence in financial remedy proceedings (Form E and replies to questionnaire apart) will be by witness statements. By rule 22.5 the court may give directions (i) as to service on the other parties of any witness statement of the oral evidence on which a party intends to rely in relation to any issues of fact to be decided at the final hearing, and (ii) as to the order in which witness statements are to be served, and whether or not the witness statements are to be filed. Directions under this rule will almost invariably be made at the first appointment.

A novelty derived from CPR rule 32.9 is the **witness summary** referred to in rule 22.9 where a party has been ordered to serve a witness statement from an intended witness for use at a hearing but has, for whatever reason, been unable to obtain it then he may apply, without notice, for permission to serve a witness summary instead. This is a summary of the evidence, if known, which would otherwise be included in a witness statement or, if the evidence is not known, the matters about which the party serving the witness summary proposes to question the witness. Where a party serves a witness summary, then so far as practicable rules 22.4(2) (form of witness statements), 22.5 (service of witness statements for use at the final hearing) and 22.6(3) (amplifying witness statements) apply to the summary.

Affidavits live on. By rule 22.12 evidence must be given by affidavit instead of or in addition to a witness statement if this is required by the court, or by a provision contained in any other rule, a practice direction or any other enactment. As stated above, Form E must be sworn (rule 9.14(20(a) states that it should be 'verified by affidavit', but the prescribed Form E contains the jurat within the body of the Form).

Current practice involves orders at the First Appointment, or in the open phase of the FDR, being made which provide for service of 'section 25 affidavits'. It is suggested that this practice may well change to ordering '*witness statements incorporating all section 25 factors relied on and all evidence in chief that is intended to be given*' (see *below* as to evidence in chief).

It is considered that verification by affidavit is only likely to be ordered where the court is concerned to pin a shifty litigant to the consequences of his or her oath. An affidavit must comply with the requirements concerning witness statements set out above. The list of persons who may administer the oath has been expanded.

As noted in Commentary on Part 9 *above*, **replies to questionnaire** must now be verified by a statement of truth (PD 9A para 5.2), but this requirement does not extend to **further chronologies** or **schedules** ordered under rule 9.15(3)(d).

Rule 22.15 allows a **Notice to Admit Facts** to be served no later than 21 days before the final hearing. Where the other party makes any admission in answer to the notice, the admission may be used against him or her only in the proceedings in which the notice to admit is served and by the party who served the notice. The court may allow a party to amend or withdraw any admission made by him or her on such terms as it thinks just. This procedure was present within the RSC, but rarely used. Its utility should not be overlooked, since there would no doubt be costs consequences of proving a fact which a person served with such a notice has not admitted. A similar procedure designed to secure an admission before the hearing of the authenticity of documents is to be found in rule 22.16, but it is not thought that this will be often used.

Hearings other than the final hearing

The general rule (rule 22.2(1)(b)) is that *at a hearing other than the final hearing* any fact which needs to be proved by the evidence of witnesses is to be proved by their evidence in writing. Thus at the hearing of any application made in the course of proceedings under Part 18 (as interlocutory hearings must now be called) oral evidence is the exception and written evidence is the rule. This general rule is repeated and reinforced by rule 22.7. It is disapplied where the court, any other rule, a practice direction or any other enactment requires otherwise. At such a hearing a party may rely on the matters set out in his or her application form, application notice or answer, if the document is verified by a statement of truth (but not otherwise).

By rule 22.8 a party may apply to the court for permission to cross-examine the person giving the written evidence. If the court gives permission but the person in question does not attend, then that person's evidence may not be used unless the court directs otherwise. Rule 22.8 does not give any steer as to when cross-examination might be ordered on a Part 18 hearing. Old civil authorities have suggested that it should only be in 'extreme cases', but as in so many instances it must all depend on the facts at large.

The final hearing

The general rule (rule 22.2(1)(a)) is that *at the final hearing* any fact which needs to be proved by the evidence of witnesses is to be proved by their oral evidence. The new scheme now rigorously limits **evidence in chief**. By rule 22.6 where a party wishes to rely on the evidence of a witness who has made a witness statement (including himself) then he must call the witness to give oral evidence unless the court directs otherwise or the party puts the statement in as hearsay evidence. *The witness statement of a witness called to give oral evidence is to stand as the evidence in chief of that witness unless the court directs otherwise* (rule 22.6(2)). Some mitigation is afforded by rule 22.6(3) which allows a witness giving oral evidence at the final hearing with the permission of the court to amplify his witness statement, and/or to give evidence in relation to new matters which have arisen since the witness statement was served; but the court will give permission only if it considers that there is *good reason* not to confine the evidence of the witness to the contents of the witness statement (rule 22.6(4)).

Thus evidence in chief is the exception. In civil cases evidence in chief is now rare and it remains to be seen whether this cultural change will be adopted in family proceedings. When considering its power to order amplification or to give evidence on new matters it is considered that the court should bear in mind that in a financial remedy application it is conducting a statutory inquisition and not an adversarial trial.

If a party who has served a witness statement does not call the witness to give evidence at the final hearing, or put the witness statement in as hearsay evidence, any other party may put the witness statement in as hearsay evidence (rule 22.6(5) – see Commentary on Part 23 *below* for the rules on hearsay evidence).

A witness who is called to give evidence at the final hearing may be cross-examined on the witness statement, whether or not reference to the statement or any part of it was made during the witness's evidence in chief (rule 22.11).

By rule 22.3 the court may allow a witness to give evidence through a video link or by other means. Annex 3 to PD 22A contains elaborate and lengthy Video Conferencing Guidance to which reference should be made.

PART 22: EVIDENCE

CHAPTER 1: GENERAL RULES

Power of court to control evidence

22.1.—(1) The court may control the evidence by giving directions as to—

(a) the issues on which it requires evidence;
(b) the nature of the evidence which it requires to decide those issues; and
(c) the way in which the evidence is to be placed before the court.

(2) The court may use its power under this rule to exclude evidence that would otherwise be admissible.

(3) The court may permit a party to adduce evidence, or to seek to rely on a document, in respect of which that party has failed to comply with the requirements of this Part.

(4) The court may limit cross-examination.

Evidence of witnesses – general rule

22.2.—(1) The general rule is that any fact which needs to be proved by the evidence of witnesses is to be proved—

(a) at the final hearing, by their oral evidence; and
(b) at any other hearing, by their evidence in writing.

(2) The general rule does not apply—

(a) to proceedings under Part 12 for secure accommodation orders, interim care orders or interim supervision orders; or
(b) where an enactment, any of these rules, a practice direction or a court order provides to the contrary.

(Section 45(7) of the Children Act 1989 (emergency protection orders) is an example of an enactment which makes provision relating to the evidence that a court may take into account when hearing an application.)

Evidence by video link or other means

22.3. The court may allow a witness to give evidence through a video link or by other means.

Witness statements

22.4.—(1) A witness statement is a written statement signed by a person which contains the evidence which that person would be allowed to give orally.

(2) A witness statement must comply with the requirements set out in the Practice Direction 22A.

(Part 17 requires a witness statement to be verified by a statement of truth.)

Service of witness statements for use at the final hearing

22.5.—(1) The court may give directions as to service on the other parties of any witness statement of the oral evidence on which a party intends to rely in relation to any issues of fact to be decided at the final hearing.

(2) The court may give directions as to—

(a) the order in which witness statements are to be served; and

(b) whether or not the witness statements are to be filed.

(3) Where the court directs that a court officer is to serve a witness statement on the other parties, any reference in this Chapter to a party serving a witness statement is to be read as including a reference to a court officer serving the statement.

Use at the final hearing of witness statements which have been served

22.6.—(1) If a party—

(a) has served a witness statement; and

(b) wishes to rely at the final hearing on the evidence of the witness who made the statement,

that party must call the witness to give oral evidence unless the court directs otherwise or the party puts the statement in as hearsay evidence.

(Part 23 (miscellaneous rules about evidence) contains provisions about hearsay evidence.)

(2) The witness statement of a witness called to give oral evidence under paragraph (1) is to stand as the evidence in chief of that witness unless the court directs otherwise.

(3) A witness giving oral evidence at the final hearing may with the permission of the court—

(a) amplify his witness statement; and

(b) give evidence in relation to new matters which have arisen since the witness statement was served on the other parties.

(4) The court will give permission under paragraph (3) only if it considers that there is good reason not to confine the evidence of the witness to the contents of the witness statement.

(5) If a party who has served a witness statement does not—

(a) call the witness to give evidence at the final hearing; or

(b) put the witness statement in as hearsay evidence,

any other party may put the witness statement in as hearsay evidence.

Evidence at hearings other than the final hearing

22.7.—(1) Subject to paragraph (2), the general rule is that evidence at hearings other than the final hearing is to be by witness statement unless the court, any other rule, a practice direction or any other enactment requires otherwise.

(2) At hearings other than the final hearing, a party may rely on the matters set out in that party's—

(a) application form;

(b) application notice; or

(c) answer,

if the application form, application notice or answer, as the case may be, is verified by a statement of truth.

Order for cross-examination

22.8.—(1) Where, at a hearing other than the final hearing, evidence is given in writing, any party may apply to the court for permission to cross-examine the person giving the evidence.

(2) If the court gives permission under paragraph (1) but the person in question does not attend, that person's evidence may not be used unless the court directs otherwise.

(Rules 35.3 and 35.4 contain rules in relation to evidence arising out of mediation of cross-border disputes.)

Witness summaries

22.9.—(1) A party who—

(a) is required to serve a witness statement for use at any hearing; but

(b) is unable to obtain one,

may apply, without notice, for permission to serve a witness summary instead.

(2) A witness summary is a summary of—

(a) the evidence, if known, which would otherwise be included in a witness statement; or

(b) if the evidence is not known, the matters about which the party serving the witness summary proposes to question the witness.

(3) Unless the court directs otherwise, a witness summary must include the name and address of the intended witness.

(4) Unless the court directs otherwise, a witness summary must be served

within the period in which a witness statement would have had to be served.

(5) Where a party serves a witness summary, so far as practicable rules 22.4(2) (form of witness statements), 22.5 (service of witness statements for use at the final hearing) and 22.6(3) (amplifying witness statements) apply to the summary.

Consequence of failure to serve witness statement

22.10. If a witness statement for use at the final hearing is not served in respect of an intended witness within the time specified by the court, then the witness may not be called to give oral evidence unless the court gives permission.

Cross-examination on a witness statement

22.11. A witness who is called to give evidence at the final hearing may be cross-examined on the witness statement, whether or not the statement or any part of it was referred to during the witness's evidence in chief.

Affidavit evidence

22.12.—(1) Evidence must be given by affidavit instead of or in addition to a witness statement if this is required by the court, a provision contained in any other rule, a practice direction or any other enactment.

(2) In relation to proceedings which are pending or treated as pending in a divorce county court or civil partnership county court, section 58(1)(c) of the County Courts Act 1984, shall have effect as if after paragraph (c) there were inserted—

"or

(d) a district judge of the principal registry; or

(e) any officer of the principal registry authorised by the President under section 2 of the Commissioner for Oaths Act 1889([81]); or

(f) any clerk in the Central Office of the Royal Courts of Justice authorised to take affidavits for the purposes of proceedings in the Supreme Court."

(Rule 7.3 sets out when proceedings are treated as pending in a divorce county court or civil partnership proceedings county court.)

Form of affidavit

22.13. An affidavit must comply with the requirements set out in the Practice Direction 22A.

Affidavit made outside the jurisdiction

22.14. A person may make an affidavit outside the jurisdiction in accordance with—

(a) this Part; or
(b) the law of the place where the affidavit is made.

Notice to admit facts

22.15.—(1) A party may serve notice on another party requiring the other party to admit the facts, or the part of the case of the serving party, specified in the notice.

(2) A notice to admit facts must be served no later than 21 days before the final hearing.

(3) Where the other party makes any admission in answer to the notice, the admission may be used against that party only—

(a) in the proceedings in which the notice to admit is served; and
(b) by the party who served the notice.

(4) The court may allow a party to amend or withdraw any admission made by that party on such terms as it thinks just.

Notice to admit or produce documents

22.16.—(1) A party to whom a document is disclosed is deemed to admit the authenticity of that document unless notice is served by that party that the party wishes the document to be proved at the final hearing.

(2) A notice to prove a document must be served—

(a) by the latest date for serving witness statements; or
(b) within 7 days beginning with the date of service of the document, whichever is later.

Notarial acts and instruments

22.17. A notarial act or instrument may be received in evidence without further proof as duly authenticated in accordance with the requirements of law unless the contrary is proved.

CHAPTER 2: RULES APPLYING ONLY TO PARTICULAR PROCEEDINGS

Scope of this Chapter

22.18. This Chapter of this Part applies to affidavits and affirmations as it applies to witness statements.

Availability of witness statements for inspection during the final hearing

22.19.—(1) This rule applies to proceedings under Part 7 (matrimonial and civil partnership proceedings).

(2) A witness statement which stands as evidence in chief is open to inspection during the course of the final hearing unless the court directs otherwise.

(3) Any person may ask for a direction that a witness statement is not open to inspection.

(4) The court will not make a direction under paragraph (2) unless it is satisfied that a witness statement should not be open to inspection because of—

(a) the interests of justice;
(b) the public interest;
(c) the nature of any expert medical evidence in the statement;
(d) the nature of any confidential information (including information relating to personal financial matters) in the statement; or
(e) the need to protect the interests of any child or protected party.

(5) The court may exclude from inspection words or passages in the witness statement.

Use of witness statements for other purposes

22.20.—(1) This rule applies to proceedings under Part 7 (matrimonial and civil partnership proceedings) or Part 9 (financial remedies).

(2) Except as provided by this rule, a witness statement may be used only for the purpose of the proceedings in which it is served.

(3) Paragraph (2) does not apply if and to the extent that—

(a) the court gives permission for some other use; or
(b) the witness statement has been put in evidence at a hearing held in public.

Practice Direction 22A supplements FPR Part 22 (Written evidence)

PRACTICE DIRECTION 22A – WRITTEN EVIDENCE

This Practice Direction supplements FPR Part 22

Evidence in general

1.1 Rule 22.2(1) sets out the general rule as to how evidence is to be given and facts are to be proved. This is that, at the final hearing, witnesses will normally give oral evidence and, at any hearing other than the final hearing, by evidence in writing (which under rule 22.7(1) will usually be by witness statement).

1.2 Rule 22.2(2) excludes the general rule—

(a) from proceedings under Part 12 (Children) for secure accommodation orders, interim care orders or interim supervision orders; or
(b) where an enactment, any rule in the FPR, a practice direction or a court order provides to the contrary.

1.3 Application forms, application notices and answers except an application for a matrimonial order or a civil partnership order or an answer to such an application may also be used as evidence provided that their contents have been verified by a statement of truth (see Part 17 for information about statements of truth).

(For information regarding evidence by deposition see Part 24 and the practice direction which supplements it.)

1.4 Affidavits must be used as evidence—

(a) where sworn evidence is required by an enactment, rule, order or practice direction; and

(b) in any application for an order against anyone for alleged contempt of court.

1.5 If a party believes that sworn evidence is required by a court in another jurisdiction for any purpose connected with the proceedings, he may apply to the court for a direction that evidence shall be given only by affidavit on any applications to be heard before the final hearing.

1.6 The court may give a direction under rule 22.12 that evidence shall be given by affidavit instead of or in addition to a witness statement—

(a) on its own initiative; or

(b) after any party has applied to the court for such a direction.

1.7 An affidavit, where referred to in the FPR or a practice direction, also means an affirmation unless the context requires otherwise.

Affidavits and Witness Statements

Meaning of "deponent" and "witness"

2.1 For the purposes of the FPR—

a "deponent" is a person who gives evidence by affidavit, affirmation or deposition; and

a "witness" is a person who gives evidence by witness statement.

2.2 References in the following paragraphs to "the maker of", or "making", an affidavit, affirmation, deposition or witness statement are to be construed accordingly.

Heading and format

3.1 The affidavit/statement should be headed with the title of the proceedings where the proceedings are between several parties with the same status it is sufficient to identify the parties, subject to paragraph 4.2, as follows—

Number:

A.B. (and others) Applicants

C.D. (and others) Respondents

3.2 Subject to paragraph 4.2, at the top right-hand corner of the first page (and on the backsheet) there should be clearly written—

(a) the party on whose behalf it is made;

(b) the initials and surname of the maker;

(c) the number of the affidavit/statement in relation to its maker;

(d) the identifying initials and number of each exhibit referred to; and

(e) the date made.

3.3 The affidavit/statement should—

(a) be produced on durable quality A4 paper with a 3.5 cm margin;

(b) be fully legible and should normally be typed on one side of the paper only;

(c) where possible, should be bound securely in a manner which would not hamper filing or, where secure binding is not possible, each page should be endorsed with the case number and should bear the following initials—

   (i) in the case of an affidavit, of the maker and of the person before whom it is sworn; or

   (ii) in the case of a witness statement, of the maker and, where the maker is unable to read or sign the statement, of the authorised person (see paragraphs 7.3 and 7.4 below);

(d) have the pages numbered consecutively as a separate document (or as one of several documents contained in a file);

(e) be divided into numbered paragraphs;

(f) have all numbers, including dates, expressed in figures; and

(g) give the reference to any document or documents mentioned either in the margin or in bold text in the body of the affidavit/statement.

Body

4.1 Subject to paragraph 4.2 and rules 14.2 and 29.1, the affidavit/statement must, if practicable, be in the maker's own words, it should be expressed in the first person, and the maker should—

(a) commence—

   (i) in an affidavit, "I (full name) of (residential address) state on oath ...";

   (ii) in a statement, by giving his or her full name and residential address;

(b) if giving evidence in a professional, business or other occupational capacity, give the address at which he or she works in (a) above, the position held and the name of the firm or employer;

(c) give his or her occupation or (if none) description; and

(d) if it be the case that the maker is a party to the proceedings or is employed by a party to the proceedings, state that fact.

4.2 If, in proceedings to which Part 14 (Adoption, placement and related proceedings) applies, a serial number has been assigned under rule 14.2, the affidavit/statement must be framed so that it does not disclose the identity of the applicant.

(Rule 29.1 provides that, unless the court directs otherwise, a party to family proceedings is not required to reveal the address of his or her private residence or other contact details.)

4.3 An affidavit/statement must indicate—

(a) which of the statements in it are made from the maker's own knowledge and which are matters of information and belief; and

(b) the source for any matters of information and belief.

4.4 It is usually convenient to follow the chronological sequence of events or matters dealt with. Each paragraph should as far as possible be confined to a distinct portion of the subject.

4.5 The maker should, when referring to an exhibit or exhibits, state "there is now shown to me marked " ... " the (description of exhibit)".

Alterations to affidavits and witness statements

5.1 Any alteration to an affidavit must be initialled by both the maker and the person before whom the affidavit is sworn.

5.2 Any alteration to a witness statement must be initialled by the maker or by the authorised person where appropriate (see paragraphs 7.3 and 7.4 below).

5.3 An affidavit/statement which contains an alteration that has not been initialled in accordance with paragraphs 5.1 and 5.2 may be filed or used in evidence only with the permission of the court.

Swearing an affidavit or verifying a witness statement

6.1 An affidavit is the testimony of the person who swears it. A witness statement is the equivalent of the oral evidence which the maker would, if called, give in evidence.

6.2 The jurat of an affidavit is a statement set out at the end of the document which authenticates the affidavit. It must—

(a) be signed by all deponents;

(b) be completed and signed by the person before whom the affidavit was sworn whose name and qualification must be printed beneath his signature;

(c) contain the full address of the person before whom the affidavit was sworn; and

(d) follow immediately on from the text and not be put on a separate page.

6.3 An affidavit must be sworn before a person independent of the parties or their representatives. Only the following may administer oaths and take affidavits—

(a) a Commissioner for Oaths (Commissioners for Oaths Acts 1889 and 1891);

(b) other persons specified by statute (sections 12 and 18 of, and Schedules 2 and 4 to, the Legal Services Act 2007);

(c) certain officials of the Senior Courts (section 2 of the Commissioners for Oaths Act 1889);

(d) a circuit judge or district judge (section 58 of the County Courts Act 1984);

(e) any justice of the peace (section 58 of the County Courts Act 1984); and

(f) certain officials of any county court appointed by the judge of that court for the purpose (section 58 of the County Courts Act 1984).

6.4 A witness statement must include a statement of truth by the intended maker as follows:

"I believe that the facts stated in this witness statement are true."

(Attention is drawn to rule 17.6 which sets out the consequences of verifying a witness statement containing a false statement without an honest belief in its truth.)

(For information regarding statements of truth, see Part 17 (Statements of truth) and Practice Direction 17A.)

(Paragraphs 7.1 to 7.4 below set out the procedures to be followed where the intended maker of an affidavit or witness statement is unable to read or sign the affidavit/statement.)

6.5 If, in proceedings under Part 14 (Adoption, placement and related proceedings), a serial number has been assigned under rule 14.2 or the name of the maker of the affidavit/statement is not being revealed in accordance with rule 29.1, the signature of the maker will be edited from the affidavit/statement before it is served on the other party.

Inability of maker to read or sign affidavit/statement

7.1 Where an affidavit is sworn by a deponent who is unable to read or sign it, the person before whom the affidavit is sworn must certify in the jurat that—

(a) that person read the affidavit to the deponent;

(b) the deponent appeared to understand it; and

(c) the deponent signed, or made his mark, in that person's presence.

7.2 If that certificate is not included in the jurat, the affidavit may not be used in evidence unless the court is satisfied that it was read to the deponent and that the deponent appeared to understand it. Annex 1 to this practice direction sets out forms of the jurat with the certificate for an affidavit and an affirmation respectively.

7.3 Where a witness statement is made by a person who is unable to read or sign the statement, it must contain a certificate made by an authorised person. An authorised person is a person able to administer oaths and take affidavits but need not be independent of the parties or their representatives.

7.4 The authorised person must certify—

(a) that the witness statement has been read to the witness;
(b) that the witness appeared to understand it and approved its content as accurate;
(c) that the statement of truth has been read to the witness;
(d) that the witness appeared to understand the statement of truth and the consequences of making a false witness statement; and
(e) that the witness signed or made his or her mark in the presence of the authorised person.

The form of the certificate is set out at Annex 2 to this practice direction.

Filing of affidavits and witness statements

8.1 If the court directs that an affidavit/statement is to be filed, it must be filed in the court or Division, or office or Registry of the court or Division, where the action in which it was or is to be used, is proceeding or will proceed.

8.2 Where the affidavit/statement is in a foreign language—

(a) the party wishing to rely on it must—
    (i) have it translated; and
    (ii) must file the foreign language affidavit/statement with the court; and
(b) the translator must sign the translation to certify that it is accurate.

Exhibits

Manner of Exhibiting Documents

9.1 A document used in conjunction with an affidavit/statement should be—

(a) shown to and verified by the maker, and remain separate from the affidavit/statement; and
(b) identified by a declaration of the person before whom the affidavit/statement was sworn.

9.2 The declaration should be headed with the name of the proceedings in the same way as the affidavit/statement is headed.

9.3 The first page of each exhibit should be marked—

(a) as in paragraph 3.2 above; and
(b) with the exhibit mark referred to in the affidavit/statement in accordance with paragraph 4.5 above.

9.4 Where the maker makes more than one affidavit/statement, to which there are exhibits, in the same proceedings, the numbering of the exhibits should run consecutively throughout and not start again with each affidavit/statement.

Letters

10.1 Copies of individual letters should be collected together and exhibited in a bundle or bundles. They should be arranged in chronological order with the earliest at the top, and firmly secured.

10.2 When a bundle of correspondence is exhibited, the exhibit should have a front page attached stating that the bundle consists of original letters and copies. They should be arranged and secured as above and numbered consecutively.

Other documents

11.1 Photocopies instead of original documents may be exhibited provided the originals are made available for inspection by the other parties before the hearing and by the court at the hearing.

11.2 Court documents must not be exhibited (official copies of such documents prove themselves).

11.3 Where an exhibit contains more than one document, a front page should be attached setting out a list of the documents contained in the exhibit. The list should contain the dates of the documents.

Exhibits other than documents

12.1 Items other than documents should be clearly marked with an exhibit number or letter in such a manner that the mark cannot become detached from the exhibit.

12.2 Small items may be placed in a container and the container appropriately marked.

General provisions

13.1 Where an exhibit contains more than one document—

  (a) the bundle should not be stapled but should be securely fastened in a way that does not hinder the reading of the documents; and
  (b) the pages should be numbered consecutively at bottom centre.

13.2 Every page of an exhibit should be clearly legible; typed copies of illegible documents should be included, paginated with "a" numbers.

13.3 Where affidavits/statements and exhibits have become numerous, they should be put into separate bundles and the pages numbered consecutively throughout.

13.4 Where on account of their bulk the service of exhibits or copies of exhibits on the other parties would be difficult or impracticable, the directions of the court should be sought as to arrangements for bringing the exhibits to the attention of the other parties and as to their custody pending trial.

Miscellaneous

Defects in affidavits, witness statement and exhibits
14.1 Where—

- (a) an affidavit;
- (b) a witness statement; or
- (c) an exhibit to either an affidavit or a witness statement,

does not comply with Part 22 or this practice direction in relation to its form, the court may refuse to admit it as evidence and may refuse to allow the costs arising from its preparation.

14.2 Permission to file a defective affidavit or witness statement or to use a defective exhibit may be obtained from the court where the case is proceeding.

Affirmations
15.1 All provisions in this or any other practice direction relating to affidavits apply to affirmations with the following exceptions—

- (a) the deponent should commence "I (full name) of (residential address) do solemnly and sincerely affirm ..."; and
- (b) in the jurat the word "sworn" is replaced by the word "affirmed".

Certificate of court officer
16.1 In proceedings under Part 7 (Matrimonial and Civil Partnership Proceedings), where the court has ordered that a witness statement, affidavit, affirmation or deposition is not be open to inspection by the public (see rule 22.19(2) and (3)) or that words or passages in the statement etc are not to be open to inspection (see rule 22.19(5)), the court officer will so certify on the statement etc and make any deletions directed by the court under rule 22.19(3).

Video Conferencing
17.1 Guidance on the use of video conferencing in the family courts is set out at Annex 3 to this practice direction.

A list of the sites which are available for video conferencing can be found on Her Majesty's Court Service's website at www.hm-courts-service.gov.uk.

Annex 1

Certificate to be used where a deponent to an affidavit is unable to read or sign it
Sworn at ... this ... day of ... Before me, I having first read over the contents of this affidavit to the deponent [if there are exhibits, add "and explained the nature and effect of the exhibits referred to in it"] who appeared to understand it and approved its content as accurate, and made his/her* mark on the affidavit in my presence. Or, (after "Before me") the witness to the mark of the deponent having been first sworn that the witness had read

over etc. (as above) and that the witness saw the deponent make his/her* mark on the affidavit. (Witness must sign.)

   * *delete as appropriate*

Certificate to be used where a deponent to an affirmation is unable to read or sign it

Affirmed at ... this ... day of ... Before me, I having first read over the contents of this affirmation to the deponent [if there are exhibits, add "and explained the nature and effect of the exhibits referred to in it"] who appeared to understand it and approved its content as accurate, and made his/her* mark on the affirmation in my presence. Or, (after "Before me") the witness to the mark of the deponent having been first sworn that the witness had read over etc. (as above) and that the witness saw the deponent make his/her* mark on the affirmation. (Witness must sign.)

   * *delete as appropriate*

Annex 2

Certificate to be used where a witness is unable to read or sign a witness statement

I certify that I [name and address of authorised person] have read over the contents of this witness statement and the statement of truth to the witness [if there are exhibits, add "and explained the nature and effect of the exhibits referred to in it"] who (a) appeared to understand the witness statement and approved its content as accurate and (b) appeared to understand the statement of truth and the consequences of making a false witness statement, and [signed the statement] [made his/her mark]* in my presence.

   * *delete as appropriate.*

Annex 3

Video Conferencing Guidance

1 This guidance is for the use of video conferencing (VCF) in proceedings to which the Family Procedure Rules apply. It is in part based, with permission, upon the protocol of the Federal Court of Australia. It is intended to provide a guide to all persons involved in the use of VCF, although it does not attempt to cover all the practical questions which might arise.

   Any reference in this guide to a judge is to be taken as including a district judge or justices of the peace if the proceedings are before a magistrates' court.

Video conferencing generally

2 The guidance covers the use of VCF equipment both (a) in a courtroom, whether via equipment which is permanently placed there or via a mobile unit, and (b) in a separate studio or conference room. In either case, the

location at which the judge sits is referred to as the 'local site'. The other site or sites to and from which transmission is made are referred to as 'the remote site' and in any particular case any such site may be another courtroom. The guidance applies to cases where VCF is used for the taking of evidence and also to its use for other parts of any legal proceedings

3 VCF may be a convenient way of dealing with any part of proceedings— it can involve considerable savings in time and cost. Its use for the taking of evidence from overseas witnesses will, in particular, be likely to achieve a material saving of costs, and such savings may also be achieved by its use for taking domestic evidence. It is, however, inevitably not as ideal as having the witness physically present in court. Its convenience should not therefore be allowed to dictate its use. A judgment must be made in every case in which the use of VCF is being considered not only as to whether it will achieve an overall cost saving but as to whether its use will be likely to be beneficial to the efficient, fair and economic disposal of the litigation. In particular, it needs to be recognised that the degree of control a court can exercise over a witness at the remote site is or may be more limited than it can exercise over a witness physically before it.

4 When used for the taking of evidence, the objective should be to make the VCF session as close as possible to the usual practice in court where evidence is taken in open court. To gain the maximum benefit, several differences have to be taken into account. Some matters, which are taken for granted when evidence is taken in the conventional way, take on a different dimension when it is taken by VCF – for example, the administration of the oath, ensuring that the witness understands who is at the local site and what their various roles are, the raising of any objections to the evidence and the use of documents.

5 It should not be presumed that all foreign governments are willing to allow their nationals or others within their jurisdiction to be examined before a court in England or Wales by means of VCF. If there is any doubt about this, enquiries should be directed to the Foreign and Commonwealth Office (International Legal Matters Unit, Consular Division) with a view to ensuring that the country from which the evidence is to be taken raises no objection to it at diplomatic level. The party who is directed to be responsible for arranging the VCF (see paragraph 8) will be required to make all necessary inquiries about this well in advance of the VCF and must be able to inform the court what those inquiries were and of their outcome.

6 Time zone differences need to be considered when a witness abroad is to be examined in England or Wales by VCF. The convenience of the witness, the parties, their representatives and the court must all be taken into account. The cost of the use of a commercial studio is usually greater outside normal business hours.

7 Those involved with VCF need to be aware that, even with the most advanced systems currently available, there are the briefest of delays

between the receipt of the picture and that of the accompanying sound. If due allowance is not made for this, there will be a tendency to 'speak over' the witness, whose voice will continue to be heard for a millisecond or so after he or she appears on the screen to have finished speaking.

8 With current technology, picture quality is good, but not as good as a television picture. The quality of the picture is enhanced if those appearing on VCF monitors keep their movements to a minimum.

Preliminary arrangements

9 The court's permission is required for any part of any proceedings to be dealt with by means of VCF. Before seeking a direction, the applicant should notify the listing officer, diary manager or other appropriate court officer of the intention to seek it, and should enquire as to the availability of court VCF equipment for the day or days of the proposed VCF. If all parties consent to a direction, permission can be sought by letter, fax or e-mail, although the court may still require an oral hearing. All parties are entitled to be heard on whether or not such a direction should be given and as to its terms. If a witness at a remote site is to give evidence by an interpreter, consideration should be given at this stage as to whether the interpreter should be at the local site or the remote site. If a VCF direction is given, arrangements for the transmission will then need to be made. The court will ordinarily direct that the party seeking permission to use VCF is to be responsible for this. That party is hereafter referred to as 'the VCF arranging party'.

10 Subject to any order to the contrary, all costs of the transmission, including the costs of hiring equipment and technical personnel to operate it, will initially be the responsibility of, and must be met by, the VCF arranging party. All reasonable efforts should be made to keep the transmission to a minimum and so keep the costs down. All such costs will be considered to be part of the costs of the proceedings and the court will determine at such subsequent time as is convenient or appropriate who, as between the parties, should be responsible for them and (if appropriate) in what proportions.

11 The local site will, if practicable, be a courtroom but it may instead be an appropriate studio or conference room. The VCF arranging party must contact the listing officer, diary manager or other appropriate officer of the court which made the VCF direction and make arrangements for the VCF transmission. Details of the remote site, and of the equipment to be used both at the local site (if not being supplied by the court) and the remote site (including the number of ISDN lines and connection speed), together with all necessary contact names and telephone numbers, will have to be provided to the listing officer, diary manager or other court officer. The court will need to be satisfied that any equipment provided by the parties for use at the local site and also that at the remote site is of sufficient quality for a satisfactory transmission. The VCF arranging party must

ensure that an appropriate person will be present at the local site to supervise the operation of the VCF throughout the transmission in order to deal with any technical problems. That party must also arrange for a technical assistant to be similarly present at the remote site for like purposes.

12 It is recommended that the judge, practitioners and witness should arrive at their respective VCF sites about 20 minutes prior to the scheduled commencement of the transmission.

13 If the local site is not a courtroom, but a conference room or studio, the judge will need to determine who is to sit where. The VCF arranging party must take care to ensure that the number of microphones is adequate for the speakers and that the panning of the camera for the practitioners' table encompasses all legal representatives so that the viewer can see everyone seated there.

14 If the local site is to be a studio or conference room, the VCF arranging party must ensure that it provides sufficient accommodation to enable a reasonable number of members of the public to attend if appropriate.

15 In cases where the local site is a studio or conference room, the VCF arranging party should make arrangements, if practicable, for the royal coat of arms to be placed above the judge's seat.

16 In cases in which the VCF is to be used for the taking of evidence, the VCF arranging party must arrange for recording equipment to be provided by the court which made the VCF direction so that the evidence can be recorded. An associate will normally be present to operate the recording equipment when the local site is a courtroom. The VCF arranging party should take steps to ensure that an associate is present to do likewise when it is a studio or conference room. The equipment should be set up and tested before the VCF transmission. It will often be a valuable safeguard for the VCF arranging party also to arrange for the provision of recording equipment at the remote site. This will provide a useful back-up if there is any reduction in sound quality during the transmission. A direction from the court for the making of such a back-up recording must, however, be obtained first. This is because the proceedings are court proceedings and, save as directed by the court, no other recording of them must be made. The court will direct what is to happen to the back-up recording.

17 Some countries may require that any oath or affirmation to be taken by a witness accord with local custom rather than the usual form of oath or affirmation used in England and Wales. The VCF arranging party must make all appropriate prior inquiries and put in place all arrangements necessary to enable the oath or affirmation to be taken in accordance with any local custom. That party must be in a position to inform the court what those inquiries were, what their outcome was and what arrangements have been made. If the oath or affirmation can be administered in the manner

normal in England and Wales, the VCF arranging party must arrange in advance to have the appropriate holy book at the remote site. The associate will normally administer the oath.

18 Consideration will need to be given in advance to the documents to which the witness is likely to be referred. The parties should endeavour to agree on this. It will usually be most convenient for a bundle of the copy documents to be prepared in advance, which the VCF arranging party should then send to the remote site.

19 Additional documents are sometimes quite properly introduced during the course of a witness's evidence. To cater for this, the VCF arranging party should ensure that equipment is available to enable documents to be transmitted between sites during the course of the VCF transmission. Consideration should be given to whether to use a document camera. If it is decided to use one, arrangements for its use will need to be established in advance. The panel operator will need to know the number and size of documents or objects if their images are to be sent by document camera. In many cases, a simpler and sufficient alternative will be to ensure that there are fax transmission and reception facilities at the participating sites.

The hearing

20 The procedure for conducting the transmission will be determined by the judge. He will determine who is to control the cameras. In cases where the VCF is being used for an application in the course of the proceedings, the judge will ordinarily not enter the local site until both sites are on line. Similarly, at the conclusion of the hearing, he will ordinarily leave the local site while both sites are still on line. The following paragraphs apply primarily to cases where the VCF is being used for the taking of the evidence of a witness at a remote site.

21 At the beginning of the transmission, the judge will probably wish to introduce himself or herself and the advocates to the witness. He will probably want to know who is at the remote site and will invite the witness to introduce himself or herself and anyone else who is with the witness. The judge may wish to give directions as to the seating arrangements at the remote site so that those present are visible at the local site during the taking of the evidence and to explain to the witness the method of taking the oath or of affirming, the manner in which the evidence will be taken, and who will be conducting the examination and cross-examination. The judge will probably also wish to inform the witness of the matters referred to in paragraphs 7 and 8 (co-ordination of picture with sound, and picture quality).

22 The examination of the witness at the remote site should follow as closely as possible the practice adopted when a witness is in the courtroom. During examination, cross-examination and re-examination, the witness must be able to see the legal representative asking the question and also any

other person (whether another legal representative or the judge) making any statements in regard to the witness's evidence. It will in practice be most convenient if everyone remains seated throughout the transmission.

* * * * *

Part 23

Commentary on Part 23:
MISCELLANEOUS RULES ABOUT EVIDENCE

There is no PD supporting Part 23.

CPR counterparts
Part 23 is modelled on CPR Part 33. The corresponding provisions are as follows:

	FPR	CPR
Scope and interpretation of this Part	Rule 23.1	Rule 33.1
Notice of intention to rely on hearsay evidence	Rule 23.2	Rule 33.2
Circumstances in which notice of intention to rely on hearsay evidence is not required	Rule 23.3	Rule 33.3
Power to call witness for cross-examination on hearsay evidence	Rule 23.4	Rule 33.4
Credibility	Rule 23.5	Rule 33.5
Use of plans, photographs and models etc as evidence	Rule 23.6	Rule 33.6
Evidence of finding on question of foreign law	Rule 23.7	Rule 33.7
Evidence of consent of trustee to act	Rule 23.8	Rule 33.8
Note of oral evidence in magistrates' courts	Rule 23.9	

The only provision within CPR Part 33 which does not find its way into FPR Part 23 is CPR rule 33.9 which provides:

(1) This rule applies where a claim is—

    (a) for a remedy under section 7 of the Human Rights Act 1998 in respect of a judicial act which is alleged to have infringed the claimant's Article 5 Convention rights; and

    (b) based on a finding by a court or tribunal that the claimant's Convention rights have been infringed.

(2) The court hearing the claim—

(a) may proceed on the basis of the finding of that other court or tribunal that there has been an infringement but it is not required to do so, and

(b) may reach its own conclusion in the light of that finding and of the evidence heard by that other court or tribunal.

This provision has not been replicated as it is impossible for a claim under section 7 of the Human Rights Act 1998 to be made within family proceedings.

Hearsay evidence

Part 23 is concerned principally with the admission of hearsay evidence. The admissibility of hearsay evidence is governed by the Civil Evidence Act 1995. Hitherto the procedure applicable to the admission of hearsay evidence in family proceedings has, strictly speaking, been governed by RSC Ord 38, rules 20 to 24 (and the corresponding provisions in the CCR), but it is fair to say that practitioners generally followed the procedure specified in CPR Part 33 notwithstanding that this was not in fact applied by the 1991 Rules to ancillary relief proceedings. The FPR 2010 regularise the position.

Civil Evidence Act 1995

This provides that:

2 Notice of proposal to adduce hearsay evidence

(1) A party proposing to adduce hearsay evidence in civil proceedings shall, subject to the following provisions of this section, give to the other party or parties to the proceedings—

(a) such notice (if any) of that fact, and

(b) on request, such particulars of or relating to the evidence,

as is reasonable and practicable in the circumstances for the purpose of enabling him or them to deal with any matters arising from its being hearsay.

(2) Provision may be made by rules of court—

(a) specifying classes of proceedings or evidence in relation to which subsection (1) does not apply, and

(b) as to the manner in which (including the time within which) the duties imposed by that subsection are to be complied with in the cases where it does apply.

(3) Subsection (1) may also be excluded by agreement of the parties; and compliance with the duty to give notice may in any case be waived by the person to whom notice is required to be given.

(4) A failure to comply with subsection (1), or with rules under subsection

(2)(b), does not affect the admissibility of the evidence but may be taken into account by the court—

(a) in considering the exercise of its powers with respect to the course of proceedings and costs, and

(b) as a matter adversely affecting the weight to be given to the evidence in accordance with section 4.

3 Power to call witness for cross-examination on hearsay statement

Rules of court may provide that where a party to civil proceedings adduces hearsay evidence of a statement made by a person and does not call that person as a witness, any other party to the proceedings may, with the leave of the court, call that person as a witness and cross-examine him on the statement as if he had been called by the first-mentioned party and as if the hearsay statement were his evidence in chief.

4 Considerations relevant to weighing of hearsay evidence

(1) In estimating the weight (if any) to be given to hearsay evidence in civil proceedings the court shall have regard to any circumstances from which any inference can reasonably be drawn as to the reliability or otherwise of the evidence.

(2) Regard may be had, in particular, to the following—

(a) whether it would have been reasonable and practicable for the party by whom the evidence was adduced to have produced the maker of the original statement as a witness;

(b) whether the original statement was made contemporaneously with the occurrence or existence of the matters stated;

(c) whether the evidence involves multiple hearsay;

(d) whether any person involved had any motive to conceal or misrepresent matters;

(e) whether the original statement was an edited account, or was made in collaboration with another or for a particular purpose;

(f) whether the circumstances in which the evidence is adduced as hearsay are such as to suggest an attempt to prevent proper evaluation of its weight.

The old rule rendering hearsay inadmissible save in prescribed circumstances was thus swept away. All hearsay became admissible, but parties were expected to give notice in accordance with rules of court (section 2(1) and (2)) although such notice could be waived consensually. However, by section 2(4) failure to comply with the notice rules *does not affect the admissibility* of the hearsay evidence, but may affect the weight to be given to it in the weighing exercise under section 4. This provides that the court may take into account a variety of rather obvious factors in assessing the weight to be attributed to admissible hearsay evidence.

Section 3 grants the court power to order the maker of a hearsay statement to attend and be cross-examined.

The hearsay rules in Part 23

FPR Part 23 now replaces the old rules in RSC Ord 38, rules 20 to 24 concerning notice and suchlike although it is fair to say that little substantive change is effected other than a modernisation of language. The rules are the same as in CPR Part 33

Rule 23.2 addresses two different scenarios where a party is seeking to rely on hearsay evidence *at the final hearing*. The first is where the hearsay evidence is to be given by a witness giving oral evidence. This is where a proposed *viva voce* witness wants to say that a person had told him something. The second scenario is where a party wishes to rely on a witness statement of a person who is not being called to give oral evidence.

In each case the party must serve a witness statement on the other parties in accordance with the court's directions. In the first scenario it will be a witness statement from the proposed viva voce witness incorporating the hearsay. In the second scenario it is the witness statement of the absent witness.

In the second scenario the party intending to rely on the hearsay evidence must, when serving the witness statement, inform the other parties that the witness is not being called to give oral evidence and give the reason why the witness will not be called.

In the former scenario, and in any other case where a party intends to rely on hearsay evidence at the final hearing, he or she must serve a notice on the other parties which (a) identifies the hearsay evidence, (b) states that the party serving the notice proposes to rely on the hearsay evidence at the final hearing, and (c) gives the reason why the witness will not be called. He or she must do this no later than the latest date for serving witness statements, and if the hearsay evidence is to be in a document, supply a copy to any party who requests it.

These requirements *do not apply to evidence at hearings other than final hearings* (rule 23.3).

As mentioned above section 3 allows the court to order the maker of a hearsay statement to attend for cross-examination. Thus by rule 23.4 where a party proposes to rely on hearsay evidence, and does not propose to call the person who made the original statement to give oral evidence, the court may on the application of any other party permit that party to call the maker of the statement to be cross-examined on the contents of the statement. However, an application for permission to cross-examine under this rule must be made no later than 14 days following the date on which the notice of intention to rely on the hearsay evidence was served on the applicant. The rule is silent as to what happens if a person ordered to attend fails to do so: the court would be well justified in excluding the (admissible) evidence under rule 22.1 (see Commentary on Part 22 *above*).

A counter-notice must be served in the following circumstances. Where a party (A) has served a notice indicating that he intends to rely on hearsay evidence and another party (B) wishes to call evidence to attack the credibility of the person who made the statement, then B must give notice of that intention to A within 14 days after the date on which the hearsay notice was served by A on B (rule 23.5).

The use of plans, photographs and models etc. as evidence

Rule 23.6 deals with the 'use of plans, photographs and models etc. as evidence. In fact under the old regime by virtue of RSC Ord 38, rule 5 such evidence could only be admitted by agreement, but no one has paid even the slightest attention to this rule for years and such evidence has been freely admitted in ancillary relief proceedings for decades. Under the new prescription the requirement to give notice under the 1995 Act is waived but such evidence is 'not receivable' unless there has been service of the evidence either at the time of service of witness statements or, if there are none, 21 days before the hearing. It is hard to envisage compliance with this rule being frequent or its enforcement rigorous.

Foreign law

Rule 23.7 sets out the procedure which must be followed by a party who intends to put in evidence a finding on a question of foreign law by virtue of section 4(2) of the Civil Evidence Act 1972. This follows RSC Ord 38, rule 7. It is a procedure that has rarely, if ever, been followed in ancillary relief proceedings and there is little reason to suppose that it will be in the future.

Evidence of consent of trustee to act

Rule 23.8 provides that in Part 9 financial remedy proceedings a document purporting to contain the written consent of a person to act as trustee and to bear that person's signature, verified by some other person, is evidence of such consent.

Note of oral evidence in magistrates' courts

Rule 23.9 stipulates that in proceedings in a magistrates' court the justices' clerk or the court shall keep a note of the substance of the oral evidence given at a directions appointment or at a hearing of any proceedings.

PART 23: MISCELLANEOUS RULES ABOUT EVIDENCE

Scope and interpretation of this Part

23.1. Rules 23.2 to 23.6 apply to evidence to which the Children (Admissibility of Hearsay Evidence) Order 1993[82] does not apply.

Notice of intention to rely on hearsay evidence

23.2.—(1) Where a party intends to rely on hearsay evidence at the final hearing and either—

(a) that evidence is to be given by a witness giving oral evidence; or
(b) that evidence is contained in a witness statement of a person who is not being called to give oral evidence,

that party complies with section 2(1)(a) of the Civil Evidence Act 1995[83] by serving a witness statement on the other parties in accordance with the court's directions.

(2) Where paragraph (1)(b) applies, the party intending to rely on the hearsay evidence must, when serving the witness statement—

(a) inform the other parties that the witness is not being called to give oral evidence; and
(b) give the reason why the witness will not be called.

(3) In all other cases where a party intends to rely on hearsay evidence at the final hearing, that party complies with section 2(1)(a) of the Civil Evidence Act 1995 by serving a notice on the other parties which—

(a) identifies the hearsay evidence;
(b) states that the party serving the notice proposes to rely on the hearsay evidence at the final hearing; and
(c) gives the reason why the witness will not be called.

(4) The party proposing to rely on the hearsay evidence must—

(a) serve the notice no later than the latest date for serving witness statements; and
(b) if the hearsay evidence is to be in a document, supply a copy to any party who requests it.

Circumstances in which notice of intention to rely on hearsay evidence is not required

23.3. Section 2(1) of the Civil Evidence Act 1995 (duty to give notice of intention to rely on hearsay evidence) does not apply—

(a) to evidence at hearings other than final hearings;
(b) to an affidavit or witness statement which is to be used at the final hearing but which does not contain hearsay evidence; or

(c) where the requirement is excluded by a practice direction.

Power to call witness for cross-examination on hearsay evidence
23.4.—(1) Where a party—

(a) proposes to rely on hearsay evidence; and
(b) does not propose to call the person who made the original statement to give oral evidence,

the court may, on the application of any other party, permit that party to call the maker of the statement to be cross-examined on the contents of the statement.

(2) An application for permission to cross-examine under this rule must be made within 14 days beginning with the date on which a notice of intention to rely on the hearsay evidence was served on the applicant.

(Rules 35.3 and 35.4 contain rules in relation to evidence arising out of mediation of cross-border disputes.)

Credibility
23.5.—(1) Where a party proposes to rely on hearsay evidence, but—

(a) does not propose to call the person who made the original statement to give oral evidence; and
(b) another party wishes to call evidence to attack the credibility of the person who made the statement,

the party who so wishes must give notice of that intention to the party who proposes to give the hearsay statement in evidence.

(2) A party must give notice under paragraph (1) within 14 days after the date on which a hearsay notice relating to the hearsay evidence was served on that party.

Use of plans, photographs and models etc as evidence
23.6.—(1) This rule applies to—

(a) evidence (such as a plan, photograph or model) which is not—
    (i) contained in a witness statement, affidavit or expert's report;
    (ii) to be given orally at the final hearing; or
    (iii) evidence of which prior notice must be given under rule 23.2; and
(b) documents which may be received in evidence without further proof under section 9 of the Civil Evidence Act 1995.

(2) Except as provided below, section 2(1)(a) of the Civil Evidence Act 1995 (notice of proposal to adduce hearsay evidence) does not apply to evidence falling within paragraph (1).

(3) Such evidence is not receivable at the final hearing unless the party intending to rely on it (in this rule, "the party") has—

(a) served it or, in the case of a model, a photograph of it with an invitation to inspect the original, on the other party in accordance with this rule; or

(b) complied with such directions as the court may give for serving the evidence on, or for giving notice under section 2(1)(a) of the Civil Evidence Act 1995 in respect of the evidence to, the other party.

(4) Where the party intends to use the evidence as evidence of any fact then, except where paragraph (6) applies, the party must serve the evidence not later than the latest date for serving witness statements.

(5) The party must serve the evidence at least 21 days before the hearing at which the party proposes to rely on it if—

(a) there are not to be witness statements; or
(b) the party intends to put in the evidence solely in order to disprove an allegation made in a witness statement.

(6) Where the evidence forms part of expert evidence, the party must serve the evidence when the expert's report is served on the other party.

(7) Where the evidence is being produced to the court for any reason other than as part of factual or expert evidence, the party must serve the evidence at least 21 days before the hearing at which the party proposes to rely on it.

(8) Where the court directs a party to give notice that the party intends to put in the evidence, the court may direct that every other party be given an opportunity to inspect it and to agree to its admission without further proof.

Evidence of finding on question of foreign law

23.7.—(1) This rule sets out the procedure which must be followed by a party (in this rule, "the party") who intends to put in evidence a finding on a question of foreign law by virtue of section 4(2) of the Civil Evidence Act 1972.

(2) The party must give any other party notice of that intention.

(3) The party must give the notice—

(a) if there are to be witness statements, not later than the latest date for serving them; or
(b) otherwise, not less than 21 days before the hearing at which the party proposes to put the finding in evidence.

(4) The notice must—

(a) specify the question on which the finding was made; and
(b) enclose a copy of a document where it is reported or recorded.

Evidence of consent of trustee to act

23.8. In proceedings to which Part 9 (financial remedies) applies, a document purporting to contain the written consent of a person to act as trustee and to bear that person's signature verified by some other person is evidence of such consent.

Note of oral evidence in magistrates' courts

23.9. In proceedings in a magistrates' court, the justices' clerk or the court shall keep a note of the substance of the oral evidence given at a directions appointment or at a hearing of any proceedings.

Part 24

Commentary on Part 24:
WITNESSES, DEPOSITIONS GENERALLY AND TAKING OF
EVIDENCE OF MEMBER STATES OF THE EUROPEAN UNION

Summary
Chapter 1 of this Part deals with witnesses and depositions in the High Court and county court. With the exception of rule 24.10(2) to (4) it does not apply to magistrates' courts.

Chapter 2 deals with the taking of evidence in the Member States of the European Union for use in domestic proceedings under Council Regulation (EC) No 1206/2001 of 28 May 2001 on cooperation between the courts of the Member States in the taking of evidence in civil or commercial matters (OJ L174 of 27.06.2001: 'The Taking of Evidence Regulation').

There is one associated Practice Direction, PD 24A, unimaginatively though catchily entitled *Witnesses, Depositions and Taking of Evidence in Member States of the European Union.*

CPR counterparts
The corresponding rules of the CPR, on which Part 24 is very closely modelled, are CPR rules 34.1 to 34.15 (Witnesses and depositions) and 34.22 to 34.24 (Taking of evidence – Member States of the European Union). A comparative table is set out below.

Subject matter	*FPR 2010*	*CPR 1998*
Scope	24.1	34.1
Witness summonses	24.2	34.2
Issue of a witness summons	24.3	34.3
Time for serving a witness summons	24.4	34.5
Who is to serve witness summons	24.5	34.6
Right of witness to travelling expenses and compensation for loss of time	24.6	34.7
Evidence by deposition	24.7	34.8
Conduct of examination	24.8	34.9

Witness summons

A single term, 'witness summons', is now used for any order that a witness attend court, whether to give evidence or to produce documents, in both the High Court and the county court. This is the term formerly used for such orders in the county court (see CCR Ord 20, rule 12). The terms for the corresponding procedures in the High Court, a writ *subpoena ad testificandum* and a writ of *subpoena duces tecum* (see RSC Ord 38, rules 13 to 18) are abolished. The language used in the new rules is identical to that used in the CPR.

The FPR 1991 did not make direct provision for any of the matters set out in Part 24 (save in relation to inspection appointments (FPR rule 2.62(7) to (9)). The applicable rules were RSC Ords 38 and 39 and CCR Ord 20, as applied to family proceedings (in the form in which they were in force prior to 26 April 1999: see FPR 1991 rule 1.3(1)).

In welcome contrast to the position under the 1991 rules the procedure governing witness summonses is now identical in the High Court and the county court.

Service of witness summons

Probably the most important change relates to the time for service of a witness summons.

Under RSC Ord 38, rule 17 the default period for service of a writ of *subpoena* was four days, while under CCR Ord 20, rule 12(4) the time for service of a witness summons was 7 days.

By rule 24.4(1) the general rule now is that a witness summons is binding if it is served at least 7 days before the required attendance date, although the court may direct that a summons is binding even though served less than 7 days before the required court attendance date (rule 24.4(2)).

A party requires *permission* to issue a witness summons where he wishes to have a witness summons issued (a) less than 7 days before the date of the final hearing; (b) for any date except the final hearing date; or (c) for any hearing except the final hearing (rule 24.3(2)).

The important power to order a witness to attend to produce documents in advance of the final hearing is preserved by rule 24.2(4)(b). The so-called *Khanna* hearing (*Khanna v Lovell White Durrant* [1995] 1 WLR 121) has proved to be a useful case management tool facilitating the production, in advance of the final hearing, of documents which if produced for the first time at trial might necessitate an adjournment.

The inspection appointment procedure in FPR 1991 rule 2.62(7) to (9) is not replicated here or in Part 9, but analogous relief is obtainable and the same objective served by rule 21.2 (orders for disclosure against a person not a party). There is plainly an overlap between rule 21.2 and rule 24.2(4)(b) and (c) but it is suggested that the procedure under 21.2 be followed in cases where an application would have been made for an inspection appointment under the 1991 rules.

Note that the substance of FPR 1991 rule 2.62(8) is preserved by rule 24.2(5), to the effect that the only documents that a witness summons may require a person to produce *before* a hearing are documents which that person could be required to produce *at* the hearing.

The rules on the offering or payment to the witness of travel expenses and compensation for loss of time should be noted with care (rule 24.6 and PD 24A paras 3.1 to 3.2).

Witnesses within the jurisdiction – depositions

A deposition (in civil proceedings) is oral evidence given by a witness within the jurisdiction other than at a court hearing. Depositions are ordered in cases where for good reason, such as illness, a witness is unable to attend court to give oral evidence. In family proceedings their use is rare.

A more common alternative to the giving of a deposition is that a witness (whether within or outside the jurisdiction) who is unable to attend court to give oral evidence is required or permitted to give evidence by video link (see rule 22.3, to the same effect as rule 4.1(3)(e)). Extensive guidance for video-conferencing is curiously sited within *PD 22 – Written Evidence* (Annex 3).

PD 24A paras 4.1 to 4.13 set out the procedural detail governing the taking of depositions, and related matters.

Witnesses outside the jurisdiction – non-EU cases

Where a deposition is to be taken from a person outside the jurisdiction (other than in an EU member state, as to which see *below*), this is achieved by means of a 'letter of request', which is a *'request to a judicial authority to take the evidence of [the proposed deponent], or arrange for it to be taken'* (rule 24.12(3)).

Only the High Court has the power to order the issue of a letter of request (rule 24.12 (2)), although the High Court may also make such an order in county court proceedings (rule 24.12(4)). A special examiner may be appointed by the High Court if examination by a special examiner is permitted by the requested country (rule 24.12(5)). Failing that, the examination will be conducted by an examiner appointed under the law of that country.

A letter of request may request the production of documents as well as the taking of oral evidence (*Charman v Charman* [2006] 2 FLR 422, CA).

The procedural detail is set out at PD 24A paras 5.1 to 5.9. A pro forma letter of request is set out at Annex A to the PD. The Treasury Solicitor's Department has issued a helpful and comprehensive guide to letters of request in civil proceedings, available at www.tsol.gov.uk/Publications/Scheme_Publications/letter_of_request.pdf.

The powers of the court in financial proceedings to order non-parties to give evidence and/or to produce documents in advance of the final hearing, and the court's power to order the issue of a letter of request, were comprehensively reviewed in *Charman v Charman* [2006] 2 FLR 422, CA. See also *Zakay v Zakay* [1998] 3 FCR 35, Gib Sup Ct, and *Wadman v Dick* [1998] 3 FCR 9.

Witnesses out of the jurisdiction – EU cases

Where the person whose evidence is sought to be taken is resident in an EU member state letters of request may not be issued. Instead the procedures under Council Regulation (EC) No 1206/2001 of 28 May 2001 on cooperation between the courts of the Member States in the taking of evidence in civil or commercial matters (OJ L174 of 27.06.2001: 'The Taking of Evidence Regulation') must be followed (rules 24.15 and 24.16 and PD 24A paras 6.1 to 9.7). The text of the Regulation is reproduced as Annex B to PD 24A.

Forms

The only Form prescribed by *Practice Direction 5A – Forms* is FP1 (Witness summons).

PART 24: WITNESSES, DEPOSITIONS GENERALLY AND TAKING OF EVIDENCE IN MEMBER STATES OF THE EUROPEAN UNION

CHAPTER 1: WITNESSES AND DEPOSITIONS

Scope of this Chapter

24.1.—(1) This Chapter provides—

(a) for the circumstances in which a person may be required to attend court to give evidence or to produce a document; and

(b) for a party to obtain evidence before a hearing to be used at the hearing.

(2) This Chapter, apart from rule 24.10(2) to (4), does not apply to proceedings in a magistrates' court.

(Rules 34.16 to 34.21 and 34.24 of the CPR apply to incoming requests for evidence.)

Witness summonses

24.2.—(1) A witness summons is a document issued by the court requiring a witness to—

(a) attend court to give evidence; or

(b) produce documents to the court.

(2) A witness summons must be in the form set out in Practice Direction 24A.

(3) There must be a separate witness summons for each witness.

(4) A witness summons may require a witness to produce documents to the court either—

(a) on the date fixed for a hearing; or

(b) on such date as the court may direct.

(5) The only documents that a summons under this rule can require a person to produce before a hearing are documents which that person could be required to produce at the hearing.

(Rules 35.3 and 35.4 contain rules in relation to evidence arising out of mediation of cross-border disputes.)

Issue of a witness summons

24.3.—(1) A witness summons is issued on the date entered on the summons by the court.

(2) A party must obtain permission from the court where that party wishes to—

(a) have a summons issued less than 7 days before the date of the final hearing;

(b) have a summons issued for a witness to attend court to give evidence or to produce documents on any date except the date fixed for the final hearing; or

(c) have a summons issued for a witness to attend court to give evidence or to produce documents at any hearing except the final hearing.

(3) A witness summons must be issued by—

(a) the court where the case is proceeding; or

(b) the court where the hearing in question will be held.

(4) The court may set aside or vary a witness summons issued under this rule.

Time for serving a witness summons

24.4.—(1) The general rule is that a witness summons is binding if it is served at least 7 days before the date on which the witness is required to attend before the court.

(2) The court may direct that a witness summons is binding although it is served less than 7 days before the date on which the witness is required to attend before the court.

(3) A witness summons which is—

(a) served in accordance with this rule; and
(b) requires the witness to attend court to give evidence,

is binding until the conclusion of the hearing at which the attendance of the witness is required.

(Rules 35.3 and 35.4 contain rules in relation to evidence arising out of mediation of cross-border disputes.)

Who is to serve a witness summons

24.5.—(1) Subject to paragraph (2), a witness summons is to be served by the party on whose behalf it is issued unless that party indicates in writing, when asking the court to issue the summons, that that party wishes the court to serve it instead.

(2) In proceedings to which Part 14 (procedure for applications in adoption, placement and related proceedings) applies, a witness summons is to be served by the court unless the court directs otherwise.

(3) Where the court is to serve the witness summons, the party on whose behalf it is issued must deposit, in the court office, the money to be paid or offered to the witness under rule 24.6.

Right of witness to travelling expenses and compensation for loss of time

24.6. At the time of service of a witness summons the witness must be offered or paid—

(a) a sum reasonably sufficient to cover the expenses of the witness in travelling to and from the court; and
(b) such sum by way of compensation for loss of time as may be specified in Practice Direction 24A.

Evidence by deposition

24.7.—(1) A party may apply for an order for a person to be examined before the hearing takes place.

(2) A person from whom evidence is to be obtained following an order

under this rule is referred to as a 'deponent' and the evidence is referred to as a 'deposition'.

(3) An order under this rule is for a deponent to be examined on oath before—

(a) a judge;
(b) an examiner of the court; or
(c) such other person as the court appoints.

(Rule 24.14 makes provision for the appointment of examiners of the court.)

(4) The order may require the production of any document which the court considers is necessary for the purposes of the examination.

(5) The order must state the date, time and place of the examination.

(6) At the time of service of the order the deponent must be offered or paid—

(a) a sum reasonably sufficient to cover the expenses of the deponent in travelling to and from the place of examination; and
(b) such sum by way of compensation for loss of time as may be specified in Practice Direction 24A.

(7) Where the court makes an order for a deposition to be taken, it may also order the party who obtained the order to serve a witness statement or witness summary in relation to the evidence to be given by the person to be examined.

(Part 22 (evidence) contains the general rules about witness statements and witness summaries.)

(Rules 35.3 and 35.4 contain rules in relation to evidence arising out of mediation of cross-border disputes.)

Conduct of examination

24.8.—(1) Subject to any directions contained in the order for examination, the examination must be conducted in the same way as if the witness were giving evidence at a final hearing.

(2) If all the parties are present, the examiner may conduct the examination of a person not named in the order for examination if all the parties and the person to be examined consent.

(3) In defended proceedings under Part 7 (matrimonial and civil partnership proceedings), the examiner may conduct the examination in private if of the view that it is appropriate to do so.

(4) Save in proceedings to which paragraph (3) applies, the examiner will conduct the examination in private unless of the view that it is not appropriate to do so.

(5) The examiner must ensure that the evidence given by the witness is recorded in full.

(6) The examiner must send a copy of the deposition—

(a) to the person who obtained the order for the examination of the witness; and

(b) to the court where the case is proceeding.

(7) The court will give directions as to service of the deposition on the other party.

Enforcing attendance of witness

24.9.—(1) If a person served with an order to attend before an examiner—

(a) fails to attend; or

(b) refuses to be sworn for the purpose of the examination or to answer any lawful question or produce any document at the examination,

a certificate of that person's failure or refusal, signed by the examiner, must be filed by the party requiring the deposition.

(2) On the certificate being filed, the party requiring the deposition may apply to the court for an order requiring that person to attend or to be sworn or to answer any question or produce any document, as the case may be.

(3) An application for an order under this rule may be made without notice.

(4) The court may order the person against whom an order is made under this rule to pay any costs resulting from that person's failure or refusal.

(Rules 35.3 and 35.4 contain rules in relation to evidence arising out of mediation of cross-border disputes. Rule 35.4(1)(d) relates specifically to this rule.)

Use of deposition at a hearing

24.10.—(1) A deposition ordered under rule 24.7 may be given in evidence at a hearing unless the court orders otherwise.

(2) A party intending to put in evidence a deposition at a hearing must file notice of intention to do so on the court and the court will give directions about serving the notice on every other party.

(3) The party must file the notice at least 21 days before the day fixed for the hearing.

(4) The court may require a deponent to attend the hearing and give evidence orally.

(5) Where a deposition is given in evidence at the final hearing, it is treated as if it were a witness statement for the purposes of rule 22.19 (availability of witness statements for inspection).

(Rules 35.3 and 35.4 contain rules in relation to evidence arising out of mediation of cross-border disputes. Rule 35.4(1)(e) relates specifically to this rule.)

Restrictions on subsequent use of deposition taken for the purpose of any hearing except the final hearing

24.11.—(1) This rule applies to proceedings under Part 7 (matrimonial and civil partnership proceedings) or Part 9 (financial remedies).

(2) Where the court orders a party to be examined about that party's or any other assets for the purpose of any hearing except the final hearing, the deposition may be used only for the purpose of the proceedings in which the order was made.

(3) However it may be used for some other purpose—

(a) by the party who was examined;

(b) if the party who was examined agrees; or

(c) if the court gives permission.

Where a person to be examined is out of the jurisdiction – letter of request

24.12.—(1) This rule applies where a party wishes to take a deposition from a person who is—

(a) out of the jurisdiction; and

(b) not in a Regulation State within the meaning of Chapter 2 of this Part.

(2) The High Court may order the issue of a letter of request to the judicial authorities of the country in which the proposed deponent is.

(3) A letter of request is a request to a judicial authority to take the evidence of that person, or arrange for it to be taken.

(4) The High Court may make an order under this rule in relation to county court proceedings.

(5) If the government of a country allows a person appointed by the High Court to examine a person in that country, the High Court may make an order appointing a special examiner for that purpose.

(6) A person may be examined under this rule on oath or affirmation or in accordance with any procedure permitted in the country in which the examination is to take place.

(7) If the High Court makes an order for the issue of a letter of request, the party who sought the order must file—

(a) the following documents and, except where paragraph (8) applies, a translation of them—

(i) a draft letter of request;

(ii) a statement of the issues relevant to the proceedings; and

(iii) a list of questions or the subject matter of questions to be put to the person to be examined; and

(b) an undertaking to be responsible for the Secretary of State's expenses.

(8) There is no need to file a translation if—

(a) English is one of the official languages of the country where the examination is to take place; or

(b) a practice direction has specified that country as a country where no translation is necessary.

(Rules 35.3 and 35.4 contain rules in relation to evidence arising out of mediation of cross-border disputes. Rule 35.4(1)(f) relates specifically to this rule.)

PD24A contains at Annex A a form of draft letter of request

Fees and expenses of examiner of the court

24.13.—(1) An examiner of the court may charge a fee for the examination.

(2) The examiner need not send the deposition to the court unless the fee is paid.

(3) The examiner's fees and expenses must be paid by the party who obtained the order for examination.

(4) If the fees and expenses due to an examiner are not paid within a reasonable time, the examiner may report that fact to the court.

(5) The court may order the party who obtained the order for examination to deposit in the court office a specified sum in respect of the examiner's fees and, where it does so, the examiner will not be asked to act until the sum has been deposited.

(6) An order under this rule does not affect any decision as to the party who is ultimately to bear the costs of the examination.

Examiners of the court

24.14.—(1) The Lord Chancellor will appoint persons to be examiners of the court.

(2) The persons appointed must be barristers or solicitor-advocates who have been practising for a period of not less than 3 years.

(3) The Lord Chancellor may revoke an appointment at any time.

CHAPTER 2: TAKING OF EVIDENCE – MEMBER STATES OF THE EUROPEAN UNION

Interpretation

24.15. In this Chapter—

"designated court" has the meaning given in Practice Direction 24A;

"Regulation State" has the same meaning as 'Member State' in the Taking of Evidence Regulation, that is all Member States except Denmark;

"the Taking of Evidence Regulation" means Council Regulation (EC) No. 1206/2001 of 28 May 2001 on co-operation between the courts of the Member States in the taking of evidence in civil or commercial matters.

Where a person to be examined is in another Regulation State

24.16.—(1) This rule applies where a party wishes to take a deposition from a person who is—

(a) outside the jurisdiction; and
(b) in a Regulation State.

(2) The court may order the issue of a request to a designated court ('the requested court') in the Regulation State in which the proposed deponent is.

(3) If the court makes an order for the issue of a request, the party who sought the order must file—

(a) a draft Form A as set out in the annex to the Taking of Evidence Regulation (request for the taking of evidence);
(b) except where paragraph (4) applies, a translation of the form;
(c) an undertaking to be responsible for costs sought by the requested court in relation to—
   (i) fees paid to experts and interpreters; and
   (ii) where requested by that party, the use of special procedures or communications technology; and
(d) an undertaking to be responsible for the court's expenses.

(4) There is no need to file a translation if—

(a) English is one of the official languages of the Regulation State where the examination is to take place; or
(b) the Regulation State has indicated, in accordance with the Taking of Evidence Regulation, that English is a language which it will accept.

(5) Where article 17 of the Taking of Evidence Regulation (direct taking of evidence by the requested court) allows evidence to be taken directly in another Regulation State, the court may make an order for the submission of a request in accordance with that article.

(6) If the court makes an order for the submission of a request under paragraph (5), the party who sought the order must file—

(a) a draft Form I as set out in the annex to the Taking of Evidence Regulation (request for direct taking of evidence);
(b) except where paragraph (4) applies, a translation of the form; and
(c) an undertaking to be responsible for the court's expenses.

Practice Direction 24A supplements FPR Part 24 (Witnesses, depositions and taking of evidence in Member States of the European Union)

PRACTICE DIRECTION 24A – WITNESSES, DEPOSITIONS AND TAKING OF EVIDENCE IN MEMBER STATES OF THE EUROPEAN UNION

This Practice Direction supplements FPR Part 24

Witness summonses

Issue of witness summons

1.1 A witness summons may require a witness to—

(a) attend court to give evidence;
(b) produce documents to the court; or
(c) both,

on either a date fixed for the hearing or such date as the court may direct (see rule 24.2).

(In relation to cases to which the Mediation Directive applies, rules 35.3 and 35.4 contain rules in relation to mediation evidence)

1.2 Two copies of the witness summons should be filed with the court for sealing, one of which will be retained on the court file.

1.3 A mistake in the name or address of a person named in a witness summons may be corrected if the summons has not been served.

1.4 The corrected summons must be re-sealed by the court and marked "Amended and Re-Sealed'.

Magistrates' courts proceedings

2.1 An application for the issue of a summons or warrant under section 97 of the Magistrates' Courts Act 1980 may be made by the applicant in person or by his legal representative.

2.2 An application for the issue of such a summons may be made by delivering or sending the application in writing to the court officer for the magistrates' court.

Travelling expenses and compensation for loss of time

3.1 When a witness is served with a witness summons the witness must be offered a sum to cover travelling expenses to and from the court and compensation for loss of time (see rule 24.6).

3.2 If the witness summons is to be served by the court, the party issuing the summons must deposit with the court—

(a) a sum sufficient to pay for the witness's expenses in travelling to the court and in returning to his or her home or place of work; and
(b) a sum in respect of the period during which earnings or benefit are lost, or such lesser sum as it may be proved that the witness will lose as a result of attendance at court in answer to the witness summons.

3.3 The sum referred to in paragraph 3.2(b) is to be based on the sums payable to witnesses attending the Crown Court (fixed pursuant to the Prosecution of Offences Act 1985 and Costs in Criminal Cases (General) Regulations 1986).

Depositions to be taken in England and Wales for use as evidence in proceedings in courts in England and Wales

4.1 A party may apply for an order for a person to be examined on oath before—

(a) a judge;
(b) an examiner of the court; or
(c) such other person as the court may appoint (see rule 24.7(3)).

(This is subject to rules about mediation evidence in cases to which the Mediation Directive applies: see rules 35.3 and 35.4)

4.2 The party who obtains an order for the examination of a deponent (see rule 24.7(2)) before an examiner of the court must—

(a) apply to the Foreign Process Section of the Masters' Secretary's Department at the Royal Courts of Justice for the allocation of an examiner;
(b) when allocated, provide the examiner with copies of all documents in the proceedings necessary to inform the examiner of the issues; and
(c) pay the deponent a sum to cover travelling expenses to and from the examination and compensation for loss of time (see rule 24.7(6)).

4.3 In ensuring that the deponent's evidence is recorded in full, the court or the examiner may permit it to be recorded on audiotape or videotape, but the deposition (see rule 24.7(2)) must always be recorded in writing by the examiner or by a competent shorthand writer or stenographer.

4.4 If the deposition is not recorded word for word, it must contain, as nearly as may be, the statement of the deponent. The examiner may record word for word any particular questions and answers which appear to have special importance.

4.5 If a deponent objects to answering any question or where any objection is taken to any question, the examiner must—

(a) record in the deposition or a document attached to it—
    (i) the question;
    (ii) the nature of and grounds for the objection;
    (iii) any answer given; and
(b) give the examiner's opinion as to the validity of the objection and must record it in the deposition or a document attached to it.

The court will decide as to the validity of the objection and any question of costs arising from it.

4.6 Documents and exhibits must—

(a) have an identifying number or letter marked on them by the examiner; and
(b) be preserved by the party or legal representative (see rule 2.3) who obtained the order for the examination, or as the court or the examiner may direct.

4.7 The examiner may put any question to the deponent as to—

(a) the meaning of any of the deponent's answers; or
(b) any matter arising in the course of the examination.

4.8 Where a deponent—

(a) fails to attend the examination; or
(b) refuses to—
    (i) be sworn; or
    (ii) answer any lawful question; or
    (iii) produce any document,

the examiner will sign a certificate (see rule 24.9) of such failure or refusal and may include in the certificate any comment as to the conduct of the deponent or of any person attending the examination.

4.9 The party who obtained the order for the examination must file the certificate with the court and may apply for an order that the deponent attend for examination or produce any document, as the case may be (see rule 24.9(2) and (3)). The application may be made without notice.

4.10 The court will make such order on the application as it thinks fit including an order for the deponent to pay any costs resulting from the failure or refusal (see rule 24.9(4)).

4.11 A deponent who wilfully refuses to obey an order of the High Court or the county court made under Part 24 may be proceeded against for contempt of court. (Where a person fails to attend before a magistrates' court in answer to a summons issued under section 97 of the Magistrates' Court Act 1980, the court may, under certain circumstances, issue a warrant for that party's arrest and to bring that party before the court at a time and place specified in the warrant: see section 97(3) of the 1980 Act.)

4.12 A deposition must—

(a) be signed by the examiner;
(b) have any amendments to it initialled by the examiner and the deponent;
(c) be endorsed by the examiner with—
    (i) a statement of the time occupied by the examination; and
    (ii) a record of any refusal by the deponent to sign the deposition and of the deponent's reasons for not doing so; and

(d) be sent by the examiner to the court where the proceedings are taking place for filing on the court file.

4.13 Rule 24.13 deals with the fees and expenses of an examiner.

Depositions to be taken abroad for use as evidence in proceedings before courts in England and Wales (where the Taking of Evidence Regulation does not apply)

5.1 Where a party wishes to take a deposition from a person outside the jurisdiction, the High Court may order the issue of a letter of request to the judicial authorities of the country in which the proposed deponent is (see rule 24.12).

(Rule 35.4(1)(f) deals with letters of request where the Mediation Directive applies)

5.2 An application for an order referred to in paragraph 5.1 should be made by application notice in accordance with Part 18 (Procedure for other applications in proceedings).

5.3 The documents which a party applying for an order for the issue of a letter of request must file with the application notice are set out in rule 24.12(7). They are as follows—

(a) a draft letter of request in the form set out in Annex A to this practice direction;

(b) a statement of the issues relevant to the proceedings;

(c) a list of questions or the subject matter of questions to be put to the proposed deponent;

(d) a translation of the documents in (a), (b) and (c), unless the proposed deponent is in a country of which English is an official language; and

(e) an undertaking to be responsible for the expenses of the Secretary of State.

In addition to the documents listed above the party applying for the order must file a draft order.

5.4 The above documents should be filed with the Masters' Secretary in Room E214, Royal Courts of Justice, Strand, London WC2A 2LL.

5.5 The application will be dealt with by the Senior Master of the Queen's Bench Division of the Senior Courts who will, if appropriate, sign the letter of request.

5.6 Attention is drawn to the provisions of rule 18.11 (Application to set aside or vary order made without notice).

5.7 If parties are in doubt as to whether a translation under paragraph 5.3(d) is required, they should seek guidance from the Foreign Process Section of the Masters' Secretary's Department.

5.8 A special examiner appointed under rule 24.12(5) may be the British Consul or the Consul-General or his deputy in the country where the evidence is to be taken if—

(a) there is in respect of that country a Civil Procedure Convention providing for the taking of evidence in that country for the assistance of proceedings in the High Court or other court in this country; or

(b) the Secretary of State has consented.

5.9 The provisions of paragraphs 4.1 to 4.12 apply to the depositions referred to in this paragraph.

Taking of evidence between EU Member States

Taking of Evidence Regulation

6.1 Where evidence is to be taken from a person in another Member State of the European Union for use as evidence in proceedings before courts in England and Wales Council Regulation (EC) No 1206/2001 of 28 May 2001 on co-operation between the courts of the Member States in the taking of evidence in civil or commercial matters ('the Taking of Evidence Regulation') applies.

6.2 The Taking of Evidence Regulation is annexed to this practice direction as Annex B.

6.3 The Taking of Evidence Regulation does not apply to Denmark. In relation to Denmark, therefore, rule 24.12 will continue to apply.

(Article 21(1) of the Taking of Evidence Regulation provides that the Regulation prevails over other provisions contained in bilateral or multilateral agreements or arrangements concluded by the Member States.)

Originally published in the official languages of the European Community in the Official Journal of the European Communities by the Office for Official Publications of the European Communities.

Meaning of 'designated court'

7.1 In accordance with the Taking of Evidence Regulation, each Regulation State has prepared a list of courts competent to take evidence in accordance with the Regulation indicating the territorial and, where appropriate, special jurisdiction of those courts.

7.2 Where Chapter 2 of this Part refers to a 'designated court' in relation to another Regulation State, the reference is to the court, referred to in the list of competent courts of that State, which is appropriate to the application in hand.

7.3 Where the reference is to the 'designated court' in England and Wales, the reference is to the appropriate competent court in the jurisdiction. The designated courts for England and Wales are listed in Annex C to this practice direction.

Central Body

8.1 The Taking of Evidence Regulation stipulates that each Regulation State must nominate a Central Body responsible for—

(a) supplying information to courts;

(b) seeking solutions to any difficulties which may arise in respect of a request; and

(c) forwarding, in exceptional cases, at the request of a requesting court, a request to the competent court.

8.2 The United Kingdom has nominated the Senior Master of the Queen's Bench Division, to be the Central Body for England and Wales.

8.3 The Senior Master, as Central Body, has been designated responsible for taking decisions on requests pursuant to Article 17 of the Regulation. Article 17 allows a court to submit a request to the Central Body or a designated competent authority in another Regulation State to take evidence directly in that State.

Evidence to be taken in another Regulation State for use in England and Wales

9.1 Where a person wishes to take a deposition from a person in another Regulation State, the court where the proceedings are taking place may order the issue of a request to the designated court in the Regulation State (rule 24.16 (2)). The form of request is prescribed as Form A in the Taking of Evidence Regulation.

9.2 An application to the court for an order under rule 24.16(2) should be made by application notice in accordance with Part 18 (Procedure for other applications in proceedings).

9.3 Rule 24.16(3) provides that the party applying for the order must file a draft form of request in the prescribed form. Where completion of the form requires attachments or documents to accompany the form, these must also be filed.

9.4 If the court grants an order under rule 24.16(2), it will send the form of request directly to the designated court.

9.5 Where the taking of evidence requires the use of an expert, the designated court may require a deposit in advance towards the costs of that expert. The party who obtained the order is responsible for the payment of any such deposit which should be deposited with the court for onward transmission. Under the provisions of the Taking of Evidence Regulation, the designated court is not required to execute the request until such payment is received.

9.6 Article 17 permits the court where proceedings are taking place to take evidence directly from a deponent in another Regulation State if the conditions of the article are satisfied. Direct taking of evidence can only take place if evidence is given voluntarily without the need for coercive measures. Rule 24.16(5) provides for the court to make an order for the submission of a request to take evidence directly. The form of request is Form I annexed to the Taking of Evidence Regulation and rule 24.16(6) makes provision for a draft of this form to be filed by the party seeking the order. An application for an order under rule 24.16(5) should be by application notice in accordance with Part 18.

9.7 Attention is drawn to the provisions of rule 18.11 (Application to set aside or vary order made without notice).

Annex A

Draft Letter of Request (where the Taking of Evidence Regulation does not apply) (see paragraph 5.3(a) above)
To the Competent Judicial Authority of in the of [*name*] Senior Master of the Queen's Bench Division of the Senior Courts of England and Wales respectfully request the assistance of your court with regard to the following matters.

2 An application is now pending in the Division of the High Court of Justice in England and Wales entitled as follows [*set out full title and case number*] in which [*name*] of [*address*] is the applicant and [*name*] of [*address*] is the respondent.

3 The names and addresses of the representatives or agents of [*set out names and addresses of representatives of the parties*].

4 The application by the applicant is for—

(a) [set out the nature of the application]
(b) [the order sought] and
(c) [a summary of the facts.]

5 It is necessary for the purposes of justice between the parties that you cause the following witnesses, who are resident within your jurisdiction, to be examined. The names and addresses of the witnesses are as follows:

6 The witnesses should be examined on oath or if that is not possible within your laws or is impossible of performance by reason of the internal practice and procedure of your court or by reason of practical difficulties, they should be examined in accordance with whatever procedure your laws provide for in these matters.

7 Either/
The witnesses should be examined in accordance with the list of questions annexed hereto.

Or/
The witnesses should be examined regarding [set out full details of evidence sought]

N.B. Where the witness is required to produce documents, these should be clearly identified.

8 I would ask that you cause me, or the agents of the parties (if appointed), to be informed of the date and place where the examination is to take place.

9 Finally, I request that you will cause the evidence of the said witnesses to be reduced into writing and all documents produced on such examinations to be duly marked for identification and that you will further be pleased to authenticate such examinations by the seal of your court or in

such other way as is in accordance with your procedure and return the written evidence and documents produced to me addressed as follows—

Senior Master of the Queen's Bench Division
Royal Courts of Justice
Strand
London
WC2A 2LL
England

Annex B

Taking of evidence regulation
http://www.justice.gov.uk/civil/procrules_fin/contents/form_section_images
/practice_directions/pd34_pdf_tif_gif/pd34_cr_1206_2001.pdf

Annex C

Designated courts in England and Wales under the Taking of Evidence Regulation (see paragraph 7.3 above)

Area	Designated court
London and South Eastern Circuit (Queen's Bench Division)	Royal Courts of Justice
Midland Circuit	Birmingham Civil Justice Centre
Western Circuit	Bristol County Court
Wales and Chester Circuit	Cardiff Civil Justice Centre
Northern Circuit	Manchester County Court
North Eastern Circuit	Leeds County Court

* * * * *

Part 25

Commentary on Part 25:
EXPERTS AND ASSESSORS

CPR counterparts

Part 25 is the counterpart to CPR Part 35 on which it is very closely modelled. The rules incorporated by Part 25 are nothing new in ancillary relief proceedings. Old FPR 1991 rule 2.61C provided that 'CPR rules 35.1 to 35.14 relating to expert evidence (with the appropriate modifications), except CPR rules 35.5(2) and 35.8(4)(b) apply to all ancillary relief proceedings'. CPR rule 35.5(2) concerned claims allocated to the small claims track or fast track, and was therefore irrelevant to ancillary relief proceedings. Rule 35.8(4)(b) allowed the court to direct that prior to the instruction of an expert the parties (or some of them) must pay his fees into court. There is no obvious reason why this power was omitted; but the omission has been carried into FPR Part 25.

Although the CPR rules on expert evidence only expressly applied to ancillary relief proceedings and not to those other financial proceedings now designated as a financial remedy, in practice the CPR regime was applied to all financial proceedings, and indeed to children proceedings.

The corresponding provisions are as follows:

	FPR	*CPR*
Duty to restrict expert evidence	Rule 25.1	Rule 35.1
Interpretation	Rule 25.2	Rule 35.2
Experts – overriding duty to the court	Rule 25.3	Rule 35.3
Court's power to restrict expert evidence	Rule 25.4	Rule 35.4
General requirement for expert evidence to be given in a written report	Rule 25.5	Rule 35.5
Written questions to experts	Rule 25.6	Rule 35.6
Court's power to direct that evidence is to be given by a single joint expert	Rule 25.7	Rule 35.7
Instructions to a single joint expert	Rule 25.8	Rule 35.8

Power of court to direct a party to provide information	Rule 25.9	Rule 35.9
Contents of report	Rule 25.10	Rule 35.10
Use by one party of expert's report disclosed by another	Rule 25.11	Rule 35.11
Discussions between experts	Rule 25.12	Rule 35.12
Expert's right to ask court for directions	Rule 25.13	Rule 35.14
Assessors	Rule 25.14	Rule 35.15

The rules in FPR 2010 Part 25 are an almost exact replication of those in CPR Part 35; only minor alterations have been made. Even grammatical errors have been faithfully preserved – see FPR rule 25.10(2)/CPR rule 35.10(2) which provides that 'At the end of an expert's report there must be a statement that the expert understands and has complied with their (sic) duty to the court.'

The only CPR rule wholly omitted from the FPR is rule 35.13, which as applied to the 1991 Rules provided that a party who fails to disclose an expert's report may not use the report at the trial or call the expert to give evidence orally unless the court gives permission. It is unclear why this eminently sensible provision (which was incorporated within the old FPR 1991 code) has been omitted. Perhaps it was felt that it added nothing to the court's powers to exclude admissible evidence under rule 22.1 (see Commentary on Part 22 *above*) although it would have sent out a strong message as to what the default position would be in the case of late production or nondisclosure of an expert's report. Perhaps on the other hand this provision would have constituted a sanction and thus engaged rule 4.6 (Relief from sanctions): see Commentary on Part 4 *above* where it is suggested that it may be unlikely that a court exercising an inquisitorial function will adopt quite so rigorous an approach as would its civil counterpart.

Reams have been written about CPR Part 35 both in the civil sphere and in its application to ancillary relief. It is not intended in this short Commentary to do other than set out the main principles.

The basic rules

The *first basic rule* is that the court can receive expert evidence on any subject, apart from the effect of English law. The court will not allow a distinguished lawyer to write a report and give sworn evidence about, say, the impact of copyright law on a piece of intellectual property owned by the parties. This rule is often forgotten as it is not uncommon for a party to seek to introduce 'expert evidence' from an accountant as to the impact of UK revenue law on the parties' assets or their distribution. This is quite irregular. Such material should be imparted from the bar by counsel having educated himself on the matter or by tax counsel duly instructed. There is nothing, however, to prevent the parties agreeing to instruct an accountant to do tax calculations on various hypotheses.

The *second basic rule* is that in financial proceedings no party may call an expert or put in evidence an expert's report without the court's permission (rule 25.4). There is no restriction on a party *instructing* an expert in financial proceedings in order to inform himself better of the issues at large. This is in contrast to proceedings relating to children. By rule 12.74(1) (in Chapter 7 entitled 'communication of information: proceedings relating to children') it is provided that 'no party may instruct an expert for any purpose relating to proceedings [relating to children], including to give evidence in those proceedings, without the permission of the court'.

This raises the question how far proceedings can be said to 'relate' to children. Do 'proceedings relating to children' include proceedings simply for variation of a child maintenance order made in divorce proceedings? Do they include proceedings under Schedule 1 to the Children Act 1989? By PD 25A para 1.2(b) 'family proceedings' include proceedings which are brought under the Children Act 1989 in any family court, or which are brought in the High Court and county courts and 'otherwise relate wholly or mainly to the maintenance or upbringing of a minor'. Section 25 of the MCA 1973 enjoins the court deciding financial issues to give 'first consideration ... to the welfare while a minor of any child of the family who has not attained the age of eighteen'.

The reason for a bar on even being allowed to *instruct* an expert in 'proceedings relating to children' is explained in para 1.6 as follows:

(a) proceedings relating to children are confidential and, in the absence of the court's permission, disclosure of information and documents relating to such proceedings may amount to a contempt of court or contravene statutory provisions protecting this confidentiality.

(b) for the purposes of the law of contempt of court, information relating to such proceedings (whether or not contained in a document filed with the court or recorded in any form) may be communicated only to an expert whose instruction by a party has been permitted by the court.

It will come as a surprise to many financial remedy practitioners to learn that in Schedule 1 proceedings the permission of the court is needed before instructing, say, an estate agent as to the cost of future housing or an accountant as to the liquidity within the father's economy. This rule was in fact present under the old regime, but was never complied with in money proceedings concerning children nor imposed by the court. It is considered that an early amendment to PD 25A should be made.

The *third basic rule* is that expert evidence will be restricted to that which is reasonably required to resolve the proceedings (rule 25.1). This reflects a number of facets: the overriding objective; the court's general case-management powers under Part 4: and the court's powers to exclude otherwise admissible evidence under rule 22.1.

The *fourth basic rule* is that it is the duty of experts to help the court on matters within their expertise; and this duty overrides any obligation to the person from whom experts have received instructions or by whom they are paid (rule 25.3). PD 25A puts it this way in para 3.1: 'An expert in family proceedings has an overriding duty to the court that takes precedence over any obligation to the person from whom the expert has received instructions or by whom the expert is paid'. This important rule, present from the inception of the CPR in 1999, was intended to thwart and arrest the phenomenon where experts were often little better than paid mercenaries or ancillary advocates in the cause of their paying clients. This was described in vivid language by Thorpe LJ in *Vernon v Bosley (Expert Evidence)* [1998] 1 FLR 297 thus:

> The area of expertise in any case may be likened to a broad street with the plaintiff walking on one pavement and the defendant walking on the opposite one. Somehow the expert must be ever-mindful of the need to walk straight down the middle of the road and to resist the temptation to join the party from whom his instructions come on the pavement.

PD 25A elaborates (but does not exhaust) the list of the expert's duties at para 3.2 to include obligations:

- to assist the court in accordance with the overriding duty;
- to provide advice to the court that conforms to the best practice of the expert's profession;
- to provide an opinion that is independent of the party or parties instructing the expert;
- to confine the opinion to matters material to the issues between the parties and in relation only to questions that are within the expert's expertise (skill and experience);
- where a question has been put which falls outside the expert's expertise, to state this at the earliest opportunity and to volunteer an opinion as to whether another expert is required to bring expertise not possessed by those already involved or, in the rare case, as to whether a second opinion is required on a key issue and, if possible, what questions should be asked of the second expert;
- in expressing an opinion, to take into consideration all of the material facts including any relevant factors arising from ethnic, cultural, religious or linguistic contexts at the time the opinion is expressed;
- to inform those instructing the expert without delay of any change in the opinion and of the reason for the change.

The *fifth basic rule* is that wherever possible expert evidence should be obtained from a single joint expert (SJE) instructed by both or all the parties (PD 25A para 5.1). See *below* for the rules and guidance applicable to the instruction of an SJE. The parties may agree to instruct separate experts, but in that case they 'they should agree in advance that the reports will be disclosed' (PD 5.5(a)). This should not be taken to mean that if a party instructs an expert but decides not to rely on the report he is nonetheless bound to disclose it: the report would remain covered by privilege (although the position may be different in children proceedings – see *Re L (A Minor) (Police Investigation: Privilege)* [1996] 2 WLR 395, HL; *Vernon v Bosley (No 2)* [1998] 1 FLR 304, CA).

Applying for permission

By PD 25A para 1.11 any application (or proposed application) for permission to instruct an expert, or to use expert evidence, should be raised with the court and, where appropriate with the other parties, as soon as possible. This normally means in financial proceedings by or at the First Appointment (see rule 9.15). The applicant must identify (a) the field in which the expert evidence is required, and (b) where practicable, the name of the proposed expert. If permission is granted it will be in relation only to the stated field and the expert, if named (rule 25.4).

Instructions to the expert

Although Section 4 of PD 25A is concerned with proceedings relating to children, by para 5.5(b) 'the instructions to each expert should comply, so far as appropriate, with paragraphs 4.5 to 4.7'. These require that the letter of instruction shall:

(a) set out the context in which the expert's opinion is sought (including any ethnic, cultural, religious or linguistic contexts);

(b) set out the specific questions which the expert is required to answer, ensuring that they:

   (i) are within the ambit of the expert's area of expertise;

   (ii) do not contain unnecessary or irrelevant detail;

   (iii) are kept to a manageable number and are clear, focused and direct; and

   (iv) reflect what the expert has been requested to do by the court.

(c) list the documentation provided, or provide for the expert an indexed and paginated bundle which shall include—

   (i) a copy of the order (or those parts of the order) which gives permission for the instruction of the expert, immediately the order becomes available;

   (ii) an agreed list of essential reading; and

   (iii) a copy of this guidance;

(d) identify any materials provided to the expert which have not been produced either as original medical (or other professional) records or in response to an instruction from a party, and state the source of that material (such materials may contain an assumption as to the standard of proof, the admissibility or otherwise of hearsay evidence, and other important procedural and substantive questions relating to the different purposes of other enquiries, for example, criminal or disciplinary proceedings);

(e) identify all requests to third parties for disclosure and their responses, to avoid partial disclosure, which tends only to prove a case rather than give full and frank information;

(f) identify the relevant people concerned with the proceedings (for example, the treating clinicians) and inform the expert of his or her right to talk to them provided that an accurate record is made of the discussions;

(g) identify any other expert instructed in the proceedings and advise the expert of their right to talk to the other experts provided that an accurate record is made of the discussions;

(h) subject to any public funding requirement for prior authority, define the contractual basis upon which the expert is retained and in particular the funding mechanism including how much the expert will be paid (an hourly rate and overall estimate should already have been obtained), when the expert will be paid, and what limitation there might be on the amount the expert can charge for the work which they will have to do. In cases where the parties are publicly funded, there should also be a brief explanation of the costs and expenses excluded from public funding by Funding Code criterion 1.3 and the detailed assessment process.

It is fair to observe that such detailed instructions have seldom, if ever, been given to an expert in financial proceedings in the past.

The instructions to the expert are *not* privileged against disclosure (rule 25.10(3)). They should be disclosed with the report.

By PD 25A para 4.7 as often as may be necessary the expert should be provided promptly with a copy of any new document filed at court, together with an updated document list or bundle index.

Power of court to direct a party to provide information

Sometimes an expert will not have all the necessary material in order to write his report. Often, such material will be in the hands of the other party. By rule 25.9 where a party has access to information which is not reasonably available to another party, the court may direct the party who has access to the information to prepare, file and serve a document recording the information. It is considered that it will be rare for this power to be invoked in financial remedy proceedings as surely such information will have been sought and answered under the questionnaire procedure provided for under rules 9.14(5)(c) and 9.15(2).

Expert's right to ask court for directions

Similarly situations may arise when prior to writing his report (or indeed afterwards) the expert considers that he needs the court's assistance to fulfil his task. So by rule 25.13 an expert may file a written request for directions for the purpose of assistance in carrying out his functions. Such an expert applicant must, unless the court directs otherwise, provide copies of the proposed request for directions to the party instructing him at least 7 days before he files the request, and to all other parties at least 4 days before he files them. The court when it gives directions may also direct that a party be served with a copy of the directions.

Form and content of expert's report

Expert evidence is to be given in a written report unless the court directs otherwise (para 25.5(1)). By rule 25.10(2): 'at the end of an expert's report there must be a statement that the expert understands and has complied with their (sic) duty to the court'. PD 25A elaborates further the requirements concerning the contents of the reports at para 3.3. First and foremost this requires that the expert's report shall be addressed to the court and prepared and filed **in accordance with the court's timetable** (emphasis in original). The report must:

(a) give details of the expert's qualifications and experience;

(b) include a statement identifying the document(s) containing the material instructions and the substance of any oral instructions and, as far as necessary to explain any opinions or conclusions expressed in the report, summarising the facts and instructions which are material to the conclusions and opinions expressed;

(c) state who carried out any test, examination or interview which the expert has used for the report and whether or not the test, examination or interview has been carried out under the expert's supervision;

(d) give details of the qualifications of any person who carried out the test, examination or interview;

(e) in expressing an opinion to the court—

    (i) take into consideration all of the material facts including any relevant factors arising from ethnic, cultural, religious or linguistic contexts at the time the opinion is expressed, identifying the facts, literature and any other material including research material that the expert has relied upon in forming an opinion;

    (ii) describe their own professional risk assessment process and process of differential diagnosis, highlighting factual assumptions, deductions from the factual assumptions, and any unusual, contradictory or inconsistent features of the case;

(iii) indicate whether any proposition in the report is an hypothesis (in particular a controversial hypothesis), or an opinion deduced in accordance with peer-reviewed and tested technique, research and experience accepted as a consensus in the scientific community;

(iv) indicate whether the opinion is provisional (or qualified, as the case may be), stating the qualification and the reason for it, and identifying what further information is required to give an opinion without qualification;

(f) where there is a range of opinion on any question to be answered by the expert—

   (i) summarise the range of opinion;

   (ii) identify and explain, within the range of opinions, any 'unknown cause', whether arising from the facts of the case (for example, because there is too little information to form a scientific opinion) or from limited experience or lack of research, peer review or support in the relevant field of expertise;

   (iii) give reasons for any opinion expressed: the use of a balance sheet approach to the factors that support or undermine an opinion can be of great assistance to the court;

(g) contain a summary of the expert's conclusions and opinions;

(h) contain a statement that the expert—

   (i) has no conflict of interest of any kind, other than any conflict disclosed in his or her report;

   (ii) does not consider that any interest disclosed affects his or her suitability as an expert witness on any issue on which he or she has given evidence;

   (iii) will advise the instructing party if, between the date of the expert's report and the final hearing, there is any change in circumstances which affects the expert's answers to (i) or (ii) above;

   (iv) understands their duty to the court and has complied with that duty; and

   (v) is aware of the requirements of Part 25 and this practice direction;

(i) be verified by a statement of truth in the following form—

'I confirm that I have made clear which facts and matters referred to in this report are within my own knowledge and which are not. Those that are within my own knowledge I confirm to be true. The opinions I have expressed represent my true and complete professional opinions on the matters to which they refer.'

Written questions to an expert

By rule 25.6 a party may put written questions about an expert's report to an expert. The questions must be proportionate. They may be put on a single occasion only and must be put within 10 days beginning with the date on which the expert's report was served, and must be for the purpose only of clarification of the report. *Note that the period of 28 days provided for in CPR rule 35.6 and incorporated in the old ancillary relief code has been shortened to 10 days.* A copy of the questions must, at the same time, be sent to the other party or parties (PD 25A para 6.1).

An expert's answers to such questions are treated as part of his report. Where a party has put a written question to an expert instructed by another party and the expert does not answer that question, the court may make use of one or both of the following orders in relation to the party who instructed the expert: (i) that the party may not rely on the evidence of that expert or (ii) that the party may not recover the fees and expenses of that expert from any other party.

Where written questions are put to an expert the court will specify the timetable according to which the expert is to answer the written questions (PD 25A para 6.1).

Discussions between experts

In the past it has been very common in ancillary relief proceedings for the court to direct a discussion between experts under CPR rule 35.12 to encourage agreement between them or at least to narrow issues. This power now extends to all financial remedy proceedings by rule 25.12, and may be exercised at any stage. Where such an order is made the court may specify the issues which the experts must discuss; further it may, and usually will, direct that following a discussion between the experts they must prepare a statement for the court setting out those issues on which they agree and they disagree, with a summary of their reasons for disagreeing. PD 25A para 6.2 provides that the specified issues will be expected to include the reasons for disagreement on any expert question and what, if any, action needs to be taken to resolve any outstanding disagreement or question; and, an explanation of existing evidence or additional evidence in order to assist the court to determine the issues. It is stated that 'one of the aims of specifying the issues for discussion is to limit, wherever possible, the need for the experts to attend court to give oral evidence' (as to which, see *below*).

Para 6.3 sets out very detailed and lengthy provisions concerning the arrangements to be made for an experts' meeting. The focus is principally on children's cases. It is not thought that a mandatory meeting within 15 days' of reports being filed is likely to be insisted on in all moncy cases.

Rule 25.12 *does not* replicate CPR rule 35.12 (4) and (5). These provide that:

(4) The content of the discussion between the experts shall not be referred to at the trial unless the parties agree.

(5) Where experts reach agreement on an issue during their discussions, the agreement shall not bind the parties unless the parties expressly agree to be bound by the agreement.

Sub-rule (4) perpetuated the previous rule in RSC Ord 38, rule 38 that meetings with experts were 'without prejudice'. Its omission in rule 25.12 must raise the suggestion that this longstanding rule has been abrogated in financial remedy (indeed in all family) proceedings. An authoritative decision must be awaited. The omission of sub-rule (5) is to be welcomed. One party should not be able to veto agreements reached between experts at their meeting.

SJEs

Rule 25.7 supplies the Court's power to direct that evidence is to be given by a single joint expert. As noted *above* PD 25A para 5.1 stipulates that wherever possible expert evidence should be obtained from an SJE instructed by both or all the parties. Rule 25.7(2) provides that where the parties cannot agree who should be the SJE the court may select the expert from a list prepared or identified by the instructing parties, or may direct that the expert be selected in some other manner (see also PD 25A para 5.1, to the same effect). Within 10 days after receipt of the list of proposed experts, the other party or parties should indicate any objection to one or more of the named experts and, if they do so, supply the name(s) of one or more experts whom they consider suitable (para 5.2). Each party should disclose whether they have already consulted any of the proposed experts about the issue(s) in question (para 5.3). Where the parties cannot agree on the identity of the expert, each party should think carefully before instructing their own expert because of the costs implications. Disagreements about the use and identity of an expert may be better managed by the court in the context of an application for directions (para 5.4).

The instructions to the SJE should comply, so far as appropriate, with PD 25A paras 4.5 to 4.7 (see *above*).

Jointly instructed experts should not attend any meeting or conference which is not a joint one, unless all the parties have agreed in writing or the court has directed that such a meeting may be held, and it is agreed or directed who is to pay the expert's fees for the meeting or conference. Any meeting or conference attended by a jointly instructed expert should be proportionate to the case (para 6.4).

Use of an expert's report, and attendance by an expert, at a hearing

Where a party has disclosed an expert's report, any party may use that expert's report as evidence at any relevant hearing (rule 25.11).

By rule 25.5(2) the court will not direct an expert to attend a hearing unless it is necessary to do so in the interests of justice. This differs from CPR rule 35.5(2) which confines this principle to 'a claim on the small claims track or the fast track', with the implication that experts should attend the hearing of multi-track claims. In all family proceedings the presumption is that experts should not attend any hearings, big or small.

Assessors

Rule 25.14 and PD 25A para 10 deal with the power to appoint assessors. As para 10.1 points out the only known instances of such appointments in practice has been in appeals from a district judge or costs judge in costs assessment proceedings.

PART 25: EXPERTS AND ASSESSORS

Duty to restrict expert evidence

25.1. Expert evidence will be restricted to that which is reasonably required to resolve the proceedings.

Interpretation

25.2.—(1) A reference to an "expert" in this Part—

   (a) is a reference to a person who has been instructed to give or prepare expert evidence for the purpose of family proceedings; and

   (b) does not include—

     (i) a person who is within a prescribed description for the purposes of section 94(1) of the 2002 Act (persons who may prepare a report for any person about the suitability of a child for adoption or of a person to adopt a child or about the adoption, or placement for adoption, of a child); or

     (ii) an officer of the Service or a Welsh family proceedings officer when acting in that capacity.

(Regulation 3 of the Restriction on the Preparation of Adoption Reports Regulations 2005 (S.I. 2005/1711) sets out which persons are within a prescribed description for the purposes of section 94(1) of the 2002 Act.)

(2) "Single joint expert" means an expert instructed to prepare a report for the court on behalf of two or more of the parties (including the applicant) to the proceedings.

Experts – overriding duty to the court

25.3.—(1) It is the duty of experts to help the court on matters within their expertise.

(2) This duty overrides any obligation to the person from whom experts have received instructions or by whom they are paid.

Court's power to restrict expert evidence

25.4.—(1) No party may call an expert or put in evidence an expert's report without the court's permission.

(2) When parties apply for permission they must identify—

(a) the field in which the expert evidence is required; and

(b) where practicable, the name of the proposed expert.

(3) If permission is granted it will be in relation only to the expert named or the field identified under paragraph (2).

(4) The court may limit the amount of a party's expert's fees and expenses that may be recovered from any other party.

General requirement for expert evidence to be given in a written report

25.5.—(1) Expert evidence is to be given in a written report unless the court directs otherwise.

(2) The court will not direct an expert to attend a hearing unless it is necessary to do so in the interests of justice.

Written questions to experts

25.6.—(1) A party may put written questions about an expert's report (which must be proportionate) to—

(a) an expert instructed by another party; or

(b) a single joint expert appointed under rule 25.7.

(2) Written questions under paragraph (1)—

(a) may be put once only;

(b) must be put within 10 days beginning with the date on which the expert's report was served; and

(c) must be for the purpose only of clarification of the report,
unless in any case—

    (i) the court directs otherwise; or

    (ii) a practice direction provides otherwise.

(3) An expert's answers to questions put in accordance with paragraph (1) are treated as part of the expert's report.

(4) Where—

(a) a party has put a written question to an expert instructed by another party; and

(b) the expert does not answer that question,

the court may make use of one or both of the following orders in relation to the party who instructed the expert—

(i) that the party may not rely on the evidence of that expert; or

(ii) that the party may not recover the fees and expenses of that expert from any other party.

Court's power to direct that evidence is to be given by a single joint expert

25.7.—(1) Where two or more parties wish to submit expert evidence on a particular issue, the court may direct that the evidence on that issue is to be given by a single joint expert.

(2) Where the parties who wish to submit the evidence ("the relevant parties") cannot agree who should be the single joint expert, the court may—

(a) select the expert from a list prepared or identified by the instructing parties; or

(b) direct that the expert be selected in such other manner as the court may direct.

Instructions to a single joint expert

25.8.—(1) Where the court gives a direction under rule 25.7(1) for a single joint expert to be used, the instructions are to be contained in a jointly agreed letter unless the court directs otherwise.

(2) Where the instructions are to be contained in a jointly agreed letter, in default of agreement the instructions may be determined by the court on the written request of any relevant party copied to the other relevant parties.

(3) Where the court permits the relevant parties to give separate instructions to a single joint expert, each instructing party must, when giving instructions to the expert, at the same time send a copy of the instructions to the other relevant parties.

(4) The court may give directions about—

(a) the payment of the expert's fees and expenses; and

(b) any inspection, examination or assessments which the expert wishes to carry out.

(5) The court may, before an expert is instructed, limit the amount that can be paid by way of fees and expenses to the expert.

(6) Unless the court directs otherwise, the relevant parties are jointly and severally liable for the payment of the expert's fees and expenses.

Power of court to direct a party to provide information

25.9.—(1) Subject to paragraph (2), where a party has access to information which is not reasonably available to another party, the court may direct the party who has access to the information to prepare, file and serve a document recording the information.

(2) In proceedings under Part 14 (procedure for applications in adoption, placement and related proceedings),—

    (a) the court may direct the party with access to the information to prepare and file a document recording the information; and

    (b) a court officer will send a copy of that document to the other party.

Contents of report

25.11.—(1) An expert's report must comply with the requirements set out in Practice Direction 25A.

(2) At the end of an expert's report there must be a statement that the expert understands and has complied with their duty to the court.

(3) The instructions to the expert are not privileged against disclosure.

(Rule 21.1 explains what is meant by disclosure.)

Use by one party of expert's report disclosed by another

25.12. Where a party has disclosed an expert's report, any party may use that expert's report as evidence at any relevant hearing.

Discussions between experts

25.13.—(1) The court may, at any stage, direct a discussion between experts for the purpose of requiring the experts to—

    (a) identify and discuss the expert issues in the proceedings; and

    (b) where possible, reach an agreed opinion on those issues.

(2) The court may specify the issues which the experts must discuss.

(3) The court may direct that following a discussion between the experts they must prepare a statement for the court setting out those issues on which—

    (a) they agree; and

    (b) they disagree,

with a summary of their reasons for disagreeing.

Expert's right to ask court for directions

25.14.—(1) Experts may file written requests for directions for the purpose of assisting them in carrying out their functions.

(2) Experts must, unless the court directs otherwise, provide copies of the proposed request for directions under paragraph (1)—

    (a) to the party instructing them, at least 7 days before they file the requests; and

    (b) to all other parties, at least 4 days before they file them.

(3) The court, when it gives directions, may also direct that a party be served with a copy of the directions.

Assessors

25.15.—(1) This rule applies where the court appoints one or more persons under section 70 of the Senior Courts Act 1981 or section 63 of the County Courts Act 1984[84] as an assessor

(2) An assessor will assist the court in dealing with a matter in which the assessor has skill and experience.

(3) The assessor will take such part in the proceedings as the court may direct and in particular the court may direct an assessor to—

(a) prepare a report for the court on any matter at issue in the proceedings; and

(b) attend the whole or any part of the hearing to advise the court on any such matter.

(4) If the assessor prepares a report for the court before the hearing has begun—

(a) the court will send a copy to each of the parties; and

(b) the parties may use it at the hearing.

(5) Unless the court directs otherwise, an assessor will be paid at the daily rate payable for the time being to a fee-paid deputy district judge of the principal registry and an assessor's fees will form part of the costs of the proceedings.

(6) The court may order any party to deposit in the court office a specified sum in respect of an assessor's fees and, where it does so, the assessor will not be asked to act until the sum has been deposited.

(7) Paragraphs (5) and (6) do not apply where the remuneration of the assessor is to be paid out of money provided by Parliament.

PRACTICE DIRECTION 25A – EXPERTS AND ASSESSORS IN FAMILY PROCEEDINGS

This Practice Direction supplements FPR Part 25

Introduction

1.1.1. Sections 1 to 9 of this Practice Direction deal with the use of expert evidence and the instruction of experts, and section 10 deals with the appointment of assessors, in all types of family proceedings. The guidance incorporates and supersedes the *Practice Direction on Experts in Family Proceedings relating to Children* (1 April 2008) and other relevant guidance with effect on and from 6 April 2011.

Where the guidance refers to "an expert" or "the expert", this includes a reference to an expert team.

1.2. For the purposes of this guidance, the phrase "proceedings relating to children" is a convenient description. It is not a legal term of art and has no statutory force. In this guidance it means—

    (a) placement and adoption proceedings; or

    (b) family proceedings which—

        (i) relate to the exercise of the inherent jurisdiction of the High Court with respect to children;

        (ii) are brought under the Children Act 1989 in any family court; or

        (iii) are brought in the High Court and county courts and "otherwise relate wholly or mainly to the maintenance or upbringing of a minor".

Aims of the guidance on experts and expert evidence

1.3. The aim of the guidance in sections 1 to 9 is to:

    (a) provide the court with early information to determine whether expert evidence or assistance will help the court;

    (b) help the court and the parties to identify and narrow the issues in the case and encourage agreement where possible;

    (c) enable the court and the parties to obtain an expert opinion about a question that is not within the skill and experience of the court;

    (d) encourage the early identification of questions that need to be answered by an expert; and

    (e) encourage disclosure of full and frank information between the parties, the court and any expert instructed.

1.4. The guidance does not aim to cover all possible eventualities. Thus it should be complied with so far as consistent in all the circumstances with the just disposal of the matter in accordance with the rules and guidance applying to the procedure in question.

Permission to instruct an expert or to use expert evidence

1.5. The general rule in family proceedings is that the court's permission is required to call an expert or to put in evidence an expert's report: see rule 25.4(1). In addition, in proceedings relating to children, the court's permission is required to instruct an expert: see rule 12.74(1).

1.6. The court and the parties must have regard in particular to the following considerations:

    (a) proceedings relating to children ...

    (b) ...

    (c) ...

1.7. ... in proceedings relating to children ...

1.8. ... in proceedings relating to children ...

1.9. Section 4 (*Proceedings relating to children*) ...

1.10. In proceedings other than those relating to children, the court's permission is not required to instruct an expert. Section 5 (*Proceedings other than those relating to children*) gives guidance on instructing an expert, and on seeking the court's permission to use expert evidence, prior to and in such proceedings. Section 5 emphasises that the use of a single joint expert should be considered in all cases where expert evidence is required.

When should the court be asked for permission?

1.11. Any application (or proposed application) for permission to instruct an expert or to use expert evidence should be raised with the court – and, where appropriate, with the other parties – as soon as possible. This will normally mean—

(a) ...
(b) ...
(c) ...
(d) in financial proceedings, by or at the First Appointment: see rule 9.15;
(e) ...

In this practice direction the "relevant hearing" means any hearing at which the court's permission is sought to instruct an expert or to use expert evidence.

General matters

Scope of the Guidance

2.2.1 Sections 1 to 9 of this guidance apply to all experts who are or may be instructed to give or prepare evidence for the purpose of family proceedings in a court in England and Wales. The guidance also applies to those who instruct, or propose to instruct, an expert for such a purpose. Section 10 applies to the appointment of assessors in family proceedings in England and Wales.

2.2. This guidance does not apply to proceedings issued before 6 April 2011 but in any such proceedings the court may direct that this guidance will apply either wholly or partly. This is subject to the overriding objective for the type of proceedings, and to the proviso that such a direction will neither cause further delay nor involve repetition of steps already taken or of decisions already made in the case.

Pre-application instruction of experts

2.3. When experts' reports are commissioned before the commencement of proceedings, it should be made clear to the expert that he or she may in due course be reporting to the court and should therefore consider himself or herself bound by this guidance. A prospective party to family proceedings relating to children (for example, a local authority) should always write a letter of instruction when asking a potential witness for a report or an opinion, whether that request is within proceedings or pre-proceedings (for example, when commissioning specialist assessment materials, reports from a treating expert or other evidential materials); and the letter of instruction should conform to the principles set out in this guidance.

Emergency and urgent cases

2.4. In emergency or urgent cases – for example, where, before formal issue of proceedings, a without-notice application is made to the court during or out of business hours; or where, after proceedings have been issued, a previously unforeseen need for (further) expert evidence arises at short notice – a party may wish to call expert evidence without having complied with all or any part of this guidance. In such circumstances, the party wishing to call the expert evidence must apply forthwith to the court – where possible or appropriate, on notice to the other parties – for directions as to the future steps to be taken in respect of the expert evidence in question.

Orders

2.5. Where an order or direction requires an act to be done by an expert, or otherwise affects an expert, the party instructing that expert – or, in the case of a jointly instructed expert, the lead solicitor – must serve a copy of the order or direction on the expert forthwith upon receiving it.

Adults who may be protected parties

2.6. The court will investigate as soon as possible any issue as to whether an adult party or intended party to family proceedings lacks capacity (within the meaning of the Mental Capacity Act 2005) to conduct the proceedings. An adult who lacks capacity to act as a party to the proceedings is a protected party and must have a litigation friend to conduct the proceedings on their behalf. The expectation of the Official Solicitor is that the Official Solicitor will only be invited to act for the protected party as litigation friend if there is no other person suitable or willing to act.

2.7. Any issue as to the capacity of an adult to conduct the proceedings must be determined before the court gives any directions relevant to that adult's role in the proceedings.

2.8. Where the adult is a protected party, that party's representative should be involved in any instruction of an expert, including the instruction of an expert to assess whether the adult, although a protected party, is competent to give evidence. The instruction of an expert is a significant step in the proceedings. The representative will wish to consider (and ask the expert to consider), if the protected party is competent to give evidence, their best interests in this regard. The representative may wish to seek advice about "special measures". The representative may put forward an argument on behalf of the protected party that the protected party should not give evidence.

2.9. If at any time during the proceedings there is reason to believe that a party may lack capacity to conduct the proceedings, then the court must be notified and directions sought to ensure that this issue is investigated without delay.

Child likely to lack capacity to conduct the proceedings on when he or she reaches 18

2.10. Where it appears that a child is—

(a) a party to the proceedings and not the subject of them;
(b) nearing age 18; and
(c) considered likely to lack capacity to conduct the proceedings when 18,

the court will consider giving directions for the child's capacity in this respect to be investigated.

The Duties of Experts

Overriding Duty

3.3.1. An expert in family proceedings has an overriding duty to the court that takes precedence over any obligation to the person from whom the expert has received instructions or by whom the expert is paid.

Particular Duties

3.2. An expert shall have regard to the following, among other, duties:

(a) to assist the court in accordance with the overriding duty;
(b) to provide advice to the court that conforms to the best practice of the expert's profession;
(c) to provide an opinion that is independent of the party or parties instructing the expert;
(d) to confine the opinion to matters material to the issues between the parties and in relation only to questions that are within the expert's expertise (skill and experience);
(e) where a question has been put which falls outside the expert's expertise, to state this at the earliest opportunity and to volunteer an opinion as to whether another expert is required to bring expertise not possessed by those already involved or, in the rare case, as to whether a second opinion is required on a key issue and, if possible, what questions should be asked of the second expert;
(f) in expressing an opinion, to take into consideration all of the material facts including any relevant factors arising from ethnic, cultural, religious or linguistic contexts at the time the opinion is expressed;

(g) to inform those instructing the expert without delay of any change in the opinion and of the reason for the change.

Content of the Expert's Report

3.3. The expert's report shall be addressed to the court and prepared and filed **in accordance with the court's timetable** and shall—

(a) give details of the expert's qualifications and experience;
(b) include a statement identifying the document(s) containing the material instructions and the substance of any oral instructions and, as far as necessary to explain any opinions or conclusions expressed in the report, summarising the facts and instructions which are material to the conclusions and opinions expressed;
(c) state who carried out any test, examination or interview which the expert has used for the report and whether or not the test, examination or interview has been carried out under the expert's supervision;
(d) give details of the qualifications of any person who carried out the test, examination or interview;
(e) in expressing an opinion to the court—
    (i) take into consideration all of the material facts including any relevant factors arising from ethnic, cultural, religious or linguistic contexts at the time the opinion is expressed, identifying the facts, literature and any other material including research material that the expert has relied upon in forming an opinion;
    (ii) describe their own professional risk assessment process and process of differential diagnosis, highlighting factual assumptions, deductions from the factual assumptions, and any unusual, contradictory or inconsistent features of the case;
    (iii) indicate whether any proposition in the report is an hypothesis (in particular a controversial hypothesis), or an opinion deduced in accordance with peer-reviewed and tested technique, research and experience accepted as a consensus in the scientific community;
    (iv) indicate whether the opinion is provisional (or qualified, as the case may be), stating the qualification and the reason for it, and identifying what further information is required to give an opinion without qualification;
(f) where there is a range of opinion on any question to be answered by the expert—
    (i) summarise the range of opinion;
    (ii) identify and explain, within the range of opinions, any "unknown cause", whether arising from the facts of the case (for example, because there is too little information to form a scientific opinion) or from limited experience or lack of research, peer review or support in the relevant field of expertise;

(iii) give reasons for any opinion expressed: the use of a balance sheet approach to the factors that support or undermine an opinion can be of great assistance to the court;

(g) contain a summary of the expert's conclusions and opinions;

(h) contain a statement that the expert—

    (i) has no conflict of interest of any kind, other than any conflict disclosed in his or her report;

    (ii) does not consider that any interest disclosed affects his or her suitability as an expert witness on any issue on which he or she has given evidence;

    (iii) will advise the instructing party if, between the date of the expert's report and the final hearing, there is any change in circumstances which affects the expert's answers to (i) or (ii) above;

    (iv) understands their duty to the court and has complied with that duty; and

    (v) is aware of the requirements of Part 25 and this practice direction;

(i) be verified by a statement of truth in the following form—

> "I confirm that I have made clear which facts and matters referred to in this report are within my own knowledge and which are not. Those that are within my own knowledge I confirm to be true. The opinions I have expressed represent my true and complete professional opinions on the matters to which they refer."

(Part 17 deals with statements of truth. Rule 17.6 sets out the consequences of verifying a document containing a false statement without an honest belief in its truth.)

Proceedings relating to children
Preparation for the relevant hearing

Preliminary Enquiries of the Expert
4.1. In good time for the information requested to be available for the relevant hearing or for the advocates' meeting or discussion where one takes place before the relevant hearing, the solicitor for the party proposing to instruct the expert (or lead solicitor or solicitor for the child if the instruction proposed is joint) shall approach the expert with the following information—

(a) the nature of the proceedings and the issues likely to require determination by the court;

(b) the questions about which the expert is to be asked to give an opinion (including any ethnic, cultural, religious or linguistic contexts);

(c) the date when the court is to be asked to give permission for the instruction (or if – unusually – permission has already been given, the date and details of that permission);

(d) whether permission is to be asked of the court for the instruction of another expert in the same or any related field (that is, to give an opinion on the same or related questions);

(e) the volume of reading which the expert will need to undertake;

(f) whether or not permission has been applied for or given for the expert to examine the child;

(g) whether or not it will be necessary for the expert to conduct interviews – and, if so, with whom;

(h) the likely timetable of legal and social work steps;

(i) in care and supervision proceedings, any dates in the Timetable for the Child which would be relevant to the proposed timetable for the assessment;

(j) when the expert's report is likely to be required;

(k) whether and, if so, what date has been fixed by the court for any hearing at which the expert may be required to give evidence (in particular the Final Hearing); and whether it may be possible for the expert to give evidence by telephone conference or video link: see section 8 *(Arrangements for experts to give evidence)* below;

(l) the possibility of making, through their instructing solicitors, representations to the court about being named or otherwise identified in any public judgment given by the court.

It is essential that there should be proper co-ordination between the court and the expert when drawing up the case management timetable: the needs of the court should be balanced with the needs of the expert whose forensic work is undertaken as an adjunct to his or her main professional duties.

Expert's Response to Preliminary Enquiries
4.2. In good time for the relevant hearing or for the advocates' meeting or discussion where one takes place before the relevant hearing, the solicitors intending to instruct the expert shall obtain confirmation from the expert—

(a) that acceptance of the proposed instructions will not involve the expert in any conflict of interest;

(b) that the work required is within the expert's expertise;

(c) that the expert is available to do the relevant work within the suggested time scale;

(d) when the expert is available to give evidence, of the dates and times to avoid and, where a hearing date has not been fixed, of the amount of notice the expert will require to make arrangements to come to court (or to give evidence by telephone conference or video link) without undue disruption to his or her normal professional routines;

(e) of the cost, including hourly or other charging rates, and likely hours

to be spent, attending experts' meetings, attending court and writing
the report (to include any examinations and interviews);

(f) of any representations which the expert wishes to make to the court
about being named or otherwise identified in any public judgment
given by the court.

Where parties have not agreed on the appointment of a single joint expert
before the relevant hearing, they should obtain the above confirmations in
respect of all experts whom they intend to put to the court for the purposes
of rule 25.7(2)(a) as candidates for the appointment.

The proposal to instruct an expert

4.3. Any party who proposes to ask the court for permission to instruct an
expert shall, **by 11 a.m. on the business day before the relevant hearing**, file
and serve a written proposal to instruct the expert, in the following detail—

(a) the name, discipline, qualifications and expertise of the expert (by
way of C.V. where possible);

(b) the expert's availability to undertake the work;

(c) the relevance of the expert evidence sought to be adduced to the
issues in the proceedings and the specific questions upon which it is
proposed that the expert should give an opinion (including the
relevance of any ethnic, cultural, religious or linguistic contexts);

(d) the timetable for the report;

(e) the responsibility for instruction;

(f) whether or not the expert evidence can properly be obtained by the
joint instruction of the expert by two or more of the parties;

(g) whether the expert evidence can properly be obtained by only one
party (for example, on behalf of the child);

(h) why the expert evidence proposed cannot be given by social services
undertaking a core assessment or by the Children's Guardian in
accordance with their respective statutory duties;

(i) the likely cost of the report on an hourly or other charging basis:
where possible, the expert's terms of instruction should be made
available to the court;

(j) the proposed apportionment (at least in the first instance) of any
jointly instructed expert's fee; when it is to be paid; and, if applicable,
whether public funding has been approved.

Draft Order for the relevant hearing

4.4. Any party proposing to instruct an expert shall, **by 11 a.m. on the
business day before the relevant hearing**, submit to the court a draft order
for directions dealing in particular with—

(a) the party who is to be responsible for drafting the letter of instruction
and providing the documents to the expert;

(b) the issues identified by the court and the questions about which the expert is to give an opinion;

(c) the timetable within which the report is to be prepared, filed and served;

(d) the disclosure of the report to the parties and to any other expert;

(e) the organisation of, preparation for and conduct of an experts' discussion;

(f) the preparation of a statement of agreement and disagreement by the experts following an experts' discussion;

(g) making available to the court at an early opportunity the expert reports in electronic form;

(h) the attendance of the expert at court to give oral evidence (alternatively, the expert giving his or her evidence in writing or remotely by video link), whether at or for the Final Hearing or another hearing; unless agreement about the opinions given by the expert is reached at or before the Issues Resolution Hearing ("IRH") or, if no IRH is to be held, by a specified date prior to the hearing at which the expert is to give oral evidence ("the specified date").

Letter of Instruction

4.5. The solicitor or party instructing the expert shall, **within 5 business days after the relevant hearing,** prepare (in agreement with the other parties where appropriate), file and serve a letter of instruction to the expert which shall—

(a) set out the context in which the expert's opinion is sought (including any ethnic, cultural, religious or linguistic contexts);

(b) set out the specific questions which the expert is required to answer, ensuring that they—

(i) are within the ambit of the expert's area of expertise;

(ii) do not contain unnecessary or irrelevant detail;

(iii) are kept to a manageable number and are clear, focused and direct; and

(iv) reflect what the expert has been requested to do by the court.

(The Annex to this guidance sets out suggested questions in letters of instruction to (1) child mental health professionals or paediatricians, and (2) adult psychiatrists and applied psychologists, in Children Act 1989 proceedings.)

(c) list the documentation provided, or provide for the expert an indexed and paginated bundle which shall include—

(i) a copy of the order (or those parts of the order) which gives permission for the instruction of the expert, immediately the order becomes available;

(ii) an agreed list of essential reading; and

(iii) a copy of this guidance;

(d) identify any materials provided to the expert which have not been produced either as original medical (or other professional) records or in response to an instruction from a party, and state the source of that material (such materials may contain an assumption as to the standard of proof, the admissibility or otherwise of hearsay evidence, and other important procedural and substantive questions relating to the different purposes of other enquiries, for example, criminal or disciplinary proceedings);

(e) identify all requests to third parties for disclosure and their responses, to avoid partial disclosure, which tends only to prove a case rather than give full and frank information;

(f) identify the relevant people concerned with the proceedings (for example, the treating clinicians) and inform the expert of his or her right to talk to them provided that an accurate record is made of the discussions;

(g) identify any other expert instructed in the proceedings and advise the expert of their right to talk to the other experts provided that an accurate record is made of the discussions;

(h) subject to any public funding requirement for prior authority, define the contractual basis upon which the expert is retained and in particular the funding mechanism including how much the expert will be paid (an hourly rate and overall estimate should already have been obtained), when the expert will be paid, and what limitation there might be on the amount the expert can charge for the work which they will have to do. In cases where the parties are publicly funded, there should also be a brief explanation of the costs and expenses excluded from public funding by Funding Code criterion 1.3 and the detailed assessment process.

Asking the court to settle the letter of instruction to a single joint expert
4.6. Where possible, the written request for the court to consider the letter of instruction referred to in rule 25.8(2) should be set out in an e-mail to the court and copied by e-mail to the other instructing parties. The request should be sent to the relevant court or (by prior arrangement only) directly to the judge dealing with the proceedings; in the magistrates' court, the request should be sent to the legal adviser who will refer it to the appropriate judge or justices, if necessary. The court will settle the letter of instruction, usually without a hearing to avoid delay; and will send (where practicable, by e-mail) the settled letter to the lead solicitor for transmission forthwith to the expert, and copy it to the other instructing parties for information.

Keeping the expert up to date with new documents
4.7. As often as may be necessary, the expert should be provided promptly

with a copy of any new document filed at court, together with an updated document list or bundle index.

Proceedings other than those relating to children

5.1. Wherever possible, expert evidence should be obtained from a single joint expert instructed by both or all the parties ("SJE"). To that end, a party wishing to instruct an expert should first give the other party or parties a list of the names of one or more experts in the relevant speciality whom they consider suitable to be instructed.

5.2. Within 10 days after receipt of the list of proposed experts, the other party or parties should indicate any objection to one or more of the named experts and, if so, supply the name(s) of one or more experts whom they consider suitable.

5.3. Each party should disclose whether they have already consulted any of the proposed experts about the issue(s) in question.

5.4. Where the parties cannot agree on the identity of the expert, each party should think carefully before instructing their own expert because of the costs implications. Disagreements about the use and identity of an expert may be better managed by the court in the context of an application for directions. (see paragraphs 5.8 and 5.9 below).

Agreement to instruct separate experts

5.5. If the parties agree to instruct separate experts—

(a) they should agree in advance that the reports will be disclosed; and
(b) the instructions to each expert should comply, so far as appropriate, with paragraphs 4.5 to 4.7 above (*Letter of instruction*).

Agreement to instruct an SJE

5.6. If there is agreement to instruct an SJE, **before instructions are given** the parties should—

(a) so far as appropriate, comply with the guidance in paragraphs 4.1 (Preliminary inquiries of the expert) and 4.2 (Expert's confirmation in response to preliminary enquiries) above;
(b) have agreed in what proportion the SJE's fee is to be shared between them (at least in the first instance) and when it is to be paid; and
(c) if applicable, have obtained agreement for public funding.

5.7. The instructions to the SJE should comply, so far as appropriate, with paragraphs 4.5 to 4.7 above (*Letter of instruction*).

Seeking the court's directions for the use of an SJE

5.8. Where the parties seek the court's directions for the use of an SJE, they should comply, so far as appropriate, with paragraphs 4.1 to 4.4 (*Preparation for the relevant hearing*) above.

5.9. The instructions to the SJE should comply, so far as appropriate, with paragraphs 4.5 to 4.7 above (*Letter of instruction*).

The Court's control of expert evidence: consequential issues

Written Questions
6.1. Where—

- (a) written questions are put to an expert in accordance with rule 25.6, the court will specify the timetable according to which the expert is to answer the written questions;
- (b) a party sends a written question or questions under rule 25.6 direct to an expert, a copy of the questions must, at the same time, be sent to the other party or parties.

Experts' Discussion or Meeting: Purpose
6.2. In accordance with rule 25.12, the court may, at any stage, direct a discussion between experts for the purpose outlined in paragraph (1) of that rule. Rule 25.12(2) provides that the court may specify the issues which the experts must discuss. The expectation is that those issues will include—

- (a) the reasons for disagreement on any expert question and what, if any, action needs to be taken to resolve any outstanding disagreement or question;
- (b) explanation of existing evidence or additional evidence in order to assist the court to determine the issues.

One of the aims of specifing the issues for discussion is to limit, wherever possible, the need for the experts to attend court to give oral evidence.

Experts' Discussion or Meeting: Arrangements
6.3. Subject to the directions given by the court under rule 25.12, the solicitor or other professional who is given the responsibility by the court ("the nominated professional") shall – **within 15 business days after the experts' reports have been filed and copied to the other parties** – make arrangements for the experts to meet or communicate. Subject to any specification by the court of the issues which experts must discuss under rule 25.12(2), the following matters should be considered as appropriate—

- (a) where permission has been given for the instruction of experts from different disciplines, a global discussion may be held relating to those questions that concern all or most of them;
- (b) separate discussions may have to be held among experts from the same or related disciplines, but care should be taken to ensure that the discussions complement each other so that related questions are discussed by all relevant experts;
- (c) **5 business days prior to a discussion or meeting**, the nominated professional should formulate an agenda including a list of questions for consideration. The agenda should, subject always to the provisions of rule 25.12(1), focus on those questions which are intended to clarify areas of agreement or disagreement.

Questions which repeat questions asked in the letter of instruction or which seek to rehearse cross-examination in advance of the hearing should be rejected as likely to defeat the purpose of the meeting.

The agenda may usefully take the form of a list of questions to be circulated among the other parties in advance and should comprise all questions that each party wishes the experts to consider.

The agenda and list of questions should be sent to each of the experts **not later than 2 business days before the discussion;**

(d) the nominated professional may exercise his or her discretion to accept further questions after the agenda with list of questions has been circulated to the parties. **Only in exceptional circumstances should questions be added to the agenda within the 2-day period before the meeting. Under no circumstances should any question received on the day of or during the meeting be accepted.** This does not preclude questions arising during the meeting for the purposes of clarification. Strictness in this regard is vital, for adequate notice of the questions enables the parties to identify and isolate the expert issues in the case before the meeting so that the experts' discussion at the meeting can concentrate on those issues;

(e) the discussion should be chaired by the nominated professional. A minute must be taken of the questions answered by the experts. Where the court has given a direction under rule 25.12(3) and subject to that direction, a Statement of Agreement and Disagreement must be prepared which should be agreed and signed by each of the experts who participated in the discussion. In accordance with rule 25.12(3) the statement must contain a summary of the experts' reasons for disagreeing. The statement should be served and filed **not later than 5 business days after the discussion has taken place;**

(f) in each case, whether some or all of the experts participate by telephone conference or video link to ensure that minimum disruption is caused to professional schedules and that costs are minimised.

Meetings or conferences attended by a jointly instructed expert
6.4. Jointly instructed experts should not attend any meeting or conference which is not a joint one, unless all the parties have agreed in writing or the court has directed that such a meeting may be held, and it is agreed or directed who is to pay the expert's fees for the meeting or conference. Any meeting or conference attended by a jointly instructed expert should be proportionate to the case.

Court-directed meetings involving experts in public law Children Act cases
6.5. ...

Positions of the Parties

7.1. Where a party refuses to be bound by an agreement that has been reached at an experts' discussion or meeting, that party must inform the court and the other parties in writing, **within 10 business days after the discussion or meeting or, where an IRH is to be held, not less than 5 business days before the IRH,** of his or her reasons for refusing to accept the agreement.

Arrangements for Experts to give evidence

Preparation

8.1. Where the court has directed the attendance of an expert witness, the party who is responsible for the instruction of the expert shall, **by the specified date or, where an IRH is to be held, by the IRH,** ensure that—

(a) a date and time (if possible, convenient to the expert) are fixed for the court to hear the expert's evidence, substantially in advance of the hearing at which the expert is to give oral evidence and no later than a specified date prior to that hearing or, where an IRH is to be held, than the IRH;

(b) if the expert's oral evidence is not required, the expert is notified as soon as possible;

(c) the witness template accurately indicates how long the expert is likely to be giving evidence, in order to avoid the inconvenience of the expert being delayed at court;

(d) consideration is given in each case to whether some or all of the experts participate by telephone conference or video link, or submit their evidence in writing, to ensure that minimum disruption is caused to professional schedules and that costs are minimised.

Experts attending Court

8.2. Where expert witnesses are to be called, all parties shall, **by the specified date or, where an IRH is to be held, by the IRH,** ensure that—

(a) the parties' advocates have identified (whether at an advocates' meeting or by other means) the issues which the experts are to address;

(b) wherever possible, a logical sequence to the evidence is arranged, with experts of the same discipline giving evidence on the same day;

(c) the court is informed of any circumstance where all experts agree but a party nevertheless does not accept the agreed opinion, so that directions can be given for the proper consideration of the experts' evidence and opinion and of the party's reasons for not accepting the agreed opinion;

(d) in the exceptional case the court is informed of the need for a witness summons.

Action after the Final Hearing

9.1. Within 10 business days after the Final Hearing, the solicitor instructing the expert shall inform the expert in writing of the outcome of the case, and of the use made by the court of the expert's opinion.

9.2. Where the court directs preparation of a transcript, it may also direct that the solicitor instructing the expert shall send a copy to the **expert within 10 business days after receiving the transcript.**

9.3. After a Final Hearing in the Family Proceedings Court, the (lead) solicitor instructing the expert shall send the expert a copy of the court's written reasons for its decision **within 10 business days after receiving the written reasons.**

Appointment of assessors in family proceedings

10.1. The power to appoint one or more assessors to assist the court is conferred on the High Court by section 70(1) of the Senior Courts Act 1981, and on a county court by section 63(1) of the County Courts Act 1984. In practice, these powers have been used in appeals from a district judge or costs judge in costs assessment proceedings – although, in principle, the statutory powers permit one or more assessors to be appointed in any family proceedings where the High Court or a county court sees fit.

10.2. Not less than 21 days before making any such appointment, the court will notify each party in writing of the name of the proposed assessor, of the matter in respect of which the assistance of the assessor will be sought and of the qualifications of the assessor to give that assistance.

10.3. Any party may object to the proposed appointment, either personally or in respect of the proposed assessor's qualifications.

10.4. Any such objection must be made in writing and filed and served **within 7 business days of receipt of the notification from the court of the proposed appointment,** and will be taken into account by the court in deciding whether or not to make the appointment.

Annex

(drafted by the Family Justice Council)

Suggested questions in letters of instruction to child mental health professional or paediatrician in Children Act 1989 proceedings ....

* * * * *

PART 26: CHANGE OF SOLICITOR

* * * * *

Part 27

Commentary on Part 27:
HEARINGS AND DIRECTIONS APPOINTMENTS

Part 27 deals with a range of matters concerning hearings and directions appointments (referred to for convenience in this commentary as 'hearings' because no distinction appears to be drawn between hearings and directions appointments in the rules or Practice Directions) including who – not least the gentlefolk of the press and the representatives of other media organisations – may or must attend; what happens if a party fails to attend a hearing; and court bundles and shorthand notes (which have, astonishingly, survived as the default means by which proceedings are to be recorded).

Part 27 is supported by three practice directions:

- PD 27A on court bundles for all courts except for the Family Proceedings (i.e. magistrates') Court;
- PD 27B on the attendance of media representatives at family proceedings otherwise held in private; and
- in almost identical terms, PD 27C in relation to the attendance of the media at proceedings under the Children Act 1989.

PDs 27B and 27C are unaltered re-issues of Practice Directions dated 20 April 2009 and refer to the 1991 Rules. However by virtue of the '*Practice Direction – Practice Directions Relating to Family Proceedings in force before 6 April 2011 which support The Family Proceedings Rules 2010*' they are to be read as if references to the FPR 2010 and its PDs were present. The versions of these PDs included in this book incorporate (so far as possible) these updating amendments. However we are also enjoined to read [sic] these PDs 'as if amended by *Re X (a child) (residence and contact: rights of media attendance)* [2009] EWHC 1798 Fam at [87]' which does risk causing most litigants in person (and maybe some other rule-users) to feel somewhat illiterate.

Rule 27.2 imposes upon justices or a single justice sitting in the magistrates' court the obligations to make decisions 'as soon as is practicable' (rule 27.2(2)) and to give written reasons (rule 27.2(3)). Where the magistrates' court comprises lay justices, notes must be taken of the names of the justice(s) and the reason for the decision before an order is made or an application refused (rule 27.2(5)). A magistrates' court must announce its decision with reasons, or at least a short explanation (rule 27.2(7)), and supply a copy of the order and the reasons for the decision by close of business the same day, or in any event within 72 hours, to the parties (rule 27.2(8), (9)).

An innovation under rule 27.3 is that the default position now is that parties are required to attend every hearing of which that party has notice. The court may direct otherwise, i.e. excuse a party from attendance. Previously parties were only specifically required to attend a First Appointment and FDR unless relieved of that obligation. Strictly interpreted, as it may be, this change will mean that any third party (such as trustees, or a party to whom a disposition has been made which one party seeks to set aside) to whom notice of a hearing has been given will be required to attend, so thought should be given in advance of each hearing as to whether compulsory attendance should be dispensed with – no doubt in furtherance of the overriding objective and not least to mitigate the expense and inconvenience of unnecessary attendance.

Rules 27.4 and 27.5 are respectively concerned with the consequences when one or more parties fail to attend a hearing, including the circumstances in which an order can be made and those in which such an order may later be set aside: these rules have equivalent counterparts in CPR rule 39.3.

Excluding parties from a hearing

Rule 27.4(1) contains a power for the court to exclude a party (including but not limited to a child) from all or part of the proceedings if the court considers that it would be in the interests of that party not to be present having regard to the subject matter under discussion and the evidence to be given. It appears that the purpose of the provision is to protect vulnerable minors and vulnerable adults from potential harm arising from what they might see unfold in the proceedings. The power can only be exercised if the party is represented; in the case of a child by a guardian or a solicitor and in the case of an adult party by a solicitor. A child so excluded has the right to make representations himself (if of sufficient understanding and the court thinks it appropriate) or through his guardian or through his solicitor in relation to the question whether it is in his interests to be excluded. An adult does not apparently have any such right although it is hard to imagine that the rule would be construed and applied in practice so as to preclude the solicitor representing that party from objecting to the exclusion of the litigant.

Continuing with a hearing when a party fails to attend

Rule 27.4(2) empowers the court to continue with a hearing at which one or more of the respondents have failed to attend, provided that the court is satisfied that the absent respondent had 'reasonable notice' and that the circumstances of the case justify proceeding in his absence (rule 27.4(3)).

Corresponding provisions empower the court to deal with a hearing attended by the respondent but from which the applicant is absent, either by refusing the application or if sufficient evidence has already been given by dealing with the application (rule 27.4(4)); and when none of the parties attend in which case the application may be refused (rule 27.4(5)).

Unsurprisingly, where the court would be obliged to stay the proceedings pursuant to obligations under a European regulation or international convention because the respondent in another State has not been properly served in accordance with that regulation or convention, then the hearing may not continue in the absence of that respondent: rule 27.4(7). This obligation will no doubt persist even in a case where the court is satisfied that the party in question has in fact been given what our courts would regard as adequate notice of the hearing. For such EU States, including in this instance Denmark (by separate agreement), service must be effected by the means prescribed in the EU Service Regulation. More detail concerning the EU Service Regulation and the Hague Convention of 15 November 1965 on the Service Abroad of Judicial and Extrajudicial Documents in Civil or Commercial Matters can be found in the Commentary on Part 4 *above*.

Setting aside an order following failure to attend

Where an order has been made or refused in the absence of the party against whom such a decision works, an application may be made, but which must (rule 27.5(2)) be supported by evidence, to set aside the decision. However the court may only (rule 27.5(3)) set the decision aside if the applicant acts promptly after learning of the adverse decision *and* had good reason for failing to attend *and* has a reasonable prospect of success at a restored hearing. However this rule does not apply in the magistrates' court where, it surprisingly seems, a decision made in the absence of a party will be final (rule 27.5(4)).

The requirement to act 'promptly' has been considered in the context of the CPR, and is a deliberately flexible term. In *Regency Rolls Ltd v Carnall* [2000] EWCA 379, [2000] All ER (D) 1417, 4 weeks was too long, whereas in *Watson v Bluemoor Properties Ltd* [2002] EWCA Civ 1875, [2002] All ER (D) 117 6 weeks was not. In the former case Simon Brown LJ said that to act promptly requires *'not that an applicant has been guilty of no needless delay whatever, but rather that he has acted with all reasonable celerity in the circumstances'*.

Court bundles and retention of documents

Rule 27.6 and the familiar PD 27A (which is in identical terms to the President's Practice Direction of 27 July 2006) deal with the preparation and lodging of court bundles, and do not apply to magistrates' courts.

Strict adherence to paras 4.2 to 4.5 and 8.2(a) of PD 27A requires six separate preliminary documents to be prepared and lodged by 11 a.m. on the day before the hearing and that the parties should if practicable agree the content of the most potentially contentious of them. Experience in financial remedy cases is that the documents are often repetitive and unmanageable and that attempts to agree the contents are costly but almost always fail.

Judges are generally content to accept a composite note from each side containing the information specified in para 4.2(i) to (iv). However, some judges have indicated that they expect the chronology, schedule of assets and bundle of authorities to be agreed. Whilst an agreed bundle of authorities can and should be produced, agreed chronologies and asset schedules remain impracticable for the reasons suggested.

Most judges welcome email filing, referred to in para 6.4 of PD 27A.

In relation to cases at the RCJ filing the combined note by 11 a.m. on the day before the hearing has proved in the past to be sometimes fruitless as cases are often not allocated to a judge until after lunch on that day. The practice has developed of filing the preliminary documents at 11 a.m. in order to obtain the necessary receipt (see para 8.1(a)), and then at 2 p.m. sending duplicate copies direct to the allocated judge's clerk (in accordance with para 8.2(b)) whether or not the judge received the original documents.

For PRFD hearings listed for longer than one hour at First Avenue House the usual practice is to lodge the preliminary documents immediately after lunch on the day before the hearing, direct to the allocated district judge. In the case of hearings listed there for one hour or less and therefore outside the scope of the PD (para 2.4(a)) advocates generally supply analogous documents immediately prior to the hearing.

For fair warning of the potential sanctions (including naming and shaming) for non-compliance see *Re X and Y (bundles)* [2008] 2 FLR 2058.

Rule 27.7 provides (in identical terms to CPR rule 39.6) that, if the court gives permission, any company or other corporate entity may be represented by a duly authorised employee (i.e. it is not necessary, subject to such permission, for the company to be represented by a director or by a solicitor).

Rule 27.8 (which is in identical terms to its counterpart CPR rule 39.7) concerns the release of documents impounded by the court, and (rule 27.8(3)) their inspection. These succinct provisions may be relevant in the context of financial remedy proceedings particularly where one party's documents have been wrongly obtained by the other party and subsequently lodged with the court (as in *Imerman v Tchenguiz and Others*

[2010] 2 FLR 814). Such documents cannot be released without a court order or (expressly but surely only exceptionally) following a written request by the DPP or a Law Officer (rule 27.8(1)), and also cannot be inspected except by a person authorised by a court order (rule 27.8(3)). Where leave to inspect is given it may or may not include leave to make copies (*Re A Solicitor* (1892) 65 LT 584).

The recording and transcribing of proceedings in open court in the High Court is governed by rule 27.9, and although the rule refers throughout to the taking of a note in shorthand, by rule 27.9(7) this term includes the more usual mechanical (i.e. electronic) recording.

Hearings in private and access to them and to the court file

By rule 27.10 proceedings governed by the FPR are to be held 'in private' unless specifically provided otherwise in some other part of the FPR or by any statute, or if the court directs otherwise. Examples of proceedings heard in open court are matrimonial proceedings under Part 7 (i.e. defended divorces) (rule 7.16), and committal proceedings, including judgment summonses (CPR Practice Direction RSC 52 and CCR 29 – Committal Applications para 9). 'In private' means that the general public has no right to be present, and not that only the parties and their representatives may be present.

Rule 27.11 (which is in almost identical terms to the previous FPR 1991 rule 10.28), together with PD 27B and 27C (which are in almost identical terms to the *President's Guidance* [2009] 2 FLR 157) regulate access to private proceedings within the meaning of rule 27.10.

In principle accredited media representatives have access to hearings, but subject to rule 27.11(4) (and rule 27.11(1) which excepts the FDR). The press can be excluded *'in the interests of any child concerned in, or connected with, the proceedings; or for the safety or protection of a party, a witness in the proceedings, or a person connected with such a party or witness; or for the orderly conduct of the proceedings; or where justice will otherwise be impeded or prejudiced.'*

Before an exclusion order is made rule 27.11(5) provides that the press must be given *'an opportunity to make representations'*. Contrary to what had been widely anticipated in April 2009 when media access was first introduced, there has been no welter of high profile cases with parties seeking to exclude the press. Indeed reporters have been almost entirely absent from proceedings they are now entitled to attend. Nowhere do the Rules, the Practice Directions or the Guidance offer any indication how these exclusionary criteria should be applied.

The test *'where justice will otherwise be impeded or prejudiced'* must be interpreted in conformity with the European Convention on Human Rights. PD 27B gives only two examples of situations where this criterion may arise namely:

(1) a hearing relating to the parties' finances where the information being considered includes price sensitive information (such as confidential information which could affect the share price of a publicly quoted company); or

(2) any hearing at which a witness (other than a party) states for credible reasons that he or she will not give evidence in front of media representatives, or where there appears to the court to be a significant risk that a witness will not give full or frank evidence in their presence.

The court file surely remains closed to public perusal, subject to leave. The effect (in contrast to the procedure in the Court of Appeal) is that the press do not have access to skeleton arguments or any other written materials save with the express permission of the court. PD 27B confirms this in para 2.3. This replaces the reference in the original Practice Direction of 27 July 2006 to FPR 1991 Part 11 by a reference to Part 12 Chapter 7 FPR 2010 and PD 12G.

These provisions (as was the case with the previous FPR 1991 Part 11) are confined to proceedings concerning children: the general prohibition of access by strangers to the court file in FPR 1991 rule 10.20 seems to have escaped reproduction in FPR 2010. This must be regarded as an accidental omission, for it is inconceivable that from 6 April 2011 the general public will have an unfettered right to inspect the court file. It is noted that rule 29.12 provides for access to copies of an order made in open court (i.e. corresponding to former rule 10.16) and it may be that the implication is to be drawn from this is that third parties are entitled to access *only* to open court orders, and thus entitled to see neither (a) the court file upon which they are placed nor (b) court orders made in private. It is suggested that the position is unclear and should rapidly be put beyond doubt in an early FPR Amendment Rule.

In *Clibbery v Allen* [2002] 1 FLR 565 Butler-Sloss P and Thorpe LJ reiterated the long-standing and well-recognised implied undertaking of non-disclosure of the other party's documents obtained under compulsion. From this they extrapolated the proposition that no information about any aspect of ancillary relief (now financial remedy) proceedings could be published in the press without leave. Arguably, the same reasoning cannot apply to information about the affairs of the parties obtained by the press at a financial remedy hearing that they are entitled to attend. Such information would include the names, addresses and occupations of the parties and everything said in court. The press will not have received such information in complicit breach of the implied undertaking and cannot thereby be fixed with contempt. Rather, they have received it by virtue of listening to it in court. At first instance in *Clibbery v Allen* [2001] 2 FLR 819 Munby J held that the Judicial Proceedings (Regulation of Reports) Act

1926 applies to ancillary relief (now financial remedy) proceedings. If this dictum is correct then the press may only publish:

(i) the names, addresses and occupations of the parties and witnesses;
(ii) a concise statement of the charges, defences and counter-charges in support of which evidence has been given;
(iii) submissions on any point of law arising in the course of the proceedings, and the decision of the court thereon;
(iv) the judgment of the court and observations made by the judge in giving judgment.

There is however a view that the press can only publish anonymous reports of proceedings observed by them. No such inhibition attaches to Court of Appeal financial remedy hearings, and the basis for this proposition is not evident.

Rule 27.11 does not address the key issues of anonymity, confidentiality, access to documentation, and the parameters of any right to report. These the judges will have to resolve. In *Spencer v Spencer* [2009] 2 FLR 1416 Munby J held that the issue whether or not the media should be excluded involved the familiar 'parallel analysis' leading to the 'ultimate balancing test': see *In re S (A Child) (Identification: Restrictions on Publication)* [2005] 1 AC 593. Thus the court has to weigh, evaluate and balance the conflicting interests protected by ECHR Articles 6, 8 and 10. In *Spencer* neither the fact that the case had begun long before the advent of the new rule, nor the mundane quotidian nature of the dispute, nor the fact that the press interest derived solely from their fascination with the particular parties tipped the balance in favour of a general exclusion. Moreover, the question of exclusion needs to be seen in the light of the fact that in both *D v D (Divorce: Media Presence)* [2009] 2 FLR 324 and *Spencer* the court held that it had power to grant an injunction preventing publication of material where its release would violate a Convention right of an adult party.

If the financial remedy hearing is related wholly or mainly to the maintenance of a minor then by section 12 of the Administration of Justice Act 1960 any publication of information concerning the proceedings not authorised by rules 12.73 and 12.75 is a contempt.

PART 27: HEARINGS AND DIRECTIONS APPOINTMENTS

Application of this Part

27.1. This Part is subject to any enactment, any provision in these rules or a practice direction.

(Rule 27.4(7) makes additional provision in relation to requirements to stay proceedings where the respondent does not appear and a relevant European regulation or international convention applies)

Reasons for a decision of the magistrates' courts

27.2.—(1) This rule applies to proceedings in a magistrates' court.

(2) After a hearing, the court will make its decision as soon as is practicable.

(3) The court must give written reasons for its decision.

(4) Paragraphs (5) and (6) apply where the functions of the court are being performed by—

(a) two or three lay justices; or
(b) by a single lay justice in accordance with these rules and Practice Direction 2A.

(5) The justices' clerk must, before the court makes an order or refuses an application or request, make notes of—

(a) the names of the justice or justices constituting the court by which the decision is made; and
(b) in consultation with the justice or justices, the reasons for the court's decision.

(6) The justices' clerk must make a written record of the reasons for the court's decision.

(7) When making an order or refusing an application, the court, or one of the justices constituting the court by which the decision is made, will announce its decision and—

(a) the reasons for that decision; or
(b) a short explanation of that decision.

(8) Subject to any other rule or practice direction, the court officer will supply a copy of the order and the reasons for the court's decision to the persons referred to in paragraph (9)—

(a) by close of business on the day when the court announces its decision; or
(b) where that time is not practicable and the proceedings are on notice, no later than 72 hours from the time when the court announced its decision.

(9) The persons referred to in paragraph (8) are—

(a) the parties (unless the court directs otherwise);
(b) any person who has actual care of a child who is the subject of proceedings, or who had such care immediately prior to the making of the order;

(c) in the case of an emergency protection order and a recovery order, the local authority in whose area the child lives or is found;

(d) in proceedings to which Part 14 applies—

    (i) an adoption agency or local authority which has prepared a report on the suitability of the applicant to adopt a child;

    (ii) a local authority which has prepared a report on the placement of the child for adoption;

(e) any other person who has requested a copy if the court is satisfied that it is required in connection with an appeal or possible appeal.

(10) In this rule, "lay justice" means a justice of the peace who is not a District Judge (Magistrates' Courts).

(Rule 12.16(5) provides for the applicant to serve a section 8 order and an order in emergency proceedings made without notice within 48 hours after the making of the order. Rule 10.6(1) provides for the applicant to serve the order in proceedings under Part 4 of the 1996 Act. Rule 4.1(3)(a) permits the court to extend or shorten the time limit for compliance with any rule. Rule 6.33 provides for other persons to be supplied with copy documents under paragraph (8).)

Attendance at hearing or directions appointment
27.3. Unless the court directs otherwise, a party shall attend a hearing or directions appointment of which that party has been given notice.

Proceedings in the absence of a party
27.4.—(1) Proceedings or any part of them shall take place in the absence of any party, including a party who is a child, if—

(a) the court considers it in the interests of the party, having regard to the matters to be discussed or the evidence likely to be given; and

(b) the party is represented by a children's guardian or solicitor,

and when considering the interests of a child under sub-paragraph (a) the court shall give the children's guardian, the solicitor for the child and, if of sufficient understanding and the court thinks it appropriate, the child, an opportunity to make representations.

(2) Subject to paragraph (3), where at the time and place appointed for a hearing or directions appointment the applicant appears but one or more of the respondents do not, the court may proceed with the hearing or appointment.

(3) The court shall not begin to hear an application in the absence of a respondent unless—

(a) it is proved to the satisfaction of the court that the respondent received reasonable notice of the date of the hearing; or

(b) the court is satisfied that the circumstances of the case justify proceeding with the hearing.

(4) Where, at the time and place appointed for a hearing or directions appointment, one or more of the respondents appear but the applicant does not, the court may refuse the application or, if sufficient evidence has previously been received, proceed in the absence of the applicant.

(5) Where, at the time and place appointed for a hearing or directions appointment, neither the applicant nor any respondent appears, the court may refuse the application.

(6) Paragraphs (2) to (5) do not apply to a hearing to which paragraphs (5) to (8) of rule 11.33 do not apply by virtue of paragraph (9) of that rule.

(7) Nothing in this rule affects any provision of a European regulation or international convention by which the United Kingdom is bound which requires a court to stay proceedings where a respondent in another State has not been adequately served with proceedings in accordance with the requirements of that regulation or convention.

Application to set aside judgment or order following failure to attend

27.5.—(1) Where a party does not attend a hearing or directions appointment and the court gives judgment or makes an order against him, the party who failed to attend may apply for the judgment or order to be set aside.

(2) An application under paragraph (1) must be supported by evidence.

(3) Where an application is made under paragraph (1), the court may grant the application only if the applicant—

(a) acted promptly on finding out that the court had exercised its power to enter judgment or make an order against the applicant;
(b) had a good reason for not attending the hearing or directions appointment; and
(c) has a reasonable prospect of success at the hearing or directions appointment.

(4) This rule does not apply to magistrates' courts.

Court bundles and place of filing of documents and bundles

27.6.—(1) The provisions of Practice Direction 27A must be followed for the preparation of court bundles and for other related matters in respect of hearings and directions appointments.

(2) Paragraph (3) applies where the file of any family proceedings has been sent from one designated county court or registry to another for the purpose of a hearing or for some other purpose.

(3) A document needed for the purpose for which the proceedings have been sent to the other court or registry must be filed in that court or registry.

(Practice Direction 27A (Family Proceedings: Court Bundles (Universal Practice to be applied in All Courts other than the Family Proceedings Courts)) does not apply to magistrates' courts.)

Representation of companies or other corporations

27.7. A company or other corporation may be represented at a hearing or directions appointment by an employee if—

(a) the employee has been authorised by the company or corporation to appear at the hearing or directions appointment on its behalf; and

(b) the court gives permission.

Impounded documents

27.8.—(1) Documents impounded by order of the court must not be released from the custody of the court except in compliance with—

(a) a court order; or

(b) a written request made by a Law Officer or the Director of Public Prosecutions.

(2) A document released from the custody of the court under paragraph (1)(b) must be released into the custody of the person who requested it.

(3) Documents impounded by order of the court, while in the custody of the court, may not be inspected except by a person authorised to do so by a court order.

Official shorthand note etc of proceedings

27.9.—(1) Unless the judge directs otherwise, an official shorthand note will be taken at the hearing in open court of proceedings pending in the High Court.

(2) An official shorthand note may be taken of any other proceedings before a judge if directions for the taking of such a note are given by the Lord Chancellor.

(3) The shorthand writer will sign the note and certify it to be a correct shorthand note of the proceedings and will retain the note unless directed by the district judge to forward it to the court.

(4) On being so directed, the shorthand writer will furnish the court with a transcript of the whole or such part of the shorthand note as may be directed.

(5) Any party, any person who has intervened in the proceedings, the Queen's Proctor or, where a declaration of parentage has been made under section 55A of the 1986 Act, the Registrar General is entitled to require from the shorthand writer a transcript of the shorthand note, and the shorthand writer will, at the request of any person so entitled, supply that person with a transcript of the whole or any part of the note on payment of the shorthand writer's charges authorised by any scheme in force providing for the taking of official shorthand notes of legal proceedings.

(6) Save as permitted by this rule, the shorthand writer will not, without the permission of the court, furnish the shorthand note or a transcript of the whole or any part of it to anyone.

(7) In these rules, references to a shorthand note include references to a

record of the proceedings made by mechanical means and in relation to such a record references to the shorthand writer include the person responsible for transcribing the record.

Hearings in private

27.10.—(1) Proceedings to which these rules apply will be held in private, except—

    (a) where these rules or any other enactment provide otherwise;

    (b) subject to any enactment, where the court directs otherwise.

(2) For the purposes of these rules, a reference to proceedings held "in private" means proceedings at which the general public have no right to be present.

Attendance at private hearings

27.11.—(1) This rule applies when proceedings are held in private, except in relation to—

    (a) hearings conducted for the purpose of judicially assisted conciliation or negotiation;

    (b) proceedings to which the following provisions apply—

        (i) Part 13 (proceedings under section 54 of the Human Fertilisation and Embryology Act 2008);

        (ii) Part 14 (procedure for applications in adoption, placement and related proceedings); and

        (iii) any proceedings identified in a practice direction as being excepted from this rule.

(2) When this rule applies, no person shall be present during any hearing other than—

    (a) an officer of the court;

    (b) a party to the proceedings;

    (c) a litigation friend for any party, or legal representative instructed to act on that party's behalf;

    (d) an officer of the service or Welsh family proceedings officer;

    (e) a witness;

    (f) duly accredited representatives of news gathering and reporting organisations; and

    (g) any other person whom the court permits to be present.

(3) At any stage of the proceedings the court may direct that persons within paragraph (2)(f) shall not attend the proceedings or any part of them, where satisfied that—

    (a) this is necessary—

        (i) in the interests of any child concerned in, or connected with, the proceedings;

(ii) for the safety or protection of a party, a witness in the proceedings, or a person connected with such a party or witness; or

(iii) for the orderly conduct of the proceedings; or

(b) justice will otherwise be impeded or prejudiced.

(4) The court may exercise the power in paragraph (3) of its own initiative or pursuant to representations made by any of the persons listed in paragraph (5), and in either case having given to any person within paragraph (2)(f) who is in attendance an opportunity to make representations.

(5) At any stage of the proceedings, the following persons may make representations to the court regarding restricting the attendance of persons within paragraph (2)(f) in accordance with paragraph (3)—

(a) a party to the proceedings;

(b) any witness in the proceedings;

(c) where appointed, any children's guardian;

(d) where appointed, an officer of the service or Welsh family proceedings officer, on behalf of the child the subject of the proceedings;

(e) the child, if of sufficient age and understanding.

(6) This rule does not affect any power of the court to direct that witnesses shall be excluded until they are called for examination.

(7) In this rule "duly accredited" refers to accreditation in accordance with any administrative scheme for the time being approved for the purposes of this rule by the Lord Chancellor.

PRACTICE DIRECTION 27A – FAMILY PROCEEDINGS: COURT BUNDLES (UNIVERSAL PRACTICE TO BE APPLIED IN ALL COURTS OTHER THAN THE FAMILY PROCEEDINGS COURT)

1.1. The President of the Family Division has issued this practice direction to achieve consistency across the country in all family courts (other than the Family Proceedings Court) in the preparation of court bundles and in respect of other related matters.

Application of the practice direction

2.1. Except as specified in paragraph 2.4, and subject to specific directions given in any particular case, the following practice applies to—

(a) all hearings of whatever nature (including but not limited to hearings in family proceedings, CPR Part 7 and Part 8 claims and appeals) before a judge of the Family Division of the High Court wherever the court may be sitting;

(b) all hearings in family proceedings in the Royal Courts of Justice ('RCJ');

(c) all hearings in the Principal Registry of the Family Division ('PRFD') at First Avenue House; and

(d) all hearings in family proceedings in all other courts except for Family Proceedings Courts.

2.2. 'Hearings' includes all appearances before a judge or district judge, whether with or without notice to other parties and whether for directions or for substantive relief.

2.3. This practice direction applies whether a bundle is being lodged for the first time or is being re-lodged for a further hearing (see paragraph 9.2).

2.4. This practice direction does not apply to—

(a) cases listed for one hour or less at a court referred to in paragraph 2.1(c) or 2.1(d); or

(b) the hearing of any urgent application if and to the extent that it is impossible to comply with it.

2.5. The Designated Family Judge responsible for any court referred to in paragraph 2.1(c) or 2.1(d) may, after such consultation as is appropriate (but in the case of hearings in the PRFD at First Avenue House only with the agreement of the Senior District Judge), direct that in that court this practice direction shall apply to all family proceedings irrespective of the length of hearing.

Responsibility for the preparation of the bundle

3.1. A bundle for the use of the court at the hearing shall be provided by the party in the position of applicant at the hearing (or, if there are cross-applications, by the party whose application was first in time) or, if that person is a litigant in person, by the first listed respondent who is not a litigant in person.

3.2. The party preparing the bundle shall paginate it. If possible the contents of the bundle shall be agreed by all parties.

Contents of the bundle

4.1. The bundle shall contain copies of all documents relevant to the hearing, in chronological order from the front of the bundle, paginated and indexed, and divided into separate sections (each section being separately paginated) as follows—

(a) preliminary documents (see paragraph 4.2) and any other case management documents required by any other practice direction;

(b) applications and orders;

(c) statements and affidavits (which must be dated in the top right corner of the front page);

(d) care plans (where appropriate);

(e) experts' reports and other reports (including those of a guardian, children's guardian or litigation friend); and

(f) other documents, divided into further sections as may be appropriate.

Copies of notes of contact visits should normally not be included in the bundle unless directed by a judge.

4.2. At the commencement of the bundle there shall be inserted the following documents ('the preliminary documents')—

(i) an up to date summary of the background to the hearing confined to those matters which are relevant to the hearing and the management of the case and limited, if practicable, to one A4 page;

(ii) a statement of the issue or issues to be determined (1) at that hearing and (2) at the final hearing;

(iii) a position statement by each party including a summary of the order or directions sought by that party (1) at that hearing and (2) at the final hearing;

(iv) an up to date chronology, if it is a final hearing or if the summary under (i) is insufficient;

(v) skeleton arguments, if appropriate, with copies of all authorities relied on; and

(vi) a list of essential reading for that hearing.

4.3. Each of the preliminary documents shall state on the front page immediately below the heading the date when it was prepared and the date of the hearing for which it was prepared.

4.4. The summary of the background, statement of issues, chronology, position statement and any skeleton arguments shall be cross-referenced to the relevant pages of the bundle.

4.5. The summary of the background, statement of issues, chronology and reading list shall in the case of a final hearing, and shall so far as practicable in the case of any other hearing, each consist of a single document in a form agreed by all parties. Where the parties disagree as to the content the fact of their disagreement and their differing contentions shall be set out at the appropriate places in the document.

4.6. Where the nature of the hearing is such that a complete bundle of all documents is unnecessary, the bundle (which need not be repaginated) may comprise only those documents necessary for the hearing, but—

(i) the summary (paragraph 4.2(i)) must commence with a statement that the bundle is limited or incomplete; and

(ii) the bundle shall if reasonably practicable be in a form agreed by all parties.

4.7. Where the bundle is re-lodged in accordance with paragraph 9.2, before it is re-lodged—

(a) the bundle shall be updated as appropriate; and
(b) all superseded documents (and in particular all outdated summaries, statements of issues, chronologies, skeleton arguments and similar documents) shall be removed from the bundle.

Format of the bundle

5.1. The bundle shall be contained in one or more A4 size ring binders or lever arch files (each lever arch file being limited to 350 pages).

5.2. All ring binders and lever arch files shall have clearly marked on the front and the spine—

(a) the title and number of the case;
(b) the court where the case has been listed;
(c) the hearing date and time;
(d) if known, the name of the judge hearing the case; and
(e) where there is more than one ring binder or lever arch file, a distinguishing letter (A, B, C etc).

Timetable for preparing and lodging the bundle

6.1. The party preparing the bundle shall, whether or not the bundle has been agreed, provide a paginated index to all other parties not less than 4 working days before the hearing (in relation to a case management conference to which the provisions of the Public Law Protocol [2003] 2 FLR 719 apply, not less than 5 working days before the case management conference).

6.2. Where counsel is to be instructed at any hearing, a paginated bundle shall (if not already in counsel's possession) be delivered to counsel by the person instructing that counsel not less than 3 working days before the hearing.

6.3. The bundle (with the exception of the preliminary documents if and insofar as they are not then available) shall be lodged with the court not less than 2 working days before the hearing, or at such other time as may be specified by the judge.

6.4. The preliminary documents shall be lodged with the court no later than 11 am on the day before the hearing and, where the hearing is before a judge of the High Court and the name of the judge is known, shall at the same time be sent by e-mail to the judge's clerk.

Lodging the bundle

7.1. The bundle shall be lodged at the appropriate office. If the bundle is lodged in the wrong place the judge may—

(a) treat the bundle as having not been lodged; and
(b) take the steps referred to in paragraph 12.

7.2. Unless the judge has given some other direction as to where the bundle in any particular case is to be lodged (for example a direction that the bundle is to be lodged with the judge's clerk) the bundle shall be lodged—

(a) for hearings in the RCJ, in the office of the Clerk of the Rules, Room TM 9.09, Royal Courts of Justice, Strand, London WC2A 2LL (DX 44450 Strand);

(b) for hearings in the PRFD at First Avenue House, at the List Office counter, 3rd floor, First Avenue House, 42/49 High Holborn, London, WC1V 6NP (DX 396 Chancery Lane); and

(c) for hearings at any other court, at such place as may be designated by the Designated Family Judge or other judge at that court and in default of any such designation at the court office of the court where the hearing is to take place.

7.3. Any bundle sent to the court by post, DX or courier shall be clearly addressed to the appropriate office and shall show the date and place of the hearing on the outside of any packaging as well as on the bundle itself.

Lodging the bundle – additional requirements for cases being heard at First Avenue House or at the RCJ

8.1. In the case of hearings at the RCJ or First Avenue House, parties shall—

(a) if the bundle or preliminary documents are delivered personally, ensure that they obtain a receipt from the clerk accepting it or them; and

(b) if the bundle or preliminary documents are sent by post or DX, ensure that they obtain proof of posting or despatch.

The receipt (or proof of posting or despatch, as the case may be) shall be brought to court on the day of the hearing and must be produced to the court if requested. If the receipt (or proof of posting or despatch) cannot be produced to the court the judge may (i) treat the bundle as having not been lodged and (ii) take the steps referred to in paragraph 12.

8.2. For hearings at the RCJ—

(a) bundles or preliminary documents delivered after 11 am on the day before the hearing will not be accepted by the Clerk of the Rules and shall be delivered—

(i) in a case where the hearing is before a judge of the High Court, directly to the clerk of the judge hearing the case;

(ii) in a case where the hearing is before a Circuit Judge, Deputy High Court Judge or Recorder, directly to the messenger at the Judge's entrance to the Queen's Building (with telephone notification to the personal assistant to the Designated Family Judge, 020 7947 7155, that this has been done).

(b) upon learning before which judge a hearing is to take place, the clerk to counsel, or other advocate, representing the party in the position of applicant shall no later than 3pm the day before the hearing—

(i) in a case where the hearing is before a judge of the High Court, telephone the clerk of the judge hearing the case;

(ii) in a case where the hearing is before a Circuit Judge, Deputy High Court Judge or Recorder, telephone the personal assistant to the Designated Family Judge;

to ascertain whether the judge has received the bundle (including the preliminary documents) and, if not, shall organise prompt delivery by the applicant's solicitor.

Removing and re-lodging the bundle

9.1. Following completion of the hearing the party responsible for the bundle shall retrieve it from the court immediately or, if that is not practicable, shall collect it from the court within five working days. Bundles which are not collected in due time may be destroyed.

9.2. The bundle shall be re-lodged for the next and any further hearings in accordance with the provisions of this practice direction and in a form which complies with paragraph 4.7.

Time estimates

10.1. In every case a time estimate (which shall be inserted at the front of the bundle) shall be prepared which shall so far as practicable be agreed by all parties and shall—

(a) specify separately (i) the time estimated to be required for judicial pre-reading and (ii) the time required for hearing all evidence and submissions and (iii) the time estimated to be required for preparing and delivering judgment; and

(b) be prepared on the basis that before they give evidence all witnesses will have read all relevant filed statements and reports.

10.2. Once a case has been listed, any change in time estimates shall be notified immediately by telephone (and then immediately confirmed in writing)—

(a) in the case of hearings in the RCJ, to the Clerk of the Rules;

(b) in the case of hearings in the

(c) in the case of hearings elsewhere, to the relevant listing officer.

Taking cases out of the list

11.1. As soon as it becomes known that a hearing will no longer be effective, whether as a result of the parties reaching agreement or for any other reason, the parties and their representatives shall immediately notify the court by telephone and by letter. The letter, which shall wherever possible be a joint letter sent on behalf of all parties with their signatures applied or appended, shall include—

(a) a short background summary of the case;
(b) the written consent of each party who consents and, where a party does not consent, details of the steps which have been taken to obtain that party's consent and, where known, an explanation of why that consent has not been given;
(c) a draft of the order being sought; and
(d) enough information to enable the court to decide (i) whether to take the case out of the list and (ii) whether to make the proposed order.

Penalties for failure to comply with the practice direction

12.1. Failure to comply with any part of this practice direction may result in the judge removing the case from the list or putting the case further back in the list and may also result in a 'wasted costs' order in accordance with CPR Part 48.7 or some other adverse costs order.

Commencement of the practice direction and application of other practice directions

13.1. This practice direction replaces *President's Direction (Family Proceedings: Court Bundles)* [2000] 1 FLR 536 and shall have effect from 2 October 2006.

14.1. Any reference in any other practice direction to *President's Direction (Family Proceedings: Court Bundles)* [2000] 1 FLR 536 shall be read as if substituted by a reference to this practice direction.

15.1. This practice direction should where appropriate be read in conjunction with *President's Direction (Human Rights Act 1998)* [2000] 2 FLR 429 *[now PD 29B, below]* and with *Practice Direction (Care Cases: Judicial Continuity and Judicial Case Management)* appended to the Public Law Protocol [2003] 2 FLR 719. In particular, nothing in this practice direction is to be read as removing or altering any obligation to comply with the requirements of the Public Law Protocol.

* * * * *

PRACTICE DIRECTION 27B – ATTENDANCE OF MEDIA REPRESENTATIVES AT HEARINGS IN FAMILY PROCEEDINGS

(This practice direction should be read as if amended by Re X (a child) (residence and contact: rights of media attendance) [2009] EWHC 1728 (Fam) [87])

Introduction

1.1. This Practice Direction supplements rule 27.11 of the Family Procedure Rules 2010 and deals with the right of representatives of news gathering and reporting organisations ('media representatives') to attend at hearings of family proceedings which take place in private subject to the discretion of the court to exclude such representatives from the whole or part of any hearing on specified grounds.[1] It takes effect on 27 April 2009.

Matters unchanged by the rule

2.1. Rule 27.11(1)(a) contains an express exception in respect of hearings which are conducted for the purpose of judicially assisted conciliation or negotiation and media representatives do not have a right to attend these hearings. Financial Dispute Resolution hearings will come within this exception. First Hearing Dispute Resolution appointments in private law Children Act cases will also come within this exception to the extent that the judge plays an active part in the conciliation process. Where the judge plays no part in the conciliation process or where the conciliation element of a hearing is complete and the judge is adjudicating upon the issues between the parties, media representatives should be permitted to attend, subject to the discretion of the court to exclude them on the specified grounds. Conciliation meetings or negotiation conducted between the parties with the assistance of an officer of the service or a Welsh Family Proceedings officer, and without the presence of the judge, are not 'hearings' within the meaning of this rule and media representatives have no right to attend such appointments.

The exception in rule 27.11 does not operate to exclude media representatives from—

(a) Hearings to consider applications brought under Parts IV and V of the Children Act 1989, including Case Management Conferences and Issues Resolution Hearings

(b) Hearings relating to findings of fact

(c) Interim hearings

(d) Final hearings.

The rights of media representatives to attend such hearings are limited only by the powers of the court to exclude such attendance on the limited grounds and subject to the procedures set out in paragraphs (3) to (5) of rule 27.11.

2.2. During any hearing, courts should consider whether the exception in rule 27.11(1)(a) becomes applicable so that media representatives should be directed to withdraw.

2.3. The provisions of the rules permitting the attendance of media representatives and the disclosure to third parties of information relating to the proceedings do not entitle a media representative to receive or peruse court documents referred to in the course of evidence, submissions or judgment without the permission of the court or otherwise in accordance with Part 12, Chapter 7 of the Family Procedure Rules 2010 and Practice Direction 12G (rules relating to disclosure to third parties). (This is in contrast to the position in civil proceedings, where the court sits in public and where members of the public are entitled to seek copies of certain documents[2])

2.4. The question of attendance of media representatives at hearings in family proceedings to which rule 27.11 and this guidance apply must be distinguished from statutory restrictions on publication and disclosure of information relating to proceedings, which continue to apply and are unaffected by the rule and this guidance.

2.5. The prohibition in section 97(2) of the Children Act 1989, on publishing material intended to or likely to identify a child as being involved in proceedings or the address or school of any such child, is limited to the duration of the proceedings.[3] However, the limitations imposed by section 12 of the Administration of Justice Act 1960 on publication of information relating to certain proceedings in private[4] apply during and after the proceedings. In addition, in proceedings to which s.97(2) of the Children Act 1989 applies the court should continue to consider at the conclusion of the proceedings whether there are any outstanding welfare issues which require a continuation of the protection afforded during the course of the proceedings by that provision.

Aims of the guidance

3.1. This Practice Direction is intended to provide guidance regarding—

(a) the handling of applications to exclude media representatives from the whole or part of a hearing: and

(b) the exercise of the court's discretion to exclude media representatives whether upon the court's own motion or any such application

3.2. While the guidance does not aim to cover all possible eventualities, it should be complied with so far as consistent in all the circumstances with the just determination of the proceedings.

Identification of media representatives as 'accredited'

4.1. Media representatives will be expected to carry with them identification sufficient to enable court staff, or if necessary the court itself, to verify that they are 'accredited' representatives of news gathering or reporting organisations within the meaning of the rule.

4.2. By virtue of paragraph (7) of the rule, it is for the Lord Chancellor to approve a scheme which will provide for accreditation. The Lord Chancellor has decided that the scheme operated by the UK Press Card Authority provides sufficient accreditation; a card issued under that scheme will be the expected form of identification, and production of the Card will be both necessary and sufficient to demonstrate accreditation.

4.3. A media representative unable to demonstrate accreditation in accordance with the UK Press Card Authority scheme, so as to be able to attend by virtue of paragraph (2)(f) of the rule, may nevertheless be permitted to attend at the court's discretion under paragraph (2)(g).

Exercise of the discretion to exclude media representatives from all or part of the proceedings

5.1. The rule anticipates and should be applied on the basis that media representatives have a right to attend family proceedings throughout save and to the extent that the court exercises its discretion to exclude them from the whole or part of any proceedings on one or more of the grounds set out in paragraph (3) of the rule.

5.2. When considering the question of exclusion on any of the grounds set out in paragraph (4) of the rule the court should—

(a) specifically identify whether the risk to which such ground is directed arises from the mere fact of media presence at the particular hearing or hearings the subject of the application or whether the risk identified can be adequately addressed by exclusion of media representatives from a part only of such hearing or hearings;

(b) consider whether the reporting or disclosure restrictions which apply by operation of law, or which the court otherwise has power to order will provide sufficient protection to the party on whose behalf the application is made or any of the persons referred to in paragraph (3)(a) of the rule;

(c) consider the safety of the parties in cases in which the court considers there are particular physical or health risks against which reporting restrictions may be inadequate to afford protection;

(d) in the case of any vulnerable adult or child who is unrepresented before the court, consider the extent to which the court should of its own motion take steps to protect the welfare of that adult or child.

5.3. Paragraph (3)(a)(iii) of the rule permits exclusion where necessary 'for the orderly conduct of proceedings'. This enables the court to address practical problems presented by media attendance. In particular, it may be difficult or even impossible physically to accommodate all (or indeed any) media representatives who wish to attend a particular hearing on the grounds of the restricted size or layout of the court room in which it is being heard. Court staff will use their best efforts to identify more suitable accommodation in advance of any hearing which appears likely to attract particular media attention, and to move hearings to larger court rooms where possible. However, the court should not be required to adjourn a hearing in order for larger accommodation to be sought where this will involve significant disruption or delay in the proceedings.

5.4. Paragraph (3)(b) of the rule permits exclusion where, unless the media are excluded, justice will be impeded or prejudiced for some reason other than those set out in sub-paragraph (a). Reasons of administrative inconvenience are not sufficient. Examples of circumstances where the impact on justice of continued attendance might be sufficient to necessitate exclusion may include—

(a) a hearing relating to the parties' finances where the information being considered includes price sensitive information (such as confidential information which could affect the share price of a publicly quoted company); or

(b) any hearing at which a witness (other than a party) states for credible reasons that he or she will not give evidence in front of media representatives, or where there appears to the court to be a significant risk that a witness will not give full or frank evidence in the presence of media representatives.

5.5. In the event of a decision to exclude media representatives, the court should state brief reasons for the decision.

Applications to exclude media representatives from all or part of proceedings

6.1. The court may exclude media representatives on the permitted grounds of its own motion or after hearing representations from the interested persons listed at paragraph (5) of the rule. Where exclusion is proposed, any media representatives who are present are entitled to make representations about that proposal. There is, however, no requirement to adjourn proceedings to enable media representatives who are not present to attend in order to make such representations, and in such a case the court should not adjourn unless satisfied of the necessity to do so having regard to the additional cost and delay which would thereby be caused.

6.2. Applications to exclude media representatives should normally be dealt with as they arise and by way of oral representations, unless the court directs otherwise.

6.3. When media representatives are expected to attend a particular hearing (for example, where a party is encouraging media interest and attendance) and a party intends to apply to the court for the exclusion of the media, that party should, if practicable, give advance notice to the court, to the other parties and (where appointed) any children's guardian, officer of the service or Welsh Family Proceedings officer, NYAS or other representative of the child of any intention to seek the exclusion of media representatives from all or part of the proceedings. Equally, legal representatives and parties should ensure that witnesses are aware of the right of media representatives to attend and should notify the court at an early stage of the intention of any witness to request the exclusion of media representatives.

6.4. Prior notification by the court of a pending application for exclusion will not be given to media interests unless the court so directs. However, where such an application has been made, the applicant must where possible, notify the relevant media organisations.

Footnotes

1. It does not, accordingly, apply where hearings are held in open court where the general public including media representatives may attend as of right, such as committal hearings or the hearing of matrimonial or civil partnership causes.
2. See *GIO Services Ltd v Liverpool and London Ltd* [1999] 1 WLR 984
3. See *Clayton v Clayton* [2006] EWCA Civ 878
4. In particular proceedings which – (a) relate to the exercise of the inherent jurisdiction of the High Court with respect to minors; (b) are brought under the Children Act 1989; or (c) otherwise relate wholly or mainly to the maintenance or upbringing of a minor.

* * * * *

PRACTICE DIRECTION 27C – ATTENDANCE OF MEDIA REPRESENTATIVES AT HEARINGS IN FAMILY PROCEEDINGS

(This practice direction should be read as if amended by Re X (a child) (residence and contact: rights of media attendance) [2009] EWHC 1728 (Fam) [87])

Introduction

1.1. This Practice Direction supplements rule 27.11 of the Family Procedure Rules 2010 ('the Rules') and deals with the right of representatives of news gathering and reporting organisations ('media representatives') to attend at hearings of relevant proceedings[1] subject to the discretion of the court to exclude such representatives from the whole or part of any hearing on specified grounds[2]. It takes effect on 27th April 2009. References to a 'hearing' within this Practice Direction include reference to a directions appointment, whether conducted by the justices, a district judge or a justices' clerk.

Matters unchanged by the rule

2.1. Rule 27.11(1) contains an express exception in respect of hearings which are conducted for the purpose of judicially assisted conciliation or negotiation and media representatives do not have a right to attend these hearings. First Hearing Dispute Resolution appointments in private law Children Act cases will come within this exception to the extent that the justices, a district judge or a justices' clerk play an active part in the conciliation process. Where the justices, a district judge or a justices' clerk play no part in the conciliation process or where the conciliation element of a hearing is complete and the court is adjudicating upon the issues between the parties, media representatives should be permitted to attend subject to the discretion of the court to exclude them on the specified grounds. Conciliation meetings or negotiation conducted between the parties with the assistance of an officer of the service or a Welsh Family Proceedings officer, and without the presence of the justices, a district judge or a justices' clerk, are not 'hearings' within the meaning of this rule and media representatives have no right to attend such appointments.

The exception in rule 27.11(1) does not operate to exclude media representatives from—

(a) Hearings to consider applications brought under Parts IV and V of the Children Act 1989, including Case Management Conferences and Issues Resolution Hearings

(b) Hearings relating to findings of fact

(c) Interim hearings

(d) Final hearings.

The rights of media representatives to attend such hearings are limited only by the powers of the court to exclude such attendance on the limited grounds and subject to the procedures set out in paragraphs (3) to (5) of rule 27.11.

2.2. During any hearing, the court should consider whether the exception in rule 27.11(1) becomes applicable so that media representatives should be directed to withdraw.

2.3. The provisions of the rules permitting the attendance of media representatives and the disclosure to third parties of information relating to the proceedings do not entitle a media representative to receive or peruse court documents referred to in the course of evidence, submissions or decisions of the court (in particular, written reasons) without the permission of the court or otherwise in accordance with Part 12, Chapter 7 of the Family Procedure Rules 2010 and Practice Direction 12G.

2.4. The question of attendance of media representatives at hearings in family proceedings to which rule 27.11 and this guidance apply must be distinguished from statutory restrictions on publication and disclosure of information relating to proceedings, which continue to apply and are unaffected by the rule and this guidance.

2.5. The prohibition in section 97(2) of the Children Act 1989, on publishing material intended to or likely to identify a child as being involved in proceedings or the address or school of any such child, is limited to the duration of the proceedings[3]. However, the limitations imposed by section 12 of the Administration of Justice Act 1960 on publication of information relating to certain proceedings in private[4] apply during and after the proceedings. In addition, in the course of proceedings to which s.97(2) of the Children Act 1989 applies the court should consider whether at the conclusion of the proceedings there may be outstanding welfare issues which may require a continuation of the protection afforded during the course of the proceedings by s. 97 (2) of the Children Act 1989 and which are not fully met by a direction under section 39 Children and Young Persons Act 1933[5], so that any party seeking such protection has an opportunity to apply to the county court or High Court for the appropriate order before the proceedings are finally concluded.

Aims of the guidance

3.1. This Practice Direction is intended to provide guidance regarding —

(a) the handling of applications to exclude media representatives from the whole or part of a hearing: and

(b) the exercise of the court's discretion to exclude media representatives whether upon the court's own motion or any such application.

3.2. While the guidance does not aim to cover all possible eventualities, it should be complied with so far as consistent in all the circumstances with the just determination of the proceedings.

Identification of media representatives as 'accredited'

4.1. Media representatives will be expected to carry with them identification sufficient to enable court staff, or if necessary the court itself, to verify that they are 'accredited' representatives of news gathering or reporting organisations within the meaning of the rule.

4.2. By virtue of paragraph (7) of the rule, it is for the Lord Chancellor to approve a scheme which will provide for accreditation. The Lord Chancellor has decided that the scheme operated by the UK Press Card Authority provides sufficient accreditation: a card issued under that scheme will be the expected form of identification, and production of the Card will be both necessary and sufficient to demonstrate accreditation.

4.3. A media representative unable to demonstrate accreditation in accordance with the UK Press Card Authority scheme so as to be able to attend by virtue of paragraph (2)(f) of the rule may nevertheless be permitted to attend at the court's discretion under paragraph (2)(g).

Exercise of the discretion to exclude media representatives from all or part of the proceedings

5.1. The rule anticipates and should be applied on the basis that media representatives have a right to attend family proceedings throughout save and to the extent that the court exercises its discretion to exclude them from the whole or part of any proceedings on one or more of the grounds set out in paragraph (3) of the rule.

5.2. When considering the question of exclusion on any of the grounds set out in paragraph (3) of the rule the court should—

(a) specifically identify whether the risk to which such ground is directed arises from the mere fact of media presence at the particular hearing or hearings the subject of the application or whether the risk identified can be adequately addressed by exclusion of media representatives from a part only of such hearing or hearings;

(b) consider whether the reporting or disclosure restrictions which apply by operation of law, or which the court otherwise has power to order will provide sufficient protection to the party on whose behalf the application is made or any of the persons referred to in paragraph (3)(a) of the rule;

(c) consider the safety of the parties in cases in which the court considers there are particular physical or health risks against which reporting restrictions may be inadequate to afford protection;

(d) in the case of any vulnerable adult or child who is unrepresented before the court, consider the extent to which the court should of its own motion take steps to protect the welfare of that adult or child.

5.3. Paragraph (3)(a)(iii) of the rule permits exclusion where necessary 'for the orderly conduct of proceedings'. This enables the court to address practical problems presented by media attendance. In particular, it may be difficult or even impossible physically to accommodate all (or indeed any) media representatives who wish to attend a particular hearing on the grounds of the restricted size or layout of the court room in which it is being heard. Court staff will use their best efforts to identify more suitable accommodation in advance of any hearing which appears likely to attract particular media attention, and to move hearings to larger court rooms where possible. However, the court should not be required to adjourn a hearing in order for larger accommodation to be sought where this will involve significant disruption or delay in the proceedings.

5.4. Paragraph (3)(b) of the rule permits exclusion where, unless the media are excluded, justice will be impeded or prejudiced for some reason other than those set out in sub-paragraph (a). Reasons of administrative inconvenience are not sufficient. An example of circumstances where the impact on justice of continued attendance might be sufficient to necessitate exclusion would be any hearing at which a witness (other than a party) states for credible reasons that he or she will not give evidence in front of media representatives, or where there appears to the court to be a significant risk that a witness will not give full or frank evidence in the presence of media representatives.

5.5. In the event of a decision to exclude media representatives, the court should state brief reasons for the decision.

Applications to exclude media representatives from all or part of proceedings

6.1. The court may exclude media representatives on the permitted grounds of its own motion or after hearing representations from the interested persons listed at paragraph (5) of the rule. Where exclusion is proposed, any media representatives who are present are entitled to make representations about that proposal. There is, however, no requirement to adjourn proceedings to enable media representatives who are not present to attend in order to make such representations, and in such a case the court should not adjourn unless satisfied of the necessity to do so having regard to the additional cost and delay which would thereby be caused.

6.2. Applications to exclude media representatives should normally be dealt with as they arise and by way of oral representations, unless the court directs otherwise.

6.3. When media representatives are expected to attend a particular hearing (for example, where a party is encouraging media interest and attendance) and a party intends to apply to the court for the exclusion of the media, such party should, if practicable, give advance notice to the court, to the other parties and (where appointed) any children's guardian, officer of the service or Welsh Family Proceedings officer, NYAS or other representative of the child of any intention to seek the exclusion of media representatives from all or part of the proceedings. Equally, legal representatives and parties should ensure that witnesses are aware of the right of media representatives to attend and should notify the court at an early stage of the intention of any witness to request the exclusion of media representatives.

6.4. Prior notification by the court of a pending application for exclusion will not be given to media interests unless the court so directs. However, where such an application has been made, the applicant must where possible, notify the relevant media organisations.

Footnotes
1. 'Relevant proceedings' are defined in rule 1 of the Rules by reference to section 93(3) of the Children Act 1989.
2. It does not, accordingly, apply where hearings are held in open court where the general public including media representatives attend as of right.
3. See *Clayton v Clayton* [2006] EWCA Civ 878.
4. In particular proceedings which – (a) relate to the exercise of the inherent jurisdiction of the High Court with respect to minors; (b) are brought under the Children Act 1989; or (c) otherwise relate wholly or mainly to the maintenance or upbringing of a minor.
5. Power of court to prohibit.

* * * * *

Part 28

Commentary on Part 28:
COSTS

The basic rule

The court may at any time make such order as to costs as it thinks just (rule 28.1). The CPR general rule in CPR rule 44.3(2)(a) that the unsuccessful party will be ordered to pay the costs of the successful party does not apply to any family proceedings. It will be recalled that in *Gojkovic v Gojkovic (No. 2)* [1991] 2 FLR 233, [1992] 1 All ER 267, CA Butler-Sloss LJ held that in ancillary relief proceedings, notwithstanding the disapplication in family proceedings of the general 'costs follow the event' rule in RSC Ord 62, rule 3(5), 'prima facie costs should follow the event'. As will be seen there is a sizeable number of types of financial proceedings that are not covered by the 'no order' principle which first found expression in FPR 1991 rule 2.71 with effect from April 2006 and is now to be found expressed in FPR 2010 rule 28.3. Whether the rule in *Gojkovic* will apply to those proceedings remains to be decided.

Application of CPR regime

Under the former FPR 1991 rule 10.27 swathes of the CPR costs regime were applied to family proceedings, save that by rule 2.71 a different prescription was devised for ancillary relief applications. That scheme is replicated almost identically in Part 28, save that a number of parts of the relevant CPR rules are omitted or amended.

By Part 28 all of CPR Parts 43 (Scope of Costs Rules and Definitions), 47 (Procedure for Detailed Assessment of Costs and Default Provisions) and 48 (Costs – Special Cases) are applied to all family proceedings, save that Part 47 shall not apply to proceedings in magistrates' courts. The following rules within CPR Parts 44 and 45 are also applied, save where noted:

Part 44

Scope of this Part	Rule 44.1
Solicitor's duty to notify client	Rule 44.2

Court's discretion and circumstances to be taken into account when exercising its discretion as to costs	Rule 44.3 except (2) and (3)
Costs orders relating to funding arrangements	Rule 44.3A
Limits on recovery under funding arrangements	Rule 44.3B
Orders in respect of pro bono representation	Rule 44.3C but not in FPC
Basis of assessment	Rule 44.4
Factors to be taken into account in deciding the amount of costs	Rule 44.5
Fixed costs	Rule 44.6
Procedure for assessing costs	Rule 44.7
Time for complying with an order for costs	Rule 44.8
Special situations	Rule 44.13 except (1A) and (1B)
Court's powers in relation to misconduct	Rule 44.14
Providing information about funding arrangements	Rule 44.15
Adjournment where legal representative seeks to challenge disallowance of any amount of percentage increase	Rule 44.16
Application of costs rules	Rule 44.17
Part 45	
Fixed enforcement costs	Rule 45.6 but not in FPC

For Part 44 in the form in which it is applied by FPR 2010 rule 28(2), see *@eGlance*.

This application of the CPR regime is subject to rule 28.3, which reproduces the existing FPR 1991 rule 2.71 prescription for (some) financial remedy proceedings. It should be noted that the definition of 'financial remedy proceedings' within rule 2(3) is altered for the purposes of rule 28.3. See *below*.

PD 28A applies the CPR Costs PD with modifications that do no more than reflect that certain parts of the CPR regime have not been applied. Specifically the CPR Costs PD applies as follows:

- to family proceedings generally, other than in magistrates' courts, with the exception of sections 6, 15, 16, 17 and 23A;
- to family proceedings generally, in magistrates' courts only, with the exception of sections 6, 15, 16, 17, 23A and sections 28 to 49A;
- to financial remedy proceedings, other than in magistrates' courts, with the exception of section 6, paragraphs 8.1 to 8.4 of section 8 and sections 15, 16, 17 and 23A;
- to financial remedy proceedings in magistrates' courts only, with the

exception of section 6, paragraphs 8.1 to 8.4 of section 8, sections 15, 16, 17, 23A and sections 28 to 49A.

Essentially, the old costs regime is unchanged, although as is noted *below* there are some important changes concerning which kinds of financial applications do and do not fall within rule 28.3, which incorporates the principle of no order as to costs for certain financial applications.

It is not within the scope of this Commentary to seek to explain or even to summarise at any length the CPR costs regime as applied, in part, to family proceedings generally, and specifically to those financial applications not covered by rule 28.3. The applications which are not covered are:

- an order for maintenance pending suit or an order for maintenance pending outcome of proceedings;
- an interim periodical payments order;
- any other interim order made within financial order proceedings (apart from an interim variation order). An example would be an order on a preliminary issue;
- an order under Schedule 1 to the Children Act 1989;
- an order under section 27 of the Matrimonial Causes Act 1973 or under Part 9 of Schedule 5 to the Civil Partnership Act 2004 (failure to maintain);
- an order under section 35 of the Matrimonial Causes Act 1973 under paragraph 69 of Schedule 5 to the Civil Partnership Act 2004 (variation of maintenance agreement);
- an order under Part 1 of the Domestic Proceedings and Magistrates' Courts Act 1978 or under Schedule 6 to the Civil Partnership Act 2004 (maintenance proceedings in magistrates' court);
- an order under section 36 Matrimonial Causes Act 1973 or para 73 of Schedule 5 to the Civil Partnership Act 2004 (alteration of maintenance agreement after death of one party);
- an order under section 17 of the Married Women's Property Act 1882 or section 66 of the Civil Partnership Act 2004 (question as to property to be decided in summary way);
- an order under section 13 of the Matrimonial and Family Proceedings Act 1984 or para 4 of Schedule 7 to the Civil Partnership Act 2004 (permission to apply for a financial remedy after overseas proceedings);
- an order for the transfer of a tenancy under section 53 of, and Schedule 7 to the Family Law Act 1996;
- an order preventing avoidance under section 32L of the Child Support Act 1991.

The no order principle in rule 28.3 will not apply to the costs of a person joined to the proceedings against his will (*KSO v MJO and JMO (PSO intervening)* [2009] 1 FLR 1036) nor to the costs of a person who intervenes in the proceedings (*Baker v Rowe* [2010] 1 FLR 761, CA). Nor does it apply to the costs of civil proceedings heard together with the ancillary relief proceedings (*Ben Hashem v Ali Shayif and Radfan Ltd* [2009] 2 FLR 896); nor to an application made to set aside an ancillary relief order on the grounds of mistake and/or non-disclosure (*Judge v Judge* [2009] 1 FLR 1287, CA).

In these proceedings the following key parts of CPR rule 44.3 apply:

(4) In deciding what order (if any) to make about costs, the court must have regard to all the circumstances, including—

   (a) the conduct of all the parties;

   (b) whether a party has succeeded on part of his case, even if he has not been wholly successful; and

   (c) any payment into court or admissible offer to settle made by a party which is drawn to the court's attention, and which is not an offer to which costs consequences under Part 36 apply.

(5) The conduct of the parties includes—

   (a) conduct before, as well as during, the proceedings and in particular the extent to which the parties followed the Practice Direction (Pre-Action Conduct) or any relevant pre-action protocol;

   (b) whether it was reasonable for a party to raise, pursue or contest a particular allegation or issue;

   (c) the manner in which a party has pursued or defended his case or a particular allegation or issue; and

   (d) whether a claimant who has succeeded in his claim, in whole or in part, exaggerated his claim.

It should be *very clearly noted indeed* that by virtue of sub-rule (4)(c), *Calderbank* letters are admissible in the costs phase of the proceedings listed above; and, following well understood principle should then strongly influence if not dictate the outcome of the costs application.

The removal of maintenance pending suit and comparable orders from the regime of no order as to costs is a significant change designed to meet the complaint that the 'no order' principle effectively emasculated the economic value of many such orders. It is slightly surprising that the same distinction has not been carried through to variation orders, whether interim or final, where similar concerns have been raised, although PD 28A para 4.4 supplies a strong steer in favour of making orders for costs in such proceedings.

Costs in (some) financial remedy proceedings

Rule 28.3 replicates FPR rule 2.71 save that, as already noted, it excludes orders for maintenance pending suit and comparable orders, but not orders for variation, whether interim or final. The list of financial remedies subject to rule 28.3 is as follows:

- a financial order, except an order for maintenance pending suit or an order for maintenance pending outcome of proceedings or an interim periodical payments order or any other interim order made within financial order proceedings (apart from an interim variation order);
- an order under Part 3 of the Matrimonial and Family Proceedings Act 1984 Act or under Schedule 7 to the Civil Partnership Act 2004; or
- an order under section 10(2) of the Matrimonial Causes Act 1973 or under section 48(2) of the Civil Partnership Act 2004.

The rule incorporates and explains the no order rule in the following way:

(5) Subject to paragraph (6), the general rule in financial remedy proceedings is that the court will not make an order requiring one party to pay the costs of another party.

(6) The court may make an order requiring one party to pay the costs of another party at any stage of the proceedings where it considers it appropriate to do so because of the conduct of a party in relation to the proceedings (whether before or during them).

(7) In deciding what order (if any) to make under paragraph (6), the court must have regard to—

  (a) any failure by a party to comply with these rules, any order of the court or any practice direction which the court considers relevant;

  (b) any open offer to settle made by a party;

  (c) whether it was reasonable for a party to raise, pursue or contest a particular allegation or issue;

  (d) the manner in which a party has pursued or responded to the application or a particular allegation or issue;

  (e) any other aspect of a party's conduct in relation to proceedings which the court considers relevant; and

  (f) the financial effect on the parties of any costs order.

(8) No offer to settle which is not an open offer to settle is admissible at any stage of the proceedings, except as provided by rule 9.17.

PD 28A elaborates this rule: in considering the conduct of the parties for the purposes of rule 28.3(6) and (7) (including any open offers to settle), the court will have regard to the obligation of the parties to help the court to further the overriding objective (see rules 1.1 and 1.3) and will take into account the nature, importance and complexity of the issues in the case. This may be of particular significance in applications for variation orders and interim variation orders or other cases where there is a risk of the costs becoming disproportionate to the amounts in dispute (para 4.4).

In *M v M* [2010] 1 FLR 256 emphasis was placed on the requirement of reasonableness in litigating particular issues: a party who had behaved unreasonably in relation to a number of issues was condemned to pay approximately 20% of the other party's overall costs.

Parties who intend to seek a costs order against another party in proceedings to which rule 28.3 applies should ordinarily make this plain in open correspondence or in skeleton arguments before the date of the hearing. In any case where a summary assessment of costs to be awarded under rule 28.3 would be appropriate parties are under an obligation to file a statement of costs in CPR Form N260 (PD 28A para 4.5). This must be filed 24 hours before the date fixed for hearing (CPR Costs PD para 13.4(4)).

Reported cases and practitioners' experience demonstrates that the 'no order' principle is by no means absolute and does not apply across the board.

The starting point is that at the final hearing unpaid costs will be 'taken off the top' as a debt of the party in question. For this purpose a much more detailed costs estimate in Form H1 is now required at trial. The approach in *Leadbeater v Leadbeater* [1985] FLR 789 (of adding back costs already paid) is now outmoded.

What of the position where there is a striking disparity in the costs each party incurs? In *RH v RH* [2008] 2 FLR 2142, a case proceeding under the old rules, W had incurred £265,000 costs and H £486,000. When calculating the relevant assets, and the award, Singer J had in effect notionally increased H's assets by £225,000 (by disregarding his unpaid costs of £65,000 and adding back £160,000 of costs already paid). The lump sum awarded to H would otherwise have been greater. In the judgment leading to the award he had stated:

> That is intended as an entirely neutral adjustment and is subject to the submissions I will no doubt hear about costs. At this stage I can only attempt to mitigate the distorting effect on my award of the unequal costs burden, as the reasons for this very large difference between the liabilities incurred on each side have not been fully explored.

In the reported costs judgment, Singer J concluded that the disparity had not been justified, and therefore that the approach adopted was not unfair to H, 'nor to W who would otherwise be saddled with a half-share of what I do now conclude was his unreasonable and excessive costs expenditure.' Whether this approach of adding back excessive costs applies under the current regime will have to be decided, but there would seem to be no reason why it should not be adopted where warranted.

Calderbank offers are no longer admissible when determining an application for costs in proceedings governed by Rule 28.3. 'Without Prejudice' offers can still be made but can be referred to only at the FDR hearing. The terms of open proposals to settle are however expressly to be considered in determining whether or not litigation misconduct has occurred. Clearly the court in determining the outcome should not be influenced by the parties' open positions, and should be ready to penalise in costs a party who has adopted an open position that is manifestly unreasonable or who has failed to make an open offer at all.

An important provision is FPR rule 28.3(7)(f) which requires the court to have regard to the financial effect of a costs order upon a party: for instance where an adverse costs order might undermine the judicial objective of the order, such as to provide secure housing.

Provisions common to both regimes

The following important provisions of the CPR regime are common to costs proceedings whether governed by rule 28.3, or not.

- CPR rule 44.3(8) and Costs PD para 12.3: payment on account of costs.
- CPR rule 44.7 and Costs PD para 13: summary assessment of costs.
- CPR rule 44.8: time for compliance with an order for costs is set at 14 days after judgment.

Under the CPR Costs PD para 13.2 the general rule is that there should be a summary assessment of costs where the case has lasted not more than one day. The statement of costs must follow as closely as possible CPR Form N260 (para 13.3) and must be served not less than 24 hours before the date fixed for the hearing (para 13.4).

Costs allowance

By PD 28A para 4.6 an interim financial order which includes an element to allow a party to deal with legal fees is an order made pursuant to section 22 of the Matrimonial Causes Act 1973 or an order under para 38 of Schedule 5 to the 2004 Act, and is not a 'costs order' within the meaning of rule 28.3. The principles applicable to a claim for a costs allowance are set out in *Currey v Currey (No 2)* [2007] 1 FLR 946, CA. The applicant must show that he or she cannot reasonably procure legal advice and representation by any other means. Moreover, the subject matter of the application will always be relevant as will the reasonableness of the applicant's stance in the proceedings.

PART 28: COSTS

Costs

28.1. The court may at any time make such order as to costs as it thinks just.

Application of other rules

28.2.—(1) Subject to rule 28.3 and to paragraph (2), Parts 43, 44 (except rules 44.3(2) and (3), 44.9 to 44.12C, 44.13(1A) and (1B) and 44.18 to 20), 47 and 48 and rule 45.6 of the CPR apply to costs in proceedings, with the following modifications—

  (a) in rule 43.2(1)(c)(ii), "district judge" includes a district judge of the principal registry;
  (b) in rule 48.7(1) after "section 51(6) of the Senior Courts Act 1981" insert "or section 145A of the Magistrates' Courts Act 1980[113]";
  (c) in accordance with any provisions in Practice Direction 28A; and
  (d) any other necessary modifications.

  (2) Part 47 and rules 44.3C and 45.6 of the CPR do not apply to proceedings in a magistrates' court.

Costs in financial remedy proceedings

28.3.—(1) This rule applies in relation to financial remedy proceedings.

  (2) Rule 44.3(1), (4) and (5) of the CPR do not apply to financial remedy proceedings.

  (3) Rule 44.3(6) to (9) of the CPR apply to an order made under this rule as they apply to an order made under rule 44.3 of the CPR.

  (4) In this rule—

  (a) "costs" has the same meaning as in rule 43.2(1)(a) of the CPR; and
  (b) "financial remedy proceedings" means proceedings for—
      (i) a financial order except an order for maintenance pending suit, an order for maintenance pending outcome of proceedings, an interim periodical payments order or any other form of interim order for the purposes of rule 9.7(1)(a), (b), (c) and (e);
      (ii) an order under Part 3 of the 1984 Act;
      (iii) an order under Schedule 7 to the 2004 Act;
      (iv) an order under section 10(2) of the 1973 Act [114];
      (v) an order under section 48(2) of the 2004 Act.

  (5) Subject to paragraph (6), the general rule in financial remedy proceedings is that the court will not make an order requiring one party to pay the costs of another party.

  (6) The court may make an order requiring one party to pay the costs of another party at any stage of the proceedings where it considers it

appropriate to do so because of the conduct of a party in relation to the proceedings (whether before or during them).

(7) In deciding what order (if any) to make under paragraph (6), the court must have regard to—

(a) any failure by a party to comply with these rules, any order of the court or any practice direction which the court considers relevant;
(b) any open offer to settle made by a party;
(c) whether it was reasonable for a party to raise, pursue or contest a particular allegation or issue;
(d) the manner in which a party has pursued or responded to the application or a particular allegation or issue;
(e) any other aspect of a party's conduct in relation to proceedings which the court considers relevant; and
(f) the financial effect on the parties of any costs order.

(8) No offer to settle which is not an open offer to settle is admissible at any stage of the proceedings, except as provided by rule 9.17.

Wasted costs orders in the magistrates' court: appeals

28.4. A legal or other representative against whom a wasted costs order is made in the magistrates' court may appeal to the Crown Court.

PRACTICE DIRECTION 28A – COSTS

This Practice Direction supplements FPR Part 28

Application and modification of the CPR

1.1 Rule 28.2 provides that subject to rule 28.3 of the FPR and to paragraph (2) of rule 28.2, Parts 43, 44 (except rules 44.3(2) and(3), 44.9 to 44.12C, 44.13(1A) and (1B) and 44.18 to 20), 47 and 48 and rule 45.6 of the CPR apply to costs in family proceedings with the modifications listed in rule 28.2(1)(a) to (d). Rule 28.2(1)(c) refers to modifications in accordance with this Practice Direction.

1.2 In addition to the modifications to the CPR listed in rule 28.2(1), in rule 48.1(1)(b) after paragraph (ii) insert "(iii) section 68A of the Magistrates' Courts Act 1980.".

1.3 Rule 28.2(2) provides that Part 47 and rules 44.3C and 45.6 of the CPR do not apply to proceedings in a magistrates' court.

Application and modification of the Practice Direction supplementing CPR Parts 43 to 48

2.1 For the purpose of proceedings to which these Rules apply, the Practice Direction about costs which supplements Parts 43 to 48 of the CPR ("the costs practice direction") will apply, but with the exclusions and modifications explained below to reflect the exclusions and modifications to those Parts of the CPR as they are applied by Part 28 of these Rules.

2.2 Rule 28.2(1) applies, with modifications and certain exceptions, Parts 43 to 48 of the CPR to costs in family proceedings. Paragraph 1.2 of this Practice Direction modifies rule 48.1(1)(b) when it applies to family proceedings. Rule 28.2(2), by way of exception, disapplies Part 47, rules 44.3C and 45.6 of the CPR in the case of family proceedings in a magistrates' court. Rule 28.3, again by way of exception, additionally disapplies CPR rule 44.3(1), (4) and (5) in the case of financial remedy proceedings, regardless of court.

2.3 The costs practice direction does not, therefore, apply in its entirety but with the exclusion of certain sections reflecting the non-application of certain rules of the CPR which those sections supplement.

2.4 The costs practice direction applies as follows—

- to family proceedings generally, other than in magistrates' courts, with the exception of sections 6, 15, 16, 17 and 23A;
- to family proceedings generally, in magistrates' courts only, with the exception of sections 6, 15, 16, 17, 23A and sections 28–49A;
- to financial remedy proceedings, other than in magistrates' courts, with the exception of section 6, paragraphs 8.1 to 8.4 of section 8 and sections 15, 16, 17 and 23A;
- to financial remedy proceedings in magistrates' courts only, with the exception of section 6, paragraphs 8.1 to 8.4 of section 8, sections 15, 16, 17, 23A and sections 28–49A.

2.5 All subsequent editions of the costs practice direction as and when they are published and come into effect shall in the same way extend to all family proceedings.

2.6 The costs practice direction includes provisions applicable to proceedings following changes in the manner in which legal services are funded pursuant to the Access to Justice Act 1999. It should be noted that although the cost of the premium in respect of legal costs insurance (section 29) or the cost of funding by a prescribed membership organisation (section 30) may be recoverable, family proceedings (within section 58A(2) of the Courts and Legal Services Act 1990) cannot be the subject of an enforceable conditional fee agreement.

2.7 Paragraph 1.4 of section 1 of the costs practice direction shall be modified as follows—

in the definition of "counsel" for "High court or in the county courts" substitute "High Court, county courts or in a magistrates' court".

General Interpretation of references in CPR

3.1 References in the costs practice direction to "claimant" and "defendant" are to be read as references to equivalent terms used in proceedings to which these Rules apply and other terms and expressions used in the costs practice direction shall be similarly treated.

3.2 References in CPR Parts 43 to 48 to other rules or Parts of the CPR shall be read, where there is an equivalent rule or Part in these Rules, to that equivalent rule or Part.

Costs in financial remedy proceedings

4.1 Rule 28.3 relates to the court's power to make costs orders in financial remedy proceedings. For the purposes of rule 28.3, "financial remedy proceedings" are defined in accordance with rule 28.3(4)(b). That definition, which is more limited than the principal definition in rule 2.3(1), includes:

(a) an application for a financial order, except:
    (i) an order for maintenance pending suit or an order for maintenance pending outcome of proceedings;
    (ii) an interim periodical payments order or any other form of interim order for the purposes of rule 9.7(1)(a),(b),(c) and (e);
(b) an application for an order under Part 3 of the Matrimonial and Family Proceedings Act 1984 or Schedule 7 to the Civil Partnership Act 2004; and
(c) an application under section 10(2) of the Matrimonial Causes Act 1973 or section 48(2) of the Civil Partnership Act 2004.

4.2 Accordingly, it should be noted that:

(a) while most interim financial applications are excluded from rule 28.3, the rule does apply to an application for an interim variation order within rule 9.7(1)(d),
(b) rule 28.3 does not apply to an application for any of the following financial remedies:
    (i) an order under Schedule 1 to the Children Act 1989;
    (ii) an order under section 27 of the Matrimonial Causes Act 1973 or Part 9 of Schedule 5 to the Civil Partnership Act 2004;
    (iii) an order under section 35 of the Matrimonial Causes Act 1973 or paragraph 69 of Schedule 5 to the Civil Partnership Act 2004; or
    (iv) an order under Part 1 of the Domestic Proceedings and Magistrates' Courts Act 1978 or Schedule 6 to the Civil Partnership Act 2004.

4.3 Under rule 28.3 the court only has the power to make a costs order in financial remedy proceedings when this is justified by the litigation conduct of one of the parties. When determining whether and how to exercise this power the court will be required to take into account the list of factors set out in that rule. The court will not be able to take into account any offers to settle expressed to be "without prejudice" or "without prejudice save as to costs" in deciding what, if any, costs orders to make.

4.4 In considering the conduct of the parties for the purposes of rule 28.3(6) and (7) (including any open offers to settle), the court will have regard to the obligation of the parties to help the court to further the overriding objective (see rules 1.1 and 1.3) and will take into account the nature, importance and complexity of the issues in the case. This may be of particular significance in applications for variation orders and interim variation orders or other cases where there is a risk of the costs becoming disproportionate to the amounts in dispute.

4.5 Parties who intend to seek a costs order against another party in proceedings to which rule 28.3 applies should ordinarily make this plain in open correspondence or in skeleton arguments before the date of the hearing. In any case where summary assessment of costs awarded under rule 28.3 would be appropriate parties are under an obligation to file a statement of costs in CPR Form N260.

4.6 An interim financial order which includes an element to allow a party to deal with legal fees (see *A v A (maintenance pending suit: provision for legal fees)* [2001] 1 WLR 605, [2001] 1 FLR 377; *G v G (maintenance pending suit; costs)* [2002] EWHC 306 (Fam), [2003] 2 FLR 71; *McFarlane v McFarlane, Parlour v Parlour* [2004] EWCA Civ 872, [2004] 2 FLR 893; *Moses-Taiga v Taiga* [2005] EWCA Civ 1013, [2006] 1 FLR 1074; *C v C (Maintenance Pending Suit: Legal Costs)* [2006] Fam Law 739; *Currey v Currey (No 2)* [2006] EWCA Civ 1338, [2007] 1 FLR 946) is an order made pursuant to section 22 of the Matrimonial Causes Act 1973 or an order under paragraph 38 of Schedule 5 of the 2004 Act, and is not a "costs order" within the meaning of rule 28.3.

4.7 By virtue of rule 28.2(1), where rule 28.3 does not apply, the exercise of the court's discretion as to costs is governed by the relevant provisions of the CPR and in particular rule 44.3 (excluding r 44.3(2) and (3)).

* * * * *

Part 29

Commentary on Part 29:
MISCELLANEOUS

The basic rule

Part 29 gathers together a gallimaufry of disparate rules which the framers were not able to place elsewhere. Another apt description would be a pot pourri. It has no specific counterpart in the CPR as such although most of the rules are to be found somewhere in the CPR. For example rule 29.7 concerning the stamping or sealing of court documents is to be found in CPR rule 2.6.

A number of the rules in Part 29 have no conceivable relevance to financial remedy proceedings and are omitted from this work.

Those relevant rules which are included and commented on here are:

Personal details	Rule 29.1
Disclosure of information under the 1991 Act	Rule 29.2
Method of giving notice	Rule 29.3
Withdrawal of applications in proceedings	Rule 29.4
The Human Rights Act 1998	Rule 29.5
Stamping or sealing court documents	Rule 29.7
Standard requirements	Rule 29.10
Drawing up and filing of judgments and orders	Rule 29.11
Copies of orders made in open court	Rule 29.12
Service of judgments and orders	Rule 29.13
Power to require judgment or order to be served on a party as well as the party's solicitor	Rule 29.14
When judgment or order takes effect	Rule 29.15
Correction of errors in judgments and orders	Rule 29.16

Part 29 is supported by *PD 29A – Human Rights, Joining the Crown* (which is modelled on CPR PD 19A Section 6), and *PD 29B – Human Rights Act 1998* (which replicates CPR PD 39A Section 8).

Personal details (rule 29.1)

For the purposes of financial remedy proceedings rule 29.1 provides that, subject to a contrary direction from the court, a party is not required to reveal his or her home address or other contact details, or the address or other contact details of any child. Where a party does not wish to reveal any such information he or she must give notice of the particulars to the court and they will not be revealed to any person unless the court directs otherwise.

PD 22A para 4.1(a)(ii) (see Commentary on Part 22 *above*) requires a witness statement to give the maker's full name and residential address. This can be avoided under rule 29.1 by adopting the specified procedure *above*.

Where a party changes home address during the course of proceedings, that party must give notice of the change to the court.

Disclosure of information under the Child Support Act 1991 (rule 29.2)

By rule 29.2 where C-MEC requires a person mentioned in regulations 3(1), 4(2) or 6(2)(a) of the Child Support Information Regulations 2008 to furnish information or evidence for a purpose mentioned in regulation 4(1) of those Regulations, nothing in the FPR prevents that person from furnishing the information or evidence sought or requires that person to seek permission of the court before doing so.

Method of giving notice (rule 29.3)

For the purposes of financial remedy proceedings rule 29.3 provides that, subject to contrary direction by the court, a notice which is required by the FPR to be given to a person must be given in writing, and in a manner in which service may be effected in accordance with Part 6.

Withdrawal of applications in proceedings (rule 29.4)

For the purposes of financial remedy proceedings rule 29.4 stipulates that where either of the parties is a protected party an application may only be withdrawn with the permission of the court. Unless the parties are present in court, when the application may be made orally, the application must be in writing setting out the reasons for the request. The court may deal with a written request without a hearing if the other parties, and any other persons directed by the court, have had an opportunity to make written representations to the court about the request.

The Human Rights Act 1998 (HRA) (rule 29.5)

Rule 29.5 provides the procedural rules where a provision or right under the HRA has arisen. A party who seeks to rely on any provision of or right arising under the HRA or who seeks a remedy available under that Act must inform the court in his or her application or otherwise in writing specifying (i) the Convention right which it is alleged has been infringed, (ii) details of the alleged infringement, (iii) the relief sought, and (iv) whether this includes a declaration of incompatibility.

The High Court may not make a declaration of incompatibility unless 21 days' notice, or such other period of notice as the court directs, has been given to the Crown. By PD 29A para 1.3 the notice must be served on the person named in the list published under section 17 of the Crown Proceedings Act 1947. This list can be accessed via www. tsol.gov.uk/Publications/Scheme_Publications/crown_proceedings_act.pdf.

Where notice has been given to the Crown, a Minister, or other person permitted by the HRA, will be joined as a party on giving notice to the court.

Where a claim is made under section 7(1) of the HRA (claim that public authority acted unlawfully) in respect of a judicial act then it must be set out in the application form or the appeal notice, and notice must be given to the Crown. By PD 29A section 2 notice must be given to the Lord Chancellor and should be served on the Treasury Solicitor on his behalf.

The notice must give details of the judicial act which is the subject of the claim for damages, and of the court that made it.

On any application concerning a committal order, if the court ordering the release of the person concludes that that person's Convention rights have been infringed by the making of the order to which the application or appeal relates, the judgment or order should so state, but if the court does not do so that failure will not prevent another court from deciding the matter.

By PD 29B section 3 the determination of a claim for a declaration of incompatibility under section 4 of the HRA, or of any an issue which may lead to the court considering making such a declaration, must be heard by a High Court Judge.

The determination of a claim made under the Act in respect of a judicial act must be heard in the High Court by a full time High Court judge and in county courts by a circuit judge (*ibid*).

Section 2 of PD 29B deals with the citation of HRA authorities. When an authority referred to in section 2 of the HRA is to be cited at a hearing the authority to be cited must be an authoritative and complete report. Copies of the complete original texts issued by the European Court and Commission, either paper-based or from the Court's judgment database (HUDOC which is available on the internet) may be used.

The court must be provided with a list of authorities it is intended to cite and copies of the reports, in cases to which PD 27A (Family Proceedings: Court Bundles (Universal Practice to be Applied in all Courts other than the Family Proceedings Court)) applies, as part of the bundle; otherwise, not less than 2 clear days before the hearing. Copies of the complete original texts issued by the European Court and Commission, either paper-based or from the Court's judgment database (HUDOC) may be used.

Stamping or sealing court documents (rule 29.7)

A court officer must, when issuing an application form, an order, or any other document which a rule or practice direction requires the court officer to seal or stamp, seal, or otherwise authenticate it with the stamp of the court. He or she may place the seal or the stamp on the document by hand or by printing a facsimile of the seal on the document whether electronically or otherwise. A document purporting to bear the court's seal or stamp will be admissible in evidence without further proof but, plainly, the court will permit an allegation of forgery of a court document to be investigated.

Standard requirements concerning judgments and orders (rule 29.10)

Every judgment or order must be sealed and must (i) state the name and judicial title of the person who made it and (ii) bear the date on which it is given or made.

Drawing up and filing of judgments and orders (rule 29.11)

Except as provided by a rule or a practice direction, every judgment or order will be drawn up by the court unless the court orders a party to draw it up, or a party with the permission of the court agrees to draw it up, or the court dispenses with the need to draw it up. The invariable practice in the High Court and PRFD is for counsel to agree and draw the order and to submit it by email to the Associate, Judge's Clerk or Court Clerk.

The court may direct that (i) a judgment or an order drawn up by a party must be checked by the court before it is sealed· or (ii) before a judgment or an order is drawn up by the court, the parties must file an agreed statement of its terms.

Where a judgment or an order is to be drawn up by a party he or she must file it no later than 7 days after the date on which the court ordered or gave permission for the order to be drawn up so that it can be sealed by the court and if that party fails to file it within that period, any other party may draw it up and file it. This time limit should be strictly adhered to as there are too many instances of the drawing of financial orders by counsel being delayed for days or even weeks. It is to be supposed that if a party has drawn up an order, but that order has not been agreed by the other party or parties, then he or she may file it without further reference to them.

Copies of orders made in open court (rule 29.12)

A copy of an order made in open court will be issued to any person who requests it on payment of the prescribed fee.

Service of judgments and orders (rule 29.13)

The court officer must, unless the court directs otherwise, serve a copy of a judgment or an order made in family proceedings to every party affected by it. Where a judgment or an order has been drawn up by a party and is to be served by the court officer the party who drew it up must file a copy to be retained at court together with sufficient copies for service on all the parties.

A party in whose favour an order is made need not prove that a copy of the order has reached a party to whom it is required to be sent under this rule.

Rule 29.13 does not affect the operation of any rule or enactment which requires an order to be served in a particular way

Power to require judgment or order to be served on a party as well as the party's solicitor (rule 29.14)

Where the party on whom a judgment or order is served is acting by a solicitor, the court may order the judgment or order to be served on the party as well as on the party's solicitor.

When judgment or order takes effect (rule 29.15)

A judgment or order takes effect from the day when it is given or made, or such later date as the court may specify.

The slip rule (rule 29.16)

The court may at any time correct an accidental slip or omission in a judgment or order. A party may apply for a correction without notice.

PART 29: MISCELLANEOUS

Personal details

29.1.—(1) Unless the court directs otherwise, a party is not required to reveal—

(a) the party's home address or other contact details;
(b) the address or other contact details of any child;
(c) the name of a person with whom the child is living, if that person is not the applicant; or
(d) in relation to an application under section 28(2) of the 2002 Act (application for permission to change the child's surname), the proposed new surname of the child.

(2) Where a party does not wish to reveal any of the particulars in paragraph (1), that party must give notice of those particulars to the court and the particulars will not be revealed to any person unless the court directs otherwise.

(3) Where a party changes home address during the course of proceedings, that party must give notice of the change to the court.

Disclosure of information under the 1991 Act

29.2. Where the Commission requires a person mentioned in regulation

3(1), 4(2) or 6(2)(a) of the Child Support Information Regulations 2008[85] to furnish information or evidence for a purpose mentioned in regulation 4(1) of those Regulations, nothing in these rules will—

(a) prevent that person from furnishing the information or evidence sought; or
(b) require that person to seek permission of the court before doing so.

Method of giving notice

29.3.—(1) Unless directed otherwise, a notice which is required by these rules to be given to a person must be given—

(a) in writing; and
(b) in a manner in which service may be effected in accordance with Part 6.

(2) Rule 6.33 applies to a notice which is required by these rules to be given to a child as it applies to a document which is to be served on a child.

Withdrawal of applications in proceedings

29.4.—(1) This rule applies to applications in proceedings—

(a) under Part 7;
(b) under Parts 10 to 14 or under any other Part where the application relates to the welfare or upbringing of a child or;
(c) where either of the parties is a protected party.

(2) Where this rule applies, an application may only be withdrawn with the permission of the court.

(3) Subject to paragraph (4), a person seeking permission to withdraw an application must file a written request for permission setting out the reasons for the request.

(4) The request under paragraph (3) may be made orally to the court if the parties are present.

(5) A court officer will notify the other parties of a written request.

(6) The court may deal with a written request under paragraph (3) without a hearing if the other parties, and any other persons directed by the court, have had an opportunity to make written representations to the court about the request.

The Human Rights Act 1998

29.5.—(1) In this rule—

"the 1998 Act" means the Human Rights Act 1998;

"Convention right" has the same meaning as in the 1998 Act; and

"declaration of incompatibility" means a declaration of incompatibility under section 4 of the 1998 Act[86].

(2) A party who seeks to rely on any provision of or right arising under

the 1998 Act; or seeks a remedy available under that Act must inform the court in that party's application or otherwise in writing specifying—

(a) the Convention right which it is alleged has been infringed and details of the alleged infringement; and

(b) the relief sought and whether this includes a declaration of incompatibility.

(3) The High Court may not make a declaration of incompatibility unless 21 days' notice, or such other period of notice as the court directs, has been given to the Crown.

(4) Where notice has been given to the Crown, a Minister, or other person permitted by the 1998 Act, will be joined as a party on giving notice to the court.

(5) Where a claim is made under section 7(1) of the 1998 Act; (claim that public authority acted unlawfully) in respect of a judicial act—

(a) that claim must be set out in the application form or the appeal notice; and

(b) notice must be given to the Crown.

(6) Where paragraph (4) applies and the appropriate person (as defined in section 9(5) of the 1998 Act;) has not applied within 21 days, or such other period as the court directs, beginning with the date on which the notice to be joined as a party was served, the court may join the appropriate person as a party.

(7) On any application concerning a committal order, if the court ordering the release of the person concludes that that person's Convention rights have been infringed by the making of the order to which the application or appeal relates, the judgment or order should so state, but if the court does not do so, that failure will not prevent another court from deciding the matter.

(8) Where by reason of a rule, practice direction or court order the Crown is permitted or required—

(a) to make a witness statement;

(b) to swear an affidavit;

(c) to verify a document by a statement of truth; or

(d) to discharge any other procedural obligation,

that function will be performed by an appropriate officer acting on behalf of the Crown, and the court may if necessary nominate an appropriate officer.

(Practice Direction 29A (Human Rights – Joining the Crown) makes provision for the notices mentioned in this rule.)

Practice Direction 29A supplements FPR Part 29, rule 29(5) (Human rights, joining the Crown)

* * * * *

Stamping or sealing court documents

29.7.—(1) A court officer must, when issuing the following documents, seal, or otherwise authenticate them with the stamp of the court—

(a) the application form;
(b) an order; and
(c) any other document which a rule or practice direction requires the court officer to seal or stamp.

(2) The court officer may place the seal or the stamp on the document—

(a) by hand; or
(b) by printing a facsimile of the seal on the document whether electronically or otherwise.

(3) A document purporting to bear the court's seal or stamp will be admissible in evidence without further proof. ...

Standard requirements

29.10.—(1) Every judgment or order must state the name and judicial title of the person who made it.

(2) Every judgment or order must—

(a) bear the date on which it is given or made; and
(b) be sealed by the court.

Drawing up and filing of judgments and orders

29.11.—(1) Except as provided by a rule or a practice direction, every judgment or order will be drawn up by the court unless—

(a) the court orders a party to draw it up;
(b) a party, with the permission of the court, agrees to draw it up; or
(c) the court dispenses with the need to draw it up.

(2) The court may direct that—

(a) a judgment or an order drawn up by a party must be checked by the court before it is sealed; or
(b) before a judgment or an order is drawn up by the court, the parties must file an agreed statement of its terms.

(3) Where a judgment or an order is to be drawn up by a party—

(a) that party must file it no later than 7 days after the date on which the court ordered or gave permission for the order to be drawn up so that it can be sealed by the court; and
(b) if that party fails to file it within that period, any other party may draw it up and file it.

Copies of orders made in open court

29.12. A copy of an order made in open court will be issued to any person who requests it on payment of the prescribed fee.

Service of judgments and orders

29.13.—(1) The court officer must, unless the court directs otherwise, serve a copy of a judgment or an order made in family proceedings to every party affected by it.

(2) Where a judgment or an order has been drawn up by a party and is to be served by the court officer the party who drew it up must file a copy to be retained at court and sufficient copies for service on all the parties.

(3) A party in whose favour an order is made need not prove that a copy of the order has reached a party to whom it is required to be sent under this rule.

(4) This rule does not affect the operation of any rule or enactment which requires an order to be served in a particular way

Power to require judgment or order to be served on a party as well as the party's solicitor

29.14. Where the party on whom a judgment or order is served is acting by a solicitor, the court may order the judgment or order to be served on the party as well as on the party's solicitor.

When judgment or order takes effect

29.15. A judgment or order takes effect from the day when it is given or made, or such later date as the court may specify.

Correction of errors in judgments and orders

29.16.—(1) The court may at any time correct an accidental slip or omission in a judgment or order.

(2) A party may apply for a correction without notice.

PRACTICE DIRECTION 29A – HUMAN RIGHTS, JOINING THE CROWN

This Practice Direction supplements FPR Part 29, rule 29.5

(The Human Rights Act 1998)

Section 4 of the Human Rights Act 1998

1.1 Where a party has informed the court about—

(a) a claim for a declaration of incompatibility in accordance with section 4 of the Human Rights Act 1998; or
(b) an issue for the court to decide which may lead to the court considering making a declaration,

then the court may at any time consider whether notice should be given to the Crown as required by that Act and give directions for the content and service of the notice. The rule allows a period of 21 days before the court will make the declaration but the court may vary this period of time.

1.2 The court will normally consider the issues and give the directions referred to in paragraph 1.1 at a directions hearing.

1.3 The notice must be served on the person named in the list published under section 17 of the Crown Proceedings Act 1947.

1.4 The notice will be in the form directed by the court and will normally include the directions given by the court. The notice will also be served on all the parties.

1.5 The court may require the parties to assist in the preparation of the notice.

1.6 Unless the court orders otherwise, the Minister or other person permitted by the Human Rights Act 1998 to be joined as a party must, if he or she wishes to be joined, give notice of his or her intention to be joined as a party to the court and every other party. Where the Minister has nominated a person to be joined as a party the notice must be accompanied by the written nomination.

(Section 5(2)(a) of the Human Rights Act 1998 permits a person nominated by a Minister of the Crown to be joined as a party. The nomination may be signed on behalf of the Minister.)

Section 9 of the Human Rights Act 1998

2.1 The procedure in paragraphs 1.1 to 1.6 also applies where a claim is made under sections 7(1)(a) and 9(3) of the Human Rights Act 1998 for damages in respect of a judicial act.

2.2 Notice must be given to the Lord Chancellor and should be served on the Treasury Solicitor on his behalf.

2.3 The notice will also give details of the judicial act, which is the subject of the claim for damages, and of the court that made it.

(Section 9(4) of the Human Rights Act 1998 provides that no award of damages may be made against the Crown as provided for in section 9(3) unless the appropriate person is joined in the proceedings. The appropriate person is the Minister responsible for the court concerned or a person or department nominated by him or her (section 9(5) of the Act).)

* * * * *

PRACTICE DIRECTION 29B – HUMAN RIGHTS ACT 1998

Human Rights Act 1998

1.1. It is directed that the following practice shall apply as from 2 October 2000 in all family proceedings:

Citation of authorities

2.1. When an authority referred to in s 2 of the Human Rights Act 1998 ('the Act') is to be cited at a hearing—

    (a) the authority to be cited shall be an authoritative and complete report;

    (b) the court must be provided with a list of authorities it is intended to cite and copies of the reports—

        (i) in cases to which *Practice Direction (Family Proceedings: Court Bundles)* (10 March 2000), [2000] 1 FLR 536 applies, as part of the bundle;

[**Editors' note:** but by virtue of paras 13.1 and 14.1 of PD 27A (*above*) 'this practice direction [i.e. PD 27A] replaces *President's Direction (Family Proceedings: Court Bundles)* (10 March 2000) [2000] 1 FLR 536 and shall have effect from 2 October 2006'; and 'any reference in any other practice direction to *President's Direction (Family Proceedings: Court Bundles)* [2000] 1 FLR 536 shall be read as if substituted by a reference to this practice direction' [i.e. to PD 27A].]

        (ii) otherwise, not less than 2 clear days before the hearing; and

    (c) copies of the complete original texts issued by the European Court and Commission, either paper based or from the Court's judgment database (HUDOC) which is available on the internet, may be used.

Allocation to judges

3.1. The hearing and determination of the following will be confined to a High Court judge—

    (a) a claim for a declaration of incompatibility under s 4 of the Act; or

    (b) an issue which may lead to the court considering making such a declaration.

3.2. The hearing and determination of a claim made under the Act in respect of a judicial act shall be confined in the High Court to a High Court judge and in county courts to a circuit judge.

* * * * *

Part 30

Commentary on Part 30:
APPEALS

Summary

Part 30 of FPR 2010 is modelled very closely on CPR Part 52. With its accompanying Practice Direction PD 30A Part 30 creates for the first time a comprehensive procedural code governing appeals to the High Court and the county court in all types of family proceedings (rule 30.1(1)(a) and (b)). A very minor exception is an appeal against a decision of an authorised court officer in detailed assessment proceedings to which CPR rules 47.20 to 47.23 apply (rule 30.1(2)).

Appeals to the Court of Appeal in family as in other civil proceedings continue to be governed by CPR Part 52. So too are appeals in non-family proceedings which may be heard in the Family Division such as those under the Inheritance (Provision for Family and Dependants) Act 1975 and the Trusts of Land and Appointment of Trustees Act 1996. There is no change to the existing routes of appeal. They are set out in PD 30A para 2.1. See also the Access to Justice Act 1999 (Destination of Appeals) (Family Proceedings) Order 2011 (SI 2011 No. 1044).

PD 30A contains a mass of important procedural detail. It is 25 pages long and this Commentary can do no more than highlight those provisions which are new and/or particularly relevant to financial remedy proceedings.

The provisions of Part 30 are stated to be subject to any rule, enactment or practice direction which sets out special provisions with regard to any particular category of appeal (rule 30.1(4)). PD 30A makes special provision for a number of categories of financial appeals which are or may be of relevance to financial proceedings: these are listed under the heading **Specific appeals** *below*.

The main changes brought about by Part 30 are as follows:

(i) A unified procedural code replaces the several regimes which were set out (for the most part) in Part 8 of FPR 1991. These were rule 8.1 (appeals from District Judges); rule 8.2 (appeals to a county court and appeals from District Judges under the Children Act 1989 or Parts 4 and 4A of the Family Law Act 1996 or relating to deduction order appeals); rule 8.3 (appeals under section 13 of the Administration of Justice Act 1960); rule 8.4 (appeals under section 8(1) of the Gender Recognition Act 2004); rule 3.22 (appeal under section 20 of the Child Support Act 1991); and rule 3.23 (appeal from the Upper Tribunal).

(ii) Permission to appeal must now be obtained except in the case of committal and secure accommodation orders.

(iii) The same appellate test now applies whether the decision appealed against is interlocutory or final. That test is whether that decision was (a) wrong or (b) unjust because of a serious procedural or other irregularity.

(iv) There is now only one route by which a consent order may be challenged, namely appeal (as to this see **Appeals against consent orders** *below*).

Permission to appeal

An important innovation is that permission to appeal is now required in all cases (a) where the decision appealed against was made by a District Judge or costs judge, or (b) as provided by PD 30A (rule 30.3(1)). The only categories of appeal where no permission is needed are those against committal and secure accommodation orders (rule 30.3(2) and PD 30A para 4.1). This rule corresponds (save that it omits reference to habeas corpus) to CPR rule 52.3(1)(a) and aligns the position in family proceedings with that under the CPR, thus removing the 'strange quirk' to which Ward LJ referred in *Bright v Bright* [2002] EWCA Civ 1412.

Permission to appeal may be given only where either (a) the court considers that the appeal would have a real prospect of success (rule 30.3(7)(a)); or (b) there is some other compelling reason why the appeal should be heard (rule 30.3(7)(b)). This wording is identical to that used in CPR rule 52.3(6) and thus in interpreting rule 30.3(7) the CPR jurisprudence will be the starting point.

In the great majority of appeals the application for permission will rely on the first limb of the test. In *Swain v Hillman* [2001] 1 All ER 91, a case concerning identical wording under CPR rule 24.2 (summary judgment), Lord Woolf MR held that:

> The words 'no real prospect of succeeding' do not need any amplification, they speak for themselves. The word 'real' distinguishes fanciful prospects of success or ... they direct the court to the need to see whether there is a 'realistic' as opposed to a 'fanciful' prospect of success.

In *Tanfern Ltd v Cameron-MacDonald (Practice Note)* [2000] 1 WLR 1311 at [21] the Court of Appeal cited this test with approval.

In *Re W (permission to appeal)* [2008] 1 FLR 406 at [16] the Court of

Appeal said that the only matter for that court on an application for permission to appeal was whether or not the applicant had an arguable case, fit to present to the full court on appeal, that the order below was 'plainly wrong' (as to which, see **The appellate test** *below*). The 'realistic prospect of success' test is at first sight stricter. It remains to be seen whether the 'arguable case' test propounded in *Re W* is still good law.

Applications in family proceedings for permission to appeal based on the second limb ('some other compelling reason') are likely to be rare, and likely to succeed only where these is some important point of law which (irrespective of the prospects of success of the appeal itself) needs to be clarified by the Court of Appeal and/or the Supreme Court: see for example *Smith v Cosworth Casting Processes* [1997] 1 WLR 1538.

Clarification of the first instance decision

Prior to these new Rules it was already incumbent on the parties and their advisers to raise with the lower court any ambiguity or deficiency in the judgment rather than to leave the matter to be dealt with on appeal: *Re M (fact finding: burden of proof)* [2008] EWCA Civ 1261, [2009] 1 FLR 1177 where Wall LJ (as he then was) stated at [38]:

> I wish to make it as clear as possible that after a judge has given judgment, counsel have a positive duty to raise with the judge not just any alleged deficiency in the judge's reasoning process but any genuine query or ambiguity which arises on the judgment. Judges should welcome this process, and any who resent it are likely to find themselves the subject of criticism in this court. The object, of course, is to achieve clarity and – where appropriate – to obviate the need to come to this court for a remedy.

See also *English v Emery Reimbold & Strick Ltd; DJ & C Withers (Farms) Ltd v Ambic Equipment Ltd; Verrechia (trading as Freightmaster Commercials) v Commissioner of Police of the Metropolis (Practice Note)* [2002] 1 WLR 2409; *Re B (Appeal: Lack of Reasons)* [2003] 2 FLR 1035; *Re T (Contact: Alienation: Permission to Appeal)* [2003] 1 FLR 531.

The important provisions of PD 30A paras 4.6 to 4.9 are designed to ensure that any assertion of a material omission from a judgment of the lower court is addressed by that court *before* an application for permission to appeal is considered.

Making the application for permission

The application for permission to appeal may (and, according to PD 30A para 4.2, should) be made to the lower court at the hearing at which the order was made (rule 30.3(3)(a)) or to the appeal court by means of an appeal notice (rule 30.3(3)(b) and rule 30.4(1)).

If the applicant for permission requires more time to present his application to the lower court, the court may grant an adjournment for that purpose (PD 30A para 4.4).

In cases governed by the CPR, permission to appeal against case management decisions is granted more sparingly than where it is sought to appeal a final order. See e.g. *Walbrook Trustee (Jersey) Ltd v Fattal* [2008] EWCA Civ 427 at [33] where Lawrence Collins LJ (as he then was) stated:

> I do not need to cite authority for the obvious proposition that an appellate court should not interfere with case management decisions by a judge who has applied the correct principles and who has taken into account matters which should be taken into account and left out of account matters which are irrelevant, unless the court is satisfied that the decision is so plainly wrong that it must be regarded as outside the generous ambit of the discretion entrusted to the judge.

PD 30A contains no provision corresponding to CPR Part 52 PD 4.5, which requires the court, when considering applications for permission to appeal against case management decisions, to take into account specific matters: (a) whether the issue is of insufficient importance to justify the costs of an appeal; (b) whether the procedural consequence of an appeal (e.g. loss of trial date) outweigh the significance of the case management decision; and (c) whether it would be more convenient to determine the issue at or after trial. Despite this lack of corresponding provision in the FPR 2010 it is likely that in financial proceedings the court will adopt a similar approach.

PD 30A paras 4.10 to 4.24 set out detailed procedural requirements governing applications for permission to appeal.

An order granting permission may (a) limit the issues to be heard or (b) impose conditions (rule 30.3(8)). In *Radmacher v Granatino* [2009] 1 FLR 1566 the Court of Appeal, applying the corresponding CPR provisions (rule 52.3(7)), imposed conditions requiring the wife to bring a sum of money into the jurisdiction and to comply with existing periodical payments orders, including the payment of arrears.

PD 30A makes further provision about the grant of limited permission at paras 4.18 to 4.21.

The role of the respondent at the permission stage

The role of the respondent at the permission stage was considered by the Court of Appeal in *Jolly v Jay* [2002] EWCA Civ 277 which is, it is suggested, still good law. The Court held (*per curiam*) at [44] that:

> a respondent should only file submissions at this early stage if they are addressed to the point that the appeal would not meet the relevant threshold test or tests, or if there is some material inaccuracy in the papers placed before the court. By this phrase we mean an inaccuracy which might reasonably be expected to lead the court to grant permission when it would not have done so if it had received correct information on the point.

If the respondent was present at the hearing in the lower court at which the initial application for permission was made he will have had an opportunity to oppose the grant of permission. However it should be noted that if he was present he may not subsequently apply to the appeal court for orders setting aside permission to appeal or for the imposition or variation of conditions upon which the appeal may be brought (rule 30.10(3)).

If an application for permission is to be determined by the appeal court at a hearing, the respondent will be notified and be informed of the essence of the appellant's case (PD 30A para 4.14) but is not required to attend unless requested by the court to do so (PD 30A para 4.15).

Applications for permission to appeal will normally be determined without the court requesting submissions from or attendance by the respondent (PD 30A para 4.22). PD 30A paras 4.23 and 4.24 make detailed provisions about the respondent's costs of permission applications.

Refusal of permission

Where the lower court allows or refuses permission to appeal, there is no right of appeal against that decision (PD 30A para 4.5). If however no application for permission is made to the lower court or that court refuses permission a (further) application for permission may be made to the appeal court (rule 30.3(4) and PD 30A para 4.3). Such an application may be determined without a hearing (PD 30A para 4.10). If the appeal court refuses permission the appellant may within 7 days of service of notice of refusal of the application (rule 30.3(6)) request reconsideration of the application for permission at a hearing (rule 30.3(5) and PD 30A para 4.12 and 4.13). The hearing may be before the judge who refused permission on paper.

The respondent has no right of appeal against an order granting permission to appeal.

Where the appeal court refuses permission without a hearing there is no provision corresponding to CPR rule 52.3(4A) which empowers the Court of Appeal in cases not covered by FPR 2010 to make an order that the applicant for permission may not request the decision to be reconsidered at an oral hearing if it considers such an application to be totally without merit.

Appellant's and respondent's notices

Appellant's and respondent's notices are collectively referred to as 'appeal notices' (rule 30.1(3)). The respondent's notice is an innovation introduced from CPR Part 52.

The appellant's notice must be filed, unless the lower court stipulates a different period, within 21 days of the decision against which the appellant seeks to appeal (rule 30.4(2)). This default time limit is the same as under the CPR, and more generous than the 14-day limit prescribed for the filing of an appeal under FPR 1991 rule 8.1(4). Any application to vary the time for filing an appeal notice must be made to the appeal court and not the lower court (rule 30.7(1)). The parties may not between themselves agree to extend time (rule 30.7(2)).

The appeal notice must state the grounds of appeal (rule 30.6) and may not be amended without permission of the appeal court (rule 30.9). Applications to amend will normally be dealt with at the hearing of the appeal unless that would cause unnecessary expense or delay (PD 30A para 5.44). The grounds of appeal should (a) set out clearly why the decision of the lower court was wrong or (as the case may be) unjust because of a serious procedural irregularity in the lower court (PD 30A para 3.2(a)). In respect of each ground the notice should specify whether the ground raises an appeal on a point of law or is an appeal against a finding of fact (PD 30A para 3.2(b)).

Unless the appeal court orders otherwise, the notice must be served as soon as practicable and in any event within 7 days after filing (rule 30.4(4)). PD 30A paras 5.35 to 5.43 make further provision about filing and service.

At the appeal hearing a party may not rely on a matter not contained in his appeal notice without permission (rule 30(12(5))).

In relation to the appellant's notice, PD 30A makes detailed provisions as to, inter alia: applications for extension of time (paras 5.4 to 5.6); documents to be filed (paras 5.8 to 5.12); skeleton arguments (paras 5.13 to 5.22); and records of the judgment and evidence in the court below (paras 5.23 to 5.34).

The respondent may file a respondent's notice (rule 30.5). He is obliged to do so only where (a) he himself seeks permission to appeal from the appeal court (rule 30.5(2)(a)), in which case he must seek permission in the notice (rule 30.5(3)); or (b) he wishes to uphold the decision of the lower court for reasons different from or additional to those given by the lower court (rule 30.5(2)(b)). Rule 30.5 and PD 30A paras 7.1 to 7.19 make further provision relating to respondent's notices.

Stay pending appeal

An appeal notice does not operate as a stay of any order or decision of the lower court unless the appeal court or appeal court orders otherwise (rule 30.8). This provision replicates FPR 1991 rule 8.1(6). In deciding whether or not to grant a stay the essential question is whether there is a risk of injustice to one or other or both parties if the court grants or refuses a stay: *Hammond Suddard v Agrichem International Holdings Limited* [2001] EWCA Civ 2065. The court must thus carry out a balancing exercise. A stay may be granted on terms: see e.g. *Hammond, above,* and *Contract Facilities Ltd v Estate of Rees (deceased)* [2003] EWCA Civ 465.

Variation and extensions of time and applications for permission to appeal out of time

As noted *above,* an application to vary the time for filing an appeal notice must be made to the appeal court (rule 30.7(1)). The application must be made in the appeal notice, which should state the reason for the delay and the steps taken prior to the application being made (PD 30A paras 5.4 and 7.6).

Where the application for an extension of time is *prospective*, the discretion should be exercised by simply having regard to the overriding objective of enabling the court to deal with cases justly including, so far as practicable, the matters set out in rule 1.1(2): *Robert v Momentum Services* [2003] 2 All ER 74, a CPR case.

Where however the application for permission to appeal is *made out of time*, the court should apply the checklist in rule 4.6: *Sayers v Clarke Walker* [2002] 3 All ER 490. Specific criteria apply where it is sought to appeal out of time on the ground that a fundamental assumption on which an order was based has been invalidated by a supervening event (the *Barder* jurisdiction). (See further **Appeals against consent orders** *below*.)

Striking out appeal notice and setting aside or imposing conditions on permission to appeal

The appeal court is empowered (a) to strike out the whole or part of an appeal notice (rule 30.10(1)(a)); (b) to set aside permission in whole or in part (rule 30.10(1)(b)); (c) to impose or vary conditions upon which an appeal may be brought (rule 30.10(1)(c)). The court will only exercise these powers where there is a compelling reason to do so (rule 30.10(2)). It is important to note that a party who was present at a hearing at which permission was given may not subsequently apply to set aside permission to appeal or for an order imposing or varying conditions (rule 30.10(3)). It may therefore be appropriate in some circumstances for a respondent wishing to seek such orders to apply for an adjournment of the application for permission to appeal if he is not in a position to make the application there and then.

In *Charman v Charman (No 3)* [2007] 1 FLR 1237 the Court of Appeal, applying CPR rule 52.9(1) and (2) (the rule corresponding to rule 30.10(1)(c)) declined to superimpose conditions on permission that had already been granted.

Owing to the high threshold that has to be surmounted it is anticipated that applications to strike out under rule 30.10 will be rare. (See also Commentary on rule 4.4 *above*.)

Where the appeal court refuses an application for permission to appeal, strikes out an appellant's notice or dismisses an appeal, and moreover considers that the application, appeal notice or appeal is totally without merit, it must record that fact and consider whether it is appropriate to make a civil restraint order (as to which see Part 4): rule 30.11(4) and (5). (See *B v B (unmeritorious applications)* [1999] 1 FLR 505, a case where the High Court exercised its inherent jurisdiction to make an order on *Grepe v Loam* principles barring the wife from making any further applications without leave.)

Powers of the appeal court

The court's powers on appeal are specified in rule 30.11. Those powers are wide-ranging. First, the court has (subject to any specific enactment) all the powers of the lower court (rule 30.11(1)). Second, it can affirm, set aside or vary any order of judgment of the lower court; refer any application or issue for determination by the lower court; order a new hearing; make orders for the payment of interest; and/or make a costs order (rule 30.11(2)).

The appellate test

Rule 30.12(3) sets out the test governing appeals to which Part 30 applies and is in identical terms to CPR rule 52.11(3). It provides that the appeal court will allow an appeal where the decision of the lower court was (a) wrong; or (b) unjust because of a serious procedural or other irregularity in the proceedings in the lower court. In the now revoked FPR 1991 rule 8.1 the appellate test was not spelled out. Nevertheless, the applicable law had been clearly established by the Court of Appeal in *Cordle v Cordle* [2002] 1 FLR 207 (overruling *Marsh v Marsh* [1993] 1 FLR 467, CA, and as followed and applied in, e.g. *Akintola v Akintola* [2002] 1 FLR 701; *V v V (financial relief)* [2005] 2 FLR 697) in these terms at [32]:

> … any appeal from a decision of a district judge in ancillary relief shall only be allowed by the circuit judge if it is demonstrated that there has been some procedural irregularity or that in conducting the necessary balancing exercise the district judge has taken into account matters which were irrelevant, or ignored matters which were relevant, or has otherwise arrived at a conclusion that is plainly wrong.

An important innovation is that, as under the CPR, the rule 30.12(3) test applies to final orders and interlocutory orders alike. By contrast, under the FPR 1991 regime, appeals against interlocutory orders in ancillary relief (now financial order) proceedings were governed by the principle in *Evans v Bartlam* [1937] 2 All ER 646 which empowered the appellate court to substitute its own discretion for that of the lower court. The appeal judge was *'entitled to exercise [his discretion] as though the matter came before him for the first time. He will, of course, give the weight it deserves to the previous decision of the [court below], but he is in no way bound by it.'* As part of this logical and welcome rationalisation, the obscure references in FPR 1991 rule 8.1(1) and (2) to CCR Ords 13 and 37 have been swept away.

The 'wrong' test

In *Re W (permission to appeal)* [2008] 1 FLR 406 at [20] Wall LJ (as he then was) considered that the question whether or not an order was plainly wrong could be broken down to the following:

(1) Did the judge arguably make any error of law in reaching his conclusion?

(2) Was there, arguably, insufficient material on which the judge could properly make the findings of fact and the assessments of the witness which he did make?

(3) Is it arguable that the order he made was not properly open to him in the exercise of his judicial discretion?

(4) Is there, arguably, any error in the exercise of that discretion which enables us to say that his order was, arguably, plainly wrong?

Note that terms such as 'plainly wrong', 'blatant error', 'clearly wrong', 'plainly wrong', or simply 'wrong' all bear the same meaning when used in context of an appeal against the exercise of a discretion by a lower court (*G v G (minors: custody appeal)* [1985] FLR 894 at 899, per Lord Fraser of Tullybelton):

> They emphasise the point that the appellate court should only interfere when they consider that the judge of first instance has not merely preferred an imperfect solution which is different from an alternative imperfect solution which the Court of Appeal might or would have adopted, but has exceeded the generous ambit within which a reasonable disagreement is possible.

The appellate court will be especially cautious in interfering with findings of fact made by the court below: see e.g. *Clarke-Hunt v Newcombe* (1983) 4 FLR 482 at 486 (Cumming-Bruce LJ); *Piglowska v Piglowski* [1999] 2 FLR 763 at 784 (Lord Hoffmann); and the useful analysis in *Assicurazioni Generali SpA v Arab Insurance Group (BSC)* [2002] EWCA Civ 1642 at [14] to [16].

An insufficiency of reasons may also render a judgment 'plainly wrong': see *Fielden v Cunliffe* [2006] 1 FLR 745 where Wall LJ (as he then was) stated at [23]:

> … In my judgment, the proper exercise of judicial discretion requires the judge to explain how he has exercised it. This is the well-known 'balancing exercise'. The judge has not only to identify the factors he has taken into account, but to explain why he has given more weight to some, rather than to others. Either a failure to undertake this exercise, or for it to be impossible to discern from the terms of the judgment that it has been undertaken, vitiates the judicial conclusion, which remains unexplained. [But see *above* **Clarification of the first instance decision.**]

The 'serious irregularity' test

The second limb of the test is: was the decision unjust because of a serious procedural or other irregularity in the proceedings in the lower court? The irregularity must be (a) serious and (b) have caused injustice. In *Hayes v Transco plc* [2003] EWCA Civ 1261 it was said:

> … the question in this part of the case is whether the decision of the judge was

unjust because of a serious procedural or other irregularity in the proceedings. It is not, however, sufficient that a serious irregularity should be shown or even that some collateral injustice should be established. The decision must be unjust. As I see it, whether the decision is unjust or not will depend upon all the circumstances of the case.

In that case the refusal of an application to adduce excluded evidence, together with restriction on cross-examination, amounted to a serious procedural irregularity resulting in injustice such that permission to appeal was given. This basis for allowing an appeal is in the alternative to the 'wrong' test and as such applies even where the decision of the lower court was not otherwise wrong: see e.g. *Storer v British Gas plc* [2000] 1 WLR 1237.

Nature of the hearing: review or rehearing?

Rule 30.12(1) is in identical terms to CPR rule 52.11(1) and provides that every appeal will be limited to a review of the decision of the lower court unless:

(a) an enactment or practice direction makes different provision for a particular category of appeal; or
(b) the court considers that in the circumstances of an individual appeal it would be in the interests of justice to hold a re-hearing.

Rule 30.12(1) effects no change to the existing law. The Court of Appeal had held in *Cordle v Cordle* [2002] 1 FLR 207 that the principles governing appeals in family proceedings from district judge to circuit (or to High Court) judge in ancillary relief cases should be aligned with those governing appeals to which the CPR applied: inter alia, appeals against ancillary relief (now financial) orders should be by way of review rather than rehearing. This principle was enshrined in FPR 1991 rule 8.1(3)(a) (as amended by rules 14 and 15, Family Proceedings (Amendment) Rules 2003, SI 2003 No. 184), which, mirroring the wording of CPR rule 52.11(1)(b), provided that:

the appeal shall be limited to a review of the decision or order of the district judge unless the judge considers that in the circumstances of the case it would be in the interests of justice to hold a rehearing.

The starting point is therefore that the appeal will be a review. The onus will be on the appellant to show why it should be a rehearing.

The difference between a rehearing and a review was considered by the Court of Appeal in *EI Du Pont De Nemours & Company v S.T. Dupont* [2003] EWCA Civ 1368 at [93] to [98]:

... it cannot be a matter of simple discretion how an appellate court approaches the matter. ... Subject to exceptions, every appeal is limited to a review of the decision of the lower court. ...The review will engage the merits of the appeal. It will accord appropriate respect to the decision of the lower court. Appropriate respect will be tempered by the nature of the lower court and its decision making process. There will also be a spectrum of appropriate respect depending on the nature of the decision of the lower court which is challenged. At one end of the spectrum will be decisions of primary fact reached after an evaluation of oral evidence where credibility is in issue and purely discretionary decisions. Further along the spectrum will be multi-factorial decisions often dependent on inferences and an analysis of documentary material. Rule 52.11(4) expressly empowers the court to draw inferences ... Submissions to the effect that an appeal hearing should be a rehearing are often motivated by the belief that only thus can sufficient reconsideration be given to elements of the decision of the lower court. In my judgment, this is largely unnecessary given the scope of a hearing by way of review under rule 52.11(1) ... On ... a rehearing the court will hear the case again. It will if necessary hear evidence again and may well admit fresh evidence. It will reach a fresh decision unconstrained by the decision of the lower court, although it will give to the decision of the lower court the weight that it deserves. The circumstances in which an appeal court hearing an appeal from within the court system will decide to hold such a rehearing will be rare ...

PD 30A provides no guidance on when an appeal should be by way of a review and when by way of a rehearing. How the discretion to hold a rehearing should be exercised was considered in *Audergon v La Baguette Ltd and others* [2002] EWCA Civ 10 at [83] where Jonathan Parker LJ set out the correct approach:

(a) The general rule is that appeals at all levels will be by way of review of the decision of the lower court; (b) A decision to hold a rehearing will only be justified where the appeal court considers that in the circumstances of the individual appeal it is in the interests of justice to do so; (c) it is undesirable to attempt to formulate criteria to be applied by the appeal court in deciding whether to hold a rehearing. There are two main reasons for this. The first reason is that the decision to hold a rehearing must inevitably rest on the circumstances of the particular appeal. The second reason is that any attempt to formulate such criteria would in effect be to rewrite the rule in more specific terms, thereby restricting the flexibility which is inherent in the general terms in which the rule is framed; (d) In a case involving some procedural or other irregularity in the lower court it will be material for the appeal court, when considering whether to hold a rehearing, to have regard to the fact that an appeal will be allowed where the decision of the lower court is rendered 'unjust because of serious procedural or other irregularity' (see CPR r.52.11(3)(b)). Thus, where in such a case the decision of the lower court was made in the exercise of its discretion, the appeal court will be free to exercise the discretion afresh, without the need to hold a rehearing. However, what weight (if any) this factor may have will depend on the circumstances of the particular case; (e) The word 'will' in the opening words of CPR r.52.11(3) ('The appeal court will allow ...') throws no light on the approach to be adopted in deciding whether to hold a rehearing under CPR 52.11(1)(b).

(The FPR provisions corresponding to CPR rules 52.11(3) and 52.11(1)(b) are rules 30.12(3) and 30.12(1(b).)

Fresh evidence on appeal

Unless it orders otherwise the appeal court will not receive (a) oral evidence; or (b) evidence which was not before the lower court (rule 30.12(2)). This wording replicates CPR rule 52.11(2). By contrast, the old FPR rule 8.1(3)(b) provided that:

> oral evidence or evidence which was not before the district judge may be admitted if in all circumstances of the case it would be in the interests of justice to do so, irrespective of whether the appeal be by way of review or rehearing.

In *Cordle* Thorpe LJ had said at [32]:

> ... it seems to me that a circuit judge hearing an appeal from a district judge should not admit fresh evidence, unless there is a need to do so on the application of the more liberal rules for the admission of fresh evidence that are recognised as necessary in family proceedings.

It remains to be seen whether rule 30.12(2) will result in a more restrictive approach to fresh evidence in financial cases than under the FPR 1991.

The approach in civil proceedings derives from the principles set out by the Court of Appeal in *Ladd v Marshall* [1954] FLR Rep 422, [1954] 3 All ER 745: leave would be given to adduce fresh evidence on appeal only where three conditions are met:

> first, it must be shown that the evidence could not have been obtained with reasonable diligence for use at the trial; secondly, the evidence must be such that, if given, it would probably have an important influence on the result of the case, though it need not be decisive; thirdly, the evidence must be such as is presumably to be believed, or in other words, it must be apparently credible, though it need not be incontrovertible.

These criteria, and the status of the test itself since the advent of the CPR, have been reviewed in numerous later cases. In *Hertfordshire Investments Limited v Bubb* [2000] 1 WLR 2318 Hale LJ stated at [37] that:

> it cannot be a simple balancing exercise as the judge in this case seemed to think. He had to approach it on the basis that strong grounds were required. The *Ladd* v *Marshall* criteria are principles rather than rules but, nevertheless, they should be looked at with considerable care ...

In *Sharab v Al Saud* [2009] EWCA Civ 353 at [52] Richards LJ said:

> The court must of course seek to give effect to the overriding objective of

doing justice, but in that respect the pre-CPR cases, including *Ladd* v *Marshall*, remain of relevance and indeed of powerful persuasive authority.

See also *Hamilton v Al Fayed* [2000] EWCA Civ 3012 at [11] and [13] (pre-CPR cases remain powerful persuasive authority, for they illustrate the attempts of the courts to strike a fair balance between the need for concluded litigation to be determinative of disputes and the desirability that the judicial process should achieve the right result; *Ladd v Marshall* principles have been followed by the Court of Appeal for nearly half a century and are in no way in conflict with the overriding objective. In particular it will not normally be in the interests of justice to reopen a concluded trial in order to introduce fresh evidence unless that evidence will probably influence the result); *Muscat v Health Professions Council* [2009] EWCA Civ 1090, [2009] All ER (D) 209 (Oct) (since the introduction of the CPR, a decision to admit fresh evidence was not to be confined within the old *Ladd v Marshall* straightjacket); *Transview Properties Ltd v City Site Properties Ltd* [2009] EWCA Civ 1255, [2009] All ER (D) 255 (Nov) (permission should only be granted if, in accordance with the overriding objective, it is just to admit evidence on appeal which was not produced at trial. The party bringing forward more evidence on an appeal must have a very good reason for not having obtained it in time to use at the trial).

The *Ladd v Marshall* principles have been applied more liberally in family proceedings, especially those involving children (see, e.g. *Re K (non accidental injuries: perpetrator: new evidence)* [2005] 1 FLR 285). The Court of Appeal has addressed this issue in two recent financial cases. In *Robson v Robson* [2010] EWCA Civ 1171, Ward LJ said at [57]:

> As CPR 52.11 makes clear, the appeal is limited to a review of the decision below, and not by way of re-hearing except where the interests of justice demand it. Accordingly the court does not receive evidence which was not before the lower court save where the desirability of achieving a fair result outweighs the public interest in the finality of judgment. Whilst, therefore, the demands of the overriding objective to deal with cases justly may dominate the decision, the well established criteria of *Ladd v Marshall* [1954] 1 W.L.R. 1489 still prevail.

In *Kaur v Matharu* [2010] EWCA Civ 930 Thorpe LJ, having reviewed *Ladd v Marshall, Cordle* and *Zeiderman v Zeiderman* [2008] EWCA Civ 760 (unreported), stated at [21]:

> The message, it seems to me, drawing these threads of rule and authority together, is that where there is an appeal in ancillary relief from district judge to circuit judge, the circuit judge always exercises a discretion which is not strictly bound by the principles enunciated in *Ladd v Marshall*. However, it will only be in exceptional cases that that discretion will be exercised in favour of the admission of fresh evidence.

Decisions on whether to allow fresh evidence do not depend on whether the appeal is by way of review or rehearing: see *El Du Pont De Nemours & Company v S.T. Dupont* [2003] EWCA Civ 1368 at [95] (May LJ):

> As to fresh evidence, under rule 52.11(2) on an appeal by way of review the court will not receive evidence which was not before the lower court unless it orders otherwise. There is an obligation on the parties to bring forward all the evidence on which they intend to rely before the lower court, and failure to do this does not normally result in indulgence by the appeal court. The principles on which the appeal court will admit fresh evidence under this provision are now well understood and do not require elaboration here. They may be found, for instance, in the judgment of Hale LJ in *Hertfordshire Investments Limited v Bubb* [2000] 1 WLR 2318 at 2325D–H. Rule 52.11(2) also applies to appeals by way of rehearing under rule 52.11(1)(b), so that decisions on fresh evidence do not depend on whether the appeal is by way of review or rehearing.

Appeals against consent orders

Para 14.1 of PD 30A makes it plain that Part 30 applies equally to consent orders. Moreover, it goes further by providing that '*An appeal is the only way in which a consent order may be challenged*'. It thus appears that under the new rules a challenge to a consent order must be by appeal (which will of course in some cases require an application for permission for leave to appeal out of time), whether (a) an error on the part of the court is alleged; (b) a supervening event has occurred invalidating a fundamental assumption on which the order was based (*Barder v Caluori* [1988] AC 20); or (c) the basis of challenge is some other vitiating factor such as duress, mutual mistake, non-disclosure, misrepresentation or fraud (see, for example, *Judge v Judge* [2009] 1 FLR 1287 at [59]).

Thus has a single short sentence in PD 30A rendered otiose a great deal of sterile case law in which the correct procedure governing challenges to consent orders was considered: see e.g. the cases (the headnotes to many of which can be found in **@eGlance's** Leading Cases) of *B-T v B-T (Divorce: Procedure)* [1990] 2 FLR 1; *Re C (financial provision: leave to appeal)* [1993] 2 FLR 799; *T v T (consent order procedure to set aside)* [1996] 2 FLR 640; *Harris v Manahan* [1997] 1 FLR 205; *Shaw v Shaw* [2002] 2 FLR 1204 at [44(iii)] per Thorpe LJ (a party seeking to challenge a consent order could do so by applying for leave to appeal out of time: (*Barder, above*; *Livesey v Jenkins* [1985] FLR 813, HL); by application to set aside (in the county court, by CCR 1981 Ord 37, rule 1); or by fresh action (*de Lasala v de Lasala* (1979) FLR Rep 223); *Robinson v Robinson (Disclosure)* (1983) 4 FLR 102). This long overdue reform is much to be welcomed.

Specific appeals

PD 30A makes specific provision for the following categories of appeal which relate (or may relate) to financial proceedings:

- Appeals from a magistrates' court to the county court under section 111A of the Magistrates' Courts Act 1980: paras 9.2 to 9.12.
- Deduction order appeals to a county court from the Child Maintenance and Enforcement Commission: paras 9.13 to 9.34.
- Appeals against pension sharing order and pension compensation sharing orders: paras 11.1 to 11.3.
- Appeals under section 20 of the Child Support Act 1991: paras 12.1 to 12.3.

Assignment of appeals to the Court of Appeal and reopening of final appeals

Where a High Court or county court appeal (but not one from a magistrates' court) raises an important point of principle or practice the court hearing the appeal may order it to be transferred to the Court of Appeal (rule 30.13). Such transfers are likely to be rare.

PD 30A paras 18.1 to 18.7 contains detailed provisions supplementing rule 30.12 (reopening of final appeals).

Summary assessment of costs

PD 30A para 17 warns that it is likely that costs will be summarily assessed at (a) contested directions hearings on appeals; (b) applications for permission to appeal where the respondent is present; (c) appeals from case management decisions or decisions made at directions hearings; and (d) appeals listed for one day or less. Parties at such hearings are expected to be prepared to deal with summary assessment. (See also CPR Part 44, PD section 13.)

Forms

The following Forms are prescribed by *PD 5A – Forms*:

N161	Appellant's Notice
N161A	Guidance Notes on Completing the Appellant's Notice
N161B	Important Notes for Respondents
N162	Respondent's Notice
N162A	Guidance Notes for Completing the Respondent's Notice
N163	Skeleton Argument
N164	Appellant's Notice (note however that this last is a CPR Form to be used in Small Claims Track cases. Its inclusion is thought therefore to be an error).

PART 30: APPEALS

Scope and interpretation

30.1.—(1) The rules in this Part apply to appeals to—

(a) the High Court; and

(b) a county court.

(2) This Part does not apply to an appeal in detailed assessment proceedings against a decision of an authorised court officer.

(Rules 47.20 to 47.23 of the CPR deal with appeals against a decision of an authorised court officer in detailed assessment proceedings.)

(3) In this Part—

"appeal court" means the court to which an appeal is made;

"appeal notice" means an appellant's or respondent's notice;

"appellant" means a person who brings or seeks to bring an appeal;

"lower court" means the court from which, or the person from whom, the appeal lies; and

"respondent" means—

(a) a person other than the appellant who was a party to the proceedings in the lower court and who is affected by the appeal; and

(b) a person who is permitted by the appeal court to be a party to the appeal.

(4) This Part is subject to any rule, enactment or practice direction which sets out special provisions with regard to any particular category of appeal.

Parties to comply with the practice direction

30.2. All parties to an appeal must comply with Practice Direction 30A.

Permission

30.3.—(1) An appellant or respondent requires permission to appeal—

(a) against a decision in proceedings where the decision appealed against was made by a district judge or a costs judge, unless paragraph (2) applies; or

(b) as provided by Practice Direction 30A.

(2) Permission to appeal is not required where the appeal is against—

(a) a committal order; or

(b) a secure accommodation order under section 25 of the 1989 Act.

(3) An application for permission to appeal may be made—

(a) to the lower court at the hearing at which the decision to be appealed was made; or

(b) to the appeal court in an appeal notice.

(Rule 30.4 sets out the time limits for filing an appellant's notice at the appeal court. Rule 30.5 sets out the time limits for filing a respondent's notice at the appeal court. Any application for permission to appeal to the appeal court must be made in the appeal notice (see rules 30.4(1) and 30.5(3).)

(4) Where the lower court refuses an application for permission to appeal, a further application for permission to appeal may be made to the appeal court.

(5) Where the appeal court, without a hearing, refuses permission to appeal, the person seeking permission may request the decision to be reconsidered at a hearing.

(6) A request under paragraph (5) must be filed within 7 days beginning with the date on which the notice that permission has been refused was served.

(7) Permission to appeal may be given only where—

(a) the court considers that the appeal would have a real prospect of success; or

(b) there is some other compelling reason why the appeal should be heard.

(8) An order giving permission may—

(a) limit the issues to be heard; and

(b) be made subject to conditions.

(9) In this rule "costs judge" means a taxing master of the Senior Courts.

Appellant's notice

30.4.—(1) Where the appellant seeks permission from the appeal court it must be requested in the appellant's notice.

(2) Subject to paragraph (3), the appellant must file the appellant's notice at the appeal court within—

(a) such period as may be directed by the lower court (which may be longer or shorter than the period referred to in sub-paragraph (b)); or

(b) where the court makes no such direction, 21 days after the date of the decision of the lower court against which the appellant wishes to appeal.

(3) Where the appeal is against an order under section 38(1) of the 1989 Act, the appellant must file the appellant's notice within 7 days beginning with the date of the decision of the lower court.

(4) Unless the appeal court orders otherwise, an appellant's notice must be served on each respondent and the persons referred to in paragraph (5)—

(a) as soon as practicable; and

(b) in any event not later than 7 days,

after it is filed.

(5) The persons referred to in paragraph (4) are—

(a) any children's guardian, welfare officer, or children and family reporter;

(b) a local authority who has prepared a report under section 14A(8) or (9) of the 1989 Act;

(c) an adoption agency or local authority which has prepared a report on the suitability of the applicant to adopt a child;

(d) a local authority which has prepared a report on the placement of the child for adoption; and

(e) where the appeal is from a magistrates' court, the court officer.

Respondent's notice

30.5.—(1) A respondent may file and serve a respondent's notice.

(2) A respondent who—

(a) is seeking permission to appeal from the appeal court; or

(b) wishes to ask the appeal court to uphold the order of the lower court for reasons different from or additional to those given by the lower court,

must file a respondent's notice.

(3) Where the respondent seeks permission from the appeal court it must be requested in the respondent's notice.

(4) A respondent's notice must be filed within—

(a) such period as may be directed by the lower court; or

(b) where the court makes no such direction, 14 days beginning with the date referred to in paragraph (5).

(5) The date referred to in paragraph (4) is—

(a) the date on which the respondent is served with the appellant's notice where—
    (i) permission to appeal was given by the lower court; or
    (ii) permission to appeal is not required;

(b) the date on which the respondent is served with notification that the appeal court has given the appellant permission to appeal; or

(c) the date on which the respondent is served with notification that the application for permission to appeal and the appeal itself are to be heard together.

(6) Unless the appeal court orders otherwise, a respondent's notice must be served on the appellant, any other respondent and the persons referred to in rule 30.4(5)—

(a) as soon as practicable; and

(b) in any event not later than 7 days,

after it is filed.

(7) Where there is an appeal against an order under section 38(1) of the 1989 Act—

(a) a respondent may not, in that appeal, bring an appeal from the order or ask the appeal court to uphold the order of the lower court for reasons different from or additional to those given by the lower court; and

(b) paragraphs (2) and (3) do not apply.

Grounds of appeal

30.6. The appeal notice must state the grounds of appeal.

Variation of time

30.7.—(1) An application to vary the time limit for filing an appeal notice must be made to the appeal court.

(2) The parties may not agree to extend any date or time limit set by—

(a) these rules;

(b) Practice Direction 30A; or

(c) an order of the appeal court or the lower court.

(Rule 4.1(3)(a) provides that the court may extend or shorten the time for compliance with a rule, practice direction or court order (even if an application for extension is made after the time for compliance has expired).)

(Rule 4.1(3)(c) provides that the court may adjourn or bring forward a hearing.)

Stay

30.8. Unless the appeal court or the lower court orders otherwise, an appeal does not operate as a stay of any order or decision of the lower court.

Amendment of appeal notice

30.9. An appeal notice may not be amended without the permission of the appeal court.

Striking out appeal notices and setting aside or imposing conditions on permission to appeal

30.10.—(1) The appeal court may—

(a) strike out the whole or part of an appeal notice;

(b) set aside permission to appeal in whole or in part;

(c) impose or vary conditions upon which an appeal may be brought.

(2) The court will only exercise its powers under paragraph (1) where there is a compelling reason for doing so.

(3) Where a party was present at the hearing at which permission was

given that party may not subsequently apply for an order that the court exercise its powers under paragraphs (1)(b) or (1)(c).

Appeal court's powers

30.11.—(1) In relation to an appeal the appeal court has all the powers of the lower court.

(Rule 30.1(4) provides that this Part is subject to any enactment that sets out special provisions with regard to any particular category of appeal.)

(2) The appeal court has power to—

(a) affirm, set aside or vary any order or judgment made or given by the lower court;
(b) refer any application or issue for determination by the lower court;
(c) order a new hearing;
(d) make orders for the payment of interest;
(e) make a costs order.

(3) The appeal court may exercise its powers in relation to the whole or part of an order of the lower court.

(Rule 4.1 contains general rules about the court's case management powers.)

(4) If the appeal court—

(a) refuses an application for permission to appeal;
(b) strikes out an appellant's notice; or
(c) dismisses an appeal,

and it considers that the application, the appellant's notice or the appeal is totally without merit, the provisions of paragraph (5) must be complied with.

(5) Where paragraph (4) applies—

(a) the court's order must record the fact that it considers the application, the appellant's notice or the appeal to be totally without merit; and
(b) the court must at the same time consider whether it is appropriate to make a civil restraint order.

Hearing of appeals

30.12.—(1) Every appeal will be limited to a review of the decision of the lower court unless—

(a) an enactment or practice direction makes different provision for a particular category of appeal; or
(b) the court considers that in the circumstances of an individual appeal it would be in the interests of justice to hold a re-hearing.

(2) Unless it orders otherwise, the appeal court will not receive—

(a) oral evidence; or

(b) evidence which was not before the lower court.

(3) The appeal court will allow an appeal where the decision of the lower court was—

(a) wrong; or

(b) unjust because of a serious procedural or other irregularity in the proceedings in the lower court.

(4) The appeal court may draw any inference of fact which it considers justified on the evidence.

(5) At the hearing of the appeal a party may not rely on a matter not contained in that party's appeal notice unless the appeal court gives permission.

Assignment of appeals to the Court of Appeal

30.13.—(1) Where the court from or to which an appeal is made or from which permission to appeal is sought ("the relevant court") considers that—

(a) an appeal which is to be heard by a county court or the High Court would raise an important point of principle or practice; or

(b) there is some other compelling reason for the Court of Appeal to hear it,

the relevant court may order the appeal to be transferred to the Court of Appeal.

(2) This rule does not apply to proceedings in a magistrates' court.

Reopening of final appeals

30.14.—(1) The High Court will not reopen a final determination of any appeal unless—

(a) it is necessary to do so in order to avoid real injustice;

(b) the circumstances are exceptional and make it appropriate to reopen the appeal; and

(c) there is no alternative effective remedy.

(2) In paragraphs (1), (3), (4) and (6), "appeal" includes an application for permission to appeal.

(3) This rule does not apply to appeals to a county court.

(4) Permission is needed to make an application under this rule to reopen a final determination of an appeal.

(5) There is no right to an oral hearing of an application for permission unless, exceptionally, the judge so directs.

(6) The judge will not grant permission without directing the application

to be served on the other party to the original appeal and giving that party an opportunity to make representations.

(7) There is no right of appeal or review from the decision of the judge on the application for permission, which is final.

(8) The procedure for making an application for permission is set out in Practice Direction 30A.

PRACTICE DIRECTION 30A – APPEALS

This Practice Direction supplements FPR Part 30

1.1 This practice direction applies to all appeals to which Part 30 applies.

Routes of appeal

2.1 The following table sets out to which court or judge an appeal is to be made (subject to obtaining any necessary permission)—

Decision of:	*Appeal made to:*
Magistrates' Court	Circuit judge
District judge of a county court	Circuit judge
District judge of the High Court	High Court judge
District judge of the principal registry of the Family Division	High Court judge
Costs judge	High Court Judge
Circuit judge or recorder	Court of Appeal
High Court judge	Court of Appeal

(Provisions setting out routes of appeal include section 16(1) of the Senior Courts Act 1981 (as amended); section 77(1) of the County Courts Act 1984 (as amended) and the Access to Justice Act 1999 (Destination of Appeals) (Family Proceedings) Order 2009 (see paragraphs 9.1 to 9.12 below. The Family Proceedings (Allocation to Judiciary) (Appeals) Directions 2009 provide for an appeal from a magistrates' court to be heard by a Circuit judge.

The routes of appeal from an order or decision relating to contempt of court of a magistrates' court under section 63(3) of the Magistrates' Courts Act 1980 and of a county court and the High Court are set out in section 13(2) of the Administration of Justice Act 1960. Appeals under section 8(1) of the Gender Recognition Act 2004 lie to the High Court (see section 8 of the 2004 Act). The procedure for appeals to the Court of Appeal is governed by the Civil Procedure Rules 1998, in particular CPR Part 52.

2.2 Where the decision to be appealed is a decision in a Part 19 (Alternative Procedure For Applications) application on a point of law in a case which did not involve any substantial dispute of fact, the court to which the appeal lies, where that court is the High Court or a county court and unless the appeal would lie to the Court of Appeal in any event, must consider whether to order the appeal to be transferred to the Court of Appeal under rule 30.13 (Assignment of Appeals to the Court of Appeal).

Grounds for appeal

3.1 Rule 30.12 (hearing of appeals) sets out the circumstances in which the appeal court will allow an appeal.

3.2 The grounds of appeal should—

(a) set out clearly the reasons why rule 30.12(3)(a) or (b) is said to apply; and
(b) specify in respect of each ground, whether the ground raises an appeal on a point of law or is an appeal against a finding of fact.

Permission to appeal

4.1 Rule 30.3 (Permission) sets out the circumstances when permission to appeal is required. At present permission to appeal is required where the decision appealed against was made by a district judge or a costs judge. However, no permission is required where rule 30.3(2) (appeals against a committal order or a secure accommodation order under section 25 of the Children Act 1989) applies.

(The requirement of permission to appeal may be imposed by a practice direction – see rule 30.3(1)(b) (Permission).)

Court to which permission to appeal application should be made

4.2 An application for permission should be made orally at the hearing at which the decision to be appealed against is made.

4.3 Where—

(a) no application for permission to appeal is made at the hearing; or
(b) the lower court refuses permission to appeal,

an application for permission to appeal may be made to the appeal court in accordance with rules 30.3(3) and (4) (Permission).

(Rule 30.1(3) defines 'lower court'.)

4.4 Where no application for permission to appeal has been made in accordance with rule 30.3(3)(a) (Permission) but a party requests further time to make such an application the court may adjourn the hearing to give that party an opportunity to do so.

4.5 There is no appeal from a decision of the appeal court to allow or refuse permission to appeal to that court (although where the appeal court, without a hearing, refuses permission to appeal, the person seeking permission may request that decision to be reconsidered at a hearing – see section 54(4) of the Access to Justice Act 1999 and rule 30.3(5) (Permission)).

Material omission from a judgment of the lower court

4.6 Where a party's advocate considers that there is a material omission from a judgment of the lower court or, in a magistrates' court, the written reasons for the decision of the lower court (including inadequate reasons for the lower court's decision), the advocate should before the drawing of the order give the lower court which made the decision the opportunity of considering whether there is an omission and should not immediately use the omission as grounds for an application to appeal.

4.7 Paragraph 4.8 below applies where there is an application to the lower court for permission to appeal on the grounds of a material omission from a judgment of the lower court. Paragraph 4.9 below applies where there is an application for permission to appeal to the appeal court on the grounds of a material omission from a judgment of the lower court. Paragraphs 4.8 and 4.9 do not apply where the lower court is a magistrates' court.

4.8 Where the application for permission to appeal is made to the lower court, the court which made the decision must—

(a) consider whether there is a material omission and adjourn for that purpose if necessary; and
(b) where the conclusion is that there has been such an omission, provide additions to the judgment.

4.9 Where the application for permission to appeal is made to the appeal court, the appeal court—

(a) must consider whether there is a material omission; and
(b) where the conclusion is that there has been such an omission, may adjourn the application and remit the case to the lower court with an invitation to provide additions to the judgment.

Consideration of Permission without a hearing

4.10 An application for permission to appeal may be considered by the appeal court without a hearing.

4.11 If permission is granted without a hearing the parties will be notified of that decision and the procedure in paragraphs 6.1 to 6.8 will then apply.

4.12 If permission is refused without a hearing the parties will be notified of that decision with the reasons for it. The decision is subject to the appellant's right to have it reconsidered at an oral hearing. This may be before the same judge.

4.13 A request for the decision to be reconsidered at an oral hearing must be filed at the appeal court within 7 days after service of the notice that permission has been refused. A copy of the request must be served by the appellant on the respondent at the same time.

Permission hearing

4.14 Where an appellant, who is represented, makes a request for a decision to be reconsidered at an oral hearing, the appellant's advocate must, at least 4 days before the hearing, in a brief written statement—

(a) inform the court and the respondent of the points which the appellant proposes to raise at the hearing;

(b) set out the reasons why permission should be granted notwithstanding the reasons given for the refusal of permission; and

(c) confirm, where applicable, that the requirements of paragraph 4.17 have been complied with (appellant in receipt of services funded by the Legal Services Commission).

4.15 The respondent will be given notice of a permission hearing, but is not required to attend unless requested by the court to do so.

4.16 If the court requests the respondent's attendance at the permission hearing, the appellant must supply the respondent with a copy of the appeal bundle (see paragraph 5.9) within 7 days of being notified of the request, or such other period as the court may direct. The costs of providing that bundle shall be borne by the appellant initially, but will form part of the costs of the permission application.

Appellants in receipt of services funded by the Legal Services Commission applying for permission to appeal

4.17 Where the appellant is in receipt of services funded by the Legal Services Commission (or legally aided) and permission to appeal has been refused by the appeal court without a hearing, the appellant must send a copy of the reasons the appeal court gave for refusing permission to the relevant office of the Legal Services Commission as soon as it has been received from the court. The court will require confirmation that this has been done if a hearing is requested to re-consider the question of permission.

Limited permission

4.18 Where a court under rule 30.3 (Permission) gives permission to appeal on some issues only, it will—

(a) refuse permission on any remaining issues; or

(b) reserve the question of permission to appeal on any remaining issues to the court hearing the appeal.

4.19 If the court reserves the question of permission under paragraph 4.18(b), the appellant must, within 14 days after service of the court's order, inform the appeal court and the respondent in writing whether the appellant intends to pursue the reserved issues. If the appellant does intend to pursue the reserved issues, the parties must include in any time estimate for the appeal hearing, their time estimate for the reserved issues.

4.20 If the appeal court refuses permission to appeal on the remaining issues without a hearing and the applicant wishes to have that decision reconsidered at an oral hearing, the time limit in rule 30.3(6) (Permission) shall apply. Any application for an extension of this time limit should be made promptly. The court hearing the appeal on the issues for which permission has been granted will not normally grant, at the appeal hearing, an application to extend the time limit in rule 30.3 (6) for the remaining issues.

4.21 If the appeal court refuses permission to appeal on remaining issues at or after an oral hearing, the application for permission to appeal on those issues cannot be renewed at the appeal hearing (see section 54(4) of the Access to Justice Act 1999).

Respondents' costs of permission applications

4.22 In most cases, applications for permission to appeal will be determined without the court requesting—

(a) submissions from; or
(b) if there is an oral hearing, attendance by,
the respondent.

4.23 Where the court does not request submissions from or attendance by the respondent, costs will not normally be allowed to a respondent who volunteers submissions or attendance.

4.24 Where the court does request—

(a) submissions from; or
(b) attendance by the respondent,

the court will normally allow the costs of the respondent if permission is refused.

Appellant's notice

5.1 An appellant's notice must be filed and served in all cases. Where an application for permission to appeal is made to the appeal court it must be applied for in the appellant's notice.

Human Rights

5.2 Where the appellant seeks—

(a) to rely on any issue under the Human Rights Act 1998; or
(b) a remedy available under that Act,

for the first time in an appeal the appellant must include in the appeal notice the information required by rule 29.5(2).

5.3 Practice Direction 29A (Human Rights, Joining the Crown) will apply as if references to the directions hearing were to the application for permission to appeal.

Extension of time for filing appellant's notice

5.4. If an extension of time is required for filing the appellant's notice the application must be made in that notice. The notice should state the reason for the delay and the steps taken prior to the application being made.

5.5 Where the appellant's notice includes an application for an extension of time and permission to appeal has been given or is not required the respondent has the right to be heard on that application and must be served with a copy of the appeal bundle (see paragraph 5.9). However, a respondent who unreasonably opposes an extension of time runs the risk of being ordered to pay the appellant's costs of that application.

5.6 If an extension of time is given following such an application the procedure at paragraphs 6.1 to 6.8 applies.

Applications

5.7 Notice of an application to be made to the appeal court for a remedy incidental to the appeal (e.g. an interim injunction under rule 20.2 (Orders for interim remedies)) may be included in the appeal notice or in a Part 18 (Procedure For Other Applications in Proceedings) application notice.

(Paragraph 13 of this practice direction contains other provisions relating to applications.)

Documents

5.8 The appellant must file the following documents together with an appeal bundle (see paragraph 5.9) with his or her appellant's notice—

(a) two additional copies of the appellant's notice for the appeal court;
(b) one copy of the appellant's notice for each of the respondents;
(c) one copy of the appellant's skeleton argument for each copy of the appellant's notice that is filed;
(d) a sealed or stamped copy of the order being appealed or a copy of the notice of the making of an order;
(e) a copy of any order giving or refusing permission to appeal, together with a copy of the court's reasons for allowing or refusing permission to appeal;
(f) any witness statements or affidavits in support of any application included in the appellant's notice.

5.9 An appellant must include the following documents in his or her appeal bundle—

(a) a sealed or stamped copy of the appellant's notice;
(b) a sealed or stamped copy of the order being appealed, or a copy of the notice of the making of an order;
(c) a copy of any order giving or refusing permission to appeal, together with a copy of the court's reasons for allowing or refusing permission to appeal;
(d) any affidavit or witness statement filed in support of any application included in the appellant's notice;
(e) where the appeal is against a consent order, a statement setting out

the change in circumstances since the order was agreed or other circumstances justifying a review or re-hearing;

(f) a copy of the appellant's skeleton argument;

(g) a transcript or note of judgment or, in a magistrates' court, written reasons for the court's decision (see paragraph 5.23), and in cases where permission to appeal was given by the lower court or is not required those parts of any transcript of evidence which are directly relevant to any question at issue on the appeal;

(h) the application form;

(i) any application notice (or case management documentation) relevant to the subject of the appeal;

(j) any other documents which the appellant reasonably considers necessary to enable the appeal court to reach its decision on the hearing of the application or appeal; and

(k) such other documents as the court may direct.

5.10 All documents that are extraneous to the issues to be considered on the application or the appeal must be excluded. The appeal bundle may include affidavits, witness statements, summaries, experts' reports and exhibits but only where these are directly relevant to the subject matter of the appeal.

5.11 Where the appellant is represented, the appeal bundle must contain a certificate signed by the appellant's solicitor, counsel or other representative to the effect that the appellant has read and understood paragraph 5.10 and that the composition of the appeal bundle complies with it.

5.12 Where it is not possible to file all the above documents, the appellant must indicate which documents have not yet been filed and the reasons why they are not currently available. The appellant must then provide a reasonable estimate of when the missing document or documents can be filed and file them as soon as reasonably practicable.

Skeleton arguments

5.13 The appellant's notice must, subject to paragraphs 5.14 and 5.15, be accompanied by a skeleton argument. Alternatively the skeleton argument may be included in the appellant's notice. Where the skeleton argument is so included it will not form part of the notice for the purposes of rule 30.9 (Amendment of appeal notice).

5.14 Where it is impracticable for the appellant's skeleton argument to accompany the appellant's notice it must be filed and served on all respondents within 14 days of filing the notice.

5.15 An appellant who is not represented need not file a skeleton argument but is encouraged to do so since this will be helpful to the court.

5.16 A skeleton argument must contain a numbered list of the points which the party wishes to make. These should both define and confine the areas of controversy. Each point should be stated as concisely as the nature of the case allows.

5.17 A numbered point must be followed by a reference to any document on which the party wishes to rely.

5.18 A skeleton argument must state, in respect of each authority cited—

(a) the proposition of law that the authority demonstrates; and
(b) the parts of the authority (identified by page or paragraph references) that support the proposition.

5.19 If more than one authority is cited in support of a given proposition, the skeleton argument must briefly state the reason for taking that course.

5.20 The statement referred to in paragraph 5.19 should not materially add to the length of the skeleton argument but should be sufficient to demonstrate, in the context of the argument—

(a) the relevance of the authority or authorities to that argument; and
(b) that the citation is necessary for a proper presentation of that argument.

5.21 The cost of preparing a skeleton argument which—

(a) does not comply with the requirements set out in this paragraph; or
(b) was not filed within the time limits provided by this Practice Direction (or any further time granted by the court),

will not be allowed on assessment except to the extent that the court otherwise directs.

5.22 The appellant should consider what other information the appeal court will need. This may include a list of persons who feature in the case or glossaries of technical terms. A chronology of relevant events will be necessary in most appeals.

Suitable record of the judgment

5.23 Where the judgment to be appealed has been officially recorded by the court, an approved transcript of that record should accompany the appellant's notice. Photocopies will not be accepted for this purpose. However, where there is no officially recorded judgment, the following documents will be acceptable—

Written judgments – Where the judgment was made in writing a copy of that judgment endorsed with the judge's signature.

Written reasons – in a magistrates' court, a copy of the written reasons for the court's decision.

Note of judgment – When judgment was not officially recorded or made in writing a note of the judgment (agreed between the appellant's and respondent's advocates) should be submitted for approval to the judge whose decision is being appealed. If the parties cannot agree on a single note of the judgment, both versions should be provided to that judge with an explanatory letter. For the purpose of an application for permission to appeal the note need not be approved by the respondent or the lower court judge.

Advocates' notes of judgments where the appellant is unrepresented – When the appellant was unrepresented in the lower court it is the duty of any advocate for the respondent to make the advocate's note of judgment promptly available, free of charge to the appellant where there is no officially recorded judgment or if the court so directs. Where the appellant was represented in the lower court it is the duty of the appellant's own former advocate to make that advocate's note available in these circumstances. The appellant should submit the note of judgment to the appeal court.

5.24 An appellant may not be able to obtain an official transcript or other suitable record of the lower court's decision within the time within which the appellant's notice must be filed. In such cases the appellant's notice must still be completed to the best of the appellant's ability on the basis of the documentation available. However it may be amended subsequently with the permission of the appeal court in accordance with rule 30.9 (Amendment of appeal notice).

Advocates' notes of judgments

5.25 Advocates' brief (or, where appropriate, refresher) fee includes—

(a) remuneration for taking a note of the judgment of the court;
(b) having the note transcribed accurately;
(c) attempting to agree the note with the other side if represented;
(d) submitting the note to the judge for approval where appropriate;
(e) revising it if so requested by the judge,
(f) providing any copies required for the appeal court, instructing solicitors and lay client; and
(g) providing a copy of the note to an unrepresented appellant.

Appeals from decision made by a family proceedings court under Parts 4 and 4A of the Family Law Act 1996

5.26 ...

Appeals under section 8(1) of the Gender Recognition Act 2004

5.27 ...

Transcripts or Notes of Evidence

5.31 When the evidence is relevant to the appeal an official transcript of the relevant evidence must be obtained. Transcripts or notes of evidence are generally not needed for the purpose of determining an application for permission to appeal.

Notes of evidence

5.32 If evidence relevant to the appeal was not officially recorded, a typed version of the judge's (including a district judge (magistrates' courts) or justices' clerk's /assistant clerk's notes of evidence must be obtained.

Transcripts at public expense

5.33 Where the lower court or the appeal court is satisfied that—

(a) an unrepresented appellant; or
(b) an appellant whose legal representation is provided free of charge to the appellant and not funded by the Community Legal Service,

is in such poor financial circumstances that the cost of a transcript would be an excessive burden the court may certify that the cost of obtaining one official transcript should be borne at public expense.

5.34 In the case of a request for an official transcript of evidence or proceedings to be paid for at public expense, the court must also be satisfied that there are reasonable grounds for appeal. Whenever possible a request for a transcript at public expense should be made to the lower court when asking for permission to appeal.

Filing and service of appellant's notice

5.35 Rule 30.4 (Appellant's notice) sets out the procedure and time limits for filing and serving an appellant's notice. Subject to paragraph 5.36, the appellant must file the appellant's notice at the appeal court within such period as may be directed by the lower court, which should not normally exceed 14 days or, where the lower court directs no such period within 21 days of the date of the decision that the appellant wishes to appeal.

5.36 Rule 30.4(3) (Appellant's notice) provides that unless the appeal court orders otherwise, where the appeal is against an order under section 38(1) of the 1989 Act, the appellant must file the appellant's notice within 7 days beginning with the date of the decision of the lower court.

5.37 Where the lower court announces its decision and reserves the reasons for its judgment or order until a later date, it should, in the exercise of powers under rule 30.4 (2)(a))(Appellant's notice), fix a period for filing the appellant's notice at the appeal court that takes this into account.

5.38 Except where the appeal court orders otherwise a sealed or stamped copy of the appellant's notice, including any skeleton arguments must be served on all respondents and other persons referred to in rule 30.4(5) (Appellant's notice) in accordance with the timetable prescribed by rule 30.4(4)) (Appellant's notice) except where this requirement is modified by paragraph 5.14 in which case the skeleton argument should be served as soon as it is filed.

5.39 Where the appellant's notice is to be served on a child, then rule 6.33 (supplementary provision relating to service on children) applies and unless the appeal court orders otherwise a sealed or stamped copy of the appellant's notice, including any skeleton arguments must be served on the persons or bodies mentioned in rule 6.33(2). For example, the appeal notice must be served on any children's guardian, welfare officer or children and family reporter who is appointed in the proceedings.

5.40 Unless the court otherwise directs, a respondent need not take any action when served with an appellant's notice until such time as notification is given to the respondent that permission to appeal has been given.

5.41 The court may dispense with the requirement for service of the notice on a respondent.

5.42 Unless the appeal court directs otherwise, the appellant must serve on the respondent the appellant's notice and skeleton argument (but not the appeal bundle),where the appellant is applying for permission to appeal in the appellant's notice.

5.43 Where permission to appeal—

(a) has been given by the lower court; or
(b) is not required,

the appellant must serve the appeal bundle on the respondent and the persons mentioned in paragraph 5.39 with the appellant's notice.

Amendment of Appeal Notice
5.44 An appeal notice may be amended with permission. Such an application to amend and any application in opposition will normally be dealt with at the hearing unless that course would cause unnecessary expense or delay in which case a request should be made for the application to amend to be heard in advance.

Procedure after permission is obtained
6.1 This paragraph sets out the procedure where—

(a) permission to appeal is given by the appeal court; or
(b) the appellant's notice is filed in the appeal court and—
  (i) permission was given by the lower court; or
  (ii) permission is not required.

6.2 If the appeal court gives permission to appeal, the appeal bundle must be served on each of the respondents within 7 days of receiving the order giving permission to appeal.

6.3 The appeal court will send the parties—

(a) notification of the date of the hearing or the period of time (the 'listing window') during which the appeal is likely to be heard;
(b) where permission is granted by the appeal court a copy of the order giving permission to appeal; and
(c) any other directions given by the court.

6.4 Where the appeal court grants permission to appeal, the appellant must add the following documents to the appeal bundle—

(a) the respondent's notice and skeleton argument (if any);
(b) those parts of the transcripts of evidence which are directly relevant to any question at issue on the appeal;
(c) the order granting permission to appeal and, where permission to appeal was granted at an oral hearing, the transcript (or note) of any judgment which was given; and
(d) any document which the appellant and respondent have agreed to add to the appeal bundle in accordance with paragraph 7.16.

6.5 Where permission to appeal has been refused on a particular issue, the appellant must remove from the appeal bundle all documents that are relevant only to that issue.

Time estimates

6.6 If the appellant is legally represented, the appeal court must be notified, in writing, of the advocate's time estimate for the hearing of the appeal.

6.7 The time estimate must be that of the advocate who will argue the appeal. It should exclude the time required by the court to give judgment.

6.8 A court officer will notify the respondent of the appellant's time estimate and if the respondent disagrees with the time estimate the respondent must inform the court within 7 days of the notification. In the absence of such notification the respondent will be deemed to have accepted the estimate proposed on behalf of the appellant.

Respondent

7.1 A respondent who wishes to ask the appeal court to vary the order of the lower court in any way must appeal and permission will be required on the same basis as for an appellant.

(Paragraph 3.2 applies to grounds of appeal by a respondent.).

7.2 A respondent who wishes to appeal or who wishes to ask the appeal court to uphold the order of the lower court for reasons different from or additional to those given by the lower court must file a respondent's notice.

7.3 A respondent who does not file a respondent's notice will not be entitled, except with the permission of the court, to rely on any reason not relied on in the lower court. This paragraph and paragraph 7.2 do not apply where the appeal is against an order under section 38(1) of the 1989 Act (see rule 30.5(7) (Respondent's notice)).

7.4 Paragraphs 5.3 (Human Rights and extension for time for filing appellant's notice) and 5.4 to 5.6 (extension of time for filing appellant's notice) of this practice direction also apply to a respondent and a respondent's notice.

Time limits

7.5 The time limits for filing a respondent's notice are set out in rule 30.5(4) and (5) (Respondent's notice).

7.6 Where an extension of time is required the extension must be requested in the respondent's notice and the reasons why the respondent failed to act within the specified time must be included.

7.7 Except where paragraphs 7.8 and 7.10 apply, the respondent must file a skeleton argument for the court in all cases where the respondent proposes to address arguments to the court. The respondent's skeleton argument may be included within a respondent's notice. Where a skeleton argument is included within a respondent's notice it will not form part of the notice for the purposes of rule 30.9 (Amendment of appeal notice).

7.8 A respondent who—

(a) files a respondent's notice; but

(b) does not include a skeleton argument with that notice,

must file the skeleton argument within 14 days of filing the notice.

7.9 A respondent who does not file a respondent's notice but who files a skeleton argument must file that skeleton argument at least 7 days before the appeal hearing.

(Rule 30.5(4) (Respondent's notice) sets out the period for filing a respondent's notice.).

7.10 A respondent who is not represented need not file a skeleton argument but is encouraged to do so in order to assist the court.

7.11 The respondent must serve the skeleton argument on—

(a) the appellant; and

(b) any other respondent;

at the same time as the skeleton argument is filed at court. Where a child is an appellant or respondent the skeleton argument must also be served on the persons listed in rule 6.33(2) unless the court directs otherwise.

7.12 A respondent's skeleton argument must conform to the directions at paragraphs 5.16 to 5.22 with any necessary modifications. It should, where appropriate, answer the arguments set out in the appellant's skeleton argument.

Applications within respondent's notices
7.13 A respondent may include an application within a respondent's notice in accordance with paragraph 5.7.

Filing respondent's notices and skeleton arguments
7.14 The respondent must file the following documents with the respondent's notice in every case—

(a) two additional copies of the respondent's notice for the appeal court; and

(b) one copy each for the appellant, any other respondents and any persons referred to in paragraph 5.39.

7.15 The respondent may file a skeleton argument with the respondent's notice and—

(a) where doing so must file two copies; and
(b) where not doing so must comply with paragraph 7.8.

7.16 If the respondent considers documents in addition to those filed by the appellant to be necessary to enable the appeal court to reach its decision on the appeal and wishes to rely on those documents, any amendments to the appeal bundle should be agreed with the appellant if possible.

7.17 If the representatives for the parties are unable to reach agreement, the respondent may prepare a supplemental bundle.

7.18 The respondent must file any supplemental bundle so prepared, together with the requisite number of copies for the appeal court, at the appeal court—

(a) with the respondent's notice; or
(b) if a respondent's notice is not filed, within 21 days after the respondent is served with the appeal bundle.

7.19 The respondent must serve—

(a) the respondent's notice;
(b) the skeleton argument (if any); and
(c) the supplemental bundle (if any),

on—

(i) the appellant; and
(ii) any other respondent;

at the same time as those documents are filed at the court. Where a child is an appellant or respondent the documents referred to in paragraphs (a) to (c) above must also be served on the persons listed in rule 6.33(2) unless the court directs otherwise.

Appeals to the High Court

Application
8.1 The appellant's notice must be filed in—

(a) the principal registry of the Family Division; or
(b) the district registry which is nearest to the court from which the appeal lies.

8.2 A respondent's notice must be filed at the court where the appellant's notice was filed.

8.3 In the case of appeals from district judges of the High Court, applications for permission and any other applications in the appeal, appeals may be heard and directions in the appeal may be given by a High

Court Judge or by any person authorised under section 9 of the Senior
Courts Act 1981 to act as a judge of the High Court.

Appeals to a county court

Appeals to a judge of a county court from a district judge
9.1 The Designated Family Judge in consultation with the Family Division
Liaison Judges has responsibility for the allocation of appeals from
decisions of district judges to circuit judges.

Appeals to a county court from a magistrates' court

*Appeals under section 111A of the Magistrates' Courts Act 1980 ("the
1980 Act") from a magistrates' court to a county court on the ground
that the decision is wrong in law or in excess of jurisdiction*
9.2 As a result of an amendment to section 111 of the 1980 Act by the
Access to Justice Act 1999 (Destination of Appeals) (Family Proceedings)
Order 2009 ("the Destination Order") an application to have a case stated
for the opinion of the High Court under section 111 of that Act may not be
made in relation to family proceedings. Family proceedings for those
purposes are defined as—

(a) proceedings which, by virtue of section 65 of the 1980 Act, are or
    may be treated as family proceedings for the purposes of that Act;
    and
(b) proceedings under the Child Support Act 1991.

9.3 Section 111A of the 1980 Act, which is inserted by article 4(3) of the
Destination Order, provides that in family proceedings as defined in
paragraph 9.2 above a person may appeal to a county court on the ground
that a decision is wrong in law or is in excess of jurisdiction; this appeal to
a county court replaces the procedure for making an application to have a
case stated. Section 111A(3)(a) provides that no appeal may be brought
under section 111A if there is a right of appeal to a county court against the
decision otherwise than under that section.
9.4 Subject to section 111A of the 1980 Act and any other enactment,
the following rules in Part 30 apply to appeals under section 111A of the
1980 Act—

(a) 30.1 (scope and interpretation);
(b) 30.2 (parties to comply with the practice direction);
(c) 30.4 (appellant's notice);
(d) 30.6 (grounds of appeal);
(e) 30.8 (stay); and
(f) 30.9 (amendment of appeal notice).

9.5 Section 111A(4) of the 1980 Act provides that the notice of appeal
must be filed within 21 days after the day on which the decision of the

magistrates' court was given. The notice of appeal should also be served within this period of time. The time period for filing the appellant's notice in rule 30.4 (2) does not apply. There can be no extension of this 21 day time limit under rule 4.1(3)(a).

Other statutory rights of appeal from a magistrates' court and the court at which the appellant's notice is to be filed-provisions applying to those appeals and appeals under section 111A of the 1980 Act
9.6 The effect of the Destination Order is that appeals against decisions of magistrates' courts in family proceedings shall lie to a county court instead of to the High Court. In addition to replacing appeals by way of case stated by amending the 1980 Act as outlined above, the Destination Order amends the statutory provisions listed in paragraph 9.7 below to provide for the appeals under those provisions to lie to a county court instead of to the High Court Paragraph 9.7 also refers to the amendment to the 1980 Act for completeness.

9.7 Paragraph 9.8 and 9.9 below apply to appeals under—

(a) section 4(7) of the Maintenance Orders Act 1958;
(b) section 29 of the Domestic Proceedings and Magistrates' Courts Act 1978;
(c) section 60(5) of the Family Law 1986;
(d) section 94(1) to (9) of the Children Act 1989;
(e) section 61 of the Family Law Act 1996;
(f) sections 10(1)(a) to (3) and 13 (1) and (2) of the Crime and Disorder Act 1998; or
(g) section 111A of the 1980 Act.

9.8 Subject to any enactment or to any directions made by the President of the Family Division in exercise of the powers conferred on him under section 9 of the Courts and Legal Services Act 1990, a district judge may—

(a) dismiss an appeal;
    (i) for want of prosecution; or
    (ii) with the consent of the parties; or
(b) give leave for the appeal to be withdrawn,

and may deal with any question of costs arising out of the dismissal or withdrawal.

Unless the court directs otherwise, any interlocutory application in an appeal under the statutory provisions listed in paragraph 9.7 may be made to a district judge.

9.9 Subject to paragraph 9.10 below, the appellant's notice and other documents required to be filed by rule 30.4 and this practice direction shall where the appeal is against the making by a magistrates' court of any order or any refusal by a magistrates' court to make such an order—

(a) in proceedings listed in Schedule 1 to this Practice Direction, be filed in a care centre within the meaning of article 2 (b) of the Allocation and Transfer of Proceedings Order 2008;

(b) in proceedings under the Adoption and Children Act 2002, be filed in an adoption centre or an intercountry adoption centre within the meaning of article 2 (c) and (d) of the Allocation and Transfer of Proceedings Order 2008; and

(c) in any other case, be filed in a family hearing centre within the meaning of article 2(a) of that Order.

9.10 Where the appeal is an appeal from a decision of a magistrates' court under section 94 of the 1989 Act or section 61 of the Family Law Act 1996, the documents required to be filed by rule 30.4 and this practice direction may be filed in the principal registry of the Family Division of the High Court.

9.11 Article 11 of the Destination Order amends article 3 of the Allocation and Transfer of Proceedings Order 2008 to provide that the principal registry of the Family Division of the High Court is treated as a county court for the purposes of appeals from decisions of a magistrates' court under section 94 of the Children Act 1989 and section 61 of the Family Law Act 1996.

9.12 This practice direction applies to appeals under the statutory provisions listed in paragraph 9.7 with the following modifications and any other necessary modifications—

(a) after paragraph 5.6 insert—

"5.6A Paragraphs 5.4 to 5.6 do not apply to an appeal to a county court under section 111A of the Magistrates' Courts Act 1980."

(b) in paragraph 5.35, insert "and 5.36A" after " subject to paragraph 5.36";

(c) after paragraph 5.36 insert—

"5.36A Where the appeal is to a judge of a county court under section 111A of the Magistrates' Courts Act 1980, the appellant's notice must be filed and served within 21 days after the day on which the decision of the lower court was given.".

Appeals to a county court from the Child Maintenance and Enforcement Commission ("the Commission"): Deduction order appeals

9.13 A "deduction order appeal" is an appeal under regulation 25AB(1)(a) to (d) of the Child Support (Collection and Enforcement) Regulations 1992 (S.I. 1992/1989) ("the Collection and Enforcement Regulations"). A deduction order appeal is an appeal against—

(a) the making of a regular deduction order under section 32A of the Child Support Act 1991 ("the 1991 Act");

(b) a decision on an application to review a regular deduction order;

(c) a decision to withhold consent to the disapplication of sections 32G(1) and 32H(2)(b) of the 1991 Act which has the effect of unfreezing funds in the liable person's account; or

(d) the making of a final lump sum deduction order under section 32F of the 1991 Act.

A deduction order appeal lies to a county court from the Commission as a result of regulation 25AB(1) of the Collection and Enforcement Regulations.

9.14 The rules in Part 30 apply to deduction order appeals with the amendments set out in paragraphs 9.15 to 9.27 and 9.29 and 9.30 below. The rules in Part 30 also apply to appeals against the decision of a district judge in proceedings relating to a deduction order appeal with the amendments set out in paragraph 9.28 below.

9.15 "The respondent" means—

(a) the Commission and any person other than the appellant who was served with an order under section 32A(1), 32E(1) or 32F(1) of the 1991 Act; and

(b) a person who is permitted by the appeal court to be a party to the appeal.

9.16 The appellant will serve the appellant's notice on the Commission and any other respondent.

9.17 The appellant shall file and serve the appellant's notice, within 21 days of—

(a) where the appellant is a deposit-taker, service of the order;

(b) where the appellant is a liable person, receipt of the order; or

(c) where the appellant is either a deposit-taker or a liable person, the date of receipt of notification of the decision.

9.18 For the purposes of paragraph 9.17—

(a) references to "liable person" and "deposit-taker" are to be interpreted in accordance with section 32E of the 1991 Act and regulation 25A(2) of the Collection and Enforcement Regulations and section 54 of the 1991 Act, respectively; and

(b) the liable person is to be treated as having received the order or notification of the decision 2 days after it was posted by the Commission.

9.19 Rule 4.1(3)(a) (court's power to extend or shorten the time for compliance with a rule, practice direction or court order) does not apply to an appeal against the making of a lump sum deduction order under section 32F of the 1991 Act in so far as that rule gives the court power to extend the time set out in paragraph 9.17 for filing and serving an appellant's notice after the time for filing and serving the that notice set out in paragraph 9.17 has expired.

9.20 The Commission shall provide to the court and serve on all other parties to the appeal any information and evidence relevant to the making of the decision or order being appealed, within 14 days of receipt of the appellant's notice.

9.21 Subject to paragraph 9.23, a respondent who wishes to ask the appeal court to uphold the order or decision of the Commission for reasons different from or in additional to those given by the Commission must file a respondent's notice.

9.22 A respondent's notice must be filed within 14 days of receipt of the appellant's notice.

9.23 Where the Commission as a respondent, wishes to contend that its order or decision should be—

(a) varied, either in any event or in the event of the appeal being allowed in whole or in part; or
(b) affirmed on different grounds from those on which it relied when making the order or decision,

it shall, within 14 days of receipt of the appellant's notice, file and serve on all other parties to the appeal a respondent's notice.

9.24 In so far as rule 30.7 (Variation of time) may permit any application for variation of the time limit for filing an appellant's notice after the time for filing the appellant's notice has expired, that rule shall not apply to an appeal made against an order under section 32F(1) of the Act of 1991.

9.25 Rule 30.8 (stay) shall not apply to an appeal made against an order under section 32F(1) of the Act of 1991.

9.26 A district judge may hear a deduction order appeal.

9.27 Rule 30.11 (appeal court's powers) does not apply to deduction order appeals.

9.28 Rule 30.11(2)(d) (making orders for payment of interest) does not apply in the case of an appeal against a decision of a district judge in proceedings relating to a deduction order appeal.

9.29 In the case of a deduction order appeal—

(a) the appeal court has power to—
    (i) affirm or set aside the order or decision;
    (ii) remit the matter to the Commission for the order or decision to be reconsidered, with appropriate directions;
    (iii) refer any application or issue for determination by the Commission;
    (iv) make a costs order; and
(b) the appeal court may exercise its powers in relation to the whole or part of an order or decision of the Commission.

9.30 In rule 30.12 (Hearing of appeals)—

(a) at the beginning of paragraph (1), for "Every" substitute "Subject to paragraph (2A), every";
(b) at the beginning of paragraph (2), for "Unless" substitute "Subject to paragraph (2A), unless";
(c) after paragraph (2), insert—

"(2A) In the case of a deduction order appeal, the appeal will be a re-hearing, unless the appeal court orders otherwise.";

(d) in paragraph (3), after "lower court" insert "or, in a deduction order appeal, the order or decision of the Commission"; and
(e) for sub-paragraph (b) of paragraph (3), substitute—

"(b) unjust because of a serious procedural or other irregularity in—

(i) the proceedings in the lower court; or

(ii) the making of an order or decision by the Commission."

Information about the Commission's decision

9.31 In relation to the deduction order appeals listed in column 1 of the table in Schedule 2 to this Practice Direction—

(a) the documents to be filed and served by the appellant include the documents set out in Column 3; and
(b) the relevant information to be provided by the Commission in accordance with paragraph 9.20 above includes the information set out in Column 4.

The court at which the appeal notice is to be filed

9.32 In relation to a deduction order appeal, the appellant's notice and other documents required to be filed with that notice shall be filed in a county court (the Collection and Enforcement Regulations 25AB(1)).

The Commission's address for service

9.33 For the purposes of a deduction order appeal the Commission's address for service is—

Commission Legal Adviser
Deduction Order Team
Legal Enforcement (Civil)
Antonine House
Callendar Road
Falkirk
FK1 1XT

All notices or other documents for CMEC relating to a deduction order appeal should be sent to the above address.

9.34 This practice direction applies to deduction order appeals and appeals against the decision of a district judge in proceedings relating to a deduction order appeal with the following modifications and any other necessary modifications—

(a) in paragraph 5.35, insert "and 5.36B" after "subject to paragraph 5.36A";

(b) after paragraph 5.36A insert—

"5.36A Where the appeal is a deduction order appeal, the appellant's notice must be filed and served within 21 days of—

(a) where the appellant is a deposit-taker, service of the order;

(b) where the appellant is a liable person, receipt of the order; or

(c) where the appellant is either a deposit-taker or a liable person, the date of receipt of notification of the decision the lower court was given.".

Appeal against the court's decision under rules 31.10, 31.11 or 31.14

10.1 ...

Appeals against pension orders and pension compensation sharing orders

11.1 Paragraph 11.2 below applies to appeals against—

(a) a pension sharing order under section 24B of the Matrimonial Causes Act 1973 or the variation of such an order under section 31 of that Act;

(b) a pension sharing order under Part 4 of Schedule 5 to the Civil Partnership Act 2004 or the variation of such an order under Part 11 of Schedule 5 to that Act;

(c) a pension compensation sharing order under section 24E of the Matrimonial Causes Act 1973 or a variation of such an order under section 31 of that Act; and

(d) a pension compensation sharing order under Part 4 of Schedule 5 to the Civil Partnership Act 2004or a variation of such an order under Part 11 of Schedule 5 to that Act.

11.2 Rule 4.1(3)(a) (court's power to extend or shorten the time for compliance with a rule, practice direction or court order) does not apply to an appeal against the making of the orders referred to in paragraph 11.1 above in so far as that rule gives the court power to extend the time set out in rule 30.4 for filing and serving an appellant's notice after the time for filing and serving that notice has expired.

11.3 In so far as rule 30.7 (Variation of time) may permit any application for variation of the time limit for filing an appellant's notice after the time for filing the appellant's notice has expired, that rule shall not apply to an appeal made against the orders referred to in paragraph 11.1 above.

Appeals to a court under section 20 of the 1991 Act (appeals in respect of parentage determinations)

12.1 ...

Applications

13.1 Where a party to an appeal makes an application whether in an appeal notice or by Part 18 (Procedure For Other Applications in Proceedings) application notice, the provisions of Part 18 will apply.

13.2 The applicant must file the following documents with the notice—

(a) one additional copy of the application notice for the appeal court, one copy for each of the respondents and the persons referred to in paragraph 5.39;

(b) where applicable a sealed or stamped copy of the order which is the subject of the main appeal or a copy of the notice of the making of an order;

(c) a bundle of documents in support which should include—
  (i) the Part 18 application notice; and
  (ii) any witness statements and affidavits filed in support of the application notice.

Appeals against consent orders

14.1 The rules in Part 30 and the provisions of this Practice Direction apply to appeals relating to orders made by consent in addition to orders which are not made by consent. An appeal is the only way in which a consent order can be challenged.

Disposing of applications or appeals by consent

15.1 An appellant who does not wish to pursue an application or an appeal may request the appeal court for an order that the application or appeal be dismissed. Such a request must state whether the appellant is a child, or a protected person.

15.2 The request must be accompanied by a consent signed by the other parties stating whether the respondent is a child, or a protected person and consents to the dismissal of the application or appeal.

Allowing unopposed appeals or applications on paper

16.1 The appeal court will not normally make an order allowing an appeal unless satisfied that the decision of the lower court was wrong, but the appeal court may set aside or vary the order of the lower court with consent and without determining the merits of the appeal, if it is satisfied that there are good and sufficient reasons for doing so. Where the appeal court is requested by all parties to allow an application or an appeal the court may consider the request on the papers. The request should state whether any of the parties is a child, or protected person and set out the relevant history of the proceedings and the matters relied on as justifying the proposed order and be accompanied by a copy of the proposed order.

Summary assessment of costs

17.1 Costs are likely to be assessed by way of summary assessment at the following hearings—

(a) contested directions hearings;
(b) applications for permission to appeal at which the respondent is present;
(c) appeals from case management decisions or decisions made at directions hearings; and
(d) appeals listed for one day or less.

(Provision for summary assessment of costs is made by section 13 of the Practice Direction supplementing CPR Part 44)

17.2 Parties attending any of the hearings referred to in paragraph 17.1 should be prepared to deal with the summary assessment.

Reopening of final appeals

18.1 This paragraph applies to applications under rule 30.14 (Reopening of final appeals) for permission to reopen a final determination of an appeal.

18.2 In this paragraph, "appeal" includes an application for permission to appeal.

18.3 Permission must be sought from the court whose decision the applicant wishes to reopen.

18.4 The application for permission must be made by application notice and supported by written evidence, verified by a statement of truth.

18.5 A copy of the application for permission must not be served on any other party to the original appeal unless the court so directs.

18.6 Where the court directs that the application for permission is to be served on another party, that party may within 14 days of the service on him or her of the copy of the application file a written statement either supporting or opposing the application.

18.7 The application for permission, and any written statements supporting or opposing it, will be considered on paper by a single judge, and will be allowed to proceed only if the judge so directs.

Schedule 1: Description of proceedings

[Editors' note: none of the proceedings listed are for financial orders of any description.]

Schedule 2

APPEAL	RELEVANT LEGISLATION	APPELLANT INFORMATION	COMMISSION INFORMATION
Appeal against the making of a regular deduction order (under section 32A of the 1991 Act)	Section 32C(4)(a) of the 1991 Act The Collection and Enforcement Regulations 25AB(1)(a) (appeals)	A copy of the order; A covering letter explaining that the order has been made and the reasons for the order namely that there are arrears of child maintenance and/or no other arrangements have been made for the payment of child maintenance, including arrears	The amount of the current maintenance calculation, the period of debt and the total amount of arrears (including account breakdown if appropriate) and the reasons for the Commission's decision, details of all previous attempts to negotiate payment i.e. phone calls and letters to the non resident parent, details of any previous enforcement action taken
Appeal against a decision on an application for a review of a regular deduction order	Sections 32C(4)(b) 32C(2)(k) of the 1991 Act The Collection and Enforcement Regulations 25G (review of a regular deduction order) and 25AB(1)(b) (appeals)	A decision notification setting out whether or not the review has been agreed by the Commission and the resulting action to be taken if agreed; with an enclosure setting out the specific reasons for the Commission's decision	The reasons for the Commission's decision in respect of the application for review and any evidence supporting that decision
Appeal against the withholding of consent to the disapplication of sections 32G(1) and 32H(2)(b) of the 1991 Act	Section 32I(4) of the 1991 Act The Collection and Enforcement Regulations 25N (disapplication of sections 32G(1) and 32H(2)(b) of the 1991 Act) and 25AB(1)(c) (appeals)	A decision notification setting out that either: a) consent has been refused; or b) consent has been given in relation to part of the application i.e. that only some of the funds which were requested to be released have been agreed to be released (the right of	The reasons for the Commission's decision in respect of the application for consent and any evidence supporting that decision

		appeal will lie in respect of the part of the application which has been refused) There will be an enclosure with the notification setting out the reasons for the decision on the application	
Appeal against the making of a final lump sum deduction order (under section 32F of the 1991 Act)	Section 32J(5) of the 1991 Act The Collection and Enforcement Regulations 25AB(1)(d) (appeals)	A copy of the order; A covering letter explaining that the order has been made and the reasons for the order namely that there are arrears of child maintenance and/or no other arrangements have been made for the payment of child maintenance, including arrears	The amount of the current maintenance calculation (if applicable), the period of debt and the total amount of arrears (including account breakdown if appropriate) and the reasons for the Commission's decision, details of all previous attempts to negotiate payment i.e. phone calls and letters to the non resident parent, details of any previous enforcement action taken.

* * * * *

PART 31: REGISTRATION OF ORDERS UNDER THE COUNCIL REGULATION, THE CIVIL PARTNERSHIP (JURISDICTION AND RECOGNITION OF JUDGMENTS) REGULATIONS 2005 AND UNDER THE HAGUE CONVENTION 1996

* * * * *

Part 32

Commentary on Part 32:
REGISTRATION AND ENFORCEMENT OF ORDERS

Summary

Despite the breadth of its title, Part 32 deals with only two discrete areas of financial enforcement, namely:

- Chapter 2: Registration of maintenance orders under the Maintenance Orders Act 1950.
- Chapter 3: Registration of maintenance orders under the Maintenance Orders Act 1958.

(Chapter 4 of Part 32 deals with the registration and enforcement of custody orders under the Family Law Act 1986, and is beyond the scope of this Commentary.)

No Practice Direction has been made to supplement Part 32. On one view, this is unsurprising, as the financial Chapters of the Part are largely devoted to the role of the court. Moreover, those procedural provisions that place obligations on applicants are comprehensive and require no further explanation or guidance. However, some guidance on topics such as the variation and discharge of orders registered under the Maintenance Orders Act 1958 would have been useful.

Part 32 makes no material change to the procedures previously set out in FPR 1991 rules 7.18 to 7.29. The language has been modernised and in a number of instances the procedure is explained more clearly.

The only Form prescribed by *PD 5A – Forms* is D151 (Application for registration of maintenance order in a magistrates' court) (the renamed Form M33).

The Maintenance Orders Act 1950, Part II

Part II of the MOA 1950 creates a regime for the reciprocal registration, for enforcement purposes, of maintenance orders between England and Wales, Scotland and Northern Ireland (MOA 1950 sections 16(1) and 28(1)), such that a maintenance order made in one of those three jurisdictions shall, when registered in another of them, be enforceable in all respects as if made by the original court (MOA 1950 section 18(1)). The Act applies to English and Welsh High Court, county court and magistrates' court maintenance orders and to their Scottish and Northern Irish counterparts.

Viewed from the English and Welsh perspective the Act applies to maintenance orders made under sections 22, 23 and 27 of the Matrimonial Causes Act 1973; sections 14 and 17 of the Matrimonial and Family Proceedings Act 1984; Part 1 of the Domestic Proceedings and Magistrates' Courts Act 1978; Schedule 1 to the Children Act 1989; and corresponding provisions under the Civil Partnership Act 2004 (MOA 1950 section 16(2)(a)).

Registration of English and Welsh maintenance orders

Where it is sought to register an English or Welsh High Court or county court order in Scotland or Northern Ireland, the application is made to the court which made the order (MOA 1950 section 17(1)(c) and rule 32.3 (High Court orders) and rule 32.6 (county court orders)).

In the case of a magistrates' court order, the application is made to the magistrates' court for the same place as the court which made the order (MOA 1950 section 17(1)(a)). Procedure is governed by the Maintenance Orders Act 1950 (Summary Jurisdiction) Rules 1950, which are beyond the scope of this Commentary.

It is a precondition to registration (a) that the payer under the order resides in the jurisdiction in which it is sought to register, and (b) that it is convenient that the order should be enforceable there (MOA 1950 section 17(2)). Registration is thus discretionary.

The destination courts in the other jurisdictions are: the Court of Session (Scotland) and the Court of Judicature of Northern Ireland (in the case of High Court orders); and the sheriff court (Scotland) and the court of summary jurisdiction (Northern Ireland) (in the case of county court orders): MOA 1950 section 17(3) and rules 32.3(2) and 32.6(b) and (c).

Effects of registration

Once registered, the order may not be registered in any other court under the 1950 Act (MOA 1950 section 17(7)). (It may however be registered in another court in the *same* jurisdiction under the MOA 1958: see *below.*) A registered order may be enforced by the court in the jurisdiction of registration in all respects as if it had been made by that court and as if that court had had jurisdiction to make it; and proceedings for, or with respect to, the enforcement of the order may be taken accordingly (MOA 1950 section 18(1)). However no court in England and Wales in which an order is registered under Part 2 of the 1950 Act may enforce the order to the extent that it is for the time being registered in another court in England or Wales under Part 1 of the MOA 1958 (MOA 1950 section 18(3A)). Moreover, no proceedings other than those provided for in the 1950 Act may be taken for, or with respect to, the enforcement of the order while it is registered (MOA 1950 section 18(6)).

Procedure

The procedure stipulated by rules 32.3 and 32.6 is straightforward and requires little elucidation. As was the case under FPR 1991 rule 7.19, it seems that the application is dealt with on paper. Presumably the court will list the matter for a hearing if it sees fit, and the applicant may seek a hearing in the event that the application is refused on paper.

The prescribed Form (see *PD 5A – Forms*) is D151 (Application for registration of maintenance order in a magistrates' court), formerly named Form M33.

Registration of Scottish and Northern Irish orders

Orders received from the other jurisdictions are registered in the Senior Courts (formerly known as the Supreme Court of England and Wales), that is, the principal registry of the High Court if made by a 'superior court' in the other jurisdiction (i.e. the Court of Session or the Court of Judicature of Northern Ireland) (MOA 1950 section 17(3)(a)), and in any other case (i.e. if the order was made by the sheriff court in Scotland or a court of summary jurisdiction in Northern Ireland) in the magistrates' court (MOA 1950 section 17(3)(b)).

Variation and discharge of registered orders

Where a maintenance order is registered in a superior court (in England, the High Court) the original court retains exclusive power to vary or discharge the order (MOA 1950 section 21(1)). Note however the specific provisions that apply to an application brought by a payer to vary a Scottish maintenance order registered in the High Court (MOA 1950 section 21(2) and rule 32.8).

By contrast, courts of summary jurisdiction may vary a registered order: see MOA 1950 section 22(1) and the Maintenance Orders Act 1950 (Summary Jurisdiction) Rules 1950.

The Maintenance Orders Act 1958, Part 1

The MOA 1958 creates a scheme for the registration, for the purpose of enforcement, of (a) High Court and county court maintenance orders in a magistrates' court and (b) magistrates' courts' maintenance orders in the High Court. By contrast, it is not possible to register a magistrates' court maintenance order in the county court.

The key feature of the scheme is that, on registration: (a) the court of registration acquires exclusive jurisdiction to enforce (MOA 1958 section 3(4)); and (b) the order may be enforced as though made by the court of registration. The consequence is that after registration the order becomes susceptible to the entire range of enforcement methods available to the latter court (MOA 1958 sections 1(1), 3(1)).

A 'maintenance order' for these purposes is a maintenance order made under one of the statutes listed in Schedule 8 to the Administration of Justice Act 1970 (MOA 1958 section 1(1A)), which includes maintenance orders made in Scotland and Northern Ireland and registered in a court in England and Wales under the Maintenance Orders Act 1950 (MOA 1958 section 1(2A)(b)), and such orders are then deemed to have been made by the court of registration (MOA 1958 section 1(2)).

The Act also applies to orders registered under the Maintenance Orders (Reciprocal Enforcement) Act 1972 Part 1, the Civil Jurisdiction and Judgments Act 1982 Part 1, and Council Regulation (EC) No 44/2001 ('Brussels I') (MOA 1958 section 1(4)).

'Maintenance order' includes a lump sum order, if such an order may be made under the relevant statute listed in AJA 1970 Schedule 8. Sums due under an order for costs made in connection with a maintenance order prior to registration are deemed to form part of the maintenance order (MOA 1958 section 1(3)).

The Maintenance Orders Act 1958 applies to all orders made on financial remedy applications except those made under section 10(2) of the Matrimonial Causes Act 1973 and their counterparts under section 48(2) of the Civil Partnership Act 2004.

Registration of maintenance orders in magistrates' courts

The procedure governing applications to register in the magistrates' court is set out clearly in rules 32.15 and 32.16.

Practice Direction (maintenance: registration of orders) [1980] 1 All ER 1007 stated that interim maintenance orders should not be registered in the magistrates' court save in exceptional circumstances. The PD has not been preserved, whether by design or through oversight, by the 'saving' *Practice Direction – Practice Directions relating to Family Proceedings in force before 6th April 2011 which support the Family Procedure Rules 2010.* Nevertheless we suggest that the principle remains sound and should be followed as a matter of good practice. PD 9A paras 9.1 and 9.2 counsel against applying to register maintenance orders which require payment direct to children.

Neither the Act nor the rules state whether the application should be considered at a hearing. The inference to be drawn from rule 32.15 is that applications are determined on paper. If so, it is suggested that it must be open to the applicant to require an oral hearing in the event that the application is refused.

Registration is not automatic but discretionary, as the court may grant the application *'if it thinks fit'* (MOA 1958 section 2(1)). It is suggested that one reason for declining to grant an application to register may be the fact that a variation application is pending in the original court.

It should be noted that once the application for registration has been granted no enforcement proceedings may be begun or enforcement process issued until the registration has taken effect or until 14 days have elapsed from the grant of the application, whichever is the earlier (MOA 1958 section 2(2)(a) and rule 32.14). If an attachment of earnings order made by the original court is in force, it will lapse on the grant of the application for registration, even if the grant subsequently becomes void (Attachment of Earnings Act 1971 section 11(1)(a) and (2)).

For so long as the order remains registered, the magistrates' court has exclusive jurisdiction to enforce (MOA 1958 section 3(4)).

Variation and discharge of orders registered in magistrates' courts

It might be thought from reading rule 32.19 (2) and (3) that the powers of the magistrates' court and the original court to vary registered orders are coterminous. In fact that is not so.

The original court has no power to vary the order while it remains registered (MOA 1958 section 4(2)(b)), save in two limited cases: (a) where either party to the order is not present in England or Wales when the application to vary is made; and (b) when an application is made to the original court to vary a provision of the order which does not specify a rate of payment. In both these cases the original court may vary the order as to the rate of payment (MOA 1958 section 4(5)). By contrast, the power of a magistrates' court to vary extends both to means and to the rate of payment (MOA 1958 section 4(2)(a) and (b)).

Note that if the magistrates' court considers it appropriate to remit a variation application to the original court, it must do so. The original court will then deal with the application as though the order were not registered (MOA 1958 section 4(4)). The criteria which should guide the magistrates in deciding whether or not to remit were set out in *Gsell v Gsell* [1971] 1 All ER 559n and *Goodall v Jolly* [1984] FLR 143: in essence magistrates should consider remitting where they have insufficient time and/or where discovery is important.

No application to vary a registered order may be made to any court while proceedings to vary the order are pending in any other court (MOA 1958 section 4(6)). The magistrates have no power to vary a registered order for periodical or other payments made under Part 3 of the Matrimonial and Family Proceedings Act 1984 (MOA 1958 section 4(6B)). The variation application must thus be made to the original court.

Note, too, the limits placed on the magistrates' court jurisdiction to vary orders made by the Court of Session or the High Court in Northern Ireland and registered under the MOA 1950 (MOA 1958 section 4(6A)).

The original court retains full jurisdiction to discharge an order registered in the magistrates' court (MOA 1958 section 5(2)).

Registration of maintenance orders in the High Court

The application to register is made to the magistrates' court under the Magistrates' Courts (Maintenance Orders Act 1958) Rules 1959. The FPR

2010 rules relating to such applications are almost entirely confined to prescribing the steps to be taken by the court itself.

On grant of the application, no enforcement of any kind is permitted until the order is registered (MOA 1958 section 2(4)(a)). Once the order is registered, and for so long as it remains so, the High Court has exclusive jurisdiction to enforce (MOA 1958 section 3(4)).

Variation and discharge of maintenance orders registered in the High Court

The implication to be drawn from MOA 1958 sections 1(b)(ii) and 4A, is that the High Court has no power to vary a registered order as to quantum, and that the application to vary should therefore be made to the magistrates' court. However, the High Court does have jurisdiction to make, revoke, suspend, revive or vary provisions relating to the means of payment attaching to a registered order, such as payment by standing order or by attachment of earnings (MOA 1958 section 4A(2)). The magistrates' court (but not, it is suggested, the High Court) is empowered to discharge a magistrates' court order registered in the High Court (MOA 1958 section 5(3)).

Cancellation of registration

Section 5 of the 1958 Act contains detailed provisions regarding cancellation of registration. Probably the most important is the bar on enforcement in the period between giving notice of cancellation and the cancellation taking effect (MOA 1958 section 5(4)(a)). This echoes the moratorium on enforcement proceedings imposed in the period between grant of the application to register and actual registration (as to which see *above*).

PART 32: REGISTRATION AND ENFORCEMENT OF ORDERS

CHAPTER 1: SCOPE AND INTERPRETATION OF THIS PART

Scope and interpretation

32.1.—(1) This Part contains rules about the registration and enforcement of maintenance orders and custody orders.

(2) In this Part—

"the 1950 Act" means the Maintenance Orders Act 1950[87];

"the 1958 Act" means the Maintenance Orders Act 1958[88].

(3) Chapter 2 of this Part relates to—

(a) the registration of a maintenance order, made in the High Court or a county court, in a court in Scotland or Northern Ireland in accordance with the 1950 Act; and

(b) the registration of a maintenance order, made in Scotland or Northern Ireland, in the High Court in accordance with the 1950 Act.

(Provision in respect of proceedings in the magistrates' court under the 1950 Act is in rules made under section 144 of the Magistrates' Courts Act 1980).

(4) Chapter 3 of this Part contains rules to be applied in the High Court or a county court in relation—

(a) The registration of a maintenance order, made in the Hight Court or a county court, in a magistrates' court in accordance with the 1958 Act; and

(b) The registration of a maintenance order, made in a magistrates' court, in the High Court in accordance with the 1958 Act.

(Provision in respect of proceedings in the magistrates' court under the 1958 Act is in rules made under section 144 of the Magistrates' Courts Act 1980).

(5) Chapter 4 of this Part relates to the registration and enforcement of custody orders in accordance with the 1986 Act.

CHAPTER 2: REGISTRATION ETC. OF ORDERS UNDER THE 1950 ACT

SECTION 1:
Interpretation of this Chapter

Interpretation
32.2. In this Chapter—

"the clerk of the Court of Session" means the deputy principal clerk in charge of the petition department of the Court of Session;

"county court order" means a maintenance order made in a county court;

"High Court order" means a maintenance order made in the High Court;

"maintenance order" means a maintenance order to which section 16 of the 1950 Act applies;

"Northern Irish order" means a maintenance order made by the Court of Judicature of Northern Ireland;

"the register" means the register kept for the purposes of the 1950 Act;

"the registrar in Northern Ireland" means the chief registrar of the Queen's Bench Division (Matrimonial) of the High Court of Justice in Northern Ireland;

"registration" means registration under Part 2 of the 1950 Act and "registered" is to be construed accordingly; and

"Scottish Order" means a maintenance order made by the Court of Session.

SECTION 2:
Registration etc of High Court and county court orders

Registration of a High Court order

32.3.—(1) An application for the registration of a High Court order may be made by sending to a court officer at the court which made the order—

(a) a certified copy of the order; and
(b) a statement which—
   (i) contains the address in the United Kingdom, and the occupation, of the person liable to make payments under the order;
   (ii) contains the date on which the order was served on the person liable to make payments, or, if the order has not been served, the reason why service has not been effected;
   (iii) contains the reason why it is convenient for the order to be enforced in Scotland or Northern Ireland, as the case may be;
   (iv) contains the amount of any arrears due to the applicant under the order;
   (v) confirms that the order is not already registered; and
   (vi) is verified by a statement of truth.

(2) If it appears to the court that—

(a) the person liable to make payments under the order resides in Scotland or Northern Ireland; and
(b) it is convenient for the order to be enforced there,

the court officer will send the documents filed under paragraph (1) to the clerk of the Court of Session or to the registrar in Northern Ireland, as the case may be.

(3) On receipt of a notice of the registration of a High Court order in the Court of Session or the Court of Judicature of Northern Ireland, the court officer (who is the prescribed officer for the purposes of section 17(4) of the 1950 Act) will—

(a) enter particulars of the notice of registration in the register;

(b) note the fact of registration in the court records; and

(c) send particulars of the notice to the principal registry.

Notice of Variation etc. of a High Court order

32.4.—(1) This rule applies where a High Court order, which is registered in the Court of Session or the Court of Judicature of Northern Ireland, is discharged or varied.

(2) A court officer in the court where the order was discharged or varied will send a certified copy of that order to the clerk of the Court of Session or the registrar in Northern Ireland, as the case may be.

Cancellation of registration of a High Court order

32.5.—(1) This rule applies where—

(a) the registration of a High Court order registered in the Court of Session or the Court of Judicature of Northern Ireland is cancelled under section 24(1) of the 1950 Act; and

(b) notice of the cancellation is given to a court officer in the court in which the order was made (who is the prescribed officer for the purposes of section 24(3)(a) of the 1950 Act[89]).

(2) On receipt of a notice of cancellation of registration, the court officer will enter particulars of the notice in Part 1 of the register.

Application of this Chapter to a county court order

32.6. Rules 32.3 to 32.5 apply to an application to register a county court order as if—

(a) references to a High Court order were references to a county court order;

(b) where the order is to be registered in Scotland, references to the Court of Session and the clerk of the Court of Session were references to the sheriff court and the sheriff-clerk of the sheriff court respectively; and

(c) where the order is to be registered in Northern Ireland, references to the Court of Judicature of Northern Ireland and the registrar of Northern Ireland were references to the court of summary jurisdiction and the clerk of the court of summary jurisdiction respectively.

SECTION 3:
Registration etc. of Scottish and Northern Irish orders

Registration of Scottish and Northern Irish orders

32.7. On receipt of a certified copy of a Scottish order or a Northern Irish order for registration, a court officer in the principal registry (who is the prescribed officer for the purposes of section 17(2) of the 1950 Act) will—

(a) enter particulars of the order in Part 2 of the register;
(b) notify the clerk of the Court of Session or the registrar in Northern Ireland, as the case may be, that the order has been registered; and
(c) file the certified copy of the order and any statutory declaration, affidavit or statement as to the amount of any arrears due under the order.

Application to adduce evidence before High Court

32.8. The Part 18 procedure applies to an application by a person liable to make payments under a Scottish order registered in the High Court to adduce before that court any evidence on which that person would be entitled to rely in any proceedings brought before the court by which the order was made for the variation or discharge of the order.

Notice of variation etc. of Scottish and Northern Irish orders

32.9.—(1) This rule applies where—

(a) a Scottish order or a Northern Irish order, which is registered in the High Court, is discharged or varied; and
(b) notice of the discharge or variation is given to a court officer in the High Court (who is the prescribed officer for the purposes of section 23(1)(a) of the 1950 Act[90]).

(2) On receipt of a notice of discharge or variation, the court officer will enter particulars of the notice in Part 2 of the register.

Cancellation of registration of Scottish and Northern Irish orders

32.10.—(1) The Part 18 procedure applies to an application for the cancellation of the registration of a Scottish order or a Northern Irish order in the High Court.

(2) The application must be made without notice to the person liable to make payments under the order.

(3) If the registration of the order is cancelled, the court officer will—

(a) note the cancellation in Part II of the register; and
(b) send written notice of the cancellation to—
   (i) the clerk of the Court of Session or the registrar in Northern Ireland, as the case may be; and
   (ii) the court officer in any magistrates' court in which the order has been registered in accordance with section 2(5) of the 1958 Act.

Enforcement

32.11.—(1) The Part 18 procedure applies to an application for or with respect to the enforcement of a Scottish order or a Northern Irish order registered in the High Court.

(2) The application may be made without notice to the person liable to make payments under the order.

Inspection of register and copies of order

32.12. Any person—

(a) who is entitled to receive, or liable to make, payments under a maintenance order made by the High Court, the Court of Session or the Court of Judicature of Northern Ireland; or

(b) with the permission of the court,

may—

(i) inspect the register; or

(ii) request a copy of any order registered in the High Court under Part 2 of the 1950 Act and any statutory declaration, affidavit or statement filed with the order.

CHAPTER 3: REGISTRATION OF MAINTENANCE ORDERS UNDER THE 1958 ACT

Interpretation

32.13. In this Chapter "the register" means the register kept for the purposes of the 1958 Act.

Registration of orders – prescribed period

32.14. The prescribed period for the purpose of section 2(2) of the 1958 Act is 14 days.

(Section 2(2) sets out the period during which an order, which is to be registered in a magistrates' court, may not be enforced)

Application for registration of a maintenance order in a magistrates' court

32.15.—(1) An application under section 2(1) of the 1958 Act may be made by sending to the court officer at the court which made the order—

(a) a certified copy of the maintenance order; and

(b) two copies of the application.

(2) When, on the grant of an application, the court officer sends the certified copy of the maintenance order to the magistrates' court in accordance with section 2(2), the court officer must—

(a) note on the order that the application for registration has been granted; and

(b) send to the magistrates' court a copy of the application for registration of the order.

(3) On receiving notice that the magistrates' court has registered the order, the court officer must enter particulars of the registration in the court records.

Registration in a magistrates' court of an order registered in the High Court

32.16.—(1) This rule applies where—

- (a) a maintenance order is registered in the High Court in accordance with section 17(4) of the 1950 Act; and
- (b) the court officer receives notice that the magistrates' court has registered the order in accordance with section 2(5) of the 1958 Act.

(2) The court officer must enter particulars of the registration in Part II of the register.

Registration in the High Court of a magistrates' court order

32.17.—(1) This rule applies where a court officer receives a certified copy of a magistrates' court order for registration in accordance with section 2(4)(c) of the 1958 Act.

(2) The court officer must register the order in the High Court by—

- (a) filing the copy of the order; and
- (b) entering particulars in—
  - (i) the register; or
  - (ii) if the order is received in a district registry, the cause book or cause card.

(3) The court officer must notify the magistrates' court that the order has been registered.

Registration in the High Court of an order registered in a magistrates' court

32.18.—(1) This rule applies where—

- (a) an order has been registered in the magistrates' court in accordance with section 17(4) of the 1950 Act; and
- (b) a sheriff court in Scotland or a magistrates' court in Northern Ireland has—
  - (i) made an order for the registration of that order in the High Court; and
  - (ii) sent a certified copy of the maintenance order to the court officer of the High Court in accordance with section 2(4)(c) of the 1958 Act.

(2) The court officer must register the order in the High Court by—

- (a) filing the copy of the order; and
- (b) entering particulars in the register.

(3) The court officer must notify—

- (a) the court which made the order; and

(b) the magistrates' court in which the order was registered in accordance with section 17(4) of the 1950 Act,

that the order has been registered in the High Court.

Variation or discharge of an order registered in a magistrates' court

32.19—(1) This rule applies where a maintenance order is registered in a magistrates' court under Part 1 of the 1958 Act.

(2) If the court which made the order makes an order varying or discharging that order the court officer must send a certified copy of the order of variation or discharge to the magistrates' court.

(3) If the court officer receives from the magistrates' court a certified copy of an order varying the maintenance order the court officer must—

(a) file the copy of the order; and
(b) enter the particulars of the variation in the place where the details required by rule 32.15(3) were entered.

Variation or discharge of an order registered in the High Court

32.20.—(1) This rule applies where a maintenance order is registered in the High Court under Part 1 of the 1958 Act.

(2) If the court officer receives from the magistrates' court a certified copy of an order varying or discharging the maintenance order the court officer must—

(a) file the copy of the order;
(b) enter the particulars of the variation or discharge in—
   (i) the register; or
   (ii) if the order is received in a district registry, the cause book or cause card; and
(c) send notice of the variation or discharge to the court officer of a county court—
   (i) who has notified the court officer of enforcement proceedings in that court relating to the maintenance order; or
   (ii) to whom a payment is to be made under an attachment of earnings order made by the High Court for the enforcement of the registered order.

Cancellation of registration – orders registered in the High Court

32.21.—(1) This rule applies where an order is registered in the High Court.

(2) A person giving notice under section 5(1) of the 1958 Act must give the notice to the court officer.

(3) The court officer must take the steps mentioned in paragraph (4) if—

(a) notice is given under section 5 of the 1958 Act; and
(b) the court officer is satisfied, by a witness statement by the person entitled to receive payments under the order that no enforcement

proceedings in relation to the order, that were started before the giving of the notice, remain in force.

(4) The court officer must, if satisfied as mentioned in paragraph (3)—

(a) cancel the registration by entering particulars of the notice in the register or cause book (or cause card) as the case may be; and
(b) send notice of the cancellation to—
  (i) the court which made the order; and
  (ii) where applicable, to the magistrates' court in which the order was registered in accordance with section 17(4) of the 1950 Act.

(5) Where the cancellation results from a notice given under section 5(1) of the 1958 Act, the court officer must state that fact in the notice of cancellation sent in accordance with paragraph (4)(b).

(6) If notice is received from a magistrates' court that the registration in that court under the 1958 Act of an order registered in the High Court in accordance with section 17(4) of the 1950 Act has been cancelled, the court officer must note the cancellation in Part II of the register.

Cancellation of registration – orders registered in a magistrates' court

32.22.—(1) Where the court gives notice under section 5(2) of the 1958 Act, the court officer must endorse the notice on the certified copy of the order of variation or discharge sent to the magistrates' court in accordance with rule 32.19(2).

(2) Where notice is received from a magistrates' court that registration of an order made by the High Court or a county court under Part 1 of the 1958 Act has been cancelled, the court officer must enter particulars of the cancellation in the place where the details required by rule 32.15(3) were entered.

Part 33

Commentary on Part 33:
ENFORCEMENT

Summary

In the FPR 1991 the High Court and county court enforcement rules were contained in a single Part, Part 7. By contrast there are three Parts in the 2010 Rules dealing with enforcement although the scope of two of them is not immediately self-evident from their titles. These Parts are:

- Part 32 entitled **Registration and enforcement of orders** but in fact limited in scope to the registration and enforcement of financial and custody orders within the United Kingdom, and the registration of maintenance orders between different levels of court in England and Wales under the Maintenance Orders Act 1958.
- Part 33 entitled simply **Enforcement** but in fact limited to committals and domestic financial enforcement.
- Part 34, **Reciprocal enforcement of maintenance orders,** providing for the international reciprocal enforcement of maintenance orders.

Part 33 breaks new ground in a number of respects:

(i) It imports further provisions from the CPR which mainly relate to specific enforcement methods.
(ii) It makes express provision for the enforcement of undertakings for the payment of money.
(iii) It creates a new type of enforcement process whereby the applicant simply applies to enforce and the court itself selects the appropriate method of enforcement.

The sole scope of accompanying *Practice Direction 33A (Enforcement of Undertakings)* concerns, as its name suggests, the enforcement of undertakings.

One other relevant pre-FPR 2010 Practice Direction is preserved by *Practice Direction – Practice Directions relating to Family Proceedings in force before 6th April 2011 which support the Family Procedure Rules*

2010, namely *PD 6C: Practice Direction (Disclosure of Addresses by Government Departments)* which brings earlier manifestations on the same topic up-to-date and has been incorporated with the other PDs accessible in this module.

Also preserved and potentially of assistance is an item of *Guidance from the President's Office: Disclosure Orders against the Inland Revenue* (November 2003).

The RSC 1965 and the CCR 1981

Under the former FPR 1991 financial enforcement in family proceedings was largely governed, procedurally, by the Rules of the Supreme Court 1965 and the County Court Rules 1981, in each case in the form in which they were in force immediately prior to 26 April 1999 (Family Proceedings (Miscellaneous Amendments) Rules 1999 rule 3, and FPR 1991 rule 1.3(1)), and in some cases subject to modification by the FPR 1991 themselves.

Under the 2010 regime the 'old' RSC and CPR are no longer applied. In their place, the versions of the RSC and CCR set out (by virtue of CPR Part 50) respectively in CPR Schedule 1 and Schedule 2, are applied (by FPR 2010 rule 33.1(2); and see also rule 2.3(1)).

In some instances, CPR Parts governing specific enforcement methods are applied for the first time directly to family proceedings, in lieu of the 'old' RSC and CCR. These are: CPR Part 69 (Court's power to appoint a receiver), Part 71 (Orders to obtain information from judgment debtors), Part 72 (Third party debt orders) and Part 73 (Charging orders, stop orders and stop notices).

While of course one of the aims of the 2010 rules is to harmonise the FPR with the CPR as far as possible, it is disappointing that the opportunity was not seized to create a single unified and non-CPR-dependent code of enforcement in family proceedings and thus to break free at last from the RSC 1965 (now 46 and going strong) and CCR 1981 (a more stripling but yet 30 year old).

Applying to enforce without specifying the method

A welcome procedural innovation is the application for enforcement where no specific remedy is sought.

The applicant for financial enforcement is now given the choice of (a) applying for a specific method of enforcement (rule 33.3(2)(a)); or (b) applying 'for an order for such method of enforcement as the court may consider appropriate' (rule 33.3(2)(b)). If the latter option is taken the court will make an order (containing a penal notice) requiring the judgment debtor to attend court and produce such documents as may be described in the order (rule 33.3(3) and CPR rule 71.2(6) and (7) (order to attend court)). This is the procedure formerly known as 'oral examination'. (See the 'old' RSC Ord 48, rule 1(1) and CCR Ord 25, rule 3(1), superseded by

CPR Part 71 in civil proceedings (orders to obtain information from judgment debtors) and now applied to family proceedings by rule 33.23.)

The application is made in Form D50K (notice of application for enforcement by such method of enforcement as the court may consider appropriate) (rule 5.1(1) and PD 5A). It requires a statement of truth to be signed by or on behalf of the applicant.

At the ensuing hearing the judgment debtor may be required to answer questions on oath as to his means (CPR rule 71.6(1)). The questioning will be carried out by a court officer unless the court has ordered that the hearing shall be before a judge. The judgment creditor or his representative (a) may attend and ask questions where the questioning takes place before a court officer; and (b) must attend and conduct the questioning if the hearing is before a judge (CPR rule 71.6(2) and (3)). If the questioning is conducted by a court officer a standard series of questions will be put (see CPR PD 71 para 4.1 and Appendix A (Form EX140)).

Penal sanctions may follow if the judgment debtor fails to attend court or bring the required documents with him, or refuses answer the questions put to him (CPR rule 71.8).

Examination in standard form before a court officer is unlikely to be efficacious in eliciting useful information about the debtor's means save in the most straightforward case. Faced with a recalcitrant and/or non-disclosing judgment debtor the applicant is likely to opt for examination before a judge.

There is no guidance in PD 33A as to how this new procedure is intended to operate in practice and in particular as to the court's powers at the conclusion of the examination before a judge. The latter may be gleaned however from Form D50K, which puts the respondent on notice that at the hearing of the application the court:

> may make an order for enforcement by any of the following methods, as it considers appropriate:
>
> - An attachment of earnings order
> - A third party debt order
> - A charging order, stop order or stop notice
> - A writ or warrant of execution (seizure and sale of personal property)
> - The appointment of a receiver.

Unsurprisingly, the menu of orders listed above does not include committal to prison under section 5 of the Debtors Act 1869, as in such proceedings the debtor cannot be compelled to give evidence (rule 33.14(2)). (See *Mubarak v Mubarak (No 2)* [2001] 1 FLR 698, which led to amendment both of the 1991 rules and of section 5 of the Debtors Act 1869 so as to render the judgment summons procedure compliant with ECHR.) A separate application will also be required in the event that the creditor seeks to invoke the draconian and highly exceptional remedy of sequestration (under RSC Ord 45(1)(i)).

If the examination is conducted by a court officer, his functions are limited to taking the evidence, reading the record of evidence to the person being questioned and asking him to sign it (and noting any refusal to do so) and providing a record of the evidence (CPR PD 71 paras 41 to 4.3).

The use of the CPR rule 71.2 procedure suggests that the process is likely to be in at least two stages: first, the debtor will be required to attend court and bring with him the documents described in the order. At the hearing he may be cross examined as to his means. Then, at the conclusion of the hearing the judge will decide, having heard submissions on behalf of the judgment creditor, what enforcement remedy to apply.

As to the nature and scope of the 'examination', in *Republic of Costa Rica v Strousberg* (1880) 16 ChD 8 at 12, it was said that the examination is '*not only intended to be an examination but to be a cross-examination, and that of the severest kind*'. The judgment debtor may be compelled to answer questions about his assets outside the jurisdiction (*Interpool Ltd v Galani* 1988] QB 738, [1987] 2 All ER 981, CA). An order will not be made requiring the attendance of a person who is outside the jurisdiction (*Re Tucker (a bankrupt), ex p Tucker* [1990] Ch 148, [1988] 1 All ER 603, CA) (although the court may issue letters of request to a foreign court to obtain the evidence of such a person (see rule 24.12).

The debtor may only be compelled to produce documents that are 'in his control' (CPR rule 71.2(6)(b)). In *Mubarak v Mubarak* [2002] EWHC 2171 (Fam), [2003] 2 FLR 553, it was held that to be in a judgment debtor's 'possession or power' (the wording used in the now defunct RSC Ord 48) the document must be one which he has the right (if necessary enforceable) to call for, and in his personal capacity not merely *qua* director or agent.

The new process is likely to be of particular assistance to judgment creditors in cases where (a) there is no up to date evidence of a judgment debtor's means; (b) there is no obvious asset or income against which to direct enforcement; and/or (c) there is a need to deal firmly and swiftly with an obstructive judgment debtor.

Committal proceedings

The main changes effected by the new rules are, first, that Part 50 of and Schedules 1 and 2 to the CPR are now expressly applied to family proceedings by rule 33.1(2). CPR Schedule 1 includes RSC Ord 52 governing committals in the High Court, and Schedule 2 contains CCR Ord 29 which applies in the county court. However, these rules are stated to apply 'with the necessary modifications'. It is unfortunate, given the seriousness of committal proceedings, that those modifications are not spelled out. Presumably, differences in nomenclature and the like are what are contemplated.

Second, the *President's Direction (committal applications and proceedings in which a committal order may be made)* [2001] 1 FLR 949 [2001] 2 All ER 704 no longer applies (by virtue of its absence from the pre 6 April 2011 Practice Directions preserved by *Practice Direction – Practice Directions relating to Family Proceedings in force before 6th April 2011 which support the Family Procedure Rules 2010*).

CPR Practice Direction RSC 52 and CCR 29 – Committal Applications, which applied previously by virtue of the above-mentioned and now revoked 2001 President's Direction, continues to apply, but now by virtue of the application of CPR Part 50 itself. No substantive change to existing procedure appears to have resulted from the application of CPR Part 50.

The lack of a single comprehensive body of rules, contained in the FPR themselves, is an unsatisfactory state of affairs, particularly given the increasing number of respondents to committal applications who are litigants in person.

Committal – forms

The text of PD 5A, in so far as it relates to committals, is set out in full below:

> Rule 33.1(2) applies Part 50 of, and Schedules 1 and 2 to the CPR, in so far as they are relevant and with necessary modification (including the modification referred to in rule 33.7), to an application made in the High Court and a county court to enforce an order made in family proceedings. The CPR Practice Direction 'RSC52 and CCR 29–Committal Applications' therefore applies with necessary modifications to the enforcement of such an order. The form to be used for a committal application is set out in that Practice Direction. Accordingly, where a committal application is made in existing proceedings, it must be commenced by filing an application notice under Part 18 in those proceedings (a form C2 where there are existing proceedings under the Children Act 1989, a form D11 where the existing proceedings are matrimonial or civil partnership proceedings, financial remedy proceedings and proceedings under Part 8 or otherwise a form FP2). Otherwise a committal application must be commenced by the issue of a Part 19 application notice (a form FP1).

In existing financial remedy proceedings, therefore, the committal application notice must be issued in Form D11. The application will be governed by Part 18.

Committal – undertakings

PD 33A, para 1.3 makes it clear that (subject to the Debtors Act 1869, as to which see *below*) CPR Part 50 and Schedules 1 and 2 apply to undertaking as they do to orders, with necessary modifications.

The wording of the notice warning of the possible consequences of a breach, and of the signed statement to be made by the person giving the undertaking confirming his understanding of the undertaking and its implications, are spelled out in PD 33A paras 1.4 and 1.5. They are in terms identical to those contained in the existing N117 (General form of undertaking).

Note that the statement need not be given before the court in person and may be endorsed on the court copy of the undertaking or filed in a separate document such as a letter (para 1.6). Presumably, para 1.6 envisages that the undertaking itself (and not simply the statement) need not be given to the court in person, and that no attendance before the court is required. If so, this is welcome confirmation that undertakings of this kind may be enforced as though given directly to the court.

Whether or not the rules as to the service of undertakings set out in CCR Ord 29, rule 1A apply to these 'out of court' undertakings is unclear. To avoid any argument as to enforceability, it is suggested that they be followed.

Enforcement of undertakings for the payment of money

For the first time, express provision is made for the enforcement of financial undertakings. Somewhat surprisingly, this innovation is not referred to at all in Part 33 itself but only in PD 33A (paras 2.1 to 2.4).

PD 33A does not create new law. It is clear that a financial undertaking may be tantamount to a judgment or order for the purpose of enforcement by garnishee order (now third party debt order): *Gandolfo v Gandolfo* [1981] QB 359, sub nom *Gandolfo v Gandolfo (Standard Chartered Bank Ltd, garnishee)* [1980] 1 All ER 833, CA (husband's undertaking to pay school fees held equivalent to an order for their payment within CCR Ord 27, rule 1, as being an integral part of the original ancillary relief order). It is also well established that, while an undertaking to pay money may not be enforced by an application to commit for contempt of court (*Buckley v Crawford* [1893] 1 QB 105), the court has the power to commit by way of judgment summons under section 5 of the Debtors Act 1869 for breach of a financial undertaking, if (following *Gandolfo*), the undertaking is an integral and indivisible part of the order: *Symmons v Symmons* [1993] 1 FLR 317 (undertakings to pay school fees and a monthly maintenance supplement held to be enforceable); *M v M (Enforcement: Judgment Summons)* [1993] Fam Law 469 (undertaking to discharge capital gains tax due on a share transfer held enforceable).

Para 2.1 of PD 33A provides:

> Any undertaking for the payment of money that has effect as if it is an order made under Part 2 of the Matrimonial Causes Act 1973 may be enforced as if it was an order and Part 33 applies accordingly.

The reference to an *undertaking for the payment of money that has effect as if it is an order made under Part 2 of the Matrimonial Causes Act 1973* echoes the reference in the Administration of Justice Act 1970 section

28(1), Schedule 8, para 2A to an order for periodical or other payments made, *or having effect as if made*, under the Matrimonial Causes Act 1973 Part 2. (Schedule 8 to the AJA lists those orders for periodical and other payments that may be enforced under section 5 of the Debtors Act 1869.)

The wording of the required form of undertaking suggests, however, that the new power is intended to apply *only* to proceedings under Part 2 of the Matrimonial Causes Act 1973. If so, that is unfortunate. Financial undertakings are frequently given in other types of financial remedy proceedings, and it would be regrettable if, as result of this restrictive language, it were held that enforcement (whether by judgment summons or otherwise) of undertakings that are an integral and indivisible part of an order was not possible.

PD 33A para 2 stipulates that the form of undertaking must be endorsed with a penal notice as follows:

> If you fail to pay any sum of money which you have promised the court that you would pay, a person entitled to enforce the undertaking may apply to the court for an order. If it is proved that you have had the means to pay the sum but you have refused or neglected to pay that sum, you may be sent to prison.

This wording differs slightly from the corresponding wording in rule 33.14(1), which provides that:

> No person may be committed on an application for a judgment summons unless – ...
>
> (c) the judgment creditor proves that the debtor—
>
> (i) has, or has had, since the date of the order the means to pay the sum in respect of which the debtor has made default; and
>
> (ii) has refused or neglected, or refuses or neglects, to pay that sum

See also section 5 of the Debtors Act 1869, as amended, which is in like terms. It may be thought that the distinction is one without a difference. However, to avoid any argument about the correct test to be applied, it would have been preferable if the wording of the undertaking had mirrored that of rule 33.14.

The person giving the undertaking must make a signed statement confirming his understanding of the undertaking and the consequences of a failure to comply (para 2.3), in these prescribed terms:

> I understand the undertaking that I have given, and that if I break my promise to the court to pay any sum of money, I may be sent to prison.

Presumably, any reference in the statement to the possibility of enforcement by other means has been omitted on the basis that a penal notice is only required where it may be sought to enforce by committal.

The statement need not be given in person before the court, but may be endorsed on the court copy of the undertaking or may be filed in a separate document such as a letter (para 2.4). (See the comment made *above* under **Committal – undertakings.**)

CPR Part 70 (General rules about enforcement of judgments and orders)
CPR Part 70 is for the first time applied to family proceedings, by rule 33.2. It contains a number of potentially important provisions.

CPR PD 70 paras 1.1 and 1.2 list the permitted methods by which money judgments may be enforced. By CPR rule 70.2(2) *a judgment creditor may, except where an enactment, rule or practice direction provides otherwise – (a) use any method of enforcement which is available; and (b) use more than one method of enforcement, either at the same time or one after another.*

CPR rule 70.3 deals with the transfer of proceedings for enforcement and must be read in conjunction with rule 33.4.

CPR rule 70.4 provides for the enforcement of a judgment or order by or against a non-party.

CPR rule 70.5 is disapplied. CPR rule 70.6 states that '*If a judgment or order is set aside, any enforcement of the judgment or order shall cease to have effect unless the court otherwise orders.*'

'Judgment or order for the payment of money' includes a judgment or order for the payment of costs, and specifically (by contrast with the position under the CPR) includes a judgment or order for the payment of money into court (rule 33.2(d)).

Specific enforcement methods
A number of CPR Parts dealing with specific enforcement methods are now directly applied to family proceedings in place of the relevant provisions of the RSC and CCR.

They are:

- Part 69 (Court's power to appoint a receiver), replacing RSC Ords 30 and 51 and CCR Ord 32;
- Part 71 (Orders to obtain information from judgment debtors) (as noted *above*), replacing RSC Ord 48 and CCR Ord 25;
- Part 72 (Third party debt orders), replacing RSC Ord 49 and CCR Ord 30 (garnishee orders);
- Part 73 (Charging orders, stop orders and stop notices), replacing RSC Ord 50 and CCR Ord 31.

The rules governing all other methods of financial enforcement are contained in Schedules 1 and 2 to the CPR (RSC and CCR respectively) and are applied to family proceedings by rule 33.1(2).

Forms

The following are the Forms relevant to Part 33, prescribed by *Practice Direction 5A – Forms*:

D62	Request for issue of Judgment Summons
N56	Form for replying to an attachment of earnings application
N323	Request for Warrant of Execution
N336	Request and result of search in the attachment of earnings index
N337	Request for attachment of earnings order
N349	Application for third party debt order
N379	Application for charging order on land or property
N380	Application for charging order on securities

Other CPR forms will be prescribed by reason of the application of CPR Part 50.

PART 33: ENFORCEMENT

CHAPTER 1: GENERAL RULES

Application

33.1.—(1) The rules in this Part apply to an application made in the High Court and a county court to enforce an order made in family proceedings.

(2) Part 50 of, and Schedules 1 and 2 to, the CPR apply, as far as they are relevant and with necessary modification (including the modifications referred to in rule 33.7), to an application made in the High Court and a county court to enforce an order made in family proceedings.

SECTION 1:
Enforcement of orders for the payment of money

Application of the Civil Procedure Rules

33.2. Part 70 of the CPR applies to proceedings under this Section as if—

(a) in rule 70.1, in paragraph (2)(d), "but does not include a judgment or order for the payment of money into court" is omitted; and

(b) rule 70.5 is omitted.

How to apply

33.3.—(1) Except where a rule or practice direction otherwise requires, an application for an order to enforce an order for the payment of money must be made in a notice of application accompanied by a statement which must—

(a) state the amount due under the order, showing how that amount is arrived at; and
(b) be verified by a statement of truth.

(2) The notice of application may either—

(a) apply for an order specifying the method of enforcement; or
(b) apply for an order for such method of enforcement as the court may consider appropriate.

(3) If an application is made under paragraph (2)(b), an order to attend court will be issued andrule 71.2(6) and (7) of the CPR will apply as if the application had been made under that rule.

Transfer of orders

33.4.—(1) This rule applies to an application for the transfer—

(a) to the High Court of an order made in a designated county court; and
(b) to a designated county court of an order made in the High Court.

(2) The application must be—

(a) made without notice; and
(b) accompanied by a statement which complies with rule 33.3(1).

(3) The transfer will have effect upon the filing of the application.

(4) Where an order is transferred from a designated county court to the High Court—

(a) it will have the same force and effect; and
(b) the same proceedings may be taken on it,

as if it were an order of the High Court.

(5) This rule does not apply to the transfer of orders for periodical payments or for the recovery of arrears of periodical payments.

SECTION 2:
Committal and injunction

General rule – committal hearings to be in public

33.5.—(1) The general rule is that proceedings in the High Court for an order of committal will be heard in public.

(2) An order of committal may be heard in private where this is permitted by rule 6 of Order 52 of the RSC (cases in which a court may sit in private).

Proceedings in the principal registry treated as pending in a designated county court

33.6.—(1) This rule applies where an order for the warrant of committal of any person to prison has been made or issued in proceedings which are—

(a) in the principal registry; and

(b) treated as pending in a designated county court or a county court.

(2) The person subject to the order will, wherever located, be treated for the purposes of section 122 of the County Courts Act 1984[91] as being out of the jurisdiction of the principal registry.

(3) Where—

(a) a committal is for failure to comply with the terms of an injunction; or

(b) an order or warrant for the arrest or committal of any person is made or issued in proceedings under Part 4 of the 1996 Act in the principal registry which are treated as pending in a county court,

the order or warrant may, if the court so directs, be executed by the tipstaff within any county court.

Specific modifications of the CCR

33.7.—(1) CCR Order 29, rule 1 (committal for breach of an order or undertaking) applies to—

(a) section 8 orders, except those referred to in paragraph (2)(a); and

(b) orders under the following sections of the 1989 Act[92]—

    (i) section 14A (special guardianship orders);

    (ii) section 14B(2)(b) (granting of permission on making a special guardianship order to remove a child from the United Kingdom);

    (iii) section 14C(3)(b) (granting of permission to remove from the United Kingdom a child who is subject to a special guardianship order); and

    (iv) section 14D (variation or discharge of a special guardianship order),

as if paragraph (3) of that rule were substituted by the following paragraph—

"(3) In the case of a section 8 order (within the meaning of section 8(2) of the Children Act 1989) or an order under section 14A, 14B(2)(b), 14C(3)(b) or 14D of the Children Act 1989 enforceable by committal order under paragraph (1), the judge or the district judge may, on the application of the person entitled to enforce the order, direct that the proper officer issue a copy of the order, endorsed with or incorporating a notice as to the consequences of disobedience, for service in accordance with paragraph (2), and no copy of the order shall be issued with any such notice endorsed or incorporated save in accordance with such a direction.".

(2) CCR Order 29, rule 1 applies to—

(a) contact orders to which a notice has been attached under section 11I of the 1989 Act[93] or under section 8(2) of the Children and Adoption Act 2006;
(b) orders under section 11J of the 1989 Act (enforcement orders); and
(c) orders under paragraph 9 of Schedule A1 to the 1989 Act (orders following breach of enforcement orders),

as if paragraph (3) were omitted.

Section 118 County Courts Act 1984 and the tipstaff

33.8. For the purposes of section 118 of the County Courts Act 1984[94] in its application to the hearing of family proceedings at the Royal Courts of Justice or the principal registry, the tipstaff is deemed to be an officer of the court.

CHAPTER 2: COMMITTAL BY WAY OF JUDGMENT SUMMONS

Interpretation

33.9. In this Chapter, unless the context requires otherwise—

"order" means an order made in family proceedings for the payment of money;

"judgment creditor" means a person entitled to enforce an order under section 5 of the Debtors Act 1869;

"debtor" means a person liable under an order; and

"judgment summons" means a summons under section 5 of the Debtor's Act 1869[95] requiring a debtor to attend court.

Application

33.10.—(1) An application for the issue of a judgment summons may be made—

(a) in the case of an order of the High Court—
    (i) where the order was made in matrimonial proceedings, to the principal registry, a district registry or a divorce county court, whichever in the opinion of the judgment creditor is most convenient;
    (ii) where the order was made in civil partnership proceedings, to the principal registry, a district registry or a civil partnership

proceedings county court, whichever in the opinion of the judgment creditor is the most convenient; and
- (iii) in any other case, to the principal registry, a district registry or a designated county court, whichever in the opinion of the judgment creditor is most convenient;
- (b) in the case of an order of a divorce county court, to whichever divorce county court is in the opinion of the judgment creditor most convenient; and
- (c) in the case of an order of a civil partnership proceedings county court, to whichever civil partnership proceedings county court is in the opinion of the judgment creditor most convenient,

having regard (in any case) to the place where the debtor resides or carries on business and irrespective of the court or registry in which the order was made.

(2) An application must be accompanied by a statement which—

- (a) complies with rule 33.3(1);
- (b) contains all the evidence on which the judgment creditor intends to rely; and
- (c) has exhibited to it a copy of the order.

Judgment summons

33.11.—(1) If the debtor is in default under an order of committal made on a previous judgment summons in respect of the same order, a judgment summons must not be issued without the court's permission.

(2) A judgment summons must—

- (a) be accompanied by the statement referred to in rule 33.10(2) and
- (b) be served on the debtor personally not less than 14 days before the hearing.

(3) A debtor served with the judgment summons under paragraph (2)(b) must be paid or offered a sum reasonably sufficient to cover the expenses of travelling to and from the court at which the debtor is summoned to appear.

Successive judgment summonses

33.12. Subject to rule 33.11(1), successive judgment summonses may be issued even if the debtor has ceased to reside or carry on business at the address stated in the application for the issue of a judgment summons since the issue of the original judgment summons.

Requirement for personal service

33.13. In proceedings for committal by way of judgment summons, the following documents must be served personally on the debtor—

- (a) where the court has summonsed the debtor to attend and the debtor has failed to do so, the notice of the date and time fixed for the adjourned hearing; and

(b) copies of the judgment summons and the documents mentioned in rule 33.10(2).

Committal on application for judgment summons

33.14.—(1) No person may be committed on an application for a judgment summons unless—

(a) where the proceedings are in the High Court, the debtor has failed to attend both the hearing that the debtor was summonsed to attend and the adjourned hearing;

(b) where the proceedings are in a county court, an order is made under section 110(2) of the County Courts Act 1984[(96)]; or

(c) the judgment creditor proves that the debtor—
 (i) has, or has had, since the date of the order the means to pay the sum in respect of which the debtor has made default; and
 (ii) has refused or neglected, or refuses or neglects, to pay that sum.

(2) The debtor may not be compelled to give evidence.

Orders for the benefit of different persons

33.15. Where an applicant has obtained one or more orders in the same application but for the benefit of different persons—

(a) where the judgment creditor is a child, the applicant may apply for the issue of a judgment summons in respect of those orders on behalf of the judgment creditor without seeking permission to act as the child's litigation friend; and

(b) only one judgment summons need be issued in respect of those orders.

Hearing of judgment summons

33.16.—(1) On the hearing of the judgment summons the court may—

(a) where the order is for lump sum provision or costs; or

(b) where the order is an order for maintenance pending suit, an order for maintenance pending outcome of proceedings or an order for other periodical payments and it appears to the court that the order would have been varied or suspended if the debtor had made an application for that purpose,

make a new order for payment of the amount due under the original order, together with the costs of the judgment summons, either at a specified time or by instalments.

(2) If the court makes an order of committal, it may direct its execution to be suspended on terms that the debtor pays to the judgment creditor—

(a) the amount due;
(b) the costs of the judgment summons; and
(c) any sums accruing due under the original order,

either at a specified time or by instalments.

(3) All payments under a new order or an order of committal must be made to the judgment creditor unless the court directs otherwise.

(4) Where an order of committal is suspended on such terms as are mentioned in paragraph—

(a) all payments made under the suspended order will be deemed to be made—
   (i) first, in or towards the discharge of any sums from time to time accruing due under the original order; and
   (ii) secondly, in or towards the discharge of a debt in respect of which the judgment summons was issued and the costs of the summons; and

(b) the suspended order must not be executed until the judgment creditor has filed a statement of default on the part of the debtor.

Special provisions as to judgment summonses in the High Court

33.17.—(1) The court may summons witnesses to give evidence to prove the means of the debtor and may issue a witness summons for that purpose.

(2) Where the debtor appears at the hearing, the court may direct that the travelling expenses paid to the debtor be allowed as expenses of a witness.

(3) Where the debtor appears at the hearing and no order of committal is made, the court may allow the debtor's proper costs including compensation for any loss of earnings.

(4) When the court makes—

(a) a new order; or
(b) an order of committal,

a court officer must send notice of the order to the debtor and, if the original order was made in another court, to that court.

(5) An order of committal must be directed—

(a) where the order is to be executed by the tipstaff, to the tipstaff; or
(b) where the order is to be executed by a deputy tipstaff, to the county court within the district of which the debtor is to be found.

Special provisions as to judgment summonses in designated county courts

33.18.—(1) Rules 1, 2, 3(2), 5, 7(3) and 9(2) of Order 28 of the CCR (which deal with the issue of a judgment summons in a county court and the subsequent procedure) do not apply to judgment summons issued in a designated county court.

(2) Rule 9(1) of Order 28 of the CCR (notification of order on judgment of High Court) applies to such a summons as if for the words "the High Court" there were substituted the words—

(a) "any other court" where they first appear; and
(b) "that other court" where they next appear.

(3) Rule 7(1) and (2) of Order 28 of the CCR (suspension of a committal order) apply to such a summons subject to rule 32.16(2) and (3).

CHAPTER 3: ATTACHMENT OF EARNINGS

Proceedings in the Principal Registry
33.19. The Attachment of Earnings Act 1971[97] and Order 27 of the CCR (attachment of earnings) apply to the enforcement of an order made in family proceedings in the principal registry which are treated as pending in a designated county court as if they were an order made by such a court.

CHAPTER 4: WARRANT OF EXECUTION

Applications to vary existing orders
33.20. Where an application is pending for a variation of—

(a) a financial order;
(b) an order under section 27 of the 1973 Act; or
(c) an order under Part 9 of Schedule 5 to the 2004 Act,

no warrant of execution may be issued to enforce payment of any sum due under those orders, except with the permission of the district judge.

Section 103 County Courts Act 1984
33.21. Where a warrant of execution has been issued to enforce an order made in family proceedings pending in the principal registry which are treated as pending in a designated county court, the goods and chattels against which the warrant has been issued must, wherever they are located, be treated for the purposes of section 103 of the County Courts Act 1984[98] as being out of the jurisdiction of the principal registry

CHAPTER 5: COURT'S POWER TO APPOINT A RECEIVER

Application of the CPR
33.22. Part 69 of the CPR applies to proceedings under this Part.

CHAPTER 6: ORDERS TO OBTAIN INFORMATION FROM JUDGMENT DEBTORS

Application of the CPR

33.23. Part 71 of the CPR applies to proceedings under this Part.

CHAPTER 7: THIRD PARTY DEBT ORDERS

Application of the CPR

33.24.—(1) Part 72 of the CPR applies to proceedings under this Part with the following modifications.

(2) In rule 72.4—

(a) in paragraph (1), for "a judge" there is substituted "the court"; and
(b) in paragraph (2), for "judge" there is substituted "court".

(3) In rule 72.7, in paragraph (2)(a), after "the Royal Courts of Justice" insert ", or the principal registry".

(4) Rule 72.10 is omitted.

CHAPTER 8: CHARGING ORDER, STOP ORDER, STOP NOTICE

Application of the CPR

33.25.—(1) Part 73 of the CPR applies to proceedings under this Part with the following modifications.

(2) In rule 73.1, paragraph (2), sub-paragraphs (b) and (c) are omitted.

(3) For rule 73.2, there is substituted "This Section applies to an application by a judgment creditor for a charging order under section 1 of the 1979 Act[99].".

(4) In rule 73.3, paragraph (2), sub-paragraphs (b) and (c) are omitted.

(5) In rule 73.4—

(a) in paragraph (1), for "a judge" there is substituted "the court,"; and
(b) in paragraph (2), for "judge" there is substituted "court".

(6) In rule 73.9, in the parenthesis after paragraph (1)—

(a) "and regulation 51.4 of the 1992 Regulations" is omitted;
(b) for "provides" there is substituted "provide", and
(c) ", or (where the 1992 Regulations apply) of the authority," is omitted.

(7) In rule 73.10—

(a) in paragraph (1), for "a claim" there is substituted "an application";

(b) in paragraph (2) and the parenthesis following it, for "A claim" each time it appears there is substituted "An application";

(c) in paragraph (3), for "claimant" there is substituted "applicant";

(d) in paragraph (4), for "claim form" there is substituted "application"; and

(e) in paragraph (5), for "claimant's" there is substituted "applicant's".

(8) In rule 73.11, "funds in court or" is omitted.

(9) In rule 73.12—

(a) paragraph (1)(a) is omitted;

(b) in paragraph (1)(b) "other than securities held in court" is omitted;

(c) in paragraph (2), in sub-paragraph (b), for "claim form" there is substituted "application notice"; and

(d) in paragraph (3)—

    (i) "or claim form" is omitted; and

    (ii) for sub-paragraph (b) there is substituted "the person specified in rule 73.5(1)(d)".

(10) Rule 73.13 is omitted.

(11) In rule 73.14, in paragraph (1), "other than securities held in court" is omitted.

(12) In rule 73.16—

(a) in paragraph (a) for "; and" there is substituted "."; and

(b) paragraph (b) is omitted.

Practice Direction 33A supplements FPR Part 33 (Enforcement of undertakings)

PRACTICE DIRECTION 33A – ENFORCEMENT OF UNDERTAKINGS

This Practice Direction supplements FPR Part 33

Enforcement of undertaking to do or abstain from doing any act other than the payment of money

1.1 Rule 33.1(2) provides that Part 50 of, and Schedules 1 and 2 to, the CPR (which contain the Rules of the Supreme Court (RSC) and County Court Rules (CCR) respectively) apply, as far as they are relevant and with necessary modification, to an application made in the High Court and a county court to enforce an order made in family proceedings.

1.2 Subject to the Debtors Act 1869 (which makes provision in relation to orders for the payment of money), RSC Order 45.5 and CCR Order 29.1 enable a judgment or order to be enforced by committal for contempt of court where—

(a) a person who is required by a judgment or order to do an act has refused or neglected to do that act within the specified time; or

(b) a person disobeys a judgment or order requiring him to abstain from doing an act.

1.3 These Rules apply to undertakings as they apply to orders, with necessary modifications.

1.4 The form of an undertaking to do or abstain from doing any act must be endorsed with a notice setting out the consequences of disobedience, as follows:

> "You may be sent to prison for contempt of court if you break the promises that you have given to the court."

1.5 The person giving the undertaking must make a signed statement to the effect that he or she understands the terms of the undertaking being given and the consequences of failure to comply with it, as follows:

> "I understand the undertaking that I have given, and that if I break any of my promises to the court I may be sent to prison for contempt of court."

1.6 The statement need not be given before the court in person. It may be endorsed on the court copy of the undertaking or may be filed in a separate document such as a letter.

Enforcement of undertaking for the payment of money

2.1 Any undertaking for the payment of money that has effect as if it was an order made under Part 2 of the Matrimonial Causes Act 1973 may be enforced as if it was an order and Part 33 applies accordingly.

2.2 The form of an undertaking for the payment of money that has effect as if it were an order under Part 2 of the Matrimonial Causes Act 1973 must be endorsed with a notice setting out the consequences of disobedience, as follows:

> "If you fail to pay any sum of money which you have promised the court that you would pay, a person entitled to enforce the undertaking may apply to the court for an order. If it is proved that you have had the means to pay the sum but you have refused or neglected to pay that sum, you may be sent to prison."

2.3 The person giving the undertaking must make a signed statement to the effect that he or she understands the terms of the undertaking being given and the consequences of failure to comply with it, as follows:

> "I understand the undertaking that I have given, and that if I break my promise to the court to pay any sum of money, I may be sent to prison".

2.4 The statement need not be given before the court in person. It may be endorsed on the court copy of the undertaking or may be filed in a separate document such as a letter.

Part 34

Commentary on Part 34:
RECIPROCAL ENFORCEMENT OF MAINTENANCE ORDERS

Summary

Part 34 deals with the *international* enforcement of maintenance orders. The reciprocal enforcement of orders *within the United Kingdom* (i.e. England and Wales, Scotland and Northern Ireland) under the scheme created by the Maintenance Orders Act 1950, is governed by Part 32 *above*.

Part 34 replaces the reciprocal enforcement rules in FPR 1991 Part 7, Chapter 4. There are two associated Practice Directions:

- *PD 34A Reciprocal enforcement of maintenance orders;*
- *PD 34B Tracing Payers Overseas.*

Part 34 contains rules relating to the reciprocal enforcement of maintenance orders under several different regimes. The vast bulk of the rules and of the provisions of PD 34A are devoted to a detailed exposition of the procedure to be followed in each case. That procedure is clear and requires no especial elucidation. The layout of the new rules is presented in a much more digestible form than that of their 1991 counterparts, and the language has been modernised.

Chapter 1: The Maintenance Orders (Facilities for Enforcement) Act 1920 (1920 Act)

The rules governing applications under the 1920 Act are contained in Chapter 1 of Part 34.

The countries and territories which have reciprocal enforcement arrangements with the various jurisdictions of the United Kingdom under that Act are: Antigua and Barbuda, The Bahamas, Belize, Botswana, certain parts of Canada (Prince Edward Island, the Yukon Territory), Cayman Islands, Christmas Island, Cocos (Keeling) Islands, Cyprus, Dominica, The Gambia, Grenada, Guernsey, Guyana, Jamaica, Jersey, Kiribati, Lesotho, Malawi, Malaysia, Mauritius, Montserrat, Nigeria, St Christopher and Nevis, St Lucia, St Vincent and the Grenadines, Seychelles, Sierra Leone,

Solomon Islands, Sri Lanka, Swaziland, Trinidad and Tobago, Tuvalu, Uganda, Virgin Islands, Zambia and Zanzibar: see the Maintenance Orders (Facilities for Enforcement) Order 1959 (as amended).

Chapter 2: The Maintenance Orders (Reciprocal Enforcement) Act 1972 (1972 Act)

Chapter 2 is devoted to applications under Part 1 of the 1972 Act. It should be noted that there are four distinct enforcement regimes under the overall 'umbrella' of Part 1. The basic scheme (see rules 34.12 to 34.25) relates to the so-called **reciprocating countries**, which are: Anguilla, Australia (including Norfolk Island but excluding Christmas Island and the Cocos (Keeling) Islands), Barbados, Bermuda, Brunei Darussalam, the Canadian Provinces of Alberta, British Columbia, Manitoba, New Brunswick, Newfoundland and Labrador (formerly known as Newfoundland), Nova Scotia, Ontario, Saskatchewan and the Northwest Territories, the Falkland Islands and Dependencies, Fiji, Ghana, Gibraltar, Hong Kong, India, the Isle of Man, Jersey, Kenya, Malta, Nauru, New Zealand, Nunavut, Papua New Guinea, St Helena, Singapore, South Africa, Tanzania (excluding Zanzibar), the Turks and Caicos Islands and Zimbabwe: see the Reciprocal Enforcement of Maintenance Orders (Designation of Reciprocating Countries) Orders 1974, 1979, 1983, 2001, 2002 and 2008.

The Part 1 scheme applies in modified form to three other countries or groups of countries. The modifications relevant to each of the three are set out both in the rules themselves and in PD 34A, principally in its three Annexes. The modified regimes apply to:

- The **Republic of Ireland**: see the Reciprocal Enforcement of Maintenance Orders (Republic of Ireland) Order 1993 and FPR 2010 rule 34.26, PD 34A paras 4.3 and 4.4, and Annex 1.
- The so-called **Hague Convention** countries: see Schedule 1 to the Reciprocal Enforcement of Maintenance Orders (Hague Convention Countries) Order 1993, as amended and FPR 2010 rule 34.27, PD 34A paras 4.5 to 4.7 and Annex 2. They are: Australia, the Czech Republic, Denmark, Estonia, Finland, France, Germany, Italy, Luxembourg, the Netherlands (and Antilles), Norway, Poland, Portugal, Slovakia, Spain, Sweden, Switzerland and Turkey.
- The **United States of America**: see the Reciprocal Enforcement of Maintenance Orders (United States of America) Order 2007 and FPR 2010 rule 34.28, PD 34A paras 4.8 to 4.11 and Annex 3. (Note the obscure, and laboriously worded 'saving' under *PD 36A – Transitional Provisions* para 3.6 whereby in some circumstances, namely that the application for enforcement was made before 1 October 2007, the reciprocal enforcement of maintenance orders made in the United States will continue to be governed in the magistrates' court by the rules promulgated in 1995 as if they had

not been amended in 2007! Such litigation is very much a minority sport minority evidently consisting of lengthy halves, but players (if any survive) and their spectator magistrates and district judges will be relieved that for pending applications the goalposts have not been moved and they need not yet grapple with the complexities of construing the now current set of provisions (listed *above*).)

Note that the Hague Convention on the International Recovery on Child Support and Other Forms of Family Maintenance concluded on 23 November 2007 will, when in force, replace both the 1958 and 1973 Hague Conventions to which Part 1 of the 1972 Act gives effect, as well as the 1956 New York Convention to which Part 2 of that Act gives effect. (Part 2 creates an entirely distinct regime to facilitate the making of maintenance claims by United Kingdom resident applicants against respondents resident or having assets in other signatory states and vice versa.)

Chapter 3: The Civil Jurisdiction and Judgments Act 1982 (1982 Act), the Judgments Regulation (i.e. the 'Brussels I Regulation') and the Lugano Conventions

Chapter 3 of Part 34 is given over to the rules governing the registration and enforcement of maintenance orders under three distinct international instruments.

The Brussels I Regulation

By far the most important of these is Council Regulation (EC) No 44/2001 of 22 December 2000 on jurisdiction and the recognition and enforcement of judgments in civil and commercial matters (Council Regulation (EC) No 44/2001). This is referred to in the rules, as in the CPR, as 'the Judgments Regulation' but is better known to family practitioners as the **Brussels I Regulation**. It applies to all the EU Member States, namely, Austria, Belgium, Bulgaria, Cyprus, Czech Republic, Denmark (since 1 July 2007: see Council Decision 2006/325/EC of 27 April 2006 (OJ L 120/22, 5.5.2006) and the Civil Jurisdiction and Judgments Regulations 2007, SI 2007 No. 1655), Estonia, Finland, France, Germany, Greece, Hungary, Republic of Ireland, Italy, Latvia, Lithuania, Luxembourg, Malta, Netherlands, Poland, Portugal, Romania, Slovakia, Slovenia, Spain and Sweden.

It should be noted that the maintenance and jurisdictional provisions of Brussels I (and those of the EEO Regulation: see *below*) will be superseded (save in relation to Denmark) by Council Regulation (EC) No 4/2009 of 18 December 2008 on jurisdiction, applicable law, recognition and enforcement of decisions and cooperation in matters relating to maintenance obligations (OJ L7/1, 10.1.2009: 'the EU Maintenance Regulation'), from the date when it applies. The EU Maintenance Regulation extends to all member states except Denmark and comes into force from 18 June 2011.

The EU Maintenance Regulation abolishes the so-called *exequatur* (declaration of enforceability, or, in the UK, registration) as a pre-condition to enforcement, and creates a rule of mutual enforceability of maintenance orders. The fundamental principle is set out in article 17: if a maintenance order is enforceable in the state in which it was made, then it will be enforceable as of right in any other state. However, the principle of direct enforceability does not apply to decisions made in states not bound by the 2007 Hague Protocol (art 26). As the United Kingdom has not opted in to that Protocol, it appears that incoming maintenance orders from other member states will be directly enforceable, whereas outgoing orders will still need a 'declaration of enforceability' in the receiving state as a prerequisite to enforcement. The Brussels I regime (and where applicable the EEO Regulation: see *below*) will thus continue to apply to orders made by UK courts.

It is anticipated that rules governing the enforcement provisions of the EU Maintenance Regulation will be inserted into Part 34 once the Regulation enters into force, and will be included in **@eGlance** as soon as practicable thereafter.

The 1968 Brussels Convention

The second instrument is the **1968 Brussels Convention**. It is of vestigial relevance, as it continues to apply only to judgments given or orders made prior to 1 March 2002, the date on which the Brussels I Regulation entered into force (see art 70(2) of the Regulation) or, in the case of Denmark, prior to 1 July 2007.

The 2007 Lugano Convention

The third instrument is the **2007 Lugano Convention** (and its predecessor the **1988 Lugano Convention**). The 1968 Brussels Convention and the 2007 Lugano Convention are given force of law by sections 2 and 3 respectively of the 1982 Act. Hence the reference to that Act in the rules. (The Brussels I Regulation, by contrast, requires no implementing legislation to make it effective under domestic law.)

The 2007 Lugano Convention on jurisdiction and the recognition and enforcement of judgments in civil and commercial matters was signed on 30 October 2007 by the European Community, Denmark and the EFTA countries (except Liechtenstein; that is to say by Iceland, Norway and Switzerland). Its scheme is modelled on the Brussels I Regulation. On entry into force with respect to a particular country, it replaces the 1988 Lugano Convention with regard to that country (see Council Decision 2007/712/EC of 15 October 2007 (OJ L 339/1, 21.12.2007) and Council Decision 2009/430/EC (OJ L147/1, 10.6.2009)). The 2007 Convention was ratified by the EU on 18 May 2009 and entered into force with respect to Norway on 1 January 2010 and to Switzerland on 1 January 2011. Pending ratification by Iceland, which is understood to be imminent, the 1988 Lugano Convention will continue to apply to that country.

Domestic law was amended to give effect to the 2007 Lugano Convention by the Civil Jurisdiction and Judgments Regulations 2009, which entered into force on 1 January 2010.

Rules 34.29 to 34.36 govern applications for registration of maintenance orders in England and Wales (which will in the first instance be in the magistrates' court). Rules 34.37 to 34.39 deal with applications for maintenance orders under this Part and with applications to enforce maintenance orders in another state.

Regulation creating a European Enforcement Order

One other EU Regulation requires mention here. It is the Regulation creating a European Enforcement Order (EEO) for uncontested claims (European Parliament and Council Regulation (EC) No 805/2004 of 21 April 2004 creating a European Enforcement Order for uncontested claims (OJ L 143, 30.4.04)), which has applied since 21 October 2005. It enables judgments, court settlements and authentic instruments arising from *uncontested* claims (i.e. including consent orders) to be enforced between EU states (apart from Denmark) without the need for the enforcing party to obtain a 'declaration of enforceability' (or, in the UK, obtain registration) in the destination state. The enforcing party may invoke the enforcement process under Brussels I in the alternative.

It is clear that the scope of the Regulation encompasses maintenance orders, as: the Regulation applies in civil and commercial matters generally (art 2(1)); maintenance claims are not excluded by art 2(2); and maintenance obligations are referred to in the definition of 'authentic instrument' (art 4(3)(b)).

A court settlement for the purpose of the Regulation is a settlement concerning a claim which has been approved or concluded before a court in the course of proceedings and is enforceable in the Member State in which it was approved or concluded (arts 4(2) and 24(1)). An authentic instrument is, in relation to maintenance, an arrangement relating to maintenance obligations concluded with administrative authorities or authenticated by them (art 4(3)(b)). A child support maintenance calculation would appear to fall within this definition.

Note that the EEO Regulation has been amended with effect from 24 November 2005 by Commission Regulation (EC) No 1869/2005 of 16 November 2005 (OJ L 300, 17.11.05). It replaces the Annexes to the EEO Regulation, following the accession of new Member States on 1 May 2004. These Annexes are important as they contain the application forms to be used in proceedings under the Regulation.

Curiously, Part 34 makes no reference to the EEO Regulation. However, detailed provisions are made by CPR rules 74.27 to 74.33 (European Enforcement Orders) and the associated PD 74B. It is suggested that even though Part 74 has not been applied to family proceedings, the procedure set out there should be followed in maintenance cases.

An application under rule 74.28 for a certificate of a High Court or county court judgment for enforcement in another Regulation State must be made using Form N219 or Form N219A. While it is clear to whom the application should be made in the case of a judgment given in the Chancery or Queen's Bench Divisions of the High Court (a Master or District Judge), the rules and PD are silent about orders made in the Family Division or PRFD. Common sense suggests that the application be made to a District Judge of the Family Division. In the case of a county court judgment, application is to be made to a district judge (see PD 74B para 2.1).

The concept of maintenance

Note that 'maintenance' for the purpose of EU maintenance legislation has its own autonomous meaning, as developed by the jurisprudence of the European Court of Justice (see Case 143/78 *de Cavel v de Cavel (No 1)* [1979] ECR 1055; Case 120/79 *de Cavel v de Cavel (No 2)* [1980] ECR 731; Case C-220/95 *van den Boogaard v Laumen* [1997] 2 FLR 399, [1997] ECR I-1147, [1997] QB 759). The relevant propositions were distilled by the Court of Appeal in *Moore v Moore* [2007] EWCA Civ 361, [2007] 2 FLR 339, at [80]:

> ... first, whether a claim is for maintenance depends upon an autonomous interpretation of the term, and the label given to the claim by national law is not decisive;
>
> second, payment of a lump sum or transfer of property may be in the nature of maintenance if it is intended to ensure the support of a spouse;
>
> third, payment of a lump sum or transfer of property which serves only the purpose of a division of property or compensation for non-material damage is not in the nature of maintenance;
>
> fourth, a payment or transfer of property intended as a division of assets will concern 'rights in property arising out of a matrimonial relationship';
>
> fifth, whether a claim relates to maintenance will depend on its purpose, and in particular whether it is designed to enable one spouse to provide for himself or herself or if the needs and resources of each of the spouses are taken into consideration in the determination of its amount, or where the capital sum set is designed to ensure a predetermined level of income;
>
> sixth, where the provision is solely concerned with dividing property between the spouses, the decision will be concerned with rights in property arising out of a matrimonial relationship and will not therefore be enforceable under Brussels I.

See also *Traversa v Freddi* [2011] EWCA Civ 81, at [36] and [59] to [64].

PD 34B tracing payers overseas

This reproduces the provisions of the Practice Note of 10 February 1976 which establishes arrangements for tracing the whereabouts of maintenance payers in Australia, Canada, New Zealand and South Africa for the purpose of obtaining or enforcing a maintenance order under the Maintenance Orders (Facilities for Enforcement) Act 1920 or Part I of the Maintenance Orders (Reciprocal Enforcement) Act 1972.

Forms

The only Forms prescribed by *Practice Direction 5A – Forms* are REMO 1 and REMO 2.

PART 34: RECIPROCAL ENFORCEMENT OF MAINTENANCE ORDERS

Scope and interpretation of this Part

34.1.—(1) This Part contains rules about the reciprocal enforcement of maintenance orders.

(2) In this Part—

"the 1920 Act" means the Maintenance Orders (Facilities for Enforcement) Act 1920[100];

"the 1972 Act" means the Maintenance Orders (Reciprocal Enforcement) Act 1972;

"the 1982 Act" means the Civil Jurisdiction and Judgments Act 1982;

"the 1988 Convention" means the Convention on jurisdiction and the enforcement of judgments in civil and commercial matters done at Lugano on 16th September 1988;

"the Judgments Regulation" means Council Regulation (EC) No. 44/2001 of 22nd December 2000 on jurisdiction and the recognition and enforcement of judgments in civil and commercial matters; and

"the Lugano Convention" means the Convention on jurisdiction and the recognition and enforcement of judgments in civil and commercial matters, between the European Community and the Republic of Iceland, the Kingdom of Norway, the Swiss Confederation and the Kingdom of Denmark signed on behalf of the European Community on 30th October 2007.

(3) Chapter 1 of this Part relates to the enforcement of maintenance orders in accordance with the 1920 Act.

(4) Chapter 2 of this Part relates to the enforcement of maintenance orders in accordance with Part 1 of the 1972 Act.

(5) Chapter 3 of this Part relates to the enforcement of maintenance orders in accordance with—

(a) the 1982 Act;
(b) the Judgments Regulation; and
(c) the Lugano Convention.

Meaning of prescribed officer in a magistrates' court

34.2.—(1) For the purposes of the 1920 Act, the prescribed officer in relation to a magistrates' court is the designated officer for that court.

(2) For the purposes of Part 1 of the 1972 Act and section 5(2) of the 1982 Act, the prescribed officer in relation to a magistrates' court is the justices' clerk for the local justice area in which the court is situated.

Registration of maintenance orders in magistrates' courts in England and Wales

34.3. Where a magistrates' court is required by any of the enactments referred to in rule 34.1(2) to register a foreign order the court officer must—

(a) enter and sign a memorandum of the order in the register kept in accordance with rules made under section 144 of the Magistrates' Courts Act 1980; and
(b) state on the memorandum the statutory provision under which the order is registered.

CHAPTER 1: ENFORCEMENT OF MAINTENANCE ORDERS UNDER THE MAINTENANCE ORDERS (FACILITIES FOR ENFORCEMENT) ACT 1920

Interpretation

34.4.—(1) In this Chapter—

"payer", in relation to a maintenance order, means the person liable to make the payments for which the order provides; and

"reciprocating country" means a country or territory to which the 1920 Act extends.

(2) In this Chapter, an expression defined in the 1920 Act has the meaning given to it in that Act.

Confirmation of provisional orders made in a reciprocating country

34.5.—(1) This rule applies where, in accordance with section 4(1) of the 1920 Act[101], the court officer receives a provisional maintenance order.

(2) The court must fix the date, time and place for a hearing.

(3) The court officer must register the order in accordance with rule 34.3.

(4) The court officer must serve on the payer—

(a) certified copies of the provisional order and accompanying documents; and

(b) a notice—
   (i) specifying the time and date fixed for the hearing; and
   (ii) stating that the payer may attend to show cause why the order should not be confirmed.

(5) The court officer must inform—

(a) the court which made the provisional order; and

(b) the Lord Chancellor,

whether the court confirms, with or without modification, or decides not to confirm, the order.

Payment of sums due under registered orders

34.6. Where an order made by a reciprocating country is registered in a magistrates' court, the court must order payments due to be made to the court officer.

(Practice Direction 34A contains further provisions relating to the payment of sums due under registered orders.)

Enforcement of sums due under registered orders

34.7.—(1) This rule applies to—

(a) an order made in a reciprocating country which is registered in a magistrates' court; and

(b) a provisional order made in a reciprocating country which has been confirmed by a magistrates' court.

(2) The court officer must—

(a) collect the monies due under the order in the same way as for a magistrates' court maintenance order; and

(b) send the monies collected to—
   (i) the court in the reciprocating country which made the order; or
   (ii) such other person or authority as that court or the Lord Chancellor may from time to time direct.

(3) The court officer may take proceedings in that officer's own name for enforcing payment of monies due under the order.

Prescribed notice for the taking of further evidence

34.8.—(1) This rule applies where a court in a reciprocating country has sent a provisional order to a magistrates' court for the purpose of taking further evidence.

(2) The court officer must send a notice to the person who applied for the provisional order specifying—

(a) the further evidence required; and
(b) the time and place fixed for taking the evidence.

Transmission of maintenance orders made in a reciprocating country to the High Court

34.9. A maintenance order to be sent by the Lord Chancellor to the High Court in accordance with section 1(1) of the 1920 Act[102] will be—

(a) sent to the senior district judge who will register it in the register kept for the purpose of the 1920 Act; and
(b) filed in the principal registry.

Transmission of maintenance orders made in the High Court to a reciprocating country

34.10.—(1) This rule applies to maintenance orders made in the High Court.

(2) An application for a maintenance order to be sent to a reciprocating country under section 2 of the 1920 Act[103] must be made in accordance with this rule.

(3) The application must be made to a district judge in the principal registry unless paragraph (4) applies.

(4) If the order was made in the course of proceedings in a district registry, the application may be made to a district judge in that district registry.

(5) The application must be—

(a) accompanied by a certified copy of the order; and
(b) supported by a record of the sworn written evidence.

(6) The written evidence must give—

(a) the applicant's reason for believing that the payer resides in the reciprocating country;
(b) such information as the applicant has as to the whereabouts of the payer; and
(c) such other information as may be set out in Practice Direction 34A.

Inspection of the register in the High Court

34.11.—(1) A person may inspect the register and request copies of a registered order and any document filed with it if the district judge is satisfied that that person is entitled to, or liable to make, payments under a maintenance order made in—

(a) the High Court; or
(b) a court in a reciprocating country.

(2) The right to inspect the register referred to in paragraph (1) may be exercised by—

(a) a solicitor acting on behalf of the person entitled to, or liable to make, the payments referred to in that paragraph; or
(b) with the permission of the district judge, any other person.

CHAPTER 2: ENFORCEMENT OF MAINTENANCE ORDERS UNDER PART 1 OF THE 1972 ACT

Interpretation

34.12.—(1) In this Chapter—

(a) "reciprocating country" means a country to which Part 1 of the 1972 Act extends; and
(b) 'relevant court in the reciprocating country' means, as the case may be—
    (i) the court which made the order which has been sent to England and Wales for confirmation;
    (ii) the court which made the order which has been registered in a court in England and Wales;
    (iii) the court to which an order made in England and Wales has been sent for registration; or
    (iv) the court to which a provisional order made in England and Wales has been sent for confirmation.

(2) In this Chapter, an expression defined in the 1972 Act has the meaning given to it in that Act.

(3) In this Chapter, "Hague Convention Countries" means the countries listed in Schedule 1 to the Reciprocal Enforcement of Maintenance Orders (Hague Convention Countries) Order 1993.

[**Editors' note**: the reference to 1973 is a typographical error. The Order in question is dated 1993.]

Scope

34.13.—(1) Section 1 of this Chapter contains rules relating to the reciprocal enforcement of maintenance orders under Part 1 of the 1972 Act.

(2) Section 2 of this Chapter modifies the rules contained in Section 1 of this Chapter in their application to—

(a) the Republic of Ireland;
(b) the Hague Convention Countries; and
(c) the United States of America.

(Practice Direction 34A sets out in full the rules for the Republic of

Ireland, the Hague Convention Countries and the United States of America as modified by Section 2 of this Chapter.)

SECTION 1:
Reciprocal enforcement of maintenance orders under Part 1 of the 1972 Act

Application for transmission of maintenance order to reciprocating country

34.14. An application for a maintenance order to be sent to a reciprocating country under section 2 of the 1972 Act must be made in accordance with Practice Direction 34A.

Certification of evidence given on provisional orders

34.15. A document setting out or summarising evidence is authenticated by a court in England and Wales by a certificate signed, as the case may be, by—

(a) one of the justices; or
(b) the District Judge (Magistrates' Courts),

before whom that evidence was given.

(Section 3(5)(b), 5(4) and 9(5) of the 1972 Act require a document to be authenticated by the court.)

Confirmation of a provisional order made in a reciprocating country

34.16.—(1) This rule applies to proceedings for the confirmation of a provisional order made in a reciprocating country.

(2) Paragraph (3) applies on receipt by the court of—

(a) a certified copy of the order; and
(b) the documents required by the 1972 Act to accompany the order.

(3) On receipt of the documents referred to in paragraph (2)—

(a) the court must fix the date, time and place for a hearing or a directions appointment; and
(b) the court officer must send to the payer notice of the date, time and place fixed together with a copy of the order and accompanying documents.

(4) The date fixed for the hearing must be not less than 21 days beginning with the date on which the court officer sent the documents to the payer in accordance with paragraph (2).

(5) The court officer will send to the relevant court in the reciprocating country a certified copy of any order confirming or refusing to confirm the provisional order.

(6) This rule does not apply to the confirmation of a provisional order made in a reciprocating country varying a maintenance order to which sections 5(5) or 9(6) of the 1972 Act applies.

(Section 5(5) and 7 of the 1972 Act provide for proceedings for the confirmation of a provisional order.)

(Provision in respect of confirmation of a provisional order varying a maintenance order under the 1972 Act is in rules made under section 144 of the Magistrates' Courts Act 1980).

(Rule 34.22 provides for the transmission of documents to a court in a reciprocating country.)

Consideration of revocation of a provisional order made by a magistrates' court

34.17.—(1) This rule applies where—

(a) a magistrates' court has made a provisional order by virtue of section 3 of the 1972 Act;

(b) before the order is confirmed, evidence is taken by the court or received by it as set out in section 5(9) of the 1972 Act; and

(c) on consideration of the evidence the court considers that the order ought not to have been made.

(Section 5(9) of the 1972 Act provides that a magistrates' court may revoke a provisional order made by it, before the order has been confirmed in a reciprocating country, if it receives new evidence.)

(2) The court officer must serve on the person who applied for the provisional order ("the applicant") a notice which must—

(a) set out the evidence taken or received by the court;

(b) inform the applicant that the court considers that the order ought not to have been made; and

(c) inform the applicant that the applicant may—
 (i) make representations in relation to that evidence either orally or in writing; and
 (ii) adduce further evidence.

(3) If an applicant wishes to adduce further evidence—

(a) the applicant must notify the court officer at the court which made the order;

(b) the court will fix a date for the hearing of the evidence; and

(c) the court officer will notify the applicant in writing of the date fixed.

Notification of variation or revocation of a maintenance order by the High Court or a county court

34.18.—(1) This rule applies where—

(a) a maintenance order has been sent to a reciprocating country in pursuance of section 2 of the 1972 Act; and

(b) the court makes an order, not being a provisional order, varying or revoking that order.

(2) The court officer must send a certified copy of the order of variation or revocation to the relevant court in the reciprocating country.

(Rule 34.22 provides for the transmission of documents to a court in a reciprocating country.)

Notification of confirmation or revocation of a maintenance order by a magistrates' court

34.19.—(1) This rule applies where a magistrates' court makes an order—

(a) not being a provisional order, revoking a maintenance order to which section 5 of the 1972 Act[104] applies;

(b) under section 9 of the 1972 Act, revoking a registered order; or

(c) under section 7(2) of the 1972 Act[105], confirming an order to which section 7 of that Act applies.

(2) The court officer must send written notice of the making, revocation or confirmation of the order, as appropriate, to the relevant court in the reciprocating country.

(3) This rule does not apply to a provisional order varying a maintenance order to which sections 5 or 9 of the 1972 Act apply.

(Section 5 of the 1972 Act applies to a provisional order made by a magistrates' court in accordance with section 3 of that Act which has been confirmed by a court in a reciprocating country.)

(Provision in respect of notification of variation of a maintenance order by a magistrates' court under the 1972 Act is made in rules made under section 144 of the Magistrates' Courts Act 1980.)

(Rule 34.22 provides for the transmission of documents to a court in a reciprocating country.)

Taking of evidence for court in reciprocating country

34.20.—(1) This rule applies where a request is made by or on behalf of a court in a reciprocating country for the taking of evidence for the purpose of proceedings relating to a maintenance order to which Part 1 of the 1972 Act applies.

(Section 14 of the 1972[106] Act makes provision for the taking of evidence needed for the purpose of certain proceedings.)

(2) The High Court has power to take the evidence where—

(a) the request for evidence relates to a maintenance order made by a superior court in the United Kingdom; and

(b) the witness resides in England and Wales.

(3) The county court has power to take the evidence where—

(a) the request for evidence relates to a maintenance order made by a county court; and

(b) the maintenance order has not been registered in a magistrates' court under the 1958 Act.

(4) The following magistrates' courts have power to take the evidence, that is—

(a) where the proceedings in the reciprocating country relate to a maintenance order made by a magistrates' court, the court which made the order;

(b) where the proceedings relate to an order which is registered in a magistrates' court, the court in which the order is registered; and

(c) a magistrates' court to which the Secretary of State sends the request to take evidence.

(5) A magistrates' court not mentioned in paragraph (4) has power to take the evidence if the magistrates' court which would otherwise have that power consents because the evidence could be taken more conveniently.

(6) The evidence is to be taken in accordance with Part 22.

Request for the taking of evidence by a court in a reciprocating country

34.21.—(1) This rule applies where a request is made by a magistrates' court for the taking of evidence in a reciprocating country in accordance with section 14(5) of the 1972 Act.

(2) The request must be made in writing to the court in the reciprocating country.

(Rule 34.22 provides for the transmission of documents to a court in a reciprocating country.)

Transmission of documents

34.22.—(1) This rule applies to any document, including a notice or request, which is required to be sent to a court in a reciprocating country by—

(a) Part 1 of the 1972 Act; or

(b) Section 1 of Chapter 2 of this Part of these rules.

(2) The document must be sent to the Lord Chancellor for transmission to the court in the reciprocating country.

Method of payment under registered orders

34.23.—(1) Where an order is registered in a magistrates' court in accordance with section 6(3) of the 1972 Act, the court must order that the payment of sums due under the order be made—

(a) to the court officer for the registering court; and

(b) at such time and place as the court officer directs.

(Section 6(3) of the 1972 Act makes provision for the registration of maintenance orders made in a reciprocating country.)

(2) Where the court orders payments to be made to the court officer, whether in accordance with paragraph (1) or otherwise, the court officer must send the payments—

(a) by post to either—
 (i) the court which made the order; or
 (ii) such other person or authority as that court, or the Lord Chancellor, directs; or
(b) if the court which made the order is a country or territory specified in the Practice Direction 34A.—
 (i) to the Crown Agents for Overseas Governments and Administrations for transmission to the person to whom they are due; or
 (ii) as the Lord Chancellor directs.

(Practice Direction 34A contains further provisions relating to the payment of sums due under registered orders.)

Enforcement of payments under registered orders

34.24.—(1) This rule applies where a court has ordered periodical payments under a registered maintenance order to be made to the court officer.

(2) The court officer must take reasonable steps to notify the payee of the means of enforcement available.

(3) Paragraph (4) applies where periodical payments due under a registered order are in arrears.

(4) The court officer, on that officer's own initiative—

(a) may; or
(b) if the sums due are more than 4 weeks in arrears, must,

proceed in that officer's own name for the recovery of the sums due unless of the view that it is unreasonable to do so.

Notification of registration and cancellation

34.25.—(1) The court officer must send written notice to the Lord Chancellor of the due registration of orders registered in accordance with section 6(3), 7(5), or 10(4) of the 1972 Act.

(2) The court officer must, when registering an order in accordance with section 6(3), 7(5), 9(10), 10(4) or (5) or 23(3) of the 1972 Act[107], send written notice to the payer stating—

(a) that the order has been registered;
(b) that payments under the order should be made to the court officer; and

(c) the hours during which and the place at which the payments should be made.

(3) The court officer must, when cancelling the registration of an order in accordance with section 10(1) of the 1972 Act, send written notice of the cancellation to the payer.

SECTION 2:
Modification of rules in Section 1 of this Chapter

Sub-section 1: Republic of Ireland

Application of Section 1 of this Chapter to the Republic of Ireland
34.26.—(1) In relation to the Republic of Ireland, Section 1 of this Chapter has effect as modified by this rule.

(2) A reference in this rule and in any rule which has effect in relation to the Republic of Ireland by virtue of this rule to—

(a) the 1972 Act is a reference to the 1972 Act as modified by Schedule 2 to the Reciprocal Enforcement of Maintenance Orders (Republic of Ireland) Order 1993[108]; and

(b) a section under the 1972 Act is a reference to the section so numbered in the 1972 Act as so modified.

(3) A reference to a reciprocating country in rule 34.12(1) and Section 1 of this Chapter is a reference to the Republic of Ireland.

(4) In the words in brackets at the end of rule 34.15 (certification of evidence given on provisional orders), for the sections mentioned substitute "section 3(5)(b) or 5(3)".

(5) Rules 34.16 (confirmation of provisional orders) and 34.21 (request for the taking of evidence by a court in a reciprocating country) do not apply.

(6) For rule 34.17 (consideration of revocation of a provisional order made by a magistrates' court) substitute—

"**Consideration of confirmation of a provisional order made by a magistrates' court**

34.17.—(1) This rule applies where—

(a) a magistrates' court has made a provisional order by virtue of section 3 of the 1972 Act;

(b) the payer has made representations or adduced evidence to the court; and

   (c) the court has fixed a date for the hearing at which it will consider
       confirmation of the order.

(2) The court officer must serve on the applicant for the provisional order—

   (a) a copy of the representations or evidence; and

   (b) written notice of the date fixed for the hearing.".

(7) For rules 34.18 and 34.19 (notification of variation or revocation)
substitute—

"Notification of variation or revocation of a maintenance order by the High Court

34.18. Where the High Court makes an order varying or revoking an order to
which section 5 of the 1972 Act applies the court officer must send—

(a) a certified copy of the order of variation or revocation; and

(b) a statement as to the service on the payer of the documents mentioned in
    section 5(3) of the 1972 Act,

to the court in the Republic of Ireland.

(Rule 34.22 provides for the transmission of documents to a court in a
reciprocating country.)

Notification of revocation of a maintenance order by a magistrates' court

34.19. Where a magistrates' court makes an order revoking an order to which
section 5 of the 1972 Act applies, the court officer must send written notice
of the making of the order to the Lord Chancellor.

(Section 5 of the 1972 Act applies to a maintenance order sent to the Republic
of Ireland in accordance with section 2 of that Act and a provisional order
made by a magistrates' court in accordance with section 3 of that Act which
has been confirmed by such a court.)

(Provision in respect of notification of variation of a maintenance order by
magistrates' court under the 1972 Act is made in rules made under section 144
of the Magistrates' Courts Act 1980.)".

(8) For rule 34.23(2) (method of payment under registered orders),
substitute—

"(2) Where the court orders payment to be made to the court officer, the court
     officer must send the payments by post—

   (a) to the payee under the order; or

   (b) where a public authority has been authorised by the payee to receive
       the payments, to that public authority.".

(9) For rule 34.24 (enforcement of payments under registered orders),
substitute—

"Enforcement of payments under registered orders

34.24.—(1) This rule applies where periodical payments under a registered order are in arrears.

(2) The court officer must, on the written request of the payee, proceed in that officer's own name for the recovery of the sums due unless of the view that it is unreasonable to do so.

(3) If the sums due are more than 4 weeks in arrears the court officer must give the payee notice in writing of that fact stating the particulars of the arrears.".

(10) For rule 34.25 (notification of registration and cancellation) substitute—

"Notification of registration and cancellation

34.25. The court officer must send written notice to—

(a) the Lord Chancellor, on the due registration of an order under section 6(3) or 10(4) of the 1972 Act; and

(b) to the payer under the order, on—

    (i) the registration of an order under section 10(4) of the 1972 Act; or

    (ii) the cancellation of the registration of an order under section 10(1) of that Act.".

(11) After rule 34.25 insert—

"Other notices under section 6 of the 1972 Act[109]

34.25A.—(1) A notice required under section 6(6) or (10) of the 1972 Act must be in the form referred to in a practice direction.

(2) Where a magistrates' court sets aside the registration of an order following an appeal under section 6(7) of the 1972 Act, the court officer must send written notice of the court's decision to the payee.

(Section 6(6) of the 1972 Act provides for notice of registration in a United Kingdom court of a maintenance order made in the Republic of Ireland, and section 6(10) of that Act for notice that a maintenance order made in the Republic of Ireland has not been registered in a United Kingdom court.)"

Sub-section 2: Hague Convention countries

Application of Section 1 of this Chapter to the Hague Convention Countries

34.27.—(1) In relation to the Hague Convention Countries, Section 1 of this Chapter has effect as modified by this rule.

(2) A reference in this rule, and in any rule which has effect in relation to the Hague Convention Countries by virtue of this rule to—

(a) the 1972 Act is a reference to the 1972 Act as modified by Schedule

2 to the Reciprocal Enforcement of Maintenance Orders (Hague Convention Countries) Order 1993[110]; and

(b) a section under the 1972 Act is a reference to the section so numbered in the 1972 Act as so modified.

(3) A reference to a reciprocating country in rule 34.12(1) and Section 1 of this Chapter is a reference to a Hague Convention Country.

(4) Rules 34.15 (certification of evidence given on provisional orders), 34.16 (confirmation of provisional orders), 34.19 (notification of confirmation or revocation of a maintenance order by a magistrates' court) and 34.21 (request for the taking of evidence by a court in a reciprocating country) do not apply.

(5) For rule 34.17 (consideration of revocation of a provisional order made by a magistrates' court) substitute—

"Consideration of revocation of a maintenance order made by a magistrates' court

34.17.—(1) This rule applies where—

(a) an application has been made to a magistrates' court by a payee for the revocation of an order to which section 5 of the 1972 Act applies; and

(b) the payer resides in a Hague Convention Country.

(2) The court officer must serve on the payee, by post, a copy of any representations or evidence adduced by or on behalf of the payer.

(Provision relating to consideration of variation of a maintenance order made by a magistrates' court to which section 5 of the 1972 Act applies is made in rules made under section 144 of the Magistrates' Courts Act 1980.)".

(6) For rule 34.18 (notification of variation or revocation of a maintenance order by the High Court or county court) substitute—

"Notification of variation or revocation of a maintenance order by the High Court or a county court

34.18.—(1) This rule applies if the High Court or a county court makes an order varying or revoking a maintenance order to which section 5 of the 1972 Act applies.

(2) If the time for appealing has expired without an appeal having been entered, the court officer will send to the Lord Chancellor—

(a) the documents required by section 5(8) of the 1972 Act; and

(b) a certificate signed by the district judge stating that the order of variation or revocation is enforceable and no longer subject to the ordinary forms of review.

(3) A party who enters an appeal against the order of variation or revocation must, at the same time, give written notice to the court officer.".

(7) For rule 34.23(2) (method of payment under registered orders) substitute—

"(2) Where the court orders payment to be made to the court officer, the court officer must send the payments by post to the payee under the order.".

(8) For rule 34.25 (notification of registration and cancellation) substitute—

"**Notification of registration and cancellation**

34.25. The court officer must send written notice to—

(a) the Lord Chancellor, on the due registration of an order under section 10(4) of the 1972 Act; and

(b) the payer under the order, on—

    (i) the registration of an order under section 10(4) of the 1972 Act; or

    (ii) the cancellation of the registration of an order under section 10(1) of the 1972 Act.".

(9) After rule 34.25 insert—

"**General provisions as to notices**

34.25A.—(1) A notice to a payer of the registration of an order in a magistrates' court in accordance with section 6(3) of the 1972 Act must be in the form referred to in a practice direction.

(Section 6(8) of the 1972 Act requires notice of registration to be given to the payer.)

(2) If the court sets aside the registration of a maintenance order following an appeal under section 6(9) of the 1972 Act, the court officer must send written notice of the decision to the Lord Chancellor.

(3) A notice to a payee that the court officer has refused to register an order must be in the form referred to in a practice direction.

(Section 6(11) of the 1972 Act requires notice of refusal of registration to be given to the payee.)

(4) Where, under any provision of Part 1 of the 1972 Act, a court officer serves a notice on a payer who resides in a Hague Convention Country, the court officer must send to the Lord Chancellor a certificate of service.".

Sub-section 3: United States of America

Application of Section 1 of this Chapter to the United States of America

34.28.—(1) In relation to the United States of America, Section 1 of this Chapter has effect as modified by this rule.

(2) A reference in this rule and in any rule which has effect in relation to the United States of America by virtue of this rule to—

(a) the 1972 Act is a reference to the 1972 Act as modified by Schedule 1 to the Reciprocal Enforcement of Maintenance Orders (United States of America) Order 2007[111]; and

(b) a section under the 1972 Act is a reference to the section so numbered in the 1972 Act as so modified.

(3) A reference to a reciprocating country in rule 34.12(1) and Section 1 of this Chapter is a reference to the United States of America.

(4) Rules 34.15 (certification of evidence given on provisional orders), 34.16 (confirmation of provisional orders), 34.19 (notification of confirmation or revocation of a maintenance order made by a magistrates' court) and 34.21 (request for the taking of evidence in a reciprocating country) do not apply.

(5) For rule 34.17 (consideration of revocation of a provisional order made by a magistrates' court) substitute—

"Consideration of revocation of a maintenance order made by a magistrates' court

34.17.—(1) This rule applies where—

(a) an application has been made to a magistrates' court by a payee for the revocation of an order to which section 5 of the 1972 Act applies; and

(b) the payer resides in the United States of America.

(2) The court officer must serve on the payee by post a copy of any representations or evidence adduced by or on behalf of the payer.

(Provision relating to consideration of variation of a maintenance order made by a magistrates' court to which section 5 of the 1972 Act applies is made in rules made under section 144 of the Magistrates' Courts Act 1980.)".

(6) For rule 34.18 (notification of variation or revocation), substitute—

"Notification of variation or revocation

34.18. If the High Court or a county court makes an order varying or revoking a maintenance order to which section 5 of the 1972 Act applies, the court officer will send to the Lord Chancellor the documents required by section 5(7) of that Act.".

(7) For rule 34.23(2) (method of payment under registered orders) substitute—

"(2) Where the court orders payment to be made to the court officer, the court officer must send the payments by post to the payee under the order.".

(8) For rule 34.25 (notification of registration and cancellation) substitute—

"Notification of registration and cancellation

34.25. The court officer must send written notice to—

(a) the Lord Chancellor, on the due registration of an order under section 10(4) of the 1972 Act; or

(b) the payer under the order, on—

  (i) the registration of an order under section 10(4) of the 1972 Act; or

  (ii) the cancellation of the registration of an order under section 10(1) of that Act."

CHAPTER 3: ENFORCEMENT OF MAINTENANCE ORDERS UNDER THE CIVIL JURISDICTION AND JUDGMENTS ACT 1982, THE JUDGMENTS REGULATION AND THE LUGANO CONVENTION

SECTION 1:
Registration and Enforcement in a Magistrates' Court of Maintenance Orders made in a Contracting State to the 1968 Convention, a Contracting State to the 1988 Convention, a Regulation State or a State bound by the Lugano Convention

Interpretation
34.29. In this Section—

  (a) an expression defined in the 1982 Act has the meaning given to it in that Act; and
  (b) "the 1958 Act" means the Maintenance Orders Act 1958.

Registration of maintenance orders
34.30.—(1) In this rule, "assets to which the 1958 Act applies" means assets against which, after registration in the High Court, the maintenance order could be enforced under Part 1 of the 1958 Act.

(2) This rule applies where the court officer for a magistrates' court receives—

  (a) an application under Article 31 of the 1968 Convention for the enforcement of a maintenance order made in a Contracting State other than the United Kingdom;

[Editors' note: the reference to 'the 1968 Convention' is to the Convention on jurisdiction and the enforcement of judgments in civil and commercial matters (including the Protocol annexed to that Convention), signed at Brussels on 27th September 1968.]

   (b) an application under Article 31 of the 1988 Convention for the enforcement of a maintenance order made in a State bound by the 1988 Convention other than a Member State of the European Union;

   (c) an application under Article 38 of the Judgments Regulation for the enforcement of a maintenance order made in a Regulation State other than the United Kingdom; or

   (d) an application under Article 38 of the Lugano Convention for the enforcement of a maintenance order made in a State bound by the Lugano Convention other than a Member State of the European Union.

(3) The court officer must—

   (a) take such steps as appear appropriate for ascertaining whether the payer resides within the local justice area for which the court acts; and

   (b) consider any available information as to the nature and location of the payer's assets.

(4) If the court officer is satisfied that the payer—

   (a) does not reside within the local justice area for which the court acts; and

   (b) does not have assets to which the 1958 Act applies,

the court officer must refuse the application and return the application to the Lord Chancellor stating the information the court officer has as to the whereabouts of the payer and the nature and location of the payer's assets.

(5) If the court officer is satisfied that the payer—

   (a) does not reside within the local justice area for which the court acts; but

   (b) has assets to which the 1958 Act applies,

then either—

   (i) the court officer must register the order; or

   (ii) if the court officer believes that the payer is residing within the local justice area in which another magistrates' court acts, the court officer may refuse the application and return the documents to the Lord Chancellor with the information referred to in paragraph (4) above.

(6) Except where paragraphs (4) or (5) apply, the court officer must register the order unless—

   (a) in the case of an application under Article 31 of the 1968 Convention, Articles 27 or 28 of that Convention apply; and

(b) in the case of an application under Article 31 of the 1988 Convention, Articles 27 or 28 of that Convention apply.

(7) If the court officer refuses to register an order to which this rule relates the court officer must notify the applicant.

(8) If the court officer registers an order the court officer must send written notice of that fact to—

(a) the Lord Chancellor;
(b) the payer; and
(c) the applicant.

(9) If the court officer considers that it would be appropriate for all or part of a registered order to be enforced in the High Court the court officer must notify the applicant—

(a) that the court officer so considers it appropriate; and
(b) that the applicant may apply under the 1958 Act for the order to be registered in the High Court.

Appeal from a decision relating to registration

34.31.—(1) This rule applies to an appeal under—

(a) Article 36 or Article 40 of the 1968 Convention;
(b) Article 36 or Article 40 of the 1988 Convention;
(c) Article 43 of the Judgments Regulation; or
(d) Article 43 of the Lugano Convention.

(2) The appeal must be to the magistrates' court—

(a) in which the order is registered; or
(b) in which the application for registration has been refused,
as the case may be.

Payment of sums due under a registered order

34.32.—(1) Where an order is registered in accordance with section 5(3) of the 1982 Act or Article 38 of the Judgments Regulation or Article 38 of the Lugano Convention, the court must order that payment of sums due under the order be made—

(a) to the court officer for the registering court; and
(b) at such time and place as the court officer directs.

(2) Where the court orders payments to be made to the court officer, whether in accordance with paragraph (1) or otherwise, the court officer must send the payments by post either—

(a) to the court which made the order; or
(b) to such other person or authority as that court, or the Lord Chancellor, directs.

(Practice Direction 34A contains further provisions relating to the payment of sums due under registered orders.)

Enforcement of payments under registered orders

34.33.—(1) This rule applies where a court has ordered periodical payments under a registered maintenance order to be made to the court officer for a magistrates' court.

(2) The court officer must take reasonable steps to notify the payee of the means of enforcement available.

(3) Paragraph (4) applies where periodical payments due under a registered order are in arrears.

(4) The court officer, on that officer's own initiative—

(a) may; or
(b) if the sums due are more than 4 weeks in arrears, must,

proceed in that officer's own name for the recovery of the sums due unless of the view that it is unreasonable to do so.

Variation and revocation of registered orders

34.34.—(1) This rule applies where the court officer for a registering court receives notice that a registered maintenance order has been varied or revoked by a competent court in a Contracting State to the 1968 Convention, a Contracting State to the 1988 Convention (other than a Member State of the European Union), a Regulation State or a State bound by the Lugano Convention, other than a Member State of the European Union.

(2) The court officer for the registering court must—

(a) register the order of variation or revocation; and
(b) send notice of the registration by post to the payer and payee under the order.

Transfer of registered order

34.35.—(1) This rule applies where the court officer for the court where an order is registered considers that the payer is residing within the local justice area in England and Wales for which another magistrates' court acts.

(2) Subject to paragraph (4), the court officer must transfer the order to the other court by sending to that court—

(a) the information and documents relating to the registration;
(b) a certificate of arrears, if applicable, signed by the court officer;
(c) a statement giving such information as the court officer possesses as to the whereabouts of the payer and the nature and location of the payer's assets; and
(d) any other relevant documents which the court officer has relating to the case.

(3) The information and documents referred to in paragraph (2)(a) are those required, as appropriate, under—

(a) Articles 46 and 47 of the 1968 Convention;
(b) Articles 46 and 47 of the 1988 Convention;
(c) Article 53 of the Judgments Regulation; or
(d) Article 53 of the Lugano Convention.

(4) If an application is pending in the registering court for the registration of the whole or part of the order in the High Court under Part 1 of the 1958 Act, the court officer must not transfer the order, or the part to which the application relates, under paragraph (2).

(5) The court officer must give notice of the transfer of an order to—

(a) the payee; and
(b) the Lord Chancellor.

(6) If an order is transferred, the court officer for the court to which it is transferred must register the order.

Cancellation of registered orders

34.36.—(1) Where the court officer for the registering court—

(a) has no reason to transfer a registered order under rule; and
(b) considers that the payer under the registered order is not residing within the local justice area for which the court acts and has no assets to which the 1958 Act applies,

the court officer must cancel the registration of the order.

(2) The court officer must—

(a) give notice of cancellation to the payee; and
(b) send the information and documents relating to the registration and the other documents referred to in rule 34.35(2) to the Lord Chancellor.

SECTION 2:
Reciprocal enforcement in a Contracting State or Regulation State of Orders of a court in England and Wales

Application in a magistrates' court for a maintenance order, or revocation of a maintenance order, to which the 1982 Act, the Judgment Regulations or the Lugano Convention applies

34.37.—(1) This rule applies where a person applies to a magistrates' court for a maintenance order, or for the revocation of a maintenance order, in relation to which the court has jurisdiction by virtue of the 1982 Act, the

Judgments Regulation or the Lugano Convention, and the respondent is outside the United Kingdom.

(2) On the making of the application the court officer shall send the following documents to the Lord Chancellor—

(a) notice of the proceedings, including a statement of the grounds of the application;

(b) a statement signed by the court officer giving such information as he has regarding the whereabouts of, and information to assist in identifying, the respondent; and

(c) where available, a photograph of the respondent.

(3) In considering whether or not to make a maintenance order pursuant to an application to which paragraph (1) applies, where the respondent does not appear and is not represented at the hearing the court shall take into account any written representations made and any evidence given by the respondent under these rules.

(Part 27 makes provision relating to attendance at hearings and directions appointments.)

(Part 9 makes provision for applications relating to financial remedies including those under Schedule 1 to the 1989 Act, Part 1 of the 1978 Act, and Schedule 6 to the 2004 Act.)

(Rules made under section 144 of the Magistrates' Courts Act 1980 make provision for applications to vary maintenance orders made in magistrates' courts.)

Admissibility of Documents

34.38.—(1) This rule applies to a document, referred to in paragraph (2) and authenticated in accordance with paragraph (3), which comprises, records or summarises evidence given in, or information relating to, proceedings in a court in another part of the UK, another Contracting State to the 1968 Convention or the 1988 Convention, Regulation State or State bound by the Lugano Convention, and any reference in this rule to "the court", without more, is a reference to that court.

(2) The documents referred to at paragraph (1) are documents which purport to—

(a) set out or summarise evidence given in the court;

(b) have been received in evidence the court;

(c) set out or summarise evidence taken in the court for the purpose of proceedings in a court in England and Wales to which the 1982 Act applies; or

(d) record information relating to payments made under an order of the court.

(3) A document to which paragraph (1) applies shall, in any proceedings in a magistrates' court in England and Wales relating to a maintenance

order to which the 1982 Act applies, be admissible as evidence of any fact stated in it to the same extent as oral evidence of that fact is admissible in those proceedings.

(4) A document to which paragraph (1) applies shall be deemed to be authenticated—

    (a) in relation to the documents listed at paragraph 2(a) or (c), if the document purports to be—
       (i) certified by the judge or official before whom the evidence was given or taken; or
      (ii) the original document recording or summarising the evidence, or a true copy of that document;
    (b) in relation to a document listed at paragraph (2)(b), if the document purports to be certified by a judge or official of the court to be, or to be a true copy of, the document received in evidence; and
    (c) in relation to the document listed at paragraph (2)(d), if the document purports to be certified by a judge or official of the court as a true record of the payments made under the order.

(5) It shall not be necessary in any proceedings in which evidence is to be received under this rule to prove the signature or official position of the person appearing to have given the certificate referred to in paragraph (4).

(6) Nothing in this rule shall prejudice the admission in evidence of any document which is admissible in evidence apart from this rule.

(7) Any request by a magistrates' court in England and Wales for the taking or providing of evidence by a court in another part of the United Kingdom or in another Contracting State to the 1968 Convention or the 1988 Convention or the Lugano Convention (other than a Member State of the European Union) for the purpose of proceedings to which the 1982 Act applies shall be communicated in writing to the court in question.

(Chapter 2 of Part 24 makes provision for taking of evidence by a court in another Regulation State).

Enforcement of orders of a magistrates' court

34.39.—(1) This rule applies to applications to a magistrates' court under—

    (a) section 12 of the 1982 Act[112];
    (b) article 54 of the Judgments Regulation; or
    (c) article 54 of the Lugano Convention.

(2) A person who wishes to enforce in a Contracting State to the 1968 Convention, a Contracting State to the 1988 Convention (other than a Member State of the European Union), a Regulation State or a State bound by the Lugano Convention (other than a Member State of the European Union) a maintenance order obtained in a magistrates' court must apply for a certified copy of the order.

(3) An application under this rule must be made in writing to the court officer and must specify—

(a) the names of the parties to the proceedings;

(b) the date, or approximate date, of the proceedings in which the maintenance order was made and the nature of those proceedings;

(c) the Contracting State or Regulation State in which the application for recognition or enforcement has been made or is to be made; and

(d) the postal address of the applicant.

(4) The court officer must, on receipt of the application, send a copy of the order to the applicant certified in accordance with a practice direction.

(5) Paragraph (6) applies where—

(a) a maintenance order is registered in a magistrates' court in England and Wales; and

(b) a person wishes to obtain a certificate giving details of any payments made or arrears accrued under the order while it has been registered, for the purposes of an application made or to be made in connection with that order in—

(i) another Contracting State to the 1968 Convention;

(ii) another Contracting State to the 1988 Convention (other than a Member State of the European Union);

(iii) another Regulation State;

(iv) another State bound by the Lugano Convention (other than a Member State of the European Union); or

(v) another part of the United Kingdom.

(6) The person wishing to obtain the certificate referred to in paragraph (5) may make a written application to the court officer for the registering court.

(7) On receipt of an application under paragraph (6) the court officer must send to the applicant a certificate giving the information requested.

(Rule 74.12 (application for certified copy of a judgment) and 74.13 (evidence in support) of the CPR apply in relation to the application for a certified copy of a judgment obtained in the High Court or a county court.)

PRACTICE DIRECTION 34A – RECIPROCAL ENFORCEMENT OF MAINTENANCE ORDERS

This Practice Direction supplements FPR Part 34

Noting Record of Means of Payment

1.1 Where a magistrates' court orders payments under a maintenance order to which Part 34 applies to be made in a particular way, the court must record that on a copy of the order.

1.2 If the court orders payment to be made to the court officer of a magistrates' court by a method referred to in section 59(6) of the Magistrates' Courts Act 1980, the court may vary the method of payment on the application of an interested party and where it does so the court must record the variation on a copy of the order.

(Section 59(6) refers to payment by standing order or other methods which require transfer between accounts of a specific amount on a specific date during the period for which the authority to make the payment is in force.)

Notification by court officer

2.1 The court officer must, as soon as practicable, notify in writing the person liable to make the payments of the method by which they must be made.

2.2 If the court orders payment to be made to the court officer of a magistrates' court by a method referred to in section 59(6) of the Magistrates' Courts Act 1980 the court officer must inform the person liable to make the payments of the number and location of the account to which the payments must be made.

2.3 If the court varies the method of payment on the application of an interested party the court officer must, as soon as practicable, notify all interested parties in writing of the result of an application (including a decision to refer it to the court).

Applications under section 2 of the 1920 Act

3.1 This paragraph refers to an application for the transmission of a maintenance order to a reciprocating country under section 2 of the 1920 Act in accordance with rule 34.10.

3.2 The applicant's written evidence must include such information as may be required by the law of the reciprocating country for the purpose of enforcement of the order.

3.3 If, in accordance with section 2 of the 1920 Act, the court sends a maintenance order to the Lord Chancellor for transmission to a reciprocating country, it shall record the fact in the court records.

Applications under section 2 of the 1972 Act (rule 34.14)

Introduction

4.1 An application for a maintenance order to be sent to a reciprocating country under section 2 of the 1972 Act is made by lodging specified documents with the court. The documents to be lodged vary according to which country it is intended that the maintenance order is be sent and the requirements are set out in this paragraph.

General provision

4.2 The general requirement is that the following documents should be lodged with the court—

- (a) an affidavit by the applicant stating—
  - (i) the reason that the applicant has for believing that the payer under the maintenance order is residing in the reciprocating country; and
  - (ii) the amount of any arrears due to the applicant under the order, the date to which those arrears have been calculated and the date on which the next payment under the order falls due;
- (b) a certified copy of the maintenance order;
- (c) a statement giving such information as the applicant has as to the whereabouts of the payer;
- (d) a statement giving such information as the applicant has for facilitating the identification of the payer, (including, if known to the applicant, the name and address of any employer of the payer, his occupation and the date and place of issue of any passport of the payer); and
- (e) if available to the applicant, a photograph of the payer.

Republic of Ireland

4.3 If the country to which it is intended to send the maintenance order is the Republic of Ireland, then the following changes to the general requirements apply.

4.4 The applicant must lodge the following documents with the court in addition to those set out in paragraph 4.2—

- (a) a statement as to whether or not the payer appeared in the proceedings in which the maintenance order was made;
- (b) if the payer did not so appear—
  - (i) the original of a document which establishes that notice of the institution of proceedings was served on the payer; or
  - (ii) a copy of such a document certified by the applicant or the applicant's solicitor to be a true copy;
- (c) a document which establishes that notice of the order was sent to the payer; and
- (d) if the payee received legal aid in the proceedings in which the order was made, a copy certified by the applicant or the applicant's solicitor to be a true copy of the legal aid certificate.

Hague Convention Country

4.5 If the country to which it is intended to send the maintenance order is a Hague Convention country, then the following changes to the general requirements apply.

4.6 In addition to the matters stated in that paragraph, the affidavit referred to in paragraph 4.2(a) must also state whether the time for appealing against the maintenance order has expired and whether an appeal is pending.

4.7 The applicant must lodge the following documents with the court in addition to those set out in paragraph 4.2—

(a) a statement as to whether or not the payer appeared in the proceedings in which the maintenance order was made;

(b) if the payer did not so appear—

    (i) the original of a document which establishes that notice of the institution of proceedings, including notice of the substance of the claim, was served on the payer; or

    (ii) a copy of such a document certified by the applicant or the applicant's solicitor to be a true copy;

(c) a document which establishes that notice of the order was sent to the payer;

(d) a written statement as to whether or not the payee received legal aid in the proceedings in which the order was made, or in connection with the application under section 2 of the 1972 Act; and

(e) if the payee did receive legal aid, a copy certified by the applicant or the applicant's solicitor to be a true copy of the legal aid certificate.

United States of America

4.8 If the country to which it is intended to send the maintenance order is a specified State of the United States of America, then the following changes to the general requirements apply.

4.9 There is no requirement to lodge a statement giving information as to the whereabouts of the payer since this information must be contained in the affidavit as mentioned in paragraph 4.10.

4.10 In addition to the matters stated in that paragraph, the affidavit referred to in paragraph 4.2(a) must also state—

(a) the address of the payee;

(b) such information as is known as to the whereabouts of the payer; and

(c) a description, so far as is known, of the nature and location of any assets of the payer available for execution.

4.11 The applicant must lodge three certified copies of the maintenance order.

Notification to the Lord Chancellor

5.1 Where, in accordance with Part 1 of the 1972 Act, a magistrates' court registers a maintenance order sent to it from a Hague Convention Country, the court officer must sent written notice of the registration to the Lord Chancellor.

Notification of means of enforcement

6.1 The court officer of a magistrates' court must take reasonable steps to notify the person to whom payments are due under a registered order of the means of enforcement available in respect of it.

6.2 Notification of the means of enforcement includes, where appropriate, notification of the possibility of registration of the order in the High Court under Part I of the Maintenance Orders Act 1958.

Certified copies of orders issued under rule 34.39

7.1 In an application under rule 34.39 by a person wishing to enforce abroad a maintenance order obtained in a magistrates' court, the certified copy of the order will be a sealed copy and will be accompanied by a certificate signed by the court officer.

7.2 In an application under the 1982 Act, the certificate signed by the court officer must state that it is a true copy of the order concerned and must give particulars of the proceedings in which it was made.

7.3 In an application under the Judgments Regulation, the certificate will be in the form of Annex V to the Regulation.

7.4 In an application under the Lugano Convention, the certificate will be in the form of Annex V to the Convention.

Countries and Territories in which Sums are Payable through Crown Agents for Overseas Governments and Territories (rule 34.23)

8.1 Gibraltar, Barbados, Bermuda, Ghana, Kenya, Fiji, Hong Kong, Singapore, Turks and Caicos Islands, United Republic of Tanzania (except Zanzibar), Anguilla, Falkland Islands and Dependencies, St Helena.

Part 1 of the 1972 Act – Modified Rules

9.1 The annexes to this Practice Direction set out rules 34.14 to 34.25 as they are modified—

(a) in relation to the Republic of Ireland, by rule 34.26 (Annex 1);
(b) in relation to the Hague Convention Countries, by rule 34.27 (Annex 2); and
(c) in relation to Specified States of the United States of America, by rule 34.28 (Annex 3).

9.2 The statutory references in the annexes are construed in accordance with rule 34.26(2), 34.27(2) or 34.28(2) as the case may be.

Annex 1: application of section 1 of Chapter 2 of Part 34 to the Republic of Ireland

Application for transmission of maintenance order to the Republic of Ireland

34.14 An application for a maintenance order to be sent to the Republic of Ireland under section 2 of the 1972 Act must be made in accordance with Practice Direction 34A.

Certification of evidence given on provisional orders

34.15 A document setting out or summarising evidence is authenticated by a court in England and Wales by a certificate signed, as appropriate, by—

(a) one of the justices; or
(b) the District Judge (Magistrates' Courts),

before whom that evidence was given.

(Section 3(5)(b) or 5(3) of the 1972 Act require a document to be authenticated by the court.)

Confirmation of a provisional order

34.16 [This rule does not apply to the Republic of Ireland]

Consideration of confirmation of a provisional order made by a magistrates' court

34.17.—(1) This rule applies where—

(a) a magistrates' court has made a provisional order by virtue of section 3 of the 1972 Act;
(b) the payer has made representations or adduced evidence to the court; and
(c) the court has fixed a date for the hearing at which it will consider confirmation of the order.

(2) The court officer must serve on the applicant for the provisional order—

(a) a copy of the representations or evidence; and
(b) written notice of the date fixed for the hearing.

Notification of variation or revocation of a maintenance order by the High Court

34.18 Where the High Court makes an order varying or revoking an order to which section 5 of the 1972 Act applies the court officer must send—

(a) a certified copy of the order of variation or revocation; and
(b) a statement as to the service on the payer of the documents mentioned in section 5(3) of the 1972 Act;

to the court in the Republic of Ireland.

(Rule 34.22 provides for the transmission of documents to a court in a reciprocating country.)

Notification of revocation of a maintenance order by a magistrates' court

34.19 Where a magistrates' court makes an order revoking an order to which section 5 of the 1972 Act applies, the court officer must send written notice of the making of the order to the Lord Chancellor.

(Section 5 of the 1972 Act applies to a maintenance order sent to the Republic of Ireland in accordance with section 2 of that Act and a provisional order made by a magistrates' court in accordance with section 3 of that Act which has been confirmed by such a court.)

(Provision in respect of notification of variation of a maintenance order by a magistrates' court under the 1972 Act is made in Rules made under section 144 of the Magistrates' Courts Act 1980.)

Taking of evidence for court in the Republic of Ireland

34.20—(1) This rule applies where a request is made by or on behalf of a court in the Republic of Ireland for the taking of evidence for the purpose of proceedings relating to a maintenance order to which Part 1 of the 1972 Act applies.

(Section 14 of the 1972 Act makes provision for the taking of evidence needed for the purpose of certain proceedings.)

(2) The High Court has power to take the evidence where—

(a) the request for evidence relates to a maintenance order made by a superior court in the United Kingdom; and
(b) the witness resides in England and Wales.

(3) The county court has power to take the evidence where—

(a) the request for evidence relates to a maintenance order made by a county court; and
(b) the maintenance order has not been registered in a magistrates' court under the 1958 Act.

(4) The following magistrates' courts have power to take the evidence, that is—

(a) where the proceedings in the Republic of Ireland relate to a maintenance order made by a magistrates' court, the court which made the order;
(b) where the proceedings relate to an order which is registered in a magistrates' court, the court in which the order is registered; and
(c) a magistrates' court to which the Secretary of State sends the request to take evidence.

(5) A magistrates' court not mentioned in paragraph (4) has power to take the evidence if the magistrates' court which would otherwise have that power consents because the evidence could be taken more conveniently.

(6) The evidence is to be taken in accordance with Part 22.

Request for the taking of evidence by a court ...

34.21 [This rule does not apply to the Republic of Ireland]

Transmission of documents

34.22—(1) This rule applies to any document, including a notice or request, which is required to be sent to a court in the Republic of Ireland by—

(a) Part 1 of the 1972 Act; or

(b) Section 1 of Chapter 2 of this Part of these Rules.

(2) The document must be sent to the Lord Chancellor for transmission to the court in the Republic of Ireland.

Method of payment under registered orders

34.23—(1) Where an order is registered in a magistrates' court in accordance with section 6(3) of the 1972 Act, the court must order that the payment of sums due under the order be made—

(a) to the court officer for the registering court; and

(b) at such time and place as the court officer directs.

(Section 6(3) of the 1972 Act makes provision for the registration of maintenance orders made in the Republic of Ireland.)

(2) Where the court orders payment to be made to the court officer, the court officer must send the payments by post—

(a) to the payee under the order; or

(b) where a public authority has been authorised by the payee to receive the payments, to that public authority.

(Practice Direction 34A contains further provisions relating to the payment of sums due under registered orders.)

Enforcement of payments under registered orders

34.24—(1) This rule applies where periodical payments under a registered order are in arrears.

(2) The court officer must, on the written request of the payee, proceed in that officer's own name for the recovery of the sums due unless of the view that it is unreasonable to do so.

(3) If the sums due are more than 4 weeks in arrears the court officer must give the payee notice in writing of that fact stating the particulars of the arrears.

Notification of registration and cancellation

34.25 The court officer must send written notice to—

(a) the Lord Chancellor, on the due registration of an order under section 6(3) or 10(4) of the 1972 Act; and

(b) to the payer under the order, on—

   (i) the registration of an order under section 10(4) of the 1972 Act; or

   (ii) the cancellation of the registration of an order under section 10(1) of that Act.

Other notices under section 6 of the 1972 Act
34.25A—(1) A notice required under section 6(6) or (10) of the 1972 Act must be in the form referred to in a practice direction.

(2) Where a magistrates' court sets aside the registration of an order following an appeal under section 6(7) of the 1972 Act, the court officer must send written notice of the court's decision to the payee.

(Section 6(6) of the 1972 Act provides for notice of registration in a United Kingdom court of a maintenance order made in the Republic of Ireland, and section 6(10) of that Act for notice that a maintenance order made in the Republic of Ireland has not been registered in a United Kingdom court.)

Annex 2: application of section 1 of Chapter 2 of Part 34 to the Hague Convention countries

Application for transmission of maintenance order to a Hague Convention Country
34.14 An application for a maintenance order to be sent to a Hague Convention Country under section 2 of the 1972 Act must be made in accordance with Practice Direction 34A.

Certification of evidence given on provisional orders
34.15 [This rule does not apply to the Hague Convention Countries]

Confirmation of a provisional order made in a reciprocating country
34.16 [This rule does not apply to the Hague Convention Countries]

Consideration of revocation of a maintenance order made by a magistrates' court
34.17—(1) This rule applies where—

(a) an application has been made to a magistrates' court by a payee for the revocation of an order to which section 5 of the 1972 Act applies; and

(b) the payer resides in a Hague Convention Country.

(2) The court officer must serve on the payee, by post, a copy of any representations or evidence adduced by or on behalf of the payer.

(Provision relating to consideration of variation of a maintenance order made by a magistrates' court to which section 5 of the 1972 Act applies is made in Rules made under section 144 of the Magistrates' Courts Act 1980.)

Notification of variation or revocation of a maintenance order by the High Court or a county court
34.18—(1) This rule applies if the High Court or a county court makes an order varying or revoking a maintenance order to which section 5 of the 1972 Act applies.

(2) If the time for appealing has expired without an appeal having been entered, the court officer will send to the Lord Chancellor—

(a) the documents required by section 5(8) of the 1972 Act; and
(b) a certificate signed by the district judge stating that the order of variation or revocation is enforceable and no longer subject to the ordinary forms of review.

(3) A party who enters an appeal against the order of variation or revocation must, at the same time, give written notice to the court officer.

Notification of confirmation or revocation of a maintenance order by a magistrates' court
34.19 [This rule does not apply to the Hague Convention Countries]

Taking of evidence for court in a Hague Convention Country
34.20—(1) This rule applies where a request is made by or on behalf of a court in a Hague Convention Country for the taking of evidence for the purpose of proceedings relating to a maintenance order to which Part 1 of the 1972 Act applies.

(Section 14 of the 1972 Act makes provision for the taking of evidence needed for the purpose of certain proceedings.)

(2) The High court has power to take the evidence where—

(a) the request for evidence relates to a maintenance order made by a superior court in the United Kingdom: and
(b) the witness resides in England and Wales.

(3) The county court has power to take the evidence where—

(a) the request for evidence relates to a maintenance order made by a county court; and
(b) the maintenance order has not been registered in a magistrates' court under the 1958 Act.

(4) The following magistrates' courts have power to take the evidence, that is—

(a) where the proceedings in the Hague Convention Country relate to a maintenance order made by a magistrates' court, the court which made the order;
(b) where the proceedings relate to an order which is registered in a magistrates' court, the court in which the order is registered; and
(c) a magistrates' court to which the Secretary of State sends the request to take evidence.

(5) A magistrates' court not mentioned in paragraph (4) has power to take the evidence if the magistrates' court which would otherwise have that power consents because the evidence could be taken more conveniently.

(6) The evidence is to be taken in accordance with Part 22.

Request for the taking of evidence by a court in a Hague Convention country

34.21 [This rule does not apply to the Hague Convention countries.]

Transmission of documents

34.22—(1) This rule applies to any document, including a notice or request, which is required to be sent to a court in a Hague Convention country by—

(a) Part 1 of the 1972 Act; or

(b) Section 1 of Chapter 2 of this Part of these Rules.

(2) The document must be sent to the Lord Chancellor for transmission to the court in the Hague Convention country.

Method of payment under registered orders

34.23—(1) Where an order is registered in a magistrates' court in accordance with section 6(3) of the 1972 Act, the court must order that the payment of sums due under the order be made—

(a) to the court officer for the registering court; and

(b) at such time and place as the court officer directs.

(Section 6(3) of the 1972 Act makes provision for the registration of maintenance orders made in a Hague Convention country.)

(2) Where the court orders payment to be made to the court officer, the court officer must send the payments by post to the payee under the order.

(Practice Direction 34A contains further provision relating to the payment of sums due under registered orders.)

Enforcement of payments under registered orders

34.24—(1) This rule applies where a court has ordered periodical payments under a registered maintenance order to be made to the court officer.

(2) The court officer must take reasonable steps to notify the payee of the means of enforcement available.

(3) Paragraph (4) applies where periodical payments due under a registered order are in arrears.

(4) The court officer, on that officer's own initiative—

(a) may; or

(b) if the sums due are more than 4 weeks in arrears, must,

proceed in that officer's own name for the recovery of the sums due unless of the view that it is unreasonable to do so.

Notification of registration and cancellation

34.25 The court officer must send written notice to—

(a) the Lord Chancellor, on the due registration of an order under section 10(4) of the 1972 Act; and

(b) the payer under the order, on—

(i) the registration of an order under section 10(4) of the 1972 Act; or

(ii) the cancellation of the registration of an order under section 10(1) of the 1972 Act.

General provisions as to notices

34.25A—(1) A notice to a payer of the registration of an order in a magistrates' court in accordance with section 6(3) of the 1972 Act must be in the form referred to in a practice direction.

(Section 6(8) of the 1972 Act requires notice of registration to be given to the payer.)

(2) If the court sets aside the registration of a maintenance order following an appeal under section 6(9) of the 1972 Act, the court officer must send written notice of the decision to the Lord Chancellor.

(3) A notice to a payee that the court officer has refused to register an order must be in the form referred to in a practice direction.

(Section 6(11) of the 1972 Act requires notice of refusal of registration to be given to the payee.)

(4) Where, under any provision of Part 1 of the 1972 Act, a court officer serves a notice on a payer who resides in a Hague Convention Country, the court officer must send to the Lord Chancellor a certificate of service.

Annex 3: application of section 1 of Chapter 2 of Part 34 to the United States of America

Application for transmission of maintenance order to the United States of America

34.14 An application for a maintenance order to be sent to the United States of America under section 2 of the 1972 Act must be made in accordance with Practice Direction 34A.

Certification of evidence given on provisional orders

34.15 [This rule does not apply to the United States of America]

Confirmation of a provisional order made in a reciprocating country

34.16 [This rule does not apply to the United States of America]

Consideration of revocation of a maintenance order made by a magistrates' court

34.17—(1) This rule applies where—

(a) an application has been made to a magistrates' court by a payee for the revocation of an order to which section 5 of the 1972 Act applies; and

(b) the payer resides in the United States of America.

(2) The court officer must serve on the payee by post a copy of any representations or evidence adduced by or on behalf of the payer.

(Provision relating to consideration of variation of a maintenance order made by a magistrates' court to which section 5 of the 1972 Act applies is made in rules made under section 144 of the Magistrates' Courts Act 1980.)

Notification of variation or revocation

34.18 If the High Court or a county court makes an order varying or revoking a maintenance order to which section 5 of the 1972 Act applies, the court officer will send to the Lord Chancellor the documents required by section 5(7) of that Act.

Notification of confirmation or revocation of a maintenance order by a magistrates' court

34.19 [This rule does not apply to the United States of America]

Taking of evidence for court in United States of America

34.20—(1) This rule applies where a request is made by or on behalf of a court in the United States of America for the taking of evidence for the purpose of proceedings relating to a maintenance order to which Part 1 of the 1972 Act applies.

(Section 14 of the 1972 Act makes provision for the taking of evidence needed for the purpose of certain proceedings.)

(2) The High Court has power to take the evidence where—

(a) the request for evidence relates to a maintenance order made by a superior court in the United Kingdom; and
(b) the witness resides in England and Wales.

(3) The county court has power to take the evidence where—

(a) the request for evidence relates to a maintenance order made by a county court; and
(b) the maintenance order has not been registered in a magistrates' court under the 1958 Act.

(4) The following magistrates' courts have power to take the evidence, that is—

(a) where the proceedings in the United States of America relate to a maintenance order made by a magistrates' court, the court which made the order;
(b) where the proceedings relate to an order which is registered in a magistrates' court, the court in which the order is registered; and
(c) a magistrates' court to which the Secretary of State sends the request to take evidence.

(5) A magistrates' court not mentioned in paragraph (4) has power to take the evidence if the magistrates' court which would otherwise have that power consents because the evidence could be taken more conveniently.

(6) The evidence is to be taken in accordance with Part 22.

Request for the taking of evidence by a court in a reciprocating country
34.21 [This rule does not apply to the United States of America]

Transmission of documents
34.22—(1) This rule applies to any document, including a notice or request, which is required to be sent to a court in the United States of America by—

(a) Part 1 of the 1972 Act; or
(b) Section 1 of Chapter 2 of this Part of these Rules.

(2) The document must be sent to the Lord Chancellor for transmission to the court in the United States of America.

Method of payment under registered orders
34.23—(1) Where an order is registered in a magistrates' court in accordance with section 6(3) of the 1972 Act, the court must order that the payment of sums due under the order be made—

(a) to the court officer for the registering court; and
(b) at such time and place as the court officer directs.

(Section 6(3) of the 1972 Act makes provision for the registration of maintenance orders made in the United States of America.)

(2) Where the court orders payment to be made to the court officer, the court officer must send the payments by post to the payee under the order.

(Practice Direction 34A contains further provisions relating to the payment of sums due under registered orders.)

Enforcement of payments under registered orders
34.24—(1) This rule applies where a court has ordered periodical payments under a registered maintenance order to be made to the court officer.

(2) The court officer must take reasonable steps to notify the payee of the means of enforcement available.

(3) Paragraph (4) applies where periodical payments due under a registered order are in arrears.

(4) The court officer, on that officer's own initiative—

(a) may; or
(b) if the sums due are more than 4 weeks in arrears, must,

proceed in that officer's own name for the recovery of the sums due unless of the view that it is unreasonable to do so.

Notification of registration and cancellation
34.25 The court officer must send written notice to—

(a) the Lord Chancellor, on the due registration of an order under section 10(4) of the 1972 Act; or
(b) the payer under the order, on—

(i) the registration of an order under section 10(4) of the 1972 Act; or

(ii) the cancellation of the registration of an order under section 10(1) of that Act.

* * * * *

PRACTICE DIRECTION 34B – TRACING PAYERS OVERSEAS

Practice Note – 10 February 1976. Difficulties can arise where a person in this country wishes to take proceedings under the Maintenance Orders (Facilities for Enforcement) Act 1920 or Part I of the Maintenance Orders (Reciprocal Enforcement) Act 1972 to obtain or enforce a maintenance order against a payer living overseas whose address is unknown to the applicant.

To mitigate those difficulties, arrangements have now been made with the appropriate authorities in Australia, Canada, New Zealand and South Africa, whereby the court may on request ask the authorities in those countries to make enquiries with a view to tracing the whereabouts of the payer. The following procedure should be followed.

On or before an application is made for a provisional maintenance order, or for transmission of an absolute maintenance order under the above Acts by an applicant who does not know the payer's actual address in either Australia, Canada, New Zealand or South Africa, there should be completed and lodged with the [district judge] a questionnaire, in duplicate, ([Principal] Registry Form D312 or county court Form D85 as appropriate) obtainable from the registry or court office, together with a written undertaking from the solicitor (or from the applicant if acting in person) that any address of the payer received in response to the enquiries will not be disclosed or used except for the purpose of proceedings.

* * * * *

Part 35

Commentary on Part 35:
MEDIATION DIRECTIVE

The Mediation Directive (Directive 2008/52/EC of the European Parliament and of the Council of 21 May 2008) is intended to facilitate access to ADR and to promote the amicable settlement of disputes by encouraging the use of mediation; it also aims to ensure a balanced relationship between mediation and judicial proceedings. It applies to all EU member states except Denmark. It applies to cross-border disputes concerning civil and commercial matters, including family disputes, except as regards 'rights and obligations which are not at the parties' disposal under the relevant applicable law'. Such rights and obligations are, of course, frequently found in the family law context. Part 35 sets out the procedure and preconditions for dealing with such cross-border mediation in the courts of England and Wales.

It is to be emphasised that the Mediation Directive and Part 35 do not affect 'domestic' mediations and other forms of alternative dispute facilitation and resolution to which Part 3 applies.

Scope
Rule 35.1 provides that this Part applies to mediated cross-border disputes that are subject to Directive 2008/52/EC of the European Parliament and of the Council of 21 May 2008 (the Directive). The most important defined terms have the meaning set out in the Directive, as follows.

A 'relevant cross-border dispute' is one in which at least one of the parties is domiciled or resident in a member state, other than that of the other party, on the date on which:

(a) the parties agree to use mediation after the dispute has arisen;
(b) mediation is ordered by a court;
(c) an obligation to use mediation arises under national law; or
(d) the court hearing an action issues an invitation to the parties to use mediation

For these purposes 'domicile' is to be determined in accordance with Arts 59 and 60 of Brussels I (Regulation (EC) No 44/2001).

'Mediation' means a structured process whereby two or more parties to a dispute attempt by themselves, on a voluntary basis, to reach an agreement on the settlement of their dispute with the assistance of a mediator. It does not matter what this process is called. Mediation of this kind may be initiated by the parties, suggested or ordered by a court, or prescribed by the law of the member state. It includes mediation conducted by a judge who is not responsible for any judicial proceedings concerning the dispute in question, e.g. on FDR. It excludes attempts made by the court or the judge seised to settle a dispute in the course of judicial proceedings concerning the dispute in question.

Mediation may be made compulsory under national law, or subject to incentives or sanctions, provided that such legislation does not prevent the parties from exercising their right of access to the judicial system. However, mediation ordered by a court or prescribed by law must still be 'voluntary' in the sense that the parties are themselves in charge of the process, and may organise it as they wish and terminate it any time (although the courts may set time-limits).

'Mediator' refers to any third person who is asked to conduct a mediation in an effective, impartial and competent way, regardless of the specific title given to that person, or the profession of that person in the member state concerned, and regardless of the way in which the third person has been appointed or requested to conduct the mediation.

The other defined terms are:

'Mediation evidence', which means evidence regarding information arising out of or in connection with a mediation process.

'Mediation administrator', which means a person involved in the administration of the mediation process.

'Relevant dispute', which means a cross-border dispute subject to the Directive.

Applications for consent orders in respect of financial remedies

Rule 35.2 applies to applications for consent orders in respect of financial remedies arising out of a relevant mediation.

The court will not include in such an order anything contrary to, or unenforceable under, the law of England and Wales. It remains to be seen whether the court will take exception, applying what might be thought to be an over-scrupulous interpretation of this provision, to proposed consent orders reciting or recording agreement about matters which are not in fact enforceable. Statements of intent, for instance, not to institute further proceedings, or not to apply to vary maintenance for a period might fall into this category.

Rule 35.2(3) to (6) deals with procedural matters. Rule 35.2(3) requires the applicant to file two copies of a draft of the order in the terms sought.

Unlike rule 9.26, which is the main rule governing ordinary applications for consent orders in respect of financial remedies, there is no requirement in rule 35.2(3) that one of these copies must be endorsed with a statement signed by the respondent to the application signifying agreement. Instead rule 35.2(4) provides that the application must be supported by evidence of the explicit consent of the respondent, unless the respondent has already written to the court consenting to the making of the order sought, in which case under rule 35.2(5) the respondent is deemed to have given explicit consent to the order. Otherwise, the provisions of rule 9.26 apply.

PD 35A supplements rules 35.2, by requiring all applications to be completed in English, or accompanied by a translation into English, and requiring the evidence of the respondent's explicit consent (or the respondent's letter to the court consenting to the making of the order) either to be in English or to be accompanied by a translation into English.

In *S v P (Settlement By Collaborative Law Process)* [2008] 2 FLR 2040 Coleridge J, with the agreement of the President, devised a short-cut procedure for the making of a consent order following an agreement reached under the collaborative law process. The application for approval of such a draft consent order may be dealt with in the 'urgent without notice' High Court applications list. A full day's notice must be given to the clerk of the High Court judge in front of whom it is proposed to list the case: such notice may be given by telephone. The Clerk of the Rules should be informed that this is taking place. Use of the shortcut process is always subject to the consent of the urgent application judge. However, provided every aspect of the documentation is agreed, the hearing is not expected to last more than 10 minutes, and the documentation has been lodged with the judge the night before the hearing, this process has been approved by the President for use by those who achieve collaborative law agreements, in order to provide as much encouragement as possible to people to resolve their difficulties in this civilised and sensible way.

It remains to be seen whether a similar streamlined procedure may be developed for cross-border mediated settlements which complies with the requirements of Part 35.

Mediation evidence: disclosure and inspection

Under rule 35.3(1) a party to proceedings who seeks disclosure or inspection of mediation evidence currently in the control of a mediator or mediation administrator must first obtain the court's permission by means of an application made in accordance with the procedure set out in Part 18. The mediator or mediation administrator in question must be named as a respondent to the application, and he or she must be served with a copy of the application notice. Evidence in support of the application must include evidence that:

(a) all parties to the mediation agree to the disclosure or inspection of the mediation evidence;
(b) disclosure to or inspection of the mediation evidence is necessary for overriding considerations of public policy (in accordance with Art 7(1)(a) of the Directive); or
(c) the disclosure or content of an agreement resulting from mediation is necessary to implement or enforce that agreement.

Parts 21 to 24 (which concern disclosure and inspection, evidence, and witnesses, depositions generally and taking of evidence in EU member states) apply to applications under rule 35.3 to the extent that the relevant Parts are consistent with the Rule.

It is foreseeable that complex issues may arise for determination if such applications are made in a case where the mediator or mediation administrator opposes disclosure and/or inspection and seeks to rely on privilege, confidentiality or the '*secret professionel*' jealously guarded by civil law jurisdictions.

Mediation evidence: witnesses and depositions

Rule 35.4 applies if a party wishes to obtain mediation evidence from a mediator or mediation administrator by means of:

- a witness summons;
- cross-examination with permission of the court (under rule 22.8 governing an order for cross-examination, or rule 23.4 governing the calling of witnesses for cross-examination on hearsay evidence);
- an order under rule 24.7 governing evidence by deposition;
- an order under rule 24.9 governing enforcing attendance of witnesses;
- an order under rule 24.10(4), concerning the court's power to require a deponent to attend the hearing and give evidence orally; or
- an order under rule 24.12, governing the examination of a person out of the jurisdiction by means of a letter of request.

In each such case, the person wishing to obtain the evidence must provide the court with evidence that:

(a) all parties to the mediation agree to obtaining of the mediation evidence;
(b) obtaining the mediation evidence is necessary for overriding considerations of public policy (in accordance with Art 7(1)(a) of the Directive); or
(c) the disclosure or content of an agreement resulting from mediation is necessary to implement or enforce that agreement.

In every case, the court may invite any person, whether or not a party, to make representations.

Parts 21 to 24 (which concern disclosure and inspection, evidence, and witnesses, depositions generally and taking of evidence in EU member states) apply to applications under rule 35.4 to the extent that the relevant Parts are consistent with the rule.

Generally

Comparison with the parallel (but not identical) provisions of the amendments to CPR Part 5 (effected from 6 April 2011 by the Civil Procedure (Amendment) Rules 2011 (SI 2011 No. 88)) and the commentary thereon in e.g. *Court Practice* may prove fruitful for those considering the implications of this EU-driven invasion of the confidentiality with which traditionally English law has (subject to very limited exceptions) protected the mediation quasi-confessional: see *D (Minors) (Conciliation: privilege)* [1993] 1 FLR 932, CA.

PART 35: MEDIATION DIRECTIVE

Scope and Interpretation

35.1.—(1) This Part applies to mediated cross-border disputes that are subject to Directive 2008/52/EC of the European Parliament and of the Council of 21 May 2008 on certain aspects of mediation in civil and commercial matters ("the Mediation Directive").

(2) In this Part—

"cross-border dispute" has the meaning given by article 2 of the Mediation Directive;

"mediation" has the meaning given by article 3(a) of the Mediation Directive;

"mediation administrator" means a person involved in the administration of the mediation process;

"mediation evidence" means evidence regarding information arising out of or in connection with a mediation process;

"mediator" has the meaning given by article 3(b) of the Mediation Directive; and

"relevant dispute" means a cross-border dispute that is subject to the Mediation Directive.

Relevant disputes: applications for consent orders in respect of financial remedies

35.2.—(1) This rule applies in relation to proceedings for a financial remedy where the applicant, with the explicit consent of the respondent, wishes to make an application that the content of a written agreement resulting from mediation of a relevant dispute be made enforceable by being made the subject of a consent order.

(2) The court will not include in a consent order any matter which is

contrary to the law of England and Wales or which is not enforceable under that law.

(3) The applicant must file two copies of a draft of the order in the terms sought.

(4) Subject to paragraph (5), the application must be supported by evidence of the explicit consent of the respondent.

(5) Where the respondent has written to the court consenting to the making of the order sought, the respondent is deemed to have given explicit consent to the order and paragraph (4) does not apply.

(6) Paragraphs (1)(b) and (2) to (6) of rule 9.26 apply to an application to which this rule applies.

Mediation evidence: disclosure and inspection

35.3.—(1) Where a party to proceedings seeks disclosure or inspection of mediation evidence that is in the control of a mediator or mediation administrator, that party must first obtain the court's permission to seek the disclosure or inspection, by an application made in accordance with Part 18.

(2) The mediator or mediation administrator who has control of the mediation evidence must be named as a respondent to the application and must be served with a copy of the application notice.

(3) Evidence in support of the application must include evidence that—

(a) all parties to the mediation agree to the disclosure or inspection of the mediation evidence;
(b) disclosure or inspection of the mediation evidence is necessary for overriding considerations of public policy, in accordance with article 7(1)(a) of the Mediation Directive; or
(c) the disclosure of the content of an agreement resulting from mediation is necessary to implement or enforce that agreement.

(4) Where this rule applies, Parts 21 to 24 apply to the extent they are consistent with this rule.

Mediation evidence: witnesses and depositions

35.4.—(1) This rule applies where a party wishes to obtain mediation evidence from a mediator or mediation administrator by—

(a) a witness summons;
(b) cross-examination with permission of the court under rule 22.8 or 23.4;
(c) an order under rule 24.7 (evidence by deposition);
(d) an order under rule 24.9 (enforcing attendance of witness);
(e) an order under rule 24.10(4) (deponent's evidence to be given orally); or
(f) an order under rule 24.12 (order for the issue of a letter of request).

(2) When applying for a witness summons, permission under rule 22.8 or 23.4 or order under rule 24.7, 24.9, 24.10(4) or 24.12, the party must provide the court with evidence that—

(a) all parties to the mediation agree to the obtaining of the mediation evidence;
(b) obtaining the mediation evidence is necessary for overriding considerations of public policy in accordance with article 7(1)(a) of the Mediation Directive; or
(c) the disclosure of the content of an agreement resulting from mediation is necessary to implement or enforce that agreement.

(3) When considering a request for a witness summons, permission under rule 22.8 or 23.4 or order under rule 24.7, 24.9, 24.10(4) or 24.12, the court may invite any person, whether or not a party, to make representations.

(4) Where this rule applies, Parts 21 to 24 apply to the extent they are consistent with this rule.

PRACTICE DIRECTION 35A: MEDIATION DIRECTIVE.

This Practice Direction supplements FPR rule 35.2
(Relevant disputes: applications for consent orders
in respect of financial remedies)

1.1 An application for an order to which rule 35.2 applies must be completed in English or accompanied by a translation into English.

1.2. Where the application is supported by evidence of explicit consent to the application by a party, the evidence must also be in English or accompanied by a translation into English.

1.3. Where a party chooses to write to the court consenting to the making of the order the correspondence must be in English or accompanied by a translation into English.

Part 36

Commentary on Part 36:
TRANSITIONAL ARRANGEMENTS AND PILOT SCHEMES

No complaint could be made about the prolixity of Part 36 itself, which merely refers to the contents of PD 36A containing '*provision for the extent to which [the FPR] shall apply to proceedings started before the day on which they come into force*', and to the possibility of further practice directions in relation to pilot schemes in relation to the modification or disapplication of the FPR. No such pilot schemes have, unsurprisingly, yet been proposed. Part 36 is an exact counterpart of CPR Part 51.

The supporting PD 36A itself is also commendably brief. In short it provides that wherever practicable the FPR will apply to existing proceedings from the date when those existing proceedings are next before the court after 6 April 2011. This is broadly the same scheme as that contained in the CPR, but without the saving that the previous rules will continue to apply to undefended cases.

The general scheme set out in para 2.1 of PD 36A is that the FPR will apply to *all* proceedings, whenever commenced so far as is practicable, but that where that is not practicable the previous rules shall continue to apply.

The 'previous rules' are defined in para 1.2 and include the RSC 1965, the CCR 1981, the FPR 1991 and 14 other identified Statutory Instruments.

Para 3 identifies the situations in which **the previous rules will normally apply,** and the general principle is that steps taken before 6 April 2011 (i.e. under the previous rules) must be responded to under those previous rules. Specific instances are given in paras 3.2 and 3.3 which deal with responses to (for example acknowledgements of service) and the filing and serving of pleadings, and para 3.4 which requires compliance with a pre-existing court order made under the previous rules even where it is inconsistent with the new FPR.

Para 3.5 ensures that parties will not be required to do again under the FPR something which they had already done under the previous rules.

There is an obscure, and laboriously worded 'saving' under para 3.6

whereby in some circumstances, namely that the application for enforcement was made before 1 October 2007, the reciprocal enforcement of maintenance orders made in the United States will continue to be governed in the magistrates' court by the rules promulgated in 1995 as if they had not been amended in 2007. Such litigation is very much a minority sport consisting of lengthy halves but players (if any survive) and their spectator magistrates and district judges will be relieved that for pending applications the goalposts have not been moved and they need not yet grapple with the complexities of construing the now current set of provisions which make FPR 2010 rule 34.28, PD 34A paras 4.8 to 4.11 and Annex 3 so absorbing.

Para 4 identifies the situations **where the FPR will normally apply,** and the general principle in para 4.1 is that any 'new step' to be taken after 6 April 2011 is normally to be taken under the FPR. Moreover, the overriding objective in Part 1 will apply to all proceedings.

Para 4.3 contains the stern warning that only new FPR-compliant Forms will be issued by the court after 6 April 2011, although para 4.3(2) provides that the court may 'in cases of urgency' direct an old type of form or process be issued as if FPR-compliant. It is presumed that this provision will be relevant and live for only a very short period to cater for urgent applications in which the drafting and preparation of the paperwork was undertaken prior to 6 April 2011 but only activated in the days immediately following.

Para 4.4(1) requires the court to consider the extent to which the FPR should apply to existing proceedings on the first court hearing after 6 April 2011 and para 4.4(2) contains a general, if rebuttable, presumption that the FPR should apply, even to the extent that under para 4.4(4) even when the first occasion after 6 April 2011 that existing proceedings are before the court is a hearing of a substantive issue, that hearing will generally be conducted in accordance with the FPR.

There is no guidance in PD 36A as to circumstances in which it might be appropriate for the court to depart from the general presumption that the FPR will apply, and it is anticipated that the power will be exercised sparingly.

* * * * *

PART 36: TRANSITIONAL ARRANGEMENTS AND PILOT SCHEMES

Transitional provisions

36.1. Practice Direction 36A shall make provision for the extent to which these rules shall apply to proceedings started before the day on which they come into force.

Pilot schemes

36.2. Practice directions may modify or disapply any provision of these rules—

(a) for specified periods; and

(b) in relation to proceedings in specified courts,

during the operation of pilot schemes for assessing the use of new practices and procedures in connection with proceedings.

Practice Direction 36A supplements FPR Part 36 (Transitional arrangements)

PRACTICE DIRECTION 36A – TRANSITIONAL ARRANGEMENTS

This Practice Direction supplements FPR Part 36

Content of this Practice Direction

1.1 This Practice Direction deals with the application of the FPR to proceedings started before 6th April 2011 ("existing proceedings").

1.2 In this Practice Direction "the previous rules" means, as appropriate, the Rules of the Supreme Court 1965 and County Court Rules 1981 as in force immediately before 26 April 1999, and—

- the Maintenance Orders (Facilities for Enforcement) Rules 1922;
- the Magistrates' Courts (Guardianship of Minors) Rules 1974;
- the Magistrates' Courts (Reciprocal Enforcement of Maintenance Orders) Rules 1974;
- the Magistrates' Courts (Reciprocal Enforcement of Maintenance Orders) (Republic of Ireland) Rules 1975;
- the Magistrates' Courts (Reciprocal Enforcement of Maintenance Orders) (Hague Convention Countries) Rules 1980;
- the Magistrates' Courts (Child Abduction and Custody) Rules 1986;
- the Magistrates' Courts (Civil Jurisdiction and Judgments Act 1982) Rules 1986;
- the Family Proceedings Rules 1991;
- the Family Proceedings Courts (Children Act 1989) Rules 1991;
- the Family Proceedings Courts (Matrimonial Proceedings etc.) Rules 1991 (in so far as those rules do not relate to enforcement or variation of orders);
- the Magistrates' Courts (Costs Against Legal Representatives in Civil

Proceedings) Rules 1991 (in so far as those rules relate to family proceedings);

- the Family Proceedings Courts (Child Support Act 1991) Rules 1993;
- the Magistrates' Courts (Reciprocal Enforcement of Maintenance Orders) (United States of America) Rules 1995 (subject to the saving in paragraph 3.6 of this Practice Direction);
- the Magistrates' Courts (Hearsay Evidence in Civil Proceedings) Rules 1999 (in so far as those rules relate to family proceedings); and
- the Family Procedure (Adoption) Rules 2005,

as in force immediately before 6th April 2011.

General scheme of transitional arrangements

2.1 The general scheme is—

(a) to apply the FPR to existing proceedings so far as is practicable; but
(b) where this is not practicable, to apply the previous rules to such proceedings.

Where the previous rules will normally apply

General principle

3.1 Where an initiating step has been taken in a case before 6th April 2011, in particular a step using forms or other documentation required by the previous rules, the case will proceed in the first instance under the previous rules. Where a party must take a step in response to something done by another party in accordance with the previous rules, that step must also be in accordance with those rules.

Responding to old process

3.2 A party who is served with an old type of originating process (for example, an originating summons) on or after 6th April 2011 must respond in accordance with the previous rules and the instructions on any forms received.

Filing and service of pleadings where old process served

3.3 Where a case has been begun by an old type of originating process (whether served before or after 6th April 2011), filing and service of pleadings will continue according to the previous rules.

Pre-commencement order inconsistent with FPR

3.4 Where a court order has been made before 6th April 2011, that order must still be complied with on or after that date.

Steps taken before commencement

3.5 Where a party has, before 6th April 2011, taken any step in the proceedings in accordance with the previous rules, that step will remain valid on or after that date, and a party will not normally be required to take any action that would amount to taking such a step again under the FPR.

Saving – Reciprocal enforcement of maintenance orders (United States of America)

3.6 Where, by virtue of article 6(2) of the Reciprocal Enforcement of Maintenance Orders (United States of America) Order 2007, the Reciprocal Enforcement of Maintenance (United States of America) Order 1995 continues in full force and effect, the Magistrates' Courts (Reciprocal Enforcement of Maintenance Orders) (United States of America) Rules 1995 shall, notwithstanding any provision in the FPR, continue to apply as if they had not been amended by the Magistrates' Courts (Reciprocal Enforcement of Maintenance Orders) (Miscellaneous Amendment) Rules 2007.

Where the FPR will normally apply

General principle

4.1 Where a new step is to be taken in any existing proceedings on or after 6th April 2011, it is to be taken under the FPR.

Part 1 (Overriding objective) to apply

4.2 Part 1 of the FPR (Overriding objective) will apply to all existing proceedings from 6th April 2011 onwards.

Issuing of application forms after the FPR come into force

4.3 (1) The general rule is that—

(a) only application forms under the FPR will be issued by the court on or after 6th April 2011; and

(b) if a request to issue an old type of form or originating process (summons, etc.) is received at the court on or after 6th April 2011, it will be returned unissued.

(2) By way of exception to the general rule, the court may in cases of urgency direct that the form or process is to be issued as if the request to issue it had been a request to issue an application form under the FPR and, if it does so, the court may make such supplementary directions as it considers appropriate.

First time before a court on or after 6th April 2011

4.4 (1) When proceedings come before a court (whether at a hearing or on paper) for the first time on or after 6th April 2011, the court may direct how the FPR are to apply to the proceedings and may disapply certain provisions of the FPR. The court may also give case management directions.

(2) The general presumption will be that the FPR will apply to the proceedings from then on unless the court directs or this practice direction provides otherwise.

(3) If an application has been issued before 6th April 2011 and the hearing of the application has been set on or after that date, the general presumption is that the application will be decided having regard to the FPR.

(4) When the first occasion on which existing proceedings are before a court on or after 6th April 2011 is a hearing of a substantive issue, the general presumption is that the hearing will be conducted according to the FPR.

Costs

4.5 (1) Any assessment of costs that takes place on or after 6th April 2011 will be in accordance with FPR Part 28 and the provisions of the Civil Procedure Rules as applied by that Part.

(2) However, the general presumption is that no costs for work undertaken before 6th April 2011 will be disallowed if those costs would have been allowed on detailed assessment before that date.

(3) The decision as to whether to allow costs for work undertaken on or after 6th April 2011 will generally be taken in accordance with FPR Part 28 and the provisions of the Civil Procedure Rules as applied by that Part.

GLOSSARY

Scope

This glossary is a guide to the meaning of certain legal expressions as used in these rules, but it does not give the expressions any meaning in the rules which they do not otherwise have in the law.

Expression	Meaning
Affidavit	A written, sworn, statement of evidence.
Cross-examination	Questioning of a witness by a party other than the party who called the witness.
Evidence in chief	The evidence given by a witness for the party who called him.
Injunction	A court order prohibiting a person from doing something or requiring a person to do something.
Official copy	A copy of an official document, supplied and marked as such by the office which issued the original.
Pre-action protocol	Statements of best practice about pre-action conduct which have been approved by the

	President of the Family Division and which are annexed to a Practice Direction.
Privilege	The right of a party to refuse to disclose a document or produce a document or to refuse to answer questions on the ground of some special interest recognised by law.
Seal	A seal is a mark which the court puts on document to indicate that the document has been issued by the court.
Service	Steps required by rules of court to bring documents used in court proceedings to a person's attention.
Set aside	Cancelling a judgment or order or a step taken by a party in the proceedings.
Stay	A stay imposes a halt on proceedings, apart from the taking of any steps allowed by the rules or the terms of the stay. Proceedings can be continued if a stay is lifted.
Strike out	Striking out means the court ordering written material to be deleted so that it may no longer be relied upon.
Without prejudice	Negotiations with a view to settlement are usually conducted "without prejudice" which means that the circumstances in which the content of those negotiations may be revealed to the court are very restricted.

I allow these Rules
Signed by authority of the Lord
Chancellor Parliamentary Under Secretary of State
Ministry of Justice

EXPLANATORY NOTE

(This note is not part of the Order)
These rules provide a new code of procedure for family proceedings in the High Court, county courts and magistrates' courts, and replace existing rules of court for family proceedings. The principal rules being replaced are the Family Proceedings Rules 1991, the Family Procedure (Adoption) Rules 2005 and, in so far as they relate to family proceedings, the Family Proceedings Courts (Children Act 1989) Rules 1991, the Family Proceedings (Matrimonial Proceedings etc) Rules 1991, and rules relating

to the reciprocal enforcement of maintenance orders, in particular the Magistrates' Courts (Reciprocal Enforcement of Maintenance Orders) Rules 1974.

The rules adopt a similar structure to the Civil Procedure Rules 1998. The introductory Parts provide for fundamental matters of general application and various preliminary matters, opening in Part 1 with the overriding objective of the rules, to enable the court to deal with cases justly, having regard to any welfare issues involved. Part 2 contains the provisions for interpreting and applying the rules including provision about the delegation of certain functions of a magistrates' court to a single justice. Part 3 contains the court's powers to encourage the use of alternative dispute resolution; Part 4 contains provision for case management powers; Part 5 provides for the forms which are to be used in family proceedings and how family proceedings are started; and Part 6 makes provision for service of documents in family proceedings (including service abroad).

The rules then make provision for procedure for the key types of family proceedings in separate Parts as follows—

- Part 7 (Procedure for applications in matrimonial and civil partnership proceedings);
- Part 8 (Procedure for miscellaneous applications such as applications for a gender recognition certificate, declarations and orders preventing avoidance under section 32L of the Child Support Act 1991 (c.48));
- Part 9 (Applications for a financial remedy);
- Part 10 (Applications under Part 4 of the Family Law Act 1996 (c.27) (domestic violence));
- Part 11 (Applications under Part 4A of the Family Law Act 1996 (forced marriage));
- Part 12 (Proceedings relating to children, except parental order proceedings and proceedings for applications in adoption, placement and related proceedings);
- Part 13 (Proceedings under section 54 of the Human Fertilisation and Embryology Act 2008 (c.22) (parental orders)); and
- Part 14 (Adoption, placement and related proceedings).

Parts 15 and 16 contain rules relating to representation of protected parties and children respectively, and Part 17 for when statements of truth are required to verify documents. Part 18 relates to the procedure for other applications in proceedings which, for example, will be used for applications for the court's permission to bring proceedings and Part 19 to the alternative procedure for applications which will be used for matters such as proceedings for an order to prevent disclosure of information to an adopted person under section 60(3) of the Adoption and Children Act 2002 (c.38).

The remaining Parts of the rules are of general application and contain procedural provisions mirroring, with modifications for family proceedings, the general procedural parts of the Civil Procedure Rules 1998, as follows—

- Part 20 makes provision for applications for interim injunctions;
- Part 21 contains miscellaneous rules about disclosure and inspection of documents;
- Parts 22 to 24 contain rules about evidence;
- Part 25 deals with experts and assessors;
- Part 26 deals with change of solicitor;
- Part 27 relates to hearings and directions appointments and includes provision relating to the giving of reasons in a magistrates' court;
- Part 28 relates to costs across all three levels of court;
- Part 29 contains miscellaneous provisions including provision for protection of personal details in proceedings and provision for Human Rights Act 1998 (c.42) questions being raised in family proceedings;
- Part 30 deals with appeals;
- Parts 31 and 32 deal with registration and enforcement of foreign or Scottish or Northern Irish orders of different sorts, and Part 34 with reciprocal enforcement of maintenance orders;
- Part 33 provides for enforcement generally;
- Part 35 relates to the Mediation Directive; and
- Part 36 contains transitional provisions.

Detailed supplementary provisions supporting many parts of the rules such as the transitional provisions in Part 36 and appeals in Part 30 are, where indicated in the rules, contained in practice directions, which do not form part of the rules.

Please note that these footnotes form part of FPR 2010 as published on issue

1. 2003 c.39. Section 75 was amended by section 15(1) and 146 of and paragraphs 308 and 338 of Schedule 4 and Part 2 of Schedule 18 to the Constitutional Reform Act 2005 (c.4). Section 76 was amended by section 12(2) of and paragraph 29 of Schedule 1 to the Constitutional Reform Act 2005 and section 261(1) of and paragraph 172 of Schedule 27 to the Civil Partnership Act 2004 (c.33) and section 62(7) of the Children Act 2004 (c.31) and section 25 of and paragraph 14 of Schedule 3 to the Children, Schools and Families Act 2010 (c.26).
2. 1972 c.18.Section 18 was amended by section 109(1) and paragraphs 155(1),(2)(a) and (3) of Schedule 8 to the Courts Act 2003.
3. 1982 c.27.
4. 1985 c.60.
5. 1989 c.41. Section 97(1) was amended by section 109(1) and paragraphs 337(1) and (2) of Schedule 8 to the Courts Act 2003 and by section 101(3) of the Adoption and Children Act 2002 (c.38).
6. 1999 c.22.

7. 2002 c. 38. Section 102 was amended by section 40 of and paragraphs 15, 16(1), (2), (3) and (4) of Schedule 3 to the Children Act 2004. Section 141(1) and (3) were amended by section 109(1) of and paragraph 413(1) and (2) of Schedule 8 to the Courts Act 2003. Sections 102(1) to (4) and(6) to (8) and 141(1) and (3) of the Adoption and Children Act 2002 were applied with modifications for the purposes of parental orders by regulation 2 of and, Schedule 1 to the Human Fertilisation and Embryology Act (Parental Orders) Regulations 2010 (S.I.2010/985).

8. Section 79 was amended by sections 15(1) and 146 of and paragraphs 308 and 341(1) of Schedule 4 and Part 2 of Schedule 18 to the Constitutional Reform Act 2005.

9. 1980 c.43.

10. 1973 c.18.

11. 1978 c.22.

12. 1984 c.42.

13. 1986 c.55.

14. 1990 c.37.

15. 1991 c.48.

16. 1996 c27.

17. 2005 c.9.

18. 2008 c 22

19. 1971 c.80.

20. Section 7(1)(a) was amended by section 74 of and paragraphs 87 and 88(a) of Schedule 7 to the Criminal Justice and Court Services Act 2000 (c.43) and section 40 of and paragraphs 5 and 6 of Schedule 3 to the Children Act 2004.

21. Section 36A was amended by article 2 of and paragraphs 5, 6(1) and (2) of Schedule 1 to the Lord Chancellor (Transfer of Functions and Supplementary Provisions) (No.2) Order 2006 (S.I. 2006/1016).

22. Section 33(1) was amended by section 15 of and paragraphs 171 and 172(1) and (2) of Schedule 4 to the Constitutional Reform Act 2005.

23. Section 21(1) was amended by section 15 of and paragraph 2 of Schedule 2 to the Family Law Act 1996 as amended by section 84(1) of and paragraphs 64 and 65(1) to (8) of Schedule 12 to the Welfare Reform and Pensions Act 1999 (c.30).

24. Section 27(6) was amended by section 63(3) of the Domestic Proceedings and Magistrates' Courts Act 1978.

25. Section 35 was amended by section 46(1) of and paragraph 13 of Schedule 1 to the Matrimonial and Family Proceedings Act 1984 and section 261(1) of and paragraph 44 of Schedule 27 to the Civil Partnership Act 2004 and section 66(1) of and paragraph 20 of Schedule 8 to the Family Law Act 1996.

26. Section 10(2) has been prospectively repealed with savings by section 66(3) of and Schedule 10 to the Family Law Act 1996.

27. Section 27(1) was amended by section 15(1) of and paragraphs 308 and 326(1) and (2) of Schedule 4 to the Constitutional Reform Act 2005.

28. 1985 c.61.

29. 2007 c.29.

30. Section 1 has been prospectively repealed by section 66(3) of and Schedule 10 to the Family Law Act 1996.

31. Section 11 was amended by section 2(4) of the Marriage Act 1983 (c.32) and section 6(4) of the Marriage (Prohibited Degrees of Relationship) Act 1986 (c.16) and section 261(1) of and paragraph 40 of Schedule 27 to the Civil Partnership Act 2004 and section 12 was amended by section 148 of and paragraph 34 of Schedule 4 to the Mental Health Act 1983 (c.20) and sections 4(4) and 11 of and paragraphs 1 and 2 of Schedule 2 and paragraphs 4 and 5 of Schedule 4 to the Gender Recognition Act 2004 (c.7).

32. Section 17 has been prospectively repealed by section 66(3) of and Schedule 10 to the Family Law Act 1996.

33. Section 22 has been prospectively repealed by section 66(3) of and Schedule 10 to the Family Law Act 1996.

34. Section 42(2)(a) was amended by section 15(1) of and paragraphs 171, 174(1) and (2) of Schedule 4 to the Constitutional Reform Act 2005.

35. Section 7(1)(b) was amended by section 40 of and paragraphs 5 and 6 of Schedule 3 to the Children Act 2004.

36. Section 19 was amended by section 6(4) and 17(2) of and Schedule 6 to the Domicile and Matrimonial Proceedings Act 1973 (c. 45) and subsection (4) has been prospectively repealed by section 66(1) of and paragraph 7 of Schedule 8 to the Family Law Act 1996.

37. 1990 c.41. Section 9 was amended by section 15(1) of and paragraphs 211 and 213 of Schedule 4 to the Constitutional Reform Act 2005.
38. Section 66 was substituted by section 78(2) of and paragraphs 26 and 27 of Schedule 11 to the Access to Justice Act 1999 (c.22) and section 109(1) of and paragraphs 215 of Schedule 8 to the Courts Act 2003. Section 67 was substituted by section 49(1) of the Courts Act 2003 and amended by section 15(1) of and paragraphs 99, 101(1), (2), (3), (4) and (5) of the Constitutional Reform Act 2005.
39. 1998 c.42. Section 4 was amended by section 40(4) of and paragraphs 66(1) and (2) of Schedule 9 to the Constitutional Reform Act 2005 and section 378(1) of and paragraph 156 of Schedule 16 to the Armed Forces Act 2006 (c.52) and section 67(1) of and paragraph 43 of Schedule 6 to the Mental Capacity Act 2005.
40. 1981 c.61.
41. Paragraph 9 of Schedule 1 was amended by section 19(5) of and paragraphs 7(1), (2), (3), (4) and (5) of Schedule 3 to the Family Law Act 1996 and regulation 4 of the European Communities (Matrimonial Jurisdiction and Judgments) Regulations 2001 (S.I. 2001/310).
42. Section 36 was amended by section 26(1) of the Inheritance (Provision for Family and Dependants) Act 1975 (c.63).
43. 1882 c.75.
44. Section 17 was amended by the Statute Law (Repeals) Act 1969 (c.52) and section 43 of the Matrimonial and Family Proceedings Act 1984.
45. Paragraph 1 of Schedule 7 to the Family Law Act 1996 was amended by section 82 of and paragraphs 16(1) and (2) of Schedule 9 to the Civil Partnership Act 2004 and article 2 of and paragraph 10(b)(i) of the Schedule to the Housing Act 1996 (Consequential Amendments) Order 1997 (S.I. 1997/74).
46. Section 32L was inserted by section 24 of the Child Maintenance and Other Payments Act 2008 (c.6).
47. Section 3(6) was amended by section 1(2) of the Child Support, Pensions and Social Security Act 2000.
48. S.I. 1981/552.
49. Sections 23(2) (a) and (b) and 23(3) have been prospectively substituted with savings by section 15 of and paragraph 4 of Schedule 2 to the Family Law Act 1996.
50. Section 25B was inserted by section 166(1) of the Pensions Act 1995 (c.26) and amended by section 21 of and paragraphs 1(1),(2),(4),(5)(a),(5)(b), (6),(7)(a),(7)(b), (8)(a), (8)(b), (8)(c) and (9) of the Welfare Reform and Pensions Act 1999 (c.30) and subsections (8) and (9) were inserted by section 16(3) of the Family Law Act 1996 and the section was modified by regulations 2 and 4(1) and (2)(b) of the Divorce etc (Pension Protection Fund) Regulations 2006 (S.I. 2006/1932). Section 25C was inserted by section 166(1) of the Pensions Act 1995 and amended by section 66(1) of and paragraph 11 of Schedule 8 to the Family Law Act 1996 and also amended by section 21 of and paragraphs 2(1), (2), (3)(a)(i) and (ii), (3)(b), (4)(a), (4)(b) and (5) of Schedule 4 to the Welfare Reform and Pensions Act 1999.
51. Paragraph 9(2) of Schedule 7 to the Civil Partnership Act 2004 was amended by section 120 of and paragraphs 14, 20(1), 20(2)(a) and (b) of the Pensions Act 2008 (c. 30).
52. Section 25F was inserted by section 120 of and paragraphs 1 and 7 of Schedule 6 to the Pensions Act 2008.
53. Section 17(1)(a)(i) was amended by section 66(1) of and paragraph 32(2) of Schedule 8 to the Family Law Act 1996 as amended by section 84(1) of and paragraphs 66(1) and (14) of Schedule 12 to the Welfare Reform and Pensions Act 1999.
54. Section 24E was inserted by section 120 of and paragraphs 1 and 3 of Schedule 6 to the Pensions Act 2008.
55. Paragraphs 9(2) and (3) of Schedule 7 to the Civil Partnership Act 2004 were amended by section 120 of and paragraphs 14 and 20(2)(b) of Schedule 6 to the Pensions Act 2008.
56. Section 24B was inserted by section 19 of and paragraphs 1 and 4 of Schedule 3 to the Welfare Reform and Pensions Act 1999.
57. Section 21C was inserted by section 120 of and paragraphs 1 and 2 of Schedule 6 to the Pensions Act 2008.
58. S.I. 2000/1048
59. S.I. 1996/1655.
60. S.I. 1996/1847 Regulation 11 was amended by regulations 5(b), 5(c), 5(d)(i) and (ii), 5(e), 5(f) and 5(g) of the Occupational Pension Scheme (Transfer Values) (Amendment) Regulations 2008 (S.I. 2008/1050) and regulations 4(a)(ii) and 4(b) of the Occupational Pension Scheme (Winding Up and Transfer Values) (Amendment) Regulations 2005 (S.I. 2005/72) and regulation 8 of the Occupational, Personal and Stakeholder Pensions (Miscellaneous Amendment) Regulations 2009 (S.I. 2009/615 and Schedule 1 was amended by regulations 7(a)(ii), (iii), (iv)(aa), (iv)(bb) and 7(b) of Occupational Pension Scheme (Transfer Values) (Amendment) Regulations 2008.

61. 1993 c.48 Section 93A was inserted by section 153 of the Pensions Act 1965 (c.26) and section 94(1)(a) and (aa) were amended by section 154(1) and (2) of the Pensions Act 1995.

62. S.I. 1987/1110.

63. S.I. 2005/2920.

64. Section 27 was amended by sections 4 and 46(1) of and paragraph 13 of Schedule 1 to the Matrimonial and Family Proceedings Act 1984 and section 63(1), (2), (3), (4) and (5) as substituted by section 33(1) of and paragraph 52 of Schedule 2 to the Family Law Reform Act 1987 (c.42) and section 89(2)(b) and Schedule 3 to the Domestic Proceedings and Magistrates' Courts Act 1978 and section 66(1) of and paragraph 13(2), (3), and (4) of Schedule 8 to the Family Law Act 1996 and section 6(1) of the Domicile and Matrimonial Proceedings Act 1973.

65. Section 35 was amended by section 46(1) of and paragraph 13 of Schedule 1 to the Matrimonial and Family Proceedings Act 1984 and by section 109(1) of and paragraph 169 of Schedule 8 to the Courts Act 2003 and section 261(1) of and paragraph 44 of Schedule 27 to the Civil Partnership Act 2004 and section 66(1) of and paragraph 20 of Schedule 8 to the Family Law Act 1996.

66. Section 20A was inserted by section 33(1) of and paragraph 69 of Schedule 2 to the Family Law Reform Act 1987 and substituted by section 108(5) of and paragraph 39 of Schedule 13 to the Children Act 1989.

67. Section 28 was inserted with savings by section 66(1) of and paragraph 28(2) and (3) of Schedule 8 to the Family Law Act 1996 and subsection (2) was repealed by Schedule 10 to that Act.

68. Section 2 was amended by sections 15(1) and 146 of and paragraphs 96(1), (2) and (3) of Schedule 4 to and Part 2 of Schedule 18 to the Constitutional Reform Act 2005.

69. Section 1 was amended by section 46(1) of and paragraph (c) of Schedule 1 to the Matrimonial and Family Proceedings Act 1984 and prospectively repealed with savings by sections 18(1) and 66(3) of and Schedule 10 to the Family Law Act 1996.

70. Section 24A was inserted by section 7 of the Matrimonial Homes and Property Act 1981 (c.24) and subsection 6 was inserted by section 46(1) of and Schedule 1 to that Act and the section was amended by section 66(1) and 66(3) of and paragraph 8 of Schedule 8 to and Schedule 10 to the Family Law Act 1996 and by section 261(1) of and paragraph 42 of Schedule 27 to the Civil Partnership Act 2004.

71. Section 27 was amended by sections 4 and 46(1) and paragraph 13 of Schedule 1 to the Matrimonial and Family Proceedings Act 1984 and sections 63(1), (2), (3) (4) and (5) and 89(2)(b) of and Schedule 3 to the Domestic Proceedings and Magistrates' Courts Act 1978 and sections 33(1) and 66(1) and paragraph 52 of Schedule 2 and paragraphs 13(2), (3) and (4) of Schedule 8 to the Family Law Act 1996 and section 6(1) of the Domicile and Matrimonial Proceedings Act 1973.

72. Section 25D(3) and (4) was amended by sections 21 and 84(1) of and paragraphs 3(1) and (5) of Schedule 4 to and paragraphs 64 and 66(1) and (4) of Schedule 12 to the Welfare Reform and Pensions Act 1999 and section 66(1) of and Schedule 8 to the Family Law Act 1996.

73. Section 46 was amended by section 320 of and Part 1 of Schedule 13 to the Pensions Act 2004 (c.35) and articles 15(1) and (4) of the Taxation of Pension Schemes (Consequential Amendments) Order 2006 (S.I. 2006/745).

74. S.I. 2005/674.

75. Paragraph 37(1) was amended by section 120 of and paragraph 14, 16(1), (5)(a)(b) and 17(10) of Schedule 6 to the Pensions Act 2008.

76. 1977 c. 32.

77. Section 7 of the Civil Procedure Act 1997 (c.12) was amended by section 261(1) of and paragraph 154 of Schedule 27 to the Civil Partnership Act 2004.

78. 1981 c.54. Section 34 was amended by section 148(3) of and Schedule 4 to the County Courts Act 1984 and article 5(b) of the Civil Procedure (Modification of Enactments) Order 1998 (S.I. 1998/2940).

79. Section 53 was amended by article 6(c)(i) of the Civil Procedure (Modification of Enactments) Order 1998 and section 10 of and paragraph 2(2) of Schedule 2 to the Civil Procedure Act 1997 (c.12) and by section 125(3) of and paragraph 44 of Schedule 18 to the Courts and Legal Services Act 1990.

80. Section 52 was amended by section 10 of and paragraph 2(2) of Schedule 2 to the Civil Procedure Act 1997 and by article 6(b) of the Civil Procedure (Modification of Enactments) Order 1998 and by section 125(3) of and paragraph 43 of Schedule 18 to the Courts and Legal Services Act 1990.

81. 1889 c.10. Section 2 was amended by section 59(5) of and paragraphs 15(1) and (2) of Schedule 11 to the Constitutional Reform Act 2005.

82. S.I. 1993/621.

83. 1995 c.38.

84. Section 63 was amended by sections 14(2) and (3) and 125(7) of and Schedule 20 to the Courts and

Legal Services Act 1990 and by articles 6(d)(i) to (iv) of the Civil Procedure (Modification of Enactments) Order 1998 (S.I. 1998/2940).

85. S.I. 2008/2551.

86. Section 4 was amended by section 40(4) of and paragraphs 66(1) and (2) of Schedule 9 to the Constitutional Reform Act 2005 and section 378(1) and paragraph 156 of Schedule 16 to the Armed Forces Act 2006 and section 67(1) of and paragraph 43 of Schedule 6 to the Mental Capacity Act 2005.

87. 1950 c.37.

88. 1958 c.39.

89. Section 24(3)(a) was amended by section 3 of and paragraph 9 of Schedule 3 to the Administration of Justice Act 1977 (c.38).

90. Section 23(1)(a) was amended by section 3 of and paragraph 8 of Schedule 3 to the Administration of Justice Act 1977.

91. Section 122 was amended by section 10 of and paragraph 2(2) of Schedule 2 to the Civil Procedure Act 1997 and sections 74(1) and (3) of the Courts and Legal Services Act 1990.

92. Sections 14A, 14B, 14C and 14D were inserted by section 115(1) of the Adoption and Children Act 2002 and amended by section 38 of the Children and Young Persons Act 2008.

93. Section 11I was inserted by section 3 of the Children and Adoption Act 2006.

94. Section 118 was amended by the Statute Law (Repeals) Act 1986 and sections 17(3) and 101(1) of and paragraph 6 of Schedule 12 to the Criminal Justice Act 1991 and section 74(6) of the Courts and Legal Services Act 1990.

95. 1869 c.62. Section 5 was amended by articles 2 and 3 of the Civil Procedure (Modification of Enactments) Order 2002 (S.I. 2002/439) and the Statute Law (Repeals) Act 2004 (c.14).

96. Section 110(2) was amended by articles 2 and 8 of the Civil Procedure (Modification of Enactments) Order 2002.

97. 1971 c.32.

98. Section 103 has been amended by section 74(1) and (3) and 125(2) and paragraph 16 of Schedule 17 to the Courts and Legal Services Act 1990 and section 10 of and paragraph 2(2) of Schedule 2 to the Civil Procedure Act 1997.

99. 1979 c. 53. Section 1 was amended by sections 34 and 37 of and paragraphs 2, 3 and 6 of Schedule 3 to the Administration of Justice Act 1982 (c.53) and section 148(1) of and paragraph 71 of Schedule 2 to the County Courts Act 1984. Subsections (6) to (8) of that section were inserted by section 93(1) and (2) of the Tribunals, Courts and Enforcement Act 2007 (c.15).

100. 1920 c.33.

101. Section 4(1) was amended by article 4(1) and (2) of the Transfer of Functions (Magistrates' Courts and Family Law) Order 1992 (S.I.1992/709) and section 1(1) of and paragraph 2(2) of Schedule 1 to the Maintenance Orders (Reciprocal Enforcement) Act 1992 (c.56).

102. Section 1(1) was amended by article 4(1) and (2) of the Transfer of Functions (Magistrates' Courts and Family Law) Order 1992.

103. Section 2 was amended by article 4(1) and (2) of the Transfer of Functions (Magistrates' Courts and Family Law) Order 1992.

104. Section 5 was amended by section 1 (2) of and paragraph 7 of Schedule 1 to the Maintenance Orders (Reciprocal Enforcement) Act 1992 and article 185(1) of and paragraph 67 of Schedule 9 to the Children (Northern Ireland) Order 1995 (S.I. 1995/755) and section 54(a) and (b) of the Domestic Proceedings and Magistrates' Courts Act 1978.

105. Section 7(2) was amended by section 1(2) of and paragraphs 8(2) to (5) of Schedule 1 to the Maintenance Orders (Reciprocal Enforcement) Act 1992.

106. Section 14 was amended by article 14(1) of and paragraph 22 of Schedule 5 to the Northern Ireland (Modification of Enactments – No 1) Order 1973 (S.I. 1973/2163) and section 154 of and paragraph 105 of Schedule 7 to the Magistrates' Courts Act 1980 and article 170(2) of and paragraph 21 of Schedule 6 to the Magistrates' Courts (Northern Ireland) Order 1981.

107. Section 23(3) was amended by section 90(1) of and paragraphs 71 and 75(1) and (2) of Schedule 13 to the Access to Justice Act 1999.

108. S.I. 1993/594.

109. Section 6 was amended by section 37 of and Schedule 11 to the Civil Jurisdiction and Judgments Act 1982 (c.27).

110. S.I. 1993/593.

111. S.I. 2007/2006.

112. Section 12 was amended by section 3 of and paragraph 7 of Schedule 2 to the Civil Jurisdiction and Judgments Act 1991 (c.12).

113. Section 145A was inserted by section 112 of the Courts and Legal Services Act 1990 and amended by section 24 of and paragraphs 15 and 19 of Schedule 4 to that Act.

114. Section 10(2) has been prospectively repealed by section 66(3) of and Schedule 10 to the Family Law Act 1996.

PRACTICE DIRECTION – PRACTICE DIRECTIONS RELATING TO FAMILY PROCEEDINGS IN FORCE BEFORE 6th APRIL 2011 WHICH SUPPORT THE FAMILY PROCEDURE RULES 2010

Introduction and the Existing Practice Directions

1.1 The Family Procedure Rules 2010 ("the FPR 2010") come into force on 6th April 2011.The purpose of this practice direction is to inform court users of the practice directions relating (only) to family proceedings which date from before 6th April 2011 ("existing Practice Directions") but will continue to apply after that date.

1.2 The table in the Annex to this practice direction lists those existing Practice Directions which will continue to apply. The listed existing Practice Directions will apply to family proceedings on and after 6th April 2011—

(a) with the modifications outlined in the Annex (in particular that the numbering of the existing Practice Directions will be as set out in column one of the table in the Annex) and any other modifications necessary in consequence of the FPR 2010 coming into force; and

(b) subject to the FPR 2010 and any other practice directions supporting those rules.

Application of Practice Direction 23B of the Civil Procedure Rules 1998

2.1 ... scientific tests to determine parentage...

[**Editors' note**: existing Practice Directions which do not relate to financial cases have been excluded from the Annex below, and are not reproduced in *@eGlance*.]

Annex

Number	Title	Date	Court	Updated rule references
Practice Direction 6C	Practice Direction (Disclosure of Addresses by Government Departments) (amending Practice Direction of	20 July 1995	High Court, county court and magistrates' court	

Number	Title	Date	Court	Updated rule references
	13th February 1989) (NB this practice direction does not apply to requests for disclosure from HMRC and related agencies which are covered by "Disclosure Orders against the Inland Revenue-Guidance from the President's Office (November 2003)"			
Practice Direction 27A	Family Proceedings: Court Bundles (Universal Practice to be applied in All Courts other than the Family Proceedings Court)	27 July 2006	High Court and county court	
Practice Direction 27B	Attendance of Media Representatives at Hearings in Family Proceedings (High Court and county courts) (This practice direction should be read as if amended by Re X (a	20 April 2009	High Court and county courts	For references to "rule 10.28 of the Family Proceedings Rules 1991", substitute "rule 27.11 of the Family Procedure Rules 2010"; in paragraph 2.2 for "paragraphs (4) to (6)", substitute "paragraphs (3) to (5)"; in paragraph 2.3, for "Part 11 of the Family Proceedings Rules 1991", substitute "Part 12, Chapter 7 of the Family Procedure Rules 2010 and Practice Direction 12G"; in paragraph 4.2, for "paragraph (8)", substitute "paragraph (7)"; in paragraph 4.3, for "paragraph (3)(f)",

	child)(residence and contact: rights of media attendance) (2009) EWHC 1728 (Fam) [87])			substitute "paragraph 2(f)" and for "paragraph 3(g)", substitute "paragraph (2)(g)"; in paragraph 5.1, for paragraph (4), substitute paragraph (3); in paragraph 5.2, for "paragraph (4)", substitute "paragraph (3)" and for "paragraph (4)(a)", substitute "paragraph 3(a)"; in paragraph 5.3, for "paragraph 4(a)(iii)", substitute "paragraph 3(a)(iii)"; in paragraph 5.4, for "paragraph 4(b)", substitute "paragraph 3(b)"; and in paragraph 6.1, for "paragraph (6)" substitute "paragraph (5)"
Practice Direction 27C:	Attendance of Media Representatives at Hearings in Family Proceedings (Family Proceedings Court) (This practice direction should be read as if amended by Re X (a child) (residence and contact: rights of media attendance) (2009) EWHC 1728 (Fam) at [87]	20 April 2009	Magistrates' courts	In paragraph 1.1, for "rule 16A of the Family Proceedings Courts (Children Act 1989) Rules 1991 ("the Rules")", substitute "rule 27.11 of the Family Procedure Rules 2010 ("the Rules")"; In paragraph 2.1, for references to "rule 16A(2)" where it occurs, substitute "rule 27.11(1)" and for "paragraphs (3) to (5) of rule 16A", substitute; "paragraphs (3) to (5) of rule 27.11"; in paragraph 2.2, for "rule 16A(2)", substitute "rule 27.11(1)"; in paragraph 2.3 for "Part 11C (rules relating to disclosure to third parties)", substitute "Part 12, Chapter 7 of the Family Procedure Rules 2010 and Practice Direction 12G"; in paragraph 2.4, for "rule 16A", substitute "rule 27.11"; and in paragraph 4.3, for "paragraph (1)(f)", substitute "paragraph 2(f)" and for "paragraph (1)(g)" substitute "paragraph 2(g)"
Practice Direction 29B	Human Rights Act 1998	24 July 2000	High Court, county court and magistrates' court	
Practice Direction 34B	Practice Note Tracing Payers Overseas	10 February 1976	High Court and county court	

Index

References are to page numbers